DATE DUE FOR RETURN

Restoring Justice after Large-scale Violent Conflicts

Restoring Justice after Large-scale Violent Conflicts

Kosovo, DR Congo and the Israeli–Palestinian Case

Edited by

Ivo Aertsen, Jana Arsovska, Holger-C. Rohne, Marta Valiñas, Kris Vanspauwen

WILLAN
PUBLISHING

Published by

Willan Publishing
Culmcott House
Mill Street, Uffculme
Cullompton, Devon
EX15 3AT, UK
Tel: +44(0)1884 840337
Fax: +44(0)1884 840251
e-mail: info@willanpublishing.co.uk
website: www.willanpublishing.co.uk

Published simultaneously in the USA and Canada by

Willan Publishing
c/o ISBS, 920 NE 58th Ave, Suite 300,
Portland, Oregon 97213-3786, USA
Tel: +001(0)503 287 3093
Fax: +001(0)503 280 8832
e-mail: info@isbs.com
website: www.isbs.com

First published 2008

ISBN 978-1-84392-302-2 hardback

British Library Cataloguing-in-Publication Data

A catalogue record for this book is available from the British Library.

Cover image
Claus Bjørn Larsen/Berlingske Tidende

Project managed by Deer Park Productions, Tavistock, Devon
Typeset by GCS, Leighton Buzzard, Bedfordshire
Printed and bound by T.J. International Ltd, Padstow, Cornwall

Contents

Acknowledgements

You must be the change you wish to see in the world.
Mahatma Gandhi

After two years of intensive work we are delighted to present this comprehensive edited volume on violent conflict and restorative justice. Compiling this volume has not been an easy project. First of all, dealing with sensitive and complex topics such as large-scale violence and mass victimisation is a notoriously difficult task in itself. Secondly, this book contains a significant number of contributors and editors, each from a different cultural background and with his/her own perception of right and wrong. Balancing these views for the 'common goal' has been a real challenge since it requires the ability to continuously adjust and change, and – as Henry Ford claims – to understand the other person's point of view and see things from that person's angle as well as from your own.

The editors would like first of all to express their enormous gratitude to the contributors of this book for their commitment and enthusiasm. The contributors were selected on the basis of their expertise and their local perspective. Despite their intricate tasks, we are extremely thankful for having worked with them in a cooperative and stimulating manner, and within a tight time frame. The editors would also like to express their gratitude to the co-editors of the different sections for their support. The co-editors have assisted throughout the whole process of putting this edited volume together and have been of valuable help to the main editors.

Secondly, the editors would like to thank all COST Action A21 members and say a few words on how this book was conceived. The book is based primarily on the analytical work done by the members of a Working Group (WG4) within COST Action A21 entitled 'Restorative Justice, Violent Conflicts and Mass Victimisation'. Founded in 1971, COST is an intergovernmental framework for European Cooperation in the field of Scientific and Technical Research, allowing the coordination of nationally funded research on a European level. The main objective of COST Action A21 was to enhance and to deepen the knowledge on theoretical and practical aspects of restorative justice in Europe. COST has enabled a number of scholars to meet and extensively exchange ideas and work on various topics. This book is also a product of the generous support and financial help of COST. We would like to express our gratitude for having been given this opportunity.

The intention of founding the WG4 within this COST Action was to explore the potential of restorative justice in dealing with the aftermath of violent conflicts in various (post-) conflict areas. The WG4 was established in August 2005, under the initiative of Kris Vanspauwen (Belgium), Ida Hydle (Norway), Ivo Aertsen (Belgium), Beni R. Jakob (Israel), Borbala Fellegi (Hungary), and Sónia Sousa Pereira (Portugal) and under the coordination of Jana Arsovska (Belgium). Moreover, WG4 throughout its existence consisted of seven additional members: Doina Balahur (Romania), Marta Valiñas (Portugal), Holger-C. Rohne (Germany), Sarah Ben-David (Israel), Finn Tschudi (Norway), Christa Pelikan (Austria) and Hanna Zagefka (UK). The editors would like to thank all of them greatly for their work and input. In the framework of COST Action A21, the WG4 has organised a series of meetings in order to discuss the progress of its work: in Maastricht, the Netherlands (October 2005), in Tel Aviv, Israel (March 2006) and finally in Warsaw, Poland (November 2006). This explorative book emerged from numerous discussions among the WG4 members and various external experts. The editors would like to thank three of these external experts – Laura Stovel (Canada), Peretz Segal (Israel) and Tyrone Savage (South Africa) – for their insightful and most valuable comments on earlier drafts of different chapters in this book. Finally, the editors are very grateful to Claus Bjørn Larsen (Denmark), a 'World Press Photo' award winner, for allowing his photograph taken during the Kosovo conflict to be used for the front cover of this volume

Examples show that peace cannot be kept by force or achieved through violence; it can only be attained through understanding

(Albert Einstein 1879–1955; Ralph Waldo Emerson 1803–82). Hence with this volume the editors hope to contribute to the efforts of understanding human relations, the complex nature of warfare and the importance of peace and dialogue for the good of humanity. In light of the devastating consequences of large-scale conflicts, the emerging discussion on the use of restorative justice in such contexts is very much needed. Thus we sincerely hope that this volume will provide a thought-provoking contribution to the related scientific debate and, certainly, for future restorative justice policy in this field.

The Editors
January 2008

List of abbreviations

ABAKO	Alliance des Bakongo
ACIL	Amsterdam Center for International Law
AFDL	Alliance des forces démocratique pour la libération du Congo-Zaire
AI	Amnesty International
AIHRC	Afghanistan Independent Human Rights Commission
ANC	Armèe Nationale Congolaise
ASADHO	Association Africaine des Droits de l'Homme
CEREBA	Centre d'Etudes et de Recherches en Education de Base pour le Développement Intégré
CEV	Communautés Ecclésiales Vivantes
CHR	Centre for Human Rights (University of Pretoria)
CLD	Code of Lekë Dukagjini (Albania)
CLK	Criminal Law of Kosovo of 1977
CLY	Criminal Law of Yugoslavia of 1977
CNS	Conférence National Souverain (Sovereign National Conference)
CPC	Commission de Pacification et de Concorde (Commission for Pacification and Harmony)
CPLY	Criminal Procedure Law of Yugoslavia of 1977
CVR	Commission Vérité et Reconciliation (Truth and Reconciliation Commission)
DRC	Democratic Republic of Congo
FAR	Forces Armées Rwandaises

FARDC	Forces Armées de la République Démocratique du Congo (Congolese National Army)
FDLR	Front Démocratique pour la Libération du Rwanda (Forces for the Democratic Liberation of Rwanda)
FGC	family group conference
HDI	Human development index
HPCC	Housing and Property Claims Commission
HPD	Housing and Property Directorate
HRW	Human Rights Watch
IAN	International Aid Network (NGO)
IANSA	International Action Network on Small Arms
ICC	International Criminal Court
ICD	Inter-Congolese Dialogue
ICG	International Crisis Group
ICTJ	International Center for Transitional Justice
ICTR	International Criminal Tribunal for Rwanda
ICTY	International Criminal Tribunal for the Former Yugoslavia
IDF	Israeli Defense Forces
IDP	Internally displaced person
IRC	International Rescue Committee
ISS	Institute for Security Studies
JNA	Yugoslav People's Army
JPS	Juvenile Probation Service (Israel)
KFOR	Kosovo Force (NATO)
KLA	Kosovo Liberation Army
KVM	Kosovo Verification Mission
KWECC	Kosovo War and Ethnic Crimes Court
LDK	Democratic League of Kosovo
LRA	Lord's Resistance Army (Uganda)
MLC	Mouvement pour la Libération du Congo
MNC	Mouvement National Congolais (Congolese National Movement)
MONUC	Mission des Nations Unies en République Démocratique du Congo (United Nations Mission in the Democratic Republic of Congo)
MPR	Mouvement Populaire de la Révolution (Popular Revolutionary Movement)
MUP	Serbian Police special forces
NATO	North Atlantic Treaty Organisation
NGO	Non-governmental organisation
NPWJ	No Peace Without Justice

OSCE	Organisation for Security and Co-operation in Europe
PA	Palestinian National Authority
PFLP	Popular Front for the Liberation of Palestine
PFM	Peace Foundation Melanesia
PLO	Palestine Liberation Army
PMG	Peace Monitoring Group
PNG	Papua New Guinea
PRCS	Palestinian Red Crescent Society
PSS	Preventive Security Services (Palestine)
PTSD	Post-traumatic stress disorder
RCD	Rassemblement Congolais pour la Démocratie
RPF	Rwandanese Patriotic Front
SAJ	Special Anti-Terror Unit
SDS	Serbian Democratic Party
SFCG	Search for Common Ground
SFRY	Socialist Federal Republic of Yugoslavia
SIDA	Swedish International Development Agency
TMG	Truce Monitoring Group
TRC	Truth and Reconciliation Commission (South Africa)
UÇK	Ushtria Çlirimtare e Kosovës – see KLA
UNCHR	United Nations Commission on Human Rights
UNDP	United Nations Development Programme
UNESC	United Nations Economic and Social Council
UNHCHR	United Nations High Commissioner for Human Rights
UNHCR	United Nations High Commissioner for Refugees
UNHRC	United Nations Human Rights Council
UNIMK	United Nations Interim Mission in Kosovo
UPEACE	University for Peace
VJ	Vojska Jugoslavije (Yugoslav Army)
VOM	Victim–offender mediation
WHO	World Health Organisation
WWSPIA	Woodrow Wilson School of Public and International Affairs

Notes on contributors

Ivo Aertsen is a Professor at the Catholic University of Leuven Institute of Criminology. His main fields of research and teaching are Victimology, Penology and Restorative Justice. His research and publications include studies on the psychological needs of victims of crime, victim assistance, victim–offender mediation and the relationship of restorative justice to criminal justice. He wrote a manual on victim assistance for the Belgian police service and cooperated in another one on implementing restorative justice in a prison context. Professor Aertsen has been chair of the European Forum for Restorative Justice from 2000 to 2004, and has coordinated COST Action A21 on Restorative Justice research in Europe from 2002 to 2006. He is a member of the editorial board of several journals and has acted as expert for various international organisations.

Michal Alberstein, SJD Harvard University, LLB, BA, Tel-Aviv University, is a senior lecturer at the Faculty of Law, Bar-Ilan University, Israel. She is a lecturer in jurisprudence and conflict resolution. Her current research deals with theories of law and conflict resolution; multiculturalism and its relation to negotiation and mediation; representations of conflict resolution in literature and film; trauma and memory. She is the co-editor (with Nadav Davidovich and Austin Sarat) of the book *Trauma and Memory: Reading, Healing and Making Law* (2007) which deals with collective trauma. Her book *Pragmatism and Law: From Philosophy to Disputes Resolution* (2002) deals with the intellectual roots of Alternative Dispute Resolution (ADR). Her book *A Jurisprudence of Mediation* is forthcoming. In 2001, Dr Alberstein was awarded the prestigious three-year Yigal Alon Scholarship.

Jana Arsovska is a PhD researcher in criminology at the Catholic University of Leuven in Belgium. She holds a BA in International Relations (Greece) and an MA in Criminology (Belgium). Her current research is on the role of cultural codes in the evolution of Albanian organised crime groups. She has done extensive field work in Albania, Kosovo and Macedonia. Arsovska is also a principal researcher in a project on the meaning of violence and crime in an Albanian context, coordinator of a working group within COST Action A21 on restorative justice and violent conflicts and guest lecturer in the New York University Skopje (Macedonia). She is a member of the Standing Group on Organised Crime executive committee and an editor of the SGOC newsletter. Prior to her PhD post, she has worked for the Euro-Atlantic Council of Macedonia and the European Forum for Restorative Justice.

Doina Balahur is Professor of Sociology of Law at Alexandru Ioan Cuza University of Iasi, Romania, Department of Sociology and Social Work and Director of the Research Centre for Social Management and Community Development. She carried out, as a project manager and partner, research projects within the framework of the European Programmes FP6 and FP7, the European COST Programme and the European AGIS Programme. In Romania she has developed several research projects on the Reform of Romanian Juvenile Justice, Restorative Justice and the Reform of the Justice System. Her recent publications include: *Sociology of Law* (2006); *Restorative Justice Developments in Romania and Great Britain. Sociological-juridical Enquiries and Applied Studies of Social Work*, co-edited with Brian Littlechild and Roger Smith (2007); 'Child and Childhood in Romania', in the *Greenwood Encyclopedia of Children's Issues Worldwide* (2007); and *Probation and Community Reintegration* (2004).

Sarah Ben-David is a senior lecturer at the Department of Criminology, Bar-Ilan University, and at the College of Judea and Samaria. She is a Senior Clinical Criminologist. Dr Ben-David is currently a chair of the Criminological Advisory Board to the Ministers of Justice and of Public Security. She is also a founder and chair of 'Shaal' – the Israeli Association of Victim Assistance (1980–90). During 1985–2006 she was Vice-President of the World Society of Victimology. Dr Ben-David is a chair of the professional committee of the first Israeli centre for the treatment of sex offenders in the community. She has many theoretical and research publications in the field of victimology and criminology, and continues to work on behalf of victims – in research on restorative justice and gender issues in victimisation and crime.

Haki Demolli completed his law studies at the University of Prishtina in Kosovo. He finished his PhD in the field of combating terrorism at the Department of Criminal Law in the same university. He has been working as a Professor in Criminalistics at the Faculty of Law of the University of Prishtina since 1987. In the period from September 1999 to April 2003, he worked as a legal instructor at the Kosovo Police School. Since May 2003 he is also the Director of the Kosovo Law Center in Prishtina, founded by OSCE Mission in Kosovo. Professor Demolli is the author of many academic articles published in national and international journals. He is also the author of two books: *Terrorism* (2002) and *Murders in Postwar Kosovo* (2006).

Borbala Fellegi is a PhD researcher at the ELTE University (Hungary), working on the implementation of restorative justice in Hungary. She obtained a Master's degree in social policy (ELTE University) and in criminology (University of Cambridge). As a researcher of the European Forum for Restorative Justice she was coordinating a project on the possibilities for implementing restorative justice in Central and Eastern Europe. Besides chairing the Research Committee of the European Forum for Restorative Justice, she is lecturing at the ELTE University and working as a consultant for the Hungarian Central Office of Justice in the field of victim–offender mediation. She is the vice chair of the London-based organisation 'Independent Academic Research Studies' and a board member of the National Society of Mediation in Hungary. Her publications primarily deal with the micro- and macro-level aspects of restorative justice.

Rexhep Gashi completed his PhD at the Law Faculty of the University of Prishtina (2001) on the 'Execution of Punishment with Imprisonment in Albania'. His LLM (1992) thesis was on 'Punishment Policy against Blood Delicts in Kosovo'. In 1984, he was appointed as a judge in the Minor Offences Court in Lipjan. Currently, he is professor in Criminology and Penology. He is member of the University's Senate and editor in chief of the journal for juridical and social issues *E drejta – Law*. Dr Gashi is political adviser to the Minister of Justice. In 2002, he was legal adviser at the Joint Advisory Council on Legislative Matters and leader of the working group drafting the Kosovo law on the execution of penal sanctions. Dr Gashi is author of more than thirty academic articles published in national and international journals. He is also author of two books: *Execution of Punishment of Imprisonment in Albania* (2001) and *Punitive Policy against Blood Delicts in Kosovo during the Period of 1980–1989* (2003).

Khalid Ghanayim is a lecturer on criminal law at the faculty of law, University of Haifa. Dr Ghanayim studied law (LLB and LLM) at the University of Cologne – Germany (1993), and LLD at the Hebrew University of Jerusalem (2002). He was visiting professor and researcher at the Max Planck Institute for Foreign and International Criminal Law, Freiburg – Germany, the University of Cologne – Germany, and the University of Toronto – Canada. Dr Ghanayim has published two books – *Incitement, not Sedition* (The Israel Democracy Institute, Jerusalem, 2002), and *The Law of Libel and Slander*, in Hebrew (The Harry Sacher Institute for Legislative Research and Comparative Law, Faculty of Law, The Hebrew University of Jerusalem, and IDI, 2005) – and many articles on criminal law defences, such as self-defence, necessity, the structure of the offence and the criminal liability of corporations.

Emile George Irani is director of the Africa and Middle East Programme for the Toledo International Centre for Peace in Madrid, Spain. Until June 2005, he was a professor in Peace and Conflict Studies at Royal Roads University (Canada). Prior to that, he was a policy analyst with the US Commission on International Religious Freedom, the Jennings Randolph Senior Fellow at the US Institute of Peace, and assistant professor at the Lebanese American University in Beirut. Professor Irani is the author of *The Papacy and the Middle East: The Role of the Holy See in the Arab-Israeli Conflict* (1989). He is co-editor of the books *Acknowledgment, Forgiveness and Reconciliation: Lessons from Lebanon* (1996) and *Workbook on Ethnopolitical Conflicts* (2007). He holds a *laurea* in political science from the Universitta Cattolica del Sacro Cuore (Italy) and an MA and PhD in international relations from the University of Southern California.

Roberto Beni Jakob is a psychologist and mediator. He obtained his PhD from the London School of Economics. He is a member of the Steering Committee of the European Forum of Family Mediation and was on the Management Committee of the COST Action A21 Project on Developments in Restorative Justice in Europe. He lectures in the LLM Programme for lawyers and judges in the Faculty of Law as well as in the Conflict Management Programme in the Criminology

Department at Bar-Ilan University, Israel. In 2006, he chaired the First International Conference in Israel on 'Serious Violence and Restorative Justice' in which delegates from 25 countries participated.

Olivier Kambala wa Kambala is a Congolese lawyer. He holds a postgraduate degree in law from the University of Kinshasa and has specialised training in post-conflict peacebuilding. He is currently completing a Master's degree in international criminal law. Since 2001, he has worked in the struggle against impunity in the Democratic Republic of Congo, as well as for the DRC's ratification of the Rome Statute of the International Criminal Court. He worked for two years as a programme officer with the Belgian NGO RCN – Justice et Démocratie, and as a campaigner for the UK-based Global Witness. He was also a Director of the International Center for Peace in Central Africa. Currently he works as a programme associate for the International Center for Transitional Justice, where his chief focus is on the Great Lakes Region.

Theodore Kasongo Kamwimbi is a Congolese lawyer at the Bar Association and an advocate to the Court of Appeal in Kinshasa (DRC). He holds an LLB and LLM from the University of Kinshasa (1996, 1999) and has studied further at the University of Cape Town (UCT). He was also a migrancy researcher at the Centre for Popular Memory at UCT, and is currently the coordinator of the Transitional Justice Fellows Programme at the Institute for Justice and Reconciliation (IJR) in Cape Town, South Africa. Kamwimbi has published numerous essays and newspaper articles on transitional justice and reconciliation with particular focus on the African Great Lakes Region.

Vesna Nikolic-Ristanovic is director of the Victimology Society of Serbia and Professor of Criminology at Belgrade University. She also teaches the MA Peace Studies course entitled 'Theories and Practice of Conflict Solving'. She is editor in chief of *Temida*, the Serbian journal on victimisation, human rights and gender; corresponding editor of *Feminist Review*; and member of the Advisory Board of *Contemporary Justice Review*. She has published largely on violence against women, war victimisation, restorative justice, sexual violence, and truth and reconciliation in Serbia. Her most important publications include: *Women, Violence and War* (ed., 2000), *Social Change, Gender and Violence: Post-Communist and War-Affected Societies* (2002), *From Remembering the Past to Positive Future* (2004, co-author) and *A Life on One's Own:*

Rehabilitation of Victims of Trafficking for Sexual Exploitation (2005, co-author).

Holger-C. Rohne, following his graduation in law (2001) at the University of Freiburg (Germany), became a researcher at the Max Planck Institute for Foreign and International Criminal Law (Freiburg). He obtained his PhD in law from the University of Freiburg (2007). He also received various mediation training (e.g. VOM). Dr Rohne researched and published on the interrelation between traditional and modern approaches to conflict resolution (with a special focus on the Middle East). He is particularly interested in identifying the impact of cultural influences on victims' attitudes in war-torn regions and to contrast them with existing domestic and international responsive instruments. Dr Rohne co-authored an international comparative survey among war victims in Asia, Africa and Europe. He conducted an in-depth study on intifada victims and authored the related book *Opferperspektiven im interkulturellen Vergleich – ('Victim perspectives in the intercultural comparison')*. Dr Rhone further co-authored the book *Victims of War* and co-edited the volume *Conflicts and Conflict Resolution in Middle Eastern Societies*.

Tyrone Savage is an independent consultant with a threefold commitment to teaching, writing and facilitating processes of transformation in societies seeking transition out of conflict. He teaches at Stellenbosch University in South Africa, and is currently working on projects with the International Centre for Transitional Justice, the United Nations Assistance Mission for Iraq (UNAMI) and, with the support of the French Institute of South Africa (IFAS), the *Institut des Sciences sociales du Politique* in Paris. Savage has worked in numerous African societies in transition, chiefly in the Great Lakes sub-region and southern Africa. A Fulbright Fellow, he holds degrees from Rhodes University, the University of Cape Town and the Maxwell School of Public Affairs, Syracuse University. Savage has published widely on dilemmas and strategic options in transitional societies.

Finn Tschudi is professor emeritus from University of Oslo where he has spent his professional life, teaching and writing on personality, cognitive and social psychology. After retiring in 1998 he was recruited to TRANSCEND by Johan Galtung, and then studied restorative justice in Australia. He has introduced conferencing in Norway and with Neimeyer published a chapter on conferencing: 'Community and Coherence' in 'Narrative and Consciousness', 2003,

New York: Oxford University Press, with Reichelt on suspected sexual abuse 'When Therapy is stuck: What about conferencing', Journal of Systemic Therapy, 2003, and with Galtung 'On the psychology of the TRANSCEND method', in Searching for Peace, 2002, London: Pluto Press. See further http://folk.uio.no/ftschudi

Marta Valiñas holds a graduate degree in Law (2002) from the Faculty of Law of the University of Porto (Portugal) and a European Master's Degree in Human Rights and Democratisation (2004) from the European Inter-University Centre for Human Rights and Democratisation (Venice, Italy). Her Master's thesis is on 'The Position of the Victim in Truth and Reconciliation Commissions: The Case of Peru'. She is currently working as a researcher at the Leuven Institute of Criminology, Catholic University of Leuven (Belgium) in a research project on 'Restorative Justice and Mass Victimisation: Case Studies in Serbia and Bosnia and Herzegovina' funded by the same university, where she is also a PhD candidate in Law. She has conducted extensive field research in Serbia and Bosnia and Herzegovina. Her research focus is on human rights, transitional justice and restorative justice.

Kris Vanspauwen is a PhD candidate in criminology at the Leuven Institute of Criminology, Catholic University of Leuven. He holds a Candidate (1999) and Licentiate Degree (2001) in Criminology from the Catholic University of Leuven. He has studied at the University of Regina (2000–1) and obtained accredited training in conflict resolution from the Justice Department of Saskatchewan (2000). He has worked as a victim–offender mediator at Suggnomè – the Forum for Victim Offender Mediation and Restorative Justice in Flanders. Before that, he was the chief researcher in a four-year project funded by the Research Foundation – Flanders on mass victimisation and restorative justice, with a case study in South Africa. In the framework of this project he has been visiting the School of Government, University of Western Cape (2003), the Department of Social Work and Criminology, University of Pretoria (2004), and the Institute for Criminology, University of Cape Town (2005).

Explanation of the COST Organisation

COST – the acronym for European **CO**operation in the field of **S**cientific and **T**echnical Research – is the oldest and widest European intergovernmental network for cooperation in research. Established by the Ministerial Conference in November 1971, COST is presently used by the scientific communities of 35 European countries to cooperate in common research projects supported by national funds.

The funds provided by COST – less than 1 per cent of the total value of the projects – support the COST cooperation networks (COST Actions) through which, with only around €20 million per year, more than 30,000 European scientists are involved in research having a total value which exceeds €2 billion per year. This is the financial worth of the European added value which COST achieves.

A 'bottom up approach' (the initiative of launching a COST Action comes from the European scientists themselves), 'à la carte participation' (only countries interested in the Action participate), 'equality of access' (participation is open also to the scientific communities of countries not belonging to the European Union) and 'flexible structure' (easy implementation and light management of the research initiatives) are the main characteristics of COST.

As precursor of advanced multidisciplinary research COST has a very important role for the realisation of the European Research Area (ERA) anticipating and complementing the activities of the Framework Programmes, constituting a 'bridge' towards the scientific communities of emerging countries, increasing the mobility of researchers across Europe and fostering the establishment of 'Networks of Excellence' in many key scientific domains such as: Biomedicine and Molecular

Biosciences; Food and Agriculture; Forests, their Products and Services; Materials, Physics and Nanosciences; Chemistry and Molecular Sciences and Technologies; Earth System Science and Environmental Management; Information and Communication Technologies; Transport and Urban Development; Individuals, Society, Culture and Health. It covers basic and more applied research and also addresses issues of pre-normative nature or of societal importance.

Web: www.cost.esf.org

ESF provides the COST Office through an EC contract

COST is supported by the EU RTD Framework programme

Part I

Introduction

Chapter 1

Challenging restorative justice – state-based conflict, mass victimisation and the changing nature of warfare

Holger-C. Rohne, Jana Arsovska and Ivo Aertsen[1]

There is no lasting hope in violence, only temporary relief from hopelessness.

Kingman Brewster Jr

Violence and conflict have always been part of human experience in one form or another and their destructive impact can be observed all over the world. However, some nineteenth-century utopian social philosophers, for example, harboured the hope that a future without war, violence and crime might be realised. Unfortunately this hope did not come about in the twentieth century (Friedrichs 1998a). The twentieth century has often been depicted as a 'post-imperial epoch', because it witnessed the collapse of the Habsburg, Ottoman, Hohenzollern, Ch'ing, British and Russian Empires. However, these splinterings have not been the end of the matter since the nationalistic spirit moved on further to divide countries (Spencer 1998: 7; Bianchini 1996: 188). Even so, many academics have argued that the Cold War period – the late 1940s to the late 1980s – often referred to as the 'Long Peace' was exceptionally stable (Human Security Report 2005: 22; Gaddis 1989). Although during this time the world indeed experienced a long period of unremitting peace between the traditional 'great powers', this trend did not mirror reality in the developing world. From the beginning of the Cold War to the early 1990s, the number of armed conflicts in developing countries rose dramatically (Human Security Report 2005: 22; Cranna 1994: xvii; Friedrichs 1998a).

Thus, seen globally and over a long period of time, we live in an increasingly violent and precarious world (see Table 1.1). Apparently the century that has just ended was the most violent that humanity has ever experienced. It has been characterised by extraordinarily high levels of war, violence and related crimes (Friedrichs 1998a). Although one should take statistical data with the necessary caution, numbers show that nearly three times as many people were killed in conflict in the twentieth century than in the previous four centuries together (Human Development Report 2005: 153). Strikingly enough, states have been complicit in a disproportionate share of such destructive activity (Friedrichs 1998a; Proall 1898; Horowitz 1989; Barak 1990; Kauzlarich *et al.* 1992; Cohen 1993, 1996).

Hence, it is the challenging task of the authors of this book to acknowledge the enormous costs that large-scale state-based conflicts[2] have on human lives and development and to search for constructive ways to deal with them. Restorative justice is a possible way – one that has attracted a great deal of scholarly attention in a very short period of time – to deal with conventional crimes (Aertsen *et al.* 2006; Daly 2004: 500); however, the potentials for this justice practice have not been explored in the context of large-scale violence and mass victimisation. Therefore, after presenting in this first chapter the main aims and methods of this book, the authors aim to investigate restorative justice possibilities in several (post-)conflict regions, by drawing on various local informal and formal practices for dealing with violent conflicts. In short, the book aims to examine if, how and to which extent restorative justice is applicable to large-scale violent conflicts in different cultural, social, political and historical contexts

Table 1.1 An overview of (armed) conflict-related deaths in the last five centuries

Period	Conflict-related deaths (millions)	World population, mid-century (millions)	Conflict-related deaths as share of world population (%)
Sixteenth century	1.6	493.3	0.32
Seventeenth century	6.1	579.1	1.05
Eighteenth century	7.0	757.4	0.92
Nineteenth century	19.4	1, 172.9	1.65
Twentieth century	109.7	2, 519.5	4.35

Sources: Human Development Report (2005: 153 table 5.1).

and whether commonalities can be identified within the different regions under analysis.

State-based crime: definitions and other challenges

Despite the fact that far more violence has been carried out in the name of states – and far more property has been destroyed – than can be ascribed to conventional offenders, state crime, as well as state-based crime,[3] is not yet a major focus of criminological investigation. According to David O. Friedrichs (1998a), the call for more criminological attention particularly to state crime is recent (Harding 1998; Chambliss 1989; Cohen 1998), although not entirely new (Proall 1998). Several criminologists have published books on political crime (Roebuck and Weeber, 1978; Ingraham 1979; Tunnell 1993; Hagan 1997; Friedrichs 1998a, 1998b) and attempts have also been made by authors from other disciplines to understand state wrongdoings (Comfort 1950; Wolfe 1973; Becker and Murray 1971; Douglas and Johnson; 1977; Macfarlane 1974). If the potential harm of state(-based) crime overshadows other forms of crime, then the challenge to criminologists should be apparent. This is one of the reasons why this book looks at the potentials of applying restorative justice practice – which, besides being part of other scientific disciplines, is also a criminological topic – to state-based crimes.

Nevertheless, it is frequently accepted that the conceptual and methodological issues in the area of state-based crimes are very daunting (Friedrichs 1998a). This links closely to the nature of the topic itself which is highly complex and sensitive and which opens a lot of definitional dilemmas. The problems of bias, establishing 'truth', double standards and 'political power' are particularly relevant in the ideological realm of state-based crimes. It is often challenging if not impossible to determine whether a state acts as aggressor or justifiably tries to defend its sovereignty and citizens against opposing military or paramilitary forces. Concepts such as state crime, political crime, genocide, politicide, terror, rebel actions, human rights violations and 'legitimate' military, diplomatic and domestic initiatives of sovereign states are intertwined in very complex ways, which is an obstacle for the methodical study of these sensitive phenomena. Interestingly, for example, international organisations collect statistics from governments on various issues; however, there is no official data on armed conflicts or human rights abuses (Human Security Report 2005: 19). Also, the challenges involved in effectively preventing or responding to state crime are enormous and they initially link to the difficulty of exposing such crimes in the first place; hence, many have argued that the immediate exposure of state crimes is very improbable (Markovits and Silverstein 1988; Friedrichs 1998a). Moreover, concepts such as 'terrorism' and 'terrorist' are also often not terms of scientific classification. They are rather imprecise and emotive; therefore, they are a source for many injustices, double standards and manipulations of present systems and regimes (O'Brien 1983). 'One man's terrorist is another man's freedom fighter' is the aphorism that strikingly illustrates this definitional problem. Having acknowledged obvious limitations, we do not intend to enter greatly into various ongoing definitional debates, but merely to explore the relevance of restorative justice principles in the context of state-based crimes using well-accepted pre-existing definitions.

Conflict trends and consequences in the bloodiest century

As noted above towards the end of the twentieth century there had been a drastic increase in state-based conflicts which in fact led to the occurrence of various state-based crimes. But what does this mean in terms of numbers and human development costs? More than fifteen years after the end of the Cold War there is still a general perception that the world is becoming more dangerous. According to public opinion polls from rich countries, this perception is linked to fears of terrorist threats as anti-state activities. However, although very significant, such attacks lead to a distorted perception of the distribution of human insecurity. For example, since 1998 'terrorism' has been responsible for approximately 20,000 fatalities globally (Human Development Report 2005: 151; UNDP 1990: 61). At the same time humanitarian tragedies such as the state-based conflicts in the Democratic Republic of the Congo (DRC) and the Darfur region of Sudan glimmer only sporadically into world news reports although they are claiming victims on a scale that dwarfs the threats facing people in industrialised countries (Human Development Report 2005: 151). In order to clarify the picture and to assess the role of states we need to examine the relation between human insecurity and conflict trends which can be interpreted in both a positive and a negative light.

Surprisingly enough, the last decade of the twentieth century witnessed a reduction of conflicts. In the early 1990s, the number of conflicts worldwide rose considerably, several wars flared in the former Soviet Union. A few years after the collapse of the Soviet Union there were more regional conflicts and civil wars than at any other time this past century (Cranna 1994). However, statistics show that from a high of 51 state-based conflicts in 1991–92 there were only 29 ongoing conflicts in 2003 (Human Development Report 2005: 153; Human Security Report 2005: 22; Kiza *et al.* 2006: 28). Although the number of conflicts in general has declined, various studies point out that the wars of the last two decades have exacted an extremely large toll in human lives (Kiza *et al.* 2006: 40).

Genocide, which the UN Genocide Convention defines as 'acts committed with intent to destroy, in whole or part, a national, ethnical, racial or religious group' and other mass murders[4] have killed enormous numbers of people in the twentieth century (Churchill 1986; Harrf and Gurr 1996; Breton and Wintrobe 1986; Friedrichs 1998a; Charny 1986; Smith 1995; Rummel 1995).[5] The Rwandan genocide in 1994 killed almost one million people and the civil war in the DRC killed approximately seven per cent of the population which amounts to nearly four million deaths. In Sudan a two-decade long civil war took more than two million lives and displaced six million people. The 1990s also saw ethnic cleansing in the heart of Europe as violent civil conflicts swept the Balkans. The ongoing bloody conflict in the Middle East is another tragedy of enormous significance. In general, it could be observed that the geographical pattern of conflict has changed over time, with a shift in security risks towards the poorest countries and also towards civilian targets (Human Development Report 2005: 153–4).

With regard to the burden of warfare for the civilian population, it could be observed that the latter in fact has become the focus of the armed struggle: whereas during the First World War the ratio between soldiers killed and civilians was nine to one, it was reversed at the end of the twentieth century with nine civilian fatalities to one killed combatant (Rohne 2006a: 80; Gutmann and Rieff 1999: 10). Hence, large-scale violent conflicts and mass victimisation have indeed become a gruesome reality with devastating consequences for millions of people, including children,[6] living in poor and troublesome regions (Singer 2005). Moreover, each major conflict from the last 60 years, such as Algeria, Korea, Vietnam, Congo and Sudan, has killed between 400,000 and two million people, amounting to more than 45 million deaths. About 78 per cent of them are identified as civilians and only 15 per cent as combatants, although these numbers are difficult to verify. According to the World Health Organisation (WHO), the estimated number of war-related deaths in the year 2000 was 310,000 of which almost 20 per cent were caused by war-related violence (Krug *et al.* 2002: 9–10; Human Security Report 2005: 30).

It is estimated that in 1950 each conflict killed 38,000 people on average (battle-deaths per conflict), but by 2002, this number dropped to 600 (Human Security Report 2005: 31; Lacina and Gleditsch 2005; see also Table 1.2[7]). These numbers have led many people to believe that wars and conflicts in the world are rapidly declining. In 2003, however, the war in Iraq and the genocidal conflict in Sudan – among the most striking examples – have again marked an increase in war victims. Around 27,000 Iraqis and Americans have died in Iraq alone as a result of continued insurgency, although the conventional war ended in 2003 (Human Security Report 2005).

In addition to the war death estimates, about 25 million people are currently internally displaced because of conflict or human rights violations and 18 million have become refugees abroad (Cranna 1994). Nine of the ten countries ranked at the bottom in the human development index (HDI) have experienced violent conflict at some point since 1990 (Human Development Report 2005: 15). In the period 1990–2003 low-income countries accounted for more than half of the countries and territories that experienced violent conflict.[7] Meanwhile, even though the number of conflicts has declined, it is a fact that today's wars last longer and, as a consequence, their impact on human development is much more severe (Human Development Report 2005: 154).

From the figures mentioned so far, it can easily be deduced that state-based large-scale violent conflict imposes extremely high human costs. Besides these immediate costs, violent conflict disrupts whole

Table 1.2 War death estimates

Year	WHO	Lacina and Gleditsch (2005)
1998	588,000	97,893
1999	269,000	134,242
2000	310,000 (changed to 235,000)	99,536
2001	230,000	42,068
2002	172,000	19,368

Note: WHO war death tolls are higher than the Lacina and Gleditsch (2005) figures.
Source: Human Security Report (2005: figure 1.7).

societies and obliterates human development gains (UN Millennium Project 2005; Human Development Report 2005: 155).[9] There are also costs which are less visible and less easy to capture in figures, i.e. collapsing food systems, disintegration of health and education services and lost income. The World Health Organisation (Krug *et al.* 2002: 3) explains that the cost of violence translates into billons of US dollars in annual health care expenditures alone. In addition, psychological stress, shame, rage and trauma also have enormous negative implications for human development, although these corollaries of conflict are often left to one side since countries lack appropriate mechanisms and institutions to deal with them. Hence statistics alone cannot reflect the full costs of such horrors (Human Development Report 2005: 154; Scheff and Retzinger 2001; Flournoy and Pan 2002).

Conflict and identity

One of the questions that deserves close attention is why it is that people kill each other in the name of their community, religion or nation, and what the world is doing – or can do – about it. As Bethany Lacina and Nils Petter Gleditsch (2005) point out in their comprehensive analysis of post-Second World War battle-deaths, 'the most cataclysmic battles of the past half century were related to the now defunct ideological polarization between East and West' (Human Security Report 2005: 31). Subsequently the late 1980s and 1990s have been marked by two mutually contradictory trends. The first is an increasing cultural, economic, environmental and political integration through 'globalisation' and the formation of international political structures such as the European Union. The second is the upsurge in separatist movements that aspire to partition states based on differences in ideological, ethnic, religious and/or cultural beliefs (Bjelic and Savic 2002; Spencer 1998; Friedrichs 1998a; Smith 1995).

Governments nowadays are challenged to provide reasonably equal opportunities to people. Among the most fundamental abuses by oppressive governments are denial of religious and cultural traditions and practices. According to some thinkers such as Huntington (1996), in the post-Cold War world the most important distinctions among peoples are cultural. People define themselves in terms of ancestry, religion, languages, history, values, customs and institutions. They identify with cultural groups, tribes, ethnic groups, religions, communities, nations and, at the broadest level, civilisations. When governments deny basic human rights to groups of people and do not recognise their 'cultural identity', then people often resort to political violence (Spencer 1998; Huntington 1996; Bjelic and Savic 2002).

In recent years, conflict reasons were almost unexceptionally attached to ethnic (or ethno-political) problems:[10] at least one conflict party claimed that its ethnicity was the reason for discrimination and oppression of its members by the opposing (ethnic) group (Wolff 2006; Huntington 1996). Today almost half the wars going on in the world are linked to ethnicity and nationalistic ideologies,[11] and are struggles for secession. According to some scholars Northern Ireland, Kosovo, Cyprus, the Israeli–Palestinian dispute, the genocide in Rwanda, the civil war in the DRC, Kashmir and Sri Lanka are all, in one way or another, ethnic conflicts since their causes and consequences became apparently ethnicised (Wolff 2006: 2; Smith 1995). Newspapers also very often refer to ethnically defined 'nations' that claim entitlement to 'self-determination' in a 'homeland' of their own (Spencer 1998: 7). In the course of such struggles for exclusive possessions, many lives have been lost. Since ethnicity is a vague concept, other scholars favour the more general term 'identity-based conflict', especially in the case of Kosovo and Israel–Palestine (Kriesberg 2003).

Hence state-based crimes are closely linked to identity (ethnic, cultural and otherwise). Some claim that differences in culture can form the basis for deep psychological distrust or enmity (Connor 1994; Horowitz 1995; Huntington 1993a, 1993b, 1996). Others emphasise how cultural differences inhibit effective communication, leading to misunderstandings and violence (Cederman 2001a, 2001b; Comor 2001; Johnston 2001). Still others see identity as an important cue for collective action (Barth 1969; Hardin 1995; Hechter 1987; Wendt 1992). Group relations may also lead to tensions, in particular when a given group is dominant in one state but politically repressed in another (Moore and Davis 1997; Moore 2002). Moreover, Huntington (1996: 28) suggests that large cultural differences divide groups, whereas Bateson (1979: 98) argues that if familiarity breeds contempt, it is often the smaller differences among many similarities that are more likely to 'make a difference'. Although the debate on identity and conflicts is a never-ending one, many have concluded that identity formation can both exacerbate and ameliorate threats (Gartzke and Gleditsch 2006: 54). However, the way we approach and treat those threats is what might bring difference in the long run.

In the search for reasons why people enter war, a quote from a famous Venetian nationalist demagogue, Dead Lagoon, has been revived: '"There can be no true friends without true enemies". Unless we hate what we are not, we cannot love what we are' (Huntington 1996: 20). Although this statement is worth discussion, it does not necessarily hold the ultimate truth. Direct dialogue gives people the opportunity to learn more about their own self and also about the other. Negative stereotypings can be deconstructed and monolithic self-representation can be replaced by a more complex understanding of the self. By discovering opposing aspects in one's self as well as similarities between the self and the other, a process of re- and deconstruction of the view of the other can be achieved (Bar-On 2005: 184). An entire research tradition renders plausible the idea that interaction with others in cross-cutting networks might reduce antagonistic feelings toward other groups within the population (Mutz 2002: 111–14) and promote tolerance (Verba *et al.* 1995: 506). Empirical research suggests that repeated interaction between people holding different convictions, or having different cultural, ethnic or religious status, will increase one's capacity to understand the perspective of opponents and thus will reduce prejudice towards that group (Allport 1954; Duckitt 1992; Sniderman *et al.* 2000). Interaction and the reconstruction of identities are highly relevant since today's 'nation-state' is often characterised by multicultural facets. In fact, centres of civilisation have always been multicultural regions where people from diverse backgrounds meet and stimulate each other through example and dialogue. Unfortunately, today cultural differences are often used by political agitators and leaders to stimulate collective stereotyping, division and hostilities. This leaves the respective societies with the danger of new intergroup conflicts as well as the revival of 'old' intergroup tensions if these conflicts were not effectively and constructively dealt with.

In recent decades there has been some research done in the field of 'long-term' prevention of state crime and armed conflict (Friedrichs 1998b; Beres 1989; Dadrian 1988; Freeman 1991; Turk 1981; Weitzer 1993; Hope 1987; Grabosky 1990), as well as on policing state crime (Walsh 1994; Buenaventura 1995) and the adjudication of state criminals (Colwill 1995; Chaney 1995; Huyse 1995). However, the policing of state crimes and imprisoning state criminals or 'terrorists' is obviously – at least according to several authors in this book – not enough for dealing with complex large-scale conflicts. Some research has been also done trying to assess the role of the international community in responding, exposing and dealing with state-based armed conflicts and state crimes (Finch 1947; Dugard 1991; Gayner 1977; Meron 1995; Friedrichs 1998b). Some believe that the role of the international community in (post-)conflict situations is crucial (Reisman 1990; Smith 1998; see Ramet 2005 on debates about intervention); others think it causes more damage than good (Koskenniemi 2001; Burg and Shoup 1999; Chomsky 2002; Jackson 2000). Authors in subsequent chapters reflect on these and other sensitive issues – subjects of a great political debate.

Nevertheless – besides the different positions – it is worth noting that in general the past decade of international experience in post-conflict assistance suggests that substantial gaps exist in the ability of the international community to assist in these areas as well as to develop an integrated strategy to promote justice and reconciliation as well as to address grievances in hope of forging a more peaceful feature (Flournoy and Pan 2002: 1). The eruption of lawlessness, corruption and crime that often accompanies post-conflict vacuums can undermine all gains that international assistance makes. Assistance to establish justice must also be timely in order to be effective. Indeed, this area has been one of poor performance, if not outright failure, in many interventions (Flournoy and Pan 2002: 1).

If one just takes the situation in the Balkans, one might assume that 'peace' has been achieved. However, how fragile this 'peace' is, it is demonstrated by the continuous eruption of violence – for example in Kosovo – and the helpless responses of the international community[12] (UNMIK). It is sad to observe that almost a century after the First World War and more than a decade after the Dayton agreement (1995), there is a 'real risk of an explosion of Kosovo, an implosion of Serbia and new fractures in the foundations of Bosnia and Macedonia' (International Commission 2005: 8). Despite the large scale of assistance efforts in the Balkans, the international community has failed to offer convincing perspectives to the societies from these regions (International Commission 2005: 8; Flournoy and Pan 2002). The UN, for example, currently spends $4.47 billion a year on all its worldwide peacekeeping operations and the US spends $5.6 billion a month for the occupation in Iraq as well as $420.7 billion per year on arms (Human Security Report 2005: 39–40; Cranna 1994: xv).[13] The main question is what have these enormous spendings achieved? The Balkan Commission acknowledges that there are no quick and easy solutions for the Balkans (as well as other regions) and that, ultimately, it is up to the people of the region – through constructive dialogues and over a longer period of time – to win their own future (International Commission 2005: 8).

Most importantly, politicians and policy-makers tend to forget that innocent people are trapped in between violent and inhumane conflicts and that post-conflict societies often lack mechanisms and institutions for upholding the rule of law and dealing with past abuses. The problem is that these victimised people might have difficulties proceeding with their lives after substantial harm has been inflicted upon them or on people around them. Particular sequences of negative emotions underline aggression: shame is evoked, which leads to rage and violence. Sadly enough the denial of shame is institutionalised in modern societies which might be very destructive and cause further aggression and violence (Scheff and Retzinger 2001: 3). Hence, in these hyper-dynamic times where every country is trying to find its place in the 'global village', 'ordinary' people remain the main victims of political and other injustices. Ignorant behaviour can be tremendously harmful in the long run since it is the potential cause for additional conflicts. Working through the past seems necessary in order to face violent history in the light of a non-violent future. This implies the inclusion of those who suffered from the violent past to overcome their hostile picture of the other and calm the desire to respond to the past in a potentially violent manner. But can this be achieved? If so, how and under which circumstances can this be done?

Challenging and defining restorative justice

Until now the discussion on restorative justice has been mainly concerned with responses to conventional crimes and interpersonal conflicts. Victim–offender mediation, family group conferences and sentencing circles are the prototypes of restorative justice in Western industrialised countries (Aertsen *et al.* 2004: 18–20; Bazemore and Umbreit 2001). Initiated in the 1970s, victim–offender mediation and other restorative justice models expanded considerably towards the late 1990s. A slow but sustainable process of official recognition accompanied this 'alternative' movement. National and international NGOs played a leading role in these developments, resulting in the official adoption of restorative justice principles and methods by international and intergovernmental institutions. The most active in this respect has been the Council of Europe, mainly by promulgating recommendations, resolutions and official statements on restorative justice since the mid-1980s. A milestone has been the adoption of the Committee of Ministers' Recommendation No. R(99)19 'concerning mediation in penal matters' (Council of Europe 2000). This recommendation has been influential on the contents and the wording of the UN Basic Principles on restorative justice programmes. The Explanatory Memorandum with the Council of Europe Recommendation contextualises the emergence of mediation towards the end of the twentieth century as:

> [...] a new type of conflict resolution [...] rivalling the traditional approach of legal settlement. Consensual models of conflict resolution are being propagated as alternatives to the classical pattern of confrontation. This development is not restricted to a particular jurisdiction or a particular branch of the law. Rather, it touches on every legal domain and proliferates in most legal systems. (Council of Europe 2000: 11)

But the Explanatory Memorandum also reminds us that consensual models of conflict resolution are not at all new. Indeed, current restorative justice practices and theories often refer to their historical roots and precursors (Weitekamp 1999), as they also – at least partly – tend to draw on their (complex) relationship with non-western legal cultures, indigenous practices and customary law (Cunneen 2007; UN Handbook 2006: 29–31). Finally, the high degree of acceptance of restorative justice programmes at the political level has been demonstrated most powerfully within the European Union, where the – binding – Council Framework Decision of 15 March 2001 on the standing of victims in criminal proceedings determined in its Article 10 that each member state must promote mediation in criminal cases 'for offences which it considers appropriate for this sort of measure'.[14]

Let us briefly review some common characteristics of restorative justice models briefly. According to the *UN Handbook on Restorative Justice Programmes* (UN Handbook 2006: 6), restorative justice is a way of responding to criminal behaviour by balancing the needs of the community, the victims and the offenders. It is an evolving concept to problem-solving that includes the victim, the offender, their social networks, justice agencies and the community (Marshall 1999: 5; Restorative Justice Consortium 1998: 3). In various – not in all – countries and societies the idea of community involvement enjoys a large consensus. Therefore these approaches may serve to strengthen the capacity of the existing justice system but may also challenge this system due to their informal and horizontal character, the personal and comprehensive involvement of conflict stakeholders and the openness to minority or deviant points of view.

Restorative justice programmes are based on the fundamental principle that criminal behaviour not only violates law, but also injures victims and the community and, therefore, both victims and offenders should be engaged in a process addressing the consequences of the criminal behaviour (Zehr 1990; Wright 1996; Van Ness and Strong 1997). In general, restorative justice refers to a process of resolving crime by focusing on redressing the harm done to the victims, holding offenders accountable for their actions and, eventually, also engaging the community in the resolution of that conflict. Participation of the parties is an essential part of the process that emphasises relationship building, reconciliation and the development of agreements around a desired outcome between victims and offenders. Most importantly restorative justice processes can be adapted to various cultural contexts and to the needs of the different communities (UN Handbook 2006: 6).

More specifically, restorative justice programmes in the subsequent contributions in this book will have the same meaning as defined in the UN Basic Principles on the Use of Restorative Justice Programmes in Criminal Matters (hereafter 'UN Basic Principles'), as adopted in 2002 under Resolution 2002/12 by the UN Economic and Social Council.[15] There, a *restorative justice programme* is defined as: 'any programme that uses restorative processes and seeks to achieve restorative outcomes'. The focus is clearly on participatory processes. A *restorative process* is defined as 'any process in which the victim and the offender, and where appropriate, any other individual or community members affected by a crime, participate together actively in the resolution of matters arising from the crime, generally with the help of a facilitator'. Restorative justice regards the process as equally important as the outcome. According to the UN Basic Principles, a *restorative outcome* is an agreement reached as a result of a restorative process. The agreement may include referrals to programmes such as reparation, restitution, and community services 'aimed at meeting the individual and collective needs and responsibilities of the parties and achieving the reintegration of the victim and the offender' (UN Handbook 2006: 7). This approach presupposes a certain degree of voluntariness, since participation in the process cannot be forced. However, there is some discussion in restorative justice literature on the necessarily voluntary or consensual character of a restorative justice outcome. According to Walgrave (2007: 564–6), a system of restorative justice should also apply when confronted with non-cooperative offenders; he argues that in such a case coercive reparative sanctions (e.g. imposed restitution or community service) must be possible, be it under strict legal control.

Moreover, the debate on restorative justice is also challenged by the question of its applicability to acts of violence occurring in the course of state-based large-scale conflicts. As indicated above, these conflicts are mainly of an intrastate nature and are labelled as 'new wars'. One of their main characteristics is the ubiquity of victimisation they produce among socially or regionally interwoven communities. The devastating effects on intergroup relations produce a deep mistrust towards the 'other' collective and its members. Looking at the aftermath of violence it is evident that restoration is needed, but restoration of what? The spontaneous answer may focus on 'peace' that has to be restored. However, what does the restoration of peace mean then? The absence of violence probably does not suffice. What role does the paradigm of *restorative justice* play in this process? Is it simply a synonym for peacemaking or peacebuilding? It is argued here that restorative justice describes a distinctive approach. As such it is not identical with but may contribute to the multifaceted and comprehensive process of peacebuilding.

Restorative justice in the context of large-scale conflicts

Various terms evolved in the context of responding to (post-)conflict situations. They often share a restorative goal. However these terms have to be clearly distinguished from a restorative justice approach. In the following we contrast restorative justice with other concepts existing in the context of responding to (post-)conflict situations, namely peacebuilding, restorative practices and transitional justice.

Restorative justice and peacebuilding

As outlined by various scholars such as John Braithwaite (2002) and John Paul Lederach (1997), a response to collective conflicts requires the healing of these societies:

> As the endeavors of the Truth and Reconciliation Commission in South Africa and those of a number of other nations now demonstrate, 'working' in terms of healing a nation is more important than working simply conceived as reducing crime. At a more micro level, 'working' as healing a workplace after sexual harassment [...], a school after bullying [...], and a family after violence [...] are exceptionally important outcomes [...]. Finally, to conceive 'working' in the traditional criminological way of reducing crime forgets victims. We conclude [...] that

> restorative justice mostly works well in granting justice, closure, restoration of dignity, transcendence of shame, and healing for victims. (Braithwaite 2002: 69)

Obviously, 'healing' is a multilayered process that cannot be imposed upon people. It describes a complex process. Some of its components concern aspects of 'peacebuilding' that include a wide range of inner and outer measures such as political agreements, judicial proceedings, amnesty, societal rapprochement, reconciliation, etc.

In the South African Community Peace Programme based on the so-called Zwelethemba model, 'peace committees' made up of local township residents undertake both peacemaking and peacebuilding (Shearing 2001; Skelton 2007). In this approach, *peacemaking* focuses on problem-solving with respect to an ongoing dispute, in order to find a solution (peace) with respect to that specific conflict. *Peacebuilding* refers to problem-solving with respect to more generic issues, and addresses underlying problems in the community, such as poverty and lack of access to services. Thus, the latter concerns more 'sustaining the process of peacemaking and peacebuilding over time'. It broadens the approach from a conflict model to a model of governance which is based on the use of local knowledge and capacity.

Restorative justice in its conventional understanding is concerned with responding to a particular interpersonal incident. In this sense restorative justice is much narrower and specific than the complex approach of peacebuilding; it relates more to peacemaking. Certainly, restorative justice might contribute to peacebuilding as well. In this case, however, it constitutes only one aspect or – metaphorically speaking – a 'tool in a tool-box' that contributes to the pursuit of overall peace. In short, in line with the philosophy of the UN Basic Principles and the Council of Europe Recommendation No. R(99)19, restorative justice can be regarded as an interpersonal response to a particular (violent) incident on the micro-level.

Restorative justice and restorative practices

Various programmes in post-conflict situations deal with the restoration of intergroup relations that suffered due to the overall conflict, such as encounter programmes. By analogy with the term launched by Ted Wachtel (USA) in the context of pedagogical and social interventions,[16] we suggest categorising such programmes as 'restorative practices'. Since the aim of restorative practices in the context of large-scale conflicts is to set up intergroup relations they are generally not focused on particular violent incidents. Here lies a major difference to traditional restorative justice programmes: the latter start from a particular (deviant) incident and deal only in second order with the general consequences of previous interpersonal or intergroup relations.

Training and evaluation of restorative practices in more classic settings such as schools, workplaces or neighbourhoods have resulted in comparative studies of various models (different types of mediation and conferencing etc.) that are based on criteria such as the 'degree of restorativeness' (Wachtel and McCold 2001) or focused on a 'restorative typology' (Hopkins 2006). The potential of restorative practices goes beyond resolving specific incidents by providing 'a general social mechanism for the reinforcement of standards of appropriate behaviour' (Wachtel and McCold 2001: 114). By doing so, social discipline policies are restructured on the basis of various degrees of control that can be exercised on the one hand, and support that can be given on the other hand. This results in a continuum of restorative practices in 'everyday life', from the very informal (affective statements between conflict parties) to the most formal (conferences in the presence of officials) (Wachtel and McCold 2001).

Restorative justice and transitional justice

In recent decades various mechanisms have emerged at a national and international level stemming from the effort to build effective and just states in a post-conflict era. These approaches have been labelled transitional justice mechanisms and are part of the search for an appropriate response to mass violence. The main approaches of transitional justice include the provision of prosecution, truth telling, reconciliation, institutional reform and reparations (Boraine 2004).[17]

Transitional justice mechanisms – starting with the South African Truth and Reconciliation Commission – are increasingly inspired by restorative justice thinking. Some truth commissions – as the primary example hereof – have offered an opportunity for (more or less mediated) encounters between victims and perpetrators, and were asked to provide recommendations for a meaningful reparation policy. In the East Timor's Community Reconciliation Programme, for example, perpetrators were asked to make amends to the victims; in return the conditions for their reintegration in the community would be created. Although these processes also refer to restorative justice principles, transitional justice cannot simply be equated with it.

Restorative justice processes – as outlined in the UN Basic Principles – are generally understood as being focused on direct communication and making amends at the interpersonal level. Although inspired by restorative justice paradigms, transitional justice mechanisms often carry a notion of being a top-down instrument applied on a societal level and implemented as an alternative to or supplement to criminal justice response as another top-down instrument. It usually offers thereby a range of options to deal with the collective and the violent past. Restorative justice, instead, is a voluntary process which all parties chose to participate in and from which they can withdraw at each stage without negative consequences. Although the implementation of restorative justice mechanisms can be promoted by top-down measures – e.g. by the lawmakers – a main characteristic of restorative justice is the voluntary participation of the parties.

It is the view at different levels – namely the individual and societal respectively – that mainly distinguishes restorative justice approaches from those of transitional justice. Transitional justice mechanisms offer a more global framework wherein a particular incident and the response to it must be placed.

Understanding restorative justice in the context of large-scale conflicts

Summing up, restorative justice is not a synonym for peacebuilding although it can certainly contribute to it – and therefore may be regarded as a part of it. In contrast to restorative practices, restorative justice is not primarily focused on repairing dysfunctional relations between members of collectives; again, a successful restorative justice process is likely to contribute to relational aspects between members of the opposing collectives due to its communicative process and the development of a consensual agreement. Restorative justice is typically a bottom-up approach and is basically concerned with the reparation of harm caused by a particular incident. The major challenge posed to restorative justice in the context of large-scale conflicts is the fact that the incident at the micro-level cannot be isolated from its more general – historical, political and social – context. In such cases, a violent incident is strongly embedded in – and therefore part of – the conflict at the macro-level. Consequently the macro conflict influences the perception as well as the resolution of the particular incident.

Due to the origin of restorative justice as a means to solve interpersonal disputes, it becomes evident that it has to be redefined in the context of large-scale conflicts, taking into account the fundamental principles, values and content of conventional restorative justice theory. In order to understand or conceptualise restorative justice in the context of large-scale conflicts, we need to reconsider and broaden up some of its constituent elements. The direct or indirect involvement of stakeholders in genocidal events for example, the non-reaction of the silent majority and the indifference of the international community will result in different notions of 'responsibility' and 'accountability'. In cases of collective conflicts and mass victimisation the notion of 'restoration' will have a particular meaning as well, referring to different levels of restoration encompassing both the interpersonal or micro-level and the collective or macro-level. The same counts for the restorative justice principle of 'active participation', which requires some (practical) rethinking. Further charactistics will be the subject of discussion in the subsequent contributions.

The aim of the present book is limited to the further development of a micro-level theory of restorative justice when placed in the context of large-scale conflicts. At the end of this study, we will examine also, whether this exploration has some relevance for a further elaboration of basic elements of restorative justice as it is applied in common crime. The above mentioned UN Basic Principles on the use of restorative justice programmes in criminal matters will provide a framework for this study and for the conceptualisation of the model proposed below. Hence, the book provides a critical analysis of these principles as far as their applicability in the context of large-scale violence is concerned and invites for further exploration of restorative justice practice in common conflict situations.

Restoring justice in Kosovo, Israel–Palestine and DR Congo

After the introductory Part 1 which reflects on the relevant aspects of gross human rights violations and the response to them – including the importance and restoration of human dignity – the book focuses on three violent large-scale conflicts: the Kosovo conflict, the Israeli–Palestinian conflict and a cut-out of the complex civil war conducted in the Democratic Republic of Congo (DRC). These regions have in common violent large-scale conflicts which over the years took high numbers of civilian lives and had detrimental effects on human development. Further, they are of an intractable and protracted nature. Finally, the chosen conflict regions are very much present on the current international agenda. The selected conflict regions are also of special interest for the European Union not only because of their political significance but also in light of the increasing deployment of forces in these regions. Thus, the book aims to contribute to the actual debate on conflict resolution by discussing related questions on the basis of relevant examples. The geographical, cultural and socio-political diversity of the selected examples allow a reflection on restorative justice against different backgrounds. It ensures a deeper understanding of possibilities and limits for the implementation of restorative justice in such unique conflict settings.

Deriving from the – rather restricted and distinct – understanding of restorative justice as a means to deal with interpersonal conflicts described above, the opportunities for and limits of restorative justice approaches are explored by analysing violent incidents (micro-level) occurring in the context of the broader large-scale conflict (macro-level). For this purpose, the contributors were provided with pre-selected case studies, typically including an interrelated chain of violent incidents. These incidents, however, serve only as an example while the authors were encouraged to add further examples to their discussion. In each case the respective formal and informal justice mechanisms available are discussed by local experts. Given the fact that subjectivity is an integral part of a conflict and its resolution, where possible a subjective view is complemented by another local contribution presenting the view of the opposing conflicting party.

The contributions of the local experts are followed by a reflection on the potentials and limits of restorative justice. A *three-level model* developed by Holger-C. Rohne served as a basis for this analysis.[18] The model – thoroughly described below – is intended to facilitate the analysis of the restorative justice potential in the respective cases. It encompasses major constituents of restorative justice but is open to further extensions. The model facilitates both the section analysis as well as the concluding comparative analysis.

Conceptualising restorative justice responses: *the three-level model*

As indicated above, the following analysis of restorative justice is closely connected to the conceptual understanding outlined in the UN Basic Principles, including those approaches that deal with a particular incident and pursue a communicative process and consensual agreement between conflicting parties. Our favour of this – somewhat limited but clearly profiled – conceptualisation of restorative justice is not to deny the legitimacy of other views on restorative justice.

At the core of the three-level model is the distinction between the levels of procedure, outcome and purpose. There is no hierarchical order between these levels; on the contrary, they constitute interacting levels. Each of them contains various sub-elements as depicted in Figure 1.1. In the following, each level and its respective sub-elements are briefly discussed.[19]

Procedural level

The first level comprises various procedural elements that constitute the characteristics of a restorative justice response. To begin with, restorative justice comprises various types of procedures. These procedures share a common restorative potential but often vary in their approach and focus (see contributions in Johnstone 2003). Accordingly, the UN principles are also not limited to a particular procedure but generally address processes and programmes that share the voluntary, communicative and inclusive approach and exemplarily mention mediation, conciliation, conferencing and sentencing circles.[20] In order to discuss possible restorative justice responses in the selected case studies, we need to explore possible types of procedure that would be feasible in the particular setting. Societal acceptance of particular processes as well as culturally rooted peculiarities in informal conflict resolution mechanisms are of crucial importance. The discussion of restorative justice in the context of large-scale conflicts should avoid making the same mistake as being observed in the field of criminal justice responses (see Drumbl 2005: 170): the often underestimated potential of conflict resolution mechanisms should be carefully explored and used. The existing range of restorative justice theory easily results in a dangerous and fairly ignorant import of 'foreign' mechanisms – most likely from westernised cultural and legal backgrounds. On the other hand, external mechanisms can also be adopted and internalised by a society. A clear example for the latter is the use of Family Group Conferencing which originates in the Maori traditions and, after being 'exported' to the Western world it found increasing implementation around the globe (see contributions in Hudson *et al.* 1996; for Israeli experiences, see, Goldstein 2006: 493). In other words, each approach – whether of indigeneous or of foreign origin – needs the acceptance of and legitimacy among the respective societies; this in turn will depend on knowledge of the respective mechanism but will probably be also influenced by other aspects, such as socio-political and cultural factors. Thus the knowledge and support of various restorative justice procedures constitutes the first element of the model's procedural level.

Knowledge of and support for a particular procedure is often related to its origin. As the Preamble of the UN Basic Principles states: '[restorative justice] initiatives often draw upon traditional and indigenous forms of justice'. Indigenous practices, as they are known from the Maori and Pacific Islanders, the American Navajos, etc. are only a few examples. Among African communities traditional tribal and customary approaches to conflict resolution are still practised. Examples are the Congolese Barza or the Rwandan Gacaca system or the Acholi practice of Mato Oput in North Uganda. The same is true for various Middle Eastern societies where we can also find traditional mechanisms of conflict resolution, such as Sulha, Jirga and others. This goes without saying that most of these traditional modes of conflict resolution are also criticised as being archaic and insensitive to gender (Fares and Khalidi 2006: 521; Shalhoub-Kevorkian 2006; Wardak 2006: 364). However, these mechanisms typically describe a genuine understanding of conflicts and a cultural approach to conflict resolution; needless to say, religion often plays a significant role in their functioning. Often these mechanisms are successively institutionalised and become a part of the formal criminal justice system; this is the case, for example, with victim–offender mediation which was integrated into some European criminal justice systems. Finally, sometimes informal practices are only partially integrated into the formal criminal justice system but interact or overlap with it,

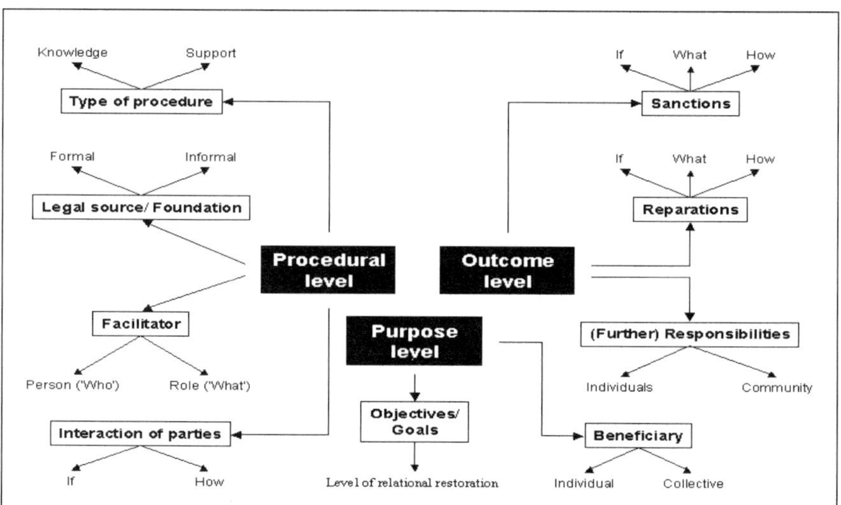

Figure 1.1 Conceptualising restorative justice – a three-level model
Source: Rohne (2006c).

e.g. in case of reparations.[21] Thus it is helpful to identify restorative elements within the different procedural (formal or informal) frameworks. It is also crucial to analyse the legitimacy and value that these frameworks presently have for the local population. Hence the differentiation between various ('legal') sources constitutes a second element on the procedural level of the model.

The third part of the procedural level is the selection and role of the facilitator. Especially in the context of large-scale conflicts and mass victimisation this is a highly sensitive issue, typically because violence occurring in these conflicts carries a strong collective notion. At the same time the opposing groups are often supported by third parties, such as foreign governments or states. Therefore it is of little surprise that even in the (track one) diplomatic sphere, the selection of a facilitator who is accepted by all sides is typically a sensitive and difficult task. Accordingly, in a restorative justice framework this becomes even more problematic due to the personal dimension and emotions in such a process. In addition, the UN Basic Principles demand that a facilitator needs to be equipped with 'a good understanding of the local cultures and communities'. For intergroup conflicts and cross-cultural settings this requirement is of special importance: the different cultural backgrounds require a sufficient consideration of other factors in the acceptance of a facilitator, such as the importance of age and gender. Closely interrelated with the selection of the facilitator is his role in the process. The UN Basic Principles require a 'fair and impartial' facilitation provided by a sufficiently qualified person (Art. I(5)) 'with due respect to the dignity of the parties' (Art. III(18)). It goes without saying that according to the particular restorative justice procedure the role of the facilitator often varies a lot. Not only the organisational or institutional context, but also cultural peculiarities shape the perception and acceptance of the facilitator. For example, in a Sulha process the acceptance of a facilitator is almost exclusively based on his social standing and age. The related authority of the facilitator goes beyond what would be accepted as a mediation mandate from a European point of view (e.g. in victim–offender mediation) (Rohne 2006b: 206).

According to Art. I(4) of the UN Basic Principles, '"*parties*" means the victim, the offender and any other individuals or community members affected by a crime who may be involved in a restorative process'. The UN Basic Principles further require a process, in which the parties 'participate together actively in the resolution of matters arising from the crime, generally with the help of a facilitator'. Thus the interaction of the parties constitutes the fourth element of the model's procedural level. Although the Basic Principles do not define the term 'together' it implies a direct cooperation between the stakeholders. But does that mean a face-to-face meeting is a precondition for a process to be called restorative? Are indirect or 'shuttle' techniques to be rejected as not restorative? What position can representatives have in cases where a collective as a whole is perceived as the enemy? And is a sentencing circle necessarily not restorative if the victim does not want to meet the offender in person? In some cultural contexts a direct encounter between the offender and the victim needs to be avoided before a settlement is reached; an untimely encounter can be perceived even as a further humiliation to the victim and would cause the confrontation to revive (for the Palestinian context, see Fares and Khalidi 2006: 511). It is argued here that the terminology used in the UN Basic Principles such as 'together' or an 'active participation' does not exclude an indirect communication between the victim and the offender. The perception of a direct communication between the parties can vary deeply depending on cultural and other factors. Therefore it is important to identify the form and degree of interaction and the importance this interaction takes in the restorative justice procedure under analysis.[22]

Outcome level

Article I(1) of the UN Basic Principles requires that a restorative justice programme seeks to achieve 'restorative outcomes'. Accordingly, the second level of the model explores possible outcomes of a restorative justice procedure. Article I(3) of the Basic Principles characterises them as 'agreements reached as a result of a restorative process'. It goes on to state that such outcomes can 'include responses and programmes such as reparation, restitution and community service, aimed at meeting the individual and collective needs and responsibilities of the parties and achieving the reintegration of the victim and the offender'. In other words, the UN Basic Principles encompass a wide range of restorative outcomes. For the purpose of the present analysis, the following typology of outcomes is suggested: Figure 1.1 differentiates between 'sanctions' as primarily offender-oriented reaction on the one hand and 'reparations' as rather victim-oriented components on the other. Obviously, there might be overlaps in some cases. However, most outcomes do in fact contain a stronger sanctioning or reparative element.

At first sight it might surprise that the model includes sanctions as a possible restorative justice outcome. However, the UN Basic

Principles explicitly label sentencing circles as restorative programmes and thereby implicitly include sentences to be of a possible restorative nature; a similar approach is taken in the literature on 'restorative punishment' (see Duff 2003). Sanctions, within the philosophy and wording of the UN Basic Principles, will only contribute to restorative justice if they are preceded by a process of well-balanced participation – where possible – by all who were affected by the crime. For this reason sanctions are included in the present conceptualisation of restorative justice constituents but are understood in a wider sense, namely not limited to imprisonment but including different types of community sanctions and (reparative) measures. The ambivalent view on sanctions among those who suffered from violence became apparent (Kiza *et al.* 2006: 112; ICTJ 2005; Rohne 2007; see also Chapter 12). Thus the question whether, and under which conditions sanctions in a wider sense can be part of restorative justice approaches under which conditions whether, and sanctions in a wider sense can be part of restorative justice approaches (and what a more precise meaning of the element of sanctioning or even punishment could be) should be included in the analysis.

The major constituents of restorative outcomes are *reparations*. We can differentiate between material and immaterial reparation. The latter consist of their symbolic content. In fact many material reparations also carry a symbolic notion to a certain extent due to the irreversibility of the losses (Evaldsson 2003: 2). Correspondingly, acknowledgement of the victimisation as injustice is central to most forms of reparation (Kiza *et al.* 2006: 118; Vandeginste 2003: 145; Minow 1998: 91).

According to Article I(3) of the UN Basic Principles a restorative outcome is 'aimed at meeting the individual and collective needs and responsibilities of the parties'. Victims might have different expectations with regard to the source of reparation which might not only be linked to the likelihood of receiving them (e.g. monetary compensation) but also to the perceptions of responsibility and guilt. This is especially true in collective conflicts when victims perceive their victimisation as part of the collective struggle. Reparation might then not be understood as an interpersonal affair but rather a debt owed by the opposing collective and sometimes maybe the 'own' community.

A major form of reparation is of a monetary nature since it can compensate at least material losses suffered by the victimisation and the process of rehabilitation. Monetary compensation has a twofold function, namely a material and an immaterial component. The latter is also fulfilled by other – purely symbolic – forms of reparation, such as memorials, sincere apologies, etc. From restorative justice in interpersonal settings we know that apology plays a crucial role for the process as well as for the final agreement (Minow 1998). In the context of large-scale conflicts the question arises of who is perceived as owing an apology: is it only the attacker or also those who backed, legitimised and organised the attack or even the opposing collective as a whole?

Whatever the form of reparation, to be 'reparative' on a symbolic level, the use of a particular measure requires that the parties attach the same content to it. This is not necessarily the case given the cultural diversity that causes i.e. different attitudes towards accepting monetary compensation due to the impression of trading off one's suffering. Each reparation requires the parties to speak a 'common language'. This in turn needs a sufficient consideration of cultural diversities and peculiarities. Cultural differences become especially relevant in cases where rituals are part of the restorative justice process. In many traditional restorative justice procedures such rituals are an integral part of making amends (e.g. Sulha or Mato Oput). The visible manifestation of resolution, the interaction of the parties as well as the (inherent) mutual acknowledgement of shared values contribute to the settling of the dispute. Hence, a thorough identification of reparative forms and their cultural context constitutes another essential element in the model (see also Tschudi, Chapter 2, this volume).

The final element of the outcome level is the identification of *responsibilities* that go beyond the particular perpetrator. As indicated above, victimisation that occurs in the context of a collective conflict is likely to be perceived not only as an individual experience that shatters the victims' perception of life (Janoff-Bulman 1992). Instead such incidences are likely to be understood also as a part of the collective struggle and regarded as a personal 'sacrifice' for the own collective.[23] Therefore the question arises of who is held to be responsible on the attacking side: is it the individual, representatives or the collective as such? Third parties might be blamed as well. This is especially true for 'bystander countries' who fail to intervene or even benefit from the conflict. The present analysis needs to examine such perceptions of (multiple) responsibilities in order to identify the parties that have to get involved in a restorative justice process.

Purpose level

The third level of the model examines various aspects with regard to the aims pursued by the particular restorative justice response, namely the spectrum of restorative objectives and the envisaged beneficiaries of the restorative justice process.

Objectives

The examples of procedures and outcomes mentioned in the UN Basic Principles also reflect a wide spectrum of objectives that restorative justice programmes can encompass. It is argued here that these objectives are characterised by their degree of relational restoration. Therefore Figure 1.2 orders restorative purposes from a *relational* point of view, suggesting the following fourfold model of relational restoration: *(material) redress – working through the past – coexistence – reconciliation*. Each of the ascending category typically includes elements of the previous categories adding a further relational aspect to it.

The least relational aspects are found in restorative justice processes that are solely focused on material redress, namely the elimination or reduction of the material consequences of the incident. This form of redress overlaps with what is often part of or induced by formal justice responses too (e.g. torts); however, in a restorative justice process a material reparation must be the result of a consensual agreement between the parties. If the parties want to settle the conflict autonomously with the help of a facilitator in an indirect mediation process, they might also want to limit this process to a material level

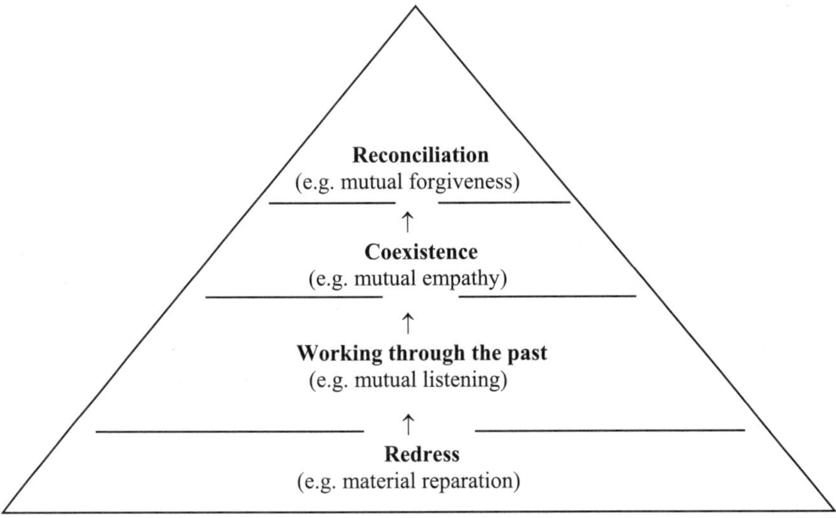

Figure 1.2 Levels of relational restoration
Source: Rohne (2006c).

without entering a more interrelational process. A victim, for example, might seek to undo the consequences without entering a dialogue with the offender. As a result of the parties' autonomy to determine the degree of restoration and due to the fact that the UN Basic Principles include indirect mediation as a restorative justice process, Figure 1.2 acknowledges the restriction to material restoration (while largely neglecting further interpersonal processes of restoration) as a minimalistic form of restoration (if resulting from the aformentioned procedural requirements outlined in the UN Basic Principles). It goes without saying that material reparation does not necessarily lead to further restoration – but material reparation can indeed constitute a basic form of restoration.

A higher degree of relational restoration is constituted by a process that is based on a mutual listening to each other's perceptions. It requires a considerable willingness to work through the past together and to understand the causes and effects of the incident. Ideally, this promotes empathy for the other. However, it does not necessarily include it. In the context of reaction to large-scale violence this degree of restoration is known from story-telling processes, such as, for example, the Truth and Reconciliation Commission in South Africa. Such a process does not necessarily reach a degree of mutual empathy. Instead, the latter is part of the next level in Figure 1.2 which is – somewhat metaphorically – termed here as 'coexistence'. It describes a higher level of restoration in which the parties are moving towards each other by not only exchanging perceptions and emotions but also sharing them in an empathetic way. It does not, however, necessarily mean that they want to interact with one another in future. The latter requires the highest degree of restoration, namely the reconciliation of the parties. Certainly, reconciliation means different things to different people and depends on the respective cultural and societal context; however, it describes the willingness for future relationships between the parties on an equal level despite the experiences of the past (Huyse 2003: 19). It can be stated that it describes the most forward-looking purpose that restorative justice can provide and requires the parties to let go of the victim–offender status and grant full rehabilitation to each other.[24]

In order to identify and to describe the restorative content of existing mechanisms and the prospects of restorative justice, the suggested continuum of relational restoration appears to be promising. This goes not without saying that the lines between the particular degrees of restoration are often blurred and that the categories could, of course, be further differentiated. However, for the present analysis this model seems to be most practicable.

Beneficiaries
Finally, the model suggests distinguishing possible beneficiaries of restorative justice responses. The UN Basic Principles indicate that restorative justice programmes are for the benefit of all parties affected by wrongdoing, namely the victim, the offender and the community. For a responsive measure it is of crucial importance to identify the prevalent perceptions about who should benefit rather than run the risk of implementing ineffective measures or leaving a party unsatisfied. These perceptions can vary a lot depending on the cultural context. For example, from a western perspective a conflict is typically understood as interpersonal. Other – especially strongly community-based – cultures perceive conflicts generally as immediately concerning the respective community, be it the family, the tribe and so forth. The perception of the conflicting parties is likely also to affect the question of who should benefit from the resolution of the conflict. It should therefore be thoroughly analysed and certainly be given special attention in a cross- or intercultural context.

Structure of the book

The present book is divided into three main parts: an introductory part, three case studies and a concluding analysis. Besides this opening chapter which describes the main aims and methods of the book, the introduction also contains a chapter by Finn Tschudi. In Chapter 2 Tschudi reflects upon a broader understanding of the concept of restorative justice which he closely links to the concepts of human dignity, pride, shame and anger.

The second part, which constitutes the main body of the book, contains three different sections dealing with three different large-scale conflicts. The three sections are constructed in the same way and each consists of: (1) an introduction to the conflict which ends with a short presentation of a specific violent incident as an illustrative and exemplary 'case study'; (2) an overview of (possible) formal and informal approaches and mechanisms as a response to the incident, presented by local or regional experts from different perspectives; and (3) a restorative justice-focused analysis. The first section is on the Kosovo conflict and is co-edited by Jana Arsovska, Marta

Valiñas and Borbala Fellegi. In Chapter 3 the co-editors introduce the 'Kosovo drama' and present the horrifying Racak killings, as well as the broader context in which they occurred. The presentation of the violent incident is followed by analyses made by local contributors. Haki Demolli, from an Albanian perspective, describes the *formal* approaches and mechanisms, both at the national and international level, available in Kosovo for dealing with violent incidents. In Chapter 4, he elaborates on the legal system of the SFR Yugoslavia in relation to the Racak massacre, and assesses the role of the international community and the International Criminal Tribunal for the former Yugoslavia (ICTY) in dealing with the crimes committed during the Kosovo conflict. In Chapter 5, Rexhep Gashi talks about possible *informal* responses to the Racak massacre – described as a crime against humanity – with reference to Albanian customary law and other cultural codes available in the Albanian context. He also reflects on the applicability of international customary principles in Kosovo. In Chapter 6, Vesna Nikolic-Ristanovic describes various *informal* mechanisms – referring mainly to contemporary examples and NGO initiatives – that exist in Serbia and Kosovo for dealing with large-scale violent conflicts. By raising the voice for 'the other side' Nikolic-Ristanovic provides a critical, thought-provoking analysis of the Racak killings. In the final chapter in this section, on the basis of the forgoing contributions by the local experts, Valiñas and Arsovska critically explore the opportunities and limits for restorative justice responses to large-scale violence in the course of the Kosovo conflict.

The second section on the Israeli–Palestinian conflict which follows is co-edited by Holger-C. Rohne, Doina Balahur, Sarah Ben-David and Beni Jakob. In Chapter 8, Rohne introduces the conflict's history and then provides for some key information for the second intifada which constitutes the focus of this section. As exemplary case study, a chain of incidents is presented that surrounded the bombing of the Mahane Yehuda market in 2003, demonstrating the vicious cycle of violence and counter-violence. On this basis, Khalid Ghanayim in Chapter 9 provides an analysis of the *formal-legal* mechanisms. Starting with an introduction to the Israeli criminal law, he provides valuable information on how the Israeli legal system deals with incidents like the Mahane Yehuda bombing. The fact that the operations against the Palestinians are carried out by the regular Israeli army excludes the application of conventional criminal law; a reflection upon the Palestinian formal criminal law is therefore not helpful. Here, only international law becomes relevant which

Ghanayim examines from the Palestinian and the Israeli viewpoint. Following this, Michal Alberstein provides an overview of existing *informal* mechanisms to deal with interpersonal violent conflicts from an Israeli-Jewish perspective. In Chapter 10 she reaches out to Jewish traditions, discusses their present importance, and introduces modern mechanisms of restorative justice that are implemented in Israel today. Finally, Alberstein reflects upon various obstacles that an application of these approaches to incidents such as the Mahane Yehuda bombing would face. Chapter 11, written by George Irani, discusses present perceptions of interpersonal conflicts within Palestinian society and introduces a traditional conflict resolution mechanism, named 'Sulha', that is still of high relevance for the Palestinian population. Irani contrasts its principles with Western approaches and discusses the relevance of Sulha principles for the Israeli–Palestinian context. In Chapter 12, Holger-C. Rohne discusses some of the findings from a recent victimological study that he conducted among Palestinian and Israeli victims of the second intifada. The victims' attitudes on how to respond to their victimisation provide for valuable insights to the applicability of restorative justice in such cases. A special emphasis is put on the identification of similarities and differences between the victim groups and the influential factors that shape their attitudes.

The third section of the book – co-edited by Kris Vanspauwen and Tyrone Savage – focuses on the conflict in the Democratic Republic of Congo. Chapter 13, by Tyrone Savage and Kris Vanspauwen, unpacks the traumatised history of the DRC, highlighting the patterns of coercive rule, failed transition, domestic decay and interconnected conflicts. It thereby attempts to foster the discussion as to how formal and informal ways of justice can be designed and implemented amid the peace that has slowly unfolded since 2002. Chapter 14, by Tyrone Savage and Olivier Kambala wa Kambala, explores the possibilities of *formal-legal* accountability mechanisms in the DRC. In light of a prosecutorial strategy, they look at the challenges and promising developments around domestic prosecutions, looking in particular at the role of the Congolese military courts and the impact of the ICC in the transitional justice process. Furthermore, they provide a critical account of the role played by the Congolese Commission *Vérité et Réconciliation.* Chapter 15 by Theodore Kamwimbi scrutinises the position and viability of the *informal* justice approaches in the DRC in the midst of the justice vs. peace debate. As informal approaches are mainly referred to as peace-enhancing structures, the author discusses the merits and limits of informal accountability mechanisms in the pursuit of justice after the violent conflict in the DRC. He thereby focuses mainly on the development of the customary courts, peace and conflict resolution mechanisms, and the established truth and reconciliation commission. And finally, in Chapter 16, Vanspauwen and Savage describe the fine line that Congo has walked in balancing peace and justice. Some significant elements in the traditional justice process lay bare the missed opportunities of the DRC to develop an integrative truth-seeking process inspired by restorative justice principles.

The third – and last – part includes a general comparative analysis and a concluding chapter. Ivo Aertsen in Chapter 17 compares the applicability of restorative justice in the various regions of conflict previously discussed in this book by using elements of the three-level model and referring to international standards on restorative justice. He also explores – the other way round – whether and how restorative justice concepts and methods should be modified on the basis of the study of their practical relevance for large-scale violent conflict. This part and the book ends with Chapter 18 by Arsovska, Valiñas and Vanspauwen that reflects on the challenges for restorative justice and the options for the future.

Notes

1 The authors would like to thank Kris Vanspauwen, Marta Valiñas and Tyrone Savage for their most valuable comments on earlier drafts of this paper.

2 When referring to 'state-based' conflicts the authors normally denote armed disputes in which control over government and/or territory is contested, in which at least one of the warring parties is a state, and which result in at least 25 battle-related deaths in a year (Human Security Report 2005: 20; Uppsala/PRIO Dataset; Kiza *et al.* 2006: 24–5). The category 'battle-related deaths' includes not only combatants but also civilians which are victims of the conflict. The book also talks about 'large-scale state-based conflict' which implies that the number of battle-related deaths is much higher than the minimum of 25. Authors also refer to 'wars' which have at least 1,000 battle-related deaths in a year. One of the primary sources for armed conflict data (Human Security Report 2005) is the dataset created by Uppsala University and the International Peace Research Institute, Oslo (PRIO) which covers the entire period from 1946 to 2003. Authors occasionally refer to different types of conflicts, namely 'intrastate' and 'interstate' conflicts, as well as 'extrastate' and 'internationlised' conflicts. Although it is not always easy to clearly separate these four categories, the categories intrastate

and interstate describe conflicts within and between states. Nowadays, intrastate conflicts are the most common type of conflicts and are responsible for a large number of civilian deaths. The threefold rise in the number of armed conflicts between 1946 and the ending of the Cold War is related to the dramatic increase in conflicts within states (more than 95 per cent of all conflicts). Extrastate conflict is a conflict between a state and a non-state group outside of the state's own territory. The last category is internationalised internal conflict and describes an intrastate conflict in which the government, the opposition, or both, receive military support from another government(s), and where foreign troops actively participate in the conflict. The war in the Democratic Republic of Congo (DRC) is a recent example of such conflict (Human Security Report 2005: 20). For more detail on definitions, see the Uppsala Conflict Database at: http://www.pcr.uu.se/database/definitions_all.htm#brd.

3 David O. Friedrichs (1998a) categorises state crimes as: war-making, genocide, nuclearism, state-sponsored terrorism and crimes against citizens. In our book, besides these crimes conducted by a state, we are also interested in state-based crimes which are a result of conflict in which one of the conflicting parties is a state, but it does not necessarily mean that the state is the initial aggressor (we refer also to anti-state crimes, terrorism, paramilitary structures, etc.).

4 Some scholars have argued that the UN's definition of genocide is too limited, and have coined the term 'politicide' to describe policies that seek to destroy groups because of their political beliefs rather than their religion or ethnicity. Barbara Harff (2003) defines genocides and politicides as acts perpetrated by governments (or in civil wars, by their opponents) that are 'intended to destroy in whole or in part a communal, political or politicised ethnic group' (Harff 2003; Human Security Report 2005: 40). Genocides and politicides often take place during civil wars, as happened in Rwanda in 1994, or in their aftermath, as happened in Cambodia in 1975–79. 'Democide' includes not only genocide, politicide and other massacres, but also deaths that arise from government actions (or purposeful failures to act) that kill people indirectly.

5 For example, in the last century, between 54 and 80 million people have been killed in genocides and between 170 and 360 million people have been killed in total by governments (democide), apart from war ('The World Revolution 2006' at: http://www.worldrevolution.org/).

6 Brookings Institution analyst Peter Singer explains that the use of child soldiers has also become very common (Singer 2005). Children fight in almost 75 per cent of today's armed conflicts (Human Security Report 2005: 35). Recruitment of children (persons under 18) into military forces is prohibited by the UN's 2000 Convention on the Rights of the Child, while the 1998 Rome Statute of the International Criminal Court defines conscripting children under 15, or deploying them in battle, as a war crime.

7 In 2002 WHO revised the death total for 2000 from 310,000 down to 235,000. There are some other war death estimates (Lacina and Gleditsch 2005) which provide lower figures when compared to WHO, but it is not very clear why this is the case. In any case the disparity between the Lacina and Gleditsch data and the WHO data is striking. It seems likely that WHO estimates are higher than those of other datasets because WHO researchers take median estimates of deaths from other sources and then multiply them by an 'adjustment factor'. It is not clear what that factor is, how it is determined, why it should differ from year to year, and what the rationale behind it is.

8 In 2000 an estimated 1.6 million people worldwide died as a result of self-inflicted, interpersonal and collective violence. The vast majority of these deaths occurred in low-to-middle income countries. Less than 10 per cent of all violence-related deaths occurred in high-income countries (Krug *et al.* 2002: 10).

9 For example, the World Bank estimates that a civil war lasts approximately seven years, with the growth rate of the economy reduced by 2.2 per cent each year which is very devastating for the countries at war. Another study puts the average cost of a conflict as high as $54 billion for a low-income country, taking into account the increased risk of future conflict (Human Security Report 2005).

10 According to Thomas Hylland Eriksen (1993: 5), 'ethnicity has to do with group identification and emerges through social situations and encounters, and through people's way of coping with the demands and challenges of life'. In social anthropology ethnicity refers to 'aspects of relationships between groups that considered themselves, and are regarded by others, as being culturally distinctive' (1993: 4). The basic conditions are that the groups must have minimum contact with each other, and they must entertain ideas of each other as being culturally different from the others. Therefore – more simplistically formulated – ethnicity is 'an aspect of social relationship between agents who considered themselves as culturally distinctive from members of other groups with whom they have minimum or regular interaction. It can thus also be defined as social identity' (1993: 12). The main common features are: descendance, language, culture, traditions, religion, as well as politics, organisational aspects and symbolic features.

11 A precondition for the emergence of secessionist movements is nationalism, which has changed in character over the years. In general, nationalism has been defined as a theory of political legitimacy which requires that ethnic boundaries should not cut across political ones, and, in particular, that ethnic boundaries within a given state should not separate the power-holders from the rest (Spencer 1998).

12 March 2004 riots by ethnic Albanians when at least 15 people died in Kosovo and riots in 2007 when two people died. The international

community couldn't stop the violence and prevent the riots. More details on the Kosovo conflict are given in Chapters 3–7.

13 Washington requested $420.7 billion for fiscal 2005, an 8 per cent increase – and plans to spend $2.2 trillion over the next five years. China and Russia each spent around $50 billion in 2003, Japan and the UK $41 billion each.

14 Council Framework Decision of 15 March 2001 on the standing of victims in criminal proceedings (2001/220/JHA), *Official Journal of the European Communities*, 22 March 2001, L 82/1.

15 UN Economic and Social Council, Resolution 2002/12 of 24 July 2002 on Basic Principles on the Use of Restorative Justice Programmes in Criminal Matters, E/2002/INF/2/Add.2, Official Records of the Economic and Social Council, 2002, Supplement No. 1 (E/2002/99). See also: http://www.un.org/docs/ecosoc/documents/2002/resolutions/eres2002-12.pdf.

16 International Institute for Restorative Practices (http://www.iirp.org/): 'Restorative practices is an emerging social science that enables people to restore and build community in an increasingly disconnected world. [...] The restorative practices concept has its roots in "restorative justice," a new way of looking at criminal justice that focuses on repairing the harm done to people and relationships rather than on punishing offenders [...]. Originating in the 1970s as mediation between victims and offenders, in the 1990s restorative justice broadened to include communities of care as well, with victims' and offenders' families and friends participating in collaborative processes called "conferences" and "circles." [...] Restorative practices is the science of building social capital and achieving social discipline through participatory learning and decision-making.'

17 International Center for Transitional Justice (http://www.ictj.net/): 'The Center works in societies emerging from repressive rule or armed conflict, as well as in established democracies where historical injustices or systemic abuse remain unresolved. [...] In order to promote justice, peace, and reconciliation, government officials and nongovernmental advocates are likely to consider a variety of transitional justice approaches including both judicial and nonjudicial responses to human rights crimes.'

18 A previous three-level model was developed by Rohne for a victimological study (due to be published in 2007). Although developed in the context of criminal justice responses, the model was intended to serve as a basis for other approaches, such as restorative justice responses (see also Kiza *et al.* 2006: 95).

19 This distinction is consistent with the approach found within the UN principles (Art. I(1)) since they define 'restorative justice programmes' as 'any programme that uses restorative processes and seeks to achieve restorative outcomes'.

20 See Art. I(2). Further, Art. I(1) of the UN principles reads: '"Restorative justice programme" means any programme that uses restorative processes and seeks to achieve restorative outcomes.'

21 For the interaction of Sulha with the Palestinian and Israeli criminal justice systems, see Fares and Khalidi (2006: 517) and Tsafrir (2006). It is worth noting that even the legal concept of retribution (lat. *retribuere* 'to pay back') stems from such a transformation: it can be traced back to the idea of introducing revenge for the comparatively restorative approach of monetary compensation as a substitute.

22 The UN document contains further aspects that can be counted part of the procedural level, such as voluntariness and balance of power, other procedural safeguards to ensure fairness (e.g. legal counsel and supervision where needed), confidentiality, proportionality and provisions to ensure the implementation of the agreement as well as the relation to the criminal justice response.

23 This is closely connected to what is known from social identity research (Sherif 1966; Tajfel 1981; Turner *et al.* 1987, etc.). Similar socio-psychological dynamics in the context of collective conflicts were described by, for example, Volkan (1991) and Lederach (1997); see also Rohne: this volume, Chapter 12.

24 Reconciliation is often associated with forgiveness which is not to be equalled with forgetting or ignoring the past.

References

Aertsen, I., Daems, T. and Robert, L. (eds) (2006) *Institutionalizing Restoratve Justice*. Cullompton: Willan.

Aertsen, I., Mackay, R., Pelikan, C., Willemsens, J. and Wright, M. (2004) *Rebuilding Community Connections – Mediation and Restorative Justice in Europe*. Strasbourg: Council of Europe Publishing.

Allport, G. (1954) *The Nature of Prejudice*. Reading, MA: Addison-Wesley.

Bar-On, D. (2005) 'Empirical criteria for reconciliation in practice', *Intervention*, 3 (3): 180–91.

Barak, G. (1990) 'State, criminology and human rights: towards an understanding of state criminality', *Journal of Human Justice*, 2: 11–28.

Barth, F. (1969) *Ethnic Groups and Boundaries: The Social Organisation of Cultural Difference*. Oslo: Scandinavian University Press.

Bateson, G. (1979) *Mind and Nature: A Necessary Unity*. New York: Button.

Bazemore, G. and Umbreit, M. (2001) *A Comparison of Four Restorative Conferencing Models*. Washington, DC: Office of Juvenile Justice and Delinquency Prevention.

Becker, T.L. and Murray, V. (1971) *Government Lawlessness in America*. New York: Oxford University Press.

Beres, R.L. (1989) 'Genocide, state and self', *Denver Journal of International Law and Policy*, 18: 37–57.

Bianchini, S. (1996) 'Geopolitics and self-determination: an atlas of insecurity in Eastern Europe in the 20th century', in *Proceedings of the Summer School on Ethnic Relations*. Belgrade: Forum for Ethnic Relations, pp. 188–209.

Bjelic, D. and Savic, O. (eds) (2002) *Balkan as Metaphor. Between Globalization and Fragmentation*. London: MIT Press.

Boraine, A. (2004) *Transitional Justice as an Emerging Field*. Paper presented at the 'Repairing the Past: Reparations and Transitions to Democracy' symposium, Ottawa, Canada, 11 March.

Braithwaite, J. (2002) *Restorative Justice and Responsive Regulation*. Oxford: Oxford University Press.

Breton, A. and Wintrobe, R. (1986) 'The bureaucracy of murder revisited', *Journal of Political Economy*, 94: 905–26.

Buenaventura, S.M. (1995) 'Human rights violations in Colombia: Colombian government and military perspectives', *Low Intensity Conflict and Law Enforcement*, 4: 271–90.

Burg, S. and Shoup, S.P. (1999) *The War in Bosnia-Herzegovina: Ethnic Conflict and International Intervention*. Armonk, NY: M.E. Sharpe.

Cederman, L.E. (2001a) 'Back to Kant: reinterpreting the democratic peace as a macrohistorical learning process', *American Political Science Review*, 95 (1): 15–32.

Cederman, L.E. (2001b) 'Modeling the democratic peace as a selection process', *Journal of Conflict Resolution*, 45 (4): 470–502.

Chambliss, W.J. (1989) 'State-organized crime', *Criminology*, 27: 183–208.

Chaney, R.K. (1995) 'Pitfalls and imperatives: applying the lessons of Nuremberg to the Yugoslav war crimes trials', *Dickinson Journal of International Law*, 14: 57–94.

Charny, W.I. (1986) 'Genocide and mass destruction: doing harm to others as a missing dimension of psychopathology', *Psychiatry*, 49: 144–57.

Chomsky, N. (2002) *Pirates and Emperors, Old and New: International Terrorism in the Real World*. Cambridge, MA: South End Press.

Churchill, W. (1986) 'Genocide: towards a functional definition', *Alternatives*, XI: 403–30.

Cohen, A. (1998) *Israel and the Bomb*. New York: Columbia University Press.

Cohen, S. (1993) 'Human rights and crimes of the state: the culture of denial', *Australian and New Zealand Journal of Criminology*, 26: 97–115.

Cohen, S. (1996) 'Government responses to human rights reports: claims, denials and counterclaims', *Human Rights Quarterly*, 18: 517–43.

Collins, R. (1974) 'Three faces of cruelty: towards a comparative sociology of violence', *Theory and Society*, 1: 415–40.

Colwill, J. (1995) 'From Nuremberg to Bosnia and beyond: war crimes trials in the modern era', *Social Justice*, 22: 111–28.

Comfort, A. (1950) *Authority and Delinquency in the Modern State: A Criminological Approach to the Problem of Power*. London: Routledge & Kegan Paul.

Comor, E. (2001) 'The role of communication in global civil society', *International Studies Quarterly*, 45 (3): 389–408.

Connor, W. (1994) *Ethnonationalism: The Quest for Understanding*. Princeton, NJ: Princeton University Press.

Council of Europe (2000) *Mediation in Penal Matters. Recommendation No. R(99)19 and Explanatory Memorandum*. Strasbourg: Council of Europe Publishing.

Cranna, M. (1994) *The True Cost of Conflict*. London: Earthscan.

Crawford, A. and Goodey, J. (2000) *Integrating a Victim Perspective Within Criminal Justice. International Debates*. Aldershot: Ashgate Publishing.

Cunneen, C. (2007) 'Reviving restorative justice traditions?', in G. Johnstone and D.W. Van Ness (eds), *Handbook of Restorative Justice*. Cullompton: Willan, pp. 113–31.

Dadrian, N.V. (1988) 'The anticipation and prevention of genocide in international conflicts: some lessons from history', *International Journal of Group Tensions*, 18: 205–14.

Daly, K. (2004) 'Pile it on. More texts on restorative justice', *Theoretical Criminology*, 8 (4): 499–507.

Douglas, J. and Johnson, J. (1977) *Official Deviance: Readings in Malfeasance, Misfeasance, and Other Forms of Corruption*. Philadelphia: Lippincott.

Drumbl, M.A. (2005) 'Collective punishment and individual punishment: the criminality of mass atrocities', *Northwestern University Law Review*, 99 (2): 101–79.

Duckitt, J. (1992) *The Social Psychology of Prejudice*. New York: Praeger.

Duff, R.A. (2003) 'Restorative punishment and punitive restoration', in G. Johnstone (ed.), *A Restorative Justice Reader. Texts, Sources, Context*. Cullompton: Willan, pp. 382–97.

Dugard, J. (1991) 'The role of international law in the struggle for liberation in South Africa', *Social Justice*, 18: 83–94.

Eriksen, T. (1993) *Ethnicity and Nationalism. Anthropological Perspective*. London: Pluto Press.

Evaldsson, A.K. (2003) *Reparations after Violent Conflicts. Problems and Possibilities*. Paper presented at the training workshop 'Senses of Right and Wrong', Copenhagen, 15–16 December.

Fares, S. and Khalidi, D. (2006) 'Formal and informal justice in Palestine: Between justice and social order', in H.-J. Albrecht, J.-M. Simon, H. Rezaei, H.-C. Rohne and E. Kiza (eds), *Conflicts and Conflict Resolution in Middle Eastern Societies – Between Tradition and Modernity*. Berlin: Duncker & Humblot, pp. 507–24.

Finch, A.H. (1947) 'The Nuremberg Trial and international law', *American Journal of International Law*, 41: 20–37.

Flournoy, M. and Pan, M. (2002) 'Dealing with demons: justice and reconciliation', *Washington Quarterly*, 25 (4): 111–23.

Freeman, M. (1991) 'The theory and prevention of genocide', *Holocaust and Genocide Studies*, pp. 185–99.

Friedrichs, O.D. (ed.) (1998a) *State Crime. Defining, Delineating and Explaining Crime*. Aldershot: Ashgate, Vol. 1.

Friedrichs, O.D. (ed.) (1998b) *State Crime. Defining, Delineating and Explaining Crime*. Aldershot: Ashgate, Vol. 2.

Gaddis, L.J. (1989) *The Long Peace: Inquiries into the History of the Cold War*. New York: Oxford University Press.

Gaddis, L.J. (1992/93) 'International relations theory and the end of the Cold War', *International Security*, 17: 5–58.

Gartzke, E. and Gleditsch, S.K. (2006) 'Identity and conflict: ties that bind and differences that divide', *European Journal of International Relations*, 12 (1): 53–87.

Gayner, B.J. (1977) 'The genocide treaty', *Journal of Social and Political Studies*, 2: 235–45.

Goldstein, A. (2006) 'Family Group Conferences (FGC) in youth justice in Israel', in H.-J. Albrecht, J.-M. Simon, H. Rezaei, H.-C. Rohne and E. Kiza (eds), *Conflicts and Conflict Resolution in Middle Eastern Societies – Between Tradition and Modernity*. Berlin: Duncker & Humblot, pp. 493–506.

Grabosky, N.P. (1990) 'Citizen co-production and corruption control', *Corruption and Reforms*, pp. 125–51.

Gutmann, R. and Rieff, D. (1999) *Crimes of War: What the Public Should* Know. London: Norton.

Hagan, E.F. (1997) *Political Crime: Ideology and Criminology*. Englewood Cliffs, NJ: Prentice Hall.

Hardin, R. (1995) *One for All: The Logic of Group Conflict*. Princeton, NJ: Princeton University Press.

Harding, S. (1998) *Is Science Multicultural?* Bloomington, IN: Indiana University Press.

Harff, B. (2003) 'No lessons learned from the Holocaust? Assessing risks of genocide and political mass murder since 1955', *American Political Science Review*, 97 (1): 57–74.

Harff, B. and Gurr, T.R. (1996) 'Victims of the state: genocides, politicides and group repression from 1945 to 1995', in A.J. Jongman (ed.), *Contemporary Genocides: Causes, Consequences*. Leiden: PIOOM, pp. 35–58.

Hechter, M. (1987) *Principles of Group Solidarity*. Berkeley, CA: University of California Press.

Hope, R.K. (1987) 'Administrative corruption and administrative reform in developing states', *Corruption and Reform*, pp. 127–47.

Hopkins, B. (2006) *The 'DNA' of Restorative Justice and Restorative Approaches in Schools and Other Institutions and Organizations*. Conference paper to the European Forum for Restorative Justice, Barcelona.

Horowitz, D.L. (1995) *Ethnic Groups in Conflict*. Berkeley, CA: University of California Press.

Horowitz, L.I. (1989) 'Counting bodies: the dismal science of authorized terror', *Patterns of Prejudice*, 23: 4–15.

Hudson, J., Morris, A., Maxwell, G. and Galaway, B. (eds) (1996) *Family Group Conferences: Perspective on Policing and Practice*. Annandale, NY: Federation Press.

Human Development Report (2005) *International Cooperation at a Crossroads: Aid, Trade and Security in an Unequal World*. New York: UNDP Publications.

Human Security Report (2005) *War and Peace in the 21st Century*, Canadian Human Security Centre. New York: Oxford University Press.

Huntington, S.P. (1993a) 'The clash of civilizations', *Foreign Affairs*, 72 (3): 22–8.

Huntington, S.P. (1993b) 'If not civilizations, what? paradigms of the post-Cold War world', *Foreign Affairs*, 72 (5): 86–94.

Huntington, S.P. (1996) *The Clash of Civilizations and the Remaking of World Order*. New York: Simon & Schuster.

Huyse, L. (1995) 'Justice after transition: on the choices successor elites make in dealing with the past', *Law and Social Inquiry*, 20: 51–78.

Huyse, L. (2003) 'Justice', in D. Bloomfield, T. Barnes and L. Huyse (eds), *Reconciliation After Violent Conflict. A Handbook*. Stockholm: International Institute for Democracy and Electoral Assistance, pp. 97–115.

ICTJ (2005) *Forgotten Voices – A Population-Based Survey on Attitudes About Peace and Justice in Northern Uganda*. See: http://www.ictj.org/images/content/1/2/127.pdf (accessed 16 March 2006).

Ingraham, L.B. (1979) *Political Crime in Europe: A Comparative Study of France, Germany and England*. Berkeley, CA: University of California Press.

International Commission on the Balkans (2005) *The Balkans in Europe's Future*. Sofia: Center for Liberal Strategies.

Jackson, R. (2000) *The Global Convenant: Human Conduct in a World of States*. Oxford: Oxford University Press.

Janoff-Bulman, R. (1992) *Shattered Assumptions: Towards a New Psychology of Trauma*. New York: Free Press.

Johnston, A.I. (2001) 'Treating international institutions as social environments', *International Studies Quarterly*, 45 (4): 487–516.

Johnstone, G. (eds) (2003) *A Restorative Justice Reader: Texts, Sources, Context*. Cullompton: Willan.

Kauzlarich, D., Kramer, R.C. and Smith, B. (1992) 'Toward the study of governmental crime: nuclear weapons, foreign intervention and international law', *Humanity and Society*, 16: 543–63.

Kiza, E., Rathgeber, C. and Rohne, H.-C. (2006) *Victims of War: An Empirical Study on War-Victimization and Victims' Attitudes towards Addressing Atrocities*. Hamburg: Hamburger Institut für Sozialforschung. See: http://www.his-online.de/cms.asp?H='79'&T=0&Plugin=10&HE=10&HEP=978-3-936096-73-6.

Koskenniemi, M. (2001) 'Human rights, politics and love', *Nordic Journal of Human Rights*, 4: 33–45.

Kramer, C.R. (1994) 'State violence and violent crime', *Peace Review*, 6: 171–5.

Kriesberg, L. (2003) *Identity Issues*, July. See: http://www.beyondintractability.org/essay/identity_issues.

Krug, E.G., Dahlberg, L., Mercy, J.A., Zwi, A. and Lozano, R. (eds) (2002) *World Report on Violence and Health*. Geneva: World Health Organisation.

Lacina, B. and Gleditsch, N.P. (2005) 'Monitoring trends in global combat: a new dataset of battle deaths', *European Journal of Population*, 21 (2–3): 145–66.

Lederach, J.P. (1997) *Building Peace – Sustainable Reconciliation in Divided Societies*. Washington, DC: United States Institute of Peace.

Macfarlane, L. (1974) *Violence and the State*. London: Nelson.

Markovits, A. and Silverstein, M. (eds) (1988) *The Politics of Scandal: Power and Process in Liberal Democracies*. New York: Holmes & Meier.

Marshall, T.F. (1999) *Restorative Justice. An Overview*. London: Home Office.

Meron, T. (1995) 'International criminalization of international atrocities', *American Journal of International Law*, 89: 554–77.

Minow, M. (1998) *Between Vengeance and Forgiveness: Facing History after Genocide and Mass Violence*. Boston: Beacon Press.

Moore, W.H. (2002) 'Ethnic minorities and foreign policy', *SAISReview*, 22 (2): 77–91.

Moore, W.H. and Davis, R.D. (1997) 'Ethnicity matters: transnational ethnic alliances and foreign policy behavior', *International Studies Quarterly*, 41 (1): 171–84.

Mutz, D. (2002) 'Cross-cutting social networks. Testing democratic theory in practice', *American Political Science Review*, 96: 111–26.

O'Brien, C.C. (1983) 'Terrorism under democratic conditions: the case of the IRA', in M. Crenshaw (ed.), *Legitimacy and Power: The Consequences of Political Violence*. Middletown, CT: Wesleyan University Press.

Proall, L. (1898) 'Conclusion', in W.D. Morrison (ed.), *Political Crime*. London: T. Fisher Unwin, pp. 340–55.

Ramet, S. (2005) *Thinking about Yugoslavia*. Cambridge: Cambridge University Press.

Raley, S. (1988) 'Political scandal: a Western luxury?', *Corruption and Reform*, 3: 277–91.

Reisman, W.M. (1990) 'Sovereignity and human rights in contemporary international law', *American Journal of International Law*, 84 (4): 886.

Restorative Justice Consortium (1998) *Standards for Restorative Justice*. London: Restorative Justice Consortium.

Roebuck, J. and Weeber, C.S. (1978) *Political Crime in the United States: Analyzing Crime By and Against Government*. New York: Praeger.

Rohne, H.-C. (2006a) 'Approaches to responding to violent conflicts – victimological reflections in the context of the Al-Aqsa-intifada', in

H.-J. Albrecht, J.-M. Simon, H. Rezaei, H.-C. Rohne and E. Kiza (eds), *Conflicts and Conflict Resolution in Middle Eastern Societies – Between Tradition and Modernity*. Berlin: Duncker & Humblot, pp. 79–98.

Rohne, H.-C. (2006b) 'Cultural aspects of conflict resolution – comparing *Sulha* and Western mediation', in H.-J. Albrecht, J.-M. Simon, H. Rezaei, H.-C. Rohne and E. Kiza (eds), *Conflicts and Conflict Resolution in Middle Eastern Societies – Between Tradition and Modernity*. Berlin: Duncker & Humblot, pp. 187–214.

Rohne, H.-C. (2006c) 'Conceptualizing Restorative Justice in the Context of Large-Scale Conflicts'. Unpublished paper presented at COST Action A21 symposium 'Restorative Justice Developments in Europe', 2–3 March.

Rohne, H.-C. (2007) *Opferperspektiven im interkulturellen Vergleich. Eine viktimologische Studie im Kontext der Al-Aqsa Intifada*. Hamburg: Verlag Dr. Kovač.

Rummel, R.J. (1995) 'Democracy, power, genocide and mass murder', *Journal of Conflict Resolution*, 39: 3–26.

Scheff, J.T. and Retzinger, M.S. (2001) *Emotions and Violence. Shame and Rage in Destructive Conflicts*. Lexington, MA: Lexington Books.

Shalhoub-Kevorkian, N. (2006) 'Tribal justice and gender: perspectives in the Palestinian society', in H.-J. Albrecht, J.-M. Simon, H. Rezaei, H.-C. Rohne and E. Kiza (eds), *Conflicts and Conflict Resolution in Middle Eastern Societies – Between Tradition and Modernity*. Berlin: Duncker & Humblot, pp. 535–56.

Shearing, C. (2001) 'Transforming security: a South African experiment', in H. Strang and J. Braithwaite (eds), *Restorative Justice and Civil Society*. Cambridge: Cambridge University Press, pp. 14–34.

Sherif, M. (1966) *In Common Predicament – Social Psychology of Intergroup Conflict and Cooperation*. Boston: Houghton Mifflin.

Singer, P. (2005) *Children at War*. Berkeley, CA: University of California Press.

Skelton, A. (2007) 'Africa', in G. Johnstone and D.W. Van Ness (eds), *Handbook of Restorative Justice*. Cullompton: Willan, pp. 468–77.

Smith, M. (1998) 'Humanitarian intervention: an overview of the ethical issues', *Ethics and International Affairs*, 12: 63–76.

Smith, N.D. (1995) 'The genesis of genocide in Rwanda: the fatal dialectic of class and ethnicity', *Humanity and Society*, 19: 57–73.

Sniderman, P., Peri, P., de Figueiredo, R. and Piazza, T. (2000) *The Outsider. Prejudice and Politics in Italy*. Princeton, NJ: Princeton University Press.

Spencer, M. (1998) 'When states divide', in *Separatism: Democracy and Disintegration*. Lanham, MD: Rowman & Littlefield, pp. 7–41.

Tajfel, H. (1981) *Human Groups and Social Categories*. Cambridge: Cambridge University Press.

Tsafrir, N. (2006) 'Arab customary law in Israel: Sulha agreements and Israeli courts', *Islamic Law and Society*, 13 (1): 76–98.

Tunnell, K. (ed.) (1993) *Political Crime in Contemporary America: A Critical Approach*. New York: Garland.

Turk, T.A. (1981) 'Organisational deviance and policing', *Criminology*, pp. 231–50.

Turner, J.C., Hogg, M.A., Oakes, P.J., Reicher, S.D. and Wetherell, M.S. (1987) *Rediscovering the Social Group – A Self Categorization Theory*. Oxford: Blackwell.

UN Handbook (2006) *UN Handbook on Restorative Justice Programmes*. Vienna: United Nations Office on Drugs and Crime.

UN Millennium Project (2005) *Investing in Development*. London: Earthscan.

UNDP (1990) *Human Development Report 1990: Concept and Measurement of Human Development*. New York: Oxford University Press.

Van Ness, D. and Strong, K.H. (1997) *Restoring Justice*. Cincinnati, OH: Anderson Publishing.

Vandeginste, S. (2003) 'Reparations', in D. Bloomfield, T. Barnes, L. Huyse (eds), *Reconciliation after Violent Conflict*. Stockholm: International IDEA, pp. 145–62.

Verba, S., Schlozman, K.L. and Brady, H. (1995) *Voice and Equality. Civic Voluntarism in American Politics*. Cambridge, MA: Harvard University Press.

Volkan, V.D. (1991) 'Psychoanalytic aspects of ethnic conflicts', in J.V. Montville (ed.), *Conflict and Peacekeeping in Multiethnic Societies*. New York: Lexington Books, pp. 81–92.

Wachtel, T. and McCold, P. (2001), 'Restorative justice in every day life', in H. Strang and J. Braithwaite (eds), *Restorative Justice and Civil Society*. Cambridge: Cambridge University Press, pp. 114–29.

Walgrave, L. (2007) 'Integrating criminal justice and restorative justice', in G. Johnstone and D.W. Van Ness (eds), *Handbook of Restorative Justice*. Cullompton: Willan, pp. 559–79.

Walsh, E.L. (1994) 'Political oversight, the rule of law, and Iran-Contra', *Cleveland State Law Review*, 42: 587–97.

Wardak, A. (2006) 'Structures of authority and local dispute settlement in Afghanistan', in H.-J. Albrecht, J.-M. Simon, H. Rezaei, H.-C. Rohne and E. Kiza (eds), *Conflicts and Conflict Resolution in Middle Eastern Societies – Between Tradition and Modernity* (Berlin: Duncker & Humblot, pp. 347–70.

Weitekamp, E. (1999) 'The history of restorative justice', in G. Bazemore and L. Walgrave (eds), *Restorative Juvenile Justice: Repairing the Harm of Youth Crime*. Monsey, NY: Criminal Justice Press, pp. 75–102.

Weitzer, R. (1993) 'Transforming the South African police', *Police Studies*, pp. 1–10. Weitzer, R. and Beattie, C. (1994) 'Police killings in South Africa: criminal trials 1986–1992', *Policing and Society*, 4: 99–117.

Wendt, A. (1992) 'Collective identity formation and the international state', *American Political Science Review*, 88 (2): 384–96.

Wolfe, A. (1973) *Seamy Side of Democracy*. New York: McKay Publishing.

Wolff, S. (2006) *Ethnic Conflict. A Global Perspective*. Oxford: Oxford University Press.

Wright, M. (1996) *Justice for Victims and Offenders: A Restorative Response for Crime*. Winchester: Watergate Press.

Zehr, H. (1990) *Changing Lenses: A New Focus for Crime and Justice*. Scottdale, PA: Herald Press.

Chapter 2

Dealing with violent conflicts and mass victimisation: a human dignity approach

Finn Tschudi

This chapter looks at the inspiring role that human dignity can play in the aftermath of mass victimisation that occurs during violent conflict. It argues that people should look beyond the classic – and in my view narrow – interpretation of restorative justice. By stating this, I face two challenges. Firstly, I will engage in the ongoing debate among restorative justice scholars as to whether and how the scope and definition of restorative justice should be broadened (Roche 2001; Villa-Vicencio 2003: 47). Secondly, I will argue that restorative justice principles should be considered when dealing with violent conflicts that result in mass victimisation (Christie 2001; Cunneen 2001; Parmentier 2003).

I will therefore opt for a more integrative and holistic view of restorative justice that aims to promote change at the individual and community level. At the individual level the objective is to repair harm and thus foster dignity and empowerment for the persons involved. This requires participation of the local community. At the community level, the objective is to promote and strengthen a viable community with empathy and trust.

To date, the most commonly used responses to mass victimisation are deterrence and punishment, and negotiation. The reactions variously called defiance or reactance illustrate that the rationality assumption underlying the deterrence and punishment approach has limited validity. Hence, I will call for a restricted use of deterrence. Negotiation on the other hand – commonly seen as an alternative to deterrence – often leads to unfruitful debates. Therefore, in this chapter, I call for the use of the most important restorative value, dialogue, in negotiations.

Finally the Bougainville case is described as an ideal example of restorative justice in the case of mass victimisation. By describing this peace process in more detail, the positive implications of a human dignity approach will be illustrated. The role of the local culture, the promotion of community capacity, the inclusion of rituals, the timing of a peacebuilding process and the (complementary) role of international law will be looked at in this regard. In a final note the chapter suggests a proposed integrated and holistic view of restorative justice which is in line with Braithwaite's regulatory pyramid.

Restorative justice, dignity, *ubuntu* and empowerment

Restorative justice has been described in different ways. Johnstone and Van Ness (2007: 19) identify three conceptions of restorative justice: (1) the 'encounter conception', which they see as more limited than (2) a 'reparative' or (3) a 'transformative' conception. It may, however, be preferable to think in terms of perspectives rather than conceptions.

The first perspective – the *encounter perspective* – refers to the procedure where stakeholders, particularly those who are most affected by injustice, come together to heal the harm and thus restore dignity and empowerment for all. Such encounters usually have ritual features which are important both in facilitating and reinforcing reconciliation. The *transformative perspective* aims at promoting values such as humility and respect, and a non-hierarchical, gentle and peaceful way of life. These values are of basic importance in the present conception of restorative justice since the encounter and the transformative perspectives are best seen as intertwined and supplementary. In the integrative and holistic view presented in this chapter, the *encounter perspective* has a major focus on the immediate steps towards reparation of harm, whereas the transformative perspective mainly aims at long-term transformative goals. Furthermore, restorative encounters primarily focus on individuals involved in harmful incidents, whereas the transformative perspective aims at structural changes.

To illustrate this intertwinement: a restorative encounter presupposes that the facilitator exemplifies transformative values, both in the preparatory phase as well as in the encounter itself. Furthermore a successful outcome of a restorative encounter should lead to increased 'transformative behaviour'. When former enemies can be reconciled this facilitates the building of a more viable society.

This view implies that restorative encounters should be conducted with an eye on possible long-term consequences. Immediate goals should never have harmful consequences in the long-term. This will obviate any critique that restorative justice is merely *cosmetic* and really serves to sustain harmful structures. The present view emphasises restorative encounters as producing micro-changes which – when multiplied – can lead to macro-changes (see Braithwaite and Drahos 2000: 595–600).

Apart from the call for a broader perspective on restorative justice as opposed to the commonly agreed narrow definitions, I would like to introduce three additional values or concepts that should play a more central role in restorative justice practices. They are: dignity, *ubuntu* and empowerment.

Dignity is a central concept in human rights language and should therefore be considered as an important restorative justice value. The *Universal Declaration of Human Rights* (1948: para. 1) states that 'all human beings are born free and equal in dignity and rights. They are endowed with reason and consciousness and should act towards one another in a spirit of brotherhood.'

Let us describe the significance of dignity by starting with its antonym, namely humiliation. By doing so, we will draw on Lindner who has devoted most of her professional life to the study of human dignity and humiliation.[1] Lindner defines humiliation as 'the enforced lowering of any person or group by a process of subjugation that damages their dignity' (2006a: x). She identifies four types of reaction to humiliation: (1) accepting a legitimate, lowly place;[2] (2) depression, open anger or planning revenge; (3) mature differentiation; and (4) moderation. Accepting a lowly place is mainly a reaction of the past when hierarchical or feudal structures were taken for granted and accepted, and humiliation meant nothing worse than to lower or humble, or to show underlings their legitimate lowly place, without any connotation that this might also signify a violation, an 'honourable social medicine' (Lindner 2006b: 7, 10–11). Anger and depression (or combinations) are typical reactions to humiliation. Mature differentiation is what characterises Nelson Mandela who succeeded in transforming his feelings of humiliation – after 27 years of prison – into a constructive contribution to social and societal change.

> The core of dignity resides in the body and thus e.g. genocide is about humiliating the personal dignity of the victims, denigrating their group to a subhuman level. The Rwandan

> genocide of 1994 provides a gruesome catalogue of practices designed to bring down the victims' dignity. The most literate way of achieving this debasement as I heard described many times was cutting off the legs of tall Tutsis to shorten not only their bodies but 'bring down their alleged arrogance'. (Lindner and Walsh 2006: 9)

The second restorative justice value that I would include is the concept of *ubuntu* which is derived from the Nguni languages and captures the essence of participatory humanism (Sparks 2003: 12–13) and avoids the sexism implied by the term 'brotherhood' in the Universal Declaration quoted above. It is not easily translatable in English, but a popular Xhosa proverb could help us to understand: *Tu ngabanye abantu* means 'people are people through other people'. Archbishop Desmond Tutu (1999) likes to quote this proverb while explaining how instrumental *ubuntu* was in the South African Truth and Reconciliation Commission. He thereby promoted an African alternative to the Cartesian 'I think therefore I am'.

Ubuntu combines generosity, hospitality and compassion and can be used to describe a personal quality: a person with *ubuntu* is open and accessible for others, primed with a certainty deriving from the experience of belonging to a larger unity. This unity is diminished when others are humiliated. Harm breaks connections, and ubuntu implies restoring connections. This dovetails with Lindner's view that 'losing one's dignity means being excluded from the family of humankind' (2006a: 42). The aim of restorative justice is thus the equivalent to restoring dignity and so includes those harmed in a joint humanity, what I think of as 'global *ubuntu*'. Sullivan and Tifft similarly aim for 'taking steps so as to make us one flesh, one bone, a one-world body' (2006: 12).

The last element I add to the important restorative justice values is empowerment. Empowerment is closely related to dignity and implies a social process where people believe that their story is worth telling. If nobody will listen to a person's story, then the dignity of that person is not respected. By telling our story we not only develop a deeper sense of self, but also expand and deepen our connectedness to each other (Sullivan and Tifft 2004: 388).

After having heard the testimony of a victim who took part in a restorative justice conference[3] it became clear that this concept of empowerment is of vital importance in restorative justice practices. This particular victim suffered from long-standing sexual abuse. Upon the request of the victim a restorative conference was convened. The perpetrator, both the victim's and the perpetrator's families as well as some friends were present. The perpetrator showed no sign of remorse, but even though this conference did not lead to any apology, forgiveness or reconciliation it was highly restorative for the victim who told the author:

> 'I'm free'. Deceit and corruption officially ended that night. I'm free to perceive, decide and behave in a way appropriate to myself and not to the perpetrator of my life. This story illustrates a 'deeper sense of self'. As for 'deepen connectedness'. Everything has changed because I have changed. Before the conference friends and family didn't know how to behave towards me. The conference allowed the best of humanity to come out. [At the social mingling after the main part of the conference] there was euphoria [...] hugging all over the place [...] One of David's sons asked me to keep in touch and gave me a hug. (Quoted in Neimeyer and Tschudi 2003)

The story illustrates the importance of an audience who collectively can validate a new and preferred sense of self, and thus create an empowering effect on the victim.

A restorative encounter is a ritual that draws on indigenous customs (see below, 'Bougainville: a restorative justice success story'). Two aspects of rituals are important to mention in this respect. Firstly, the encounter should contribute to a larger discourse and should not be an isolated event. And secondly, rituals should contribute to group solidarity, collective effervescence (Rossner 2006). Usually these conditions can be established by first allowing the display of negative emotions. This is often followed by feelings of collective vulnerability (Neimeyer and Tschudi 2003) – a recognition of the joint humanity of all the stakeholders. This condition paves the way for later collaboration and the display of positive emotions. A basic condition for such a process is that the facilitator treats all participants – however obnoxious their behaviour may appear – with the utmost respect for their dignity. Violating this prescription is likely to lead to non-restorative outcomes. Preparations for such a ritual may require months of work; furthermore, diligence is required in following up any agreement made, and to utilise the created emotional energy for further rebuilding. As mentioned above this work needs to be directed by transformative values and the capacity for dialogue, respect and humility.

Dignity as the core value of restorative justice

From all the values described above, dignity should be regarded as the core value in restorative justice. Others prefer non-domination as the core value (Braithwaite and Pettit 1990; Pettit 1996, 1997). Braithwaite (2006b) writes 'I prefer non-domination to dignity, though obviously being free of domination increases dignity. One could imagine George W. Bush sincerely believing he stands for human dignity, but he could not conceivably believe he stands against domination'.

Looking at the conceptualisation of dignity as laid down in the *Universal Declaration of Human Rights* (1948), Lindner points out that equal dignity can be interpreted in two distinct ways, namely in a *Kantian* and in a *Levinasian* interpretation. The Kantian interpretation states: 'Equal dignity means that although you are poor, you can have full dignity ... provided you have political rights such as the right of free speech'. The Levinasian interpretation argues: 'You are poor and live under circumstances that violate human dignity. To ensure your dignity, you must be supported by an enabling environment that gives you the chance to work yourself into a more dignified quality of life' (Lindner 2006a: 66).

Lindner (2006a: 52) has coined the term egalisation to signify a movement towards equal dignity in our global village. Egalisation is about whether we use fear as the glue for coercive hierarchies or prefer to live in creative networks held together by mutual respect [and] equal dignity. If we take equal dignity to imply an enabling environment and fight against coercive hierarchies this should have sufficient bite to be an ideal for restorative justice. Does this, however, take us beyond the ideal of non-domination? Domination implies that someone has the power to subjugate or restrict choices for someone else, freedom can be conceptualised as anti-power, and 'maximization of anti-power should generally involve its equalization' (Pettit 1996: 595). There are several strategies for the equalisation of resources as, for instance:

- having fair laws and – as far as possible – equal access to law;
- regulating the resources of the powerful, e.g. regulations against unfair dismissal in workplaces, minimal wages and safe working conditions;
- enhancing capacities, empowerment, by supplying universal education, welfare state initiatives as social security, medical services, etc.

In a society without domination 'you do not have to live either in fear of that other or in deference to the other. You are a somebody in relation to them, not a nobody. You are a person in your own legal right' (Pettit 1996: 595). Pettit's concept of equalisation is thus identical with Lindner's egalisation, and non-domination is equivalent to equal dignity in Lindner's interpretation. Pettit sees domination as the capacity for more or less intentional interference – with impunity – in choices another person is in a position to make. This can take place either by imposing restrictions or withholding assets. For instance, environmental harm will – even if it comes about inadvertently or as the aggregate outcome of individually innocent actions – be an assault on at least the range of undominated choices, and thus 'count as a loss in the ledger book of republican liberty' (Pettit 1997: 137–8). This interpretation seems related to the concept of structural violence coined by Galtung (1969). Structural violence is seen as the discrepancy between actual and potentially possible conditions of life. A simple example might clarify: the degree of damage wrought by a tsunami that could be prevented by sophisticated warning techniques could be counted as structural violence. In my opinion restorative justice rituals might be appropriate in this context. Technicians with access to resources to construct appropriate warning systems could visit places damaged by a tsunami, and extend their regrets at previous negligence. Some local survivors could be invited to assist in constructing maximally efficient warning systems, and in line with good restorative traditions a celebration could end the ceremony. Such a happening might foreshadow a global *ubuntu*. All of us are in some sense stakeholders with the potential to contribute to set things right again, to exhibit 'moments that reframe the macro-community' (Braithwaite 2002: 69).

Restorative justice has sometimes been criticised for ignoring larger social issues. The present account on dignity and closely related concepts hopes to foster the debate for a broader conception of restorative justice so that more general social issues may be included (Villa-Vicencio 2003: 47). Before describing applications of this broader conceptualisation of restorative justice in response to mass victimisation, I first describe some of the problematic counter forces that prevent a human dignity approach to come about.

Failure of deterrence measures in response to terrorism

In the post-9/11 era terrorism is a popular and widely discussed threat to our human security. Less evident is a generally accepted definition of the phenomenon. This has been a major obstacle in the development of meaningful international countermeasures. Usually 'terrorism' is used to refer to violence towards civilians (victims of terrorism) by a group that does not officially represent a state (author's definition). A common feature of acts labelled as terrorism is that these are actions directed against a relatively powerful state who can command much bigger resources than the so-called terrorists. The often disproportionate responses to terrorism by states often result in the killing of innocent civilians (victims of collateral damage). From a victim's perspective – be it as a victim of terrorism or as a victim of collateral damage – one might rightly question the usefulness of the label 'terrorist'. The rationale for most responses to terrorism is that they have a deterrent effect on terrorists. This assumption is too often taken for granted by the states being attacked. Perhaps it is related to a belief that those with less power will show acquiescence as it was previously taken for granted that humiliation would work. An important question is whether or to what extent this assumption is warranted.

It is interesting in this respect to look at the review done by Lum *et al.* (2006) who have reviewed the more than 20,000 articles on deterrence measures. The general conclusion is that most deterrence measures fail to achieve their goal of compliance.[4] This is also supported by Harvey (1999) who has critically studied the successes and failures of coercive threats. The only possible applicability of the deterrence theory that Lum *et al.* highlight is the use of metal detectors for passengers in airports. This has been shown to have a deterrent effect on hijacking, but this is restricted to hijacking for purposes other than terror. Drawing on the above literature review, LaFree *et al.* (2006) point out that a common accepted assumption has been that actors are 'rational' in the sense of responding to punishment or the construction of barriers with compliance, i.e. decreased offending/harmful behaviour. Their general conclusion, however, is that this assumption of rationality has limited, if any, validity as interventions may be associated with an increase in the likelihood of subsequent attacks. A general tendency for government responses to terrorism is to mobilise the sympathies of would-be supporters. 'When such supporters are enraged and energized the likelihood of further terrorist strikes may increase. Responses to terrorism can be more dangerous than terrorism itself' (LaFree *et al.* 2006: 4–5). In my view the feeling of 'being enraged' can be related to anger as a response to humiliation (see above). LaFree *et al.* (2006)

further elaborate on the psychological literature of reactance (see also Brehm and Brehm 1981). Reactions such as defiance, stigmatising, shaming and reactance show that deterrence and punishment often result in the opposite of the intended effect. The crucial variables identified (in Lum *et al.* 2006) that distinguish between reactions of conformity and reactance or defiance are:

- perceived fairness: high level of fairness increases chance of conformity;
- salience of the regulation of freedom: low level will increase chance of conformity;
- social bond between sanctioning agent and the sanctioned: strong social bonds increase chance of conformity.

In situations of asymmetric warfare these variables most often lean towards reactance. The perception of fairness is low, there is a high salience of freedom (self-determination, respect for religious traditions, etc.), and there is a weak – if any – social bond between the conflicting parties.

Moreover, escalating deterrence measures are likely to have severe side effects. A useful metaphor might be to compare terrorism with malign diseases. In the medical sciences doctors are careful to check whether attempted treatments may have unfortunate side effects, or even make the health condition worse. Such considerations are practically unknown in the literature on terrorism.

Dialogue, humility and respect versus egocentrism

As mentioned before negotiation is an alternative approach to the deterrence approach. It often happens, however, that when the negotiation process fails the parties revert to the deterrence measures. This paragraph will look at the possible weaknesses of the negotiation approach and will argue for dialogue and restorative justice as a viable alternative to negotiation and deterrence.

In many cases peacebuilding can be characterised as neither deterrence nor restorative justice but simply as negotiations. However, it is not sufficient to get the contesting parties around the table, and quite often these negotiations do not solve conflicts. They often lead to adversarial situations where parties seek support from third parties, or where unsatisfactory compromises are reached, or where opposing views and interests are only confirmed. A typical reason for the failure of negotiations may be that restorative values such as humility and respect are not present in the process. A widespread assumption which is contrary to restorative values is that we are in direct, unmediated contact with reality and see things the way they really are. This assumption is the core of naive realism and leads to poor communication when we encounter others who see people and events quite differently from us. Ross and Ward (1996: 110–11) describe how the layperson will regard his or her social attitudes, beliefs, preferences and the like as dispassionate, unbiased apprehension of the evidence at hand. This gives to their perspective a privileged epistemological position vis-à-vis the other's perspective. Tschudi and Rommetveit (1982) have labelled this attitude *cognitive imperialism*. When a naive realist encounters another party with a radically different interpretation of an event, there are two ways to interpret the failure of getting to a common understanding. Firstly, the other party may be uninformed, and does not have sufficient access to the same information as you have. Or secondly, the other party may have an irrational, biased or distorted view.

This concept of naive realism is well grounded in psychological traditions. Piaget is in this respect an important source of inspiration. He describes a development from an 'egocentric' to a 'decentred' construction of the world (Piaget 1954). During the course of his development a child will gradually see the world from the point of view of the other and recognise that there are several viable perspectives. However, the social development of a person that tries to understand the social world is a never ending process. A classic example in social psychology shows how two opposing parties can have a totally different interpretation of the same event. Ross and Ward (1996: 118) quote the classic article 'They saw a game'. This concerned a movie of an American football game between Dartmouth and Princeton. It was as if the two sets of partisan viewers saw different games. The Princeton fans saw a continuing saga of Dartmouth atrocities and occasional Princeton retaliations, whereas the Dartmouth fans saw a hard-hitting contest in which both parties contributed equally to the violence.

With this knowledge in mind and looking at violent conflicts again, there seems to be little hope for fruitful interchanges if egocentrism persists among conflicting parties. Moreover there is a pronounced risk that interchanges will even increase the rifts while conciliatory proposals may be interpreted as devious manoeuvres that show the bad will of the other party. Fostering restorative values provide a valuable contrast to egocentrism. Humility implies a profound awareness of the limitations of one's own knowledge and openness to the value of insights from the other (Johnstone and Van Ness 2007: 19). This fits well with David Bohm's (1996) emphasis on the importance of dialogue. He deplored the tendency to lose understanding of a basically interconnected reality, and not be aware of how hidden intentions, assumptions and values – as, for instance, our egocentrism – control our behaviour. Bohm further discusses the distinction between dialogue and discussion or debate. The etymological meaning of dialogue is helpful to understand the difference. The Greek word δια (*dia*) means 'through' and λόγος (*logos*) means 'the meaning of the word'. Dialogue thus represents the image of a river of meaning flowing around and through the participants. This is in stark contrast with 'discussion', a word that shares its root meaning with 'percussion' and 'concussion', which refer to breaking things up.

A *Bohmian* dialogue group is not designed to solve specific problems. The aim is rather to become aware of implicit assumptions. It is then helpful to suspend immediate impulses as much as possible, and to give space to expose these reactions so that others can reflect on them. This form of dialogue requires respectful listening and it is argued that this form will lead to greater mutual understanding and possibly also towards a shared culture. A good example is a prison setting where inmates, staff and 'prison friends' regularly meet together. On many occasions this interactive process has led to a pronounced increase in mutual understanding. Is it realistic to transfer this model of Bohmian dialogue to the international scene of violent conflicts? Is dialogue applicable to ease tensions between warring parties? At least we might hope that dialogue groups between, for example, Israeli soldiers, Palestinian civilians and observers who report on possible cases of humiliation can lead towards a certain level of mutual understanding.

Some mutual respect is a necessary precondition to start a dialogue group. At the same time, (increased) respect is also an outcome in most dialogue processes. This process of gradual increase in mutual respect can facilitate joint problem-solving. While a dialogue aims at increased mutual understanding, the purpose of a debate is to defeat the opponent. A good metaphor is a boxing match. Galtung (2006) has deplored that Bohm mainly distances his approach from discussion rather than debate. A discussion refers to many interchanges not necessarily marked by any belligerence, whereas a debate clearly implies antagonism.

We can see the nature of interchanges as a continuum ranging from a war with words at the one end, then fierce debates, everyday conversations (neutral), friendly discussions and finally dialogue at the other end of the continuum. Concomitant with this continuum there is Martin Buber's (1958) celebrated *I–It* relation at the *debate*-pole. Here the other is regarded as an object to be eliminated or moulded. On the *dialogue*-pole of the continuum there is the almost mystical union which Buber describes as an *I–Thou* relation, where we are part of each other, yet retain our separate identity.

Overcoming some limitations of dialogue

Galtung (1996) convincingly argues that deep-seated conflicts usually have a bliss point which will give a better future for all parties in the conflict. Finding such a possibility, however, requires creativity. Participants in debates, however, tend to be single-minded; the aim is to defeat the other. Dialogue requires a much broader focus, a willingness to enter the world of the other and a broad interest which is one of the basic positive emotions. Studies of emotion have increasingly come to recognise the widespread beneficial effects of positive emotions (Fredericsson 2001). Negative emotions, however, will go with single-mindedness, which is typical for debates.

In some cases it may not be fruitful to try to start a dialogue between adversaries. Shuttle diplomacy is then an alternative. A relevant TRANSCEND approach is described by Galtung and Tschudi (2002). In this process the contesting parties are visited separately and the conflict worker brings back to the other party only whatever the first party agrees should be shared. The focus of the dialogue between conflict worker and one party is to explore hopes and fears in order to probe deeper into goals, and also to map advantages and disadvantages of both previous states and possible future states. The kernel is to 'open cognitive space to new outcomes not envisaged by the parties', and such new outcomes usually require reframing of the conflict, or 'dis-embedding and re-embedding' (Galtung and Tschudi 2002: 154).

With deep-seated conflicts there is a risk that attempts at dialogue may backfire. An alternative is to emphasise the building of personal relations by having the participants work together on concrete tasks. The Middle East Project for Young Leaders (2007) (MEP-project) with participants from Israel, Palestine, Jordan and Norway is a good example in this regard.[5]

Building viable relations requires mutual resonance, the rediscovering of joint humanity and global *ubuntu*. The use of music can be a facilitator by releasing positive emotions. Music has proved its positive influence in the MEP-project where a musician at some point found the right melodies (Føyen 2005). Jordanger (2006) has also reported success by using music in dialogue groups in the Caucasus region. The theoretical framework was inspired by Neimeyer and Tschudi (2003).[6]

Bougainville: a restorative justice success story

Dialogue alone is not sufficient. The examples above illustrate some supplementary ways of building viable relations characterised by transformative values. This part describes how these transformative values have contributed to the remarkable peace process in Bougainville (Papua New Guinea).[7] There are two good reasons for using Bougainville as a restorative justice example when dealing with cases of mass victimisation.

First of all, the seriousness and the massive scale on which the conflict unfolded, shows the potential of restorative justice to operate in cases of serious crimes. Few, if any, recent wars can match the cruelty and devastation of the civil wars in Bougainville from 1988 to 1997. Comparing these wars with the genocide in Rwanda, Braithwaite (2006c) wrote: 'the worst thing was that it was a slow war, so a whole generation has never seen the inside of a school'. From a population of about 200,000 estimates of the number killed in the wars range from 15,000 to 20,000.

And secondly, the Bougainville case was more or less a success story from which we can obviously draw some important lessons. After 1997 there has not been any outbreak of renewed civil war. After a recent visit to Bougainville, Braithwaite (2006a) reported that there have been thousands of reconciliation ceremonies, and that the lesson from Bougainville is that 'what may be required to return a society to peace [...] may be restorative processes that are historically sustained, deep and broad'.

In an impressive dissertation Peter Reddy (2006) gives a comprehensive account of restorative justice, specifically as applied to today's wars. To illustrate the potentiality of restorative justice he compares the operations in Bougainville and Somalia where the former illustrates a successful approach and the latter a failure. The reason for comparing Bougainville with Somalia was that there are several similarities between the backgrounds in the two countries so that differences in the peace operations can be related to differences in outcome. Unlike Somalia which received considerable media attention in the West, Bougainville is practically unknown to most Westerners. For both countries there had been inequitable treatment by remote and powerful interests, and boundaries imposed by colonial powers.

People in Bougainville were strongly dissatisfied with the central government in Papua New Guinea (PNG). Part of the reason was that the PNG government had violently evicted local landowners in the process of developing a large open-cut copper mine in the Panguna valley. The mine opened in 1964 but in 1988 the installations were destroyed 'in a wave of sabotage' (Reddy 2006: 215). Not only did this start a war with the military forces of PNG, there were also several factions in Bougainville engaged in internecine wars.

Somalia had a repressive dictatorship. In both countries there were cruel civil wars marked by irregular militias fighting, gangs of armed youth cut off from the restraints of family and community with free reign to rape and rob, old clan rivalries revived, rapid urban growth with concomitant social disruption, etc.

There were several unsuccessful peace attempts in Bougainville in the period 1988–97. In that period there was widespread war fatigue, and at the same time an offer from New Zealand to host peace talks. These peace talks – which took place in Burnham (New Zealand) – were accepted by the major fighting parties. This led to the establishment of a Truce Monitoring Group (TMG), later to be followed by a Peace Monitoring Group (PMG) in November 1997. They were scheduled to operate for a six-year period, but 'a peace process is still unfolding – regularly reinforced by indigenous restorative processes' (Reddy 2006: 228). For Bougainville the mission was defined as encouraging reconciliation, providing education and boosting confidence, whereas for Somalia the mission merely concentrated on providing humanitarian aid. In Bougainville the peace workers were invited whereas in Somalia the interventions were imposed on the people.

Respect for cultural tradition

The main difference between the peace operation in Bougainville and that in Somalia is the high level of respect for the local culture that was present in Bougainville and the lack thereof in Somalia. A unique feature of the PMG was that the participants – composed of people with both military and civilian backgrounds – were unarmed. 'The very presence of an unarmed peace force was a reminder that trying to solve conflict with the barrel of a gun is not the answer' (Reddy

2006: 236). One of the former rebel leaders 'believes that had the peace monitors been armed this would have aroused suspicion that the rebels were to be fought with, their political leaders killed and the mine reopened. In short it would have inflamed the situation. So the crucial element, it seems, was trust' (2006: 236).

In Bougainville the peace workers got to be acquainted with and respect the local culture. This was facilitated by the fact that the multicultural PMG was from the Pacific area, and the closer the cultural background the easier it was for the members 'to pick up local vibes'. A major task for the PMG was to 'encourage a space in which life could begin to return to normal' (2006: 231). The processes in Bougainville were, however, largely driven by the inhabitants themselves. In this bottom-up approach they had the ownership of the process. Local capacity was mobilised in finding paths to reconciliation and the roots for societal renewal. In Somalia, on the other hand, the process was almost exclusively a top-down approach, emphasising the imposition of coercion from outside and thus illustrating disrespect.

Training local experts – promoting restorative values

In Bougainville some 10,000 people received some form of training in restorative justice – combining local traditions with Western influences (Howley 2003). An illustration of how indigenous skills were integrated in the courses is the fact that much of the training was group work with tasks where the trainers had no fixed answers. The group often found creative solutions which amazed the trainers. These courses lasted two to three weeks and took place in public meeting places. Several of the students would be teachers to the next group.

It was a careful but well-considered approach to include also as many as possible of the former community leaders. Some of them had been quite authoritarian, not good at listening to others, and also dominant in their private lives. Howley reports cases where such persons markedly changed as a result of the courses, e.g. they stopped beating their wives, or women cut back on yelling at their children. When they learned good listening skills this had the effect of encouraging people who had usually been quiet to be active participants. Generally people learned to speak their mind and become assertive without having to resort to being subservient or aggressive (Howley 2003: 218).

The empowerment of women was another important aim of the training programme. This way women became a normal and accepted part of the emerging group of local leaders. There was a growing willingness to see women as worthwhile and equal participants, rather than a threat to men's traditional position of power and influence (Howley 2003: 251–2). Furthermore women played a crucial role in getting opposing factions to come together for reconciliation meetings.

Getting less authoritarian community leaders and achieving a more active role for women clearly illustrate the ground work for post-conflict regeneration, and the fostering of restorative values as empowerment, empathy and listening skills.

Indigenous rituals

Reconciliation meetings took place in about half of all the local villages. The issues dealt with ranged from theft, rape the the burning of houses to torture and murder. To the extent possible all the meetings were facilitated by locally trained persons. In serious cases there might be several days' work just to get the persons involved to participate in the meeting. Sometimes the facilitators would use shuttle mediation. Preliminary deliberations and negotiation might take days or weeks.

At the meeting gifts are exchanged but the symbolic aspect of the gifts is far more important than the material value. Howley (2003: 241) describes it as follows: 'A gift is intended to wash away the tears, and in no way is it intended as a payment for the loss incurred.' Furthermore there is often *tarout* which translates as 'vomiting'. This was done at the the Burnham talks in New Zealand and may last for hours. *Tarout* is where unrestrained emotional outpourings are allowed to happen. Here anything that any relevant party feels needs to be said, shouted or cried out is expressed. As with physical vomiting, where toxins are purged, this verbal equivalent gives vent to internal emotional and psychological poisons. But in either case some movement along the path to feeling better has commenced (Reddy 2006: 227). Reddy further quotes a delegate:

> The vomiting sessions united us and from then on we stood back as one [...] The women played a very important role, they would say: 'Look, I am here, there is my son over there [...] and all of you, you are all our sons'. During this time there was

> no agenda, and it was so important to vomit it all out. (2006: 228)

This ceremony produces *wan bel* which means one stomach, and is a metaphor for reconciliation. 'When two people are of *wan bel* they share one good feeling' (Reddy 2006: 232). A common feature of all such meetings is that telling what happened is necessary, whatever needs to be said is 'vomited out'. The process is not professionalised and it is the people themselves, victims, offenders and their communities of care, who carry out these restorative ceremonies (2006: 248). Other important ceremonies were to bury a rock to symbolise the departure of the weight of sorrow and bad experience, or to plant a tree to symbolise a new future (2006: 245). Usually the ceremonies are followed by admission of responsibility and explanations of the events. Apology is made, and gifts and compensation are given to survivors or victim's relatives. When forgiveness has been asked for, it is rarely, if ever, refused (2006: 245). Reconciliation closes the meeting. An important feature of reconciliation ceremonies is that they are carried out at different levels, at both a community level and an individual level.[8] Braithwaite (2003) does not regard forgiveness and reconciliation as necessary for a restorative outcome, but this idea 'was greeted with bemusement and almost derision' (Reddy 2006: 248). This extends to persons where one had been tortured but could say 'today this man is my brother and I have reconciled with him' (Reddy 2006: 247).

Time perspective

Both in Bougainville and Somalia the people had a much longer time perspective than is dominant in the West. For some of the groups sent to Somalia the time perspective for the operation was three to four months. By way of contrast the Bougainville mission was tentatively set for three years but acknowledged a more open-ended process. The UN-sponsored peace talks in Somalia were driven by an unseemly haste to conclude discussion and agree on peace. An end date had precedence over any desired end state. In Bougainville no timetable was imposed. One NGO worker informed a group of Bougainvillian leaders that his organisation might be in Bougainville for several years. The leaders responded: 'Why are you not committed to us for a hundred years. Why is there not a hundred years plan to right all wrongs and put in place all the things that should be?' (Reddy 2006: 278).

The relationship with international law

Reddy (2004: ch. 8) emphasises that in order for restorative justice and reconciliation to provide a foundation for more successful social and political processes it must be carried out at several levels. For Bougainville we mentioned three levels; major leaders of the fighting first met in New Zealand, and then there were reconciliation ceremonies at both the local community and individual levels.

The South African Truth and Reconciliation Commission (TRC) is often portrayed as an ideal model of peacebuilding after serious conflict. Both Rossner (2006) and Makhalemele (2004), however, emphasise that while the peace process was successful at the national level – starting with reconciliation between former president De Klerk and Mandela – the TRC was rather unsuccessful at the individual level. In the wake of this struggle for numerous victims and survivors of political violence the Khulumani Support Group was established in 1995 as a strong party to advocate for the inclusion of victims' needs and concerns in the process of the TRC. The TRC had promised to heal wounds at all levels, but it turned out that many victims felt ignored. The priority was given to national coverage at the expense of many victims who felt that their dignity was not respected. They were given promises of reparation which were not fulfilled. Many victims did not even get a chance to 'wash away the tears' as was the case in Bougainville. The deep disappointment of Khulumani on behalf of the many victims has led them to continue the struggle for victims to receive reparation.

As said before, in Bougainville reconciliation was carried out at different levels without any serious conflict between individual and community considerations. Furthermore, local people were always in charge of the reconciliation process whereas in South Africa the TRC – as an institution – always had a firm grip on the process. This suggests that the peace work in Bougainville should be studied more closely as it may provide important lessons for post-conflict situations.

The relationship between restorative justice practices and International Criminal Justice, and more in particular the newly established International Criminal Court (ICC), is an unresolved issue. In the context of mass victimisation and crimes against humanity, Robertson (2006) strongly argues that all such cases should be subjected to international prosecution. He sees such crimes as 'by definition, unforgivable' (2006: 327), and argues for the unacceptability of amnesties. There is a place for a truth commission but as 'a prelude to trial' (2006: 312). On the other hand we should be open to the possibility that the insistence on bringing in international law procedures may be a contemporary example of the sin of Western hubris, carrying forth an imperialistic agenda. This is currently an urgent issue in Uganda. There is a dispute whether Joseph Kony – leader of the Lord's Resistance Army or LRA, and accused of mass murder, rape, mutilation and abducting children to become soldiers – should be tried before the ICC or not. McGreal (2007) reports that African governments believe that trials should be subordinated to local peace deals and reconciliation, and further quotes local people who would rather prefer to end the war and allow people to return to their homes. Furthermore, others see the claim for prosecution as ICC grandstanding.

In line with the claim of Western hubris, Bloomfield *et al.* (2003: 46) describe a tendency, especially among Western and Northern interveners, to export conflict management mechanisms from the developed world and try to impose them in novel contexts. This form of cognitive imperialism may lead to failure when the models are not culturally appropriate and will thus be seen as alien, irrelevant and imposed from outside, and the tendency to put a one-sided emphasis on retributive justice by NGOs (such as Human Rights Watch and Amnesty International) is seen as dangerous (Huyse 2003: 107).

The experience from Bougainville shows that local procedures and peace workers trained in universal, transformative values may accomplish much more than what is possible by criminal procedures. Whereas the latter mainly leads to exclusion, reconciliation leads to inclusion in a joint community. This is not a question of universal values versus local customs but how universal values may be locally adapted. This is not to say that the ICC is useless but it should not be imposed. Peace workers should be thoroughly familiar with the communities in need of reconciliation, and may draw inspiration from the ICC and NGOs as guidelines for the development dialogue.

Conclusion

Regardless of all attempts to get to fruitful dialogue in conflicts, the world is such that there will always be situations where one must admit that dialogue will fail. This is where deterrence measures may have to be brought in. The theory of responsive regulation and a regulatory pyramid (Braithwaite 2002) prescribes that one should always start at the bottom of a pyramid, and this implies restorative, dialogical approaches. If these fail one should move up the pyramid, which implies bringing forth a tailor-made set of deterrence measures, e.g. mild to extremely pointed warnings before going to such a strong measure as a boycott. If all further attempts at deterrence fail, incapacitation (change of regime, withdrawing licences to operate in cases of serious business crimes, etc.) is called for. The basic point in the responsive regulation theory is that at the smallest sign of compliance one should 'scale down' in the pyramid, i.e. go back to basic dialogic approaches. One should always be reluctant and slow in scaling upwards and fast in scaling downwards. 'Talk softly and carry a big stick' is one of Braithwaite's favourite quotes.

From this point of view, Joseph Kony from the Lord's Resistance Army (LRA) might get a choice of restorative encounters in which it could be worked out how he could participate in the constructive rebuilding of his war-torn country. The alternative to this dialogic approach would be to face the ICC. Steinberg (2005: 234) is sharply critical of restorative justice and prefers realpolitik, where 'power balance and mutual deterrence relationships are the prime determinants of stability (and peace)'. From the point of view of the regulatory pyramid, dialogue vs. deterrence is not necessarily a question of either/or, but rather a question of complementarity. At the stage where dialogue seems to fail, realistic critique of dialogic approaches is strongly called for. This can serve to highlight undue optimism and thus lead to more efficient procedures.

Notes

1 For further information go to http://www.humiliationstudies.org.
2 Milder forms of humiliation might still be seen as 'social medicine' – ideally to be gracefully received. Unless explicitly mentioned humiliation will here refer to the strong forms, where today 'humiliation [has been] redefined as a mortal wounding of one's very being' (Lindner 2006b: 10.
3 This victim, named Cathy, took part in a programme led by the police officer and restorative justice pioneer Terry O'Connell in New South Wales (Australia). The personal communication between Cathy and the author is described in more detail in Neimeyer and Tschudi (2003).
4 It should be noted, however, that much of the research reviewed by Lum was of doubtful quality.
5 The MEP project has been going on for three years, and a preliminary report is compiled by Breivik (2006). For more detailed information on

the project, see also the website of the Middle East Programme for Young Leaders at http://mep.abildso.org.

6 In this regard the suggestion to hold a large Middle East peace concert could be worthwhile to consider. This idea was once suggested to a Palestinian singer in Ramallah. At a personal level it was very much welcomed, but never realised.

7 We also draw on the work by Pat Howley (2003) who was leader of Peace Foundation Melanesia (PFM) which was responsible for much of the training of local peace workers.

8 This is beautifully and forcefully illustrated by the UN Peace Award winning film *Breaking Bows and Arrows*. See also the website of the documentary at http://www.firelight.com.au/breakl.html.

References

Bloomfield, D., Barnes, T. and Huyse, L. (eds) (2003) *Reconciliation After Violent Conflict. A Handbook*. Stockholm: International Insititute for Democracy and Electoral Assistance.

Bohm, D. (1996) *On Dialogue*. New York: Routledge.

Braithwaite, J. (2002) *Restorative Justice and Responsive Regulation*. New York: Oxford University Press.

Braithwaite, J. (2003) 'The fundamentals of restorative justice', in S. Dinnen (ed.), *A Kind of Mending. Restorative Justice in the Pacific Islands*. Canberra: Pandanus Books, pp. 35–43.

Braithwaite, J. (2006a) *Rape, Shame and Pride*. Paper presented at Stockholm Criminology Symposium, Stockholm, Sweden, June.

Braithwaite, J. (2006b) *Subject: My Chapter*. Personal communication (online). Message to F. Tschudi, 16 July.

Braithwaite, J. (2006c) *Subject: Bougainville*. Personal communication (online). Message to F. Tschudi, 24 February.

Braithwaite, J. and Drahos, P. (2000) *Global Business Regulation*. Cambridge: Cambridge University Press.

Braithwaite, J. and Pettit, P. (1990) *Not Just Deserts: A Republican Theory of Criminal Justice*. London: Oxford University Press.

Brehm, S.S. and Brehm, J. (1981) *Psychological Reactance: A Theory of Freedom and Control*. London: Academic Press.

Breivik, N. (2006) *Intergroup Friendships in Intractable Conflicts*. Master's thesis in Peace and Conflict Studies, University of Oslo.

Buber, M. (1958) *I and Thou*, 2nd edn. Edinburgh: T. & T. Clark.

Christie, N. (2001) 'Answers to atrocities. restorative justice in extreme situations', in E.A. Fattah and S. Parmentier (eds), *Victim Policies and Criminal Justice on the Road to Restorative Justice. A Collection of Essays in Honour of Tony Peters*. Leuven, Belgium: Leuven University Press, pp. 379–92.

Cunneen, C. (2001) 'Reparations and restorative justice: responding to the gross violation of human rights', in H. Strang, and J. Braithwaite (eds), *Restorative Justice and Civil Society*. Cambridge: Cambridge University Press, pp. 83–98.

Føyen, A. (2005) Personal communication, 20 January.

Fredericsson, B.L. (2001) 'The role of positive emotions in positive psychology', *American Psychologist*, 56: 218–26.

Galtung, J. (1969) 'Violence, peace and peace research', *Journal of Peace Research*, 6: pp. 167–91.

Galtung, J. (1996) *Peace by Peaceful Means*. London: Sage.

Galtung, J. (2006) Personal communication, 12 July.

Galtung, J. and Tschudi, F. (2002) 'Crafting peace. On the psychology of the TRANSCEND approach', in J. Galtung, C.G. Jacobsen and K.F. Jacobsen (eds), *Searching for Peace. The Road to TRANSCEND*. London: Pluto Press, pp. 151–70.

Harvey, F.P. (1999) 'Practicing coercion. Revisiting successes and failures using Boolean logic and comparative methods', *Journal of Conflict Resolution*, 43 (6): 840–71.

Howley, P. (2003) 'Restorative justice in Bougainville', in S. Dinnen (ed.), *A Kind of Mending. Restorative Justice in the Pacific Islands*. Canberra: Pandanus Books.

Human Dignity and Humiliation Studies (2007) See: http://www.humiliationstudies.org.

Huyse, L. (2003) 'Justice', in D. Bloomfield, T. Barnes and L. Huyse (eds), *Reconciliation After Violent Conflict. A Handbook*. Stockholm: International Institute for Democracy and Electoral Assistance, pp. 97–115.

Johnstone, G. and Van Ness, D. (2007) 'The meaning of restorative justice', in G. Johnstone and D. Van Ness (eds), *Handbook of Restorative Justice*. Cullompton: Willan, pp. 5–23.

Jordanger, V. (2006) *Healing Cultural Violence – Collective Vulnerability through Guided Imagery with Music*. Japan: Toda Institute, forthcoming.

LaFree, G., Korte, R. and Dugan, L. (2006) *Deterrence and Defiance Models of Terrorist Violence in Northern Ireland, 1969 to 1992*. Paper presented at Stockholm Criminology Symposium, Stockholm, Sweden, June.

Lindner, E. (2006a) *Making Enemies: Humiliation and International Conflict*. Westport, CT: Praeger.

Lindner, E. (2006b) 'The Concept of Human Dignity'. Unpublished manuscript.

Lindner, E. and Walsh, N.R. (2006) 'Humiliation or dignity in the Israeli–Palestinian Conflict', in J. Kuriansky (ed.), *Psychosocial Approaches to the Israeli–Palestinian Conflict*. Westport, CT: Praeger, pp. 123–31.

Llewellyn, J.J. and Howse, R. (1999) *Restorative Justice: A Conceptual Framework*. Toronto: Law Commission of Canada.

Lum, C., Kennedy, W. and Sherley, A.J. (2006) *The Effectiveness of Counterterrorism Strategies: A Campbell Systematic Review*. See: http://www.campbellcollaboration.org/CCJG/index.asp.

McGreal, C. (2007) 'Search for peace in Africa throws world court into crisis', *The Guardian*, 12–18 January.

Makhalemele, O. (2004) *Southern Africa Reconciliation Project: Khulumani Case Study*. See: http://www.csvr.org.za/papers/papoupa2.htm.

Middle East Project for Young Leaders (2007) See: http://mep.abildso.org.

Neimeyer, R.A. and Tschudi, F. (2003) 'Community and coherence. Narrative contributions to the psychology of conflict and loss', in G. Fireman, T. McVey and J. Flannagan (eds), *Narrative and Consciousness*. New York: Oxford University Press, pp. 166–91.

Parmentier, S. (2003) 'Global justice in the aftermath of mass violence. The role of the international criminal court in dealing with political crimes', *International Annals of Criminology*, 41 (1–2): 203–24.

Pettit, P. (1996) 'Freedom as antipower', *Ethics*, 106: 576–604.

Pettit, P. (1997) *Republicanism. A Theory of Freedom and Government*. Oxford: Clarendon Press.

Piaget, J. (1954) *The Construction of Reality in the Child*. New York: Basic Books.

Reddy, P.D. (2006) *Peace Operations and Restorative Justice: Groundwork for Post-Conflict Regeneration*. PhD dissertation at the Australian National University.

Robertson, G. (2006) *Crimes against Humanity: The Struggle for Global Justice*, 3rd edn. London: Penguin.

Roche, D. (2001) 'The evolving definition of restorative justice', *Contemporary Justice Review*, 4 (3–4): 341–53.

Ross, L. and Ward, A. (1996) 'Naive realism in everyday life: implications for social conflict and misunderstanding', in T. Brown (ed.), *Values and Knowledge*. Hillsdale, NJ: Erlbaum, pp. 103–35.

Rossner, M. (2006) *Justice Rituals and Expressive Events: An Analysis of the South African TRC*. Paper presented at Stockholm Criminology Symposium, Stockholm, Sweden, June.

Sparks, A. (2003) *The Mind of South Africa. The Story of the Rise and Fall of Apartheid*. Jeppestown, South Africa: Jonathan Ball Publishers.

Steinberg, G.M. (2005) 'The UN, the ICJ and the separation barrier: war by other means', *Israel Law Review*, 38: 331–47.

Sullivan, D. and Tifft, L. (2004) 'What are the implications of restorative justice for society and our lives', in H. Zehr and B. Toews (eds), *Critical Issues in Restorative Justice*. New York: Monsey, pp. 391–404.

Sullivan, D. and Tifft, L. (2006) 'The healing dimension of restorative justice: a one-world body', in D. Sullivan and L. Tifft (eds), *Handbook of Restorative Justice*. New York: Routledge.

Tschudi, F. and Rommetveit, R. (1982) 'Sociality, intersubjectivity, and social processes: the sociality corollary', in J.C. Mancuso and J.R. Adams-Webber (eds), *The Construing Person*. New York: Praeger, pp. 235–61.

Tutu, D. (1999) *No Future without Forgiveness*. London: Rider.

Universal Declaration of Human Rights (1948) United Nations General Assembly, General Assembly Resolution 217 A(III) of 10 December 1948.

Villa-Vicencio, C. (2003) 'Restorative justice: ambiguities and limitations of a theory' in C. Villa-Vicencio and E. Doxtader (eds), *The Provocations of Amnesty. Memory, Justice and Impunity*. Claremont, South Africa: Institute for Justice and Reconciliation, pp. 30–50.

Part 2

Case studies

Section I
The Kosovo conflict

Jana Arsovska, Marta Valiñas and Borbala Fellegi

Based on UN map No. 4069 Rev. 2 (January 2004)

Chapter 3

Prologue to the Kosovo drama: causes and consequences of a violent ethno-political conflict

Jana Arsovska, Marta Valiñas and Borbala Fellegi

During the twentieth century the relationship between political systems, state borders and security has taken on a new form, particularly for people living in Central and Eastern Europe and the Balkans. Just in the period from 1908 to 1993, borders in this region have changed at least nine times, leading to various conflicts and wars (Bianchini 1996: 188). In recent years, parallel with the process of integration, half of the wars going on in the world, including the Balkans, have been struggles for secession. Since 1992, when the Yugoslav wars of secession began, there have been 51 state-based conflicts[1] around the world (UN Human Development Report 2005; Human Security Report 2005). Ethnic, or often more generally stated 'identity-based', conflict is one common form of clashes. This term refers to conflicts in which the goals of at least one of the confronted parties are defined in ethnic identity terms, and in which supposedly the primary fault line of confrontation is one of ethnic distinction (Wolff 2006: 2). Today's literature has been linking ethnicity, language and religion (as a part of people's identity) to intra and interstate dispute behaviour suggesting that cultural traits and identity influence greatly dispute patterns in various ways (Connor 1994; Horowitz 1995; Huntington 1996; Cederman 2001a, 2001b; Comor 2001; Hardin 1995; Hechter 1987; Wendt 1992, 1994).

In the last 15 years newspapers have been incessantly writing about ethnically defined 'nations' and 'culturally homogeneous' people that claim the right to self-determination in a country of their own (Spencer 1998: 7). Some of these claimants have been perpetrating 'ethnic cleansing' campaigns and even genocide

(Spencer 1998: 7; Huttenbach 2004: 24).[2] During the 1980s and 1990s growing nationalism[3] and rapid socio-political changes have led to the escalation of conflicts in the former Yugoslavia. Politicians from the different republics started arguing that ethnically homogeneous nations will progress much faster than multi-ethnic ones. According to their views, communication between the people can be better enhanced within a single territory. As they pointed out, ethnic or – more broadly – cultural diversity leads to stagnation.

As a result, a bloody decade of political tensions and killings took place. However, one might ask whether it has brought any progress to the republics of the former Yugoslavia at all.

The disintegration of Yugoslavia

The Socialist Federal Republic of Yugoslavia (SFRY) was drawn into a highly destructive armed conflict in the early 1990s. The genesis of the collapse of Yugoslavia lies in the decade of difficulties that followed Josip Broz Tito's death in 1980, during which the country failed to overcome the legacies of the past as well as to address demands for reform emanating from society (Allcock 2000: 418; Cohen 1993). One approach to the Yugoslav crisis is to trace the disintegration of Yugoslavia to economic factors. The less developed republics claimed that the federation was not doing enough for them, whereas the more developed republics argued that their own growth was being slowed by the necessity to provide support to the less developed republics (Ramet 2005: 55–6). According to some authors, the problem that led to disintegration was not so much the demand for self-determination within the complex Yugoslav institutional construction but the way in which the leadership of the republics went about resolving their grievances (Vejvoda 1996: 101; Tilly 1993). As they argued a so-called 'velvet divorce' in 1990–91 would have been plausible, had there been a decision by the presidents of the six republics to agree a moratorium on their respective demands for constitutional and territorial change (Vejvoda 1996: 101). However, this vision now appears unreal. Instead, there has been a decade of destruction in which hundreds of thousands of people ended up dead and countless numbers were displaced. As a result, frustration, fear, shame and humiliation have thrived all over the territory of the former Yugoslavia.

The collapse of the federal state culminated in the secession of the more developed republics – Slovenia and Croatia – during the spring of

1991. It was the advent of the Serbian president Slobodan Milosevic's rise to power, with the 'vision of a revived Serbian hegemony' – allied to 'a version of populist Communism' – that turned the Croats and the Slovenes against Yugoslavia (Cviic 1996: 130). However, the Brioni agreements of July 1991 ended the confrontation between the Yugoslav People's Army (JNA) and the Slovenian defence forces. Yet this agreement failed to halt the disintegration and violence, accelerating the outbreak of fighting in Croatia (Shoup 2002: 173; Cviic 1996: 130–1). The armed conflict in Croatia started when the Belgrade-backed local Serb population and military groups organised a rebellion in response to Croatia's declaration of independence in 1991 (Cruvellier and Valiñas 2006). In the months that followed, the Croat population was systematically expelled from the territories under Serbian control. Thousands of Croats were tortured and killed. However, as a result of counter-military offences, in 1995, Croatia managed to regain control of its territories. These actions caused the exodus of more than 200,000 Serbs from these territories (Dancev and Halverson 1996; Cviic 1996).

After a UN monitored ceasefire started in Croatia during the spring of 1992, Bosnian Croats and Serbs fighting in Croatia returned to Bosnia and Herzegovina to take up the struggle there. As a result, in 1992 Europe was about to experience the bloodiest war on its territory ever since the Second World War. Bosnia and Herzegovina was one of the republics of the former Yugoslavia with a highly complex ethnic structure due to the multi-ethnic composition of its population (Ignatieff 1996: xii; Malcolm 1994; Rogel 1998; Ramet 2005). Bosnian Muslims as well as Serbian and Croatian Christians have been peacefully living together for a long time on the territory of Bosnia, showing a positive example for multi-ethnic cooperation. As Michael Ignatieff (1996: xii) explains, in Western eyes this was the very picture of the multicultural dream. However, in the early 1990s, as a result of political games it became apparent that Bosnia would not remain in Yugoslavia under the leadership of Slobodan Milosevic. The Serbian Democratic Party (SDS) in Bosnia started arguing for the creation of a separate Serbian entity within the country, and, in January 1992, the Assembly of Serbian people in Bosnia adopted a Proclamation of the Serbian Republic of Bosnia and Herzegovina.[4] Faced with a mounting threat, the Bosnian government organised a referendum on independence in March 1992. The majority of Bosnian Muslims and Croats voted for independence, while Bosnian Serbs boycotted the referendum. As a response, Bosnian Serb forces began to take control of ethnically mixed areas. The international community tried to prevent the impending war by recognising the independence of Bosnia and Herzegovina; however, they failed in their mission and witnessed a devastating war (Malcolm 1994; Rogel 1998; Ramet 2005).

The war in Bosnia lasted until 1995, when the Dayton Peace Agreement was signed. During this period, 4.3 million citizens were displaced and up to a quarter of a million were killed and their properties destroyed (Cousens and Cater 2001: 25; Ramet 2005: 186). In July 1995 'the UN protected area' of Srebrenica was taken over by the Bosnian Serb Army that executed over 7,000 (some say 8,000) Bosnian Muslims in a matter of days and tried to hide the killings by reburying the bodies in secondary mass graves (ICTY 2004; Simons 2007; Federal Commission for Missing Persons 2005). In November 1995 the Dayton Peace Agreement ended the armed conflict and established an international protectorate. The war in Bosnia was soon followed by the quickly escalating conflict in Kosovo. This was partially caused by the Dayton accords that sent a message to the Albanians that you can do much more with a kind word and a gun than only with a kind word. Up to the Dayton accords, the Kosovo Albanian response to Belgrade's apartheid-like regime was a non-violent one (Shoup 2002: 173; Troebst 1998; Salla 1995).

The origin and consequences of the Serb–Albanian conflict

Historical overview

Kosovo is located in the south-western corner of the Republic of Serbia – a territory of 10,887 square kilometres called *Kosova* or *Kosova dhe Rrafshi i Dukagjinit* in Albanian and *Kosovo* or *Kosovo-Metohija* in Serbian (Troebst 1998: 6; Janjic 2003: 4).[5] It is inhabited by over two million people of which ethnic Albanians account for more than 1,800,000 (between 90 and 95 per cent of the population). The Serbian population of Kosovo is 5 to 10 per cent[6] (Janjic 2003: 5; Salla 1995; Barnett and Xharra 2007). The fact that many ethnic Albanians were living in Kosovo became a serious political problem after the death of Tito (1980). Kosovo Albanians started to demand an upgrade of their autonomous province to the seventh Yugoslav Republic. The Serbian President Milosevic not only rejected this demand, but in 1989 he sacked what was left of Kosovo's political autonomy (Troebst 1998: 6).

The seeds of confrontation between Serbs and Albanians in Kosovo were sown many decades ago although this problem was neglected by Western scholars until some years ago (Robertson 1999; Janjic 2003; Ramet 2005: 200). Only in the last decade has Kosovo become the focus of a continuing flood of books trying to understand Serb–Albanian relations (Mertus 1999; Malcolm 1998; Vickers 1998; Ramet 2005). According to Mertus (1999) the answer is to be sought in the different 'truths' nurtured by the two communities. The Kosovo conflict itself is mainly over control of the territory of Kosovo which has a great significance for the two ethnic groups. Both Serbs and Albanians had regarded Kosovo as their own historical space. In 1389, Serb forces were defeated by the Ottomans at the battle of Kosovo Polje. This event made Kosovo an integral part of the Serbian collective nationalistic ideology. For Albanians it is regarded as the birthplace of their claimed ancestors, the Illyrians, and as one of the hotbeds of Albanian culture (Janjic 2003: 4; Robertson 1999: 2). Moreover, according to Janjic (2003: 4), the Kosovo conflict reflects the tension between the Serbian majority 'opting for domination and self-isolation' and the Albanian minority 'opting for separation'. Chronologically, Serb–Albanian relations went through a number of stages, revealing the complexity of the problem.

Despite its ethnic Albanian majority, Kosovo became part of Serbia in 1913, following the Balkan wars. Later it became part of Yugoslavia. According to Janjic (2003), the period between 1918 and 1941/45 was a period of changing domination in Kosovo, accompanied by sporadic violence. First, Albanians were under Serbian domination, and than Serbs were persecuted in Kosovo in the so-called Greater Albania that was created in collaboration with Nazi Germany and fascist Italy (1941–45). The second stage (1945–66) in Janjic's (2003: 5) view, was a period of 'oscillation from occasional violence' to solutions to the disputes by 'political means'. Towards the end of the 1960s the Yugoslav policy towards Kosovo changed from repressive to more tolerant. The third phase (1966–81) was a period in which the rights of Albanians have been widely guaranteed, while the autonomy of Kosovo within Yugoslavia strengthened. Under the 1974 Yugoslav Constitution, Kosovo became an autonomous province within Serbia (Janjic 2003: 5; Robertson 1999: 2; Malcolm 1998). The fourth stage, known as the disintegration of Yugoslavia, encompasses the period between 1981 and present times. At this time both Serbian and Albanian ethno-nationalistic movements have been strengthened. The intensification of the conflict occurred between 1989 and 1998. The culmination of the disagreement arose in 1998–99 resulting in open armed conflict between the two groups and in NATO intervention (Janjic 2003: 5; Robertson 1999).

The escalation of the Kosovo conflict

During the 1980s, the Serbs in Kosovo expressed some concerns over discrimination against them by the Kosovo Albanian-led government, while Kosovo Albanians were worrying about the economic underdevelopment and their political power. According to Mertus (1999, cited in Ramet 2005) various public events encouraged further the tensions between the two communities. Given that popular consciousness centres on highly publicised events with symbolic value, Mertus[7] explains that issues such as the 1981 riots in Kosovo and the 1985 'Martinovic Affair' promoted further the hatred between the Serbs and the Albanians. In the 'Martinovic Affair', a 56-year-old Serbian peasant went to a local hospital with a bottle jammed into his anus, alleging that his predicament was the result of an attack by two Albanian men. The community leaders of Gnjilane issued a statement describing the injuries as the 'accidental consequences of a self-induced sexual practice' (Mertus 1999: 101), while the newspapers in Belgrade hyperbolically associated the case with the Jasenovac concentration camp operated by the Ustase during the Second World War (Mertus 1999: 110, cited in Ramet 2005: 201).

As a result of these and similar other politicised events, in the period 1981–86 Albanians used mass demonstrations for demanding their own state within Yugoslavia as the 'Kosovo Republic'. Their protests were suppressed by the SFRY military and police forces (Janjic 2003: 5). The accession of Slobodan Milosevic to power in 1987 fostered these tensions, since he was vigorously fomenting a Serbian nationalist sentiment (ICTY 1999). Bringing Kosovo under stronger control of the Serbian central government led to more demonstrations, which resulted in the dismissal of prominent Kosovo Albanian state officials. In 1988 Milosevic pushed through a bill declaring Serbian to be the official language of Kosovo and banning the use of Albanian for official business (Troebst 1998; Robertson 1999). Simultaneously, the first mass rallies of Serbs demanding the abrogation of the autonomy of the two Serbian provinces – Kosovo and Vojvodina – took place. Albanian demonstrations culminated in February 1989 in a hunger strike of more than one thousand miners. As a result, Belgrade sent the army in and imposed emergency measures (Ramet 1997: 147; Troebst 1998: 19).

In early 1989 the Serbian Assembly proposed amendments to the Constitution of Serbia that removed most of the autonomous power Kosovo had enjoyed since the 1974 Constitution.[8] According to this Constitution, the province was granted substantial autonomy including control over its educational system, judiciary, police and its own provincial assemblies. The Constitution of 1974 linked Kosovo with the Federal State directly referring to it as a 'constitutive element' (Janjic 2003: 4). After Kosovo's autonomy was revoked, the political situation became worse. Throughout 1990 and 1991 thousands of Kosovo Albanians lost their jobs, while Serbian police violence against them increased. During this period, the unofficial Kosovo Albanian leadership ('shadow government') practised a policy of non-violent civil resistance and established a system of unofficial, parallel institutions in the health care and education sectors (Troebst 1998; Robertson 1999: 2; Malcolm 1998; Salla 1995).

It is commonly believed that Milosevic's regime tried to establish direct jurisdiction over Kosovo by restricting the rights of the Albanians through 'a methodically pursued campaign for their marginalisation' and discrimination (Janjic 2003: 5). On the other hand, the Albanian leader Ibrahim Rugova and the Democratic League of Kosovo (LDK) tried to achieve independence for the 'Republic of Kosovo' by building parallel institutions. These two political actors maintained this status quo until 1995. According to Janjic (2003: 6) the result was a complete division within Kosovo society. However, the Dayton Peace Accord of 1995 did not deal with the Kosovo question. The Kosovo Albanian tactics of non-violent resistance to Serbian oppression were interpreted by Westerners as a guarantee against escalation into armed conflict (Troebst 1998; Salla 1995). Therefore, following the Dayton Peace Accord, two parallel processes took place: (1) official public discussion of the status of Kosovo, and (2) radicalisation of the Albanian movement and political life (Janjic 2003).

The radicalisation process among the Kosovo Albanians produced a massive student movement and a small militant underground. In 1996, among the Albanians there was a growing tendency to reject the peaceful policy of Rugova (LDK). The strengthening of the anti-Serbian attitude culminated in a series of attacks from 1996 carried out by the militant underground KLA (Kosovo Liberation Army: Ushtria Çlirimtare e Kosovës (UÇK)).[9] Following the establishment of the KLA, Kosovo Albanians started an armed rebellion against Serbian authorities, targeting Serbian police forces. Udovicki and Ridgeway (2000) give a detailed account on the rise of the KLA, where they argue that as a result of the violent activities against Serbian targets, pressure built up on the Belgrade regime to respond. Hence, Serbs responded with violence against the KLA and their supporters (Udovicki and Ridgeway 2000: 317–27; Ramet 2005: 19). Most Albanians perceived the KLA as legitimate 'freedom fighters' while the Yugoslav government called them terrorists attacking civilians. Although the US envoy Robert Gelbard once referred to the KLA as terrorists, he later admitted that they were never legally classified as a terrorist organisation by the US government (Cohen 1999; Doggett 1999). From February 1998 incidents in Kosovo rapidly intensified and turned into an internal armed conflict in August 1998 (Troebst 1998; Ramet 2005).

The violent incidents and the Rambouillet Accords

By March 1998 the situation in Kosovo became highly unstable. The KLA with an estimated strength of several hundred fighters increased the number of attacks and assassinations of Serbian officials. The regime retaliated first by police violence and long-term sentences. Later, more security forces were brought to Kosovo (Terlingen 1997: 6). According to various sources, the violent activities of the KLA guerrillas were openly applauded by Kosovo Albanian youngsters and other radicals that were unsatisfied with the peaceful methods previously used (Troebst 1998: 14).[10]

From the Serbian point of view, there was an overture of a general rebellion of Albanians against the organs of the Serbian state; hence the Supreme Defence Council decided to strengthen the army corps (Jovanovic 1998: 2; Ramet 2005). In March 1998, a battle-like clash between KLA fighters on the one side and heavily armed Special Anti-Terror Units (SAJ) on the other took place near the Drenica village of Likoshan. At least four Serbian police officers and 30 Albanian civilians were killed (Troebst 1998: 15; Foreign & Commonwealth Office 1999; Human Rights Watch 1998). Following this event the Serbian police went after the family compound of a local KLA leader in Donji Prekaz. An estimated 58 Albanians were killed, including 18 women and ten children under the age of 16 (Troebs 1998: 15; Blitzer *et al.* 1999; Foreign & Commonwealth Office 1999; Human Rights Watch 1998). On 2 March 1998 Serbian riot police cracked down on a large crowd of Albanian demonstrators in Prishtina and injured at least 289 persons. From 4 to 7 March the Serbian side directed a second blow against the Drenica villages where some families were killed (Troebst 1998: 15; Human Rights Watch 1998; Foreign & Commonwealth Office 1999). During the same month, clashes between Albanian armed groups and Serbian police occurred in several other villages resulting in many more civilian deaths (Clines 1999; Erlanger 1999; Foreign & Commonwealth Office 1999; Human Rights Watch 1998; Clinton 1999).

Despite the rapid escalation of the Kosovo conflict, there were also some positive signs. The Drenica massacre caused intergovernmental organisations and NGOs to increase their efforts to facilitate a non-violent solution to the Kosovo conflict (Troebst 1998: 14; Janjic 2003). In addition, in January 1998 the Serb Christian-Orthodox Patriarch sent a letter to the Student Union of the Albanian underground university condemning a crackdown of Serbian security forces on student demonstrators (Troebst 1998: 14). The 'Pan-Serbian Church and People Assembly' in Prishtina called on the political representatives of Kosovo Albanians and Serbs to enter immediately into negotiations: 'Only by dialogue can a solution be found, since a war would be a catastrophe for Serbs and Albanians alike' (1998: 15). In February 1998 the so-called 3+3 Group, composed of Serbian and Kosovo Albanian educational authorities, met under the patronage of the Catholic NGO Comunità di Sant'Egidio to discuss issues related to the implementation of the education agreement (1998: 15). However, despite some positive developments, the violent incidents on both sides were multiplying.

In 1998 Milosevic decided to stop offensive operations and to prepare for talks with the Albanians. However, the KLA did not stop taking over areas in Kosovo[11] and this led again to a series of Serb offensive actions. These attacks resulted in public talks hinting that a new Srebrenica massacre could possibly take place (Craig 2003: 240–55). The threats were intensifying; however, a terrifying event was needed to bring the situation to culmination. The KLA got it on September 1998 when the mutilated corpses of an Albanian family were discovered outside Gornje Obrinje. The other major issue that fostered the use of violence was supposedly the estimated 250,000 displaced Albanians, of whom 50,000 were out in the woods in winter time, without shelter (Robertson 1999: 9).

As intimidations increased, NATO's Activation Order was given for launching bomb attacks (Robertson 1999: 9).[12] However, negotiations led to the Kosovo Verification Agreement on 12 October 1998. The international community demanded an end to the fighting. A ceasefire was achieved, but it did not last long. The fighting began again in December 1998 after the KLA occupied some bunkers, not long after the Panda Bar Massacre where the KLA opened fire in a coffee bar in Pec. The KLA attacks and the Serbian reprisals continued, culminating with the Racak incident on 15 January 1999. Even before the investigation, the event was immediately condemned as a 'massacre' by Western countries and the United Nations Security Council (UN Statement 1999).[13] Later this particular incident became the basis of one of the charges of war crimes against Milosevic and his top officials. The details of what happened at Racak are still somewhat controversial (Craig 2003: 240–42; Boari 2001: 5; Gelman 1999: 6-9).[14] The authors in the subsequent chapters of this volume thoroughly discuss – from both Albanian and Serbian perspectives – some of the particularities of this incident.

Immediately afterwards, NATO concluded that the conflict could only be settled by military intervention. As a consequence, on 30 January 1999 it issued a statement announcing that it was prepared to launch air strikes against Yugoslav targets. Hence the Rambouillet talks began on 6 February 1999. The main problems were the non-negotiable principles of the international community (the Contact Group) that were unacceptable for both conflicting parties: the Albanians were unwilling to accept a solution that would keep Kosovo as part of Serbia, and the Serbs did not want to see the pre-1990 status quo restored or the international community governing the province. On 18 March 1999, the Albanian, American and British delegation signed what became known as the Rambouillet Accords,[15] while the Serbian and Russian delegations refused to do so (Robertson 1999). The accords seemed too radical for the Serbs, who responded by substituting a drastically revised text. This led to further escalation of the conflict and to the subsequent NATO intervention.

The international intervention

The NATO's bombing campaign lasted from 24 March to 11 June 1999 and was originally designed to destroy Yugoslav air defences and military targets. Just a few days after the bombing started over 300,000 Kosovo Albanians had fled into neighbouring countries and many thousands more were displaced within Kosovo. By April, the United Nations reported that 850,000 people, most of whom were Albanians, had fled from their homes (UNHCR Report).[16] The cause of the refugee exodus has been the subject of considerable controversy and it formed the basis of ICTY war crimes charges against Milosevic and other officials. The Yugoslav side and its Western supporters claimed that the refugee outflows were caused by mass panic, and that the exodus was generated principally by fear of NATO bombs (Human Rights Watch 2000a, 2000b; Craig 2003: 248–50).[17] It was also alleged that the exodus was encouraged by KLA guerrillas and that in some cases the KLA issued direct orders to Albanians to flee. Many Albanian eyewitnesses identified Serbian security forces and

KLA paramilitaries as those responsible for systematically emptying towns and villages by either forcing Albanians to flee or through executions.[18]

The former German Minister of Foreign Affairs, Joschka Fischer, claimed that the refugee crisis was initiated by a Serbian plan codenamed 'Operation Horseshoe'. While the existence of such a plan remains controversial, the United Nations and international human rights organisations were convinced that the refugee crisis was the result of a deliberate policy of ethnic cleansing (Craig 2003: 249).[19] According to some sources, possibly Milosevic wanted to achieve 'Serbianisation' of Kosovo by replacing the Albanian population with Serbian refugees from Bosnia and Croatia (see Clinton 1999; Blitzer *et al.* 1999).

Milosevic finally recognised that NATO was serious regarding the resolution of the conflict and he accepted the conditions offered by a Finnish-Russian mediation team. He also agreed to a military presence within Kosovo headed by the UN, but incorporating NATO troops. Soon afterwards, KFOR, a NATO-led force, began entering Kosovo. Towards the end of September 1999 there were 49,400 personnel deployed with KFOR (Robertson 1999: 21). When the war ended, it left Kosovo and Yugoslavia facing an unknown future. The most immediate problem was the return of refugees which was resolved promptly. According to the UN High Commissioner for Refugees, by November 1999 808,913 out of 848,100 refugees had returned. However, much of the remaining Serb population of Kosovo fled fearing revenge attacks (Human Rights Watch 1999b). The Yugoslav Red Cross had registered 247,391 mostly Serbian refugees by November 1999. According to Human Rights Watch (1999b) the rash of killings of Serbs since mid-June 1999 had shown that such fears were not unfounded. Some reports also pointed out that minorities such as Roma, Turks and Bosniaks had been seriously abused by Albanians and driven out of their homes which had been burned by men in KLA uniforms (Human Rights Watch 1999b, 2001; Craig 2003). Most terrifying was the fact that as many as 1,000 Serbs and Roma had been murdered or gone missing since 12 June 1999. According to various reports, criminal gangs or vengeful individuals may have been involved in some of these violent incidents, but elements of the KLA had been allegedly responsible for many of the crimes (Human Rights Watch Report 1999b, 2001; see Nikolic-Ristanovic: this volume, Chapter 6).

The war also inflicted many casualties. By March 1999, it had left an estimated 1,500–2,000 Yugoslav civilians and combatants dead (Human Rights Watch 2001). Yugoslavia claimed that NATO attacks caused between 1,200 and 5,700 civilian casualties but NATO acknowledged killing at most 1,500 civilians. Human Rights Watch (2000a) counted a minimum of 488 civilian deaths. The exact number of Albanian civilians killed in Kosovo is unclear. It is generally estimated around 10,000 although several foreign forensic teams were unable to verify the exact number (Ball *et al.* 2002). Some of the largest mass graves were cleared before the war ended in an effort to eliminate potential war crimes evidence. As of July 2001, the International Criminal Tribunal for the former Yugoslavia (ICTY) had ordered the exhumation of approximately 4,300 bodies believed to have been victims of unlawful killings by Serbian and Yugoslav forces in Kosovo, although the link between the killings and the involvement of the Serbian forces had not then been proven. Nonetheless, there was incontrovertible evidence of grave tampering carried out by Serbian and Yugoslav troops[20] (Human Rights Watch 2001; Spiegel and Salama 2000).

The aftermath of the Kosovo conflict: challenges for the region

Twelve years after the Dayton Agreement and eight years after the fall of the Milosevic regime, according to some, Kosovo and the Western Balkans[21] are a relatively stable region with no military conflicts. But do stability and peace merely mean the absence of military conflicts? Until a few years ago, the lack of violence-related headline news from the Balkans had convinced the international community that the status quo in Kosovo was working well. The fact that it was an illusion was demonstrated by the events that took place in Kosovo in March 2004.[22] These events vividly illustrate the more truthful state of affairs in the Balkans: the situation in Kosovo is far from peaceful (International Commission 2005: 10; Barnett and Xharra 2007; see Nikolic-Ristanovic: this volume, Chapter 6).

According to the Third International Commission on the Balkans (2005: 7), 'the region is as close to failure as it is to success. For the moment, the wars are over, but the smell of violence still hangs heavy in the air'. Their report clearly explains that economic growth in the Balkan territories is low or non-existent, unemployment is very high, corruption is pervasive and the public is pessimistic and distrustful towards its nascent democratic institutions. It is a fact that the international community has invested enormous sums of money and human resources in Kosovo and the region. It has put 25 times more money and 50 times more troops on a per capita basis in post-conflict

Kosovo than in post-conflict Afghanistan (International Commission 2005: 7). However, despite the scale of the assistance effort in the Balkans, the international community has failed to offer a convincing political perspective to the societies in the region. There is a real risk of an explosion of Kosovo and an implosion of Serbia. Moreover, the Commission acknowledges that there are no quick and easy solutions for the Balkans and that ultimately it is up to the people of the region to win their own future (2005: 8).

According to sources, the international community has failed in its attempts to bring security and development to the province. It seems that multi-ethnic Kosovo does not exist, except in the bureaucratic assessments of the international community (Human Rights Watch 1999b; Klemendi 2006; Barnett and Xharra 2007: 28; Nikolic-Ristanovic: this volume, Chapter 6). The events of March 2004 amounted to the strongest signal so far that the situation could explode. Various reports show that Serbs in Kosovo are living imprisoned in their enclaves with no freedom of movement, no jobs and neither hope nor opportunity for meaningful integration into Kosovo society. The position of the Serbian minority in Kosovo is the greatest indictment of Europe's willingness and ability to defend its proclaimed values; hence Kosovo Albanians should receive a clear message that the use of violence is the worst enemy of their dream for independence (International Commission 2005: 19; Barnett and Xharra 2007: 28).

The lack of leadership in Belgrade has also contributed to the plight of the Kosovo Serbs. Consequently, the Serbian community in Kosovo has also become hostage to the political struggles. The Albanian leadership in Kosovo must also shoulder its part of the blame for failing to show real willingness to engage in a process of reconciliation and development of multi-ethnic institutions. A survey commissioned by the International Commission on the Balkans and conducted in November–December 2004[23] indicates that a majority of Kosovars are keen on living in an 'ethnically homogeneous Kosovo' and are ready to 'seek justice through power and the army' (see Figure 3.1, 3.2 and 3.3). Most Kosovo Albanian politicians have done nothing to oppose this public mood that goes against European values.

According to some, a considerable share of the blame for the failure of the project of a multi-ethnic society in Kosovo should be attributed to the United Nations Mission in Kosovo (UNMIK) and the international community. Over the past few years UNMIK has on several occasions been actively involved in a policy of reverse discrimination in Kosovo (International Commission 2005: 19).[24]

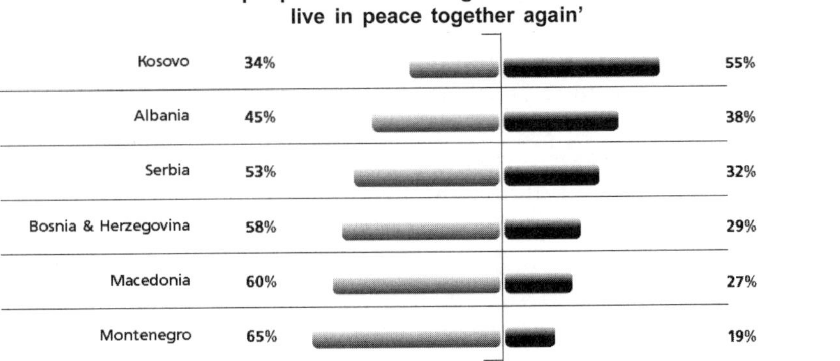

Figure 3.1 Public opinion survey
Source: International Commission on the Balkans (2005: 49).

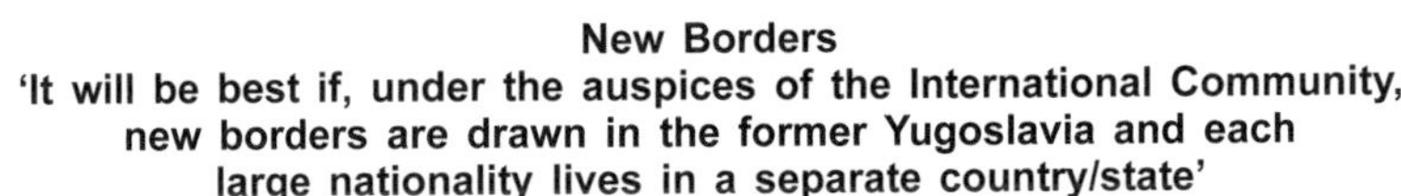

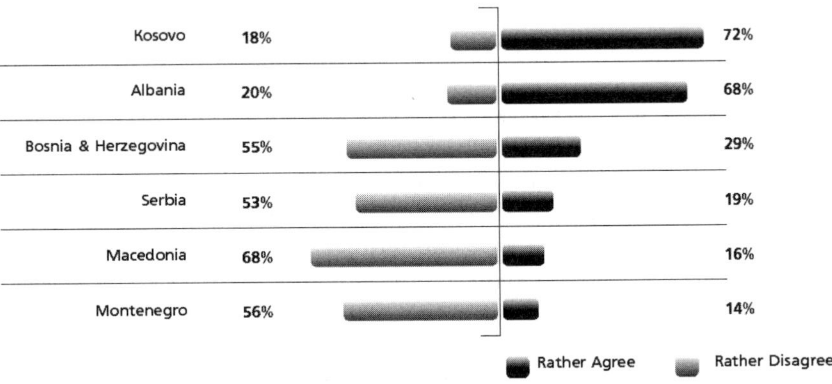

Figure 3.2 Public opinion survey
Source: International Commission on the Balkans (2005: 53).

'The international community in Kosovo is today seen by Kosovo Albanians as having gone from opening the way to now standing in the way. It is seen by Kosovo Serbs as having gone from securing the return of so many to being unable to ensure the return of so few' (Eide 2004). Kosovo Albanians and Serbs are frustrated with the unresolved status, with the economic situation and with the problems of dealing with the past (International Commission 2005: 20).

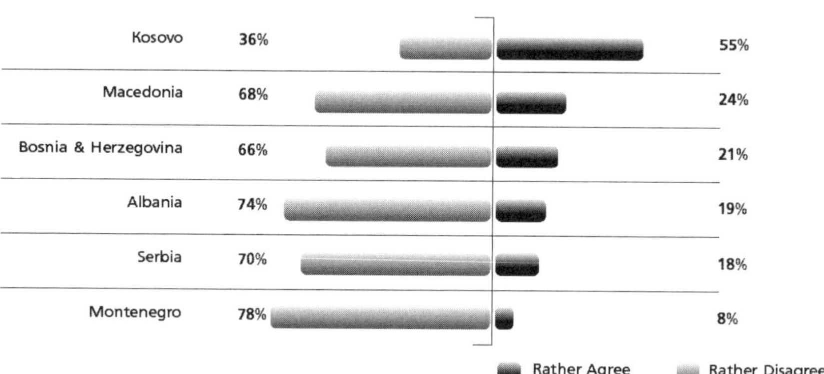

Figure 3.3 Public opinion survey
Source: International Commission on the Balkans (2005: 48).

Hence the question remains: what can be done on a national and international level in order to make Kosovo a truly better place for living and to achieve sustainable peace? How can relations between Serbs and Albanians be improved and how can multi-ethnic cooperation in Kosovo be encouraged? Will revenge killings be stopped and are people ready to reconcile and live together? Is there a possibility for restorative justice in this context? What are the most appropriate mechanisms for dealing with a violent past and mass victimisation in Kosovo? These are some – among many – questions that boggle people's minds.

In the subsequent chapters local contributors provide some details on the existing *formal* and *informal* mechanisms in Kosovo for dealing with violent large-scale incidents, such as, for example, the Racak massacre. The function of the 'Racak incident' presented to the authors was to make the contributors' analysis more focused and comparable. Haki Demolli, referring mainly to the Racak massacre as a case study, analyses the availability of the *formal* justice mechanisms existing in Kosovo. From the Albanian perspective he is examining the effectiveness of the different mechanisms dealing with violent incidents at national and international levels. Then, Rexhep Gashi sheds some light on the available *informal* mechanisms dealing with conflicts in the Kosovo Albanian context, such as for example, the Kanun laws and other cultural codes. Finally, Vesna Nikolic-Ristanovic – from the Serbian perspective – using examples from contemporary society describes the possibilities for *informal* mechanisms for dealing with the Racak and other killings that occurred during the Kosovo conflict. On the basis of their analyses Marta Valiñas and Jana Arsovska evaluate the possibilities and limits for restorative justice: namely, does an approach that intends to provide long-term solutions to violent conflicts through dialogue and participation have any potential in the Kosovo context?

In Focus: The Racak Incident*

Protests and rebellions against the Belgrade-centred Serbian rule had already started in the former autonomous province of Kosovo in the turn from the 1980s to the 1990s. However, due to the wars fought in Croatia and Bosnia, it was only during 1998 and 1999 that mass violence between the Serbian forces (the Yugoslav Army (VJ) and the special forces of the Serbian Police (MUP)) and the Kosovo Liberation Army (KLA) intensified and escalated to appalling proportions. The fighting continued until the NATO air strikes in March 1999 forced the Serbian forces to back up. In the meantime, atrocious mass violations of international humanitarian law had been committed by both sides. During this period, certain regions of Kosovo were particularly affected by the violence. The Stimlje region was one of such regions.

As the fighting between Serbian forces and the KLA escalated and spread throughout Kosovo, the KLA intensified its attacks against ethnic Serbs. During the summer of 1998 it was reported that a number of ethnic Serbs were kidnapped in the Stimlje region. In fact, in the Stimlje as well as in the Suva Reka region, a high number of kidnappings of ethnic Serbs and of summary executions have been attributed to the KLA. An example of such incidents occurred in Orahovac when the KLA started its attack on this city on 19 July 1998. In this attack, an estimated 85 ethnic Serbs were taken into custody by the KLA. Of these, 35 were later released on 22 July and another ten were released on 29–30 July. Around 40 individuals remained unaccounted for and are presumed dead. Concerning these, around the time of this attack, there were reports of ethnic Serb civilians being taken by armed ethnic Albanians and put into vans, hands tied, transported to the woods and never seen again.

One town in the Stimlje region, Racak, was the stage of numerous and severe incidents of violence, particularly in the beginning of 1999. One of the KLA's bases was in Racak. On 8 January 1999, the KLA carried out a well-prepared ambush near Dulje (west of Stimlje) in which three Serbian policemen were killed and one was wounded. Two days after, on 10 January 1999, the KLA ambushed another Serbian police patrol in Slivovo (south of Stimlje), killing one policeman. Other incidents of the same type are said to have been planned and executed by the KLA. As the fighting increased in this particular region between the KLA and the Serbian forces, the Yugoslav Army built up in the area around Stimlje, especially on the mountain road between Dulje and Caraljevo villages, allowed the Serbian forces to progressively win control of the area.

The Serbian police had already shelled Racak in August 1998. On 15 January 1999, the Serbian police forces (including local policemen), in a well coordinated action together with the Yugoslav Army forces, conducted an attack on the civilian population of Racak. This included indiscriminate attacks on civilians, torture of detainees and summary executions of civilians of Albanian ethnicity. On that day, as the Serbian forces entered the town, around 45 civilians (suspected to belong to or to support the KLA) were killed.

The police forces were said to have entered the town from different directions and started searching the houses for people and guns. In one of such houses, approximately 30 men of Albanian ethnicity and over 15 years of age that were hiding in a stable were tortured by the police in the yard of that house, rounded up and taken to a hill outside the village where they were executed. Some were shot at close range and others had their throats cut.

In the town itself, 18 people also of Albanian ethnicity were killed (of which nine were KLA soldiers). Among them were children, women and elderly people. Most of these killings happened as the civilians were trying to flee when they saw the police and army forces. Most were shot at close range; a couple were killed by a grenade. Others, as was the case with an elderly man, were killed in their own houses or in their backyards. As these killings took place, houses were being looted and burnt.

The killings in Racak and the chain of violent incidents surrounding this event reflect the vicious circle of confrontation and suffering that is experienced by the population of both sides. The following analysis will focus on the Racak killings from January 1999 while taking into close consideration the context of violent incidents it occurred in.

*The facts presented here are taken from two reports published by Human Rights Watch. See HRW (1999a) and also HRW (1998). The authors would like to emphasise that many of the facts and views presented in these reports are still today subject to controversy. The authors of this book do not necessarily endorse the reading or the wording of these accounts.

Notes

1 State-based conflicts describe a situation in which two or more actors of which one is a state pursue incompatible, yet from their individual perspectives entirely just, goals.

2 Ethnic cleansing was a term coined by a journalist to describe what he witnessed in Yugoslavia. Recognising the ethnic component of the wars and their acts of extreme violence, he linked ethnicity (as a motif) to the idea of purging (i.e. killing) – hence 'cleansing'. It was not he but others who picked up the term and made out of it a synonym for genocide. The term as an alternative to genocide has been absorbed into general everyday vocabulary but has no legal standing (Huttenbach 2004: 23–34).

3 Heywood (2000: 254), quoted in Heise (2005), defines nationalism as the belief that the nation is the central principle of political organisation. Nations are shaped by cultural, political and psychological factors. Culturally, a nation is a group of people bound together by a common language, religion, history and traditions. Politically, a nation is a group of people who regard themselves as a natural political community. Psychologically, a nation is a group of people distinguished by a shared loyalty or affection in the form of patriotism (Heywood 2000: 251–2). Nationalism as ideology includes different forms: political, cultural and ethnic nationalism. The linkage between nationalism and ethnicity, which is frequently applied in the case of Yugoslavia, derives from the organic idea of nationhood. Ethnic nationalism, often advanced by conservative nationalists, is the belief that the organic nation concept is the central principle of political organisation. This exclusive concept gives priority to a common ethnic identity and shared history. The relation between nationalism and ethnicity has been subject to different theories (e.g. primordialism, modernism and ethnicism) (see more in Heise 2005).

4 In August 1992, the Serbian Republic of Bosnia and Herzegovina changed its name to the Republic of Srpska.

5 Kosovo is officially still part of the Republic of Serbia (June 2007), but it has been administered by the UN Interim Mission in Kosovo (UNMIK) – UN Security Council Resolution 1244, 10 June 1999.

6 In the 1981 census the total population of Kosovo was approximately 1,585,000 of which 1,227,000 (77 per cent) were Kosovo Albanians and 210,000 (13 per cent) were Serbs. The last census in SFR Yugoslavia was held in 1991. General estimates are that the population of Kosovo in the period 1991–99 was between 1,800,000 and 2,100,000, of which approximately 85–90 per cent were Kosovo Albanians and 5–10 per cent were Serbs. Estimates in 1993 put the Albanian population at 87.6 per cent while Serbs made up around 6.6 per cent of the total population. Today some estimates point out that the Serbian population in Kosovo is no more than 5 per cent.

7 Mertus' book is based on a large number of interviews with Kosovo Albanians and Serbs over a period of years.

8 The territory of Kosovo became an administrative entity in the second half of the twentieth century. The 1946 Constitution of the Federal People's Republic of Yugoslavia for the first time in history gave Kosovo and Methohija the shape of an administrative and political entity – an autonomous region. The 1963 Constitution of the SFR Yugoslavia determined the status of an 'autonomous province' for Kosovo and Methohija, as well as Vojvodina in northern Serbia. Constitutional Amendments made in 1968 extended the powers of the province of Kosovo.

9 On 22 April 1996, four attacks on Serbian civilians and security personnel were carried out simultaneously in several parts of Kosovo. A hitherto unknown organisation calling itself the 'Kosovo Liberation Army' (KLA) subsequently claimed responsibility. The KLA was initially a small, mainly clan-based but not very well organised group of radicalised Albanians, many of whom came from the Drenica region of western Kosovo. The KLA at this stage consisted mainly of local farmers and unemployed workers.

10 Estimates of the number of KLA fighters vary from 350 (according to Western sources) to 1,500 (according to Serbian sources).

11 The KLA first took over the cities of Pec and Djakovica. Later the KLA capital was situated in the town of Malisevo. The KLA infiltrated Suva Reka and the areas to the north-west of Prishtina, then threatened the Belacevec coal pits and captured them in late June, threatening energy supplies in the region.

12 On 23 September the UN Security Council adopted resolution 1199 which highlighted the impending human catastrophe in Kosovo and demanded a ceasefire and the start of real political dialogue.

13 Statement by the President of the UN Security Council, 19 January 1999, S/PRST/1999/2.

14 According to Craig (2003: 249), the question of what exactly happened in Racak has been hotly contested. 'The version of events announced to the world in the immediate aftermath of the killing suggested that Serbian units in pursuit of a small KLA contingent occupied the village and massacred its inhabitants as an admonition to those tempted to offer sanctuary to the guerrillas [...] Subsequent international investigations of the incident have however failed to produce forensic evidence that would indicate that a massacre occurred, and suggest that it remains possible (as Serb observers had argued at the time) that the cadavers displayed at Racak were those of fallen resistance fighters and innocent bystanders killed in the fighting, gathered together from over a wider area by villagers under KLA direction, and presented as victims of a purposeful massacre with the express purpose of swaying international sentiment against the Serbs.' See Gelman (1999: 6–9): US CIA reports

had already specified that many KLA actions were intended to provoke reprisals in order to encourage foreign intervention.

15 The accords called for NATO administration of Kosovo as an autonomous province within Yugoslavia; a force of 30,000 NATO troops to maintain order in Kosovo; an unhindered right of passage for NATO troops on Yugoslav territory, including Kosovo; and immunity for NATO and its agents from Yugoslav law.

16 For more information on the Kosovo refugee crisis see the UNHCR website at: http://www.unhcr.org/cgi-bin/texis/vtx/home?id=search.

17 During the NATO bombing there were also many unwanted civilian causalities and the bombing itself caused a lot of infrastructural damage in the region. In May, a NATO aircraft attacked an Albanian refugee convoy, believing it was a Yugoslav military convoy, killing around 50 people. NATO admitted its mistake five days later, but the Serbs accused NATO of deliberately attacking the refugees. On 7 May, NATO bombs hit the Chinese Embassy in Belgrade, killing three Chinese journalists. NATO claimed they were firing at Yugoslav positions. In another major incident – Dubrava prison in Kosovo – the Yugoslav government attributed 85 civilian deaths to NATO bombing. Human Rights Watch research in Kosovo determined that an estimated 18 prisoners were killed by NATO bombs.

18 There were certainly some well-documented instances of mass expulsions, as happened in Prishtina at the end of March when tens of thousands of people were rounded up at gunpoint and loaded onto trains before being dumped at the Macedonian border. Other towns, such as Pec, were systematically burned and their inhabitants killed.

19 A postwar statistical analysis of the patterns of displacement, conducted by Patrick Ball of the American Association for the Advancement of Science, found that there was a direct correlation between Serbian security force operations and refugee outflows, with NATO operations having very little effect on the displacements. There was other evidence of the refugee crisis having been deliberately manufactured: many refugees reported that their identity cards had been confiscated by security forces, making it much harder for them to prove that they were bona fide Yugoslav citizens. Indeed, since the conflict ended Serbian sources have claimed that many of those who joined the refugee return were in fact Albanians from outside Kosovo (see more in American Bar Association Central and East European Law Initiative 1999).

20 Between 1,200 and 1,500 bodies were destroyed at the Trepca mine. As of July 2001, the Serbian authorities had announced the discovery of four additional graves in Serbia with as many as 1,000 Kosovar Albanian bodies. A study by *The Lancet* estimated 12,000 deaths in the total population (see more in Spiegel and Salama 2000).

21 Since it first came into use at the turn of the ninteenth century, the

Balkans have always been a fluid concept with countries being excluded and included regularly. The past 15 years have seen the region go through more contortions of geographic definition. Now the Western Balkans include Albania, Bosnia and Herzegovina, Kosovo, Macedonia, Serbia and Montenegro.

22 In these ethnic Albanian riots more than 15 people died (March 2004).

23 The Survey was conducted in November–December 2004 in Macedonia, Albania, Serbia and Montenegro and Bosnia and Herzegovina. The complete data was analysed by BBSS Gallup International.

24 Under UNMIK's leadership the number of Serbs employed in the Kosovo Electric Company has declined from more than 4,000 in 1999 to 29 now, out of a total of over 8,000 employees.

References

Allcock, J.B. (2000) 'Quo Vadis Jugoslavijo?', in *Explaining Yugoslavia*. New York: Columbia University Press, pp. 411–40.

American Bar Association Central and East European Law Initiative (1999) *Political Killings in Kosovo/Kosova*. See: http://shr.aaas.org/kosovo/pk/toc.html.

Ball, P., Berts, W., Scheuren, F., Dudukovic, J. and Asher. J. (2002) *Killings and Refugee Flow in Kosovo March–June 1999. A Report for the International Criminal Tribunal for the Former Yugoslavia*. New York and Washington: American Association for the Advancement of Science.

Barnett, M. and Xharra, J. (2007) 'Decision time', *Jane's Intelligence Review*, 19 (3): 28–35.

Bianchini, S. (1996) 'Geopolitics and self-determination: an atlas of insecurity in Eastern Europe in the 20th century', in *Proceedings of the Summer School on Ethnic Relations*. Belgrade: Forum for Ethnic Relations, pp. 188–209.

Blitzer, W., Amanpour, C., King, J. and Koppel, A. (1999) 'Clinton: Serbs must be stopped now', CNN, 23 March. see: http://www.cnn.com/US/9903/23/u.s.kosovo.04/.

Boari, T. (2001) 'Racak, bugia di Guerra', *E Manifesto*, 6 February, p. 5.

Cederman, L.E. (2001a) 'Back to Kant: reinterpreting the democratic peace as a macro-historical learning process', *American Political Science Review*, 95 (1): 15–32.

Cederman, L.E. (2001b) 'Modelling the democratic peace as a selection process', *Journal of Conflict Resolution*, 45 (4): 470–502.

Clines, F.X. (1999) 'NATO hunting for Serb forces: U.S. reports signs of genocide', *New York Times*, 30 March, p. Al.

Clinton, B. (1999) 'Press conference by the president', 25 June. See: http://clinton6.nara.gov/1999/06/1999-06-25-press-conference-by-the-president.html.

Cohen, L. (1993) *The Disintegration of Yugoslavia*. Boulder, CO: Westview.
Cohen, W. (1999) 'Secretary Cohen's press conference at NATO headquarters', *US Department of Defense*, 1 April.
Comor, E. (2001) 'The role of communication in global civil society', *International Studies Quarterly*, 45 (3): 389–408.
Connor, W. (1994) *Ethnonationalism: The Quest for Understanding*. Princeton, NJ: Princeton University Press.
Cousens, E. and Cater, K.C. (2001) *Towards Peace in Bosnia: Implementing the Dayton Accords*. Boulder, CO: Lynne Rienner.
Craig, N.R. (2003) *War in the Balkans 1991–2002*. Carlisle Barracks, PA: US Army War College.
Cruvellier, T. and Valiñas, M. (2006) *Croatia: Selected Developments in Transitional Justice*. New York: International Center for Transitional Justice.
Cviic, C. (1996) 'Slovene and Croat perspectives', in A. Danchev and T. Halverson (eds), *International Perspectives on the Yugoslav Conflict*. London: Macmillan Press.
Dancev, A. and Halverson, T. (eds) (1996) *International Perspectives on the Yugoslav Conflict*. London: Macmillan Press.
Doggett, T. (1999) 'Cohen fears 100,000 Kosovo men killed by Serbs', *Washington Post*, 16 May.
Eide, K. (2004) *The Situation in Kosovo. Report to the Secretary-General of the United Nations*. Brussels.
Erlanger, S. (1999) 'Early count hints at fewer Kosovo deaths', *New York Times*, 11 November, pp. A6.
Federal Commission for Missing Persons (2005) *Preliminary List of Missing and Killed in Srebrenica*. Sarajevo: Federal Commission for Missing Persons.
Foreign & Commonwealth Office (June 1999) *Research & Analytical Papers Kosovo Chronology: 1997 to the End of the Conflict*. London: Foreign & Commonwealth Office, Central European & Eastern Adriatic Research Group.
Gelman, B. (1999) 'How we went to war', *Washington Post*, national weekly edition, pp. 6–9.
Hardin, R. (1995) *One for All: The Logic of Group Conflict*. Princeton, NJ: Princeton University Press.
Hechter, M. (1987) *Principles of Group Solidarity*. Berkeley, CA: University of California Press.
Heise, J. (2005) *Was Nationalism the Main Cause of the Wars of Secession in the Former Yugoslavia?* Edinburgh: University of Edinburgh Press.
Heywood, A. (2000) *Key Concepts in Politics*. London: Palgrave Macmillan.
Horowitz, D.L. (1995) *Ethnic Groups in Conflict*. Berkeley, CA: University of California Press.
Human Rights Watch (1998) *Federal Republic of Yugoslavia: Humanitarian Law Violations in Kosovo*, October, 10: 9(D). See: http://www.hnv.org/reports98/kosovo/.

Human Rights Watch (1999a) *A Week of Terror in Drenica: Humanitarian Law Violations in Kosovo*, February. See: http://www.hrw.org/reports/1999/kosovo/.

Human Rights Watch (1999b) *Abuses against Serbs and Roma in the New Kosovo*, August, 11: 10. See: http://www.hrw.org/reports/1999/kosov2/.

Human Rights Watch (2000a) *Civilian Deaths in the NATO Air Campaign*, 12: 1(D). See: http://www.hrw.org/reports/2000/nato/index.htm#TopOfPage.

Human Rights Watch (2000b) *New Figures on Civilian Deaths in Kosovo War*. See: http://www.hrw.org/press/2000/02/nato207.htm.

Human Rights Watch (2001) See: http://www.hrw.org/reports/2001/kosovo/undword.htm.

Human Security Report (2005) *War and Peace in the 21st Century*, Canadian Human Security Centre. New York: Oxford University Press.

Huntington, S.P. (1996) *The Clash of Civilizations and the Remaking of World Order*. New York: Simon & Schuster.

Huttenbach, H.R. (2004) 'The genocide factor in the Yugoslav wars of dismemberment', in J.S. Morton, R.C. Nation, P. Forage and S. Bianchini (eds), *Reflections on the Balkan Wars: Ten Years After the Break Up of Yugoslavia*. New York: Palgrave MacMillan, pp. 23–34.

ICTY (1999) *Prosecutor* v. *Slobodan Milosevic and others*, IT-99-37-PT. See: http://www.un.org/icty/cases/indictindex-e.htm.

ICTY (2004) *Prosecutor* v. *Radislav Krstic*, Trial Chamber Judgement, 19 April, Case No. IT-98-33-T/IT-98-33-A. See: http://www.un.org/icty/cases/jugemindex-e.htm.

Ignatieff, M. (1996) 'Introduction: virtue by proxy', in A. Danchev and T. Halverson (eds) *International Perspectives on the Yugoslav Conflict*. London: Macmillan Press, pp. ix–xix.

International Commission on the Balkans (2005) *The Balkans in Europe's Future*. Sofia: Center for Liberal Strategies.

Janjic, D. (2003) *Kosovo Between Conflict and Dialogue*. Belgrade: Forum for Ethnic Relations.

Jovanovic, V. (1998) '"Adut" za kasnije pregovore. Priprema li se ogranicen udar na Drenicu?', *Nedeljna naaa borba*, 31 January/1 February.

Klemendi, B., Deputy Public Prosecutor of Kosovo and Head of Anti-Corruption Unit (2006) Interview by Jana Arsovska, December.

Kusovac, Z. (1998) 'Another Balkans bloodbath?', *Jane's Intelligence Review*, 2: 13–16.

Malcolm, N. (1994) *Bosnia: A Short History*. New York: New York University Press.

Malcolm, N. (1998) *Kosovo: A Short History*. New York: New York University Press.

Mertus, J. (1999) *Kosovo: How Myths and Truths Started a War*. Berkeley and Los Angeles, CA: University of California Press.

Ramet, S.P. (1997) *Whose Democracy? Nationalism, Religion, and the Doctrine of Collective Rights in Post-1989 Eastern Europe*. Lanham, MD: Rowman & Littlefield.

Ramet, S. (2005) *Thinking about Yugoslavia*. Cambridge: Cambridge University Press.

Robertson, G. (1999) *Kosovo: An Account of the Crisis*, Report by Secretary of State for Defence. Brussels: NATO Publication.

Rogel, C. (1998) *The Break-up of Yugoslavia and the War in Bosnia*. Westport, CT: Greenwood Press.

Salla, M. (1995) 'Kosovo, non-violence and the break up of Yugoslavia', *International Peace Research Institute Oslo, Security Dialogue*, 26 (4): 427–38.

Shoup, P. (2002) 'The West and the war in Bosnia: some thoughts', in S. Bianchini, G. Schopflin and P. Shoup (eds), *Post-Communist Transition as a European Problem*. Ravenna: Longo Editore, pp. 173–85.

Simons, M. (2007) 'Court declares Bosnia killings were genocide', *New York Times*, 26 February.

Spencer, M. (1998) 'When states divide', in M. Spencer (ed.), *Separatism: Democracy and Disintegration*. Lanham, MD: Rowman & Littlefield, pp. 741.

Spiegel, P.B. and Salama, P. (2000) 'War and mortality in Kosovo, 1998–99: an epidemiological testimony', *The Lancet*, 355 (9222): 2204–9.

Terlingen, Y. (1997) *Kosovo: Show Trials in Prishtina*, Amnesty International War Report 55, October.

Tilly, C. (1993) 'National self-determination as a problem for all of us', *Deadalus*, 122 (3): 29–36.

Troebst, S. (1998) *Conflict in Kosovo: Failure of Prevention? An Analytical Documentation, 1992–1998*, ECMI Working Paper 1. Flensburg: European Centre for Minority Issues (ECMI)).

Udovicki, J. and Ridgeway, J. (2000) *Burn This House: The Making and Unmaking of Yugoslavia*. Durham, NC: Duke University Press.

UN Human Development Report (2005) *International Cooperation at a Crossroads: Aid, Trade and Security in an Unequal World*. UNDP.

UN Security Council Resolution 1244 (1999) UN Documentation Centre, 10 June. See: http://www.un.org/documents.

UN Statement by the President of the Security Council (1999) S/PRST/1999/2, 19 January. See: http://www.un.org/peace/kosovo/sprst992.htm.

Vejvoda, I. (1996) 'Serbian perspectives', in A. Danchev and T. Halverson (eds), *International Perspectives on the Yugoslav Conflict*. London: Macmillan Press.

Vickers, M. (1998) *Between Serb and Albanian: A History of Kosovo*. New York: Columbia University Press.

Wendt, A. (1992) 'Collective identity formation and the international state', *American Political Science Review*, 88 (2): 384–96.

Wendt, A. (1994) 'Anarchy is what states make of it', *International Organization*, 46 (2): 391–425.

Wolff, S. (2006) *Ethnic Conflict. A Global Perspective*. Oxford: Oxford University Press.

Chapter 4

Criminal judicial qualification and prosecution in the Racak case according to national and international legislation – Albanian perspective

Haki Demolli

During the war in Kosovo (February 1998 – June 1999), the Yugoslav forces, dominated by the Serbs, executed a great number of massacres against the Albanian civilian population. There is no doubt that the case of Racak had the greatest influence, not only on regional developments, but also on international ones. This, in some ways, influenced the international community to reinforce the pressure on the Yugoslav politics of that time; the epilogue being the beginning of NATO bombing of Yugoslav military targets, pushing the Yugoslav forces to retreat from Kosovo.

The case of Racak is of interest because of the significant impact it had on the further developments of the war in Kosovo. The following analysis – among several other matters – will mainly focus on: certain characteristics of the Racak case; its criminal judicial qualification according to national and international provisions; the criminal responsibility of the perpetrators of the Racak crime; the criminal prosecution and jurisdiction over the perpetrators of the crime according to national and international law; and the importance of the criminal prosecution and punishment of the perpetrators of war crimes – especially for the victims of these crimes.

Typological characteristics of the Racak case

The attacks of the Kosovo Liberation Army (KLA) against the Yugoslav military-police forces and the subsequent reprisals of the Yugoslav forces against Albanian civilians continued during the winter of

1998–99. It is estimated that the violence among the combating parties reached its peak on 15 January 1999, with the massacre in Racak.

It is indisputable that the first shots that preceded the killings of the civilians in Racak were heard some time after 6 o'clock on the morning of 15 January 1999 (Jashari 2004: 27). Instantly after the first shots were fired, the village was consumed by real chaos. In order to stay alive, the inhabitants (2004: 50)[1] of the village began to abandon their homes. The majority took off (in small groups or individually) in the direction of the forest near the village; some gathered in the houses of their fellow countrymen,[2] others took refugee in the basements or roofs of their houses, while the rest wandered from one neighbourhood to the next in search for a safe, secure refuge.

The incident of Racak took place between 7 a.m. and 4 p.m. until the Yugoslav forces retreated from the scene (2004: 32).[3] Mostly, the murders of the civilians happened in the following ways: the largest number (24 victims) were caught at the home of Sadik Osmani, the village teacher. They were tortured and forced to walk one by one in a column in the direction of 'Kodra e Bebushit' (Hill of Bebushi) where they were subsequently executed at a distance of three to four metres – shot from the front with firearms. Then some of the victims were killed from a distance of one to three metres – shot from behind on the streets of the village. Others were killed by automatic arms, snipers, tanks and other artillery from a distance of 100 to 300 metres – shot in their yards or as they were fleeing toward the nearby forest. Some of them were executed from close-range with firearms in the yards of their homes. In general, the characteristic treatment of the Yugoslav forces toward a great number of Racak's victims included: (1) psychological and physical torture before they were murdered – generally, being beaten and bludgeoned with heavy implements (e.g. guns and wood sticks) (Jashari 2004);[4] and (2) during and after the killing, mutilation of the victims' bodies. The mutilation was performed on various parts of the body but mostly on the head by removing the eyes and brain (2004: 155),[5] cutting the ears and nose, peeling the skin (2004: 157),[6] and cutting off the head (2004: 331).[7] The chest and breasts were also often mutilated, as well as other parts. The mutilation also included the removal of organs (2004: 318).[8] The grievous sight of the cadavers prompted immediate response from various actors, as well as a statement from the OSCE Chief of the Kosovo Verification Mission, William Walker, who on 16 January 1999 declared at the scene: 'I have been in various missions and war scenes in the world, but I have never seen before a more terrible and sadder scene in my life' (in Jashari 2004: 333).

The final toll of the massacre of Racak were 45 murdered civilians, including a 12-year-old boy, three females, nine members of the KLA (Judah 2000: 193) and many wounded from firearms as well as from the tortures perpetrated by the Yugoslavian forces.

Criminal judicial qualification and responsibility

Criminal judicial qualification according to national laws

At the time the crime was perpetrated in Racak, the law applicable in Kosovo was the Criminal Law of Yugoslavia (CLY) of 1977 and the Criminal Law of Kosovo (CLK). Keeping in mind the actions, aims and consequences presented in the Racak case, it can be argued that the whole event contains elements of two criminal offences foreseen in the CLY: a war crime against the civilian population (Art. 142 of the CLY) and genocide (Art. 141 of the CLY). These two criminal offences were committed in a so-called combination of criminal acts (Art. 48 of the CLY), which exists in cases when the perpetrator who has committed one action has also committed two or more other criminal offences that can be judged simultaneously.

War crime against civilians

Article 142 of the CLY foresees that the criminal offence of a war crime against the civilian population can be committed by anyone who, in violation of rules of international law effective at the time of war, armed conflict or occupation, orders that civilian population be subject to killings, torture, inhuman treatment, dislocation or displacement, or who commits any of the foregoing acts. Based on this definition, the war offence – crime against the civilian population – can be committed in two ways: by way of giving the orders, and by way of directly committing the offences (e.g. murder, torture and infliction of psychological/physical sufferings). The principal elements of this criminal offence include the time and the circumstances surrounding the perpetration of the offence, which stipulate that this criminal offence can be committed only during circumstances of hostility, armed conflict, occupation and so on. The projective target of this criminal offence is *the civilian population*, comprised of people who are in the occupied territory, as well as those who are under the direct power of the enemy forces. Due to the difficult circumstances in which civilians may find themselves during an armed conflict, international law has offered a special criminal-judicial protection from violence that is the constitutive element of this criminal offence.

If a careful analysis of the Racak case takes place, it will be seen that the case contains in itself all the elements of the criminal offence described in Art. 142 of the CLY. In the case of Racak, one is faced with the concrete action of the Yugoslav police forces, which caused the death of 45, the wounding of twelve, and the torturing of twelve Kosovar civilians (Jashari 2004: 56–7) as well as the infliction of psychological and physical suffering on considerable numbers of Racak inhabitants (2004: 51).[9]

Out of the 54 people killed in Racak, 45 were civilians – people who, according to their physical appearance, should be treated as civilian population and not as military (2004: 61–143),[10] whereas nine of them were members of the KLA. Out of 24 wounded twelve were civilians and twelve were members of the KLA. Such facts are also confirmed by Helena Ranta, head of the forensic team from Finland, who in the report on the autopsies of the Racak victims stressed – among other things – that there was no proof that the victims were other than unarmed civilians and that the majority of them were killed from short range, in shooting-gallery style (Bellamy 2002: 114–20). This offence was committed during the time when Kosovo was engaged in the war between the Yugoslav armed forces and the KLA. The armed conflict situation is better verified by the 'ceasefire' of October 1998, for the monitoring of which the OSCE had send the 'Verification Team' consisting of 700 officials from various countries of the world.

The civilian category – be they men, women, the elderly, youth, or children – is protected by the provisions of various international conventions against murder, torture, mutilation and other suffering during times of armed conflict. Such provisions can be found in the Geneva Convention for the Protection of Civilian Persons in Time of War (1949).[11] This Convention was ratified by the former Yugoslavia in 1950. Therefore one could reasonably argue that Racak case constitutes the criminal offence of a war crime against the civilian population under Art. 142 of the CLY.

Criminal offence of genocide

According to Art. 141 of the CLY, the criminal offence of genocide can be committed by anyone who, with the intention of destroying a national, ethnic, racial or religious group, in whole or in part, orders the commission of killings or the inflicting of serious bodily injuries, or serious disturbance of physical or mental health, against members of a group, or the forcible dislocation of the population, or by an individual who with the same intent commits any of the foregoing acts. The distinct characteristics of the criminal offence of genocide are:

- The offence can be committed by way of giving orders for murdering, injuring or displacing members of a certain group.
- The offence can be committed by concrete actions through which murders, injuries and displacements of the members of certain group are carried out.
- The principal element of this criminal offence is the purpose (intent) of destroying in whole or partly a national, ethnic or religious group. Such intent is usually confirmed through the systematic and organised action directed toward a larger number of individuals. However, the criminal offence of genocide can also be committed through individual murders, if the purpose of eradicating a group is present as one of the primary characteristics of the criminal offence (see Zlatarič 1977: 74–5).
- The consequences of the criminal offence of genocide involve the peril of the existence of the national, ethnic or religious group.
- The criminal offence of genocide can be committed during hostilities, armed conflict or during peace.

All of the inherent characteristics of genocide stressed above are found in the acts of the Yugoslav forces during their execution of the crimes in Racak. The 'action' in Racak was executed under the orders of high officials of the Belgrade government. The involvement of higher officials in this action is confirmed by the telephone talks among them, tapped by Western governments, in which the officials in Belgrade had ordered the government forces to 'act harsher' (Smith 1999). These recordings demonstrate engagement of 'the commanding chain' in the relations between Belgrade and Prishtina (Bellamy 2002: 114–20).[12]

Besides the people giving the orders in the Racak's case, there were also those who executed the orders – the members of the police and military forces of Yugoslavia. The Canadian General Michel Maisonneuve – who in the beginning of 1999 was the chief of the Regional Center of the Verification Mission – stressed that the tanks and flak of the Yugoslav army, placed on the hills above the village, 'supported' the police forces composed of 100 troops who took the action of entering every house in order to clean out the area (Klarin 2002). Even though the purpose of the action is a subjective element and it is difficult to confirm all events with total assurance, there is no doubt that the Yugoslav authorities, with actions such as the one in Racak, had as their purpose the complete or partial eradication of the Albanian population from the territory of Kosovo. Regarding the conflict in Kosovo, Barry Carter, a professor at the Georgetown University Law School, said 'I think it's genocide by any definition, but specifically genocide by the definition of the convention against genocide which over 100 countries are parties to, including the United States, Europe and Yugoslavia'. The UN convention signed in 1948 says genocide involves an intent to destroy in whole or in part a national, ethnic, racial or religious group (Hana 1999: 2). Moreover, former Yugoslav President Vojislav Kostunica, in an interview with CBS's *60 minutes II* in October 2000, admitted for the first time that 'Yugoslav forces committed genocide in Kosovo', and said he was ready to take his share of responsibilities for the crimes committed by his predecessor Slobodan Milosevic (Global Policy Forum 2000: 1). The conflict in Kosovo was treated as 'the worst examples we have of genocide and ethnic cleansing in the past decade. Rwanda, Bosnia, and Kosovo, all share the element of direct personal confrontation between the violator and his victim' (Kahn 1999: 1), so 'we must press for full support for the International War Crimes Tribunal to indict as many as possible of those involved in the Serbian genocide in Kosova' (Shaw 1999).

To better understand the seriousness of the problem, it is important to see how the Kosovo issues were handled by the Serbian side. Just in the period March 1998 to June 1999, approximately 13,500 Albanians were killed by the Serbian forces in Kosovo. Most of their bodies were found in 600 mass graves in Kosovo and Serbia. In addition, almost 40 per cent of all residential houses and approximately 649 schools and 155 mosques were heavily damaged or completely destroyed. Also more than 800,000 Kosovar Albanians were expelled from Kosovo, and thousands more were internally displaced (Abrahams 2001: 20–65). According to the International Committee of the Red Cross, as of April 2001, 3,525 people remained missing as a result of the conflict – the vast majority of them Kosovar Albanians. One of the more blatant forms of civilian property destruction in Kosovo during 1998 and 1999 was the widespread practice of water well contamination, which is forbidden by the laws of war. Throughout Kosovo, Serbian and Yugoslav forces deliberately rendered water wells unusable by dumping chemicals, dead animals and even human corpses into the water. Also Serbian and Yugoslav forces placed an estimated 50,000 anti-personnel and anti-tank mines in Kosovo, especially along the borders with Macedonia and Albania. More than 3,470 people were held in detention (Abrahams 2001: 45–70). The Kosovo problem is a classic example of a territorial conflict in which claims based on history and those founded in ethnic considerations collide. 'The Serbs describe Kosovo as the "Serbian Jerusalem" in order to express their strong emotional ties to this territory' (Reuter 1999: 183).

Indicators of the Serbian government's plan for ethnic cleansing of Kosovars are the measures taken for changing the national structure of the Kosovar population – drafted and promoted by the former Deputy Prime Minister of Serbia, Vojislav Seselj in October 1995. This high-ranking functionary of the Serbian government (who is now accused of war crimes in the Hague Tribunal), in order to accomplish the ethnic cleansing of Kosovars among other things, had also pronounced the following concrete measures:

> the repatriation of Albanians temporarily working in foreign countries must be prevented, especially those who left during the 1990–1993 period (it is estimated that their number was some 300,000). All Albanians who are not Yugoslav citizens – something that can be easily proved with a census – should be fired from their work. All the Albanians who wish to leave will be given passports. Albanians of Yugoslav citizenship living abroad and/or involved in secessionist activities must lose their citizenship. Distinguished individuals who play important roles in their political life should be eliminated through scandals or by staging traffic accidents, jealousy killings or infecting them with the AIDS virus when they travel abroad. (Seselj 1995)[13]

Considering the circumstances and the very tense political and military situation in Kosovo in 1995, Seselj concludes his plan on ethnic cleansing of the Kosovars with the words: 'If we have to fight a war to defend Kosovo and Metohija, it should be fought with all possible means which we have in possession' (Seselj 1995). Indeed, during the war in Kosovo in 1998–99, the Serbian military, paramilitary and police forces acted according to such instructions, without sparing from murder Kosovo-Albanian civilians, women, old people or children.

The case of Racak presents only one link in the chain of age-old systematic and organised activities of the Yugoslav authorities, the purpose of which was the eradication of the Albanian population from Kosovo. In certain periods this activity against Albanians was extremely harsh and brutal (Malcolm 1998: 265; Demolli 2002: 150).[14] Also, the period between February 1998 and 15 January 1999 can be described as harsh for the Albanians of Kosovo. Within these eleven months more than 2,000 people were killed and nearly 300,000 other Albanians were forced to leave their houses as a consequence of the offensives of the Yugoslav forces (Kratovac 1999).

While it cannot be argued that the murdering of 45 civilians has caused the total extinction of the Albanian population in Kosovo, in essence such action has endangered the existence of the Kosovar Albanians. The act itself, as well as the consequences and the ways in which it has been executed are considered to have had a negative psychological impact, not only on the inhabitants of Racak and the surrounding localities, but also on the Albanians of Kosovo as a whole. The culmination of the impact that this act had on the existence of the Albanian population in Kosovo was reached after 24 March 1999, when the military-police and paramilitary Yugoslav forces – being unable to oppose NATOs attacks – executed thousands of innocent Albanians and expelled from their lands over 800,000 Kosovars.[15] The case of Racak also fulfils the alternative element constituting a genocide act. This element has to do with the period of time during which it was committed. On 15 January 1999, when the criminal offence was committed, a ceasefire was in force in Kosovo, a fact showing that it was a time of hostilities or armed conflict between the armed units of both parties (Yugoslav armed forces and the KLA).

On the basis of the above-mentioned explanations, we could conclude that, although still subject to political debate, the Racak massacre fulfils all the elements of the criminal offence of genocide as described in Art. 141 of the CLY, taking into consideration the consequences, the manner of perpetration, the set-up and the planning as well as the overall purpose behind the entire case.

Criminal judicial consideration according to international acts

Bearing in mind the time[16] and the place[17] where the Racak incident happened, it can be argued that judicial consideration should be carried out in accordance with the Statute of the International Criminal Tribunal for the former Yugoslavia (The Tribunal),[18] the Geneva Conventions of 1949 and the Convention on the Prevention and Punishment of the Crime of Genocide of 1948. Four types of criminal offence are foreseen in the Tribunal statute: serious violations of the Geneva Conventions of 1949 (Art. 2 of the Statute);

violations of the laws or customs of war (Art. 3 of the Statute); genocide (Art. 4 of the Statute); and crimes against humanity (Art. 5 of the Statute).

In the case of Racak, the Yugoslav military-police forces have breached parts of the provisions in four Articles (2–5) of the Statute of Hague Tribunal. These forces have committed serious violations of the Geneva Conventions of 1949 (Art. 2 of the Statute). Concretely, clause (a) intentional murdering, as well as clauses (b) and (c) of Art. 2, determine – as a criminal offence – the torture and inhuman treatment, as well as the intentional infliction of great pain, or serious injury to the body or health. Article 3(1) of the Geneva Convention relating to the Protection of Civilian Persons in Time of War highlights that each party in the conflict should guarantee the application of the convention and the minimum of provisions that have to do with the individuals who did not take an active part in the enmity (the case of the civilians of Racak). This also includes that the members of the armed forces who have handed in their weapons should in all situations, be treated humanely. Article 3(2) forbids certain actions against these individuals at any time and place, among which is (clause (a)) violence against life and body, especially murder of any kind, mutilation, dehumanised treatment and torture, and (clause (d)) pronunciation of punishment and its perpetration without preliminary judgement by the courts founded according to regulations.

According to witnesses, the Yugoslav forces exercised dehumanising violence[19] and torture against civilians which presents a violation of the provisions of Art. 3(2)(a) of the Geneva Convention relating to the Protection of Civilian Persons in Time of War. Also, there is a lot of evidence which shows that the police executed civilians without any trial, which is a direct violation of Art. 3(2)(d) of the Geneva Convention relating to the Protection of Civilian Persons in Time of War.

> After a detailed investigation, the Human Rights Watch accused Serbian special police forces and the Yugoslav army of indiscriminately attacking civilians, torturing detainees, and committing summary executions. The evidence suggests that government forces had direct orders to kill village inhabitants over the age of fifteen. Human Rights Watch confirmed that a group of approximately 40 policemen, in blue uniforms and without masks, shot from a distance of 20 metres unarmed civilians who were running through their yards.[20] (Human Rights Watch 1999: 1)

A similar pattern can be observed in the Racak massacre, where evidence shows that out of the 45 civilians killed, 36 were killed with firearms from a distance of 0.5 m to 5 m (Jashari 2004: 150). This fact is also confirmed by the declaration of the Finnish expert Helena Ranta, who stresses that 'the members of the OSCE Verification Mission were correct by verifying that the majority of the murdered were executed from nearby' (Bellamy 2002: 114–20). Also the UN report confirms that 'many of the dead appeared to have been summarily executed, shot at close range in the head and the neck' (United Nations 1999: 1).

Human Rights Watch (HRW) has documented 3,453 extrajudicial executions of Kosovo Albanians by state actors in the Kosovo conflict. HRW obtained the names of 916 people, or 27 per cent of the victims. The rest of the victims were unidentified by witnesses. Witnesses claimed to have identified the Serbian police in 1,768 executions, the Yugoslav Army in 531 cases and paramilitaries in 1,154 cases (Abrahams 2001: 65).

During the action of the Yugoslav forces there were also violations of the laws and customs of war foreseen by Art. 3 of the Tribunal Statute. More specifically, under (c) of this Article a violation of this nature consists *inter alia* of 'the attack or bombardment with any means of the cities, villages, residences or unprotected buildings'. On the critical day, beside the other police and military activities, there were also bombardments of the village of Racak by the Yugoslav army. This is confirmed by the words of Smith (1999) who argued that 'the majority of the houses were bombarded directly from three T-55 tanks of the Yugoslavian army', as well as by the declaration of a Canadian general (Klarin 2002).[21]

The Yugoslav forces also committed the criminal offence of genocide as laid down in Art. 4 of the Tribunal Statute, by having murdered 45 individuals and wounded 24 others, and having harmed psychologically and physically a large number of Albanians, with the underlying purpose of their total or partial extinction from the Kosovo territory.[22] Hence, on the basis of the arguments mentioned above, it is my strong belief that with these activities the Yugoslav forces have violated the provisions of Art. 5 of the Statute of the Criminal Tribunal for the former Yugoslavia[23] which determines that murder, extirpation, captivity, imprisonment, torture and other inhuman activities committed against civilian population during an armed conflict with an international or local character constitute crimes against humanity. Therefore we can argue that the case of Racak contains the four necessary elements of the criminal offence of crimes against humanity as laid down in Art. 5 of the Statute: (1) the actions of the Yugoslav forces were undertaken during the time of the armed conflict between the two parties (the Yugoslav forces and KLA); (2) these actions were committed against the Albanian civilian population that lives in Kosovo; (3) these actions have resulted in murders (Art. 5(a) of the Statute) and torture (Art. 5(b) of the Statute); and (4) the people responsible for these actions were members of the Yugoslav police, military and paramilitary groups.

Such actions are also punishable by the Geneva Convention related to the Protection of Civilian Persons in Time of War. Besides Art. 3 that determines the 'civilian' and the criminal offences that are forbidden against them during the armed conflict, Art. 27 lays down a special protection from all forms of violence or threat of violence for certain civilian categories (for example, women and children). Yet, as already noted, in Racak, the Yugoslav forces killed three women and one child. The majority of crimes mentioned above are qualified in indictment IT-99-37 of the Tribunal, with which Slobodan Milosevic, ex-leader of Yugoslavia and four other high-ranking officials of this country were charged. Each of them was charged according to the three clauses covering crimes against humanity and under the single clause concerning violation of the laws and customs of war.

Criminal responsibility for perpetrators

National legislation and international law lay down two categories of subjects who can be charged with the crimes against humanity and crimes against international law: persons that order the perpetration of the crimes of such nature, and persons that commit those crimes.

Article 7(3) of the Tribunal Statute regulates individual criminal responsibility, pointing out that:

> The fact that any of the acts referred to in Articles 2 to 5 of the present Statute was committed by a subordinate does not relieve his superior of criminal responsibility if he knew or had reason to know that the subordinate was about to commit such acts or had done so and the superior failed to take the necessary and reasonable measures to prevent such acts or to punish the perpetrators thereof.

These provisions are completely compatible with the criminal law/justice doctrine, which generally provides that the leader is responsible for the actions committed by his subordinate if: he knew or ought to have known that his subordinate had committed or wanted to commit the crime, and he did not undertake necessary and reasonable measures to prevent the offence or punish the subordinate (Ratner and Abrams 2001: 133).

In the case of Racak, those criminally responsible are the high political and military functionaries who gave orders for undertaking the killings in Racak. Such persons include: the Yugoslav president,[24] the Serbian president, the person in charge of affairs in Kosovo, the Commander of the General Yugoslav Military Headquarters and the Ministers of Internal Affairs of Yugoslavia and Serbia. In addition, different police and military leaders at the level of the republics and regions who participated in the planning and organisation of a crime can be held responsible. Not only should the persons giving orders be held responsible for Racak but also those who executed those orders. The order given by a leader should be in compliance with the law or special provisions. The subordinate is obliged to accomplish the order, even if it is against the law, except in cases when the order is given to commit a criminal offence. Therefore police officers and military units operating in Racak should have avoided obeying the orders that involved the murder and wounding of civilians. According to national legislation, their responsibility is the same as the responsibility of their leaders, and according to Art. 7 of the Tribunal Statute, 'The fact that an accused person acted pursuant to an order of a Government or of a superior shall not relieve him of criminal responsibility, but may be considered in mitigation of punishment if the International Tribunal determines that justice so requires.'

In this specific case, the police force numbered 100, though no precise figure for the number of military forces exist. The actual perpetrators of the murders, injuries and torture are almost impossible to recognise, considering the fact that a large number of them were wearing masks and some of them were firing from a distance. A favourable circumstance is that some of the witnesses of the crime have survived and they can identify the perpetrators, especially the police officers, from the regions of Shtimje and Ferizaj.

Criminal procedure against perpetrators

Criminal prosecution and jurisdiction over perpetrators

In general, international law recognises five grounds of jurisdiction for a criminal offence: the territorial principle, the active personality principle nationality, the protective principle, the passive personality principle and the principle of universality (Ratner and Abrams 2001: 161). Regarding the judicial jurisdiction over the Racak crime, the provisions of Art. 9 of the Tribunal Statute are very decisive. According to this article, jurisdiction over crimes against humanity and genocide committed on Yugoslav territory from January 1991 is concurrent. This means that the International Tribunal and the national courts have simultaneous jurisdiction to prosecute the perpetrators of these crimes. However, Art. 7(2) states that the International Tribunal has priority over national courts. In any procedural phase, the Tribunal can officially require that national courts delegate their competence over these cases to the Tribunal.

In terms of the jurisdiction of national courts – in the case of Racak – the court (of first instance) that is competent is the District Court in Prishtina, since applicable provisions require that courts of that level should be competent for all criminal offences for which the prescribed punishment is a sentence of over five years' imprisonment. The District Courts in Kosovo are competent to judge in the first instance the perpetrators of aggravated criminal offences such as war crimes, whereas the Municipal Courts are competent for those criminal offences for which a punishment of up to five years' imprisonment is prescribed.

For the perpetrators of a crime of genocide or a war crime against a civilian population, the CLY in 1977 had foreseen two types of punishment: punishment of at least five years imprisonment, and the death penalty. Since the Constitution of the Federal Republic of Yugoslavia from 1992 abrogated the death penalty under federal law, there was no possibility of declaring the death penalty in the case of Racak. Actually, according to the CLY and the Provisional Criminal Code of Kosovo, the punishment for those criminal offences is from five to 40 years of imprisonment. Besides imprisonment, the Tribunal can also give an order for the return of property usurped by criminal conduct, and also by force, to the legal owners (Art. 24(3) of the Statute). More specifically, up till now, in relation to the Racak massacre, two criminal indictments have been issued, one in the Hague Tribunal and the other in the District Court of Prishtina.

The ICTY investigated the Racak massacre along with other alleged crimes carried out in Kosovo during the war, and on 27 May 1999 it issued indictments for crimes against humanity and violations of the laws and customs of war against a number of senior Yugoslav and Serbian officials. Racak was specifically cited in those ICTY indictments. The other indictment is that of 9 May 2000, issued in Kosovo against Zoran Stanojevic, a former police officer who allegedly on 15 January 1999 was a member of a group of FRY Ministry of Interior police officers, who participated in the shooting of civilians as they were attempting to flee from the village of Racak. The charge on the initial indictment was murder, according to Art. 30(1) of KCC.

On the other hand, the special institutions of Serbia for war crime prosecutions (the Prosecution's Office for War Crimes and the Chamber for War Crimes under the District Court in Belgrade), established in accordance with the request of and under pressure by the international community in 2003, have so far issued two indictments for war crimes in Kosovo committed by Serbian forces (the *Podujeva* case and the *Suhareka* case), but they have not issued any indictments whatsoever regarding the Racak case.

Criminal procedure for crimes against humanity and international law

The provisions of the criminal procedural law regulate the phases and the process of criminal procedure. At the time of the criminal act in Racak, the applicable law in Kosovo was the Criminal Procedural Law of Yugoslavia (CPLY) of 1977. The perpetrators of the Racak crime can be prosecuted under either national or international criminal procedure.

National criminal procedures for perpetrators of crimes

Since the case of Racak represents a serious criminal offence (over five years of imprisonment is prescribed), according to the CPLY, the regular criminal procedure applies. This procedure is divided into two levels: criminal procedure of first instance, and appellate procedure.[25] The criminal procedure process begins by filing a petition for investigation, which is done by a prosecutor. This petition is filed only when it is suspected that a criminal offence has been committed. The investigation should be completed before the petition can be accepted and moved to a higher instance. During the investigation procedure, the facts of the existence or non-existence of the offence should be established. The investigating judge proceeds with the pre-criminal procedure. After the completion of the investigation, the investigating judge delivers all the documents and material facts to the competent prosecutor. If the prosecutor, based on the documents and facts, concludes that there are elements of a criminal offence, he makes an accusation. The pre-criminal procedure ends with the enforcement of the accusation, and then the main criminal procedure begins. In specific cases the CPLY makes exceptions from this procedure.

The most important phase is the main criminal procedure. This phase begins with the enforcement of the accusation and ends with the decision of the first instance. Unfortunately, in the Racak case, the Yugoslav judicial organs, that had jurisdiction over the region where the crime occurred had announced to the media after the investigation that there was no judicial ground for the accusation of any of the Serbian police officers regarding the incident of Racak (Rainio *et al.* 2001: 10). In June 2000, UNMIK announced the establishment of the Kosovo War and Ethnic Crimes Court (KWECC) to deal with the prosecution of war crimes committed during the conflict. The court's mandate was to cover events from January 1999. The Kosovo Court, for participation in the massacre of Racak, impeached only Zoran Stanojevic, ex-Serbian police officer. According to the indictment of the Public Prosecutor, he is accused of the criminal offence of murder. However, having in mind the seriousness of the Racak crimes and the fact that the defendant has participated in this massacre – it is my belief that he should have been accused of war crimes against the civilian population (Art. 142 of the CLY). For this criminal offence, the defendant would be judged by a trial panel composed of two international judges and one local judge, and on conviction could be sentenced to up to 15 years' imprisonment.

The criminal prosecution before the Serbian local courts for war crimes committed by the members of the Serbian forces has been hardened by the absence of political support from the Serbian government and the Serbian population in general. On the other hand, the court procedures against the war criminals in Serbia have several characteristic elements that need attention. First, among the accused there have been no individuals with high rank in the Yugoslav military or police. In addition, the punishments have been perceived as very 'soft', favouring Serbian criminals[26] and discriminating against non-Serbs such as Kosovar Albanians, Bosnians, Croatians and others. For example, in

> the first trial in Serbia which had to deal with the massacre of nearly 8,000 Muslim men and boys around Srebrenica, the Scorpions' [Serbian unit] unit leader and one of his accomplices were given 20 years each, and the others thirteen and five years. A fifth man was cleared of the murders which took place during the Srebrenica massacre in Bosnia in July 1995. Regarding this trial the relatives of the victims expressed disappointment that the maximum sentences of 40 years had not been handed down. (Traynor 2007:1)

In reaction, Alispajic Azmira, one of the relatives of the victims, said: 'There is no other place where you can kill somebody without being punished for it.' Their views were echoed by well-known Serbian lawyer Natasa Kandic who said 'Considering the seriousness of the crime committed, justice was not done with the verdict' (Traynor 2007:1).

Three other important war crime cases that were to be tried in Serbia made their way to the Supreme Court in 2004 and 2005. In 2005, 14 former paramilitaries and Yugoslav soldiers who were found guilty of taking part in the massacre at Vukovar, the first atrocity of the Balkan wars of the 1990s, won a reprieve. The court overturned the convictions citing 'incomplete facts' and a 'misapplication of substantive law'. The Supreme Court did uphold one conviction, that of Milan Bulic, but reduced his sentence to two years in prison from eight, because of his ill health. In the second case, also in 2005, the court ordered the retrial of a paramilitary policeman accused of killing 14 ethnic Albanians, mostly women and children, in the town of Podujevo in Kosovo in 1999. In that case the retrial in a district court reconvicted the suspect, Sasa Cvjetan, and gave the same sentence. In the third case, in 2004, the Supreme Court ordered the retrial of four Serbs accused of abducting and killing 16 Muslims from western Serbia in 1992 (Wood 2007: 1). On the other hand, the Serbians were more rigorous in the cases against non-Serbs. On 22 May 2000, a court in Nis (Serbia) sentenced 143 men transferred during the war from Kosovo to prisons in Serbia to a total of 1,632 years in prison (Abrahams 2001: 46).

International criminal procedures for perpetrators of crimes

The International Tribunal is the only institution accredited by the international community for criminal proceedings against individuals responsible for the violation of international humanitarian law in Yugoslavia after 1991. Regarding the jurisdiction of the Hague Tribunal, in practice, there are two aspects. For Kosovars the jurisdiction of the Hague Tribunal is uncontested, whereas the Serbian side has continuously contested the jurisdiction of the Tribunal and has not shown readiness or willingness to cooperate with it. In addition, according to the results of research carried out in the summer of 2005, the majority (around 70 per cent) of the Kosovar Albanians interviewed consider the function of and cooperation with the Hague Tribunal as a priority issue which affects the general security of Kosovo. According to them, the Tribunal helps in the establishment of peace among the parties in conflict (Irvin 2005).[27]

The attitude of the Serbian side toward the Hague Tribunal is revealed more than anything by the declaration of its main defendant (Slobodan Milosevic) who, during the presentation of his defence, repeated various times that the Tribunal at the Hague and his arrest were 'illegal'. Given the lack of concrete efforts from the Yugoslav judiciary to condemn the perpetrators of war crimes, the Tribunal represents the only extant institution for prosecuting the criminals. Nevertheless, the Yugoslav authorities have continuously contested the Tribunal's jurisdiction over the Kosovo territory, and have obstructed the work of international prosecutors by not issuing them entery visas (e.g. as in the case of prosecutor Louise Arbour) and by expelling them from the investigation.

In addition, Milosevic's successor, Vojislav Kostunica, goes further, insisting continuously that Serbs committed no war crimes because they were acting in the national defence, that Serbs are the victims, that Milosevic only made political decisions and therefore cannot be guilty for war crimes and that a civil war took place in the ex-Yugoslavia, hence all parties were equally culpable. As Kostunica told journalists in August 2000, 'There is no solid evidence suggesting that Serbs committed any war crimes' (Lukovic 2001: 1). For these reasons Judge Claude Jorda, President of the ICTY, reported the continued non-cooperation by the Federal Republic of Yugoslavia to the Security Council: 'Acting within the scope of the powers vested in me and at the request of the Prosecutor, I am officially referring to you the failure of the Federal Republic of Yugoslavia to comply with its obligations to co-operate with the International Tribunal in accordance with Art. 29 of the Statute' (Jorda 2002: 1).

The refusal to cooperate was based on the argument that 'the conflict in Kosovo was treated as an internal conflict in war against terrorists' (Abrahams 2002: 2), a standpoint which was not accepted by Kosovars, the Hague Tribunal, the Security Council of the UN and other international organisations. The negative attitude of the Serbian authorities toward the Tribunal has shown a marked change after strong pressure from the US government. The cooperation of the Yugoslav government with the Tribunal visibly improved just before 31 March 2001 – which was the deadline for a US financial support to Serbia of around $50 million. It was only during the period October 2004 – April 2005 that the Yugoslav functionaries handed over to the Hague Tribunal 14 of the accused. Among them were the Serbian general officers N. Pavkovic, V. Lazarevic and S. Lukic, accused of war crimes in Kosovo. In January 2005, the American government imposed a similar threat to block financial support (Ivanisevic 2005:

1), announcing it was withholding $10 million in aid to Serbia as 'a direct result of the Serbian government's continued lack of full and unconditional cooperation' with the ICTY (Lillis 2005: 1).

The provisions of the Rules of Procedure and Evidence (ICTY Rules), formally approved in February 1994 and amended many times afterwards, regulate procedure before the Tribunal. According to these provisions, the prosecutor initiates and presides over the investigation. He can request from a state the temporary arrest of the suspect and the preservation of the evidence. He can also request the judges to issue an order for the transfer of the suspect to the detention unit of the Tribunal. If the prosecutor is convinced he has gathered enough evidence that may lead to suspect that a crime that falls under the Tribunal's jurisdiction has been committed, he should file an accusation to the presiding judge for confirmation (Art. 47 of the ICTY Rules). After a detailed evaluation, the judge can confirm the accusation and give orders for other measures, such as an arrest and transfer order. Immediately after the transfer, the accused has to be brought 'without delay in front of the judge or a permanent panel where the accusation will be formalised' (Art. 62 of the ICTY Rules). After the first appearance of the accused, the parties can file preliminary appeals, including a refusal to accept the Tribunal's jurisdiction and a refusal of proof (Art. 72 of the ICTY Rules). Some of the appeals can be the subject of interlocutory appeals.

Before the beginning of the trial, the Court Chamber can hold a pre-examining conference (Art. 73 of the ICTY Rules). Both parties examine witnesses and the judge has also the right to bring witnesses for examination. After the presentation of evidence the Court Chamber brings a decision in a closed hearing. The accused can be declared guilty only when the majority of the panel is convinced that the guilt is proven beyond any reasonable doubt (Art. 87 of the ICTY Rules). In the only indictment before the Hague Tribunal, which includes the Racak massacre among other issues for which the perpetrators were held responsible, the defendants, besides the ex-leader of Yugoslavia, also included the four other high-ranking Serbian functionaries mentioned above. In points 98, 98(a) and 99 of the indictment the case of Racak is mentioned:

> Beginning on or about 1 January 1999 and continuing until the date of this indictment, forces of the FRY and Serbia, acting at the direction, with the encouragement, or with the support of Slobodan Milosevic, Milan Milutinovic, Nikola Sainovic, Dragoljub Ojdanic, and Vlajko Stojilkovic, have murdered

> hundreds of Kosovo Albanian civilians. These killings have occurred in a widespread or systematic manner throughout the province of Kosovo and have resulted in the deaths of numerous men, women, and children.

Moreover, among the incidents of mass killings, it included the following:

> On or about 15 January 1999, in the early morning hours, the village of Racak (Stimlje/Shtime municipality) was attacked by forces of the FRY and Serbia. After shelling by the VJ units, the Serb police entered the village later in the morning and began conducting house-to-house searches. Villagers, who attempted to flee from the Serb police, were shot throughout the village. A group of approximately 25 men attempted to hide in a building, but were discovered by the Serb police. They were beaten and then were removed to a nearby hill, where the policemen shot and killed them. Altogether, the forces of the FRY and Serbia killed approximately 45 Kosovo Albanians in and around Racak.

In the third amended indictment, the charges against Vlajko Stoijlkovic were removed due to his death. Nevertheless, with the amended indictment IT-03-70, the indictment for the case of Kosovo (including the massacre of Racak at point 32(a)), is expanded to include four more former high-ranking Serbian politicians and military and police functionaries, N. Pavkovic, V. Lazarevic, V. Djordjevic and S. Lukic. According to the indictment, the defendants have committed the following criminal offences:

> [...] planned, instigated, ordered, committed or otherwise aided and abetted the planning, preparation or execution of: (a) deportation, a crime against humanity, punishable under Art. 5(d) of the Statute of the Tribunal; (b) murder, a crime against humanity, punishable under Art. 5(a) of the Statute of the Tribunal; (c) murder, a violation of the laws or customs of war, punishable under Art. 3 of the Statute of the Tribunal and recognized by Art. 3(1)(a) (murder) of the Geneva Conventions; and (d) persecutions on political, racial and religious grounds, a crime against humanity, punishable under Art. 5(h) of the Statute of the Tribunal.

At the end of the indictment the perpetrators who committed such criminal offences in Kosovo have not been accused of the criminal offence of genocide. However, on the basis of the arguments stated above, I believe that, by their actions, they have indeed committed precisely the criminal act of genocide.

The trial against Milosevic commenced on 12 February 2002, with evidence relevant only to the charges relating to Kosovo. The prosecution concluded its case regarding Kosovo in September 2002 and the defence case commenced in August 2004. Because the accused Milosevic passed away in March 2006, the Trial Chamber terminated proceedings against him. The trial against Milan Milutinovic and others commenced on 10 July 2006. During this period in procedure a large amount of evidence and many witnesses against the defendants have been presented, among them also witnesses related to the massacre at Racak. The criminal procedure against the defendants before the Hague Tribunal is still ongoing (June 2007).

Importance of criminal prosecution and punishment for perpetrators of war crimes

Importance of punishment for war crimes

The case of Racak contains elements of war crimes and genocide and, therefore, prosecution and punishment can be fulfilled through both national and international courts. Yet there is a risk to leaving prosecution and punishment just to national courts because this can lead to non-punishment of the perpetrators (Schabas 2000: 416). One of the reasons for this duality is also mentioned by Carla Del Ponte (1999):

> The tribunal has neither mandate nor the sources to be the main investigator and prosecutorial agency in Kosovo. The vast majority of crimes committed during the armed conflict will have to be dealt with by the local Kosovo police and judiciary, currently under the mandate of the UNMIK.[28]

The goals of all the above-mentioned actions are:

- to punish the perpetrators, regardless of whether they were direct perpetrators or their leaders;
- to announce to others that if they commit such crimes they will be punished, regardless of the fact that during the perpetration

they were protected under their leadership or the government, or regardless of the fact that they committed such crimes during war in the hope that they will not be discovered and identified because of the circumstances of war;
- to give moral and human satisfaction to the families for their losses, and respectively to the ethnic, racial or religious group of the victims. By punishing the perpetrators, it will be made clear that justice is on the side of the victims and that human society does not allow their victimisation to go unpunished and unacknowledged.

Normally, the victims want the judicial system to have power which it will use against the perpetrators of such crimes. According to the relatives of the victims the only way to stop murders and revenge cycles is to take away the power of judgment from certain individuals and to give this power to the judicial system. They want these processes to proceed as soon as possible in the Tribunal in The Hague, as well as in the Serbian and Kosovo courts. They also think that the impeachment of the war criminals would accelerate the process of reconciliation between the two nations that were in conflict. The achievement of a quick reconciliation among these two nations would also save new and future generations which were not involved in the conflict (Farquhar 2005: 1).

The relatives of the victims of Racak have considerable faith in the process of the Hague Tribunal; however, simultaneously, they feel frustrated with regard to the slow proceedings of specific cases (Bala 2002: 1). Delays to the prosecutions in the Tribunal present extra torment and insecurity for them, which is accompanied with the expectancy for the verdict and the level of punishment for the defendants, or eventually even for their death as in the case of Milosevic. The death of the defendants denies satisfaction for the families of the victims, because they want the defendants to be found guilty and punished for the crimes they committed (Paçarizi 2006: 1).

The relatives of victims are aware that full justice can never be achieved, because it is impossible to catch and prosecute all those who ordered and committed the massacre. But they are not satisfied by the fact that, even seven or eight years after the crimes were committed, only a few individuals have sat in the dock. The highest criminal responsibility falls on those who organised and planned the crimes, rather than on those who committed them. Therefore they should be the first to be prosecuted, and only then the direct perpetrators (Bala 2002: 1). Relatives are ready to recall even the most painful memories as testimony in front of the judicial bodies if the criminals are to be punished and justice to be achieved. For this reason, among other things, they also need psychological support during judicial proceedings. The prosecution of the criminals presents a kind of spiritual relief for the families as well as respect for the victims (Askin 2002: 1).

Another concern is the insufficient supervision of and weak security around the defendants accused of war crimes while they are in detention, a situation which makes their escape possible and at the same time affects the continuation of criminal proceedings against them, since, according to UNMIK Regulation 2001/1, criminal procedures against individuals in absentia are not allowed (OSCE 2003: 12–28).[29] Moreover, there is also a concern related to the criminal procedure itself: there are cases where the prosecutor withdraws the prosecution of the war criminals, or the prosecution proceeds with charges of another criminal offence which are not adequate (i.e. for which a lighter sanction is prescribed) for the specific criminal offence committed. Such a situation has been seen in the one case concerning the massacre at Racak. In the Verdict of the Supreme Court of Kosovo (File Ap. nr. 1/2002) it is stated that: '[The] injured parties decided to continue the charges against Zoran Stanojeveic as private prosecutions and they filed an indictment with the accusation of attempted murder of Destan Rashiti and Nazmi Mahmuti on January 15, 1999' (OSCE 2003:19).

That the wider Serbian community has insufficient knowledge of the crimes of the Yugoslav military and police forces in Kosovo is yet another issue which brings pain for the families of the victims. The media in Serbia have not fulfilled their mission, because even nowadays a large number of the ordinary citizens in Serbia do not have a clear picture of the level of crimes and terror committed against the victims in Kosovo.

The war victims think that it is the Serbian officials who should accept responsibility and liability for the crimes committed, in order for them to forgive the acts of their neighbours, but not to forget. Such acceptance of responsibility should be done through a public search for forgiveness. The worst of the matter is that in practice often the opposite happens. The high-ranking Serbian officials, instead of asking for forgiveness from the victims of war, publicly protect those accused of war crimes in Kosovo, expressing their assurance that these people are innocent. There are also cases where certain Serbian politicians and media glorify the individuals accused of war crimes, glorifying them as national heroes, expressing no feeling of solidarity with or sharing the pain of the victims of crime (Bala 2002: 1).

The relatives of victims are sceptical with regard to the level of the pronounced punishments against the perpetrators, not only from the Hague Tribunal, but also from the national courts. In principle, they ask for very severe punishments for the perpetrators, raising the question of whether, for a person who has killed dozen of civilians, an ordinary punishment of nearly 20 years is enough (Hartman 2005: 1). Among the Kosovo population there is a common opinion that the Tribunal is applying a light sentence policy, especially towards the criminals who surrender and which are collaborating with it. Such actions of the Tribunal are treated as advantages on the account of the institution (Kocijan 2003: 1).

The relatives of the victims are hurt badly when war criminals, after guilty pleas, get very light prison sentences. The victims see it almost as an insult (Pecanin 2006: 1). It means that guilty pleas are important, but not as important for the reconciliation process as one might think. This is where the Tribunal has failed the most. The light punishment of the war criminals is a concern not only for the relatives of the war victims, but for the whole population of Kosovo. According to research done in Kosovo by the Belfast Institute for Administration, one of the three main issues which affect relations among Kosovo Albanians and Serbs is the inadequate prosecution of the war criminals which does not meet the needs of the Kosovo Albanians for justice (Irvin 2005: 4). Due to these facts some victims suspect that a possible secret agreement exists between Belgrade and UNMIK which leads to advantages for the Serbs accused of war crimes (Hartman 2005: 2).

The relatives of victims consider that the decision of the Hague Tribunal on the culpability of the defendants for war crimes would have a positive effect on the Serbian government and population, so that they would be aware and understand that in the past their police forces have committed crimes against others, and that such crimes shall not be repeated in the future (Bala 2002: 2). Also the punishment of war criminals would prevent the stigmatisation of the whole group (Serbian people) in the name of which the crimes are committed, and in this way a new path for reconciliation would be opened (Akhayan 2001: 7). The relatives of victims are conscious that nothing can be done now to bring their murdered relatives back, but the punishment of the criminals could enable them to live together with their age-old neighbours (Bala 2002: 1). However, there are also victims who have revenge against the perpetrators in mind.

Such an attitude may be found in declarations such as that made by Muharrem Hetemi, a relative of a massacred victim, in regard to the prosecution of Milosevic: 'If for each murdered individual they would get one year of imprisonment would still not be enough for them' (Bala 2002: 1).

Another goal of punishment is to preach to the authorities of certain states that war crimes and genocide deeply affect human dignity and the life of human beings in general, and that the international community is devoted to prosecuting and punishing the perpetrators, even if they are heads of state.

Beneficiaries from prosecution and punishment of the war criminals

People who directly benefit from the prosecution and punishment of war criminals are the victims' families, the victims' ethnic, racial, political and religious group and the state supporting the socio-political activities of the victims' group. Family members of the victim can morally benefit from the punishment of the persons that caused the loss of the family member, and sometimes they can even benefit in material terms because the court can decide to award compensation for some of the damages caused by the perpetrator's acts. The ethnic, religious, political or racial group and the state supporting their activities can benefit only morally from the prosecution. Those who indirectly benefit are the ethnic, religious, political and racial groups that have similar relations with the state on trial or another state, the international community and human society in general. These three categories are definitely interested in punishing war criminals because their punishment leads to the prevention of possible crimes against their members, and because their punishment shows respect for their rules which are mainly of an international character.

Taking all of the above into consideration, the international community as well as the national institutions should take into account the requests and needs of the war crime victims, because only by paying respect to them will they make it possible for the victims' relatives to be first to get involved in the reconciliation process between the parties in conflict. Otherwise, the war victims will find it difficult to undertake any steps toward reconciliation, while in Kosovo and Serbia the war criminals move freely and are sometimes even glorified.

Conclusions

From the theoretical and scientific analysis of the Racak case, we can derive several important conclusions regarding the national and international normative acts discussed. Firstly, we tried to show in this paper that there are elements of war crimes against a civilian population and genocide in the actions of the Yugoslav forces in Racak. These crimes are prescribed in the CLY (1977) as well as in the Statute of the International Tribunal and other international conventions. In the case of Racak, the Yugoslav forces violated parts of the provisions in four Articles (2–5) of the ICTY Statute. The Yugoslav forces also made serious breaches of the Geneva Conventions of 1949. Moreover, the criminal responsibility for the crimes in Racak rests upon a number of senior Yugoslav and Serbian officials such as the former President of Yugoslavia, the former President of Serbia, the former Yugoslav Deputy Prime Minister, the former Chief of the General Staff of the Yugoslav Army, the former Serbian Interior Minister, police and military commanders at different levels and their subordinates (police officers, paramilitaries and soldiers in the field). The criminal offences committed by the perpetrators fall under the jurisdiction of national courts in Kosovo and Serbia and the International Criminal Tribunal for the former Yugoslavia in The Hague. Yet until now, in relation to the massacre at Racak, only two criminal indictments have been issued, one in the Hague Tribunal, and the other in the District Court of Prishtina. It was the ICTY that investigated the Racak killings along with other alleged crimes carried out in Kosovo during the war. The initial indictment was amended a few times due to the death of the accused, in order to expand the indictment to other persons or due to other reasons. The criminal procedure against the defendants before the Hague Tribunal is still ongoing (June 2007).

Furthermore, it is important to note that for Kosovars the jurisdiction of the Hague Tribunal is uncontested, whereas the Serbian side has continuously fought against it and has not shown readiness or willingness to cooperate with it. The Kosovo courts, in relation to the massacre at Racak, have prosecuted only one former Serbian policeman, who was accused of the criminal offence of murder, although due to the fact that the defendant participated in the massacre at Racak he should have been accused of war crimes. For this criminal offence, he was sentenced to 15 years' imprisonment. On the other hand, the special institutions of Serbia for the prosecution of war crimes (the Prosecution Office for War Crimes and the Chamber for War Crimes under the District Court of Belgrade), established in

2003, until now have issued only two indictments for war crimes in Kosovo committed by Serbian forces (the Podujeva case and the Suhareka case), but have not issued any indictment whatsoever regarding the Racak massacre.

In conclusion, those who benefit from the prosecution of war criminals are the families of the victims, the ethnic, racial, political and religious groups, certain states, the international community and society in general.

Notes

1 On 15 January 1999 there were 1,140 habitants in the village.
2 For example, the house of the teacher Sadik Osmani, Mehmet Mustafa and others.
3 Statement of witness Adem Jahir Bajrami.
4 The witnesses that survived the massacres, Adem Bajrami, Burim Osmani and Nusret Shabani, who were present in the house of Sadik Osmani, witnessed the torture of the victims Mufail Hajrizi, Rame Shabani and Sadik Osmani.
5 The victim Nazmi Nuhë Imeri, after being murdered, had his brain taken out with a sharp tool.
6 The victim Ajet Brahimi, after being murdered in a barbarous way, was cut on the neck with a knife or bayonet, and then his skull was broken with a strong tool.
7 Witness Agim Kameri, while describing the cadaver of his uncle Banush Kamerit, stresses that 'for the first time in my life I saw a human without a head'.
8 Witness Rame Shabani stresses that the cadavers of 'Kodra e Bebushit' were without eyes, hearts, ears, etc.
9 As a consequence of Racak's case, there were 63 children and young people under 18 years of age that became orphans, 25 women lost their husbands, many families lost two or more family members, and a considerable number of the wounded individuals remained handicapped for life.
10 Among these were a child named Halim Rizah Beqiri who was 13 years and 6 months old on the day of the massacre, Nazmi Nuhë Imeri, who on the day of the massacre was 81 years and 6 months old, the housewife Sahide Metushi, who on the day of the massacre was 59 years old, Hanumshahe Mujota, who was less than 16 years old, and five other victims who were between 60 and 70 years old.
11 The Convention was adopted on 12 August 1949 at the Diplomatic Conference for the drawing of International Conventions regarding the Protection of War Victims held in Geneva on 12 August 1949. It came into force on 21 October 1950.

12 Two Serbian high officials have expressed their concerns regarding the high number of victims (Minister Lukič, in the discussion, reports 22 victims). Thus, with the aim of avoiding any possible international reaction, Nikola Šainovič recommended two kinds of actions for the Yugoslavian police under Minister Lukič. The first had to do with the closing of the Macedonian border in order to prevent Louise Arbour, Prosecutor of the Hague Tribunal who was on her way to Yugoslavia, to enter Kosovo; and secondly, Lukič was instructed to order his forces to retake Racak, which had fallen into the hands of the KLA on the evening of 15 January, with the purpose of hiding the results of the massacre. On 19 January, Louise Arbour was not allowed to enter into Kosovo by Yugoslav officials.

13 Parts of a statement by Serb Deputy Prime Minister, Vojislav Seselj, in *The Greater Serbia Journal*, Belgrade, 14 October 1995, 'The Serb blueprint for cleansing Kosova' published in: http://www.peacelink.nu/Jugoslavia/Seselj_ makes_clear.html.

14 See Malcolm (1995): the period between October 1912 and January 1913 alone, around 20,000 Albanians were killed by the Serbian forces; see also Demolli (2002: 150): based on the national secret files, in the period 1918–40 around 80,000 Albanians were exterminated, between 1944 and 1950, 49,000 Albanians were killed by the communist Yugoslav forces, and in the period 1981–97, 221 Albanians were killed by the Serbian police and military forces. During these periods hundred of thousands of Albanians have been forcibly displaced towards Turkey and Western European countries.

15 In the Tribunal's indictment against the former leader of Yugoslavia, the expulsion of the Kosovar Albanians is highlighted with the words: 'Serbian forces have initiated a campaign of ethnic cleansing against the Albanians of Kosovo through which approximately 800,000 Kosovar-Albanians were expelled mainly toward Albania, Macedonia and Montenegro.' According to Aleksander Roknic (2006) ethnic cleansing is also stressed by witnesses in the Hague Tribunal, as it was the case with the former Serbian politician and Secret Service agent of Serbia and Great Britain, Ratomir Tanic, who in the proceedings against Milosevic and others, declared: 'Slobodan Milosevic wanted NATO bombings of Yugoslavia, because they gave him a reason to eliminate the opposition in Serbia and to cleanse Albanians from Kosovo'. See http://www.mail-archive.com/tribunal_update_uenglish@iwpr.gn.apc.org/.

16 See Art. 8 of the Statute of the International Criminal Tribunal for the former Yugoslavia, which states that: 'The temporal jurisdiction of the International Tribunal shall extend to a period beginning on 1 January 1991.' Given that the Racak incident was committed on 15 January 1999, the Tribunal has jurisdiction over it.

17 See Art. 8 of the Statute of the ICTY: 'The territorial jurisdiction of the International Tribunal shall extend to the territory of the former Socialist Federal Republic of Yugoslavia, including its land surface, airspace and

territorial waters.' Since the village of Racak and Kosovo are part of the territory of ex-Yugoslavia, the Racak case falls within the jurisdiction of the court.

18 The UN Security Council, acting under Chapter VII of the Charter of the United Nations, established the International Tribunal for the Prosecution of Persons Responsible for Serious Violations of International Humanitarian Law committed in the Former Yugoslavia since 1991.

19 The witness Bilall Avdiu, in the ICTY proceedings against Slobodan Milosevic for war crimes in Kosovo, Bosnia Herzegovina and Croatia on 30 and 31 May 2002, has stressed: 'I have seen it how, to one of the civilians, the police took out his heart while he was still alive'.

20 They killed Riza Beqa, 44 years old, Zejnel Beqa, 22 years old, and Halim Beqa, 12 years old, and wounded two women, Zyhra Beqa, 42 years old, and her daughter Fetije, 18 years old.

21 The general got a confirmation of what he saw the following day from a Yugoslav officer. When Masonneuve made an official protest in the name of the KVM, saying that the operation violated the Holbrooke-Milosevic Agreement of October 1998, the officer told him that in Racak the actions were undertaken by the police forces and that the military had only 'supported the police force with ordnance'.

22 This offence is prescribed by Art. 4(2)(a) and (b) of the ICTY Statute.

23 Adopted on 25 May 1993 by UN Resolution 827.

24 Article 7(2) of the Statute points out that: 'The official position of any accused person, whether as Head of State or Government or as a responsible Government official, shall not relieve such person of criminal responsibility nor mitigate punishment'.

25 The criminal procedure of first instance has two phases: the pre-criminal procedure and the main criminal procedure. The pre-criminal procedure consists of the investigating phase and the accusation phase. The main criminal procedure consists of three phases: the preparation for the main court sentence, the main sentence and the decision.

26 On July 2000, a court in Pozarevac (Serbia) sentenced a Serbian policeman to four years and nine months in prison and another one to one year for the murder of three ethnic Albanians in Velika Hoca. On December 2000, a military court in Nis sentenced two Yugoslav reservists to four and a half years in prison for murdering two ethnic Albanian civilians in Susica. According to the presiding judge the sentence was lenient because the soldiers were suffering from 'war psychoses' at the time of the crime.

27 Statement by Dr Kolin Irvin (2005).

28 Press Release, 'Statement by Carla Del Ponte, Prosecutor of the International Criminal Tribunal for the Former Yugoslavia, on the Investigation and Prosecution of Crimes committed in Kosovo', 29 September 1999.

29 According to the OSCE Department of Human Rights and Rule of Law in Kosovo, up to the end of 2002, 17 indictments had been issued for

war crimes against 30 individuals (28 Serbian, 1 Kosovar Albanian and 1 Roma). Only five of them have been sentenced to imprisonment from 1 to 20 years, and 14 defendants have escaped detention.

References

Abrahams, F. (2001) *Under Orders: War Crimes in Kosovo*. New York: Human Rights Watch.

Abrahams, F. (2002) *The Tribunal*. New York: Human Rights Watch.

Akhayan, P. (2001) 'Beyond impunity: can international criminal justice prevent future atrocities?', *American Journal of International Law*, 95 (1): 7–31.

Askin, D.K. (2002) 'The Milosevic Trial, Part I'. See: http://www.crimesofwar.org/onnews/news-milosevic2.html.

Bala, B. (2002) 'Milosevic in The Hague' See: http://www.aimpress.ch/dyn/alba/archive/data/200202/20225-011-alba-pri.htm.

Bellamy, J.A. (2002) 'The Kosovo Verification Mission', in *Kosovo and International Society*. London: Palgrave Macmillan.

Demolli, H. (2002) *Terrorizmi*. Prishtinë: Law Faculty Prishtina.

Farquhar, M. (2005) 'Srebrenica: anatomy of a massacre', Institute for War and Peace Reporting. See: http://iwpr.net/?apc_state=hsrftri253777&l=en&s=f&o=253778.

Global Policy Forum (2000) 'Kostunica acknowledges Kosovo genocide', *Reuters*, 24 October. See: http://www.globalpolicy.org/wldcourt/tribunal/001 Okost.htm.

Hana, M. (1999) 'NATO, British leaders allege genocide in Kosovo', CNN, 29 March. See: http://edition.cnn.com/WORLD/europe/9903/29/refugees.01/.

Hartman, M.E. (2005) *Justice in Kosovo Unbiased, Non-political*, Special Report 451. United States Institute of Peace. See: http://www.usip.org/pubs/specialreports/sr451.html.

Human Rights Watch (1999) 'Yugoslav forces guilty of war crimes in Racak, Kosovo'. See: http://www.hrw.org/reports/1999/kosovo/Obrinje6-07.htm.

Irvin, K. (2005) *The Solution of the Problem of Kosovo: What Do People from Kosovo and Serbia Think*, Research Report. Belfast: Institute for Administration.

Ivanisevic, B. (2005) *Real Progress in The Hague*, Human Rights Watch Report. See: http://hrw.org/english/docs/2005/03/29/serbial0386.htm.

Jashari, R. (2004) *Masakra e Racakut Krim Kundër Njerëzimit*. Prishtinë: Fondi I Kompleksit Përkujtimor Masakra e Reçakut.

Judah, T. (2000) *Kosovo War and Revenge*. New Haven, CT: Yale University Press.

Kahn, W.P. (1999) 'War and sacrifice in Kosovo', *Institute for Philosophy and Public Policy*. See: http://www.puaf.umd.edu/IPPP/spring_summer99/kosovo.htm.

Klarin, M. (2002) 'Analysis: tribunal judges restrict Racak evidence', Institute for War and Peace Reporting, TU No. 268, 27 May–1 June. The Hague: Institute for War and Peace.

Kocijan, J. (2003) 'Haski Tribunal: Ko su profiteri'. See: http://www.mail-archive.eom/sin@antic.org/msg05935.html.

Kratovac, K. (1999) 'The possible falsification of the evidence on the Racak cadavers', Associated Press, 26 January.

Lalu, J.R., Penttila, K. and Penttila, A. (2001) 'Independent forensic autopsies in armed conflict: investigations of the victims from Racak, Kosovo', *Forensic Science International*, 116: 2–3.

Lillis, M. (2005) 'Srebrenica accused are finally turning up in The Hague'. See: http://www.crimesofwar.org/onnews/news-srebrenica.html.

Lukovic, P. (2001) 'Serbia and The Hague', Institute for War and Peace Reporting. See: http://www.globalpolicy.org/wldcourt/tribunal/2001/0505hagu.htm/.

Malcolm, N. (1998) *Kosovo: A Short History*. Prishtina: Koha Ditore.

OSCE (2003) *Kosovo's War Trials: A Review*. Prishtina: OSCE Mission in Kosovo, September.

Paçarizi, R. (2006) 'Kosove: Keqardhje qe Milloshevigi nuk u denua', *Koha Ditore*, 15 March.

Pecanin, S. (2006) 'Naser Oric – Moneta za potkusurivanje'. See: http://www.bhdani.com/default.asp?kat=kol&broj_id=473&tekst_rb=l.

Rainio, J., Lalu, K. and Penttila, A. (2001) 'Independent forensic autopsies in an armed conflict: investigation of the victims from Racak, Kosovo', *Forensic Science International*, 116 (2–3): 171–85.

Ratner, R.S. and Abrams, S.J. (2001) *Accountability for Human Rights Atrocities in International Law: Beyond the Nuremberg Legacy*. New York: Oxford University Press.

Reuter, J. (1999) *Kosovo 1998 – The International Community and the Kosovo Problem 1991–1997: OSCE Year Book 1998*. Baden-Baden: Institute for Peace Research and Security Policy, University of Hamburg/IFSH, p. 183.

Roknic, A. (2006) 'Witness claims Milosevic wanted NATO air strikes', Institute for War and Peace Reporting, TU No. 477, 17 November. See: http://iwpr.net/?p=tri&s=f&o=325503&apc_state=henitri2006.

Schabas, W. (2000) *Genocide in International Law*. Cambridge: Cambridge University Press.

Seselj, V. (1995) 'The Serb blueprint for cleansing Kosova', *Greater Serbia Journal* (Belgrade), 14 October. See: http://www.peacelink.nu/Jugoslavia/Seselj_makes_clear.html.

Shaw, M. (1999) *The Kosova War*. See: http://www.sussex.ac.uk/Users/hafa3/kosova.htm.

Smith, R.J. (1999) 'Serbs tried to cover up massacre; Kosovo reprisal plot bared by phone taps', *Washington Post*, 28 January.

Taylor, S.R. (2004) 'Sentencing guidelines urged – legal experts say arbitrary sentencing practices could undermine tribunal's credibility in The Hague',

Institute for War and Peace Reporting, TU No. 347, 8 March. The Hague: Institute for War and Peace.
Traynor, I. (2007) 'Serbia jails death squad men for Srebrenica killings', *The Guardian*, 11 April.
United Nations (1999) Report of the Secretary General prepared pursuant to resolutions 1160 (1998), 1199 (1998) and 1203 (1998) of the Security Council, 30 January.
Wood, N. (2007) 'To-and-fro in Serbian war crimes cases'. See: http://www.iht.sp.co.gg/.
Zlatarič, B. (1977) *Krivično pravo – opči dio*. Zagreb: Globus.

Chapter 5

Criminological views and informal responses to the Racak massacre according to Albanian customary law and the principles of international law – Albanian perspective

Rexhep Gashi

Serious crimes against humanity and international law were carried out during the Kosovo war (February 1998–June 1999), some of which amount to genocide. These atrocities against the Albanian civil population were carried out by Serb and Yugoslav police, military and paramilitary forces. Such crimes include: murder, infliction of serious physical and mental injury, torture, the forced deportation of the population, rape, hostage taking, collective punishment, sending people to concentration camps, forced labour, and the looting and destruction of homes and dwelling-places. During this period, several massacres against unprotected civilians from different age groups were carried out, such as, for example, the massacres in Likoshan, Polklek, Obri, Sushice, Gollubovc, Racak, etc. All these crimes and massacres were well organised and coordinated by the Serbian authorities in order to intimidate Albanians, create a climate of insecurity and force them to flee their ancestral homes.

Among these crimes and massacres, it's worth mentioning the massacre in Racak, which echoed throughout the world and had an impact on attracting the attention of the public and increasing the pressure on the Yugoslav authorities of that time to stop the violence; it was a turning point in the later flow of events, which eventually resulted in the NATO air strikes on Serbian targets followed by the withdrawal of the police and military forces from the territory of Kosovo.

This article presents and analyses some elements and aspects of the use of informal legal mechanisms for conflict resolution with emphasis on the massacre in Racak. It relies on the traditional rules of international law, Albanian customary law, local customs, religious, cultural and moral rules, and other traditional customs observed in the territory of Kosovo, which can provide many answers for the crimes committed throughout Kosovo, including those in Racak. In our study of the Racak case, we look for informal judicial mechanisms that can be applied in order to uncover the truth about the crimes committed in Kosovo as well as for the restoration of justice as a precondition for coexistence and reconciliation of the warring parties.

Case interpretation

The massacre at Racak occurred on 15 January 1999, in the village of Racak in the municipality of Shtimje (Kosovo). On this date, in the village of Racak, 45 Albanian civilians of different ages, including a child and three women, were massacred by members of Serb and Yugoslav police, military and paramilitary forces,[1] and many more were injured, beaten and tortured. Nine members of the Kosovo Liberation Army (KLA) were also killed (Jashari 2004: 57). According to eyewitnesses the gunfire that preceded the killing of civilians in this village was heard in the early morning hours (at 06:45) of 15 January 1999 (2004: 27). Soon afterwards, the peasants realised that the village had been surrounded and many of them fled their homes and took refuge in a nearby forest, in order to escape the worst. Others gathered in the houses of their co-villagers, looking for safe places to hide. Many people took shelter in the houses of Sadik Osmani (2004: 314–17)[2] – who was a teacher – and Mehmet Mustafa, among others. This horrible event went on from 7 a.m. until 4 p.m. when Serb and Yugoslav units withdrew from the crime scene.

Racak is a village near Shtimje and its outskirts are only 200 metres straight from the town – some 300 metres away from the police station and 350 metres from the pine trees of Shtimje where the Serb military forces were positioned. This situation made it impossible for the KLA to protect the village because it only had a small number of lightly armed soldiers. The massacre in Racak occurred at the time when the Holbrooke-Milosevic agreement was in place. This settlement included a partial withdrawal of Serb forces from Kosovo, a ceasefire and the restoration of peace (Shala 2000: 156–57).[3] In addition to this, under the terms of this settlement, the OSCE had deployed 2,000 monitors headed by the outstanding American diplomat William Walker, backed up by NATO air forces.

Bearing in mind some of the elements of this crime – such as the number of victims that were massacred, the manner and means used to carry the massacre out, the time and place of the crime, the nationality and innocence of the victims, the purpose of the crime and the executors – it becomes clear that this represents a crime against humanity and a crime of genocide. This crime is punishable both under local laws applicable at the time when it happened as well as under international provisions and instruments. It is also punishable according to traditional (local and international) customary rules, religious, moral and cultural rules, as well as other customs observed in people's day-to-day lives. Below we present some characteristics related to the qualification of this crime, its constitutive elements and the criminal responsibility of the perpetrators of this crime.

Understanding the crime in Racak and its constitutive elements

According to the Yugoslav criminal legislation in force at the time when the massacre of Racak was carried out, this crime is classified in the group of criminal offences against humanity and international law. According to the Criminal Law of the former Socialist Federal Republic of Yugoslavia (former SFRJ) of 1977, the massacre of Racak is considered a war crime against civilian population (Art. 142) and it contains some elements of the crime of genocide (Art. 141). This crime is carried out in two forms: (1) by ordering it; and (2) by carrying out the criminal acts directly (these forms of commission of criminal acts are laid down in the above mentioned provisions and will be analysed later in this chapter). For such crimes, the former criminal legislation prescribes long-term imprisonment, including the death penalty.

The massacre at Racak, in which innocent civilians were killed and massacred, is punishable under Albanian customary rules, canons and local traditional rules applicable in Kosovo. The rules of Albanian customary law (Elezi 2003; Elezi 2006)[4] contain many paragraphs regarding murders, injuries and other criminal offences against the person as well as paragraphs for other criminal acts. The law also provides sentences for offenders. In the past these canonic rules prescribed criminal offences and criminal sanctions that only applied to individuals when both offender and victim belonged to the Albanian community. But in our opinion, these rules may also apply to the individuals of other nationalities, whether offender or victim. Albanian customary law, in particular the Albanian criminal customary law, has maintained its original features throughout history, despite invasion by other nations. These original characteristics were preserved even during the Ottoman occupation which lasted almost five centuries. Many of these rules have been applied in the past as part of informal justice whenever the power and role of the state and the positive law in society weakened.

The rules of Albanian customary law consider murder as one of the most serious crimes among other crimes against the person. The Code of Lekë Dukagjini (hereinafter CLD) along with other Albanian canons pay significant attention to murder and vengeance (Gjeçovi 1933: para 822–990; Ilia 1993: paras 2736–2744).[5] These canons lay down respective punishments for murder and other criminal acts against the person. In particular, Albanian customary traditions and rules severely punish cruel murder and those causing grave consequences. By turning the ancient tradition of hospitality of the Albanian people into law, these rules provide a special protection for people's life, health, honour and dignity. Under the Albanian customary criminal law murder may be carried out directly by acting and indirectly by failing to act. The customary law also recognises the status of accomplice in carrying out a murder. The CLD distinguishes the following forms of complicity in murder: the murderer (the executer), the *simahuri* (the accomplice) and secret mediation[6] (Gjeçovi 1933: paras 843, 850, 766). According to Albanian customary law, in order for a murder to be considered a grave murder, attention is placed on particular elements: the time when it was carried out, the place where it occurred, the manner of killing, the means used to kill, the consequences of such an act, etc. Murders are classified into two groups: (1) murders targeting the lives of several people; and (2) murders targeting the life of a single person. It is understandable that murders of the first group are penalised more harshly. According to Albanian customary law, severe murders are considered those murders committed against a person who has been given a peace vow (The Truce), murdering women or children, murdering a man while he is accompanied by a woman, murdering a pregnant woman, etc. In particular, murdering a friend or cleric was considered a serious murder. The CLD also prescribes criminal offences against the health, honour, and dignity of a person, such as bodily injury,[7] beating and rape as well as other criminal offences (Gjeçovi 1933: paras 906–907).

Based on the rules of Albanian criminal customary law with regard to murders, bodily injuries and other criminal offences that are constitutive parts of the crime in Racak, one can conclude rightfully that the massacre in Racak contains enough elements to be qualified as a severe crime in accordance with Albanian customary law.

The massacre at Racak was a premeditated and intentional act, carried out through orders given and criminal acts directly committed by Serb and Yugoslav police forces. These forces executed and mutilated 45 civilians, wounded 12, tortured 12 others and brought physical and psychological suffering to the vast majority of the unprotected population of this village (Jashari 2004: 54–8). Those who suffered the most and were the main target of this crime were unprotected civilians. Thus, out of 54 people killed that day, 45 were civilians and only nine of them were members of the KLA (Jashari 2004: 54–7; Bellamy 2002: 114–20).[8] As can be seen, this was a crime carried out against civilians of different ages (Jashari 2004: 61–156),[9] including three women among those killed in the massacre. According to Albanian customary law, killing a woman is a great dishonour and carries severe punishment. Furthermore, if a man is accompanied by a woman, he does not have to fear for his life or bodily integrity (Gjeçovi 1933: para. 835). This is due to the fact that under Albanian customary law a woman is considered a saint and intact. As we mentioned above, many of those killed in the massacre at Racak were accompanied by women and children; they were afterwards separated from their families and executed. The CLD also protects the life of the unborn child of a pregnant woman (Gjeçovi 1933: para. 951).[10]

The constitutive elements that make a criminal offence worse, according to Albanian customary law, are the circumstances of the crime with respect to the place where the crime was committed, the timing of the crime, the manner in which it was carried out, the consequences of such crime, etc. As we have already mentioned, the crime in Racak occurred on 15 January 1999, at a time when war was going on in Kosovo between the KLA and Yugoslav forces. Many of the victims were tortured and then forced to walk in a row toward a place called 'Bebushi Hill' where they were executed with firearms at close range from three to four metres. Some others were shot dead in their yards in front of their family members and co-villagers. Under Albanian customary law and other local customs the use of torture and other forms of mutilation of victims carry severe penalties. Testimonies of witnesses that survived the massacre and the results of autopsies clearly show that the victims of the massacre in Racak had been subjected to psycho-physical torture prior to being killed[11] and mutilated after their death (Jashari 2004: 299–355).

Another element that makes the massacre in Racak a monstrous crime, according to Albanian customary law, is the time when it was carried out. This crime occurred at a time when a ceasefire as part of the Holbrooke-Milosevic accord was in force. Hoping that Serb forces would honour the agreement, the displaced Albanian population began returning to their homes, even though their houses were burnt to the ground by the very same Serb police and military forces. According to the CLD, murders carried out during the time when a person is granted a peace vow (The Truce), a word of honour known as 'besa' ('besa-pledge' – Gjeçovi 1933: paras 854–873),[12] are considered grave criminal offences because they have broken the 'vow' and under the customary laws during the period of vow no revenge could be exercised. The Racak crime contains elements of such killings.

According to the international legal instruments in effect at the time when the massacre was committed as well as under the laws and customs of war, the case of Racak can be qualified as a crime against humanity with elements of genocide. This crime was directed against civilians who were protected by international legal instruments which had been ratified by the former Yugoslavia. One such instrument is the Geneva Convention relative to the protection of civilian persons in time of war of 1949.[13] This crime is also punishable according to the Statute of the ICTY[14] and other international legal instruments.[15] This massacre represents a severe crime which is punishable harshly in accordance with religious norms preached by all the main faiths of the world (Buddhism, Christianity and Islam). Thus the Qur'an, the holy book of Islam, preaches peace. According to Islam, war is to be waged in the following exceptional circumstances: (1) in self-defence and to ward off unjustified aggression; (2) to resist those who oppress and persecute Muslims because of their religion; and (3) to protect holy shrines and places of religious worship (Rahman 1992: 117). This religion forbids initiating a war during the holy months of the Islamic Lunar Calendar.[16] Islamic International Law has prescribed many limitations with a view to minimising the horrors of war: it prohibits cruel murder; mistreatment and rape; the killing of women, even when women aid men (the wounded), as well as children and sick people; the killing of those who cannot protect themselves (the elderly, the blind, the paralysed, people with mental illnesses and women); killing the enemy treacherously (perfidiously); the mutilation of infidels (cutting off their noses or ears); the unnecessary continuation of war until a peace accord is reached, etc. (Stadtmüller 1961: 58; Gruda 1995: 24). There are also many other tenets in Islam that deal with other issues, including the fulfilment of a ceasefire between warring sides (Gruda 1995: 25).[17] By analysing the religious tenets of Islam it becomes very obvious that the massacre at Racak has all elements of a severe crime which is forbidden under the tenets of this faith, bearing in mind the time when it was carried out (this crime occurred during the holy month of Ramadan), the breach of the ceasefire between the parties in conflict, the category of people killed and massacred, and the manner and means used to commit this crime.

Criminal responsibility of the perpetrators of the crime in Racak

The perpetrators of the massacre at Racak should be brought to justice and held accountable for their acts in compliance with the criminal legislation in force and other international legal instruments in effect at the time when the crime was committed. This is an individual responsibility and applies to persons who order the commission of criminal offences, as well as to those who commit such acts.[18] They are responsible for this crime both under moral and legal rules prescribed by the laws and customs of war. The perpetrators of this crime are also responsible according to the Albanian criminal customary law, the local tradition and culture, and the religious rules.

Albanian customary law contains rules which regulate issues regarding the responsibility of perpetrators of criminal offences, in particular for murder. Such norms can be partially applied in determining the responsibility of perpetrators of the massacre at Racak. Under the criminal principles set forth in the CLD a person 14–15 years old capable of carrying a weapon was liable for punitive murder (Elezi 1983: 107), whereas the person responsible for criminal offences carried out by other family members, including murder, was the householder, meaning that the father was accountable for criminal offences carried out by his children (1983: 108). The elderly who had abandoned weapons were not liable for punitive murder while a woman was not liable for murder even when she executed the crime (1983: 108). When a woman has carried out a crime, her parents are responsible for her actions, or even her husband in special cases. The Code of Lekë Dukagjini, the Canon of Skenderbeu, the Canon of Labëria and other Albanian canons regard guilt as an element of accountability. The Code of Lekë Dukagjini distinguishes these forms of guilt: premeditation (para. 882), wittingly with premeditation (para. 901) and negligence (para. 932). These tenets also provide other elements of murder such as purpose and motive. According to the tenets of customary law, murders may be carried out by actions of one person or two or more persons acting together. As can be inferred, these rules recognise the principle of complicity, which is the case when a crime is committed by two or more persons, provided that there they have agreed to commit such crime.[19] According to these rules, those who have aided and abetted the commission of murder are held accountable like the executer; however, instigators are not held accountable as associates to murder, but they have to pay a certain fine, because the rule 'words don't kill people' applies (Elezi 1983: 120).

From our short presentation of the principles of Albanian customary law, with regard to the accountability of the perpetrators it becomes clear that some of these principles could be applied in the case of the massacre at Racak. According to these principles the political and military leadership of Yugoslavia who ordered the commission of the crime along with those who carried it out, i.e. the Yugoslav and Serb police and military forces, are the perpetrators of the crime in Racak. This crime was carried out deliberately, with complicity between political and military leaders, because there was a connection among participating structures in ordering and executing the crime. Again, talking from the viewpoint of Albanian customary law, this crime aimed to intimidate Albanians, creating a climate of insecurity, without perspective for living for inhabitants of Racak in particular and Albanian in general, so they would be forced to flee the homeland in which they had lived for centuries.

Outcome level

From what has been said above in our analysis of the case, it is clear that we are dealing with a serious crime against humanity that includes elements of the crime of genocide, with numerous and irretrievable consequences for the inhabitants of Racak and beyond.[20] Bearing in mind the high number of grave consequences of this crime, not to mention the other crimes committed in the territory of Kosovo, the parties in conflict should strive to find additional mechanisms in order to see justice done, uncover the truth related to this case and re-establish previous relations through compensation. In this way conditions for coexistence as well as reconciliation between the Serbs and Albanians should be established. In order to reach these goals, apart from having a formal justice system in place, an important role lies in the functioning of various informal mechanisms to achieve mutual trust between the parties in conflict.

Below we will examine the different informal mechanisms available to achieve justice and uncover the truth, and look into the possibility of restoring pre-war relationships between the warring parties, relying on the traditional rules of international law, Albanian customary law, religious rules, and cultural, moral and other local customs that are observed in the territory of Kosovo and elsewhere.

Justice

In accordance with the general principles of international law,[21] the principles of Albanian customary criminal law (see Gjeçovi 1933; Ilia 1993; Elezi 1983) and other customs practised in Kosovo, the perpetrators of the crime in Racak should be brought to justice and should be punished. This is the obligation of the state deriving from international conventions referring to war crimes and crimes against humanity, which has been signed and ratified by the state party. Such an obligation is included in the preamble of the Convention on the Non-Applicability of Statutory Limitations to War Crimes and Crimes against Humanity, 1968, which among other things points out that:

> The States Parties to the present Convention [are] convinced that the effective punishment of war crimes and crimes against humanity is an important element in the prevention of such crimes, the protection of human rights and fundamental freedoms, the encouragement of confidence, the furtherance of co-operation among peoples and the promotion of international peace and security […] Recognising that it is necessary and timely to affirm in international law, through this Convention, the principle that there is no period of limitation for war crimes and crimes against humanity, and to secure its universal application […]

It is a known fact that soon after the crime in Racak was carried out, this act was condemned by numerous international actors, representatives of governments and international organisations, all of them calling for the perpetrators to be prosecuted and tried. In its report Human Rights Watch points out that the Yugoslav forces were to blame for the war crimes in Racak (Human Rights Watch 1999; Jashari 2004: 249–55). Moreover, William Walker, the head of the OSCE's Kosovo Verification Mission (KVM) at that time, after having seen in person what had happened in Racak, described it as a massacre and a crime against humanity, and declared in a press conference:

> We must find out who ordered and carried out the orders, and justice has to prevail; with or without invitation by the Government of FRJ the representatives of the International Tribunal for war crimes in the territory of ex-Yugoslavia must come here to investigate these crimes and should be here if possible within next 24 hours.

International rules and legal regulations which comprise the laws and customs of war, along with traditional Albanian customary law and other regulations, pay significant attention to the issues of accountability and punishment of the perpetrators of criminal offences, including the perpetrators of crimes against humanity. These rules and regulations should help to implement the criminal rules stipulated in the relevant conventions and laws of particular countries. It is understandable that the implementation of these customary laws is possible only if they are not in contradiction with the other provisions of the applicable legislation.

According to Albanian customary law, for criminal offences against life and physical integrity, honour and authority, dignity and morals, and acts directed against wealth, severe punishments – and often the death penalty – apply. In cases of severe murder the main penalty was death or blood revenge, because the perpetrator was accountable according to the principle of 'blood for blood' (Gjeçovi 1933: para. 1194–1195; Elezi 1983: 128–34).[22] Women and children were exempt from the penalty. Besides the death penalty, a cumulative fine was also sanctioned for a murder case. The death penalty was usually carried out by firing squad composed of members of the village, the brotherhood and the clan. It is important to mention that Albanian customary laws did not discriminate on the basis of status in society when it came to punishment (Gjeçovi 1933: 887).[23] The CLD and other Albanian canons, following the principle of *lex talion*, provide that 'blood follow the finger', meaning that acts of vengeance should be first directed against the executor of the murder (Elezi 2003: 100). Consequently, customary laws – that are nowadays in contradiction with the applicable law – stipulate harsh punishments for perpetrators of murder, including those who committed the crime in Racak. Islamic religious rules also provide certain regulations with regard to the accountability of perpetrators and their punishment for such crimes. Thus the Qur'an provides: that the recompense for an injury is an injury equal thereto (in degree): but if a person forgives and makes reconciliation, his reward is due from Allah: for (Allah) loves not those who do wrong (see The Holy Qur'an 42: 40, in Alī 1989: 1257–8).

The issue of accountability and punishment of the perpetrators of the crime in Racak and the restoration of infringed justice deserves a special analysis for several reasons. Firstly, distinction should be made between the population as a whole, which is in general innocent of the crimes, and the political leaders and individuals who are responsible for preparing, launching and implementing the actions which resulted in these crimes. A clear line of demarcation should be drawn between the Serb people, who are not guilty, and those responsible, i.e. those who ordered and carried out this crime, in other words state leaders, political leaders, various groups and individuals.

Secondly, discussion of the issue of responsibility has to do with the request of the victims to bring the offenders to justice as a precondition for restoring the trust and peace among Albanians and Serbs. Thirdly, bringing the perpetrators before the courts and achieving their conviction would provide satisfaction for the victims and would be a preventive measure restraining other perpetrators from conducting similar criminal acts in the future. Finally, this would enable precise identification of the persons responsible for the crime at Racak. As is well known, criminal responsibility is always an individual responsibility linked to the existence of culpability. This can be clearly noted by the provisions of national and international legislation dealing with the issue of criminal responsibility and punishment for criminals, as well as the traditional rules that contain the laws and customs of war and other Albanian customary regulations.

Determining the responsibility of the perpetrators of the Racak crime represents a challenge for the formal judicial institutions, either national or international, and the institutions of informal justice. Until now, there has been little willingness to uncover the perpetrators of this crime and bring them to justice in Serbia. In addition to this, there has been little done either by the organs of international justice to capture the perpetrators of the Racak crime. Identifying the various military and paramilitary formations established by the state or by individuals – groups or nationalist political parties such as Arkan's 'Tigers' ('Arkanovi tigrovi'), the 'White Eagles' ('Beli orlovi'), the

'Scorpions' and others that operated in Kosovo – and bringing to justice those responsible for this atrocity may be very helpful.

Another particular problem in indicting the criminals linked to the Racak case and other crimes committed in Kosovo is the strong resistance put up by the Serbian state, which is trying to conceal its own illegal activities behind the issue of national sovereignty. In addition, resistance of the state to cooperate with the Hague Tribunal in bringing the criminals before the bodies of the international justice system presents another major problem. All these obstacles and challenges encountered by the judicial institutions represent serious difficulties for lasting peace, reconciliation and restoration of justice.

Truth-seeking

According to the circumstances in which the crime in Racak was carried out and according to testimonies made by witnesses – survivors from the hands of criminals the day the crime was committed – it is obvious that this crime was perpetrated following orders given by high officials of the Serb government, although it was implemented by Yugoslav police and military forces. The involvement of the Serb government in this crime has been proven by the records of telephone conversations in which the government gives orders to the police to take tougher action (Smith 1999).[24] This fact is further reinforced by the testimony of a prosecution witness, Ratomir Tanic, who appeared before the Hague Tribunal during November 2006 (*Koha Ditore* 2006: 6).[25]

The crime scene was outside the village, away from the control of the International Verification Mission. It was carried out in the suburbs of the village, away from international supervision. This was an attempt to conceal the crime. Cancellation of the International Verification Mission's work was another attempt to cover up as was the battle launched by the Yugoslav and Serb police to recover the bodies. However, because of the fact that the international institutions were quickly informed about the truth surrounding this crime and the news was made public through worldwide mass media, the Serb leadership ordered a blockade of Racak and undertook measures to transport all the bodies to the Institute of Legal Medicine in Prishtina, where a biased post mortem would be performed so that an official Serbian version could be published to hide the crime (Jashari 2004: 148).

Additional proof that the Serbs were trying to conceal the truth about this crime was the prohibition from entering into Kosovo of the expert team from the Hague Tribunal, at the Kosovar-Macedonian border, so they were not allowed to reach the crime scene and uncover the truth of the massacre against innocent and unprotected civilians (2004: 148).

Based on the statements made by witnesses, the post mortems of the victims and other evidence, it is clear that the ages of the victims ranged from the youngest aged below 14 to 81. Among the victims there were also three women, all of whom were unarmed, taken from their houses during a Muslim religious holiday (the Holy Month of Ramadan) and killed at a close range (2004: 145–56). Various weapons were used in committing this crime, such as knives, pocket-knives, axes and bayonets, and blunt or hard objects such as rifle butts, sticks and other strong objects, as well as firearms of various calibres such as sharpshooters and machine guns (2004: 152).

All the circumstances surrounding the commission of this crime, in particular the place where it was carried out, the timing when it occurred, the means used to carry it out and the battle to transport the cadavers in order to cover up the crime are strongly condemned by traditional international regulations, the rules of Albanian customary law and other religious rules. According to Albanian canons, the perpetrator of a criminal offence should send word to the victim's family notifying them that he murdered their family member and should show respect for the corpse by not desecrating it (Gjeçovi 1993: para. 846).[26] In the case of Racak not only were the villagers massacred, their corpses were also mutilated after being killed (Jashari 2004: 89).[27] Moreover, one cadaver is still missing.[28]

The attempts made by Serb forces to cover up the truth are in full contradiction to Albanian customary laws and other religious laws. In order to achieve this, Yugoslav and Serb police and military forces launched a widespread offensive to recapture Racak. After two days of fierce fighting with the KLA they eventually forced their way into the village on 17 January 1999. They then committed a second crime by forcibly picking up the bodies of the people they had massacred and performing a post mortem examination in the absence of representatives of the Hague Tribunal. They were then preparing to commit yet another crime by burying the cadavers. This was done after the peasants had collected the corpses and laid them in the village mosque, so they could be identified and have autopsies carried out by international pathologists, and then buried according to the customs of Islamic tradition. This 'game' with the cadavers lasted for almost a month, from 15 January until 11 February of 1999, when the bodies were eventually buried. A large number of citizens from

Kosovo, the mass media and representatives of humanitarian and religious associations attended the collective funeral ceremony and burial of the victims of the massacre in Racak. This funeral ceremony was enabled by the OSCE Mission in Kosovo, but due to the fact that Serb forces were positioned very close to Racak they prevented people from returning to the village to express their condolences to the families of the victims (Jashari 2004: 48–50). This humiliation of the cadavers committed by the Serbian and Yugoslav regime is a flagrant infringement of fundamental human rights and contrary to the tradition of Islamic religion. It is well-known that according to the tenets of Islamic religion and Albanian tradition it is an exclusive right of family members to organise the burial of the dead. This act of the Serbian and Yugoslav forces towards the cadavers of the Racak massacre was harshly condemned by the Albanian population and the democratic world.

There is no doubt that the implementation of the criminal law is of great importance in the process of uncovering the truth, restoring justice and establishing peace and reconciliation between the parties in conflict in Kosovo. But, it should be stressed that this process alone is insufficient to solve the conflict and restore the shaken peace. The necessary additional mechanisms should be found to contribute to achieving the goals set out above. There is a great role here for informal mechanisms containing customary and religious rules. Albanian customary law contains a number of paragraphs referring to the institutions and customary procedures for uncovering the truth and resolution of conflict resulting from various criminal offences, including murder as the most serious offence. These regulations may also apply in the case of the crime in Racak.

According to Albanian customs, the body that tried and sentenced criminal offenders was called the *pleqnia* (Council of Elders). Even though the CLD mentions no division of this Council of Elders, we have found in the literature the division into *pleqnia e madhe* (Big Council of Elders) and *pleqnia e vogel* (Small Council of Elders) (Halili 1985: 88; Sahiti 2006: 64). Big Elder Council usually implies an assembly of the clan (tribe) or an assembly of the elders in order to discuss issues of great importance including serious crimes between tribes, whereas the Small Council of Elders assembled to discuss issues and conflicts within the tribe, village or even family. Customary rules recognise the Council of Elders as a special trial body dealing with cases of parties in conflict, which was composed of tribe leaders or other adults that enjoyed a reputation of being wise, honourable and prudent. The structure of the Council of Elders was determined by the parties.[29] We shall consider later the flow of procedure before the Council of Elders and the evidential procedure involved.

Non-governmental organisations and other informal mechanisms also have a role in uncovering the truth and achieving the restoration of justice, not just in the case of Racak, but also for other crimes committed in Kosovo. In this respect, the Humanitarian Law Centre based in Belgrade is currently doing remarkable work in solving the conflicts that took place within the territory of ex-Yugoslavia. During its work this Centre has assisted several times in uncovering the truth regarding crimes committed in these ex-nests of the conflict and has helped in bringing some criminals to justice (Kandić 2006: 109–14). We think that this organisation should widen its activities and include uncovering the truth of the massacre in Racak and bringing the perpetrators to face justice. Establishing a Truth and Reconciliation Commission as has been done in other countries which have gone through similar conflicts may play an important role in restoring justice and peace between the parties in conflict in Kosovo.

Redress

In accordance with the principles and practice of international law, the victims of flagrant violence during armed conflicts should be compensated for their losses and sufferings.[30] Reparation for damage is an essential element in restoring democracy, the rule of law and reconciliation between parties in conflict. Reparation for victims that have been subject to war crimes and violence is also required by the provisions of Albanian customary law and the country's legislation. According to Albanian customary law a court of elders was set up for criminal offences, in particular murder cases, and dealt with reconciliation of the parties in conflict and provided the terms of the remuneration for reconciliation (Sahiti 2006: 68–74). This court was called the 'Elders of Blood' and it was usually comprised of representatives of both the parties in conflict and other people with good reputation who had a wide knowledge of the country's customs. On the other hand, financial compensation demanded from the family of the murderer was called 'the money of blood'. Such compensation was a sign of admission of guilt, and a gesture of care and compassion expressed by the family of the murderer, or as an equivalent price for the blood of the victim.

The idea of providing reparations to victims is not new. Aristotle, in Book V of the *Nichomachean Ethics*, articulates what was surely not a novel view even at the time, according to which 'rectificatory justice' requires the judge to 'equalise by means of the penalty, taking away from the gain of the assailant' (Aristotle V: 2–4). This view, in favour of compensation for the victims of armed conflicts, has the support of other outstanding authors of international law. However, the practice of various countries in conflict tell us that compensation of victims either does not take place at all or has been difficult to accomplish for different reasons.

As mentioned previously, those who suffered from the violence exercised by Serb and Yugoslav police in the massacre of Racak were innocent people. We think that the victims of the crime and their relatives should be compensated. This is the only way to create the preconditions for the restoration of justice and reconciliation of the parties in the conflict. In compliance with international provisions and the country's customs, the Serbian state must undertake steps towards compensating the victims of the massacre in Racak as well as the victims of other crimes committed in Kosovo. In this way Serbia will fulfil the requirements of the international community and facilitate its pathway to gaining membership of international organisations. The compensation of victims can be achieved in several ways: at the individual, group or national level.

First of all, the state of Serbia must accept the truth regarding the massacre in Racak, and express public apologies for the use of force there. Recognising the truth and publicly seeking forgiveness for the crime in Racak and other crimes in Kosovo conducted by Serb forces will be perceived as an act of good will and will enable the restoration of shaken relationship between Serbs and Albanians living in Kosovo. The families of victims of the crime in Racak do not deserve to be despised; instead, respect should be shown for them. This obligation arises from the rules of the CLD that says: 'It is not only a law but an obligation to be contemptuous of anyone in the family of the victim, even if he is poor and weak' (Gjeçovi 1933: para. 868).[31]

Secondly, Serbia should show goodwill in identifying and trying perpetrators of the crime in Racak, which will provide satisfaction for the victims of this crime. While formal courts have failed to identify and try the perpetrators, we must look into the possibility that informal bodies may exercise this duty in accordance with Albanian customary law or other informal rules. Finally, the Serbian state should compensate the victims of this crime and their relatives for the suffering it has brought to them as well as for their loss of family members.

Reparation may range from symbolic acts to financial compensation for the damage that has been done. Besides making a public apology, other forms of symbolic reparation include: the organisation of commemorative ceremonies in remembrance of the victims of this crime, erecting a monument to the victims,[32] acts leading to reconciliation, etc. These forms of reparation would be another symbolic gesture and a small satisfaction for the families of the victims and will have an impact in raising awareness of the Serbian people of the consequences of such crimes. Families of the victims of the massacre in Racak and families of all the other victims of the crimes committed in Kosovo should be given priority during their education, should receive proper healthcare service and should receive economic aid in the form of pensions or other compensation. They have the right to just compensation for the emotional damage caused by the killing of their loved ones.[33]

Procedural level

As mentioned above, in resolving conflicts and achieving reconciliation between parties, the application of formal legal procedures and measures alone is not sufficient. Various informal procedural mechanisms have an important role in restoring justice, uncovering the truth and restoring the previous situation. These informal mechanisms are applicable in accordance with the specificities of different countries.

First, the case of Racak involved different warring parties: the Yugoslav and Serbian police, military and paramilitary forces on one side and the Kosovo Liberation Army on the other. Because of the composition of the warring parties, it is understandable that Albanian customary law is difficult to apply due to the fact that these provisions have been applied and are still applied in conflict resolution only within the Albanian nation. However, since there are some similarities between Serbian and Albanian customary laws, and with other nations that have been living in these territories, some of these customs might be applied in resolving the conflict between the two nations. Below we will analyse some of the Albanian provisions and traditional customs as well as some rules and procedures of an international character that can be applied in uncovering the truth and restoring justice in the case of Racak.

Procedural provisions and local traditions

Besides the relevant laws, when identifying and trying perpetrators of the crime in Racak, informal procedures may be applied. Albanian customary law contains several rules that concern the investigation and trial of perpetrators, in particular those who have committed murder. As we have mentioned above, the body that looks into matters of criminal character and hands down sentences against perpetrators is called the *pleqnia* (Council of Elders). The procedure followed by the *pleqnia* corresponds with the accusatory procedure and as a rule begins with a public hearing (Sahiti 2006: 65). The inquiries in this procedure are conducted by a private person (a private detective) hired by the injured party; the person who conducts such an investigation is anonymous (unknown to the *pleqnia*). According to the CLD this person is called a *kapucar* (Gjeçovi 1933: paras 1079–1090). In order for this procedure to commence the injured party has to make a verbal indictment; this procedure is initiated *ex officio* only in exceptional cases when the defendant was caught red-handed or when the defendant had committed a crime against his relative in public (1933: paras 1017–1022). The most important phase of this procedure is the court hearing, in which the accuser is heard, the defendant is asked questions, evidence is analysed and finally a verdict is reached and communicated to the parties. The *pleqnia* selects one of its members, *pleqnar*, as leader (*kryepleqnar*), who presides over the trial. Because the decision taken by the *pleqnia* is not given in a written form, before the trial the *pleqnia* requires from both sides what in Albanian is called a *dorëzanë* (warrantee, guarantee) that both parties will abide by the verdict. The right to lodge an appeal against the Council's decision does not exist (1933: para. 1002).[34] The execution of the decision today is implemented with the free will of both parties. Some of the evidence used in the process of trying and proving guilt is rational, some irrational. Rational evidence includes the defendant's claim, the testimony of the witness, the opinion of the expert, the *kapucari*, the tracking of trails, recognition of the item, warrantors, looking into the crime scene, flagrancy, word of honour, documents, etc. (Sahiti 2006: 72–81). Irrational evidence includes oaths, vows, carrying a stone on the shoulder and heavenly trial (2006: 81–6).

Some of this evidence may be used in the procedure of identifying perpetrators of the crime in Racak, because they have been in use for a long time and have some similarities with Serbian customary law. It is understandable that both parties need to agree in order to apply these procedures and evidence. This would be very helpful for achieving official justice and would contribute to the restoration of peace and the settling of past injustice.

One of the forms of informal procedural reconciliation between parties in conflict is mediation for apology and reconciliation. Mediation is a century long tradition of Albanian people, passed on from generation to generation as well as encoded in Albanian canons such as the Code of Lekë Dukagjini, the Canon of Skenderbeu, the Canon of Laberia and others. Mediation is based on popular philosophy: it's better for warring parties to reconcile than to fight, it is better to prevent than to punish.

In accordance with Albanian customary law, the process of reconciliation is mediated by a well-known person, who has a good reputation in the community. Until recently, in Kosovo and other ethnic Albanian territories, a reconciliation of the blood by giving money to the house of the person killed was applicable, as a relict of customary law. Nowadays this form of reconciliation no longer exists (Çetta 1999).[35] Relying on the rich experience of the Albanian people in the reconciliation of hundreds of families involved in blood feuds, we believe that this form of reconciliation may apply in the case of Racak.

The perpetrators of such crimes and their victims, in the Racak case as well as in other war crimes, have a great role in achieving peace and reconciliation. As we have mentioned above, the political and military leadership of Serbia and Yugoslavia that ordered the commission of the crime along with those who carried it out, i.e. the Yugoslav and Serb police and military forces, are the perpetrators of the crime in Racak. The perpetrators should seek forgiveness for the massacre in Racak and appear before the court. Despite the fact that Serbian authorities have not shown readiness to bring those responsible for the massacre to face justice and the failure of the national and international institutions of justice to identify those responsible for it, the victims of this crime and the freedom-loving Albanian nation, need to be prepared to forget such crimes and the bitter past and turn towards the future. As the Dalai Lama said:

> Learning to forgive is much more useful than merely picking up a stone and throwing it at the object of one's anger, the more so when the provocation is extreme. For it is under the greatest adversity that there exists the greatest potential for doing good both for oneself and for others. (Braithwaite 2002: 3)

Forgiveness and reconciliation have always been appreciated values (features) of the Albanians, proven throughout the centuries. That is why these forms of informal reconciliation have a future in Kosovo and can be applied in conflict resolution between Albanians and Serbs.

International procedural rules and regulations

The application of procedural rules of an international character has an important role in resolving conflicts between parties and restoring peace and justice. These rules and regulations may be applied in restoring justice in the case of Racak and other crimes that took place in Kosovo during the last war. We share the opinion that international mechanisms would have a powerful effect in resolving the conflict and restoring reconciliation and the rule of law in Kosovo, given the fact that Kosovo is currently under the international supervision and administration of the United Nations Interim Administration Mission in Kosovo. The international procedural regulations are easier to apply due to the fact that the warring parties in Kosovo were the Yugoslav and Serb police on the one side and the Kosovo Liberation Army on the other.

The procedural means and methods of an international character that could be applied in resolving the case of Racak and other crimes committed in Kosovo include talks (negotiations), good services and mediations, the conducting of research (survey), reconciliation and other forms. The use of these means and forms for conflict resolution have a widespread tradition in international practice; hence, international human rights organisations and other associations have an important role in solving inter-ethnic and inter-state conflicts. These entities may help in restoring justice and achieving reconciliation between parties in conflict, as in the Kosovo conflict. These organisations can offer their help in a very painful issue such as that of missing persons; furthermore, these entities can help shed light on the fate of all missing persons, as a precondition for possible reconciliation in Kosovo (Zëri 2006: 17).[36]

A more active involvement by the International Committee of the Red Cross and by UNMIK itself has been expected. These international organisations should put more pressure on the Serb government to uncover the truth about the fate of missing people and repatriate their remains from mass graves in Serbia. At the same time, the international community should play a greater role in compelling the Serbian state to identify and try the perpetrators of the massacre at Racak as well as of other crimes committed in Kosovo. It can help and encourage the application of traditional and informal mechanisms in respect of the case in Racak and other crimes committed in Kosovo.

Purpose level

Apart from the applicable laws, many traditional rules of international law, rules of Albanian customary law, religious, moral and cultural rules, and other local customs may apply in the case of Racak. In addition, a number of traditional informal mechanisms could be applied in order to see the justice done, to uncover the truth and to compensate the victims. These traditional and informal mechanisms aim at the following:

- *Justice.* Through informal mechanisms of conflict resolution, in the case of the crime in Racak, its perpetrators should come before their victims and answer questions in order to uncover the truth and achieve reconciliation and justice. They should be held accountable for their crimes within the framework of informal justice procedures.
- *Truth.* It is important to uncover the truth in the case of Racak so that the perpetrators and victims can be successfully reintegrated into society. Due to the failure of justice and formal mechanisms to find out the truth, informal mechanisms that offer alternative possibilities for uncovering the truth of this crime and identifying its perpetrators should be applied. Our study clearly shows the seriousness of this crime and the duties and responsibilities of the different actors involved, as well as the importance of informal mechanisms in shedding light on what happened in Racak.
- *Redress.* It is very important that the victims and perpetrators of this crime try to forget the past and turn towards the future. This is a painful but necessary sacrifice that is required from the victims. But in order to achieve this goal many preconditions must be fulfilled: uncovering the truth of this crime, identifying its perpetrators, ensuring they are held accountable and awarding compensation to the victims through the application of the law and of informal rules and mechanisms.

Taking into consideration the informal mechanisms for conflict resolution between warring parties as a constitutive part of restoring justice, including the case of Racak, all three goals mentioned above are of incontrovertible importance for both the victims and perpetrators. Depending on the accomplishment of these goals, the victims and their families should benefit from compensation for the damage inflicted on them whereas the perpetrators should have the opportunity to integrate into society. In this way, the purpose of informal justice, as a constitutive part of overall justice, should be achieved.

Conclusion

Our analysis has considered the case of Racak as a crime against the civilian population, including elements of genocide. This crime is punishable under the local laws applicable in Kosovo as well as according to international instruments. From what has been said so far, we can conclude that the senior political and state leaders of Serbia and Yugoslavia who ordered the commission of this crime and the executors of those orders (the police, military and paramilitary forces following the orders of their supervisors) are responsible for the crime in Racak.

Bearing in mind the multiple and serious repercussions of this crime, the parties in conflict should try to find additional mechanisms to accomplish justice, uncover the truth and restore previous conditions by providing compensation for the damage, wherever possible. This would be a step forward in the process of restoring trust, coexistence and reconciliation between Serbs and Albanians. Besides implementing the official justice system, mechanisms of informal justice play a great role in achieving these goals.

Traditional rules of international law, the rules of Albanian customary law as well as religious, moral and cultural rules applicable in Kosovo may help in uncovering the truth of our case and bring justice. However, until now these provisions and traditional regulations have not been applied for a variety of reasons, such as exaggerated trust in formal justice hoping it will shed light on this crime, lack of goodwill between the warring parties to implement formal justice, lack of initiative on the part of national and international actors to implement these rules, lack of Serbian cooperation in identifying the perpetrators of this crime, and so on. We consider that the application of these customary laws might significantly help in restoring justice. Both the perpetrators and the victims have an important role in achieving peace and reconciliation between the parties in conflict.

Given the fact that Kosovo is currently under international administration, we think that the application of provisions and international rules of an informal character has an important role in restoring justice and bringing the parties together.

The application of informal mechanisms in the case of the massacre at Racak will help achieve the goals of justice, uncover the truth and provide some compensation. The accomplishment of these goals will be beneficial not only for the victims but also for the perpetrators and the society as a whole.

Notes

1 For more information about this massacre see Jashari (2004), *The Racak Massacre: Crime Against Humanity*, Prishtina: Skrola.

2 Referring to the statements made by eye-witnesses Nusret Shabani, Ramë Shabani, etc., around 30 women and children were gathered in the basement of Sadik Osmani's house at 08:30, while 30 males had found shelter in his cottage, so in all there were 60 people. This house was very close to the forest near the village.

3 The Holbrooke-Milosevic accord was reached on 13 October 1998, after long talks between the American diplomat Richard Holbrooke and former Serb president Milosevic. It is estimated that Holbrooke spent over 50 hours talking to Milosevic, explaining to him the difference between B52 aircraft and U2s (B52s are combat aircraft that drop bombs whereas U2 aircraft collect information) and that 2,000 verifiers in Kosovo provide a much better solution than 400 NATO aircraft in Serbia.

4 The Albanian customary criminal law is encoded in the following canons: the Code of Lekë Dukagjini (collected and codified by Shtjefën Gjeçovi), Shkodër, 1933; the Canon of Skënderbeu (collected and codified by Dom Frano Ilia), Milot, 1993; the Canon of Labëria (codified and prepared for publication by Dr Ismet Elezi), Tiranë, 2006; the Canon of Mountains (this canon was applicable in the nine mountains of the Malësia e Madhe e Mbishkodrës up to the Gjakova Highlands, Malësia e Madhe and the Kosovo Field) and other special canons. (For more information see Elezi (2003), *Information on the Pan-Albanian Customary Law*, Prishtina: no publisher)

5 See the Code of Lekë Dukagjini, paras 822–990. On the other hand the Canon of Skënderbeu prescribes murders in paras 2736–44.

6 'An accessory is he who, with criminal and secret mediation, gives aid to another in order to commit some destructive or dishonorable act against a third person in his village' (CLD, para. 766).

7 The Code of Lekë Dukagjini makes a distinction between severe bodily injuries and light bodily injuries. An injury above the belt is considered

severe whereas an injury below the belt is considered light (see paras 906 and 907 of the CLD).

8 This is confirmed by Helena Ranta, head of the forensic team (coroners) from Finland, whose report, on the basis of autopsy findings conducted on the victims of the massacre in Racak, found that most of them were unarmed civilians shot at close range.

9 The youngest victim of this crime was the 13½-year-old child Halim Rizah Beqiri, whereas the oldest was Nazmi Nuhë Imeri, aged 81½.

10 According to para. 951 of the CLD, if someone kills a pregnant women he is accountable not only for killing the woman but also for destroying the embryo.

11 Testimonies of eyewitnesses in the massacre of Racak. One of the witnesses, Bilall Avdiu, during his testimony in the criminal case according to the indictment JL/PlU403-t against Slobodan Milosevic accused of war crimes in Kosovo, Bosnia and Croatia among other things held on 30 and 31 May 2002, declared: '... I have seen the police taking out a heart from one of the civilians while he was still alive'.

12 The Code of Lekë Dukagjini deals with the institution of 'The Truce' (*Besa* – 'pledge, a word of honour') in paras 854–73.

13 This Convention was adopted on 12 August 1949 and came into force on 21 October 1950.

14 See the Statute of the International Tribunal for the Prosecution of Persons Responsible for Serious Violations of International Humanitarian Law Committed in the Territory of the Former Yugoslavia since 1991, established by the Security Council acting under Chapter VII of the Charter of the United Nations, Security Council Resolution 827, adopted on 25 May 1993, Articles 2–5.

15 Such as the Geneva Conventions of 1949, and the Convention on the Prevention and Punishment of the Crime of Genocide of 1948.

16 The months of the Islamic Lunar Calendar are: muharem, dhulkada, dhul-hidxha dhe rexheb (ramazan).

17 The Qur'an says literally: 'Allah doesn't like those who do not keep their word'.

18 The Statute of the International Tribunal contains provisions referring to individual criminal responsibility, which implies ordering and carrying out such crimes. This is best described in Article 7, point 1, of this Statute which says: 'A person who planned, instigated, ordered, committed or otherwise aided and abetted in the planning, preparation or execution of a crime referred to in Articles 2 to 5 of the present Statute, shall be individually responsible for the crime.'

19 Paragraph 839 of the CLD says: 'A gun or bread given with knowledge of the murder brings blood on the one who gave it.'

20 As a result of the crime in Racak, 63 children under 18 years were left parentless, 25 women lost their husbands, several families lost two or more family members and a considerable number of farmers became

handicapped. In addition to this, this crime inflicted much trauma and other psycho-physical suffering on the inhabitants of Racak.

21 See the Convention on the Prevention and Punishment of the Crime of Genocide, General Assembly Resolution 260A(III) of December 1948, Article 4; Convention on the Non-Applicability of Statutory Limitations to War Crimes and Crimes Against Humanity, General Assembly Resolution 2391(XXIII) of 26 November 1968, Article 4; Principles of International Co-operation in the Detection, Arrest, Extradition and Punishment of Persons Guilty of War Crimes and Crimes Against Humanity, General Assembly Resolution 3074(XXVIII) of 3 December 1973.

22 See paras 1194 and 1195 of the CLD. The punishments prescribed according to the CLD are: death penalty, revenge and blood feud, expulsion from the village, burning of house, fine, boycott and loss of some other rights (Elezi 2003: 128–34).

23 Thus para. 887 of the CLD stipulates: 'The value of the man's life is the same, whether he is handsome or ugly.'

24 Two high-ranking Serb officials had expressed their concerns over the large number of victims (22 reported by Minister Lukic at the time of the conversation). Therefore, in order to avoid any possible reaction by the international community, Nikolla Shahinovic recommended two courses of action for the police force under Lukic: the sealing-off of the border with Macedonia in order to prevent the entry of Chief Prosecutor of the Hague Tribunal, Louise Arbour, who was en route to Yugoslavia, and the restoration of control over Racak which was in the hands of the KLA on the night of 15 January with the aim of covering up the massacre.

25 The accusing witness, Ratomir Lukic, declared before the Tribunal in The Hague on 13 November 2006 that: 'There is a cassette which contains phone taps of conversations between Shahinovic and Lukic. I have heard this conversation in one of the official locations of the Intelligent State Security Service of Serbia, which had taped all conversations. During this conversation, Shahinovic has instructed general Lukic on how to remove the cadavers of the victims in Racak and for other military operations' (according to daily newspaper *Koha Ditore* 2006: 6).

26 Paragraph 846 of the CLD states: 'The murderer, if he is able to do so himself, turns the victim over on his back. If he can, well and good; if not, he must tell the first person he meets to turn the victim over on his back and place his weapon near his head.'

27 Thus, after Banush Kamberi was executed, Serb police forces had taken out their bayonets and cut off his head, and took the head with them.

28 The body of Sahide Metushi has not been found yet and her grave remains open.

29 According to the case law of *pleqnia* (Council of Elders) in Kosovo, it was comprised of twelve members in the vast majority of cases (six members for each party in dispute).

30 See Convention Against Torture and Other Cruel, Inhuman or Degrading Treatment or Punishment, 1987; Vienna Declaration of Torture, 1993.

31 There is a saying among Albanians: 'You killed him once, don't kill him again', which sends a message that the family of the victim should be respected, should not be offended and should not be caused harm.
32 Eight years after the massacre in Racak, on 15 January 2007, the construction of the Memorial Complex of Racak has begun that aims to lessen the pain of the families of the victims.
33 In accordance with the recommendation of the Resolution of the General Assembly of the United Nations of 16 December 2005, the Serbian state is bound to provide reparations for the victims of the crimes which constitute serious breaches of international humanitarian law.
34 The principle of the Kanun is: 'There is no substitution of Elder for Elder, judgment for judgment, or oath for oath' (CLD, para. 1002).
35 Reconciliation with remuneration was eliminated in Kosovo thanks to the Nationwide Movement for Reconciliation of Blood Feuds during the period 1990–92; over a short period of time from 2 February 1990 to 17 May 1992 this movement managed to reconcile 1,230 blood feuds, 542 injuries and 1,180 entanglements (see more in Çetta 1999).
36 According to the available data of October 2006, the number of persons reported missing is 2,195 (see the daily newspaper *Zëri* 2006: 17).

References

Ali, A.Y. (ed.) (1989) *The Holy Qur'an* (text, translation and commentary). Brentwood, MD: Amana Corporation.

Aristotle (n.d.) *Nichomachean Ethics*, Book V (s.l.), chapters 2–4.

Bellamy, J.A. (2002) 'The Kosovo Verification Mission', *Kosovo and International Society*. London: Palgrave Macmillan, pp. 114–20.

Bible (1994) Albanian trans. Dom Simon Filipaj. Ferizaj: Drita.

Bleeker, M. (ed.) (2006) *Dealing with the Past and Transitional Justice: Creating Conditions for Peace, Human Rights and the Rule of Law*, Conference Paper 1/6. Political Affairs Division IV, Federal Department of Foreign Affairs, Switzerland.

Braithwaite, J. (2002) *Restorative Justice and Responsive Regulation*. Oxford: Oxford University Press.

Çetta, A. (1999) *Reconciliation of Blood Feuds 1990–1991*. Prishtina: Albanological Institute.

Convention Against Torture and Other Cruel, Inhuman or Degrading Treatment or Punishment (1987). General Assembly Resolution 39/46, 10 December 1984.

Convention on the Non-Applicability of Statutory Limitations to War Crimes and Crimes Against Humanity (1968). General Assembly Resolution 2391(XXIII).

Convention on the Prevention and Punishment of the Crime of Genocide (1948). General Assembly Resolution 260A(III).

Criminal Code of the Socialist Federal Republic of Yugoslavia (1977) Adopted by the SFRJ Assembly at the session of the Federal Council held on 28 September 1976, Official Gazette of SFRJ, no. 36/77, Belgrade.

Elezi, E. (2003) *Information on the Pan-Albanian Customary Law*. Prishtina: no publisher.

Elezi, I. (1983) *Albanian Criminal Customary Law*. Tirana: 8 November.

Elezi, I. (ed.) (2006) *The Canon of Labëria*. Tirana: Toena.

Gashi, R. (2003) *Punitive Policy Against Blood Delicts in Kosovo During the Period of 1980–1989*. Prishtina: University of Prishtina.

Gjeçovi, Sh. (ed.) (1933) *The Code of Lekë Dukagjini*. Prishtina: Rilindja.

Gruda, Z. (1995) 'Islam and the international law (2)', *Islamic Erudition*, 73 (Prishtina: Dituria Islame), 73, pp. 21–5.

Gruda, Z. (2003) *International Public Law*. Prishtina: University of Prishtina.

Halili, R. (1985) *Criminal Sanctions According to the Customary Criminal Law in Kosovo*. Prishtina: Rilindja.

Human Rights Watch (1999) 'Yugoslav forces guilty of war crimes in Racak, Kosovo'. See: http://www.hrw.org/reports/1999/kosovo/Obrinje6-07.htm.

Ilia, F. (ed.) (1993) *The Canon of Skanderbeg*. Milot: Editrice La Rosa.

Jashari, R. (2004) *The Racak Massacre: Crime Against Humanity*. Prishtina: Shkrola, Memorial Complex Center of the Racak Massacre.

Kandić, N. (2006) 'A contribution to dealing with the past and transitional justice: the promotion of peace, respect of human rights and the rule of law', in M. Bleeker (ed.), *Dealing with the Past and Transitional Justice: Creating Conditions for Peace, Human Rights and the Rule of Law*, Conference Paper 1/6. Political Affairs Division IV, Federal Department of Foreign Affairs, Switzerland, pp. 109–14.

Koha Ditore (Prishtina) (2006) 14 November, p. 6.

Principles of International Co-operation in the Detection, Arrest, Extradition and Punishment of Persons Guilty of War Crimes and Crimes Against Humanity (1973). General Assembly Resolution 3074(XXVIII) of 3 December.

Rahman, H. (1992) 'Last justice', *Takvimi* (Prishtina: Dituria Islame), 1412/13 pp. 117–20.

Sahiti, E. (2006) *Reasoning in the Criminal Procedure*. Prishtina: University of Prishtina.

Shala, B. (2000) 'Years of Kosova 1998–1999', *Zëri*. Prishtina: Rilindja.

Smith, R.J. (1999) 'Serbs tried to cover up massacre: Kosovo reprisal plot bared by phone taps', *Washington Post*, 28 January.

Stadtmuller, G. (1961) *Historia del Derecho International Publico, Parte I*. Madrid: Aguilar.

Statute of the International Criminal Tribunal for the Prosecution of Persons Responsible for Serious Violations of International Humanitarian Law Committed in the Territory of the Former Yugoslavia since 1991 (1993). United Nations Security Council, Resolution 827.

Zëri (2006) 29 November, p. 17.

Chapter 6

Potential for the use of informal mechanisms and responses to the Kosovo conflict – Serbian perspective

Vesna Nikolic-Ristanovic

The qualification of the Racak killings in legal terms depends significantly on the established facts about the victims and the circumstances in which they were killed. There is no doubt that the killings occurred; this was acknowledged by both Serbs and Albanians. Also, there is no dispute that the perpetrators were Serbian police, who undertook a retaliatory attack on Racak as a reaction to the killings of Serbian policemen by the KLA (Igric 2002).[1] However, there is strong disagreement over how the incident happened and who the victims were. On the one hand, the Albanians argue that the victims were civilians and unarmed KLA members, and they accused the Serbs of putting gunpowder on the bodies in order to make them look as if they were armed soldiers. On the other hand, the Serbs argue that the victims were KLA soldiers dressed as civilians in order to accuse the Serbs and convince the West to intervene.

Thus if the victims were civilians – as the Albanians argue they were and as the location of both the bullets and the dead bodies suggests – it is obvious that a war crime or crime against humanity was committed. But if the victims were soldiers who were killed during the fight – as Serbian police and politicians argued and facts about context, place and time of the event seemed to suggest – the Racak event, in spite of its tragic consequences and brutality, could not be qualified as a war crime.

However, whatever the legal qualification is, the Racak killings, as well as other killings that occurred during the Kosovo conflict, caused enormous harm to the Kosovo people and their future relationships. This is a sufficient and at the same time highly important reason for trying negotiation and stopping further violence. Efforts that have been taken so far are far from being successful, though. The international community has taken the role of the mediator but has failed to fulfil it by taking sides and using violence itself. This resulted in more violence and increased hostilities. The cycle of violence, developed through centuries – particularly during the 1980s and 1990s – was not stopped or alleviated but it became much more intensified and even broadened so as to include the international community, i.e. Western countries themselves.

The purpose of this chapter is to elaborate on the potential in Serbia for dealing with the Racak killings through the use of informal mechanisms. After considering the main challenges and obstacles related to the establishment of truth, justice and redress, this chapter gives an overview of informal justice mechanisms that have been used in Serbia and that may be applied in the same or similar way in the Racak case and other analogous cases in Kosovo. The overview of informal mechanisms includes examples mostly from contemporary society, but illustrations from historical times are also explored.

Dealing with the outcomes

Bearing in mind the above-mentioned arguments, dealing with the outcomes of the Racak violence is extremely complicated not only with regard to the establishment of truth and attainment of justice and redress, but also in relation to narrowing the distance and establishing trustful relationships between Serbs and Albanians. The events that followed Racak, especially the bombing of the whole of Serbia, the ethnic cleansing of Serbs from Kosovo, the ongoing conflict and the unresolved status of Kosovo, are – from a Serbian point of view – some of the most important but not the only obstacles to overall progress.

The historical heritage of factors, such as living besides each other rather than together, the lack of trust, the stereotyping of the other as bad/criminal; denial of the other's sufferings; struggling over the territory; perceiving oneself only as victim; the exaggeration of differences and negative experiences along with the minimisation of similarities and positive experiences; the strong political pressure that expects 'ethnic loyalty' from individuals – all these aspects, make the related conflicts even more complicated. There are useful indicators that can illustrate the large social distances between the citizens, such as the small number of ethnically mixed marriages (fewer than between other ethnic groups in the former Yugoslavia) (NGO 'Jelena Anzujska' 2005a: 11), or the strong stigmatisation of those few Serbs who date or marry Albanians.

It is also important to bear in mind that the political and military responses to the Racak incident were not based on established facts. What happened after Racak was a series of cycles of violence, both on inter-ethnic and international levels. All these consequences make justice and the revelation of truth as well as redress extremely difficult and complicated nowadays. As a result of political and military decisions after Racak, Serbs lost control over Kosovo and the whole territory of Serbia was faced with severe destruction and killing by NATO. The result is that Serbs appear to be highly frustrated and unhappy with the current situation.

Thus, dealing with the outcomes of the Racak killings, and especially looking for solutions, makes sense only if it is put into a broader political, historical and social context. The truth about Racak is very much connected and interlaced with the truth about the subsequent events, particularly with the NATO intervention/war and the position of Serbs under the international government in Kosovo. As a consequence, discovering and recognising the truth about the Racak incident and resolving the conflict between Albanians and Serbs seem to be highly difficult without discovering the truth about what has happened afterwards and what is presently going on in Kosovo.

Truth(s)

Establishing truth about Racak seems difficult in spite of the high level of agreement about the fact that killings occurred. The main point of dispute seems to be on the interpretative level (see Cohen 2001: 22 on interpretative denial) which seems to make Racak very well embedded into the history of giving opposite meanings to the same events, including exclusive and stereotypical notions of the good and the bad, i.e. the victims and the criminals.

Serb–Albanian truth and identity dichotomy

Racak seems to be part of the historical truth and identity dichotomy, which has been feeding perpetual and persistent trans-generational cycles of violence. As Mertus points out, Kosovo is an example of a society in which the identities of two opposing groups have been in existence for a long time. They both believe in their own truths about the other (Mertus, quoted by Zdravkovic 2005: 116). 'Their' truth is actually what people believe the truth is, and this is what matters and is used in everyday life (Zdravkovic 2005: 116). This also means that individual experiences and feelings are valued only if they are politically useful. Therefore the space for open dialogue and expression of feelings is very narrow and always under political scrutiny. It creates a paradoxical situation in which politicians first shape the attitudes and beliefs of people by imposing everyday political needs (e.g. that they must protect Serbs in Kosovo); then they become afraid of losing the political support of these people if they are not successful enough in meeting the declared needs. In this way the macro- and the micro-levels intermingle and feed each other through the development of a series of wrong expectations and decisions. It all leads to revenge and a spiral of violence rather than to any rational solution. This is exactly what happened in relation to the Serbian and Albanian approach to Kosovo: political (mis)use of centuries-old myths about Kosovo have resulted in macro- and micro-level vicious circles. Consequently, it is very difficult to decide where to start looking for the truth and the solution: from macro- or from micro-level, from one or from the other group's truth?

Apart from the complexity of this issue, this may also show the way towards its alleviation, or even towards its solution. When developing mechanisms for dealing with conflict, it is important to bear in mind that the conflict that was created on the macro level cannot be solved (merely) on the micro level. Consequently, informal mechanisms need to be accompanied by advocacy for political action, i.e. for the proper use of formal mechanisms.

The struggle for each group's own truth is largely incorporated into identity conflict based on feelings of fear and being in danger (Janjic 1997: 10). Hence, any attempt for establishing only one of the truths might make the conflict even bigger instead of alleviating it. As noticed earlier by some authors (e.g. Arendt, Habermas and Bauman, in Bauman 2003: 152–3), disputing the truth is not always the best way of resolving conflict, and often it even contributes to its increase. This aspect is highly relevant in the case of Kosovo, where the conflict is embedded, lasting, prolonged and very persistent (Zdravkovic 2005: 13); where a collective memory/denial dichotomy has been overwhelming and suppressing individual memories. As a result, people have been creating their images of others based on the 'messages' passed to them from above instead of using their own direct experiences.

Moreover, abandoning historical stereotypes about the other as an enemy is seen as a direct threat to national interests or a betrayal and loss of the positive self-image. Thus establishing what really happened in Racak as well as in other parts of Kosovo will have certain political costs on both sides – Serbian and Albanian – since Serbs and Albanians were obviously involved in a chain of violence, both as victims and perpetrators. In other words, both sides have significant political stakes as well as high levels of interdependence between politicians and citizens. It makes diversion from everyone's own truth impossible. Consequently, none of the sides is interested in anything but their own truth and the political benefits connected to it.

The impact of the NATO bombing

Since the end of the NATO bombing and the establishment of the international government, violence by Albanian paramilitaries against Serbs and other non-Albanians has been going on. In the first months of the international government 200,000 Serbs and other non-Albanians were expelled. Between 1999 and 2004 about 1,000 Serbs from Kosovo were killed, more than 1,000 were abducted and 112 Serbian churches were destroyed or damaged (Milosevic and Stefanovic 2004: 14–15). Moreover, the escalation of Albanian violence against Serbs in Kosovo in March 2004 offered a final proof showing that human rights abuses have not been stopped by the intervention. Thus it seems that, instead of establishing the rule of law and building peace, the reality of the internationally governed Kosovo has become chaos and violence (Suroi 2004). Although Albanian violence had been alarming before (Parenti 2000), the simultaneous attacks on 33 sites, including almost all the Serbian enclaves in Kosovo, using the large quantity of weapons which appeared on that occasion, led to 19 killed and more than 900 wounded (Milosevic and Stefanovic 2004: 14–15). Also over 700 Serb, Ashkali and Roma homes, up to ten public buildings, 30 Serbian churches and two monasteries were damaged or destroyed. Besides the damage or the destruction of these buildings, roughly 4,500 people were displaced (Europe Report 2004) in no more than a couple of days. This clearly showed that the projects of demilitarisation, demobilisation and transformation of the Kosovo Liberation Army (KLA) into civil police as well as the establishment of a multicultural society in Kosovo have been dangerous and unsuccessful.

The outburst of Albanian violence in 2004 followed five years of almost complete denial of the atrocities committed against Serbs and other non-Albanians in Kosovo and a number of 'fairy tale' reports about the success of the multicultural project on Kosovo. A short time before the March outburst of violence, for example, the Dutch delegation showed high satisfaction with the level of multi-ethnic society achieved in Kosovo. At the same time, the KFOR commander in the town of Prizren, where the escalation of violence later was striking, estimated that the situation in that town was stable (Milosevic and Stefanovic 2004: 15), while the German commander asked for the reduction of KFOR forces. Misha Glenny – commenting on the situation in Kosovo after the March 2004 events – argued that the international forces in Kosovo should stop doing what they had been doing so far, which was actually 'nothing'. Otherwise they would, according to Glenny, promote violence and place weapons in the hands of the Albanian extremists.[2]

It seemed the long-term consequence of the humanitarian intervention was chaos rather than the protection of human rights and stable peace. This was further proved by the spreading of violence which included hostility between international soldiers and local people, as well as violence among international soldiers themselves. This is obviously the consequence of the lack of consent of the local population from one or both sides, and the lack of legitimacy of the international military forces. The result was that the international forces became another party in the conflict (for similar examples see Kaldor 2001).

Interestingly, in March 2004 a scenario very similar to the Racak incident took place: an unverified story about Albanian boys who drowned in the river served as a pretext for an outburst of Albanian violence against Serbs. The first news reports which were immediately put out by the world's media laid the blame for the incident on the Serbs.[3] This obviously further encouraged Albanian paramilitaries to kill Serbs and destroy their houses and churches.

The international community significantly contributed to strengthening the perception of the Albanian side as the 'good' one. It made the Albanians think they had indefinite and unconditional support from the international community; hence they started to exact revenge with extreme brutality. At the same time, the violence committed against the 'bad' (Serbian) side and the acceptance of this violence by the larger community was expanding together with the denigration and denial of crimes committed against it. Global denial of crimes committed against Serbs in the former Yugoslavia in general and in Kosovo in particular, a constant increase in their victimisation as well as the lack of efficient international protection, the feelings of frustration and helplessness among Serbs in Serbia because Serbia was not allowed to protect them – all these factors made Serbians feel frustrated and the victims of injustice.

The international project in Kosovo has been experienced as injustice towards Serbia and the final proof of the 'world conspiracy against us', i.e. the Serbs. This was not unusual bearing in mind that it was more than evident that, in spite of numerous NGOs working on inter-community peacebuilding projects in Kosovo, the most obvious results of humanitarian intervention seemed to be the further increase in hostility, social distance and frustration on both sides. Its primary signs were the following:

- the strengthening of extreme nationalism on both sides;
- the replacement of ethnic cleansing of Albanians by ethnic cleansing of Serbs;
- the spreading of Albanian violence in southern parts of Serbia and Macedonia;
- the strengthening of Albanian organised crime in general and organised prostitution;
- trafficking in women and drug trafficking in Kosovo (Nikolic-Ristanovic 2002; Amnesty International 2004).

In addition to the above mentioned issues a new 'truth dichotomy' was created around NATO's intervention. For Serbs it was aggression/war against Serbia, while Western countries (and Albanians as well) called it euphemistically 'humanitarian intervention'. Those who were victims for the Serbs were considered to be 'collateral damage' for Western countries and those they were protecting. All these aspects together with the selective prosecutions by the International Criminal Tribunal for the former Yugoslavia (ICTY), particularly in relation to the lack of prosecution of leading Albanian war criminals and NATO commanders, largely contributed to the further decrease of the willingness among Serbs to recognise the suffering caused by their police and other forces.

Thus the truth about Racak as well as the prospects for solving problems related to the Serb–Albanian relationship are strongly connected to the truth about the entire conflict in Kosovo. Bearing that in mind, in order to appreciate the depth and the nature of the problem that needs to be solved in the future, it is necessary to understand the impact of the truth(s) about the bombing and the subsequent international government on further relationships between Serbs and Albanians as well.

Justice and redress

Certain mechanisms that are established at both the international and national level can be useful not only for discovering the truth, but also for attaining justice, repairing the damage and bringing both sides closer to each other. Temporary international government and peace corps, international and domestic courts, truth and reconciliation and independent expert commissions are some of them. However, it seems that beside their obvious contribution to bringing peace and justice, they also have certain shortcomings.

The Kosovo experience suggests that, apart from immediate relief and some positive effects, international mechanisms have several shortcomings and counter effects. It is especially dangerous when a double standards policy is experienced or when it seems the international community is taking sides in the conflict instead of mediating and helping building trust and a multicultural society. Insisting on the 'truth' which is accepted only by one of the sides in the conflict is especially risky when it comes from the side that appears to be a mediator or as one trying to contribute to the resolution of the conflict. What is even more dangerous is when the third side is inconsistent, i.e. sending contradictory messages and, thus, constantly loosing the trust of both sides. This is exactly what happened after the Racak incident in Kosovo with regard to the role of the international community.

By the time the decision about military intervention was made, nothing was clear about Racak, except the fact that people had been killed. Both sides were consistent with their opposite versions of the same event, accusing each other of faking the killings of the civilians, i.e. the soldiers. By the time Serbs allowed the Finnish experts to have access to bodies, it was impossible to prove one or the other truth with certainty (Igric 2002). Unfortunately, this uncertainty about the truth was disclosed only much later, a long time after the military intervention was over and further cycles of violence were produced. The report itself was surrounded with many suspicious facts questioning its reliability. In his 'Complete Analysis of the Incident at Racak on 15 January 1999' Chris Soda (1999: 1) wrote:

> There are some problems which I'll state at the outset: although I have the comments and positions of many of the actual forensic experts who performed studies on the bodies, I cannot lay my hands on the actual forensic reports. No copies were to be found at the OSCE, University of Prishtina, University of Helsinki, University of Nis, NATO, UN, EU or Government of Yugoslavia websites – or anywhere else that I've looked. This absence precludes a vital cross-reference to any definitive Racak study.[4]

However, the Kosovo Verification Mission's immediate qualification of Racak as a massacre was followed by the journalists' reports about Racak. These reports – as with many others based on unverified or false facts about extreme atrocities committed by a side designated as 'bad' – served as the main trigger for the political and military decisions made by the international community. Thus, in spite of immediate doubts about the version of the event put out (Johnstone 2002), these reports were used as justification, first, for the Rambouillet conference, then for the ultimatum to Serbia, and later for its bombardment. Through reporting on what the Finnish experts called the Racak 'massacre' perpetrated by the Serbs, the *Washington Post* had the most important role in distributing inaccurate conclusions from the forensic team report. However, only two years later a few European newspapers made the real content of the Finnish report known to the public. This shed completely new light on the Racak deaths, attributing them predominantly to killings during the fight (Johnstone 2002).

Thus, in spite of increased tensions around the truth about the Racak case and the obvious increase in violence from both sides, NATO decided to bombard Serbia. Also, in its indictment against Milosevic the ICTY included the Racak incident as the only individual crime committed before the bombing. This suggests that the stakes of the international community are very much dependent on the Albanian truth about Racak. This very soon raised the question whether the international community is really as good, willing and objective a third party as it is supposed to be. The importance of the international community's role in increasing rather than decreasing the truth and identity dichotomy in Kosovo in general, and particularly in relation to the Racak killings, is perhaps best described in the following words by Soda (1999: 2):

> If the incidents which occurred at Racak really were atrocities perpetrated by the Yugoslav government, then NATO will continue to use this to claim the 'moral high ground' in past, present, and future actions in the Balkans ... If, on the other hand, the incidents at Racak were not atrocities perpetrated by the Yugoslav government, the NATO-bombers' 'house of cards' claiming moral legitimacy falls apart; as well, any past, present, and future actions by NATO in the region will be severely scrutinized for hidden agendas. And if the incidents at Racak on Jan 15/99 are shown not to be atrocities, then the whole question of self-claimed objective international legalities will be shown to be just another link in the chain of selective, biased judgment fuelling the same hidden agendas.

Another problem is the general disappointment of Serbs in the ICTY. It is largely considered a political actor having prejudices against the Serbs, thus not guaranteeing justice for them. The widespread opinion is that KLA war criminals are allowed to have high positions in Kosovo's government, while the Serbian political elite, including the former president of Serbia, were sent to The Hague. On the other hand, the increasing dependence of Serbs from Kosovo on the international government because of security reasons led them to trust international courts in Kosovo even more than Albanians. Albanians, however, seem to be disappointed by what they consider selective justice by these courts. Similarly to the Serbian perception of the ICTY, Albanians seem to think that the international courts in Kosovo use double standards. As suggested by Keljmendi (2003), instead of contributing to the peace between two communities, trials for war crimes turn Albanians against Serbs (and vice versa) even more. Moreover, they turn Albanians against the international community as well (Keljmendi 2003).

Albanians appear to believe that KLA members are given significantly higher prison sentences than Serbs, which is considered an obstacle to reconciliation. Obviously, high sentences to KLA members and a number of Serbs who are not sentenced because of the lack of evidence seem to further intensify the conflict between the two sides. For example, the former commander of the KLA Rustem Mustafa was sentenced to 17 years' imprisonment for ordering the killings of five Kosovo Albanians for their alleged collaboration with Serbs and for not preventing the illegal custody of people in the region north of Kosovo during 1998 and 1999. Local Serbs and Albanians reacted completely differently to this and other sentences. On the one hand, Serbs greeted it as a step forward towards normalisation of the situation and a contribution to a safer Kosovo to which they could return. Albanians, on the other hand, considered it selective justice and presumed that there had been a hidden agreement between UNMIK and Belgrade related to the release of Albanian prisoners from Serbian prisons in 2001.

Looking more specifically at the Racak case, it is worth mentioning that it was part of the indictment against Milosevic but also against some of the policemen directly involved. Milosevic's trial only contributed to the confusion. As pointed out in a letter sent to the magazine *Vreme* by a Serb from Sweden who had followed most of the trials online, after all the evidence had been presented one could not be sure whether it had really been a crime or it had been so well faked (Antović 2002). Due to the contested 'facts' – part of one enormous indictment and long trial – and as a result of Milosevic's death, these questions were never cleared up. In any case, during the trial prosecutors were already complaining that, just because there was no separate trial for it, they would not have enough time either to hear more than a few witnesses or to prove the case (Klarin 2002). On the other hand, the Prishtina court in Kosovo sentenced policeman Zoran Stojanovic for his role in the Racak killings. It was proven that he shot civilians who tried to escape and killed one man. He was sentenced to 15 years in prison, which is the highest penalty issued by the Kosovo international court to a Kosovo Serb.

In terms of justice and redress it is important to mention the special department for war crimes located in the Belgrade district court and its verdicts for war crimes committed by Serbs as well as by one Albanian. So far it has proved to be a highly professional court that has encouraged many Serbian witnesses to offer their testimonies and, within the framework of the new Serbian legislation about victims, set the ground for the highest standards of victim protection in comparison to other trials in Serbia.[5] This court is obviously very important in terms of the recognition of crimes committed by both Serbs and Albanians, as well as for increasing the feeling of justice within Serbian communities. Generally, Serbian people have less trust in international than in domestic courts. The lack of confidence in international justice, which is widely perceived as imposed from abroad and as being partial, was documented by recent surveys (e.g. Pavicevic 2003). Thus there is a really big potential for the domestic war crimes court to assure justice. The trials before that court are also important in terms of achieving redress for both Serbian and Albanian victims. As an example, on 24 January 2007 redress was requested by 24 family members of Albanian civilians killed in Podujevo (Kosovo) (at the time of writing the decision has not been made). Sasa Cvjetan, a reservist in the 'Scorpions', was sentenced to 20 years' imprisonment for this crime, while the other accused had escaped.

In general, the role of existing (international and national) formal mechanisms is highly important for justice and redress, especially bearing in mind that formal mechanisms in general, and retributive ones in particular, are traditionally seen as the only appropriate answer to severe crimes in Serbia. This is further intensified by most of the public discourses about the past atrocities and present-day crime problems that tend to emphasise the need for harsher treatment of criminals as the primary solution to deal with the past. Redress is expected to be obtained from the state, as compensation for the damage caused by the crimes. The problem of redress for Serbs is especially connected with expectations from the international government in Kosovo and the Serbian state to set proper conditions for the return of internationally displaced Serbs by rebuilding their houses and repairing other damage they suffered. Thus it seems crucial that proper international and national mechanisms be established that can guarantee the rule of law, unbiased prosecution, a fair trial and redress accessible to all those in need.

However, in reality, formal mechanisms are rather slow and not very efficient. In addition, the formal mechanisms, even if properly used, have limitations per se that makes them insufficient and even inappropriate to restore relationships and bring reconciliation to the affected sides. Not to mention that attending court trials is especially hard for the victims. As a consequence, informal, i.e. restorative, justice mechanisms may compensate for the limits and shortcomings of the conventional justice system.

Informal mechanisms applicable to Racak and similar cases

Main challenges and potentials

The previous analysis suggests that – bearing in mind the truth dichotomy and the related conflict between Serbs and Albanians, as well as the low efficiency of the formal mechanisms used so far – there is a lot of 'unused' space for trying informal ways in order to discover the truth, work on the resolution of the conflict and attain justice.

However, when thinking about informal ways for dealing with conflicts in Kosovo, it is necessary to bear in mind two factors that have been stressed earlier in this chapter: the significant and embedded social distance between Serbs and Albanians and the pressures put on them by politicians, i.e. their loyalty to 'higher' goals defined by their leaders. In addition, it seems that the already significant social distance between Serbs and Albanians had been further intensified during the 1990s conflicts. Also, the language barrier can be considered an important challenge in this process (NGO 'Jelena Anzujska' 2005a: 18).

Moreover, especially when thinking about (re)establishment of contacts, it is important to bear in mind that after Serbs were expelled from Kosovo (after the end of the NATO bombing), most Serbs and Albanians in Kosovo had hardly any physical contact with each other (NGO 'Jelena Anzujska' 2005a: 11). It is especially striking when the Racak incident is in the spotlight. Nowadays there are no Serbs left there and even by the time the killings occurred only three Serbian families were living in the entire area. This means that since 1999 no Serbs have been living not only in but also around Racak. Thus the police and the army who committed the alleged crimes did not have any prior relationship with Albanians from Racak, and are definitely not living near the victims' families today.

The consequence is that people from Racak look at Serbs in a very abstract way. Therefore a lot of effort and patience is needed simply even to get Albanians in contact with Serbs, let alone the difficulties of how to encourage them to start a dialogue about the events of 15 January 1999. Racak people seem to be fed up with all those who actually deepen their wounds through different forms of investigation, including the endless repetition of what happened, the bodies of their loved ones not being returned to them for a long time because of autopsy and so on (Igric 2002).[6] However, the main source of their frustration might be that their suffering has not been properly recognised and respected. The incident that occurred in March 2001 during an attempted reconstruction of the Racak events may be a good illustration of that. Apart from an accused Serbian policeman and his lawyer, the people that were present on that occasion included the Kosovo police as well as representatives of the Kosovo international court, OSCE and the Belgrade-based NGO Humanitarian Law Center that were supposed to be welcome by Albanians. However, they were all expelled by armed Albanians, who forced them all out of the village by shouting 'You all get out of the village! We do not need anyone!'[7]

The questions that one can ask are obvious: is it possible at all to establish contact and start a dialogue between Serbs and Albanians, and if so, how does one go about it? In order to come to an answer to these questions, the following sections will point out some examples to illustrate the ways in which informal mechanisms in conflict resolution have been applied in the historical and contemporary Serbian society. The selected initiatives have been organised both by the state and civil society.

State-organised informal mechanisms

The historical overview suggests that on the territory of the former Yugoslavia informal mechanisms for reconciliation between offender and victim have been used for a long time. Up to the end of the Second World War, so-called 'courts of good people' existed and were especially active in Montenegro, Herzegovina and Kosovo. They were involved in conflicts around blood revenge, damage reparation and interpersonal problems. They were used by all ethnic groups, including Serbs, for reconciliation and solving conflicts around property and other problems. In Kosovo and Montenegro they were especially successful in stopping blood revenge cases between Serbs and Albanians (Mrvic-Petrovic 2001: 165; Sahiti 1985: 177). They were focused on reconciliation rather than on the trial, i.e. establishing facts, and their result was an agreement regarding the amount which needed to be paid as compensation. This was a local mechanism in which the mediator had to be well known and respected by both parties.

Under communism, in the entire territory of the former Yugoslavia there were also informal mechanisms such as mediation. In this parties were obliged to try to come to an agreement in cases of petty offences. The so-called peace courts existed until 1985, when they were removed from the Criminal Procedure Law (Mrvic-Petrovic 2001: 165). However, peace courts were only rarely used, and most of the time they were unsuccessful in terms of achieving reconciliation (Sahiti 1985: 13). It seems that informal mechanisms from the distant past were mostly replaced by criminal sanctions and were forgotten by Serbs, especially those who have been living outside of Kosovo where the remains of old traditions lasted a long time under communism and were very successful (Sahiti 1985: 17).

Recently, mediation as well as some other restorative justice elements have again been included in Serbian legislation (2005 and 2006). Also, as part of the UNICEF programmes in Serbia during 2003–6, experimental mediation projects have been developed in two towns in Serbia, including conflict resolution between juvenile offenders and staff in correctional institutions, and victim–offender mediation in cases of less serious juvenile crimes. However, the average citizen of Serbia, including lawyers and other professionals, does not trust restorative justice, usually thinking it is a way of escaping justice. Its application is seen as problematic especially in cases of serious crimes such as Racak, where long imprisonment is seen as the only worthwhile answer. Also, it is difficult to find any connection between earlier informal mechanisms and these new restorative justice mechanisms, especially since the latter were mainly imported from abroad and do not have roots in Serbian tradition.

When speaking about informal mechanisms at the state level and their potential use in the Racak case, it is worth mentioning the Truth and Reconciliation Commission that existed in Serbia in 2001–3. The Commission spent almost three years without undertaking any substantial activity. Therefore the message that was sent to the public about the role of Truth and Reconciliation Commission was very confusing, and basically discredited the very idea of the Commission as a useful way of dealing with the past in Serbia.

However, in spite of the above-mentioned shortcomings, a restorative justice spirit has definitely been growing in Serbia, encompassing efforts for its main principles to be used much more widely than in criminal law, i.e. in work-related disputes, between litigation parties, etc. In 2005, the Victimology Society of Serbia organised an international conference 'Alternative Sanctions and Victim's Rights', which in 2006 was followed by panel discussions and the publication of the brochure *Restorative Justice and the Victim's Rights*. The main purpose of these initiatives was to raise awareness among professionals and the general public of the meaning of restorative justice and its potential in dealing with criminal offences.

It is also worth mentioning that the results of a survey on dealing with the past showed that people only rarely think that criminal sanctions should be the only answer to war atrocities (the research has been conducted by the Victimology Society of Serbia since 2004 throughout the Serbian population). Respondents often suggested using mechanisms such as or similar to truth commissions at the national or local level, as well as other mechanisms for establishing contacts and dialogue between victims and offenders. This may suggest that a truth commission or commission of inquiry which would have clear aims and support within community may be suitable for dealing with crimes such as the Racak incident, even despite the earlier experiences with the established Truth Commission.

Informal mechanisms and civil society

Informal mechanisms of dealing with war crimes that have been implemented by the civil society of Serbia mainly include initiatives aiming at bringing conflicting communities/groups in contact and establishing dialogue between them. These initiatives include various examples of inter-ethnic seminars, meetings of people from different ethnic groups that have similar war-related experiences and inter-ethnic meetings and negotiations around the topic of the returning of Serbs who were displaced from Kosovo. There are also attempts to bring other social groups together that are in conflict concerning the perception of the war.

Inter-ethnic dialogue initiatives are those dealing with Serb-Albanian relations. Analysis of experiences from these activities suggests that loyalty to one's own community and/or fear of the reaction of one's own community is a strong obstacle to their success. For example, it is often heard that people prefer to come to inter-ethnic seminars on conflict resolution and reconciliation as individuals rather than as members of organisations. Sometimes, it even happens that Albanian participants from NGOs are not allowed by their own organisation to participate in the seminars. Also, when they participate in these seminars they are often silent about the meetings when they go back to their organisations. It might mean that what they have learned has no immediate influence on the way they behave in their everyday life, since they have to be loyal to the predominant rules of their own group/political elite.

A good example is given by a member of the Association Joint Action FOR Truth and Reconciliation, who is a Serb from Kosovo. She said that Albanian war veterans do not have any problem with visiting her at home, but they are afraid to speak publicly about their contacts with Serbs. The experience of a Serbian woman from Kosovo who visited an Albanian friend and whose son was later burned by other Albanians because of it suggests that this fear is not unfounded (Nikolic-Ristanovic and Hanak 2004: 36). Some other examples also suggest politics is interwoven when dealing with conflict at an individual level. Especially striking is one example where dialogue was established about the return of Serbs into the village of Musutiste near Suva Reka. At the critical moment, when it came to concrete details about their return, Albanians asked for apologies of Serbian leaders as a condition for allowing Serbs to return.

Recent research carried out in the town of Kosovska Mitrovica gives additional evidence of the very strong impact of daily politics on how people see the other ethnic group and the possibilities for cooperation. For example, when answering the question 'Do you believe that Serbs and Albanians can live together?', both Albanian and Serbian respondents mostly gave answers that contained the predominant political messages of their communities (NGO 'Jelena Anzujska' 2005a: 12). Similarly, when answering a question about willingness to get closer to another ethnic group, Serbs and Albanians showed significantly different understanding of the notion 'getting closer'. This difference is in direct relationship with differences in the current political status of Kosovo and these two ethnic communities. Thus for Albanians 'getting closer' means that they move to the north, which would mean unification of the city, while for Serbs this means assimilation and loss of national identity. Consequently, Albanians wish for what Serbs fear very much.

However, there are good models of inter-ethnic dialogue that can be found in some initiatives for establishing contact and dialogue between people from different ethnic groups and with similar war-related experiences. So far they have mostly been carried out by organisations of war victims and war veterans. These specifically affected groups often suggest that they can communicate easier and get better understanding from similar groups from other ethnic communities than from people from their own community who did not have the same experience. The following examples may give some useful ideas about dealing with Racak and similar cases in Kosovo.

War veterans' organisations from Serbia, for example, established contacts and cooperated with war veterans from earlier enemy sides, including Albanians from the southern part of Serbia. Recently, an Albanian–Serbian seminar was organised in Bulgaria, on neutral territory, since both were afraid to come to the territory of the former enemy. Also, the recently established organisation Veterans for Peace has three Albanian members. War veterans from Croatia, Serbia and Bosnia-Herzegovina have already been cooperating for three years with very good results. They stress the importance of listening to the experiences of war veterans for establishing truth.[8] Panels have been organised by the Centre for Non-Violent Action, Belgrade-Sarajevo, and a book has been recently published titled *Oh, Where Have You Been, My Blue-eyed Son?*,[9] based on experiences of both Serbian and Albanian war veterans.

Although it is less known, similar initiatives have been successful between individual women whose husbands were killed in the war (Nikolic-Ristanovic and Hanak 2004: 67), as well as between family members of missing persons. Within the scope of its activities, the International Organisation for Families of Missing Persons has launched the implementation of the project 'Paths to Reconciliation' that is intended as an umbrella association for the families of missing persons in the area of the former Yugoslavia. This project enables the missing families' associations to meet within their national environments through a series of workshops before tackling the difficult and painful issues that burden every ethnic community. The project intends to open up the possibility of exploring various options that might ensure the implementation of justice and open space for a dialogue between victim groups at the regional and international level. It also aims at encouraging participants to exchange their experiences in searching for the truth and building trust (Masic 2004: 8).

During a small-group discussion organised by the Victimology Society of Serbia, the representatives of the Organisation for Families of Missing Persons mentioned that they had often been approached by people who were interested in giving testimonies about war crimes. Also, some of the initiatives of the organisation for families of missing persons (Serbs) from Kosovo include possible cooperation with Albanian witnesses in order to search for evidences about missing persons from both sides and start dialogue. Prisoners-of-war organisations also mentioned a similar idea: using dialogue with prisoners of war from the other side to discover the truth, recognise what was done and recover relationships.

A good example showing that dialogue between Serbs and Albanians can be painful but possible is the inter-ethnic dialogue over the return of Serb internally displaced persons (IDPs) to the village of Musutiste, in Suva Reka municipality, where serious crimes were committed. Despite the very tense discussions and even some violent incidents (the stoning of Serbs by Albanians on one occasion that prevented one of their visits to Musutiste), one very important thing was achieved very quickly: agreement by both sides that dialogue mediated by UNMIK should continue.[10] Anika Krstic, who was involved in the 'Go and See' mission in Musutiste as the representative of the NGO International Aid Network (IAN), stressed several features of the mission which were crucial for its success in getting Serbs and Albanians together:

- the Serbs and Albanians that were chosen to participate in the negotiations were those who were respected and trusted by both communities;
- good and neutral (international) mediators;
- allies in the local community, including local government;

- adaptation of the procedures to local traditions;[11]
- a careful and detailed plan;
- reasonable security;[12]
- social events.

The participation of the mayor was especially important since it provided a guarantee that speaking with Serbs was a politically acceptable behaviour. The example of Musutiste may be used as a positive model of how, when carefully planned, contact and dialogue can be established, despite the severe crimes and the high impact of global politics on the individual citizens. However, the Musutiste example also very clearly shows that political approval is a necessary precondition and guarantee for Albanian people to ensure that they do not suffer consequences as a result of their participation.

Opening a dialogue as well as listening to personal experiences at some secure and, if possible, neutral place is suggested on the basis of experience from other civil initiatives in Serbia. This is seen as a good way of learning and understanding what has happened, and building trustful relationships (Nikolic-Ristanovic and Hanak 2004: 79; Milosevic 2004: 63; NGO 'Jelena Anzujska' 2005a: 1). Many NGO activists, including war veterans and victims of war organisations, emphasised the importance of a 'third party' as a mediator in dialogues between members of two ethnic groups (Murati 2004: 18; Djurdjevic 2004: 67). They also stressed the importance of maintaining the continuity of talks through conceptualising common activities (Djurdjevic 2004: 67), as well as starting with less painful topics and then moving carefully toward those more sensitive.

Also, some other examples suggest that the establishment of contact and reconciliation between Serbs and Albanians is possible. For example, living together with very high tolerance is a reality in the community of Mikro-*naselje* in the northern part of Kosovska Mitrovica (NGO 'Jelena Anzujska' 2005b: 15). A woman activist from the NGO 'Jelena Anzujska', in a personal conversation with the author, also stressed some less known positive characteristics of Serb-Albanian relationships that may be used in the development of informal mechanisms. She explained that although Serbs and Albanians from Kosovo have always lived beside each other rather than together, they always had high respect for each other. She also stressed that Serbs and Albanians in general do not know each other very well. However, Serbs and Albanians who live close to each other (e.g. in North or South Kosovo) know each other better than they know Serbs and Albanians who live in different parts of Kosovo and they are their compatriots. Examples of friendship and solidarity between Serbs and Albanians also suggest that the situation is not as hopeless as it appears to be (Nikolic-Ristanovic and Hanak 2004: 49–52).

Apart from the above-mentioned civil society initiatives, existing informal mechanisms in Serbia also include long-term activities aimed at bringing both ethnic and other conflicting groups together in order to develop communications and restore relationships between them. Such an initiative is the Association Joint Action FOR Truth and Reconciliation, developed and coordinated by the Victimology Society of Serbia.

The Association was developed during 2005 over four consultative meetings which took place in Belgrade and in two towns located in two multi-ethnic regions in Serbia – Sandzak and Vojvodina. The Association is defined as an

> initiative, based on a continued action and open communication of individuals and organisations in a conflict and post-conflict society. Its members are unified in differences and recognised similarities. Their aim is to come closer to the truth regarding the offenders and the victims of war and political conflicts; understanding their past; establishing permanent trust and reconciliation through joint individual potentials and strengths; building international cooperation and exchanging experiences and knowledge. (Nikolic-Ristanovic and Bjelic 2006)

The Association's mission is to work towards developing a third way in dealing with the past in Serbia.

The third way stands for the belief that all perpetrators, all victims and all crimes are important, not because they should be made equal or their numbers should be counted and compared, but because it is necessary to get the complete picture about all the events during and after the conflict, to express empathy with all the victims and to condemn all crimes and all sources of human suffering. The third way tries to deal with the past in a gradual way, without additionally hurting an already traumatised society. It implies open discussion about the past, establishment of the truth not only by the courts but also in other ways (such as making known the names of all victims, research, public hearings, exhibitions, film festivals, campaigns, museums, education, etc.), as well as including all groups in society in the discussion – both victims and war veterans, no matter their national, political or any other group membership.

The Association Joint Action FOR Truth and Reconciliation represents a model of inclusion and cooperation among all parts of the society, and of mediation in reconciling differences that might lead to conflicts. Thus the activities of the Association try to demonstrate a model of reconciliation within Serbian society, which should be spread gradually throughout the whole region of the former Yugoslavia. The Association welcomes all the people who wish to deal with the past in a non-provocative way and who wish to contribute to peace in Serbia and in the region. The Association differs from similar initiatives in its inclusion of the representatives of the victims of war, ex-prisoners of war, war veterans and other persons who have, in the most direct way possible, been affected by war. It also differs from other initiatives by its decision to deal with all victims and all crimes, regardless of their national, political or other affiliations. As such, the Association may be a good framework for establishing contacts and dialogue between Serbs and Albanians from Racak.

Concluding remarks

The findings of recent research carried out in Kosovo suggest that, despite the extremely low level of mutual trust and high level of disagreement between Serbs and Albanians over several issues, there is also an agreement about some points, including support for the trials of war criminals from both sides and the need for public apology for crimes committed by both sides, as well as about the importance of defining the role of the Kosovo Serbs in talks about the status of Kosovo. Thus it is obvious that the basis for talks and negotiation on both macro and micro levels exist in Kosovo and both sides are aware that so far the exclusion of the Kosovo Serbs from negotiations has been a significant obstacle in working on just solutions and getting them accepted (Irwin 2005). In addition, the examples of existing informal mechanisms also show that, although contacts and dialogue are extremely difficult, the establishment of trustful relationships between Serbs and Albanians in Kosovo seems to be possible.

The above-mentioned examples also suggest the importance of political approval or at least the importance of tolerance towards processes building contacts and dialogue between formerly conflicting sides. However, there are some crucial preconditions for opening a larger and more relaxing dialogue about the past atrocities: the creation of a political framework accepted by both sides that guarantees the security as well as the conditions for free movement for all the citizens of Kosovo and Serbia; non-selective trials for most of the serious crimes, including recognition of the role and responsibility of NATO/the international community; and finally, providing the possibility for everyone to discover the truth and achieve reconciliation between all those who are still involved in the conflict related to Kosovo.[13]

As an example, the chances of bringing Serbian and Albanian victims or offenders/war veterans together, especially Serbian policemen and the families of Albanians who were killed, may be very difficult before agreeing on the official status of Kosovo. However, it does not mean that preparations, using both the above-mentioned principles and separate interviews with people from both sides, need to await the political decisions. Serbian and Albanian researchers and NGO activists, trained in mediation and victim issues and familiar with Kosovo's social context and restorative justice in a broader sense, may work toward establishing the foundations for starting dialogue, mediation and joint hearings. It is obvious that the people from Racak are fed up with all those who manipulate them and misuse their suffering. This means that the approach needs to be very careful and sensitive. It also means that the families of Serbian policemen killed on the eve of the Racak killings need to be heard and their suffering needs to be recognised and dealt with properly. Previous experiences show that people, especially victims with similar backgrounds, understand each other much better than others understand them. Therefore it may be worth trying to start to build communication firstly by involving the victims of the incident themselves. This process may be assisted and supported by other civil society initiatives, such as victim support, human rights and war veterans' organisations, and initiatives that tend to bring together all the stakeholders of the conflicts.

The situation in Kosovo is nowadays extremely complicated since violence against Serbs is still going on; they are living in isolation under extremely difficult conditions. The return of IDPs is completely uncertain. Serbs feel highly frustrated in relation to status talks, and they fear that the international community will again take the Albanian side. Thus the role of the international community as a mediator between Serbs and Albanians is still extremely important, and Serbs, who are especially concerned about their safety, hope that the international community will guarantee security for them. Furthermore, the international community needs to take on the role of neutral, well balanced and skilful mediator at local, national and international levels, and should stop repeating all the time that the Serbs are the guilty party.

Notes

1 The KLA was well known for ambushing Serbian policemen to provoke revenge attacks. 'I would kill my own family for a free Kosovo', a 20-year old KLA member said to Gordana Igric, then researcher for Human Rights Watch (Igric 2002).
2 Glenny, quoted in Milosevic and Stefanovic (2004: 15).
3 The report which was put out later showed that this was an accident, with the allegation that the boys were escaping from Danish KFOR soldiers who were running after them, thinking that they were stealing something (see: 'U reci zbog Danaca' [In the river because of Danish soldiers] (2004) *Vecernje novosti*, 1–3 May).
4 Retrieved from: http://www.egroups.com/group/yugoslaviainfo.
5 This is the first and so far only court in Serbia that has a victim and witness support unit.
6 Igric (2002) quoted one old man saying that even worse than his son's death was the inability to lay the body properly in the ground to rest.
7 'Naoruzani Albanci sprecili rekonstrukciju dogadaja u Racku' [Armed Albanians prevented reconstruction of events in Racak] (2001) 14 March. See: http://www.hlc.org.yu.
8 That was stressed at the public promotion of the book *Oh, Where Have You Been, My Blue-eyed Son?* (Beara and Miljanovic 2006) in Belgrade, where, apart from Serbs, Albanians from southern Serbia and Croats were present.
9 On that occasion, Gordan Bodrog, war veteran and now peace activist from Croatia, also stressed the importance of war veterans for discovering the truth about the past by saying that, in Croatia, veterans were the first to speak about ethnic cleansing; they submitted evidence to the ICTY and they were the ones who asked for the political responsibility of Croatian politicians for the war to be established.
10 Minutes from the meeting in Musutiste (2004) 10 November. See: http://www.ian.org.yu/kosovo-info/srpski/index.htm.
11 The Albanian community is much more patriarchal than the Serbian. It is especially important to bear in mind the rule that respected old men speak with respected old men from the other community. The decisions that they make have to be accepted by the other members of the community.
12 The importance of the sensitivity of the issue of security is clearly seen in the example of the visit of Serbian IDPs to Musutiste that was prevented by stoning, just as a reaction to the use of too many and too visible security forces by UNMIK.

13 It seems that there is a certain confusion about who is in conflict with whom and who is negotiating with whom. For example, Belgrade is full of graffiti claiming 'Ahtisari is the criminal', while Albanians in Kosovo are protesting against the international community. This may suggest that both sides are also in some kind of conflict with the international community, which is expected to take on the role of mediator between them.

References

Amnesty International (2004) 'Kosovo – "So Does That Mean I Have Rights?"' Unpublished report.

Antović, P.J. (2006) 'Kako sam poceo da navijam za Miloševića' [How I started to support Milosevic], *Vreme*, 26 September. See: http://www.hlc.org.yu.

Bauman, Z. (2003) *Liquid Love*. Cambridge: Polity Press.

Beara, V. and Miljanovic, P. (2006) *Oh, Where Have You Been, My Blue-eyed Son? An Existentialist Contribution to the Understanding of War Trauma and PTSD*. Novi Sad: Drustvo za zastitu mentalnog zdravlja ratnih veterana i zrtava ratova 1991–1999.

Chomsky, N. (2000) *Novi militaristicki humanizam, lekcije s Kosova* [*The New Military Humanism: Lessons from Kosovo*]. Beograd: Plato.

Cohen, S. (2001) *States of Denial*. Cambridge: Polity Press.

Djurdjevic, N. (2004) 'Koraci ka uspostavljanju dijaloga na Kosovu – iskustva Centra za nenasilni otpor' ['Steps toward establishment of dialogue in Kosovo – experiences of the centre for non-violent resistance'], *Temida*, 4: 67–9.

Europe Report (2004) 'Collapse in Kosovo', *Europe Report*, 155, 22 April. See: http://www.crisisweb.org/home/index.cfm?id=2627&l=l.

Hudson, B. (2003) *Justice in the Risk Society*. London: Sage.

Igric, G. (2002) 'Report: Milosevic challenged by Racak survivors', *Tribunal Update*, February, 255: 18–23. See: http://www.iwpr.net.

Irwin, C. (2005) *Coming to Terms with the Problem of Kosovo: The People's Views from Kosovo and Serbia*. See http://www.peacepolls.org.

Janjic, D. (1997) 'Ethnic conflicts and the break-up of former Yugoslavia', in D. Janjic (ed.), *Ethnic Conflict Management: The Case of Yugoslavia*. Ravenna: Longo, pp. 9–52.

Johnstone, D. (2002) *Fools' Crusade: Yugoslavia, NATO and Western Delusions*. London: Pluto Press.

Jokic, A. (2003) 'The aftermath of the Kosovo intervention: a proposed solution', in A. Jokic (ed.), *Lessons of Kosovo: The Dangers of Humanitarian Intervention*. Toronto: Broadview Press, pp. 173–83.

Kaldor, M. (2001) *New and Old Wars*. Cambridge: Polity Press.

Keljmendi, A. (2003) 'Suđenje članovima OVK šteti pomirenju' ['Trials against

KLA damage reconciliation process'], *IWPR Crisis Report*, 445, 18 July. See: http://www.hlc.org.yu.

Klarin, M. (2002) 'Analysis: tribunal judges restrict Racak evidence', *Tribunal Update*, 268, 27 May–1 June. See: http://www.iwpr.net.

Masic, A. (2004) 'Perspektive u Bosni i Hercegovini' ['Perspectives in Bosnia and Herzegovina'], *Temida*, 4: 7–9.

Milosevic, M. and Stefanovic, N. (2004) 'Kosovo 17 mart', *Vreme*, 25 March, pp. 14–15.

Milosevic, T. (2004) 'Topljenje leda – Projekat studenata Americkog univerziteta u Bugarskoj' ['Ice melting: project of students of American University in Bulgaria'], *Temida*, 4: 63–5.

Mrvic-Petrovic, N. (2001) *Naknada stete zrtvi krivicnog dela* [*Restitution to Crime Victims*]. Beograd: Vojnoizdavacki zavod i Institut za uporedno pravo.

Murati, G. (2004) 'Proces oporavka od rana prouzrokovanih ratom na Kosovu' ['Process of healing wounds caused by Kosovo conflict'], *Temida*, 4: 17–21.

NGO 'Jelena Anzujska' (2005a) *Da li se moze izgraditi poverenje u ratom razorenim zajednicama: uporedna analiza Mitrovice i Mostara* [*Is It Possible to Build Trust in War Affected Communities: Comparative Analysis of Mitrovica and Mostar*]. Kosovska Mitrovica: NVO 'Jelena Anzujska'.

NGO 'Jelena Anzujska' (2005b) *Kosovska Mitrovica – North 1999–2005*. Kosovska Mitrovica: NVO 'Jelena Anzujska'.

Nikolic-Ristanovic, V. (2002) *Social Change, Gender and Violence: Post-Communist and War-Affected Societies*. Dordrecht: Kluwer.

Nikolic-Ristanovic, V. and Bjelic, D. (2006) 'Asocijacija Zajednicka akcija za istinu i pomirenje – aktivnosti u 2006. godini i planovi za budućnosf' ['Association Joint Action FOR Truth and Reconciliation – activities in 2006, and plans for the future'], *Temida*, 4: 43–9.

Nikolic-Ristanovic, V. and Hanak, N. (2004) *Od secanja na proslost ka pozitivnoj buducnosti-ideje i misljenja gradjana Srbije* [*From Remembering the Past Toward a Positive Future – Ideas and Opinions of Citizens of Serbia*]. Beograd: VDS and Prometej.

Parenti, M. (2000) *To Kill a Nation*. London and New York: Verso.

Pavicevic, Dj. (2003) 'Zlocini i odgovornost' ['Crimes and responsibility'], in Z. Golubovic, I. Spasic and Dj. Pavicevic (eds), *Politika i svakodnevni zivot, Srbija 1999–2002* [*Politics and Everyday Life, Serbia 1999–2002*]. Beograd: Institut za filozofiju i drustvenu teoriju, pp. 141–61.

Pavkovic, A. (2004) 'Saving lives in nationalist conflicts: a few moral hazards', in G. Meggle (ed.), *Ethics of Humanitarian Interventions*. Frankfurt and Lancaster: Ontos/Verlag, pp. 161–89.

Sahiti, E. (1985) 'Uloga mirovnog veca u krivicnom postupku' ['The role of peace courts in criminal procedure'], *Jugoslovenska revija za kriminologiju i krivicnopravo*, 2–3: 177–85.

Soda, C. (1999) 'Complete analysis of the incident at Racak on January 15, 1999'. See: http://www.egroups.com/group/yugoslaviainfo.

Suroi, V. (2004) War and Peace Institute, Balkan Investigative Reporting Network (BIRN). See: http://www.iwpr.net.

Walzer, M. (1992) *Just and Unjust Wars*. New York: Basic Books.

Zdravkovic, H. (2005) *Politika zrtve na Kosovu* [*Politics of the Victim in Kosovo*]. Beograd: Srpski genealoski centar.

Chapter 7

A restorative approach for dealing with the aftermath of the Kosovo conflict – opportunities and limits

Marta Valiñas and Jana Arsovska

Kosovo is perhaps one of the best examples today, at least in Europe, where formal and informal mechanisms of dealing with conflict coexist but do not communicate with each other. Whereas the formal mechanisms of dealing with conflict are the result of hierarchically superior decision-making processes mostly taking place outside Kosovo, most of the informal mechanisms, and especially the traditional ones, have been rather home-grown and based on very specific cultural, historical and religious roots. The parallel and independent development of such mechanisms reveals and at the same time contributes to the tension, or at least estrangement, between the two approaches.

In the present analysis, we will focus on mechanisms or approaches – either existing or desirable – meant to deal with the large-scale violence that swept through Kosovo during the 1998–99 conflict and its aftermath. In doing so, we will centre our attention on three main types of mechanisms or processes identified on the basis of the contributions that precede this chapter: the formal mechanisms, which in this case consist almost exclusively of the current national and international legal responses to past gross human rights violations; the informal and traditional processes deeply rooted in Albanian culture that find their expression in the various cultural codes, such as that of Lekë Dukagjini; and a wider range of informal, contemporary mechanisms or initiatives aimed at addressing the legacy of the past atrocities and at rebuilding social relations, among which civil society initiatives assume the forefront. These three groups, although created for pragmatic and analytical reasons, also serve to make evident the distinction between 'informal' and 'traditional' mechanisms of justice. It is indeed worth keeping in mind that although most traditional forms of justice also share the characteristic of informality, there may be several informal[1] processes of justice that are not traditional, but – as we called them – 'contemporary'.

Our aim in this chapter is to identify the retributive and restorative elements presented in the three types of mechanisms and processes presented above. This will enable us to reflect upon the potentials and limitations of a restorative approach in dealing with past atrocities and their consequences. This suggests that in both the formal and the informal approaches of dealing with past crimes we may find retributive and restorative elements, thus avoiding a sometimes common assumption that automatically equates formal with retributive and informal with restorative. Adding on what was said before, in our analysis we will neither use 'traditional' nor 'informal' as immediate synonyms of 'restorative'. Instead we will draw on the principles and values of restorative justice as presented in the first chapter of this book in order to identify the restorative elements in each approach.

An important factor to bear in mind in this analysis is the intervention of the international community in the conflicts of the 1990s in the former Yugoslavia and the creation at a relatively early stage of these conflicts of a primarily retributive mechanism – the International Criminal Tribunal for the Former Yugoslavia (ICTY). The resolution and consensus of the international community in creating this judicial mechanism even before the atrocities in Kosovo took place, and later the investment it made in its functioning, determined very early on to whom the primacy of dealing with the conflict would be accorded. Given the centrality of individual criminal responsibility and of punishment in the modus operandi of the ICTY, this decision created an important precedent in how the conflict would be dealt with: through judicial and retributive means. This was later reinforced through the rebuilding and strengthening of the national judicial system and through the integration in it of international judges and prosecutors who are responsible for cases of inter-ethnic crimes and organised crime.[2] The emphasis placed on these externally originated, formalised and retributive mechanisms overlooked existing informal practices of conflict resolution and their age-old bases on the one hand, and seems to overshadow other less visible and small-scale grassroots initiatives on the other.

Retributive and restorative elements in the formal and informal approaches

Formal approaches

The formal mechanisms put in place in order to deal with the gross human rights violations committed during the war in Kosovo consist, as mentioned above, of international and domestic judicial mechanisms: the ICTY and the Kosovo judicial system. For the moment we will consider irrelevant whether the particular case of Racak could be qualified or not as a war crime, genocide or crime against humanity, and thus whether it would fall under the jurisdiction of the ICTY. We are now interested in analysing in more abstract terms the existing mechanisms created to deal with the atrocities committed during the war.

There has been a remarkable involvement and control on the part of the international community in the creation and functioning of the ICTY and the Kosovo judicial system. Both the ICTY and the Kosovo courts apply internationally recognised norms, and in the latter case also national legislation. In both cases the nature of the procedures is formal. In fact, they both – more or less – follow the typical procedures of judicial bodies in criminal cases present in other European countries. This means that the procedures are perpetrator-oriented, i.e. focused on the individual criminal responsibility of the defendant, in which the victim plays a merely secondary role (in both cases, at most he/she can participate in the proceedings as a witness) and that there is no interaction between the parties directly involved in the crime (victim and defendant). As far as the outcome is concerned, in both cases the final aim of the proceedings is to allow the judges to issue a verdict of guilty or non-guilty and determine the applicable punishment accordingly (which in the case of the ICTY can only be imprisonment – Art. 24(1) ICTY Statute). In other words, these mechanisms have a primarily retributive function as they are mainly concerned with determining whether punishment is applicable or not. The Statute of the ICTY is silent on reparations, except for the possibility given to the judge to order the return of property but this is not considered to be a reparation measure as such (Sarkin 2005: 177).[3] As far as the national jurisdiction is concerned, reparations may be claimed in separate, civil proceedings. Reparations have thus not been a priority of the formal, criminal judicial mechanisms of dealing with the past.

The ICTY states among its goals the following: ensuring accountability, establishing the facts, bringing justice to the victims and giving them a voice, strengthening the rule of law, and paving the way to reconciliation in the region.[4] Although some[5] would argue that several of these goals sound more like wishful thinking rather than concrete end results of the court's proceedings, it is interesting to note that this institution combines at least theoretically both retrospective and prospective objectives and hopes to benefit both individuals and communities. In this way, as many argue, this judicial body goes beyond mere retribution (Schvey 2003).

Besides the courts, other formal mechanisms have been put into place in Kosovo to deal with the issue of reparations. Concerning reparations for personal injuries, the United Nations Mission in Kosovo (UNMIK) Regulation 66 of December 2000[6] provided that both Serb and Albanian combatants and civilians would be entitled to benefits including 'financial payments to war disabled and families of those killed, free access to medical care provided in governmental health centers, and exemption from taxes and customs duties on vehicles for the disabled' (Djordjevic 2002). Furthermore, quasi-judicial, joint international and national bodies were created to deal with property issues: the Housing and Property Directorate (HPD) and Housing and Property Claims Commission (HPCC).[7] On March 2006, UNMIK Regulation 2006/10 created the Kosovo Property Agency (KPA) with the aim of addressing 'claims relating to immovable property, including residential, agricultural and commercial property disputes that resulted from the displacement of communities after the conflict'.[8] Since then, all the claims pending before the HPD are to be handled by the KPA, while those pending before the HPCC remain under its authority.

These efforts in providing reparations to the victims of the war, albeit following formal procedures in which those responsible for the harm in question either have no role to play or do not assume an active responsibility through making amends but instead comply with a judicial or administrative order, may still be seen as coming closer to the values defended by proponents of restorative justice in its 'reparative conception' (Johnstone and Van Ness 2007). According to the authors, these proponents 'also envisage the possibility of *partially* restorative solutions to problems of crime emerging outside such processes [of encounter], including through reparative *sanctions* ordered and administered by professionals employed by the formal criminal justice system' (Johnstone and Van Ness 2007: 14). Although this quote refers only to the sanctions imposed by judicial decisions, we would like to suggest that the same reasoning applies to administrative procedures with the same reparative ideal.

Informal approaches

Kanun laws: context

Besides formal justice mechanisms, the authors of the preceding chapters have identified several informal mechanisms for dealing with conflicts still present in Kosovo. One of the most significant Albanian traditional methods of exacting justice – the *gjakmarrje* (blood feud) – is promoted by the Albanian customary laws, codified in the Code of Lekë Dukagjini (CLD, also known as Kanun). As Gashi (see Chapter 5) explains, the Code of Lekë Dukagjini along with some other Albanian canons formulates the rules upon which the Albanian culture is based, primarily focusing on the concept of honour and hospitality, as well as pride, vengeance and reconciliation. Lekë Dukagjini (1410–81) formalised the oral laws regulating Albanian community life in the fifteenth century. Nevertheless, the practice of these codes potentially dates back to 2,000 to 3,000 years ago[9] and presents the fundamental customary law employed in the Middle Ages in almost all areas of Albanian settlement (Fox 1989). These codes were followed widely in Lezhe, Dukagjin, Shkoder, Gjakove, Kosovo and even among the Albanian population in parts of Serbia, Montenegro and Macedonia (Camaj 1989: xiv). As Gashi notes, the Albanian customary criminal law is encoded in different canons, but that of Lekë Dukagjini is one of the most influential.

The laws applied equally to ethnic Albanian Christians and Moslems. The impact of the CLD on ethnic Albanians has been enormous, although it has been somewhat greater among the Gegs (subculture from north Albania and Kosovo) than among the Tosks (subculture from south Albania). According to Durham, for the ethnic Albanians 'Lek said so' obtained far more obedience than the Ten Commandments. 'The teachings of Islam and of Christianity, the Sharia and Church law, all have to yield to the Canon of Lek [...]. For all their habits, laws, and customs, the people, as a rule, have but one explanation: it is in the Canon of Lek' (Durham 1994: 25; Camaj 1989: xiv). The CLD has been described as an expression of the independence and de facto autonomy particularly of the northern Albanian clans during the Ottoman Empire (Hasluk 1954: 14). The preservation of customary law was one of the most important elements in helping the Albanian people to maintain their individuality (Vickers 1997: 21; McClear 2001; Arsovska 2006).[10]

During the communist period (1944–91) the use of the Kanun laws and the practice of the blood feud as a means of resolving disputes were forbidden, particularly in Albania (Jolis 1997: 30).[11] During this period all religions were also strictly prohibited (O'Donnell 1995; Minnesota Lawyers 1992: viii). Even though the 45 years of communism caused 'mass amnesia' in some parts of the ethnic Albanian population, statistical data show that the ancient creeds remained the foundations of Albanian culture (Biberaj 1995; Neza 1997: 108; Arsovska 2006).[12] After the downfall of the communist regime – accompanied by a general decline of state authority and increase in social confusion – the Kanun morality experienced an upward revaluation (Waldmann 2001: 440; Gjoka 2000; Arsovska and Craig 2006). Throughout the centuries, both in Albania and Kosovo, the state has often been viewed as an intruder and occupier; hence many ethnic Albanians do not have real respect for state institutions and regulations, or for institutionalised forms of justice. However, in recent years Albania and Kosovo have been enormously influenced by the Western world. During the process of integration and globalisation, new laws emerging from the Western value system were steadily imposed on Kosovo and the region in general. Many of them did not emerge naturally from within society but were implemented top down, as were other laws during their troublesome past. As a result, the gap between the people and the 'state' remained wide (Arsovska and Verduyn 2008). Governments have been ratifying laws in order to initiate the integration process with and to bring the Balkan region closer to the EU; however, often it seems that neither the governments nor the civil society understands clearly the values behind those laws.

Moreover, the Westernised state regulations and laws in Albania and Kosovo are often incompatible with the other informal normative systems – such as the CLD – that exist in the country as a 'second level' of regulation that is not openly accepted by the official legal system (Arsovska and Verduyn 2008). Cultural laws such as the CLD (as well as religious laws) do not align with state laws, leaving the people lost in a 'three-way loyalty system' (state, culture and religion). However, it seems that many ethnic Albanians prefer to shun perplexing official state laws in favour of an interpretation of the ancient creeds that have been omnipresent in their society for centuries (Arsovska 2006; Arsovska and Craig 2006; Waldmann 2001). Nonetheless, many original elements of the CLD today have been degraded to the level of mere reflexes of self-defence. As we noted, the effects that the communist regime had on the Kanun morality cannot be ignored. In Albania, Kosovo and other parts of the Balkans it seems that the ethnic Albanians are acquainted to some degree with the contents of the code from oral tradition – although only a few have actually read it (Arsovska and Verduyn 2008; Riber 2003; Mortimer and Toader 2005). Hence, ethnic Albanians in Kosovo have created their own interpretations of the CLD, focusing much more on the concept of revenge and exaggerated sense of honour than on reconciliation. The society has not forgotten the violence-promoting mechanisms of the revenge codes, but has forgotten or holds it to be superfluous to put a stop to the escalation of violence (Waldmann 2001; Schwandner-Sievers 1998). Nevertheless, the aim of the original laws was to achieve social order, and the laws contained many restorative elements – seldom practised today – that encouraged reconciliation and mediation as mechanisms for solving conflicts.

Kanun laws: traditional processes

Regarding the content, the CLD is a formal expression of the deeply felt concept of honour of the Albanian people. It means the entirety of rules according to which a person can protect his own community of solidarity against attack from third parties. This protection – among many other things – includes the moral obligation to apply a series of violent retaliatory attacks, until the honour of one's own group has been re-established (Waldmann 2001: 440). 'There is no fine for an offence to honour. An offence to honour is never forgiven. The person dishonoured has every right to avenge his honour; no pledge is given, no appeal is made to the Elders, no judgment is needed, no fine is taken. The strong man collects the fine himself' (CLD 2: 600). One who meets these revenge obligations from the CLD is taken to be cleansed white, whereas one who does not fulfil it is labelled unclean and must suffer all humiliations on the part of the village community (Riber 2003; Waldmann 2001: 440; Schwandner-Sievers 1998: 80). Nonetheless, Lekë Dukagjini's intention when formalising the laws was to limit the cycles of bloodletting among the mountain tribes – which sometimes destroyed entire communities – by enabling a council of tribal elders to arrange a *besë* (principle of unity, reconciliation and trust; word of honour; pledge) once honour had been obtained. The aim was to decrease the serious social and economic dislocation that resulted from so many men being killed or forced into hiding by the cycle of revenge (McClear 2001; Arsovska and Craig 2006). Hence the original Kanun includes very specific clarifications of the manner of retaliatory killings for restoring honour to the offended when the laws are disobeyed which today are not strictly followed in the Albanian context (Waldmann 2001: 436).

> The foundation of it all is the principle of personal honour. Next comes the equality of persons. From these flows a third principle, the freedom of each to act in accordance with his own honour, within the limits of the law, without being subject to another's command. And the fourth principle is the word of honour, the besë (def.: besa), which creates a situation of inviolable trust. (Malcolm 1998: 18)

According to the CLD (2: 599) even when a murderer has killed someone, he must inform the family of the victim about the murder, so there will be no confusion regarding his/her identity. Originally the Kanun sanctioned the slaying of the murderer himself; fathers shall not be killed in place of sons, nor sons in place of fathers, but everyone will die for his own sin. Later on, the practice was extended so that male honour can be cleansed by the slaying of any male relative of the murderer: all males incur the blood feud during the 24 hours following the murder; after 24 hours, the family of the victim must give a guarantee of truce (CLD 2: 898–900).

As Gashi explains (see Chapter 5), women traditionally were also exempt from the feuds although recently there have been cases where women have been killed. During the conflict in Kosovo raping and killing women and children was one of the strategies used by the Serbian and Albanian armies which – according to the Kanun – is a highly dishonourable act; hence the CLD (according to the principle 'blood for blood') prescribes harsh punishments – such as the death penalty – for the perpetrators of such severe crimes (Gjeçovi 1933: paras 1194–95; Gashi: this volume, Chapter 5). In addition, the graveness of a murder – according to Albanian customary law – is also evaluated by analysing the time and place at which it occurred, the manner of the killing, the means used to kill and the consequences of such an act. Many of the killings that occurred during the Kosovo conflict – from a cultural perspective – seem to rank very high with regard to severity; hence retribution and vengeance is often evoked on the part of the ethnic Albanian population as a punishment for the perpetrators of such crimes.

However, the original Code of Lekë Dukagjini specifies that an offence to honour is not paid with property but by the spilling of blood or by a magnanimous pardon (through the mediation of good friends) (CLD 2: 598). Hence it states that there is a possibility of solving conflict via the mediation of good friends. The Kanun presents two ways in which the 'reconciliation of blood' is accomplished (2: 969): (1) through intercession by friends of the family of the victim and by the parish priest; and (2) through a general amnesty declared by the Chiefs, the House and the men of the Banner. Hence in general *gjakmarrje* does allow reconciliation. Traditionally this could be arranged by the family of the murderer tying him up on a donkey and leading him to the family of the murdered man. The family would ask for forgiveness, and sometimes forgiveness was given. If reconciliation had been achieved, the families would not only be reconciled but also allied. If feuding families or clans agreed to bury their differences, their wishes were respected.

The CLD also more specifically introduces the concept of mediator. 'The mediator may be a man or a woman, a boy or a girl, or even a priest' (Art. 669). The blood feud mediation is based on the rules of the mediation specified in Chapter XCIX in the Kanun (Fox 1989: 138–40):

> A mediator is one who intercedes to resolve disputes, which may cause killing or some other disaster among the contending parties (668); a mediator may go from house to house, from village to village from one Banner to another (670); the traditional words of the mediator are: 'Stop arguing, you men, I am in the middle! Put down your rifles, men, I will stand between you until you listen to me! Put down your rifles, for the village ..., the Banner ... is between you' (679); the mediator takes pledges from both sides and arranges a time and place to meet together for hearing (680); if the mediator is unable to reach reconciliation, he leaves the pledges of the two sides in the hands of men of wisdom, and he is then free of the task of mediation (681); and mediation always ends either at sunrise or sunset (682).

There are four steps identified in the CLD for reconciliation to occur: laying down the weapons, opening a dialogue, finding a solution and achieving forgiveness and reconciliation. The mediators traditionally gave four reasons why parties should reconcile: for the sake of God, for the sake of the children and next generations, for the sake of national reconciliation and for the sake of eliminating the severe act of blood feud and creating the image of brotherly tolerance (Riber 2003). Besides the mediator, there are also the concepts of truce negotiator and guarantors of blood. The negotiator goes to the parents and relatives of the murdered man in order to obtain a truce for the murderer and his family. They are protectors of the murderer and his family during the period of truce (Fox 1989: 166). The guarantor has a very similar role and that is to make sure that any repeated outbreak of hatred and conflict initiated by the families is averted (Fox 1989: 182).

Literature on Albanian customary laws also mentions the Council of Elders (small and big councils – see Chapter 5) as a special trial body. This court of elders – often called 'Elders of Blood' – was set up for criminal offences, in particular murder cases, and dealt with the reconciliation of parties in conflict as well as remuneration for reconciliation (Sahiti 2006: 68–74; Gashi: this volume, Chapter 5). It was usually comprised of representatives of both parties in conflict and other people with good reputation – who were honourable, wise and prudent – who had a wide knowledge of the country's customs. The families (sometimes clans) and the Council of Elders met for talks in a neutral place. They had to establish whether a murderer has behaved 'humanly' at any time during a chain of vendettas. If this was not the case, reconciliation was ruled out.

The CLD (2: 982) also introduces a ceremony called the 'meal of the blood'. The 'meal of the blood' occurs when the mediators of reconciliation of blood, together with some relatives and friends of the 'owner of the blood' go to the house of the murderer to reconcile the blood and eat a meal to observe that reconciliation. Ending blood feud is not a simple task, since arranging peace can take years of negotiations with the warring families. In reality peace was seldom made until the same number had been killed on both sides (Riber 2003). If a man was not killed but only wounded, and if revenge killed his enemy, the elders made sure that the wounded man pay wound money or 'blood money' – half a blood – to the family of the killed person so as to make it 'one for one'. The cost of the wound was evaluated according to the limb or the judgment of a physician in order to balance the difference (Fox 1989: 172). Equality between families was a very important element (Riber 2003). In the case of murder there is also a rule 'a head for head or blood for blood' and in reality it looks as if the families of the murdered men should not demand compensation from each other. However, often financial compensation was also demanded for murder, and such compensation – according to Gashi (see this volume, Chapter 5) – was a sign of admission of guilt, a gesture of care and compassion expressed by the family of murderer, or as an equivalent price of the blood of victim. These gestures of recognition and admission of guilt are extremely valued and appreciated elements in the Albanian 'honour' culture. In the ethnic Albanian context financial compensation was frequently given for various types of crimes, such as robbery, marriage issues, wounds, certain types of dishonour and so on. In all regions where the Kanun is observed, every stolen object was subject to double compensation. 'Two for one, as you walk with your feet' (CLD CXVI: 804).

Moreover, one of the 'odd' rules of the blood feud and the Kanun is that of asylum. If somebody from the blood feud family (i.e. the family of the murderer) entered a victim's yard, asylum was immediately given (Rieber 2003). The rival family had to show respect and give hospitality. The killer can find protection in the homes of the victims. So besides the blood feud and *besë*, the CLD comprehensively elucidates the concept of hospitality which involves the uncompromising protection of a guest, even one with whom the host is in a state of blood feud. The Kanun stipulates that the house of the Albanian belongs to God and the guest and the life of the guest should be placed before your own life (Fox 1989: VIII/18/XCVIII; Kadare 2003: 78). 'An offence against a father, a brother, and even a cousin without heirs may be forgiven, but an offence against a guest is not forgiven' (Fox 1989: 136).

Nowadays there has been a limitation of the content of the CLD and the code has had to be adapted to modern times since many parts of the printed version have little or no meaning in the twenty-first century (Fox 1989: 38). Yet in the case of traditional Kosovo, conflicts and lawlessness did not hinder various younger groups – mainly composed of ethnic Albanians – from reproducing the old model of cultural attitudes, above all in the form of an inflated sense of honour (Waldmann 2001: 441). It is worth mentioning, that in the Serbian context – although to a lesser extent – similar laws and courts made up of the good existed until the end of the Second World War and, as Nikolic-Ristanovic explains, these courts were particularly successful in stopping cases of blood revenge cases between Serbs and Albanians. Yet it seems that such traditional informal mechanisms have now been almost totally forgotten by Serbs and replaced with criminal sanctions (see Chapter 6).

Today it is also important to note that as a result of the atheistic communist past notions of forgiveness, reconciliation and truce are often left aside and are hard to enforce in both the Albanian and Serbian contexts. Yet as Gashi explains, the Islamic religious norms (and also Buddhism and Christianity) as such do provide certain regulation with regard to the accountability of perpetrators, punishment for crimes and reconciliation and forgiveness. He also argues that severe crimes – such as those committed during the

Kosovo conflict – are seriously condemned by all the main religions of the world which in principle strongly denounce violence. Yet it seems that the true customary and religious laws are still practised only by very small segments of the population, i.e. the older generations (see Chapter 5).

In general the ability to use violence and to carry and use weapons – among many other things – has been highly respected in Albanian society since this is closely associated with the notions of honour, courage, dignity and strength – cornerstones of Albanian culture (Mortimer and Toader 2005). But bearing in mind the various contextual processes, Dukajin Gorani, director of the Human Rights Center at Prishtina University in Kosovo, explains: 'you think twice before getting in an argument in Kosovo because someone always ends up dead' (Farnam 2003). He argues that a 'gun culture' that has resulted from decades of conflict and lawlessness is to be blamed for such hideous phenomena.

> In this part of the world, there is a strong belief in customary law which means an eye for an eye. It is commendable that KFOR is trying to collect weapons, but it is an impossible task. Kosovars have learned from the KLA that you get international attention if you have a gun. In our lifetime the rule of law has never achieved anything, only guns have provided a measure of justice. So you stick to your gun. (Farnam 2003)

Although these retributive elements have indeed been part of Albanian culture, there have also been many – often forgotten – restorative elements present that should be pushed forward in order to gain momentum in modern times. These restorative elements, if properly introduced, could be used to accompany justice mechanisms for dealing with violent incidents occurring in large-scale violent conflicts.

Contemporary mechanisms

We will now turn to the group of informal, contemporary processes or initiatives that try to address the legacy of the mass atrocities in Kosovo. In both contributions on the informal mechanisms that precede this chapter, the authors recognise and demonstrate the importance of the existence and strengthening of a range of informal mechanisms alongside the formal ones, not only as necessary complements to the latter which are insufficient to deal with the challenges posed by post-conflict justice (see Chapter 5), but also as more appropriate ways 'to restore relationships and bring reconciliation' (Nikolic-Ristanovic:

this volume, Chapter 6). It is worth noting, though, that both authors also recognise the essential role of international and national formal mechanisms and their contribution to 'justice and redress' (Nikolic-Ristanovic: this volume, Chapter 6) as well as to truth, peace and reconciliation (Gashi: this volume, Chapter 5), and not least because these mechanisms are widely seen by the population as an adequate means to ensure justice, particularly in cases of serious crimes. The need to ensure adjudication by either national or international courts in cases such as war crimes, genocide and crimes against humanity (including Racak in particular, for those who qualify it as such) can be found in several instances in two of the previous chapters: both because of a need to comply with international and domestic norms and customs, and because that means providing 'justice' and 'satisfaction' for the victims (Gashi: this volume, Chapter 5; Demolli: this volume, Chapter 4). In one of the contributions, however, this idea is challenged by the assertion that 'formal mechanisms are rather slow and not very efficient' and that these 'even if properly used, have limitations per se that makes them insufficient and even inappropriate to restore relationships and bring about reconciliation between the affected sides'. The author adds that 'attending court trials are especially hard for the victims' (Nikolic-Ristanovic: this volume, Chapter 6).

Among the informal and non-traditional mechanisms or initiatives proposed and praised by Nikolic-Ristanovic and Gashi, the role of international and national civil society organisations takes on a privileged position. These include non-governmental organisations aimed at creating the space for contact, dialogue and exchange among members of different ethnic groups with a view to rebuilding broken relations and trust, and others which focus on contributing to the establishment and acknowledgment of the facts of the past, either through small-scale experience-sharing initiatives, through large-scale investigations (including particularly those dealing with the issue of missing persons) or through the support of witnesses in criminal justice proceedings. In spite of the failed attempt to have a Truth and Reconciliation Commission (TRC) in Serbia in 2001, the idea of an official commission of inquiry to investigate and report on the atrocities committed in the past seems to be gaining renewed interest as a way to counter the persistant denials and multiple truths in the region (Gashi: this volume, Chapter 5; Nikolic-Ristanovic: this volume, Chapter 6). The authors also point out the importance of memorials and other forms of commemoration of the suffering of the victims as measures of symbolic reparation as well as to so-called measures of rehabilitation for victims such as healthcare and assistance in education. Finally, among the proposed informal mechanisms are also featured negotiations and mediation hosted and facilitated by international actors, which are on the one hand seen as potential neutral and objective facilitators (Gashi: this volume, Chapter 5), and on the other feared for their partiality and double-standard policies in the past (Nikolic-Ristanovic: this volume, Chapter 6).

Some important concepts that can be identified in this group of proposed approaches are those of encounter, exchange, participation, truth-seeking and truth-telling, acknowledgment, reparation and mediation. Naturally the prevalence of one or another of these elements will differ in each type of initiative. By the same token, participation and exchange will take on a different meaning whether we refer to a community-based encounter programme or to international, diplomatic negotiations. Keeping these differences in mind, however, it is important to identify the central notions in these informal approaches and analyse them against a restorative justice backdrop. Before that, one remark must be made: most of the processes now under analysis (with the exception to a certain extent of a possible TRC) are not intended to deal with one specific and concrete case where a crime was committed in terms of 'resolving that conflict' strictly speaking. Naturally, the connection with particular cases is always there, whether it be in the truth-seeking functions of NGOs working on missing persons or on other human rights violations, or when individuals come together to share their experiences of the past, but we are not talking here primarily of 'resolving a conflict between parties', i.e. between the individual victim and the respective individual perpetrator. And this fact, precisely, poses perhaps the greatest challenge in thinking about such informal mechanisms as possibly 'restorative justice' initiatives.

Nonetheless, in our view it is relevant to identify the elements and values present in these mechanisms that are shared with the restorative justice 'philosophy'.[13] In procedural terms, most of these informal processes rely on a facilitator, or are themselves a link between the individuals they work with and other institutions or processes (as is the case of NGOs that give assistance to victims in criminal proceedings). In fact, the role of the facilitator is highlighted as one of crucial importance, provided that this role is performed with balance, impartiality and objectivity and that the person or institution is respected (Nikolic-Ristanovic: this volume, Chapter 6). The participation of and interaction between the parties is at the centre of initiatives of inter-ethnic dialogue and in general terms in TRCs (although the level of interaction here differs in each commission). It has been noted how important it is that the parties feel they are participating in a safe and welcoming environment; and this is also a central concern in restorative justice encounters (Nikolic-Ristanovic: this volume, Chapter 6; Johnstone and Van Ness 2007: 9). Moreover, community dialogue initiatives and TRCs, as well as other truth-seeking projects, tend to be primarily victim-centred. One might debate how to qualify NGO programmes with war veterans aimed at experience-sharing and conflict transformation. Although such programmes work with those who actively participated in the violence, they are equally based on the belief that they too have suffered harm and need to be assisted in their reintegration – another idea that is also central to restorative justice (Nikolic-Ristanovic: this volume, Chapter 6; Van Ness and Strong 1997: 114–16). One important remark made by Nikolic-Ristanovic concerning participation is that this type of encounter might need to start by bringing together individuals with similar experiences and with similar suffering, but in any case all groups in society must be given a chance to participate in such initiatives. This points at the necessity of a broad inclusion and active participation of all those who were harmed by conflict – which again is a very familiar idea to restorative justice theories (Nikolic-Ristanovic: this volume, Chapter 6; Van Ness 2002: 2, 5; Valiñas and Vanspauwen 2006).

As far as the outcome of the mechanisms and initiatives proposed is concerned, they are clearly not aimed at handing down any sort of sanction (perhaps excluding the international negotiations, depending on which framework they are taking place in). In fact, they are aimed at re-establishing contacts and relations, contributing to establishing 'the truth', acknowledging the victims' suffering and providing certain material benefits. In one way or another, their aim seems to be reparation – of relations and individual harm. In fact, different forms of reparation as conceptualised in the *UN Basic Principles and Guidelines* are envisaged by the initiatives proposed in the two preceding chapters: 'verification of the facts and full and public disclosure of the truth'; 'the search for the whereabouts of the disappeared, for the identities of the children abducted, and for the bodies of those killed, and assistance in the recovery, identification and reburial of the bodies'; 'public apology, including acknowledgement of the facts and acceptance of responsibility'; 'commemorations and tributes to the victims'; measures of rehabilitation which 'should include medical and psychological care as well as legal and social services' (UNCHR 2005).

Accordingly, these mechanisms have primarily prospective goals as they focus on creating the basis for the rebuilding of trust between former enemies. At the core of that basis are the notions of acknowledgment of harm and exchange or dialogue – both central values in restorative justice.

The challenges to a restorative approach in Kosovo

The war in Kosovo left behind very deep scars and extremely high social tensions. Some argue that the violence that flared up in the 1990s and today's tensions are based on deeply rooted socio-cultural divisions that go back decades and even centuries, and which were ingeniously manipulated and exploited by nationalistic politicians (Sofos 1996). The intricacies of the relation between ethno-cultural identity and politics, and the role played by victimisation or 'victimhood' in that relation, poses enormous challenges not only to those who try to grasp the reality in Kosovo but also to those who are contemplating ways in which social and legal conflicts could be resolved and social bonds restored.

As long as the private spheres of individuals and interpersonal relations continue to be determined primarily and peremptorily by political affiliation and group identity, attempts to bring individuals together and create empathy between them beyond ethnic lines will face extreme difficulty to succeed. While we are not suggesting that social relations between individuals (as opposed to between groups) can or should be apolitical, it seems that a very essential element of individuality is lost when such relations are so highly politicised. That element seems crucial in restorative justice theory and practice. In fact, whereas the involvement of the social network of individuals and the so-called 'community of care' is strongly encouraged in restorative justice processes, emphasis is placed on the individual harm, on the individual needs, on each individual's human dignity and on creating empathy between those individuals. In other words, it is precisely the ability to recognise in the other his/her own human dignity as an individual that is at the basis of the replacement of feelings of anger, distrust and revenge by mutual understanding and recognition of the harm suffered by each other. The point here is that in our view restorative processes require that individuals participate primarily as such, and not as representatives of a particular ethnic group. The latter, however, seems to be more often the case in societies highly divided along ethnic lines such as Kosovo. On the one hand, the identity of the individual is overlaid by that of the group, which feeds on certain unchallengeable truths (often related to previous and ongoing victimisation and oppression) about that group and others, and which finds an almost linear representation at the political level. On the other hand, and as a result, those individuals who are willing to cross the group boundaries or challenge those truths and try to understand the others' perspective are regarded as 'traitors' and suffer immense peer pressure.

It is also important to reflect upon the role of the community or communities as such in the process of addressing past violence and overcoming tensions. Stovel has suggested that when considering the potential contribution of restorative justice to reconciliation in war-ravaged societies, restorative justice faces additional challenges when the conflict is of an inter-community rather than an intra-community nature. In her view, both victim and perpetrator have the need to heal and regain trust *in* or *of* the community, respectively. When victim and perpetrator belong to different communities who reorganise themselves internally after the conflict and are separated from each other by a major rift, the community that the victim needs to regain trust in and the community that the perpetrator needs to regain the trust of are not one and the same (Stovel 2006). What seems to be missing then is an overarching community (even if victim and perpetrator would belong to different 'groups' within that community) that could provide the necessary social cohesion as the backdrop for the re-establishment of those social bonds between the victim and the community, the perpetrator and the community, and to a greater or lesser extent between the victim and the perpetrator. This also explains how the same person will be regarded by one community as a 'war criminal' and by the other (his or her own community) as a 'war hero' and how such perceptions will remain unchallenged within the community over time and generations.

In addition to this is the fact that the parties to the conflict in Kosovo to a large extent are not living within the boundaries of Kosovo itself, and that many of those involved in the violence have never actually lived within those boundaries. When conflicting parties still regard each other with anger or distrust, but do not even share the same geographical space, distance builds a powerful barrier to any attempt at bringing the parties into contact or dialogue. Similarly, when the parties at conflict do not share the same cultural background it will be difficult to use traditional informal mechanisms of resolving conflicts that are part of the culture and history of one community, but not of the other (see Chapter 5).

As described previously, traditionally the use of violence in Albania and Kosovo has been seen as a structured phenomenon representing the archetype of social control. The ability to use violence and to take justice into your own hands has been considered the main criteria for assessing the value of the Albanian 'man of honour'. As Gashi explains, the Kanun of Lekë Dukagjini and other Albanian canons which follow the *lex talionis* principle of 'blood for blood' point out that acts of vengeance are directed against the executor of the murder (and even other males in the murderer's family). It is clear that these traditional norms stipulate harsh punishment for perpetrators and murderers such as those involved in the Racak massacre. Such punishments are nowadays in contradiction with the applicable law.

According to the Western value system the wish to avenge is considered to be a leftover of an archaic epoch (Waldmann 2001: 435; Arsovska 2006; Arsovska and Craig 2006). In Western countries the era in which self-justice on behalf of the victims was permitted is considered to be over because there are institutions for the discovery and prosecution of criminal acts. According to modern conception, it is the duty of the criminal justice authorities and the courts to combat crime. Revenge (as with envy, pride, shame and other emotions) is suppressed and often thought of as dirty (Waldmann 2001: 435). However, in Kosovo, particularly after the conflict, the wish to avenge and doubly punish someone who has done 'injustice' has been very much alive among the Albanian population, resulting in a number of retaliatory acts against the Serbs (but also Albanians) using culture as justification (Human Rights Watch 1999; Craig 2003; see also this volume, Chapter 3). For example, in a public survey conducted during 2006 with ethnic Albanian respondents from Albania, Macedonia and Kosovo (N = 864), Arsovska (2007) observed that 35 per cent (254 out of 726) of the respondents stated that an offence to honour is never forgiven and blood (revenge) must be taken. Surprisingly, 22.3 per cent of the respondents did not provide an answer to this question which points to the general confusion within the society regarding social norms,[14] while 42.7 per cent of the respondents disagreed with the statement (see Figure 7.1). The statement was directly taken from the Kanun laws (see also Arsovska and Verduyn 2008).

Similar division in opinions, and a significant percentage of negative attitudes, in relation to 'obtaining justice' in Kosovo could be observed in the results of a survey administered by the International

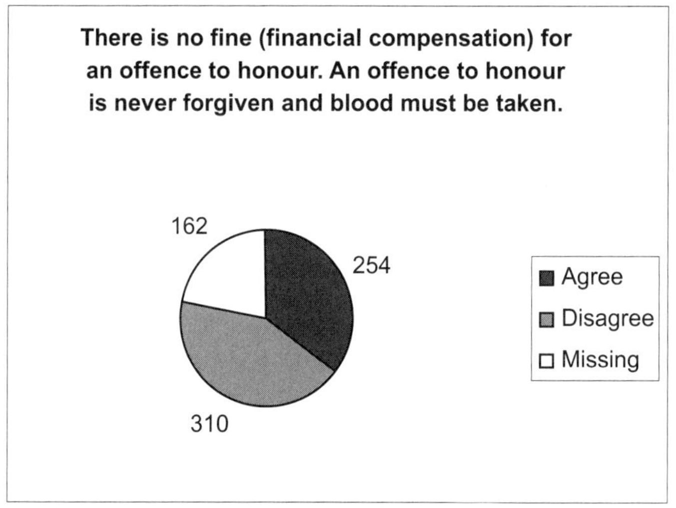

Source: Arsovska and Verduyn (2008).

Figure 7.1 Agreement with statement promoting revenge killings

Commission of the Balkans (2005) in November–December 2004 (see this volume, Chapter 3: Figures 3.1, 3.2 and 3.3). Besides the fact that the majority of Kosovars stated that they are keen to live in an 'ethnically homogeneous Kosovo' they also pointed out that they are ready to seek justice through power and the army (55 per cent of the respondents: see this volume, Chapter 3: Figure 3.3). The answers of the Serbian people from Serbia were more positive in this respect and only a minority (18 per cent) was in favour of another armed conflict.

Although a significant number of Kosovar Albanians might argue that they do not trust the justice system and therefore want to take justice into their own hands to seek revenge, this goes against the principles of the Western value system. Also, a number of other elements described in the Kanun are in complete opposition to internationally recognised human rights standards; hence the question remains how to make sure that people understand why they should give up their traditional ways of doing justice in the name of the Western institutionalised form of justice. Yet there are many justice mechanisms present in Albanian culture that are not so common in the Western world but certainly do not run in complete opposition to the Western value system.

However, in principal, the traditional justice mechanisms applied only to ethnic Albanian people and not to 'foreigners'; hence it remains unclear to what extent it might be possible to broaden their applicability to the general population in Kosovo (i.e. Albanians, Serbs, Roma and so forth). Will other ethnic groups be willing to accept the positive aspects of traditional Albanian mechanisms of doing justice that are not in complete opposition to internationally recognised human rights standards? Gashi argues that traditionally the rules of Albanian customary law promoted criminal sanctions applicable only in cases when both the offender and the victim belonged to the Albanian community. But in his opinion these rules may apply to the individuals of other nationalities as well – both as victims and offenders (Gashi: this volume, Chapter 5).

Finally, the Albanian customary laws are very harsh regarding severe murders: murders committed against a person who has been given a peace vow (The Truce), murdering women, murdering children, murdering a man while he is accompanied by a woman, murdering a pregnant woman and murdering a friend or cleric. During the Racak massacre all these brutal types of murders took place, hence the only solution – according to customary law – for exacting justice is revenge (Gashi: this volume, Chapter 5). Although, as we can observe in the graph in Figure 7.1 above, not all of the people justified revenge, it does seem a very difficult and challenging task to promote restorative justice principles for such severe types of crimes. Hence, nowadays, in Kosovo the retributive elements are much more practised than the restorative ones and the question remains how to alter this trend.

Opportunities for further development of a restorative approach in Kosovo

The potential contribution of restorative justice principles to meeting the challenges and needs of post-conflict societies has been highlighted by a growing number of authors. Among them, Browny Leebaw (2001) captured very clearly the essence of that relation in the following words:

> Restorative principles offer a promising approach to the dilemmas of political transition, where both condemnation and re-integration are essential, where desired transformation may benefit from wide-ranging involvement, and where political and economic resources to prosecute are simply unavailable. Restorative principles are uniquely appropriate to these goals

> as they are founded on an appreciation for the communicative and educative function of justice alongside a commitment to problem-solving and community reconstruction that parallels the transitional task of nation-building.

In the former Yugoslavia and in Kosovo in particular, unlike most other post-conflict countries, a powerful mechanism was put in place to deal with the most serious human rights violations that took place during the conflicts in the region. Nevertheless, the ICTY's limited scope (it deals only with certain crimes), reach (it will only try a relatively small number of perpetrators) and its failure to significantly contribute to peace in the province (Meernik 2005) demonstrate the shortcomings that a mechanism of this type is bound to have in situations such as this. The incapability of the judiciary (international and national) to deal with all the cases where crimes were committed during the conflict, and its inadequacy to actually conduce to a rebuilding of trust among citizens and sustainable peace is undoubtedly one strong argument to look for complementary or alternative responses to mass abuses. Restorative principles may indeed provide this complementary or alternative option. But what is interesting for us is to explore their potential and possible implementation, not just as second-best alternatives, but in their own right. The question is, thus, what could restorative principles bring to the resolution of the atrocities of the past and the tensions of the present in Kosovo, and is there a fertile ground in Kosovo for the application of such principles?

The present situation in Kosovo, characterised by a sharp social divide and well cemented ethnic distance, demonstrates clearly the need of the society for social reconstruction. Social reconstruction has proved to demand more than the reaffirmation of fundamental values through judicial institutions, the punishment of some of the perpetrators and the rebuilding of democratic state institutions. All of these elements of 'justice' and 'nation-building' are undoubtedly essential for a society to overcome the consequences of mass and violent conflict. However, such efforts tend to be more often than not alienated or at least very distant from the population concerned. For that reason, the impact of those efforts on the rebuilding of trust among former enemies has been revealed to be quite tenuous. In an insightful contribution, Halpern and Weinstein (2004) suggest that in order to reach reconciliation, there must be a process of creating empathy between the parties leading to 'rehumanisation' between them. The idea of fostering empathy and rehumanisation between the parties to the conflict is precisely at the core of the restorative justice philosophy especially for those who adopt an 'encounter conception' of restorative justice (Van Ness and Strong 1997: 76–8; Umbreit 2001; Johnstone and Van Ness 2007: 9–12). Indeed, the importance of engaging the parties in a more or less mediated encounter aims at creating the space in which they can express and share their views. Such exchange has the potential of allowing the parties to become aware of and eventually to understand each others' perspective. And this is expected to bring the sense of recognition and accountability that the parties are in need of. In this sense, restorative justice may be said to be more concerned with the rebuilding of relationships based on trust rather than 'restoring' the situation before the conflict (*status quo ante*) in the strict sense of the word.[15] Furthermore, in relation to what has been said before on the need to ensure a certain degree of individuality in restorative justice processes, we would like to suggest that this same element of individuality is at the basis of empathy-building which reinforces our belief that restorative justice principles are instrumental in the process of creating empathy between the parties.[16]

In spite of the high level of tension in society in Kosovo, there seem to be some positive developments that may foster an increasing interest in the application of restorative principles to conflict resolution mechanisms and initiatives. One of these developments is the growing number of civil society initiatives of inter-ethnic dialogue that try to build a bridge between the divided communities and bring them into contact in a safe and welcoming atmosphere. The fact that more and more of these initiatives are taking place, even if registering a very slow and small-scale progress, indicates that more and more people realise the need to re-establish contact and feel ready to express that need and translate it into action. In spite of the heavily hostile context, these initiatives may be important catalysts for more and larger initiatives where the conflicting parties can meet and actively participate in decision-making processes or simply engage in dialogue. Another important development is the inclusion of restorative justice elements in the legislation. This was reported to be the case in the Serbian legislation but there is no reason to doubt that the same trend will follow in Kosovo's own legislation. Although these legal developments take place to a large extent due to Western European initiatives and pressure rather than being home-grown, the acceptance and integration of such principles might open up new windows that may gain increasing interest among professionals and the population at large. Also, although such restorative elements were introduced in relation to so-called 'common crimes', and particularly to juvenile crimes, once again they may provide an important encouragement to the revival of or to a new interest in certain values when responding to crime and conflicts in more general terms. As far as the functioning of the formal criminal justice system is concerned, it is at least disputable whether its failures or shortcomings are in practice fostering the search for more restorative alternatives of conflict resolution. In fact, and along the lines of what we have discussed above, the frustrations of the population of Kosovo with the functioning of the ICTY and national courts (accused of ethnic bias and of covering only a few cases and a few perpetrators) may indeed increase interest in other forms of accountability that may bring more satisfaction to the victims. However, some also argue[17] that there needs to be a well-functioning criminal justice system in place which is capable of ensuring the accountability at least of the leaders of the heinous crimes in order to restore people's trust in the institutions and the rule of law. Only then, when some degree of accountability has been ensured, these authors argue, will individuals be willing to meet and engage in dialogue with former enemies.

On a more general political level, the decision on the status of Kosovo will end the uncertainty about the future both for Kosovo Albanians and Serbs that has been a major source of unrest and social tension. The formal end to this transitional period is an important step for the people of Kosovo to be able to focus on rebuilding relations with former enemies. This is not to suggest that the latter will necessarily and so easily follow the former, but at least the former seems indispensable to the latter.

As noted previously, the traditional Albanian justice mechanisms clearly give some space to the possibility of solving conflict via mediation through the intercession of friends of the victim's family, and through a general amnesty declared by older, respected and charismatic leaders in the society. Although today these criteria have slightly changed in some parts of the Albanian settlement (the same applies to Serbia and the Balkan region in general) and often power and respect come with money and material goods, older people are still considered wise and powerful and could help in the process of reconciliation between the different communities.

According to Gashi, there is no doubt that the implementation of criminal law is of great importance in the process of uncovering the truth, restoring justice and establishing peace and reconciliation between the parties in conflict in Kosovo. But – as Gashi argues – informal mechanisms containing customary and religious rules could play a very important role in this truth-seeking process. Albanian customary law contains many paragraphs referring to the institutions and customary procedure for uncovering the truth and achieving resolution of the conflicts arising from various criminal offences, including murder as the most serious.

Moreover, bearing in mind that the Albanian (as well as Serbian) culture places enormous significance on cultural elements such as honour and dignity, we can postulate that even a simple public acknowledgment by the perpetrators of the crimes committed during the conflict can be of great value for the process of reconciliation between the conflicting parties. As previously noted, symbolic (mutual) acknowledgments of the suffering of the victims' families and/or reparations for their losses can greatly encourage inter-ethnic cooperation and enhance dialogue. Hence there are certainly some opportunities for restorative justice in the ethnic Albanian context. However, the great challenges remain: (1) how to promote the restorative elements already used in the society for centuries (i.e. treatment of conflict and conflict resolution through reconciliation, the ways to implement reconciliation, the role of the mediator(s), the obligation of parties in conflict and the reconciliation ceremony) as a complementary method to the already existing Westernised formal justice mechanisms and to diminish the significance of elements associated with 'revenge'; and (2) how to extend the practice of these restorative mechanisms to the general population in Kosovo in order to achieve sustainable and long-term peace within the broader society.

Conclusion

Dealing with the aftermath of the Kosovo conflict has been shown to be a daunting task. The type and extent of the atrocities committed, and the complexities of both the context leading to the violence and that which followed the war, pose overwhelming challenges to any effort to address both past and present abuses and contribute to social reconstruction. Bearing in mind this highly tense and extremely sensitive context, in the present analysis we set out to explore what the opportunities and limits of integrating restorative justice principles are in the process of dealing with the conflict in Kosovo and what the contribution of such principles could be to this process.

The benchmark decision by the international community to create the ICTY in response to the violations being committed in the former

Yugoslavia set an important precedent for the retributive nature of the ensuing processes of dealing with the past in these countries. In Kosovo, reinterpretations of the rules of Albanian customary law, centred almost exclusively in notions of pure revenge and violence, not only added to a retributive approach in dealing with the conflict but also put in question the respect for internationally recognised standards of human rights and the rule of law.

However, significant elements of Albanian customary law – as originally interpreted – point out the need to ensure social order and to the contribution that mediation and pardon or reconciliation can have for it. These conciliatory and restorative elements – as deeply rooted in tradition as more retributive ones – could potentially have an important contribution to social reconstruction when properly revived and strengthened. Further attention would need to be paid to ways of fostering this revival in respect of fundamental human rights standards and to ways in which such elements could be applied to different communities in Kosovo, thus contributing to the rebuilding of trust among them. As a minimum, a reflection upon the potential contribution of such deeply culturally rooted and genuinely home-grown mechanisms of conflict resolution, or at least of some of their elements, should not be completely put aside.

The need for processes of reparation both of social relations and of individual harm that may – to say the least – make up for the shortcomings of judicial bodies in addressing the consequences of the conflict is at the basis of the increasing number of civil society initiatives of dialogue, truth-seeking, acknowledgment and victim assistance. In spite of the small-scale nature of these processes, their potential contribution to inter-community trust-building (including across the boundaries of Kosovo) should not be overshadowed by the more visible and donor-friendly judicial processes.

Kosovo still faces a long and hard road to address its legacy of violence with regard to achieving sustainable peace and social reconstruction. In this process, some measure of accountability and redress might be more significantly reached when the key restorative values of participation and acknowledgment are given a central place.

Notes

1 One helpful definition of 'informal justice' is given by Abel who defines it as being 'unofficial (dissociated from state power), noncoercive

(dependent on rhetoric rather than force), nonbureaucratic, decentralized, relatively undifferentiated, and non-professional; its substantive and procedural rules are imprecise, unwritten, democratic, flexible, ad hoc, and particularistic' (Abel 1982).

2 These constitute the so-called Regulation 64 Panels owing to the Regulation that created them: UNMIK Regulation 2000/64. See also: http://www.unmikonline.org/justice/ijsd.htm.

3 Article 24(3) ICTY Statute.

4 See: http://www.un.org/icty/glance-e/index.htm.

5 Many authors have highlighted the shortcomings of international trials to achieve the purposes they set for themselves, particularly in what concerns their contribution to deterrence and reconciliation. Teitel, for example, highlights the failure of the ICTY 'to achieve pacification through deterrence and to accomplish reconciliation through the creation of historical narratives' (Teitel 1999).

6 See: http://www.unmikonline.org/regulations/2000/reg66-00.htm.

7 The mandate of the HPD was to handle 'claims for restitution of property lost through discrimination; claims for registration of informal property transactions; and claims by refugees and internally displaced persons who have lost possession of their homes but wish to return or transfer their property', and 'to compile a Kosovo-wide inventory of abandoned and vacant housing and to supervise the temporary allocation of such property for humanitarian purposes'. The HPCC had 'the exclusive power to resolve residential property legal disputes, issue eviction orders, and hand down final and binding decisions' (Djordjevic 2002).

8 More information is available at: http://www.kpaonline.org/aboutus.asp.

9 Possibly of Illyrian origin going back to the fifth century BC.

10 The Kanun was an oral tradition and no written form existed until 1913 when a Franciscan priest Shtjefën Gjeçovi from Janjeve, Kosovo started codifying the laws and published them in 1933. The aim of the 1,262 articles of the Kanun was to regulate every aspect of the social lives of the Albanians: economic and family life, hospitality, brotherhood, clan, boundaries, marriage, land, local government, settlement of disputes and so on (Alibali 1977; Hasluk 1954: 381).

11 The communist leader Enver Hoxha (1944–85) described the blood feud as a legacy of feudalism, and officially outlawed the use of the Kanun. Under his regime it was strictly forbidden to 'defend the honour of the family'. Anyone practising the customs was severely punished; murderers were condemned to death and their families driven into isolated areas of the Prokletije Mountains.

12 Numerous statistical accounts from Albania and Kosovo point out the importance of certain segments of the Kanun laws for 'ordinary' Albanians: ORT (funded by a US AID Democracy grant) nationwide survey from 1997; a recent survey on the Kanun by the Independent

Social Studies Centre, Eureka; a study by the National Reconciliation Committee; a study by the Albanian NGO, 'MJAFT!'; estimates by the Albanian Ministry of Public Order; a survey conducted by the Law Faculty of Tirana University in March 2000; a cross-national survey from 2006 led by Arsovska (2007) in Albania, Kosovo and Macedonia.

13 The use of the term 'restorative justice philosophy', which is a synonym for 'restorative justice approach' in this chapter, goes along the line of thought of Walgrave: the author states 'restorative justice is not defined as a particular type of action, but as an option, a philosophy, a way of looking at crime and its aftermaths' (Walgrave, unpublished; see also Walgrave 2008: 621).

14 Arsovska (2007) found that a significant number of ethnic Albanian people are in favour of combining formal and informal justice mechanisms (although they do not know them well) in order to achieve best results for resolving conflicts in the Kosovo context. However, this as well as many other answers of the Albanian respondents in this survey point to the high level of social confusion that can be observed in Kosovo and the region. Arsovska (2007) explains that 51.5 per cent of the respondents (374 out of 726) agreed or strongly agreed that their country needs a strong dictator and harsher prison sentences in order to fight criminality. Additionally 15.2 per cent remained undecided and 30.7 per cent disagreed or strongly disagreed. Interestingly, 210 out of 726 respondents (28.9 per cent) respondents agreed or strongly agreed with the statement: 'The democratic legal system of the "Western world" cannot be a model for our country since it is incompatible with our culture/traditions', 70 remained undecided (23.4 per cent) and 344 respondents (47.3 per cent) disagreed (see also Arsovska and Verduyn 2008).

15 This idea derives from Zehr's widely celebrated understanding of crime as a violation of people and relationships rather than an offence against the state (Zehr 1990). See also the third paragraph of the Preamble to the UN Basic Principles on the Use of Restorative Justice Programmes in Criminal Matters, where it is stated that 'restorative justice [...] builds understanding, and promotes social harmony through the healing of victims, offenders and communities' (UNESC 2002).

16 In support of this, Halpern and Weinstein state: 'We hypothesize that one of the fundamental components of reconciliation between former enemies is the development of empathy, which we describe as a fundamentally individualizing view of another' (Halpern and Weinstein 2004).

17 In this context, Ajdukovic argues that 'A very important aspect of social context that can help the community in the healing process is the public perception of justice and accountability for crimes committed during times of violence' (Ajdukovic 2006).

References

Abel, R. (ed.) (1982) *The Politics of Informal Justice: Comparative Studies*, Vol. 2. New York: Academic Press.

Ajdukovic, D. (2006) 'Barriers to social reconstruction of communities', in U. Ewald and K. Turkovic (eds), *Large-scale Victimisation as a Potential Source of Terrorist Activities*. Amsterdam: IOS Press, pp. 269–77.

Alibali, A. (1977) 'On the current situation of Albanian law and the challenges for the next century', *International Journal of Albanian Studies*, 1 (1). See: http://albanian.com/IJAS/voll/isl/art3.html.

Arsovska, J. (2006) 'Understanding a "culture of violence and crime": the Kanun of Lek Dukagjini and the rise of the Albanian sexual-slavery rackets', *European Journal of Crime, Criminal Law and Criminal Justice*, 14 (2): 161–84.

Arsovska, J. and Craig, M. (2006) '"Honourable" behaviour and the conceptualisation of violence in ethnic-based organised crime groups: an examination of the Albanian Kanun and the code of the Chinese triads', *Global Crime*, 7 (2): 214–46.

Arsovska, J. and Verduyn, P. (2008) 'Globalisation, Conduct Norms and "Culture Conflict": Perceptions of Violence and Crime in an Ethnic Albanian Context', *British Journal of Criminology* (forthcoming, doi:10.1093/bjc/azm068).

Biberaj, E. (1995) 'Albania', in Z. Barany and I. Volgyes (eds), *The Legacies of Communism in Eastern Europe*. Baltimore, MD: Johns Hopkins University Press, pp. 245–66.

Camaj, M. (1989) *The Code of Lekë Dukagjini*, trans. Leonard Fox, compiled by Shtjefën Gjeçovi. New York: Gjonlekaj Publishing.

Craig, N.R. (2003) *War in the Balkans 1991–2002*. Carlisle Barracks, PA: US Army War College.

Djordjevic, D. (2002) *A Casualty of Politics: Overview of Acts and Projects of Reparation on the Territory of the Former Yugoslavia*. New York: ICTJ.

Durham, M.E. (1994) *High Albania*, 2nd edn. London: Edward Arnold.

Farnam, A. (2003) 'Gun culture stymies the UN in Kosovo', *Christian Science Monitor*, 26 September.

Fox, L. (trans.) (1989) *The Code of Lekë Dukagjini/Kaunui I Lekë Dukagjinit*, compiled by Shtjefën Gjeçovi. New York: Gjonlekaj Publishing.

Gjeçovi, Sh. (ed.) (1933) *The Code of Lekë Dukagjini*. Prishtina: Rilindja.

Gjoka, R. (2000) *Reality and Tradition in the Mediation Process in Albania*. Report based on presentations from a seminar on 'Albanian and Norwegian Experiences in Conflicts: Mediation in Cases of Violent Conflicts', May. Oslo: University of Oslo, pp. 5–11.

Halpern, J. and Weinstein, H.M. (2004) 'Empathy and rehumanization after mass violence', in E. Stover and H.M. Weinstein (eds), *My Neighbor, My Enemy: Justice and Community in the Aftermath of Mass Atrocity*. New York: Cambridge University Press, pp. 303–22.

Hasluck, M. (1954) *The Unwritten Law in Albania*. Cambridge: Cambridge University Press.

Human Rights Watch (1999) 'Abuses against Serbs and Roma in the New Kosovo', August, 11 (10). See: http://www.hrw.org/reports/1999/kosov2/.

International Commission on the Balkans (2005) *The Balkans in Europe's Future*. Sofia: Center for Liberal Strategies.

Johnstone, G. and Van Ness, D.W. (2007) 'The meaning of restorative justice', in G. Johnstone and D.W. Van Ness (eds), *Handbook of Restorative Justice*. Cullompton: Willan, pp. 5–23.

Jolis, B. (1997) 'Honour killing makes a comeback', *Albanian Life*, 57 (1): 25–35 (reprinted from *The Guardian*, 14 August 1996). See: http://www.gendercide.org/case_honour.html.

Kadare, I. (2003) *Broken April*. London: Vintage.

Leebaw, B. (2001) 'Restorative justice for political transitions: lessons from the South African Truth and Reconciliation Commission', *Contemporary Justice Review*, 4 (3/4): 267–89.

McClear, S. (2001) *Albanians and Their Culture: A Study of Their Defining Character and Uniqueness*. MA thesis, California State University.

Malcom, N. (1998) *Kosovo: A Short History*. New York: New York University Press.

Meernik, J. (2005) 'Justice and peace? How the International Criminal Tribunal affects societal peace in Bosnia', *Journal of Peace Research*, 42 (3): 271–89.

Minnesota Lawyers International Human Rights Committee (1992) *Trimming the Cat's Claws: The Politics of Impunity in Albania*. Minneapolis, MN: MLIHRC.

Mortimer, M. and Toader, A. (2005) 'Blood feuds blight Albanian lives', *BBC World Service*, 23 September.

Neza, A. (1997) *Albania*. Tirana: Albin Publishing House.

O'Donnell, J. (1995) 'Albania's Sigurimi. The ultimate agents of social control', *Problems of Post-Communism*, 42 (6): 18–23.

Riber, B.H. (2003) 'The Mediator of Blood'. Unpublished paper, Oslo University College.

Sahiti, E. (2006) *Reasoning in the Criminal Procedure*. Prishtina: University of Prishtina.

Sarkin, J. (2005) 'Reparations for gross human rights violations as an outcome of criminal versus civil court proceedings', in K. De Feyter, S. Parmentier, M. Bossuyt and P. Lemmens (eds), *Out of the Ashes. Reparation for Victims of Gross and Systematic Human Rights Violations*. Antwerp and Oxford: Intersentia, pp. 151–88.

Schvey, A.A. (2003) 'Striving for accountability in the former Yugoslavia', in J. Stromseth (ed.), *Accountability for Atrocities: National and International Responses*. New York: Transnational, pp. 39–85.

Schwandner-Sievers, S. (1998) 'Wer besitzt die Lizens zum Toten in Albanien? Oder Fragen zur Gruppensolidarität und Gewaltlegitimation in einer anderen Modernisierung', in J. Kohler and S. Heyer (eds), *Anthropologie der Gewalt*. Verlag für Wissenschaft und Forschung, pp. 71–88.

Sofos, S.A. (1996) 'Culture, politics and identity in former Yugoslavia', in S.A. Sofos and B. Jenkins (eds), *Nation and Identity in Contemporary Europe*. London and New York: Routledge, pp. 251–82.

Stovel, L. (2006) Presentation at COST Action A21 Final Conference 'Restorative Justice Research in Europe: Outcomes and Challenges', Warsaw, 22–24 November.

Teitel, R. (1999) 'Bringing the Messiah through the law', in C. Hesse and R. Post (eds), *Human Rights in Political Transitions: Gettysburg to Bosnia*. New York: Zone, pp. 177–94.

Umbreit, M. (2001) *The Handbook of Victim Offender Mediation: An Essential Guide to Practice and Research*. San Francisco: Jossey-Bass.

UNCHR (2005) *Basic Principles and Guidelines on the Right to a Remedy and Reparation for Victims of Gross Violations of International Human Rights Law and Serious Violations of International Humanitarian Law*, Human Rights Resolution 2005/35.

UNESC (2002) *Basic Principles on the Use of Restorative Justice Programmes in Criminal* Matters, UN Economic and Social Council Resolution 2002/12.

Valiñas, M. and Vanspauwen, K. (2006) *The Promise of Restorative Justice in the Search for Truth after a Violent Conflict. Experiences from South Africa and Bosnia-Herzegovina*. Paper presentation at the Fourth Conference of the European Forum for Restorative Justice, 'Restorative Justice and Beyond – An Agenda for Europe', Barcelona, Spain, 14–17 June.

Van Ness, D. (2002) 'The shape of things to come', in E.G.M. Weitekamp and H.-J. Kerner (eds), *Restorative Justice: Theoretical Foundations*. Cullompton: Willan, pp. 1–20.

Van Ness, D. and Strong, K.H. (1997) *Restoring Justice*. Cincinnati, OH: Anderson.

Vickers, M. (1997) *The Albanians: A Modern History*. New York: Tauris Press.

Waldmann, P. (2001) 'Revenge without rules: on the renaissance of an archaic motif of violence', *Studies in Conflict and Terrorism*, 24: 435–50.

Walgrave, L. (2008) 'Restorative Justice: An Alternative for Responding to Crime?', in S.G. Shoham, O. Beck and M. Kett (eds), *International Handbook of Penology and Criminal Justice*. Boca Raton, London and New York: CRC Press, pp. 613–89.

Walgrave, L. (n.d.) 'Restoring Peace After War Through Restorative Justice'. Unpublished.

Zehr, H. (1990) *Changing Lenses: A New Focus for Crime and Justice*. Scottdale, PA: Herald Press.

Section 2
The Israeli–Palestinian conflict

Holger-C. Rohne, Doina Balahur,
Sarah Ben-David and Beni Jakob

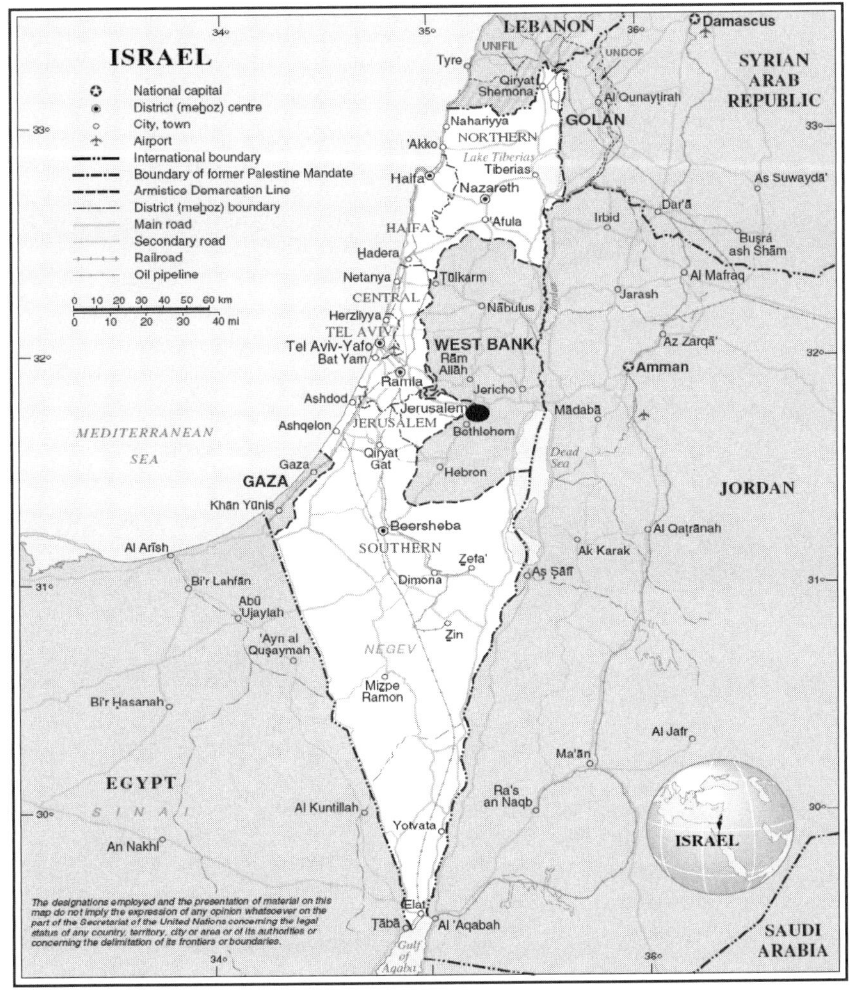

Based on UN map No. 3584 Rev. 2 (January 2004)

Chapter 8

The Israeli–Palestinian conflict and the second intifada – a cycle of violence

Holger-C. Rohne[1]

The Israeli–Palestinian conflict has been drawing the world's attention for more than half a century now. It is a protracted and multifaceted conflict. It seems to be symptomatic that the beginning of the conflict's history is already in dispute. Although the conflict can be traced back at least to the early nineteenth century, especially in the first half of the twentieth century the tensions between Arabs and Jews increased. In the second half of the century the tensions turned into a constant struggle between them. A vicious cycle of violence and counter-violence began which never really ceased; instead, it repeatedly culminated in dramatic escalations. The focus of the following chapters will be mainly set upon violence that occurred during the latest conflict period, the second intifada (also called *Al Aqsa intifada*[2]) which erupted in September 2000.

Since the historical and political complexity of the Israeli–Palestinian conflict makes it difficult to view the different periods of conflict separately, a discussion on violence during the second intifada also needs to be contextualised in the conflict's history and its burdensome legacy of previous decades. Therefore, some benchmarks of the conflict-riddled history are outlined below.

Introduction to and history of the conflict

In the beginning of the nineteenth century the Jewish population in the region was comparatively low. During the second half of the century an increasing number of Jews immigrated, and especially in the first half of the twentieth century when many fled in the course of their persecution by the Nazis. Tensions arose between the Arab majority and the growing Jewish population. Due to the developments of the First World War and the regional interests of the *entente cordiale,* Arabs and Jews alike sought for international backing for their plans to create their own sovereign state in Palestine. This led to contradictory promises – the Sykes-Picot agreement (1916) on one hand and the Balfour declaration (1917) on the other – to support the foundation of respectively an Arab and a Jewish state in the region.

On 29 November 1947, the UN General Assembly voted on the Partition Plan to establish both an Arab and a Jewish state. Although neither side was happy with it, the Partition Plan was approved by the Jewish Agency as the Jewish representation but rejected by the representatives of the neighbouring Arab states. The British mandate ended on 14 May 1948. On 15 May 1948, David Ben Gurion declared the establishment and independence of the State of Israel as it was outlined in the UN Partition Plan. In response, the armies of Lebanon, Syria, Jordan, Egypt and Iraq declared war against Israel. The following battles claimed numerous lives on both sides. Ambushes and guerrilla tactics especially caused suffering among the civilian population. A considerable part of the local – mainly Arab – population was expelled or left their homes to escape the danger of fighting. A large part of the Arab population found themselves uprooted. Thus, this period was named 'Al Nakbah' (arab. 'catastrophe'), intending to draw a parallel to the Jewish 'Shoa', the Holocaust.

Armistice agreements were signed in 1949 which resulted in a temporary cessation of the fighting. It did not, however, solve the main source of dispute, namely the partition of the territory. Moreover, the fighting during the 1948 war led to territorial changes deviating from the UN Partition Plan. Consequently, the tensions never ceased but rose again in light of inter-state tensions between Israel and its neighbouring countries on one hand and the Palestinians on the other who lived in the West Bank and the Gaza Strip under Jordanian and Egyptian administration respectively. In the following decades the region witnessed various wars, including the Suez War (1956), the Six Day War (1967), the war of Attrition (1970), the October War (or Yom Kippur War – 1973) and the Lebanon War (1982). The war in 1967 resulted in an extension of territorial control by Israel, including the West Bank, the Gaza Strip and East Jerusalem; the latter was later annexed to the State of Israel (Gelvin 2005; Gilbert 1993). Peace treaties were signed between Israel and Egypt in 1979 as well as between Jordan and Israel in 1994. The treaties stabilised the relations between the respective parties and resolved their territorial disputes. But the dispute between the Palestinians and the Israelis remained unsolved.

On 2 June 1964, the Palestine Liberation Organisation (PLO) was founded in order to engage for the right of Palestinian refugees and for the abolition of the State of Israel. The PLO was later acknowledged as the Palestinian representation. On 9 December 1987, growing tensions between the Palestinian population and Israel culminated in the eruption of a popular resistance, the first intifada. The violent confrontations lasted for seven years causing the death and injury of many, especially Palestinians but also Israelis (Abu-Amr 1994: 53; O'Ballance 1998; Noble and Efrat 1990). On 15 November 1988, an independent State of Palestine was proclaimed by the Palestinian National Council meetings in Algiers with a vote of 253 to 46. Only in the early 1990s did the violence subside after the PLO and the Israeli government entered into secret talks. The latter led to the Oslo Peace Accords (in 1993 and 1995) which officially ended the first intifada. The Oslo agreements included the mutual acknowledgment and establishment of the Palestinian National Authority (PA) as an interim Palestinian governmental body for the West Bank and the Gaza Strip.

The second intifada

Background

In the succeeding years the peace process stagnated and the relations worsened again after the Oslo agreements were not implemented to the satisfaction of either party. In the following years the Israeli–Palestinian tensions grew and the economic distress within the Palestinian population increased. In September 2000, the Camp David negotiations between Yasser Arafat and Ehud Barak failed which finally triggered the latest popular uprising, the second intifada. Memories of the first intifada awakened. The situation quickly escalated and on both sides the widespread use of massive force was seen as a legitimate means to accomplish the respective goals. International attempts to revive the peace process were manifested, for example, in the so called *road map* which is supported by the quartet of the UN, the EU, the US and Russia. Its implementation, however, has not yet been successful.

Equally, the unilateral declaration of a temporary truce by Hamas and Islamic Jihad in June 2003 was also not successful: Israel suspected this truce to be a means for the militant organisations to reorganise their considerably weakened infrastructures. Although a noticeable low in the conduct of violence was apparent (see Figure 8.1 page 221), on both sides violence was soon revived: Israel pursued to eleminate or capture wanted members of militant organisations. At the same time Islamic Jihad, the Al-Aqsa Brigades and later also Hamas have continued to conduct militant operations.

In November 2004 Yasser Arafat died and Mahmud Abbas became his successor as Palestinian president and leader of his secular Fatah party. In February 2005, Abbas met with Israel's then prime minister Ariel Sharon, the Egyptian President Hosni Mubarak and the Jordanian King Abdullah II in Sharm el-Sheikh in order to end the fighting on the basis of the road map. In separate declarations Abbas and Sharon announced the end of the second intifada. The Sharm el-Sheikh agreement was initially backed by the autonomous Palestinian organisations. However, in the following years violence continued, albeit at a lower level.[3] In January 2006, Hamas won the elections and replaced the then ruling Fatah party in the PA. This in turn led to international isolation of the Hamas-led Palestinian government due to its radical stance towards Israel and previous agreements between the PA and Israel. The relations between the PA and Israel worsened again and internal tensions between Fatah and Hamas increased. Especially in the Gaza Strip members of Hamas and Fatah confronted each other repeatedly in deadly clashes.[4]

Actors in the armed confrontations

Soon after the eruption of violence, the main actors in this new round of violence became clear. On the Israeli side, operations were generally directed by the Israeli government and conducted by state forces, especially the army (Israeli Defense Forces (IDF)). On various occasions Israeli police and border police forces were involved in violent incidents. Militant civilians played a rather marginal role in the total number of confrontations.[5]

On the Palestinian side the situation was far more complex. The role of the PA was rather ambiguous and to a certain extent unclear. Prior to the intifada the Palestinian security forces (Preventive Security Services (PSS)) partially cooperated with the Israeli security forces as agreed in the Oslo Accords. This changed immediately after the onset of the intifada. The PA and the PSS were accused of supporting the intifada at least indirectly. The PA infrastructure became a direct target for Israeli military operations which paralysed its administrative and security capacities. The tension between Israel and the PA was illustrated by Arafat's house arrest at his Muqata headquarters in Ramallah until his death in November 2004.

Besides the tension with Israel internal factors were essential for the weakening of the PA. The lack of a regular Palestinian army necessarily facilitated the involvement of paramilitary organisations in the confrontations with Israel. The PA had no means to control these organisations in the armed struggle against Israel. At the same time the PA was facing increasing internal criticism. Being accused of corruption and failure to effectively represent the public's economic and national interests, the PA aimed to prove its relevance in the struggle against Israel (Hammami and Tamari 2001: 20). However, various autonomous militant organisations gained public support due to their internal opposition to the PA but also for being the more 'effective' power in the Palestinian fight against Israel.

This was especially true for the radical Islamic Hamas (arab. *Harakat al-Muqaqamah al-Islamiyyah*).[6] Hamas was founded during the beginning of the first intifada in 1987 and originates in a Palestinian branch of the Egyptian Muslim Brotherhood. Hamas continued to pursue the social and religious philosophy of the Muslim Brotherhood, namely to reach a societal adoption of Islamic rules in all aspects of life. However, in contrast to the Muslim Brotherhood, Hamas supported the use of violent means in the struggle against Israel (Abu-Amr 1993). As indicated above, it strongly opposed the politics of the PA, especially its political dialogue with Israel and the mutual recognition between the parties (Robinson 1997: 132; Kristianasen 1999). According to the internal and external objectives Hamas pursued, it consisted of a political, a social and a military wing. Their popularity was based on the activities of each wing, namely Hamas' opposition to the PA politics, the provision of urgently needed social infrastructure and its leading role in the conduct of militant operations against Israeli targets (Jamal 2006: 245; Abu-Amr 1994; Mishal and Sela 2000). The latter were conducted by the military wing, the *Izz al-Din al-Qassam* Brigades. Their operations also included a high number of bombings against Israeli civilians (Human Rights Watch 2002: 66).

Another influential radical Islamic militant organisation is the Islamic Jihad (arab. *Harakat al-Jihad al-Islami*). It had been founded by students at the Islamic University of Gaza already before the first intifada began. It also originates from the Muslim Brotherhood. Contrary to Hamas, it did not openly question Yasser Arafat notwithstanding its opposition to the Oslo agreements. The group is said to have ties to Iran and looks up to the Iranian Islamic revolution as an example (Abu-Amr 1994: 91; Hatina 2001). The military wing of Islamic Jihad, *Saraya al-Quds*, has launched its operations either alone or in cooperation with Hamas as well as secular groups. Its attacks frequently included ambushes and the use of human bombs against civilian targets (Human Rights Watch 2002: 71).

Relevant secular organisations are the Al-Aqsa Brigades and the Popular Front for the Liberation of Palestine (PFLP). The Al-Aqsa Brigades were founded after the second intifada broke out. They claimed responsibility for numerous bombing and shooting attacks. The Al-Aqsa Brigades are said to be affiliated with the aforementioned Fatah movement. During the time of Fatah-ruled government they were therefore considered as the military arm of the PA, aiming to restore the public image of the PA and to counterbalance the military relevance of the Islamic groups in the intifada (Human Rights Watch 2002: 78; Palestinian Centre for Human Rights 2004: 27).

The PFLP was founded in 1967 as a marxist-anticapitalist organisation and has been a member of the PLO since 1968 (except for their temporary absence in protest of the Oslo agreements). During the second intifada its military wing, the Abu-Ali-Mustafa Brigades, were responsible for various bombing attacks (Human Rights Watch 2002: 87).

Fatalities on both sides

The violent clashes during the second intifada had devastating consequences for the daily life of many and for the economy of both societies. The suffering of the civilians has many facets that cannot be grasped in the limited scope of this introduction but have been the subject of earlier elaborations (Kiza *et al.* 2006: 80; Rohne 2007). The present focus is set on the worst form of victimisation, namely the loss of human lives that were claimed on both sides.

According to B'tselem, an Israeli human rights organisation, more than 4,300 people were killed in total and many more wounded from the eruption of the second intifada to the end of 2005.[7] In this period B'tselem counted 3,345 Palestinians who were killed by the IDF and other state forces; another 41 Palestinians fell victim to violence from Israeli civilians or settlers. In total, 112 people were killed by their

Palestinian fellow men for their alleged collaboration with Israel. The Palestinian Red Crescent Society (PRCS) reported a total of 3,771 Palestinian victims up to the end of 2005.[8]

Almost all of the Palestinian fatalities occurred in the West Bank and the Gaza Strip. For the aforementioned period, B'tselem reports 56 Palestinians who were killed inside Israel. Among the fatalities were 1,476 people that could be identified as not having taken part in violent confrontations at the time of their death while 985 people were involved in hostilities when being killed. Up to the end of 2005, 203 persons were killed during 'extrajudicial' (or 'targeted') killings carried out by the Israeli army in order to eliminate members of militant organisations which, due to their prior involvement in clashes, were regarded by Israel as 'ticking bombs'. Among them were leading figures of Hamas, Islamic Jihad and the PFLP.

On the Israeli side, B'tselem reported a total of 994 Israeli fatalities up to the end of 2005. As among the Palestinian fatalities, the number of killed civilians was much higher than of fallen combatants. The civilian fatalities amounted to 683, almost two-thirds of them (N = 455) being killed inside Israel. In total, 311 people were members of the Israeli army or other security forces. The majority of them (N = 225) were killed in the West Bank and the Gaza Strip. According to the Israeli government the Israeli fatalities amounted to 1,084 (up to 15 January 2006), including 761 civilians and 323 members of the IDF or other security forces.[9]

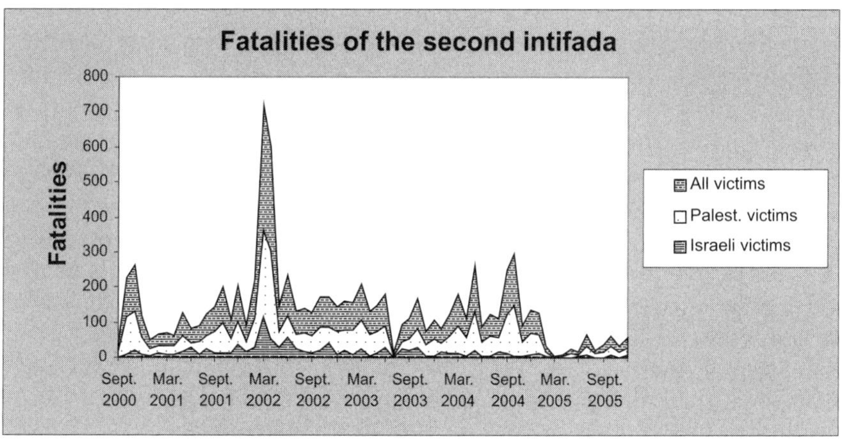

Source: Rohne (2007) data by B'tselem (2006).

Figure 8.1 Fatalities of the second intifada

Typically, on both sides the use of violence is declared retaliation for a previous attack. A review of the intifada fatalities does indeed reveal a cycle of violence. As suggested in Figure 8.1, a wave of violence from one side was typically followed by an intensification of attacks from the other side, and vice versa: a decrease in violence on one side was also frequently accompanied by a decrease in attacks from the other side. This gives reason to believe that these claims are not just rhetoric but also reflect the actual politics of conduct.

This becomes especially apparent during the aforementioned unilateral declaration of truce (*hudna*) in June 2003 by the Palestinian militant organisations: although mistrusted by Israel, the number of Palestinian fatalities were significantly declining in that time. This is also the case in the period following the Sharm el-Sheikh agreement between Sharon and Abbas in February 2005. Certainly, a too simplistic conclusion must be avoided since the figures do not take into account the failed attacks as well as concomitant national and international developments that also might have affected the conduct of violence. However, Figure 8.1 does reveal the applied logic of retaliation and also of a reciprocical interaction between attack and counter-attack.

From macro to micro: a case study as example

A discussion of the total number of casualties typically keeps the focus on the overall conflict and prevents a view at the micro-level: the interpersonal dimension. This seems logical since the macro-conflict is the *conditio sine qua non* for each attack conducted. In addition, the ever increasing number of victims tends to mask the individual tragedy in the public debate. Yet, it might be illusionary to believe that restoring peace needs only the settlement of the overall political conflict. This means largely ignoring the wounds that had already been created among individuals. Violent victimisation strongly affects lives of individuals, families and the social environment. They have severe implications for future relations between the opposing collectives and its members (Volkan 1991: 86). It is a persistent sense of victimisation that causes them to support the overall confrontation. Moreover, the motivation to get personally involved in future hostilities is often based on a personal experience of victimisation and hatred (Braithwaite 2002: 184). It is beyond doubt that a political solution is desperately needed. But it is dangerous to degrade the individual victims to numbers in the body count of 'collateral damage'. Instead, the personal experience of victimisation requires a response on a (inter-)personal level that corresponds to the needs of those who were personally involved and affected – a task that cannot be tackled at the macro level. It needs a restoration that includes but goes beyond the settlement of the overall conflict.[10]

With the following case study we leave the macro level and 'zoom' into the micro level. At the same time the case study contextualises the particular incidents in the overall conflict. In the centre of the case study is a bombing on 11 June 2003 near the Mahane Yehuda market. This bombing is closely related to other violent incidents prior and after its conduct. It is understood to be a response to earlier Israeli violence while at the same time it provokes further counter-strikes. Other examples could have been chosen with the same legitimacy. However, the embedding of the present case in a deadly 'chain of incidents' reveals the cyclical dynamics of violence in the Israeli–Palestinian conflict. It is the explicit referral to earlier violence as a means to justify further violence that characterises this case study. It therefore illustrates very well the interrelatedness of violence and counter-violence. It also shows how civilians can become part – or even the centre – of hostilities. Lastly, the 'zoom' into the micro level reveals the interpersonal dimension of violence being conducted in the course of a collective conflict. The involvement of individuals – combatant or civilian, perpetrator or victim – give reason to analyse existing mechanisms to respond to such violence as is done in the following chapters.

In Chapters 9–12 various formal and informal mechanisms of conflict resolution are introduced that can be found in the Israeli or Palestinian society. These instruments are then analysed with regard to their applicability to the violence occurring in the context of the second intifada. In Chapter 9, Khalid Ghanayim describes and critically discusses the application of domestic and international legal responses to violence occurring in the Israeli–Palestinian conflict. Following this, informal mechanisms that exist in the respective societies are explored. In Chapter 10, Michal Alberstein introduces informal approaches which exist in Jewish tradition and the present Israeli society. Correspondingly, George Irani discusses traditional approaches to conflict resolution from a Palestinian perspective (Chapter 11). Finally, the prospects for restorative justice approaches are discussed: in Chapter 12, Holger-C. Rohne first introduces empirical data giving a voice to Palestinian and Israeli intifada victims with regard to their view on how to respond to their victimisation. Based on the theoretical and empirical insight provided by all the papers in this section, Chapter 12 closes with the discussion of opportunities for and limits to restorative justice in the context of the Israeli–Palestinian conflict.

In Focus: The Mahane Yehuda bombing and its context

On 8 June 2003 various violent incidents claimed the lives of Palestinian militants and Israeli soldiers. Among them were those who were killed in a joint attack by Hamas, the Islamic Jihad and the Al-Aqsa Martyrs Brigade in which a Palestinian wearing an Israeli Defense Force (IDF) uniform opened fire on an IDF outpost near the Erez checkpoint and industrial zone in the Gaza Strip. This attack also caused the injury of four IDF soldiers.[11]

Israel responded to those attacks on 10 June 2003 when it launched a helicopter strike in Gaza City in an attempt to kill a senior Hamas official Abdel Aziz Rantisi, then leader of the Gazan Hamas, and in order to severely damage the organisational infrastructure of Hamas.[12] Rantisi was wounded; another passenger and a bystander were killed. About 27 people were injured in this attack. On the same day, three other Palestinian civilians were killed in the course of another attempted targeted killing of Hamas members next to the Jabalya refugee camp, North Gaza district.[13]

The retaliatory attack against Israel was not long in coming: on 11 June 2003 a Palestinian blew himself up in a crowded bus in downtown Jerusalem. The attack occurred during rush hour, at around 5:30 p.m. when a man dressed as an ultra-Orthodox Jew boarded a bus at the Mahane Yehuda market. A short while later, as the bus drove down the Jaffa Road, the man detonated a bomb. The bomb wrecked the bus and killed 17 people. Among the killed were 15 Israeli civilians, a female soldier and a foreign worker from Ethiopia.[14] Over 100 people were reportedly wounded in this attack, including dozens of passersby.[15] The military wing of Hamas claimed responsibility for the attack stating that it was in retaliation for the previous strike on Rantisi. According to BBC News, Hamas announced on its website that the bombing was the 'first in a new series of operations [...] targeting every Zionist usurping our land'. [16]

Israel responded swiftly when it stepped up its attacks against Hamas in the following days. Only hours after the bombing at Mahane Yehuda market, a helicopter strike was launched in Gaza City targeting and killing a senior leader of the Hamas military wing, Massoud Titi, who was believed to be behind the rocket-firing on Israel, as well as Suhil Abu Nahel, another Hamas member who was an aide to the Hamas spiritual leader Ahmed Yassin. Furthermore, six civilian bystanders were killed in this attack.[17] Following this numerous violent operations were carried out on both sides leaving many dead and many more injured and further fuelling the cycle of violence and counter-violence.

Notes

1 The data presented in this chapter stems from earlier research done by the author (Rohne 2007). The case study ('In Focus') stems from preparatory work done in cooperation with Professor Doina Balahur, Dr Sarah Ben-David and Dr Beni Jacob. The author owes thanks to Mustafa Abdelbaqi, Dr Peretz Segal and Professor Finn Tschudi for their invaluable comments on earlier drafts of this chapter.

2 The term 'al-Aqsa intifada' is sometimes objected to because of a perceived political connotation. Among the Israelis some would argue the term implies getting rid of the Israelis (or 'shaking off' = intifada) as the ultimate goal (= 'al-Aqsa'). Most Israelis, however, understand this term as pointing to a critical event in the beginning of the second intifada when the then opposition leader Ariel Sharon visited the Temple Mount on which the al-Aqsa mosque is situated.

3 Also in February 2005, the Israeli parliament decided on a unilateral withdrawal from the Gaza Strip, which was accomplished in September 2005. The withdrawal caused internal tensions among the Palestinian political factions and organisations but also among the Israeli political factions.

4 Later in 2006 Israel entered Lebanon in an attempt to fight the Lebanese Shiite militant organisation Hisbullah that prior to this had kidnapped two Israeli soldiers and launched rocket attacks on the North of Israel. The Israeli invasion led to international criticism especially due to the civilian losses among the Lebanese population.

5 See statistics presented by B'tselem on its website at: http://www.btselem.org/english/statistics/Casualties.asp.

6 As indicated above, Hamas later won the election and took over the Palestinian government with Ismael Haniyeh as prime minister. Hroub (2006) points to internal changes within Hamas in the course of its experiences as government.

7 The following numbers stem from an earlier analysis (Rohne 2007) and are based on data collected by B'tselem. Its records of incidents and fatalities make this source one of the most transparent and reliable sources available. See details at: http://www.btselem.org/english/statistics/Casualties.asp. An overview for the first three years was provided in an earlier publication (see Rohne 2006: 81–83).

8 For further information, see the PRCS website at: http://www.palestinercs.org/crisistables/table_of_figures.htm. Unfortunately, the

PRCS statistics do not provide a traceable account of incidents and fatalities.

9 See the website of the Israeli Defense Forces at: http://www1.idf.il/dover/site/mainpage.asp?sl=EN&id=22&docid=16703&clr=1&subject=14931&Pos=2&bScope=False. Like the PRCS data, these statistics do not provide a traceable account for incidents and fatalities.

10 It goes without saying that the multidimensional effects of victimisation, e.g. on psychological, physical and financial well-being cause the need for multifaceted support. Due to the scope of this volume, the following chapters are limited to approaches that primarily focus on the pursuit of 'justice'.

11 See B'tselem at http://www.btselem.org/English/Statistics/Casualties.asp; see also the protocol of the UN Security Council meeting 13 June 2003 (S/PV.4773) at: http://domino.un.org/unispal.nsf/e872be638a09135185256ed100546ae4/1648ae984bd1423c85256d48004b2322!OpenDocument.

12 For the perception of Rantisi by the Israeli government see the official website of the Israeli Ministry of Foreign Affairs at: http://www.mfa.gov.il/MFA/MFAArchive/2000_2009/2003/6/The%20Hamas%20leadership%20-%20Abd%20al-Aziz%20Rantisi.

13 See B'tselem records at: http://www.btselem.org/English/Statistics/Casualties_Data.asp?Category=1. Rantisi was assassinated on 17 April 2004, shortly after he was appointed Hamas leader after the assassination of Ahmed Yassin on 22 March 2004. Rantisi was killed in an air strike on his car hours after a bombing attack was carried out in a joint operation by Hamas and Al-Aqsa Brigades at the Erez industrial zone in Israel.

14 See: http://www.passia.org/publications/annual_seminar_reports/annual2003n.htm; for further details see B'tselem records at: http://www.btselem.org/English/Statistics/Casualties.asp.

15 See reports by the Israeli government at: http://www.mfa.gov.il/MFA/MFAArchive/2000_2009/2003/6/Suicide+bombing+of+Egged+bus+No+14A+in+Jerusalem+-.htm, and by Al-Jazeera (English) at: http://english.aljazeera.net/NR/exeres/8AF3A6E7-06E2-45A8-AF16-A7A743BE3A94.htm.

16 See http://news.bbc.co.uk/2/hi/middle_east/2983426.stm. The BBC News goes on to quote Mahmud al-Zahhar, a leading Hamas official, announcing in an interview for Qatari satellite TV station Al-Jazeera that Palestinian attacks on Israelis were imminent 'to show them that an eye is for an eye and a tooth for a tooth'.

17 For further information see: http://www.guardian.co.uk/israel/Story/0,,975640,00.html, and the protocol of UN Security Council meeting S/PV.4773 at: http://domino.un.org/unispal.nsf/e872be638a09135185256ed100546ae4/1648ae984bd1423c85256d48004b2322!OpenDocument. As indicated above, this deadly month ended with the unilateral declaration of a

temporary truce (arab. *hudna*) by Hamas and other militant organisations which Israel believed to be a manoeuvre to reorganise their weakened infrastructure.

References

Abu-Amr, Z. (1993) 'Hamas: a historical and political background', *Journal of Palestine Studies*, 22 (4): 5–19.

Abu-Amr, Z. (1994) *Islamic Fundamentalism in the West Bank and Gaza – Muslim Brotherhood and Islamic Jihad*. Bloomington, IN: Indiana University Press.

Braithwaite, J. (2002) *Restorative Justice and Responsive Regulation*. New York: Oxford University Press.

Gelvin, J.L. (2005) *The Israel-Palestine Conflict: 100 Years of War*. Cambridge: Cambridge University Press.

Gilbert, M. (1993) *The Arab-Israeli Conflict. Its History in Maps*. London: Weidenfeld & Nicolson.

Hammami, R. and Tamari, S. (2001) 'The second uprising: end or new beginning?', *Journal of Palestine Studies*, 30 (2): 5–25.

Hatina, M. (2001) *Islam and Salvation in Palestine – The Islamic Jihad Movement*. Tel Aviv: Syracuse University Press.

Hroub, K. (2006) 'A "new Hamas" through its new documents', *Journal of Palestine Studies*, 35 (4): 6–27.

Human Rights Watch (2002) *Erased in a Moment – Suicide Bombing Attacks against Israeli Civilians*. New York: Human Rights Watch.

Jamal, A. (2006) 'Political and ideological factors of conflict in Palestinian society', in H.-J. Albrecht, J.-M. Simon, H. Rezaei, H.-C. Rohne and E. Kiza (eds), *Conflicts and Conflict Resolution in Middle Eastern Societies – Between Tradition and Modernity*. Berlin: Duncker & Humblot, pp. 229–56.

Kiza, E., Rathgeber, C. and Rohne, H.-C. (2006) *Victims of War – An Empirical Study on War-Victimization and Victims' Attitudes towards Addressing Atrocities*. Hamburg: Hamburger Institut für Sozialforschung. See: http://www.his-online.de/cms.asp?H='79'&T=0&Plugin=10&HE=10&HEP=978-3-936096-73-6.

Kristianasen, W. (1999) 'Challenge and counterchallenge: Hamas's response to Oslo', *Journal of Palestine Studies*, 28 (3): 19–36.

Mishal, S. and Sela, A. (2000) *The Palestinian Hamas: Vision, Violence, and Coexistence*. New York: Columbia University Press.

Noble, A.G. and Efrat, E. (1990) 'Geography of the Intifada', *Geographical Review*, 80 (3): 288–307.

O'Ballance, E. (1998) *The Palestinian Intifada*. New York: St. Martin's Press.

Palestinian Centre for Human Rights (2004) 'Assassinations of Palestinians'. See: http://www.pchrgaza.ps/files/Reports/English/2005/kiiling7.pdf.

Robinson, G.E. (1997) *Building a Palestinian State: The Incomplete Revolution*. Bloomington, IN: Indiana University Press.

Rohne, H.-C. (2006) 'Approaches to respond to violent conflicts – victimological reflections in the context of the Al-Aqsa Intifada', in H.-J. Albrecht, J.-M. Simon, H. Rezaei, H.-C. Rohne and E. Kiza (eds), *Conflicts and Conflict Resolution in Middle Eastern Societies – Between Tradition and Modernity*. Berlin: Duncker & Humblot, pp. 79–98.

Rohne, H.-C. (2007) *Opferperspektiven im interkulturellen Vergleich. Eine viktimologische Studie im Kontext der Al-Aqsa Intifada*. Hamburg: Verlag Dr. Kovač.

Volkan, V.D. (1991) 'Psychoanalytic aspects of ethnic conflicts', in J.V. Montville (ed.), *Conflict and Peacekeeping in Multiethnic Societies*. New York: Lexington Books, pp. 81–92.

Chapter 9

Courting the intifada: discussing legal perspectives

Khalid Ghanayim

In September 2000 the latest period in the Palestinian–Israeli conflict – the second intifada – began. As outlined in Chapter 8, the intifada has been characterised by attacks, retaliation and counter-retaliation. This vicious cycle of violence has continued up until today. The present contribution discusses various legal aspects of how to respond to this cycle of violence and counter-violence. The case study of the Mahane Yehuda bombing (see Rohne: this volume, Chapter 8) serves as a starting point for the following analysis. In our examination of legal responses to the violence occurring in the context of the overall political conflict, we need to reflect upon international humanitarian law as well as on the application of domestic criminal law. The latter is of particular importance for the Israeli perspective. This is not because Israel is more affected by the violence conducted during the intifada than the Palestinian side. Instead, due to the well-established criminal justice system, Israel is challenged to balance and justify the (non-)application of its conventional criminal law on the one hand and international humanitarian law on the other. This situation is very much different in the Palestinian territories where the domestic judicial system is extremely weak.

This chapter therefore discusses not only aspects of international humanitarian law which are highly relevant for both sides, but also begins to describe the legal instruments of the Israeli legal system in order to deal with violence stemming from the second intifada, such as the Mahane Yehuda incident. It discusses the various relevant elements of crime and questions of liability. Due to the particular conduct of violence, the direct perpetrator who carried out the bombings is usually dead and can therefore no longer be subject of a legal response. Other forms of criminal liability are therefore the focus of such responses, namely the indirect perpetrator, the co-perpetrator, the instigator and the abettor.

Contextualising the case study within the Israeli legal framework

In the case of the Mahane Yehuda bombing, a member of the Hamas organisation blew himself up and caused the death and injury of many people. The Hamas organisation has been declared by Israel a terrorist organisation. With regard to attacks conducted by Hamas, there are far reaching legal implications for those who are affiliated with this organisation: leaders, members and other supporters of Hamas can be held responsible for the attacks due to various offences regulated by Israeli law, namely the prohibition of activities by unlawful – or terrorist – organisations according to the Emergency Defence Regulations 1945, the Prevention of Terrorism Ordinance 1948, the Unlawful Combatants Law 2002 and other elements of crimes in the Israeli Penal Law 1977.[1] In what follows, we analyse the relevance of these regulations for the conduct of political violence, such as the Mahane Yehuda bombing.

The Emergency Defence Regulations 1945 prohibit activities relating to an unlawful organisation,[2] including membership of and activities on behalf of such an association.[3] This comprises performing work for or providing services to such an association as well as participation in gatherings. The provision of places for the purpose of an unlawful association's gatherings, collecting money on behalf of the association and even acting as a representative of the association are prohibited. The mental element requires *mens rea*. However, in certain cases the burden of proving lack of *mens rea* is transferred to the accused in section 85.[4] 'The military case law has held that this offence includes also passive membership accompanied by consent to join the association' (quoted from Kedmi 1994: 1172). The same activities are prohibited by the Prevention of Terrorism Ordinance 1948[5] and the Penal Code 1977, sections 145–50.[6]

Due to the Mahane Yehuda bomber's affiliation to Hamas, the attack constitutes a liability for all persons connected with Hamas: this is the case for the leader of the Hamas organisation and includes persons who have influence on the organisation even if they are not official members of Hamas, e.g. the spiritual leader. But liability is also constituted for active and passive members, as well as for those who aided the organisation without holding membership. This includes, for example, those who constructed the explosive or provided materials for its construction and those who drove the bomber to the location, here the Mahane Yehuda area.

The bomber in the Mahane Yehuda incident caused the death of 17 people. Thus, the Penal Code offences of manslaughter and murder are also relevant in this case. Manslaughter is defined in section 298 of the Penal Code as 'causing the death of another person' with *mens rea*.[7] If the mental element is premeditation the offence might be qualified as murder according to section 300(a)(2) of the Penal Code.[8] Premeditation is dependent on the existence of three elements: (a) the decision to kill, i.e. an awareness of the possibility of causing death and a desire to bring it about; (b) preparation to cause the death; and (c) absence of provocation.

Provocation requires a provocative conduct of great force which takes place immediately before the act of killing. According to case law the test for determining provocation is subjective and objective, i.e. the provocative behaviour may impair the ability of a reasonable man to engage in a process of preparation and consideration of the outcome of his actions, whereas the subjective test means that the provocative behaviour actually affects the mental ability of the perpetrator to control himself.[9] In the case of the Mahane Yehuda bombing, the attack was in fact declared a retaliation for earlier Israeli strikes against Hamas leaders (see Rohne: this volume, Chapter 8). However, the attack was planned by various people and then executed by the bombers some time after the Israeli strikes were carried out. Hence, provocation cannot be assumed in this particular case. Instead, the special *mens rea* of premeditation was fulfilled by the bomber at the time of the attack. Thus, according to Israeli criminal law, the offence is qualified as murder.

In Israeli criminal law there are no clear rules relating to concurrent sentences, i.e. real and ideal concurrent sentences, as is the case in continental law. The prevailing view in the case law is that the court will impose the appropriate sentence on the convicted defendant. Generally, the courts will impose consecutive sentences for a number of offences; thus, for example, the Mahane Yehuda incident led to the death of 17 people. On being convicted of murder the punishment for the perpetrator would be 17 sentences of life imprisonment to be run consecutively.[10]

In the context of the Mahane Yehuda attack, the offence of *conspiracy* would probably also be considered relevant.[11] Conspiracy is defined in section 499 of the Penal Code as preparation in co-authorship. It is worth noting that until 1994 Israeli law adopted the doctrine of *solidarity liability* whereby a conspirator was liable for the offence even if his contribution did not exceed the stage of conspiracy (the doctrine of *actio illicita in causa*). In 1994 subsection (b) was introduced repealing the doctrine of solidarity liability and it was held that the laws of joint perpetrators would be determined in accordance with the general provisions of section 29 of the Penal Law.

Other offences connected to preparation are the 'possession of dangerous substances to commit a felony or misdemeanor' and 'providing means for the commission of a felony' according to sections 497 and 498 of the Penal Code. Both sections provide for a range of punishment of up to three years imprisonment. These offences are also relevant in the Mahane Yehuda bombing: Hamas members received the explosives and left it to the bomber to cause the death and injury of others.

Special attention should be drawn to the offence of 'incitement to violence or terror' according to section 144(d)(2) of the Penal Code. This offence was passed in 2002 in reaction to the intifada. It prohibits public calls to commit an act of violence as well as public statements that praise or sympathise with such acts of violence. Encouragement and support is prohibited as well as identification with such acts and the placing of a prohibited publication for the purpose of distribution. This offence is considered to be a 'political' crime, hence the charge needs the written consent of the Attorney General.[12] It is relevant for persons who publicly call for the commission of acts of violence against the Israeli people or who publish a statement praising or identifying with such an event. It further relates to acts that have already been committed and thereby prohibits the publication of 'martyr videos'.

As indicated above, another recent law is also relevant to the Mahane Yehuda incident: the law on the Imprisonment of Unlawful Combatants 2002.[13] This law is also a legislative reaction to the intifada. It permits the authorities to arrest an 'unlawful combatant' for a lengthy period of time. An unlawful combatant is defined as a person who has taken part in hostile acts in any way against the State of Israel or who is a member of a force which carries out hostile acts against the State of Israel and who does not have the status of prisoner of war in humanitarian international law, as specified in Article 4 of the Third Geneva Convention of 12 August 1949. According to the law, the Chief of General Staff can order the imprisonment of such a person if he has reasonable grounds to believe that his release will harm national security. The term 'unlawful combatant' and the Law of Imprisonment of Unlawful Combatants have both been subjected to sharp criticism (Mudrik-Even Chen 2005; Kremnitzer 2005; Kretzmer 2005: 171) since humanitarian international law does not recognise the category of unlawful combatants.

The military and civil system – interrelation of two Israeli legal systems

In the Israeli legal system, there are two systems, the military and the civil. The military system is composed of military courts and military prosecutors. It is headed by the Military Attorney General. The ordinary civil system consists of civil courts within the State of Israel and the State Attorney's Office headed by the Attorney General. The State of Israel can apply both legal systems to Palestinians who harm its interests, including security interests. An exclusive relationship exists between the two systems, in the sense that a defendant is only tried before one. However, no clear rules exist that distinctively determine the application of the respective system. For example, it was said that the imprisoned chairman of the Fatah movement in the West Bank and a member of the Palestinian Parliament, Marwan Barghouti, was tried before a civil court (and not a military court) because of his high political rank (Hajjar 2005: 234). On the other hand, the president of the Palestinian Parliament, Dr Aziz Dawik, and other members of the Parliament, accused of membership and leadership of a terrorist organisation, were tried before military courts. The civil system is preferable for the accused since it guarantees him several rights derived from due process such as knowing the facts leading to his conviction. Further, the judge in a military court can accept evidence which is prohibited in a civil court.

Acceptance and rejection of legal authority

The Palestinians deny the right of the State of Israel to prosecute them in Israeli courts and apply Israeli law to them. The defendants argue that Israeli courts 'represent the Israeli occupation and seek to defend the occupation'.[14] Accordingly, Marwan Barghouti declared in his trial before an Israeli court:

> I, as a Palestinian citizen, who lives in Ramallah under Israeli occupation, have the full right to oppose the Israeli occupation.

> I am against the occupation and I shall do everything to remove the occupation. [...] I do not understand why I am here. [...] I do not see that there is a single reason to arrest or to investigate or to prosecute me in this court. This is not the right way to treat leaders who were elected. I was elected in accordance with an agreement which was signed between the two parties, and in accordance with that agreement, I was elected a member of the Palestinian Parliament in free elections to the Palestinian Authority and to the Legislative Council. The Israeli court is not competent to arrest or try a Palestinian Member of Parliament, such a thing has never happened before. I live under the sovereignty of the Palestinian Authority in Ramallah; I was kidnapped in the Defensive Shield Campaign.[15]

The position taken by the Palestinians is not unfounded, as many studies show that Israeli courts – including the civil courts – automatically sanction the actions of the military regime, many of which are irreconcilable with the substantive requirements of international humanitarian law; the main aim of Israeli civil courts is not to criticise the unlawful acts of the army, but to try to find excuses for those unlawful acts. Judicial review, including that exercised by the Supreme Court, has accorded greater legitimacy to the occupying regime than protected human rights anchored in international law, even when the international legal view is different (Kretzmer 2002: 2–3, 187–8; Reichman 2004: 731, 733). This position is explained by the fact that Israeli judges perceive the courts as national courts; hence, in petitions which are perceived as part of the struggle of the State of Israel, they find it difficult to stand against the interests of the State of Israel (Kretzmer 2002: 118–19, 193–6; Reichman 2004: 751). In turn, the court is perceived as part of the occupying mechanism and not an objective judicial institution (Kretzmer 2002: 198; Reichman 2004: 751–3). The court identifies with the Zionist ethos and the Zionist narrative, i.e. Israeli and Jewish national ideology. Therefore there is a fundamental correlation between the ideology and world view of the judges and that of the general public (Barak-Erez 2003: 128–9; Barzilai *et al.* 1994: 199).

It can also be said that, generally, Palestinians are brought to court without representation. They reject the court's offer to appoint a public defender for the same reasons, namely that the public defence service represents the Israeli occupation and seeks to defend it. Even when the court does appoint a public defender, the defendants refuse to cooperate with them. They refuse to assert legal arguments and do not cross-examine witnesses (as happened, for example, in the Marwan Barghouti case).[16] The public defenders often ask to be released from representing defendants who do not wish to take advantage of their services.

Defences to criminal liability

Palestinians who perform acts which fall within the framework of criminal offences can refer to the general legal instruments of defence with regard to their criminal liability. This includes self-defence, necessity and duress. These defences are not applicable in the case of the Mahane Yehuda bombing as described by Rohne in Chapter 8 (in this volume). Instead, in such cases defences against criminal prosecution, such as immunity against prosecution and conviction, are highly relevant. These defences are examined below.

Competence to institute criminal prosecutions in Israel

The Israeli courts prosecute Palestinians who have participated in any activities against Israel in accordance with Israeli law. The application of Israeli penal law is regulated in sections 7 *et seq*. of the Penal Law. The Israeli court has the competence to try persons for domestic offences, i.e. offences committed within the jurisdiction of the State of Israel, as well as for foreign offences, i.e. persons suspected of committing offences against the State or against the Jewish people, or against a resident or citizen of Israel, and for criminal offences under international law (Kremnitzer and Cohen 2005: 364–7). The Mahane Yehuda attack was conducted in Jerusalem and is therefore a domestic offence. Accordingly, the competence of the Israeli court derives from section 9 together with section 7(a)(1).

The Palestinians generally raise the argument that by virtue of Regulation 2 of the Jurisdiction and Legal Aid Law, Israeli law is inapplicable to Palestinians. Regulation 2 states that '(a) In addition to the provisions of any law, the court in Israel will be competent to prosecute a person present in Israel in accordance with the law applicable in Israel, for his acts or omissions which took place in the territory as well as in Israel, for his acts or omissions which took place within the territory of the Palestinian Council, where the acts or omissions would have been offences had they taken place within the jurisdiction of the Israeli courts [...]' and continues to state that '(c) this regulation does not apply to a person who at the time of the act or omission was a resident of the territory of the Palestinian Council, who is not an Israeli'.

The aforementioned position claimed by many Palestinians is incorrect because the intention behind Regulation 2(a) is to apply Israeli law to the settlers in the occupied territories in respect of offences carried out there, whereas Regulation 2(c) refers to the non-application of Israeli law to Palestinians living within the territory of the Palestinian Authority and who carried out criminal offences there. Regulation 2 does not intend to derogate the jurisdiction from Israeli courts to try domestic offences under section 7(a) of the Israeli Penal Law.[17] In addition, section 7(a) of Annex IV of the Israeli–Palestinian Interim Agreement on the West Bank and Gaza Strip expresses the application of Israeli law. This agreement was signed in Washington on 28 September 1995 and was later authorised in the Application of the Interim Agreement on the West Bank and Gaza Strip Law from 1996. It stated that 'without prejudice to the criminal jurisdiction of the [Palestinian] Council, and with due regard to the principle that no person can be tried twice for the same offence, Israel has, in addition to the above provisions of this Article, criminal jurisdiction in accordance with its domestic laws over offences committed in the territory against Israel or an Israeli.' The legal system of the State of Israel is therefore vested with criminal jurisdiction for offences committed within the territory of the State of Israel (see Fares and Khalidi 2006: 507).

Immunity against prosecution

A state of war or terror – application of international humanitarian law?

Palestinians generally argue that international humanitarian law should be applied to them since under this law they are 'prisoners of war'. Accordingly, in their view, they ought not be prosecuted in an Israeli court.

International humanitarian law, such as the Geneva Conventions, applies to cases of war, armed conflict or a situation of occupation. The State of Israel has argued repeatedly that international humanitarian law does not apply in the case of the Israeli–Palestinian conflict because the West Bank and Gaza Strip are not occupied territories from a sovereign state which is a party and signatory to the conventions. It is argued that the Gaza Strip was liberated from Egypt which never claimed sovereignty over it. The territory of the West Bank – Judea and Samaria – were liberated from Jordan, which annexed it in 1950 – an annexation which was regarded as unlawful and which did not attract international recognition, except by Pakistan and Britain. Therefore it is argued that the Palestinian territories are not a state that signed the respective conventions (Meron 1979: 109; Shamgar 1982: 31–43).[18]

These arguments have been justifiably dismissed. With regard to the illegality of the separation fence dealt with at the International Court of Justice, Judge Kooijmans argued in his opinion that Jordan effectively controlled the territories (West Bank) and claimed sovereignty over them. From this point of view it was irrelevant whether the possession was lawful or unlawful because, from the Israeli perspective, the West Bank was occupied territory (Reichman 2004: 755).[19] It may also be argued that Israel's agreement to negotiate with the PLO as the representative of the Palestinian people on the basis of Resolutions 242 and 338 of the UN Security Council as well as the signing of the Oslo peace agreements testify to the fact that Israel recognises the West Bank and Gaza Strip as being occupied territory (Mudrik-Even Chen 2004: 471 and 474; Kanor 2004: 562). This position is meanwhile well reflected in the rulings of the Israeli Supreme Court, for example in the ruling that 'the belligerent activity of the army in Rafah is governed, in so far as it concerns the local residents, by the (Fourth) Hague Convention on the Laws and Customs of War on Land, 1907 [...] and the (Fourth) Geneva Convention relative to the Protection of Civilians in Times of War, 1949'.[20]

Others contend that international humanitarian law, including the issue of prisoners of war, applies only in situations of war. It is argued that the Israeli–Palestinian dispute is a fight against terror and not a state of war. Therefore the Geneva Conventions would not apply. They state that there is indeed a dispute regarding the definition of the term 'terror'; however, it would be agreed that the basic requirement of terrorism is a deliberate attack on civilian targets for the purpose of achieving political goals.[21] One of the measures used by the Palestinian organisations is attacks on civilians, as was the case in the Mahane Yehuda incident. According to this definition, they would be conducting terror. In consequence, these 'terrorists' would be considered criminals that are to be held accountable by the Israeli jurisdiction and the application of domestic criminal law.

Opposed to this position is the opinion prevailing in international law that terror is warfare. Accordingly, the laws of war apply in these cases even when the dispute is not an international one. This is viewed to be true at least in protracted conflicts in which the parties are highly organised, which would also apply to the Palestinian–Israeli dispute

(Kremnitzer 2005: 7–8).[22] Moreover, the Palestinian–Israeli dispute is partially conducted in a way that creates a military analogy of war, e.g. the use of heavy weaponry and attacks against military facilities. Accordingly, international humanitarian law, including the Geneva Conventions, applies directly (Kremnitzer 2005: 5–6).

It should be noted that the State of Israel applies international law but in a rather casuistic manner. When international law is advantageous for the State of Israel, it is applied. If, on the other hand, international law imposes obligations on the State, it will avoid applying it. For example, the State of Israel refers to the armed struggle against Palestinians as war which in consequence constitutes certain rights in the conduct of violence. At the same time, it labels the actions carried out by Palestinians in the course of the same struggle as 'terrorism' when directed against Israeli targets (Kremnitzer 2005). The State of Israel has taken a stand which enables it to enjoy the best of both worlds: to enjoy jurisdiction and legal power in the territories ensuing from international law, and concurrently to repudiate responsibility for respecting rights anchored alongside the powers ensuing from the same international law (Kretzmer 2002: 38; Reichman 2004: 758). Generally, the State of Israel does not enforce Israeli law on army and settler activities carried out against Palestinians. But if the situation is – as it is argued – a fight against terrorism and the applicability of Israeli criminal law is supported, then it is not reasonable that it is not applied to the activities of the Israeli army and the settlers.

According to international humanitarian law the State of Israel is obliged to refrain from causing physical, mental and economic harm to residents of the territories. In contrast to that, hundreds of dead, thousands of injured, the destruction of houses and the confiscation of property testify to a continuous breach of this obligation – something that has not yet been the subject of a legal hearing (Mudrik-Even Chen 2004: 499–500).[23] When Palestinian civilians are killed in such operations and it is found that this was the result of negligence, the Israeli military and political leadership have apologised. However, the civil State Attorney's Office and Military Attorney General did not investigate these incidents and consequently did not bring charges against anyone. It is hard to argue that dropping a bomb weighing one ton on a residential home is a justified means for killing a leader of a Palestinian militant organisation when it also leads to the death of another 15 civilians in the same building. Instead, it can in fact be viewed as a criminal act (Waltzer 2004: 453).[24] The aforementioned incident gave rise to a public debate and apologies but did not become the subject of a legal hearing. When the army carries out such illegal acts against Palestinians and Israeli criminal law is not applied, the question arises as to how the State of Israel can be entitled to prosecute Palestinians who harm Israelis under Israeli criminal law? The State of Israel has the moral and legal right as well as the duty to prosecute whoever has committed a criminal offence regardless of the allegiance of the perpetrator – be it a Palestinian fighter or an Israeli settler or an Israeli soldier – by uniformly applying domestic Israeli law or military law. Otherwise, Palestinian voices might argue that Israel loses its moral right to prosecute Palestinians for their offences against Israeli citizens if not equally prosecuting Israeli settlers and soldiers for their offences against Palestinians.

Prisoners of war or unlawful combatants?

The main challenge is to define and identify 'prisoners of war' who are in turn entitled to immunity against legal prosecution. The definition of a prisoner of war is found in Article 4 of the Third Geneva Convention, as well as in Articles 43 and 44 of the First Additional Protocol to the Fourth Geneva Convention.

Article 4 of the Third Geneva Convention provides that the preconditions for recognising a combatant as a prisoner of war is the person's membership of the armed forces or a party or an organisation with the following characteristics: (a) the organisation operates within a hierarchical structure, which is commanded by a person responsible for his subordinates; (b) the organisation uses a fixed distinctive sign recognisable at a distance; (c) the fighters carry arms openly; (d) the organisation conducts its operations in accordance with the laws and customs of war. According to this definition, the Palestinians who participated in attacks, such as the Mahane Yehuda incident, do not satisfy the preconditions of Article 4 of the Convention.

However, a combatant who does not satisfy the preconditions set out in Article 4 of the Third Geneva Convention may still be a prisoner of war according to Articles 43 and 44 of Protocol 1 Additional to the Fourth Geneva Convention which expand the definition of a prisoner of war.[25] Protocol 1 sought to equate the status of international disputes which do not meet the definition of war, such as fighting against occupation and situations of terrorism, to states of war by applying the laws of war to them. It intended to extend the application of the laws of war also to guerrilla fighters – 'freedom fighters' – recognising them as combatants and, consequently, as prisoners of war (Kremnitzer 2005). Accordingly, guerrilla fighters who fulfil the preconditions of freedom fighters but do not satisfy the preconditions of Article 4 of the Third Geneva Convention are entitled to the status of prisoners of war and not to the status of criminals. The conditions in the Third Geneva Convention are difficult for guerrilla fighters to meet: secrecy and concealment is an inherent characteristic for them. Article 44 of the Protocol provides that carrying arms openly – but only during military operations – is a necessary but sufficient condition for recognising a guerrilla fighter as a prisoner of war (Mudrik-Even Chen 2005: 18).

If they fulfil the requirements, these fighters enjoy the status of a prisoner of war and, hence, have to being granted immunity from being prosecuted in a domestic court for criminal offences under the respective domestic law. According to Article 44(4) of the aforementioned Protocol, a guerilla fighter who fails to meet the requirement of carrying weapons openly forfeits his right to be a prisoner of war. He shall, nevertheless, be given protections accorded to prisoners of war by the Third Convention and by this Protocol.[26] He may be tried for any offences he has committed. A combatant who does not act in accordance with the laws of war does not enjoy the protection of international humanitarian law. It is therefore possible to prosecute him according to domestic law (Dinstein 1983: 248; Mudrik-Even Chen 2005: 47).

In addition, Article 48 of the Protocol Supplementary to the Geneva Convention entitled 'basic rule' provides that: 'In order to ensure respect for and protection of the civilian population and civilian objects, the Parties to the conflict shall at all times distinguish between the civilian population and combatants, and between civilian objects and military objectives, and accordingly shall direct their operations only against military objectives.' A person who attacks civilian objects and the civilian population – as was the case in the Mahane Yehuda incident – is not entitled to the protection of international humanitarian law. In accordance with Articles 85 and 99 of the Third Geneva Convention he may be prosecuted criminally. In light of what has been said above, Palestinians who participate in attacks directed against civilians are not entitled to the status of freedom fighters or guerrilla fighters within the meaning of those terms in Protocol 1 because they do not abide by the laws of war (Gross 2001: 202–3, 2004). It is important to note that the State of Israel has not signed Protocol 1 Additional to the Fourth Geneva Convention. Therefore Article 44 of the Protocol which relates to prisoners of war does not apply (directly). The State of Israel also consistently objected to Article 44 of the Protocol. Accordingly, in the matter at hand, there is no dispute relating to the application of Article 44 of the Protocol.

It is possible to try those persons involved in an attack like the Mahane Yehuda bombing for offences under Israeli law. However, it is important to note that when a war attack is directed against soldiers during the military conflict, it is not a terrorist act (Kretzmer 2005: 171; Waltzer 2004: 452). Some even argue that the settlers are 'agents of the occupation' and that an attack against them during the conflict is also not terrorism. Instead, an attack on soldiers or settlers during the period of the dispute is viewed as a warlike act. The perpetrator should not be tried for any criminal offence due to his recognition as being a prisoner of war (Yuval 2004: 521).

It is also important to note that Israeli law is applied to Palestinians without engaging in an extensive discussion of the judicial legitimacy (Dinstein 1983: 141).[27] The courts refuse to recognise the defendant as a prisoner of war arguing that the defendant did not act in accordance with the laws of war; instead, the defendant would have deliberately targeted civilians. The courts classify the defendants as 'unlawful combatants' within the definition of section 2 of the Imprisonment of Unlawful Combatants Law 2002, who must be prosecuted according to Israeli criminal law.[28] As noted above, sharp criticism has been voiced against this law and against the term 'unlawful combatant' (Mudrik-Even Chen 2005; Kremnitzer 2005; Kretzmer 2005: 171).

In the Mahane Yehuda incident, the bomber intentionally blew himself up in a civilian bus and caused the death and injury of civilians. In light of the aforesaid, the commission of this act is against humanitarian law, namely the prohibition of intentionally harming civilians. The attack does not fulfil the criteria of an act of war and the person(s) responsible can therefore not be considered prisoners of war. Hence they do not have the defence of immunity and can be prosecuted under Israeli penal law and Israeli military law.

Liability for criminal offences[29]

In the Mahane Yehuda case many people were involved in carrying out the bombing, such as the leaders of Hamas and those involved in planning the bombing. As indicated above, all persons who supported the attack materially, logistically or with their know-how can also be held criminally accountable as co-perpetrator, indirect perpetrator, instigator or abettor. The various classes of these parties are defined in sections 29–31 of the Penal Code.

The *direct perpetrator* is the person who fulfils all the elements of the offence in person and who controls his own actions. In the Mahane

Yehuda case, it is the bomber who blew himself up. According to section 31, an *abettor* is a person who – before or during the crime committed – contributes to the offence by enabling, facilitating or ensuring its conduct or by preventing the apprehension of the offender, the discovery of the offence or its loot, or who contributes in any other way to the creation of supportive conditions.[30] The mental element of abetting requires the purpose to assist another person to commit the offence and the abettor's awareness that the other will carry out a criminal offence.[31] It is sufficient that the abettor is aware that the primary offender is about to commit a particular offence.[32] But it is not sufficient for abetting a murder to supply money or weapons for the conduct of offences that are not yet specified at the time of abetment.[33] As applied to the case study, those involved in the construction of the explosive and who assisted logistically, e.g. by driving the bomber to the Mahane Yehuda area, or who supported this particular attack are abettors; however, those who prior to events provided materials without knowing about the planned Mahane Yehuda attack cannot be abettors for related offences. They can, however, commit the offence of providing means for the commission of a felony under section 498.

An *instigator* is defined in section 30 as 'a person who prompts another person to commit an offence by demanding its commission or by urging or encouraging him using means that mount to imposing pressure'. Instigation is possible by initiating the decision to commit the offence or when this decision has been generally made but was not yet final, i.e. the act of instigation swayed the balance in finalising the decision to commit the offence. The prevailing view is that the mental element of instigation requires, first, the awareness of the act of instigation, i.e. awareness of the fact that the act is capable of causing the person being instigated to commit the offence, and, second, the intention to cause the instigated person to commit the offence.[34] Instigation can be directed with regard to a particular person or to a small, determinate, defined group.[35] In the Mahane Yehuda case, the person who recruited the bomber and convinced him to blow himself up in the bus was an instigator of the related offences committed by the bomber.

Special attention should be made to the leader of Hamas who planned and prepared the event. Is he a co-perpetrator, an indirect perpetrator or 'just' an instigator?

Joint perpetrators are defined in section 20(b) as 'persons participating in the commission of an offence by doing acts for its commission. It is immaterial whether all the acts are done together or whether some are done by one person and some by other.' Joint commission refers to the situation where the partners are considered to be a single entity and, therefore, all the acts committed are also attributed to the other partner(s). In joint commission of an offence, each partner controls the event. The essential requirements for a joint commission are a joint decision and a joint action. The allocation of contributions in the commission of the offence is an essential element in the joint commission. If the offence cannot be carried out without the contribution of a partner or where the offence would be carried out in a different manner, this contribution constitutes a joint commission of an offence. An *indirect perpetrator* is a person acting by means of another person. Section 29(c) describes him as 'a person who contributes to the doing of the act by another person, who serves as an instrument in the first person's hands, while the other person was in a condition such as one of the following, as defined in this code: (a) in a state of minority or mental incapacity; (b) without voluntariness; (c) without *mens rea*; (d) without being aware of the true state of things; or (e) under duress or with justification.' A person committing a crime by means of another does not participate physically in the commission of the crime. At least historically, the figure of indirect perpetrator is relevant when the direct perpetrator cannot be held responsibility at all or for a *mens rea* offence, i.e. the direct perpetrator is 'an instrument in his hands' as put by section 29(c).

The majority view in the case law considers an arch-criminal – i.e. the leader of a gang who prepares plans for the commission of an offence or who gives orders and instructions for its commission and supplies the means for carrying it out – as being very similar to an indirect perpetrator. It is argued that he has a superior and outstanding control over the gang members who then conduct the crimes according to his orders. According to the academics, the arch-criminal, such as the leader of the group, is an indirect perpetrator since he controls the event (controlling the organisation) (Kremnitzer 1990: 72; Gur-Aryeh 2001: 83). However, the difference between an indirect perpetrator and an arch-criminal is that in the latter case the offender bears full criminal liability for the *mens rea* offence. Since most justices of the Israeli Supreme Court want to hold the arch-criminal accountable as a perpetrator, they classify him as a joint perpetrator.[36] In a minority opinion, Justice Dorner held that an arch-criminal has to be regarded as an instigator and not as a joint perpetrator. She argues that he does not participate in the commission of the offence as such nor is he present at the scene of the crime.[37]

In our case, the Hamas leader who was responsible for the Mahane Yehuda incident would be considered a co-perpetrator by the majority of the justices (or as an instigator by Justice Dorner) or an indirect perpetrator by the academics.

The role of the victim in the prosecution

Israeli criminal procedural law does not grant an active role in the prosecution to a victim of an offence or his family, nor does it recognise the mechanism of a side-attorney (Nebenklaeger) as is customary in other legal systems such as German law. However, according to sections 63 and 64 of the Criminal Procedure Law 1982, every person – including the victim and his family – is entitled to lodge a complaint asserting the commission of an offence. If the civil State Attorney's Office decides not to investigate or not to prosecute, it must notify the complainant who is then entitled to appeal against the decision. Persons who are not complainants may submit a petition to the High Court of Justice to compel the Attorney General (the head of the civilian prosecution service) to prosecute a person for a criminal offence. The High Court of Justice does not examine whether the decision of the Attorney General is fully reasonable, but only whether the decision is unreasonable to the extreme, e.g. if a decision not to prosecute is based on political or personal motives.

Importance of out-of-court systems

Indemnification of the victim by the perpetrator of the offence in an out-of-court decision is an extra-legal measure which cannot obstruct the criminal process. Nonetheless, the Israeli criminal procedural law is constructed on the principle of opportunity in the sense that the State Attorney's Office has broad discretion regarding whether to prosecute an alleged offence. It can decide not to prosecute when there is no public interest in such a prosecution. The rule is the opportunity principle and not the duty to prosecute (legality principle). The indemnity as it occurs, e.g. in cases of *sulha* agreements, can lead to the non-prosecution of a person grounded in a lack of public interest in the prosecution (Tsafrir 2005: 76).[38] Israeli criminal law does not officially recognise informal responses, such as 'victim–offender mediation'. However, as indicated above, the Israeli legal system treats offences committed during the course of the military conflict as offences under aggravating circumstances. Even if out-of-court agreements could be implemented, due to the severity of the offences it is difficult to imagine that prosecution of such a case would ever be regarded as being outside the public interest. Therefore they are the subject of criminal prosecution.

Sanctions and reparations

The Israeli criminal courts can impose the 'classic' or conventional sanctions, i.e. imprisonment, suspended sentence of imprisonment, fines, community service and the like. The Israeli law abolished the death penalty as a criminal sanction, except in cases of high treason in war and for serious offences under Israeli military law. Generally, the courts impose sentences of imprisonment and treat offences committed within the context of the political conflict as offences with aggravating circumstances. Mitigating factors, such as economic distress or the remorse of a perpetrator, are typically given little weight. The primary consideration here is general deterrence (Kremnitzer and Ghanayim 2000: 302). Consequently, harsh punishments are the rule in these cases.

It should be noted that according to section 77 of the Penal Code, the court can also impose a duty to pay reparation to the victim or his family – but this kind of sanction is not part of the sanctions imposed on Palestinians due to the fact that they are not willing to accept paying such reparations and the absence of proper means for Israel to enforce the payment.[39]

This kind of punishment is known as 'doing formal justice' in which the State punishes the offenders – top-down justice. This is a purely criminal process and, besides the aforementioned purpose of deterring potential perpetrators in future, its purpose is to expose the truth, i.e. to declare that a person has committed a crime and should be punished. At the same time the person harmed by the crime is acknowledged as a victim who has suffered from injustice. This judicial denouncement of the offence aims at restoring the sense of justice to individuals and society as such.

Conclusion

The second intifada is characterised by attacks, retaliation and counter-retaliation; it is a conflict between the Palestinians and the State of

Israel. The Israeli civil and military courts apply Israeli domestic law and prosecute Palestinians according to Israeli laws; they mostly reject the application of international humanitarian law and accordingly also reject the recognition of Palestinians involved in hostilities as prisoners of war. Instead, they consider these Palestinians as criminals and terrorists. The Palestinians on their part consider the intifada as an international conflict, dominated by international law. They deny the right of the State of Israel to prosecute them in Israeli courts as well as the application of Israeli law to their case. Accordingly, in their view prisoners should be considered prisoners of war.

Notes

1 It should be noted that in a case similar to the Mahane Yehuda case study (Rohne: this volume, Chapter 8) a petition was submitted to the High Court of Justice to compel the Attorney General to prosecute the accessories for war crimes and crimes against humanity. However, the High Court dismissed this petition on technical grounds of tardiness, i.e. the application had been brought over a year after the filing of the original indictment. See HCJ 8797/03 *Boyar et al.* v. *Attorney General et al.*, decision of the High Court of Justice delivered on 6 April 2004 (not yet published).

2 'Unlawful association' is defined in section 84 of the Regulation.

3 See, for example, section 85. It should be noted that the Regulations have the force of statute. See also Rubinstein and Medina (1996: 262); Zur (1999); Cr.App. 49/58 *Haruti* v. *Attorney General*, 12 P.D. 1541, 1563.

4 Section 85(1)(c) prohibits the performance of work for or provision of services to an unlawful association, unless the defendant proves that he believed in good faith that the work or service was not for the unlawful association. Section 85(1)(e) prohibits giving permission to an unlawful association to hold a meeting in a place belonging to or being under the control of the person giving the permission, unless the latter proves that he did not know of the meeting and did not assist it clandestinely or that he believed in good faith that the meeting was not a meeting of an unlawful association.

5 For criticism of the use of the Prevention of Terrorism Ordinance for political purposes, see Barzilai (2000: 229).

6 See also Kedmi (1994: 1168–72). According to section 147 only the membership of an unlawful association is dependent on the relevant person being over the age of 16. This condition does not apply for memberships in other laws, such as the Emergency Defence Regulations or the Prevention of Terrorism Ordinance. See Cr.App. 88/79 *Abu Dhila et al.* v. *State of Israel*, 33(2) P.D. 148. Furthermore, according to section 150 of the Penal Code, prosecution in respect of any of the offences

relating to unlawful association in the Penal Code requires the consent of the Attorney General.

7 The *mens rea* in Israeli law is broader than, for example, in German law. In Israeli law it contains intention (*dolus directus*), the knowledge rule (*dolus indirectus*) and recklessness. The so called 'bewußte Fahrlässigkeit' (knowing negligence) in German law is therefore part of *mens rea* (recklessness) in Israeli law.

8 'Premeditation' is defined in section 301 as follows: '(a) For the purpose of section 300, a person shall be deemed to have killed another with premeditation if he resolved to kill him, and killed him in cold blood without immediate provocation in circumstances in which he was able to think and realise the result of his actions and after having prepared himself to kill him or the instrument with which he killed him.' See also Kremnitzer (1998: 627).

9 See Cr.App. 30/73 *Shmulevitch* v. *State of Israel and cross-appeal*, 27(2) P.D. 598; and Cr.App. 3071/92 *Azualos* v. *State of Israel*, 50(2) P.D. 573; Cr.App 1042/04 *Beton* v. *State of Israel* (decision of the Supreme Court, 27 November 2006, not yet published). The legal literature has criticised this combined test and suggests that the element 'absence of provocation' is a subjective test. See Feller (1996: 379); Kremnitzer (1987: 10).

10 See (T-A) 1158/02 *State of Israel* v. *Marwan Barghouti*, decision of the district court of Tel Aviv, 19 January 2003.

11 In Israeli law there are different views on whether conspiracy is an independent offence (Cr.App. 441/72 *Bashan* v. *State of Israel*, 27(2) P.D. 141, 149–51, 155–6; Feller 1978: 240–2), or whether it is derived from the commission of the primary offence – see Kremnitzer (1985: 231).

12 For details on the law of incitement, see Kremnitzer and Ghanayim (2002).

13 The source of the term 'unlawful combatant' may be found in *Ex parte Quirin et al.* 317 U.S. (1942), which dealt with four German soldiers who landed in New York during the Second World War. The soldiers were dressed in civilian attire and sought to attack targets in the USA. The court did not treat them as prisoners of war but as unlawful combatants who had to be prosecuted under criminal law. On the question of whether the category of unlawful combatants exists, see Ipsen (1995: 68, para. 302).

14 See (T-A) 1158/02 *State of Israel* v. *Marwan Barghouti*, decision of the district court of Tel Aviv, 19 January 2003, para. 2; see also Hajjar (2005: 234).

15 See (T-A) 1158/02 *State of Israel* v. *Marwan Barghouti*, decision of the district court of Tel Aviv, 19 January 2003, para. 3.

16 See (T-A) 1158/02 *State of Israel* v. *Marwan Barghouti*, decision of the district court of Tel Aviv, 19 January 2003.

17 See Cr.App. 75/91 *Ala* v. *State of Israel*, 48(1) P.D. 710, 712–13; (T-A) 1158/02 *State of Israel* v. *Marwan Barghouti*, para. 2, decision of the district court of Tel Aviv, 19 January 2003.

18 See also the position taken by the State of Israel in relation to the separation fence, *Legal Consequences of the Construction of a Wall in the Occupied Palestinian Territory – Advisory Opinion*, ICJ Report, July 2004, para. 90. Some who adopt this position indirectly apply the principles of humanitarian law found in the Hague and Geneva Conventions by analogy – see Gross (2001: 199).

19 See also ICJ Report, July 2004, *Legal Consequences of the Construction of a Wall in the Occupied Palestinian Territory – Advisory Opinion*, para. 9.

20 See HCJ 4764/04 *Doctors for Human Rights* v. *Commander of IDF Forces in Gaza*, para. 10; see also the decision of the Israeli Supreme Court on 'targeted killing', ruled on 14 December 2006 (HCJ 769/02 *The Public Committee against Torture in Israel et al.* v. *The Government of Israel et al.*), English version at: http://elyonl.court.gov.il/files_eng/02/690/007/a34/02007690.a34.htm; see also Kremnitzer and Cohen (2005: 347).

21 For definitions of terrorism, see Coll (1990: 298); Rawls (1990: 307); Kopel and Olson (1996: 247); Gross (2001: 91).

22 See also *Prosecutor* v. *Tadic*, Case No. IT-94-1, ICTY, App.C. (2 Oct. 1995) para. 70; Military and Paramilitary Activities (*Nicar.* v. *U.S.*) 1986, ICJ 4; HCJ 769/02 *The Public Committee against Torture in Israel et al.* v. *The Government of Israel et al.*, English version at: http://elyonl.court.gov.il/files_eng/02/690/007/a34/02007690.a34.htm.

23 The Attorney General and Military Attorney General have not investigated most of the breaches committed against Palestinians during the struggle. It was argued that Israel is at war and therefore there is no room to hold trials.

24 HCJ 769/02 *The Public Committee against Torture in Israel et al.* v. *The Government of Israel et al.*, English version at: http://elyon1.court.gov.il/files_eng/02/690/007/a34/02007690.a34.htm.

25 See Protocol I Additional to the Geneva Conventions of 12 August 1949, and relating to the Protection of Victims of International Armed Conflicts (7.12.1978), 1125 UNTS 3 (Protocol 1).

26 This is also the reason why Israel and the United States refused to sign the Protocol. See Mudrik-Even Chen (2005: 20–1); Meron (1994: 678); Kretzmer (2005).

27 See also (T-A) 1158/02 *State of Israel* v. *Marwan Barghouti*, decision of the district court of Tel Aviv, 19 January 2003, para. 3.

28 See also US Army's Operational Law Handbook (2004: 17) at: http://www.fas.org/irp/doddir/army/law2004.pdf, under which an unlawful combatant must be regarded as a criminal who may be prosecuted under the domestic law of the captor.

29 See further details in Kremnitzer and Cohen (2005: 373–8); Gross (2007).

30 On abetting, see the majority view in Cr.App. 325/64 *Attorney General* v. *Yarkoni*, 18(4) P.O. 20; Cr.App. 320/99 *Anon.* v. *State of Israel*, 55(3) P.O. 25.

31 See Cr.App. 807/99 *State of Israel* v. *Azizian*, 53(5) P.D. 750; Cr.App. 320/99 *Anon.* v. *State of Israel*, 55(3) P.D. 25; Cr.App. 426/67 *Be'eri* v. *State of Israel*, 22(1) P.D. 477, 481; Cr.App. 7085/93 *Najar et al.* v. *State of Israel*, 51(4) P.D. 221, 238–9.
32 See Cr.App. 320/99 *Anon.* v. *State of Israel*, 55(3) P.D. 25, 31–2; Cr.App. 426/67 *Be'eri* v. *State of Israel*, 22(1) P.D. 477, 481; Cr.App. 7085/93 *Najar et al.* v. *State of Israel*, 51(4) P.D. 221, 238–9.
33 As indicated above, in this case an offence under section 498 is possible.
34 See Cr.App. 320/99 *Plonit* v. *State of Israel*, 55(3) P.D. 22.
35 A public incitement that affects a large and indeterminate group – such as a large crowd in a demonstration – is also an incitement and constitutes an independent offence; see Kremnitzer and Ghanayim (2002).
36 Cr.F.H. 1294/96 *Meshulam et al.* v. *State of Israel*, 52(5) P.D. 1; Cr.Ap. 3596/93 *Abu Sror* v. *State of Israel*, 52(2) P.D. 481, 491.
37 Cr.F.H. 1294/96 *Meshulam et al.* v. *State of Israel*, 52(5) P.D. 1, 42–7.
38 For the *sulha* mechanism, see Tsafrir (2005: 76). A further description of *sulha* is provided by Irani (this volume, Chapter 11) and Rohne (this volume, Chapter 12).
39 Israel destroys the house or apartment of the offender, even if it is rented or the house of the perpetrator's parents. Israel has argued on many occasions that destroying the house is not a punishment but a preventive administrative means.

References

Barak-Erez, D. (2003) *Key Trials – Milestone in the Supreme Court*. Tel Aviv: Ministry of Defence.

Barzilai, G. (2000) 'Center versus periphery: "Prevention of Terrorism" laws as polities', *Plilim*, 8: 229–49.

Barzilai, G., Ya'ari-Yuchtman, A. and Segal, Z. (1994) *The Supreme Court in the Eye of Israeli Society*. Tel Aviv: University of Tel Aviv Press.

Coll, A. (1990) 'The legal and moral adequacy of military responses to terrorism', in M.P. Malloy (ed.), *American Society of International Law: Proceedings of the 81st Annual Meeting*. Washington, DC: American Society of International Law, pp. 298–307.

Dinstein, Y. (1983) *Laws of War*. Tel Aviv: University of Tel Aviv Press.

Fares, S. and Khalidi, D. (2006) 'Formal and informal justice in Palestine: between justice and social order', in H.-J. Albrecht, J.-M. Simon, H. Rezaei, H.-C. Rohne and E. Kiza (eds), *Conflicts and Conflict Resolution in Middle Eastern Societies – Between Tradition and Modernity*. Berlin: Duncker & Humblot, pp. 507–24.

Feller, S.Z. (1978) 'Criminal conspiracy versus joint perpetrators in the commission of an offence', *Mishpatim*, 7: 232–49.

Feller, S.Z. (1996) 'Preparing himself as an attribute of premeditation: a slow but a needful metamorphosis', *Mishpatim*, 26: 379–98.

Gross, E. (2001a) 'Legal aspects of tackling terrorism: the balance between the right of a democracy to defend itself and the protection of human rights', *UCLA Journal of International Law and Foreign Affairs*, 6: 89–168.

Gross, E. (2001b) 'Thwarting terrorists acts by attacking the perpetrators or their commanders as an act of self-defense: human rights *versus* the state's duty to protect its citizens', *Temple International and Comparative Law Journal*, 15: 195–246.

Gross, E. (2007) 'Participation in crime: criminal liability of leaders of criminal groups and networks in Israel', in U. Sieber (ed.), *Participation in Crime: Criminal Liability of Leaders of Criminal Groups and Networks – A Comparative Analysis*. Berlin: Duncker & Humblot, forthcoming.

Gross, M. (2004) 'Assassination: killing in the shadow of self-defense', in J. Irwin (ed.), *War and Virtual War: The Challenges to Communities*. Amsterdam: Rodopi, pp. 99–116.

Gur-Aryeh, M. (2001) 'Sides to the offence – Amendment 39 to the Penal Law in the prism of the case-law', *Criminal Trends*. Tel Aviv: Tel Aviv University Press, pp. 83–110.

Hajjar, L. (2005) *Courting Conflict: The Israeli Military Court System in the West Bank and Gaza*. Berkeley, CA: University of California Press.

Ipsen, K. (1995) 'Combatants and non-combatants', in D. Fleck (ed.), *The Handbook of Humanitarian Law in Armed Conflicts*. Oxford: Oxford University Press, pp. 65–104.

Kanor, I. (2004) 'Israel and the Territories: on private international law, public international law and what is between them', *Law and Government*, 8: 551–600.

Kedmi, J. (1994) *On Criminal Law*, Part 3. Tel Aviv: Tel Aviv University Press.

Kopel, D. and Olson, J. (1996) 'Preventing a reign of terror: civil liberties implications of terrorism legislation', *Oklahoma City University Law Review*, 21: 247–347.

Kremnitzer, M. (1985) 'On the nature of criminal conspiracy and its relationship with solicitation to commit an offence', *Mishpatim*, 14: 231–54.

Kremnitzer, M. (1987) 'Premeditation or normal intent – murder with premeditation – on the element "without provocation" in murder premeditation', *Criminal Law, Criminology and Police*, 1: 9–38.

Kremnitzer, M. (1990) 'Portrait of the perpetrator in penal law', *Plilim*, 1: 65–81.

Kremnitzer, M. (1998) 'On premeditation', *Buffalo Criminal Law Review*, 1: 627–60.

Kremnitzer, M. (2005) *Are All Actions Acceptable in the Face of Terror? On Israel's Policy of Preventive (Targeted) Killing in West Bank and Gaza Strip*. Jerusalem: Israel Democracy Institute.

Kremnitzer, M. and Cohen, M.A. (2005) 'Prosecution of international crimes in Israel', in A. Eser, U. Sieber and H. Kreicker (eds), *National Prosecution of International Crimes*, Vol. 5. Berlin: Duncker & Humblot, pp. 317–409.

Kremnitzer, M. and Ghanayim, K. (2000) 'Book review', *Israeli Law Review*, 34: 302–19.

Kremnitzer, M. and Ghanayim, K. (2002) *Incitement, not Sedition*. Jerusalem: Israel Democracy Institute.

Kretzmer, D. (2002) *The Occupation of Justice: The Supreme Court of Israel and the Occupied Territories*. Albany, NY: State University of New York Press.

Kretzmer, D. (2005) 'Targeted killing of suspected terrorists: extra-judicial execution or legitimate means of defence', *European Journal of International Law*, 16 (2): 171–212.

Meron, T. (1979) 'West Bank and Gaza: human rights and humanitarian law in the period of transition', *Israel Yearbook on Human Rights*, 9: 106–20.

Meron, T. (1994) 'The time has come for the United States to ratify Geneva Protocol 1', *American Journal of International Law*, 88 (4): 678–86.

Mudrik-Even Chen, H. (2004) 'Commitments on the border – on the obligations of an occupying state towards an occupied state', *Law and Government*, 8: 471–519.

Mudrik-Even Chen, H. (2005) *Illegal Combatants or Illegal Legislation? Analysis of the Imprisonment of Illegal Combatants Law, 2002*. Jerusalem: Israel Democracy Institute.

Rawls, J. (1990) 'Military responses to terrorism: substantive and procedural constraints in international law', in M.P. Malloy (ed.), *American Society of International Law: Proceedings of the 81st Annual Meeting*. Washington, DC: American Society of International Law, pp. 307–17.

Reichman, A. (2004) 'Judicial review, belligerent occupation and the academic discourse: on the work of Prof. David Kretzmer: the occupation of justice: the Supreme Court of Israel and the Occupied Territories', *Law and Government*, 8: 731–86.

Rubinstein, A. and Medina, B. (1996) *The Constitutional Law of the State of Israel*, 5th edn. Tel Aviv: Shoken.

Shamgar, M. (1982) 'Legal concepts and problems of the Israeli military government – the initial stage', in M. Shamgar (ed.), *Military Government in the Territories Administrated by Israel 1967–1980: The Legal Aspects*, Vol. I. Jerusalem: Hebrew University, pp. 13–60.

Tsafrir, N. (2005) 'Arab customary law in Israel: *sulha* agreements and Israeli courts', *Islamic Law and Society*, 13: 76–98.

Waltzer, M. (2004) 'Israel, law and the Territories', *Law and Government*, 8: 441–57.

Yuval, J. (2004) 'The living and the dead: equality of life and the death of equality or everyone wants to live', *Law and Government*, 8: 521–50.

Zur, M. (1999) *Emergency Defence Regulations (1945)*. Jerusalem: Israel Democracy Institute.

Chapter 10

Israeli-Jewish cultural aspects of an event of violence: between biblical codes and Zionist ideology – Israeli perspective

Michal Alberstein

On 8 June 2003 a suicide bomber blew himself up in a bus which was near a stop in front of a large office building not far from the Mahane Yehuda outdoor market in Jerusalem. This incident, one among many other violent events, is the focus of the following analysis which examines Israeli culture and its relation to restorative processes. In this attack 17 people were killed and over 100 were wounded. The event was part of a chain of violent acts, responses and counter-responses which were escalating during the second intifada period (2000–4) both in Israel and in Palestinian territories. The direct victims were the bus passengers and the driver, the surrounding bystanders who got injured and their family members. The more indirect victims were the Jerusalem citizens, the Israeli-Jewish community and to some extent the broader worldwide Jewish community which shares collective memories and imagined destiny with Israel as a Jewish state. The victims came from diverse ethnic and cultural backgrounds, including Israeli-Arabs, ultra-orthodox Jews and an immigrant worker. The direct perpetrator was the person who committed suicide by detonating the bomb, turning himself into another victim of the event. Behind him, as an indirect perpetrator, sending him for his mission stood the Hamas military wing. The Palestinian people overall supported this act as a revenge for the strikes in Gaza against the Hamas leader (Moghadam 2003). Behind them – to a certain level – stood the global Arab community striving to protect its oppressed people – the Palestinians. The violation which occurred here was the shattering of life and well-being of innocent citizens by using a disguised person who chose martyrdom and self-destruction as a method of attack. The latter produces horror for itself. The responsibility for the event in the narrow sense is on the direct and indirect perpetrators as described above. However, it is clear that it is only part of a chain of violence in which targeting and bombing become routine resulting in an endless bloody circle which entices the most extreme responses. This case will be used here as a micro-cosmos for understanding Jewish and Israeli approaches to violence and reconciliation. It can be used as foundations for weaving a restorative process which takes into account the cultural sensitivities and inspirations of both parties.

The response to the event requires understanding of the cultural perception of justice in the Israeli and Jewish society, as well as some overview of existing restorative justice mechanisms which currently operate in Israeli society. This paper aims to explore the ways in which the truth about such violent events could be revealed, in order to attain justice and to begin constructing mechanisms for redress.

Cultural perception of justice in Jewish and Jewish-Israeli society

Following the law

In Jewish tradition, there is not an equivalent process to the Arab notion of *sulha* (Irani 2006; Rohne 2006). There is not an official formal method of reconciliation which is supposed to bring together victims and offenders by using procedures which involve compensation and forgiveness. Although there are elements of restorative justice in biblical stories, there is a strong emphasis in halachic and rabbinical sources on retributive justice on legal rules that constituted the foundations of the community. The sons of Israel are commanded to obey the Hebraic Supreme court, the Sanhedrin: 'Thou shalt not turn aside from the sentence which they shall declare unto thee, to the right hand, nor to the left' (Deuteronomy 17: 11). The appeal to law and to judicial decision-making is based on a search for a divine justice which cannot be settled or compromised. Following that, some rabbinical sources forbid the judge (*dayan*) to decide a dispute by splitting the difference (Bavli Sanhedrin: 6b).[1] Others emphasised the importance of using judicial discretion instead of referring to compromising methods (Bavli, Ktubot 94a).[2]

Going beyond the law

When it comes to a prejudicial intervention, or to a discretion which goes beyond the 'black letter law', there is almost a consensus among ancient and contemporary leaders that peace and reconciliation are supreme values in Jewish culture (Bazak 1982). There is a famous expression in the Avot Mishna[3] saying: 'On three things the world is sustained: on truth, on judgment and on peace' (Mishna, Avot 1: 18) and peace is considered an inherent value in settling disputes. It is very common to mention Ahron, the brother of Moses, who represents law and justice, as the peacemaker who would bring people's hearts together and would prefer mediation and reconciliation over litigation and adversarial exchanges. The famous tale about Ahron is that when two people were fighting and not talking to one another, he would go to each of them separately without the knowledge of the other and would tell him how much his friends regrets his acts and would like to reconcile with him. They would then go to each other and fall on each other's shoulder crying and reconciling (Avot Derabi Natan 12: 3–4). Rabbi Hilel, a talmudic sage, known for his own reconciliatory approach, encouraged others 'to be the pupils of Ahron who love and pursue peace loving the people and bringing them closer to the Torah' (Mishna: Avot 1: 12).

The traditional Jewish judge is also asked to try and encourage the parties to settle peacefully before he begins the trial.[4] From ancient times, the differentiation between criminal and civil law has not been strict. Cases of injuries are treated mainly as tort cases and it can be argued that elements of restorative justice existed already during this prejudicial settlement (Segal 2006). When the criminal and civil law are considered distinct areas of law as they are today, it is more unlikely to find elements of compensation and reconciliation within the criminal justice system (Emsley and Knafla 1996). The call for the judge to use compromise in Jewish law and to decide cases 'by way of compromise' is unique since he keeps exerting authority as if it were a strict verdict. It is only to avoid the severity of applying Tora law and the consequences of misapplying it that the idea of deciding 'by way of compromise' was introduced (Bazak 1982; Tirkel 2002; Miller 2005). Compromise requires judicial skills and is equivalent with strict legality (Soloveitchik 1974). An arbitrary call to simply split the difference is considered a misuse of justice. But combining elements of justice and peace within the judicial decision is considered necessary and even a preferred method according to halachic literature (see also Deutronomy 16: 20).[5] The advice to incorporate grace and mercy into judicial decision and not to follow the strict rules if this results in imbalanced consequences is a supplementary principle for the Jewish judge. It emphasises his moral position within the community and demonstrates the value given to peace as a form of justice in Jewish thought. This principle is called 'Lifnim Mishurat Hadin' and means 'doing *more* than the Tora prescribed'. A famous Talmudic example for applying such a principle stems from a case brought before Sage Rav. A man hired two porters to carry a few barrels for him. The porters were negligent and damaged his property. Since they did not have any money to pay for the loss the man took their cloaks. They went to court and Rav ordered him first to give back their clothes. After they indicated they would not have anything to eat or to take to their families following the salary loss, Rav ordered the employer to pay them money for the unsuccessful job as well. When the employer complained and asked 'Is this the law?', Rav answered by using a verse which indicated that indeed sometimes the legal obligation is to go beyond the law – then 'lifnim mishurat Hadin' becomes the law (Bavli, Bava Metsia: 83).

It can be summed up by saying that beside the obligation to obey the law and to apply it strictly, there is also the necessity to apply the spirit of the law in judgements that are closer to compromise. There is the moral advice to go beyond the law by striving for peace, exercising mercy and grace, and enhancing solidarity.

Restorative elements in ancient Jewish law

Under Jewish law as well as in many other pre-modern legal systems a bodily injury could be financially compensated. In these cases, the expression 'an eye for an eye' (Exodus 21: 24) was not understood as conveying a basic retributive message. Instead, it was mainly interpreted as demanding a payment adequate to healing and recovery expenses (Rashi to Exodus 21: 24). This mainstream conventional interpretation is considered to have been given to Moses orally together with the written text. It indicates restorative elements in biblical thinking. In cases of (claimed) unintentional homicide and also in all unproved cases of suspected murder, there were shelter cities. In these cities, the alleged offenders were protected from revenge by the victim's family (Exodus 21: 13; Numeri 35: 6–34).[6] From this exception, we can learn about the rule: revenge was prevalent in biblical times. It was conducted by the victim's family in a personal pursuit of the offender. The cities of refuge constituted an important exception from retribution that portrays the victims as stakeholders in a crime as well as the community's responsibility to deal with it. This is a certain parallel to restorative justice approaches today, although the rule of taking refuge in cities does not transport a genuine ideal of reconciling victims and offenders.

Ethnocentrism of restorative principles

The above description is part of the internal code of the Jewish tradition. It is an intra-communal arrangement which applies – in the modern terminology of intercultural communication – inside the in-group (Rogers and Steinfatt 1999: 221–41). Grace and peacemaking are considered important values among one's fellow men. The attitude towards the Other is characterised by suspicion and negative images. This Other is perceived as a potential attacker, as was the case, for example, with the famous biblical nation of 'Amalek': they attacked the 'sons of Israel' just after their exodus from Egypt and since then have been cursed as the ultimate evil which should be extinguished (Exodus 17: 1–16). Once having persecuted Jews, the gentile neighbour (non-Jew or 'goy') can be suspicious even when acting in a friendly manner.

However, expressions in favour of respect and honour for all human beings also emerge from the Bible, especially in the first chapters of Genesis when the beginning of humanity is described. The verse 'This is the book of the generations of Adam. In the day that God created man, in the image of God made He him' (Genesis 5: 1) is interpreted as conveying a universal duty towards every human being since all people were created 'in the image' of God. This understanding is considered to be foundational in Jewish culture (Lorberbaum 2007). Nevertheless, when referring to mainstream historical and sociological perspectives, the isolation and seclusion of the Jewish people were considered preferred strategies in traditional thought, at least according to canonical interpretation. A universal perception of justice and peace between all nations was considered part of a messianic apocalyptic vision which is limited to prophetic and ceremonial expressions (Isaya 2: 1–4). This tendency became stronger over thousands of years while the Jewish people were expelled from their country and lived in the Diaspora. Seclusion became a survival mechanism for Jews living within societies that were mostly hostile to the Jewish minority. Preserving the ancient tradition and the social support systems among the secluded community became a paramount goal. It is only following the Enlightment in Western culture and its modernisation that peaceful voices in Jewish tradition were borrowed from the intra-communal context and reinterpreted as carrying a universal message.

Modernity and Zionism

Zionism was inherently a secular movement and inspired a wave of nationalism in the nineteenth century. It aspired to invent 'the new Jew' and to reread the Bible by strengthening both its national and universal messages. In Herzl's utopia *Altneuland* (Herzl 1987) friendship and fraternity were described as prevailing between Jews and Arabs, since the latter would be grateful for the civilisation brought to the land by the newcomers. In early Zionism, Israeli socialist culture was thus striving to emphasise the Jewish traditional care for the weak – the widow, the orphan, the stranger who lives among the community (Deutronomy 26: 13): establishing social institutions such as the kibbutz was part of an insertion of universal socialist ideas into the project of building a nation (Near 1992: 11). Still, the contradiction between the national agenda of establishing a Jewish state and universal fraternity was mostly resolved by enhancing more national goals. The assumed rejection of the UN partition plan in 1947 by the Arab population was considered a legitimate cause of a war for a land providing a genuine shelter for the Jewish people. Thus it can be stated that overall the Zionist culture as a modern national project was developing a socialist perception of conflicts, emphasising equality and solidarity. The collective ideology behind any conflict treatment was the main motivation for alternative processing of disputes which resembled more group trials than consensual procedures. With regard to inter-group conflicts, the national aspiration often dominated the socialist liberal. It seems that – as in the traditional Jewish experience – ethnocentric lenses influenced the application of restorative elements, restricting them to the 'own' community and diminishing their universal applicability.

Existing informal mechanisms in contemporary Israeli society

Like most modern systems, the criminal law of the present state of Israel is based on retributive and preventive concepts of justice. It reflects the norms of Jewish criminal laws to a very little extent (Segal 2006: 525). Today's Israeli criminal law is a secular legal system which is borrowed from preceding – mainly British – legal systems.

In the years after the foundation of the State of Israel in 1948 it was successively emancipated and developed further, again by taking into consideration other legal systems and jurisprudence (Barak 1992). In criminal matters, Jewish law serves only as one of the various possible supplements for Israeli jurisprudence if the positive law appears to be insufficient (Statute of the Foundations of Law 1980).

Over the past 15 years restorative practices have been introduced in the work of various Israeli government services (Farkash 2002; Segal 2006: 533–4). The interest in this field follows the implementation of civil mediation. Both restorative practices and civil mediation were implemented top-down. During the 1990s the Juvenile Probation Service (JPS) in the Ministry of Social Affairs pioneered the use of restorative justice and was later joined by other governmental services and NGOs (Segal 2006; Goldstein 2006a). Experimentation included restorative in the Juvenile Probation Service, victim offender mediation (VOM) as part of the psychosocial investigation and decision-making process regarding indictment, and family group conference (FGC) in youth justice at other junctures of the criminal proceedings (see also Goldstein 2006b). The family group conferences were especially utilised in various contexts such as child protection, fierce divorce battles, schools, adult probation service, juvenile prisoners, youth protection and other public institutions. Most of the programmes are pilot projects and are still in a preliminary stage of development, but they represent a shift in the conventional perception of justice in Israeli society (Segal 2006: 533–34; Goldstein 2006a). These modern alternatives supplement existing traditional systems of restorative justice which are to be found among the Arab population, the Druse, the Bedouin and immigrant Jews who came from Ethiopia (Goldstein 2006a). In contrast to the restorative processes described above, which are either traditional (e.g. Druse, Bedouin) or mostly modern (e.g. VOM, FGC), the Ethiopian case is an interesting effort to modernise and partly institutionalise traditional methods of dispute resolution.

The Jewish-Ethiopian approach has an additional focus on strengthening the community. This focus emphasises the potential of mediation and restorative justice to combine ancient practice with modern needs while at the same time developing a process which leads to community empowerment: Jewish-Ethiopian communities which immigrated to Israel during the 1980s and 1990s brought their own local mediators – 'Schmagloth' – into the Israeli community. Later these traditional mediators were offered training in modern mediation programmes. They also had to introduce modern law and norms into their practice. Such a training programme was offered by the 'Joint' (a Jewish philanthropic organisation) and was concluded by integrating the work of the Schmagloth into rabbinical and family courts, such as the work with divorcing couples and other family matters. The Schmagloth function as intermediators between their community and the modern legal system and, hence, assist the courts' work up to the present. However, they barely benefit financially from the work they do. It is also not yet clear whether the younger generation will take over the role of 'Schmagloth' when grown up. This role was assigned back in Ethiopia but now, since the community is in modern Israel, it is hard to imagine how it will continue to function. Interestingly, when interviewed about their work, many of the Schmagloth stated they conduct their practice in the traditional way, not incorporating modern skills they have aquired from modern training. That means they combine authority with the craft of reconciliation (Nagat 2006). To summarize, in a similar way to what has been discussed above, the ethnocentric bias has led to the fact that the existing restorative justice practices in Israel have been operating only on the intra-communal level. They do not involve an inter-cultural process between Arabs and Jews. Some of them are limited to interactions inside a small sub-community, like in the Ethiopian case.

Implications for the case study

According to the overview presented of Jewish and Israeli informal approaches to conflict resolution and reconciliation, some implications can be drawn for the case study mentioned at the beginning. The cultural Jewish approach in response to events such as the Mahane Yehuda terror attack is at first motivated by fear of the enemy, an urge for revenge and a legal impulse to redefine the boundaries of the law by punishing the perpetrator.

On top of the inherent fear of the Other and the group seclusion – which might be typical to any ethnic community – in Israeli-Jewish culture there is also the Holocaust (Shoa) trauma, which is a collective experience of persecution inscribed in the Israeli consciousness as a constitutive trauma (Zertal 2005). The fear of being abandoned, attacked, being 'thrown to the sea' or exterminated in gas chambers lies deep in almost any Israeli-Jewish heart. The effect of the Mahane Yehuda attack and the events that preceded and followed it reinforced these feeling of helplessness and retraumatisation. Not all the victims of the event experience the collective trauma in the same way and individual perception is always nuanced, reflecting a multiplicity of ideological influences (Sarat *et al.* 2007). However, the constitutive trauma of the Shoa keeps echoing through the media, public opinion and other levels of the public sphere and, hence, has inevitable influence on the perception of any terror attack. The fact that more than half of the dead victims in the present case study were immigrants (including one migrant worker) gives another indication for the diversity and fragility of a community which is still in a stage of formation, such as, for example, establishing a common language. The concrete phenomenon of suicide bombers – in this case dressed as an ultra-orthodox Jew – who sacrifice their life and become 'Shahids' in the eyes of their community is horrifying for the common Jewish spectator. It reinforces a demonised and stereotypical image of the Palestinian Other. This image is the negation of the perceived own Jewish identity – a reflection of the inverse and irreconcilable with the own social identity. In the absence of any significant other channels of interaction and communication between Palestinians and Israelis on the everyday level, it is hard to imagine a reversal of this stereotype and, hence, an emerging process of reconciliation.

From a more nuanced constructive approach, portraying the cultural sensitivities of Israelis in sharp colours might itself be misleading and oversimplistic. Israeli culture is a mosaic of cultures in itself, among diverse Jewish traditions and also between Jews and Arabs. Since the emergence of the Zionist movement the inspiration of the Arab spirit for the new pioneers from Europe was strong and substantial. The Arab way of life was considered genuine and romantic. It seemed in harmony with the aspiration to go back to nature and to the land, while living the life of farmers (Peled 2005). Imitation and borrowing from the Arabs' way of life were prevalent in the formative period of Zionism. Many Arab expressions and words penetrated the Hebrew language (Shohat 1989; Berman 2004; Herzl 1987). Among the Jews themselves, many new immigrants in the 1950s came from Arab countries, both from Africa and the Middle East. They were very much familiar with the Arab ways of life, including their methods of conflict resolution. Their efforts to integrate into Israeli society nevertheless resulted often in 'forgetting' the local cultures in which they were raised. They strived to become a 'sabra' (a native Jew in Israel) and, thus, to become part of the dominant culture in Israel. The latter was rather Europe oriented. For them being depicted as Arab was considered dangerous since Arabs were generally identified as the enemy. Some Mizrachi Jews even reclaim today the Arab identity and illustrate how much the inheritance of the immigrant Jews from Arab countries was repressed and denied as part of Zionist ideology (Hever *et al.* 2002). It is only now, a few decades after the establishment of the State of Israel that the security concerns become less acute and that these lost complex identities can be tracked. Today, some reconciliation possibilities can be imagined: when the Arab population is not per se perceived as the ultimate enemy in Israel as it was since the establishment of the state, more dialogue and better relationships can be imagined. Some cultural exchanges and counter-influences begin to develop as part of this process. These processes have an influence on relationships with the Palestinians as well. It can be claimed in summary that a closer look at the Jewish-Israeli cultural perspective, sensitive to the nuances within it, might reveal a much more multicultural mosaic of approaches to conflicts than one official retributive one. Arab sentiments, customs and sensitivities are already very much embedded in Israeli culture, whether from within the Jewish community or due to the developing dialogue with the Israeli Arab population. This phenomenon of multiplicity is a first sign of hope when evaluating the prospects of peaceful restorative processes among the diverse cultures which compose the conflict. Deconstructing the sharp image of a cultural clash and working with the differences while at the same time emphasising the similarities and not the differences might be a promising start for a shift in the violent dynamics between the two sides as reflected in the case study.

It is hard to imagine a direct encounter between the specific perpetrators and victims in this case, including their close families. First of all, the perpetrator and many of the victims are dead or severely wounded as a result of the explosion. It is hard to expect them or their relatives agreeing to sit together and develop a dialogue due to the severity of the wounds and trauma. Ripeness for conflict resolution may not develop at this life time at all, though for some people interest in a peaceful resolution of the broader conflict might intensify after such an event (Auer-Shayan and Cromer 2007).[7] Reconciliation processes might begin in the broader communities, beginning with the establishment of a new regime of rights between the national communities and with the support of the international community. This could be the only way to achieve justice in the case study presented. This would mean deconstructing the ideological framework which enabled the violence to develop and transforming the counter-projections between victim and offender into a relationship between equals. Later, or in parallel to the global arrangement, some local circles of reconciliation between representatives of the diverse groups among the societies could be developed. Finally, circles such as restorative discussions on specific violent incidents of the conflict might develop through a process equivalent to the Truth and Reconciliation Commission in South Africa. The Arab victims of the Mahane Yehuda attack can in this case serve as a preliminary bridge for communication and exchange. Establishing such a 'transitional justice' (Teitel 2000) regime requires the setting up of bilateral committees that attempt to construct a proper process for transforming the overall conflict and – within it – the micro events. Such committees should be mixed in terms of the participants' ethnic, national and professional background and other aspects of identity. They should be balanced in terms of gender and should include professionals in conflict resolution. The main emphasis of the committees in constructing a restorative process should be elicitive and not directive (Lederach 1995). In other words, an existing practice of restorative justice or conflict resolution would not be considered as sufficient to answer the concrete cultural sensitivities of the parties at stake. Developing the process to address the conflict should become an intercultural exchange in itself (Alberstein 2007) which utilises local existing practices and sensitivities, as discussed here and in other chapters of this book. At the local level, attention to the life histories of the individuals involved could be a starting point for constructing the micro-level processes. The conflict narratives which individuals tell reflect the operation of culture and communities within their own life histories. They reflect the multiplicity of the parties' identities speaking with different voices that might need to be reconciled in terms of their demand for justice and redress. A person who is a woman, an immigrant, a daughter of a human rights fighter, a mother to a soldier and a teacher can have a variety of attitudes toward a suicide bombing event, and exploring all the voices she can bring to the table while retaining their multiplicity might in itself have a reconciling effect (Alberstein 2007). Avoiding stereotypes and developing a true dialogue which is sensitive to cultural narratives that guide the parties' perceptions of entitlements and fairness (Winslade and Monk 2000) – which sometimes contradict – is a promising, opening position to transform the situation of conflict. The outlines of the process should thus be determined by the founding committees considering the existing culturally rooted practices in both societies. But enough discretion should be left for the individuals to devise their own process at the local level. The purpose of these processes would be to deconstruct the sharp stereotypical pictures of the conflict and the parties' roles within it. It would allow an exploration of similarities and diversity to give a more nuanced, realistic picture of the conflict.

In response to an incident as described in the case study, not only achieving a distributive justice but also encompassing restorative values including the rehabilitation and the rebuilding of the community, requires a combination of processes at the macro-level – e.g. political and ideological processes – and at the micro-level, e.g. interpersonal dialogues, to address the individual narratives. In the absence of such a comprehensive system for processing the event, each community will strive to reinforce and recover its own code of justice. Attempts to rehabilitate individuals will probably only reinforce the perception of the dominating inter-communal conflict. The truth about the Mahane Yehuda event can be revealed by exploring the private life histories of the victims involved and understanding the perpetrator's motivation and needs as well as by discussing the damage done to and horror of the families and the broader community. Redress for the victims was partly granted by the Israeli government in terms of a national security allowance for terror victims (Statute of Compensation for Victims of Hostile Acts 1970). This compensation – provided by the National Insurance Institute – includes a one-time payment, a monthly disability allowance (which is determined according to the level of functional incapacity of the victim), and medical and rehabilitation services as well as other benefits. The Palestinian side might have its own compensation mechanisms for the perpetrator's family as a 'shahid', but full redress will include not only monetary reimbursement. Instead, it requires a direct negotiation among the circle composed of the affected parties. It would have to conclude with reparation agreements and ideally result in future communication. Such encounters may currently seem more utopian and on consideration of the cultural perceptions discussed above, it is hard to imagine them materialising in the near future. However, it seems likely that dialogues such as these might enhance a stable and genuine reconciliation.

Conclusion

Understanding the informal approaches to a specific event of violence like the Mahane Yehuda bombing from an Israeli perspective requires a cultural analysis and understanding of both Jewish and Zionist secular traditions within Israeli society. An inquiry into Jewish resources reveals a strong emphasis on retributive justice existing alongside high evaluation of peaceful methods which go beyond the formal law when passing judgment. Taking ideas of peace and applying them in a universal context or an inter-ethnic conflict is not a common interpretation of traditional Jewish texts. However, some modern interpretations do follow this path.

The analysis of Jewish secular culture on the other hand revealed an inherent tension between a universalistic socialist message and a strong nationalist sentiment. The struggle to live peacefully among the surrounding nations is accompanied by a deep fear of remaining the persecuted Other who strives to escape from annihilation. Here again, the universal message is marginalised; solidarity and compassion are nourished inside the group but not in relation to other groups. Within the Israeli criminal justice system, restorative justice practices have been implemented in domestic criminal matters during the last decades. Some interesting insights can be gained from projects carried out in the Ethiopian community in Israel, where traditional restorative practice was incorporated and modernised to some extent by the legal system to assist family courts and to deal with internal conflicts. Extensions of these practices into the inter-ethnic conflict are hard to imagine within the broader cultural framework. However, they can inspire future efforts to develop a 'culture-sensitive' model of restorative justice.

A path to restoration might also be imagined through a specific event in which the broad binary picture becomes the names of actual people who represent very diverse identities, including Israeli Arabs, labour immigrants, Jewish immigrants from Arab countries and other representatives of minorities. Deconstructing the assumed acute ideological struggle and working in a specific context to regain humanity and interpersonal communication might be an important step to transform the conflict situation to a more constructive phase. This chapter has emphasised the need to borrow intra-communal restorative practices and sensitivities and the need to imagine a broader universal community in which these sensitivities can inspire a process of reconciliation between conflicting parties.

Notes

1 Rabbi Eliezer, son of Rabbi Jose the Galilean, says: 'It is forbidden to arbitrate in a settlement and he who arbitrates thus offends, and whoever praises such an arbitrator contemneth the Lord. But let the law cut through the mountain, for it is written: "For the judgment is God's".' For

an equivalent argument within the modern discourse of mediation, see Fiss (1984).

2 'If two deeds bear the same date, Rab ruled that they should be divided between the parties who hold them. Samuel ruled: it is up to the discretion of the judges' (Bavli, Ktubot 94a).

3 Pirkei Avot is one tractate among the 63 which make up the Mishna. It is called 'Ethics of the Fathers' and transmits the favourite moral advice and insights of the leading rabbinic scholars of different generations. See: http://www.jewishvirtuallibrary.org/jsource/Judaism/pirkei_avot.html.

4 There is a famous commentary on the opening verse to the section of the Torah which deals with the law (*mishpatim parsha*): 'Now these are the ordinances which thou shalt set before them' (Exodus 21: 1) which uses acrostics to show that the judge is obliged to try settlement before he begins the judicial process.

5 'Justice, justice shalt thou follow' (Deutronomy 16: 20). The common interpretation is one justice for the law and one for settlement – see Bavli, Sanhedrin 32: 2. See also the common commentary to the expression '[...] thou shalt do that which is right and good [...]' (Deutronomy 6: 18): 'That which is right and good' (Rashi) which implies a compromise beyond the letter of the law; and 'Do that which is good and upright in every matter' (Ramban), accepting where necessary even a compromise in a legal dispute and going beyond the letter of the law.

6 'And if a man lie not in wait, but God cause it to come to hand; then I will appoint thee a place whither he may flee' (Exodus 21: 13).

7 See, for example, Parents Circles – Families Forum at: http://www.theparentscircle.com.

References

Alberstein, M. (2007) *A Jurisprudence of Mediation*. Jerusalem: Magnes Press (in Hebrew).

Auer-Shayan, H. and Cromer, G. (2007) 'The Families Forum: from personal tragedy to political reconciliation among Israeli bereaved parents' in Y. Danieli (ed.), *International Handbook of Multigenerational Legacies of Trauma*. New York: Springer (in press).

Barak, A. (1992) *Interpretation in Law*, Vol. 1. Jerusalem: Nevo (in Hebrew).

Bazak, Y. (1982) 'Conflict resolution by way of compromise in Hebrew Law', *Sinai*, 71: 64–72 (in Hebrew).

Berman, N. (2004) 'Thoughts on Zionism in the context of German–Middle Eastern relations', *Comparative Studies of South Asia, Africa and the Middle East*, 24 (2); 133–44.

Emsley, C. and Knafla, L.A. (eds) (1996) *Crime History and Histories of Crime: Studies in the Historiography of Crime and Criminal Justice in Modern History*. Westport, CT: Greenwood Press.

Farkash, A. (2002) *Restorative Justice in the Sphere of Criminal Law. The National Center for Mediation and Conflict Resolution*. Jerusalem: Ministry of Justice, Israel (in Hebrew).

Fiss, O.M. (1984) 'Against settlement', *Yale Law Journal*, 93: 1073–90.

Goldstein, A. (2006a) *Restorative practices in Israel: The State of the Field*. See: http://www.realjustice.org/library/beth06_goldstein.html.

Goldstein, A. (2006b) 'Family group conference (FGC) in youth justice in Israel', in H.-J. Albrecht, J.-M. Simon, H. Rezaei, H.-C. Rohne and E. Kiza (eds), *Conflicts and Conflict Resolution in Middle Eastern Societies – Between Tradition and Modernity*. Berlin: Duncker & Humblot, pp. 493–506.

Herzl, T. (1987) *Old New Land: Altneuland* (trans. from German by L. Levensohn). New York: M. Wiener and Herzl Press.

Hever, H., Shenhav, Y. and Motzafi-Haller, P. (eds) (2002) *Mizrahim in Israel*. Tel Aviv: Schocken Publications (in Hebrew).

Irani, G.E. (2006) 'Lebanese and Arab methods of conflict resolution', in H.-J. Albrecht, J.-M. Simon, H. Rezaei, H.-C. Rohne and E. Kiza (eds), *Conflicts and Conflict Resolution in Middle Eastern Societies – Between Tradition and Modernity*. Berlin: Duncker & Humblot, pp. 575–92.

Lederach, J.P. (1995) *Preparing for Peace: Conflict Transformation Across Cultures*. Syracuse, NY: Syracuse University Press.

Lorberbaum, Y. (forthcoming) *In the Image of God: Theosophy and Law in Classical Judaism*. Berkeley, CA: University of California Press (forthcoming).

Miller, D. (2005) 'Compromise, law and mediation', *Tchumin*, 25: 101–18 (in Hebrew).

Moghadam, A. (2003) 'Palestinian suicide terrorism in the second intifada: motivations and organizational aspects', *Studies in Conflict and Terrorism*, 26: 65–92.

Nagat, Y. (2006) *The Shmagloth in the Ethiopian Community and Their Self-perception*. MA thesis, Bar Ilan University (in Hebrew).

Near, H. (1992) *The Kibbutz Movement: A History, Origins and Growth, 1909–1939*, Vol. 1. Oxford: Oxford University Press.

Peled, R. (2005) *'The New Man' of the Zionist Revolution: Hashomer Hazaiir and his European Roots*. Tel Aviv: Am Oved.

Rogers, E.M. and Steinfatt, T.M. (1999) *Intercultural Communication*. Prospect Heights, IL: Waveland Press.

Rohne, H.-C. (2006) 'Cultural aspects of conflict resolution – comparing *sulha* and Western mediation', in H.-J. Albrecht, J.-M. Simon, H. Rezaei, H.-C. Rohne and E. Kiza (eds), *Conflicts and Conflict Resolution in Middle Eastern Societies – Between Tradition and Modernity*. Berlin: Duncker & Humblot, pp. 187–214.

Sarat, A., Davidovitch, N. and Alberstein, M. (eds) (2007) *Trauma and Memory: Reading, Healing and Making Law*. Stanford, CA: Stanford University Press, (forthcoming).

Segal, P. (2006) 'Restorative justice in Jewish law and present Israel', in H.-J. Albrecht, J.-M. Simon, H. Rezaei, H.-C. Rohne and E. Kiza (eds),

Conflict and Conflict Resolution in Middle Eastern Societies – Between Tradition and Modernity. Berlin: Duncker & Humblot, pp. 525–34.

Shohat, E. (1989) *Israeli Cinema: East/West and the Politics of Representation*. Austin, TX: University of Texas Press.

Soloveitchik, J.D. (1974) 'The role of the judge', in J. Epstein (ed.), *Shiurei Harav: A Conspectus of the Public Lectures of Rabbi Joseph B. Soloveitchik*. New York: Hamevaser, Yeshiva University/Tova Press, pp. 48–74.

Teitel, R.G. (2000) *Transitional Justice*. Oxford: Oxford University Press.

Tirkel, Y. (2002) 'One for the law and one for compromise – on compromise and deciding by way of a compromise', *Shaarei Mishpat*, 3: 13–37 (in Hebrew).

Winslade, J. and Monk, J. (2000) *Narrative Mediation: A New Approach to Conflict Resolution*. San Francisco, CA: Jossey Bass Wiley.

Zertal, I. (2005) *Israel's Holocaust and the Politics of Nationhood*. Cambridge: Cambridge University Press.

Chapter 11

Cultural aspects in responding to violence in the Israeli–Palestinian conflict – Palestinian perspective

George Irani

The case and the underlying dimensions

The case study presented in Chapter 8 is not one of the major and bloody events in the long and tortured history between Palestinians and Israelis. However, it constitutes a point of departure to assess the cultural dimensions in a possible process of restorative justice between the two contending narratives. The assessment of historical events is always endangered to be flawed and one-sided. In the Israeli–Palestinian context this might be avoided by taking into consideration the very important works of Israeli revisionist historians such as Tom Seguev, Ilan Pappe, Benny Morris and Idith Zertal.

The Israeli–Palestinian dispute has political, socio-economic and psychological dimensions. At the core of this conflict lie the disjunctive claims of two peoples – the Israelis and the Palestinians – who, for their own historical reasons, found themselves entangled in a series of tragic events. This tension led to military conflicts between Arab and Israeli armies in 1948, 1956, 1967 and 1973 and to war between Hezbollah and the Israeli Defence Forces (IDF) in the summer of 2006.

The political causes of the dispute are based on the Zionists' determination to establish a state for the Jews in Palestine and on the rejection of Zionist schemes by the indigenous Palestinian population – a rejection later evolving into militant and military opposition. The arrival of Jewish settlers in Palestine coincided with the colonial trend that characterised the policies of some Western European countries (Britain, France, Germany and Italy) and the increased struggle for self-determination by the Arabs living under Ottoman rule.

The question of Palestine had other roots as well: (1) Britain did not honour its promises for independence made to the Arab leadership in the First World War; (2) the Palestinians perceived that the arrival of a non-indigenous population was bent on tilting the local equilibrium in its favour due to the substantial external support from Jewish and Zionist groups; and (3) Jewish settlements in Palestine were viewed as a continuation of the *mission civilisatrice* that had justified most of the European colonial endeavour (Said 1979). In fact, the Zionists convinced the British that Palestine was 'a land without people' and that it was for the Jews to settle – serving both Zionist aims and British imperial policies (Khouri 1980).

At the socio-economic level, the Israeli–Palestinian dispute is a microcosm of the ongoing struggle between the developed industrialised North and the developing countries of the South made more dramatic by the pervasive globalisation of world economies. Jewish settlers who had fought in European wars and contributed significantly to Western cultural values clashed with the Palestinian and Arab populations trying to liberate themselves from the yoke of centuries of Turkish domination. One of the key factors in the struggle was the organisational gap between a highly organised and deeply committed Jewish community in the diaspora on one side and the still disorganised and embryonic nature of Arab politics on the other.

Moreover, the Israeli–Palestinian dispute has psychological dimensions involving the importance of land as well as a sense of insecurity. Being both victims and victimisers, Israelis and Palestinians are a deformed mirror image of each other. Both peoples are continually trying to secure some kind of firm identity for themselves. For example, it is a complicated matter for Arab Christians who are also Israeli citizens to define their identity and feel part and parcel of the Israeli body politic. They are currently still considered second-class citizens despite some recent but timid strides towards integration. The same applies to Israelis who came from different countries and societies such as the United States, Russia or North Africa. Being in Israel they all share the same citizenship but their different cultural backgrounds pose an obstacle to their total assimilation into Israeli society.

The murkiness in the identity of Palestinians and Israelis creates a problem of constant insecurity, mistrust and fear of one another. This sense of insecurity is reflected in the claims and attachment that both groups have to the land of Palestine. The historical roots of the Palestinian presence in the Holy Land challenge the legitimacy of the Israeli claim.

Lastly – and for the purpose of restoring justice – we have to consider the total power imbalance between Israelis and Palestinians. On the one hand Israelis inflict disproportionate pain on the Palestinians and Arabs because of the excessive power they possess; the Palestinians on the other hand inflict pain because of the searing anger they feel: a privilege of a weaker party.

Acknowledging victimisation

During the last ten years, more and more voices of scholars and practitioners in the field of conflict resolution have been calling attention to the importance of acknowledgment and forgiveness in achieving lasting reconciliation among conflicting parties (see, for example, Barkan and Karn 2006). Many of the world's most intractable conflicts involve age-old cycles of oppression, victimisation and revenge. These conflicts, which can have dangerous and long-lasting political repercussions, are rooted in a psychological dynamic of victimisation. Racism and 'ethnic cleansing' are only the most dramatic manifestations of such cycles of victimisation and vengeance.

Montville delineates three components of victimisation. First, victimisation is the result of a personal experience: 'Some episode of physical or psychological violence occurs at the hands of an adversary, which stuns the victim or those close to the victim, creating a powerful sense of loss.' The second component is the victim's feeling that his or her civil and human rights have been unjustifiably violated. The third component, according to Montville, is that the 'continuous threat posed by the adversary group [...] generates a basic fear of annihilation in the victim or victim group' (Montville 1991a: 162 and 1991b). Rather than consciously and constructively working through these painful experiences to overcome the legacy of victimisation, victims all too often fall into despair and anger instead, ultimately inflicting violence upon those close to them, friend and foe alike. This destructive pattern of behaviour is evident in many of the conflicts raging in the world today, from the former Yugoslavia to Northern Ireland, from Rwanda and Burundi to Lebanon's civil war and, of course, such internecine violence is also evident in Israel-Palestine.

To embark upon the challenging process of reconciliation, victims and victimisers must find a way to acknowledge past hurts and suffering inflicted by the other in order to achieve forgiveness, the key component of true conflict resolution. The necessity for atonement or acknowledgment in conflict resolution was recently highlighted by Michael Ignatieff, who observed:

> The hostilities of the past few years between Serbia and Croatia might have been avoided if Croatia's leader, Franjo Tudjman, had gone to Jasenovac – site of a World War II death camp where the fascist Ustashe slaughtered scores of thousands of Serbs – and got down on his knees as Willy Brandt did at Auschwitz. If he had done so, Serbs and Croats might have begun the process of ending the past, instead of living it over and over.[1]

To be effective, however, remorse for past crimes must be reciprocal. In his book, *Blood and Belonging*, Ignatieff also notes: 'at Jasenovac, Tito's Yugoslavia remembered Croatians only as murderers, never as victims' (Ignatieff 1995: 34).

The process of forgiveness and reconciliation begins with two crucial, interrelated and necessary steps: acknowledgment and apology. Acknowledgment means that the parties recognise that something harmful has happened and has destructive repercussions for one or both. Apology entails the admission of a mistake or a violation of agreed-upon social rules or moral principles, and a sincere expression of remorse to the victim. In his pioneering book, *Mea Culpa*, Nicholas Tavuchis details three stages required for a full apology. Tavuchis defines apology as a 'speech act' that is 'any of the acts that may be performed by a speaker in making an utterance, as stating, asking, requesting, advising, warning, or persuading, considered in terms of the content of the message, the intention of the speaker, and the effect on the listener' (Tavuchis 1991: 132). Apology is usually followed by compensation and possibly forgiveness and reconciliation. Apology is mostly a process that occurs between individuals in communally based societies. We have a different process relevant to our case.

Communalism and the law

In Middle Eastern societies individuals are usually part of a larger community that includes the immediate family, the clan or the religious community. The concept of citizenship is a modern reference but still heavily influenced by communal belonging. This is due to several factors fundamentally the absence of societies where religious and political factors cannot be separated. In Israel, for instance, we have a three-dimensional perception of reality based on *eretz Israel* (land of Israel), *haam Israel* (the people of Israel) and *Torat Israel* (the Torah). In addition, the Israeli Law of Return provides automatic Israeli citizenship to any Jew immigrating to Israel while Palestinians are deprived of this right. This, of course, reflects on the justice system whereby a perpetrator's national or ethnic belonging determines his or her rights and duties.

The same applies in many Arab societies inspired by Islam. Like Judaism, Islam does not make a distinction between the secular and the religious (*al Islam houwa deen wa dawla* Islam is a religion and a state). Three types of laws co-exist: *shari'a*, Western laws (mostly French or British) and tribal laws.

Arab 'citizens' are not citizens in the Western meaning of individuals bound to one another and the state by an agreed-upon interlocking system of rights and duties. Instead, Arabs belong to communities and abide by their rules and rituals. Inhabitants of large Arab cities are more likely than villagers to resort to the official legal system to settle their disputes. The legal system, however, is backlogged and corruption is pervasive. Moreover, the interpretation of the rule of law in sectarian-based societies or societies based on tribal modes of social interaction has a different meaning than it does in Western states. The law is usually that of the powerful and the wealthy (politicians and clergy) or heads of village clans or bedouin tribes (Irani 2006).

The rule of law also has to confront the pervasive and powerful influence of patronage and its strong emphasis on asymmetrical power relationships. For example, an individual who has committed a crime, along with his immediate family, can face both the legal justice system and the tribal mode of conflict control and reduction. Unlike the Western legal system that is based on the rule of habeas corpus, in the Arab-Islamic world legal jurisdiction has three dimensions. As indicated above, the first dimension consists of state laws inherited from colonial times, the second dimension is the Islamic *shari'a* or the confessional laws of various religious communities for non-Muslims and the third dimension is the customary tradition of private justice.

This situation underlines the importance of closely studying modes of reconciliation and conflict control in an Arab-Islamic environment. The observer interested in conflict control and reduction in non-Western societies also has to look into the rituals that inform individual and community behaviour following a crime or any other illegal action.

Sulh and *musalaha* – cultural notions of reconciliation

In some Middle Eastern societies, such as Lebanon, Jordan and Palestine, rituals are used in private modes of conflict control and reduction. Private modes are processes outside state control that utilise traditional steps to restore justice. In various places both private and official justice are invoked simultaneously in fostering reconciliation (see contributions in Albrecht *et al.* 2006). This is also the case for the Palestinian context (Fares and Khalidi 2006). One such step is the process of *sulh* (settlement) and *musalaha* (reconciliation). As described by Khadduri, according to Islamic law (*shari'a*), 'the purpose of *sulh* is to end conflict and hostility among believers so that they may conduct their relationships in peace and amity [...]. In Islamic law, *sulh* is a form of contract (*'akd*), legally binding on both the individual and community levels' (Khadduri 1997: 845–6). And he goes on to state that similar to the private *sulh* between two believers, 'the purpose of [public] *sulh* is to suspend fighting between [two parties] and establish peace, called *muwada'a* (peace or gentle relationship), for a *specific period of time*' (Khadduri 1997: 845–6 – author's emphasis).

In a sense, *sulh* and *musalaha* can be considered as forms of arbitration supported by rituals. They comprise a mediation-arbitration process for communally based societies. The *sulh* ritual, which is an institutionalised form of conflict management and control, has its origins in tribal and village contexts (Jabbour 1996: 26; Abu-Hassan 2006). 'The *sulh* ritual stresses the close link between the psychological and political dimensions of communal life through its recognition that injuries between individuals and groups will fester and expand if not acknowledged, repaired, forgiven and transcended' (King-Irani 2000: 131). The judicial system in Lebanon does not include *sulh* as part of the conflict control process. Nonetheless, *sulh* rituals are approved and encouraged in rural areas where state control is not very strong. The ritual of *sulh* is used today in the rural areas of Lebanon (the Bekaa Valley, the Hermel area in eastern Lebanon and the Akkar region of north Lebanon). In the Hashemite Kingdom of Jordan, the ritual of *sulh* is officially recognised by the Jordanian government as an acceptable tradition of the Bedouin tribes. The ritual of *sulh* is also highly relevant for Palestinians living in the West Bank and the Gaza Strip as well as among the Palestinian citizens of Israel living, for example, in the villages of Galilee (Fares and Khalidi 2006; Jabbour 1996: 26). I will now describe the ritual of settlement and reconciliation – *sulh* and *musalaha* – as used in the Middle East and give concrete examples of the ritual process of reconciliation that follows blood feuds, honour crimes and cases of murder.

In order to thwart any attempt at blood revenge, the family of the murderer calls on a delegation of mediators comprised of village elders and notables, usually called *muslihs* or *jaha* (those who have gained the esteem of the community). The mediators initiate a process of fact-finding and questioning of the parties involved in the murder. As soon as the family of the guilty party calls for the mediators' intervention, a *hudna* (truce) is declared. The task of the *muslihs* or *jaha* is not to judge, punish or condemn the offending party, 'but rather, to preserve the good names of both the families involved and to reaffirm the necessity of ongoing relationships within the community. The *sulh* ritual is not a zero-sum game' (King-Irani 2000: 131). To many practitioners of *sulh* and *musalaha,* the toughest cases to settle are those involving blood feuds. Sometimes, a blood price is paid to the family of the victim that usually involves an amount of money, *diya,* set by the mediators. The *diya* (blood money) or an exchange of goods (sometimes the exchange includes animals, food, etc.) substitutes for the exchange of death.

The ritual process of *sulh* usually ends in a public ceremony of *musalaha* (reconciliation) performed in the village square. The families of both the victim and the guilty party line up on both sides of the road and exchange greetings and apologies. The ceremony includes four major stages: (1) the act of reconciliation itself; (2) the two parties shake hands under the supervision of the *muslihs* or *jaha;* (3) the family of the murderer visits the home of the victim to drink a cup of bitter coffee; and (4) the ritual concludes with a meal hosted by the family of the offender (Jabbour 1996: 51; Rohne 2006: 189).

The specific form of the ritual varies sometimes in the respective countries and regions, as is the case, for example, in Israel/Palestine, Lebanon and Jordan (see Albrecht *et al.* 2006). The basic philosophy, however, is shared and always based on *sulh* (settlement), *musalaha* (reconciliation), *musafaha* (hand-shaking), and *mumalaha* ('partaking of salt and bread,' i.e. breaking bread together).

While *sulh* in some respects resembles contemporary Western approaches to mediation and arbitration, a key difference is the process to restore communal relationships. *Sulh* does not merely take place between individuals but between *groups.* While Western theorists are just beginning to experiment with the reintroduction of non-legalistic community-based approaches to settlement and reconciliation, Arab-Islamic culture has never jettisoned such approaches, which provide a means of negotiating, symbolising and achieving a practical transformation of relationships among large numbers of people.

Towards the political level

Back to our case. It is very clear that the case study is impacted by the overall conflict opposing Israelis and Palestinians. Moreover, any attempt at restorative justice ought to take into consideration the meaning of justice under occupation and a state of power imbalance. The bombing of the Mahane Yehuda market (2003) is part of an ongoing conflict and cannot be the sole focus of a process of justice redress.

Redress will occur when international law is respected and UN resolutions implemented – fundamentally the inadmissibility of acquiring land by force. Furthermore, terrorism in all its forms ought to be stopped and condemned in no uncertain terms by political, religious and communal leaders throughout the Arab and Islamic world. On the Israeli side there ought to be a condemnation of the land grabbing going on in the occupied West Bank and Gaza Strip and the building of walls. How can we talk about restorative justice when rights are being violated on a daily basis?

At the conclusion of a conference I organised in 1994 with my wife Dr Laurie King-Irani on 'Acknowledgment, Forgiveness and Reconciliation: Alternative Approaches to Conflict Resolution in Lebanon', a suggestion was made by some participants to adapt the ritual of *sulh* in order to facilitate acknowledgment, apology and forgiveness at the national, not just communal, level in postwar Lebanon. Ghassan Mokheiber, a prominent Lebanese attorney and Member of the Lebanese Parliament who has written about traditional reconciliation rituals in Lebanon, stated that modified processes of *sulh* and *musalaha* could play a similar role to that of truth and reconciliation commissions in Latin America and South Africa. In this context, Mokheiber pondered the following:

> [There is the] question of the transferability of a process from the interpersonal to the national level, from dealing with personal problems between two individuals, to political problems involving a much wider community. This issue is tied up with larger processes, which are more or less political in nature, particularly the issue of war crimes tribunals. [...] In the *sulh* ritual, you have to identify the specific parties to

> the dispute, and even if you manage to do that, you need accepted mediators who will be able to undertake the fact-finding mission of identifying right and wrong, accompanied by the voicing and venting of people's grief and anger, which ultimately leads to acknowledgment and the emotional process of catharsis [...] and the reconciliation of the parties through a mutual exchange of apology and forgiveness. Now, transferring all of this to a national, political level – well, I really can't see it happening except in the context of a war crime tribunal. This, of course is very controversial. [...] It would have to be carried out by civil society, not the Lebanese government. Universally respected and credible members of Lebanese civil society would symbolically 'try' the people responsible for the war [in Lebanon] and it should be a trial not only of individuals but of social, political and economic causes of the war. Identifying the people and factors that brought about the war, putting them under the scrutiny of respectable people, finding liabilities, validating people's experiences of suffering – all of this should happen. I am a strong advocate of such a process. We cannot go on forever sweeping history under the carpet in Lebanon. Instead of just sanctioning it all in the end, it should lead to a process of forgiveness.

The importance of Arab-Islamic rituals for conflict resolution lies in their communal nature (King-Irani 2000: 143–4).

The application of the principles of *sulh* to the Arab-Israeli conflict would be challenging but, in the long term, rewarding. Before the ritual of *sulh* can be adapted for Track Two conflict resolution efforts between societies, principles of *sulh* must first be applied at the inter-state level. There is a need for an effective guarantor of the peacemaking and reconciliation process. The guarantor must respect the consensus of the international community, balance power relationships, demonstrate a nuanced appreciation of local histories and cultural values, and engender a context of common security and *equity.*

The international community and its facilitating role

The Arab-Israeli conflict is one of competing claims to justice, marked by competing needs, fears and insecurities. Many Arab Muslims and Christians feel that their claims have not been heard or have even been ignored. A recurring question in the Arab body politic today is: 'Who will guarantee the implementation of peace?' Before this is a key question in light of the fact that for the last twenty years only one superpower, the United States of America, has taken upon itself the role of 'honest broker' and 'mediator'. Unfortunately, the overall perception of public opinion in the Arab Middle East is that the United States is not an unbiased and fair broker in the Arab-Israeli–Palestinian conflict. While Arabs appreciate the ideal of an unbiased, even-handed mediator, their conception of the preferred third party emphasises the role of the principled guarantor who ensures a settlement based on values of equity and just compensation.

In this regard, it would be helpful for the United States to articulate more clearly the principles underlying its mediation efforts, above and beyond the frequently voiced commitments to preserving the security of Israel and fighting terrorism. Mainstream public opinion in the Arab-Islamic world has accepted that Israel is in the Middle East to stay, and most states and individuals are willing to recognise Israel provided that Israel recognises and compensates the Palestinians, and provided that mediation between Arabs and Israelis is conducted on the basis of values which all hold to be legitimate. For the US role to be legitimised in Arab eyes, diplomats must adopt a more neutral stance – a stance that guarantees the fundamental human needs and the essential aspirations *of all parties* for self-determination, security and development.

The United States has an opportunity to reframe its role in the Middle East. Rather than merely viewing itself as a force for stability, as was the case post Second World War, or as a destabilising force, as has been the case since the US adopted the principle of pre-emption in 2002, the United States could instead conceive of its role as active facilitator – helping to empower peoples in the region to develop culturally relevant models of reconciliation, democracy and development. This would help to ameliorate perceived tensions between modernity and tradition as well as between secularism and religion.

Notes

1 Quoted in Aryeh Neier, 'Watching rights', in *The Nation*, 13 July/7 August 1995, p. 119. See also Michael Ignatieff, *Blood and Belonging* (1995: 33–4). A recent groundbreaking book on the importance of apologies and reconciliation is co-edited by Eleazar Barkan and Alexander Karn (2006) *Taking Wrongs Seriously: Apologies and Reconciliation*.

References

Abu-Hassan, M. (2006) 'Tribal reconciliation (el-sulh) in Jordan', in H.-J. Albrecht, J.-M. Simon, H. Rezaei, H.-C. Rohne, and E. Kiza (eds), *Conflicts and Conflict Resolution in Middle Eastern Societies – Between Tradition and Modernity*. Berlin: Duncker & Humblot, pp. 557–74.

Albrecht, H.-J., Simon, J.-M., Rezaei, H., Rohne, H.-C. and Kiza, E. (eds) (2006) *Conflicts and Conflict Resolution in Middle Eastern Societies – Between Tradition and Modernity*. Berlin: Duncker & Humblot.

Barkan, E. and Karn, A. (2006) *Taking Wrongs Seriously: Apologies and Reconciliation*. Stanford, CA: Stanford University Press.

Fares, S. and Khalidi, D. (2006) 'Formal and informal justice in Palestine: between justice and social order', in H.-J. Albrecht, J.-M. Simon, H. Rezaei, H.-C. Rohne, and E. Kiza (eds), *Conflicts and Conflict Resolution in Middle Eastern Societies – Between Tradition and Modernity*. Berlin: Duncker & Humblot, pp. 507–24.

Ignatieff, M. (1995) *Blood and Belonging*. New York: Noonday Press.

Irani, G.E. (2006) 'Apologies and reconciliation: Middle Eastern rituals', in E. Barkan and A. Karn (eds), *Taking Wrongs Seriously: Apologies and Reconciliation*. Stanford, CA: Stanford University Press, pp. 132–50.

Jabbour, E.J. (1996) *Sulha – Palestinian Traditional Peacemaking Process*. Montreal: House of Hope Publications.

Khadduri, M. (1997) 'Sulh', in C.E. Bosworth et al. (eds), *The Encyclopedia of Islam*, Vol. IX. Leiden: Brill, pp. 845–6.

Khouri, F.J. (1980) *The Arab-Israeli Dilemma*, 2nd edn. Syracuse, NY: Syracuse University Press.

King-Irani, L. (2000) 'Rituals of forgiveness and process of empowerment in Lebanon', in W. Zartman (ed.), *Traditional Cures for Modern Conflicts: African Conflict 'Medicine'*. Boulder, CO: Lynne Rienner, pp. 129–40.

Montville, V.J. (1991a) 'The arrow and the olive branch: a case for Track Two diplomacy', in V.D. Volkan, J.V. Montville and J.A. Demetrius (eds), *The Psychodynamics of International Relations*, Vol. II. Lexington, MA: Lexington Books, pp. 161–75.

Montville, V.J. (1991b) 'Transnationalism and the role of "Track Two" diplomacy', in W.S. Thompson and K.M. Jensen (eds), *Approaches to Peace: An Intellectual Map*. Washington, DC: United States Institute of Peace, pp. 259–69.

Rohne, H.-C. (2006) 'Cultural aspects of conflict resolution – comparing sulha and Western mediation', in H.-J. Albrecht, J.-M. Simon, H. Rezaei, H.-C. Rohne and E. Kiza (eds), *Conflicts and Conflict Resolution in Middle Eastern Societies – Between Tradition and Modernity*. Berlin: Duncker & Humblot, pp. 187–214.

Said, E.W. (1979) *The Question of Palestine*. New York: Times Books.

Tavuchis, N. (1991) *Mea Culpa: A Sociology of Apology and Reconciliation*. Stanford, CA: Stanford University Press.

Chapter 12

Opportunities and limits for applying restorative justice in the context of the Israeli–Palestinian conflict

Holger-C. Rohne

The discussion of appropriate responses to the violence occurring in the second intifada encompasses various approaches at the macro and micro level. Some of them have been introduced and analysed in the preceding Chapters 9–11. Probably the most popular response in this respect is the criminal prosecution. At the macro level, only a few alternatives have been discussed (Cohen 1995). At the grassroots level, there are numerous programmes and institutions that promote dialogue and encounter between Palestinians and Israelis (Bar-On 2005; Maoz 2004; Auer-Shayan and Cromer 2007). Unfortunately, they are not given the degree of attention they deserve. At the same time restorative justice programmes as they are defined in the UN Basic Principles on the Use of Restorative Justice Programmes in Criminal Matters (henceforth UN Basic Principles) are hardly – if at all – implemented in the context of the Israeli–Palestinian conflict.[1] The question arises if restorative justice approaches are of any relevance for violent incidents occurring in the course of the intifada and to what extent the definitions of the UN Basic Principles can be applied in such cases.

The present chapter aims to contribute to this discussion. On an empirical and comparative basis, it analyses the potential of various restorative justice elements in the context of the intifada. In the first part, some findings of a recent survey among intifada victims are presented. The survey explored attitudes of Palestinian and Israeli victims on how to respond to their victimisation (Rohne 2007).[2] In the second part, the paper contrasts the empirical results with the findings from Chapters 9–11 and critically discusses the potential and challenges of restorative justice in the context of intifada violence. The respective parts follow the three-level model outlined in Chapter 1.

Research methods

As indicated above, the following data stems from a survey among victims of the second intifada (Rohne 2007). Given the difficult access to the respondent group and the sensitivity of the survey topic, it was decided to use convenience sampling by exclusively addressing clients of local, non-governmental victims' assistance organisations. In cooperation with the latter, the respondents were provided with a standardised questionnaire in Arabic or Hebrew containing 27 questions.[3] In the period of June to December 2004 a total of 298 persons were surveyed on the basis of full anonymity. Among them were 119 Israelis and 179 Palestinians (69 Gaza, 110 West Bank). All respondents reported either physical and/or financial victimisation in the course of the second intifada and were recognised as intifada victims by the respective organisation. Most respondents were physically injured (N = 150; 52.1 per cent)[4] and half of those surveyed (N = 149; 50 per cent)[5] experienced the loss of at least one relative due to the intifada clashes. The vast majority of the respondents reported (additional) financial losses due to their victimisation (N = 239; 80.2 per cent). About one-third of the Palestinian participants reported solely a financial victimisation (N = 62; 36.3 per cent).[6] The survey data was supplemented by in-depth interviews with nine experienced Palestinian and Israeli local experts who were personally working with intifada victims.

Giving a voice to intifada victims – some findings

The original survey explored the expectations and attitudes of intifada victims concerning favourable responses to their victimisation (Rohne 2007). The study primarily focused on elements of criminal prosecution as the most discussed mechanism. But it also included various aspects that usually characterise informal or 'non-judicial' responses. Some of the main findings are presented in the following. They provide valuable indicators for the subsequent discussion on the prospects of restorative justice approaches.

Procedural level

Criminal prosecution and alternatives

In order to explore the relevance of particular responsive mechanisms the Israeli and Palestinian victims were asked about their respective support. In light of the ongoing confrontations at the time of the survey it was expected that those who were victimised during these clashes would strongly support the idea of a criminal prosecution. This expectation was confirmed: in both victim groups an overwhelming majority expressed their desire to prosecute the victimisers. Such a prosecution was supported by 148 Palestinians (92.5 per cent) and 109 Israelis (99.1 per cent).[7]

As a possible alternative or supplement to criminal prosecution the survey also explored the attitudes towards the implementation of a truth commission. Truth commissions have been implemented in numerous countries albeit in various forms (Avruch and Vejarano 2001; Hayner 1994). Hence it is probably the best known mechanism accompanying or replacing a criminal justice response. The respondents were asked about their general knowledge about truth commissions and – if having heard of them before – about their support for such an approach in their case.

Compared to the support for criminal justice response, the picture was very different. Among those who provided a decisive answer, most respondents stated they had never heard of 'truth commissions' before (N = 276; 78.6 per cent). This unawareness was found to be slightly higher among the Palestinian respondents (N = 133; 82.6 per cent) than within the Israeli group (N = 84; 73 per cent). Corresponding to the little knowledge on truth commissions in general, only a few persons expressed their view on the usefulness of a truth commission in their own case (N = 99). The group consisted of mainly Palestinian respondents (N = 78); only a few Israelis provided a decisive answer in this respect (N = 21). About half of them (N = 48; 48.5 per cent) thought a truth commission would be helpful in their situation. This support was stronger among the Israeli respondents (N = 13, 61.9 per cent) than within the Palestinian group (N = 35, 44.9 per cent). However, the low numbers require a very careful interpretation. In total, almost half of the supportive group (47.2 per cent) consisted of those who before had reported their ignorance of truth commissions in general.[8] Apparently, the term 'truth commission' awakened associations of revealing and exposing the truth. The answers indicate a related desire among these victims.[9]

In contrast to criminal prosecution, the support for a truth commission was surprisingly low which possibly results from widespread ignorance of truth commissions in general. This assumption is supported by the fact that in the Palestinian sample the data revealed a correlation between knowledge of truth commissions on the one hand and support on the other.[10] Due to the weak knowledge about truth commissions, the following discussion uses criminal prosecution as a point of departure.

Support for international and domestic institutions

The collective dimension of large-scale conflicts such as the Israeli–Palestinian dispute requires the determination of certain procedural constituents such as the judicial responsibility, the legal or moral basis for taking action and the degree to which victims participate in the process. Especially in the context of collective conflicts various combinations and nuances of the aforementioned aspects are conceivable (Findlay and Henham 2005). The following paragraphs explore the related attitudes of the intifada victims.

To start with, the participants were asked about who should be responsible for prosecuting the offender. In a multiple response set the respondents were offered six answer options as displayed in Figure 12.1.

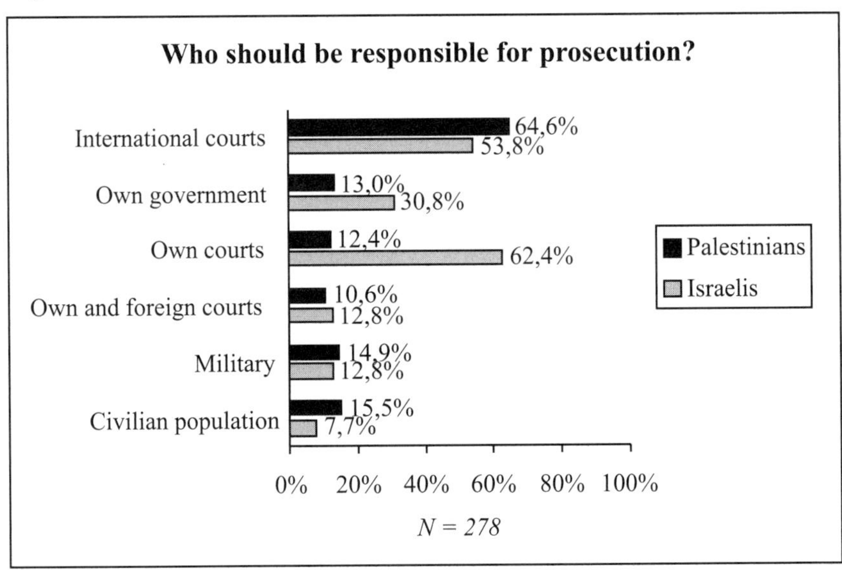

Figure 12.1 Judicial responsibilities

Figure 12.1 reveals two interesting aspects. First, it indicates that the support for a certain authority strongly depends on trust in their capability and effectiveness. As described in the contribution by Khalid Ghanayim (Chapter 9, in this volume), both the Israeli judicature and executive are taking action against those who are believed to be responsible for attacks on Israelis. This corresponds with the strong support for domestic state institutions among the Israeli victims, namely national courts (N = 73; 62.4 per cent) and the government (N = 36; 30.8 per cent). Obviously, the Israeli respondents perceived their domestic institutions to be a safeguard to effectively deal with the perpetrators.[11] On the Palestinian side the support for PA-based institutions, namely domestic courts (N = 20; 12 per cent) and governmental institutions (N = 21; 13 per cent), was significantly lower.[12] Again, this can be attached to a related (mis-)trust. At the time of the survey the PA was still headed by Yasser Arafat and his Fatah party. The PA infrastructure was severely weakened due to the damage it faced, especially in the first year of the intifada. The PA was further weakened by the growing pressure from other rival political factions such as Hamas. As indicated in Chapter 8, the PA increasingly lost support among the local population and was publicly suspected of being corrupt and ineffective (Jamal 2006: 242; Roy 2001: 8; Robinson 1997a: 174; see also Irani: this volume, Chapter 11). The survey data correlates with this scepticism towards the PA-led institutions effectively taking action against the offenders.

A second remarkable observation is the widespread acceptance of international involvement. This was especially true for the Palestinian respondents (N = 104; 64.6 per cent). Support for international bodies appears as an alternative to the domestic instances. In light of the aforementioned mistrust among the Palestinian respondents towards domestic institutions this finding could have been expected. But international involvement was also strongly supported among the Israeli participants: the majority of them (N = 63; 53.8 per cent) opted for the jurisdiction of an international court. This result was somewhat surprising due to the negative Israeli experience with various UN Resolutions, legal opinions and so forth.[13] It could have been expected that the Israeli victims would have welcomed international involvement with lesser enthusiasm. A surprising amount of support for international responsibilities was also found among those Israelis who wanted domestic instances to be in charge of a prosecution: About a third of them also supported the implementation of an international jurisdiction (N = 37; 31.6 per cent). These results suggest that international involvement is generally welcome, at least as long as it effectively prosecutes the responsible.

Legal foundation

A second layer of the procedural framework is very much connected with judicial responsibility, namely the question on which (legal) foundation such responsive mechanisms should be based. In the sense of legal pluralism the study included not only formal but also informal legal sources. As indicated in Chapter 1 of this volume, formal and informal mechanisms typically coexist and often interact with one another depending on the cultural context (see also Rohne 2006a: 92). This is also true for the Middle Eastern context and was described in the previous Chapters 9–11. In the search for appropriate responses to violence, it is necessary to explore the relevance that the different legal sources have for the victims (see Figure 12.2).

To the question what a prosecution should be based on, the victims' responses remarkably correspond to the findings in the context of judicial responsibility: most of the respondents showed a readiness to let the violence be reviewed and judged by international legal standards. The vast majority in both samples supported international law as the basis for a prosecution (N = 88 Israelis (79.3 per cent) and N = 118 Palestinians (74.7 per cent)). The support for domestic law was significantly lower among the Palestinian respondents

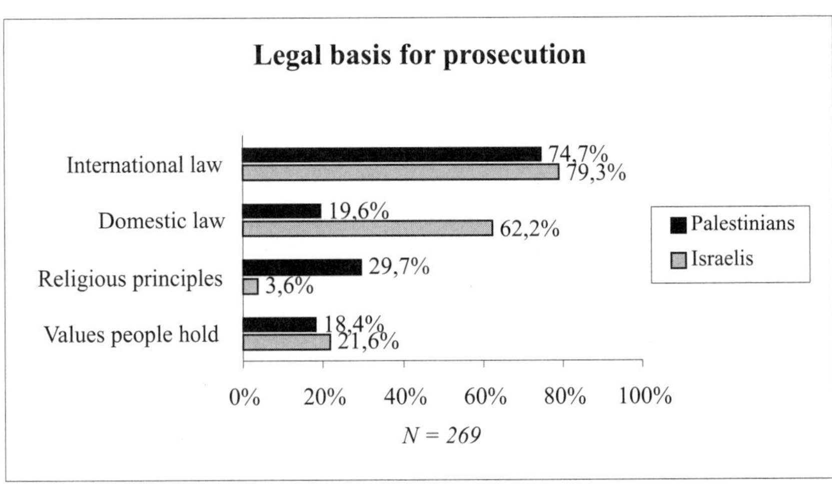

Figure 12.2 Legal sources

(N = 31; 19.6 per cent) than within the Israeli sample (N = 69; 62.2 per cent).[14] For the majority of the Israeli participants the application of domestic law was viewed as an appropriate basis for taking action. Again, domestic and international elements were frequently combined within the Israeli sample (N = 53; 47.4 per cent).

This confirms the aforementioned assumptions that international legal sources are not rejected in either group. However, among the Palestinians, international law offers an alternative to a deficient domestic legal system that is largely mistrusted to effectively prosecute the victimisers. It is noteworthy that the aforementioned mistrust against the PA is apparently not only attached to a particular government but to the system as such. This might be due to a perception that the present formal law is only an 'externalised' legal system (Drumbl 2007: 127) that was developed and imposed by foreign rulers since the Ottoman period (see also Fares and Khalidi 2006: 513; Robinson 1997b). For the Israeli victims, international sources seem – at least partially – to be perceived as supplementary to the domestic legal system that is generally trusted to effectively pursue the prosecution of the responsible.

Another important difference in the victims' responses is the application of religious principles. Among the Israelis almost nobody supported the idea of basing the offender's prosecution on religious principles (N = 4; 3.6 per cent).[15] This extraordinary low support cannot only be explained by a widespread secularism among the Israeli population (see also Landau 2006: 267). Instead, it seems that even among the religious respondents recourse to religious principles was not viewed as an appropriate basis for prosecuting the offender. Within the Palestinian sample the importance of religious principles in prosecuting perpetrators was valued much higher: almost a third of the respondents (N = 47; 29.7 per cent) supported the idea of basing the offender's prosecution on religious principles.[16] According to the reported religious affiliation the respondents were referring to Islamic principles.[17] For these persons, religion provides a vital source for dealing with their victimisation. Although they were the minority in the sample, responsive mechanisms should not neglect this finding but carefully explore the relevance of religion for a considerable number of victims.

Participation of victims

Another relevant aspect of the procedural level concerns the involvement of the victim in a responsive process. When being asked whether victims should generally participate in the prosecution, the vast majority of respondents agreed (N = 242; 91 per cent).[18] Generally, the degree and the form of the desired involvement may vary significantly depending on the respective context (Joutsen 1991: 771). Thus in a multiple response set the participants were asked about particular ways they would like to see victims involved. The answers displayed in Figure 12.3 show differences between the Israeli and Palestinian victims but also a considerable overlap between them.

The option to hear the victims as witnesses found the highest support among all victims. In both groups the majority supported this option (with N = 65 Israelis (61.2 per cent) and N = 87 Palestinians (55.8 per cent)). This support might be influenced by the fact that this form of participation is the usual way victims are integrated into a criminal prosecution. The option to involve victims by enabling them to tell the story of their victimisation was also considerably supported; almost half of all respondents opted for this item (N = 125; 47.9 per cent). Among the Palestinians it found equal support as the option 'to be heard as a witness' (N = 86; 55.1 per cent) and was often combined with it (N = 36; 23.1 per cent). In the Israeli sample the support was lower (N = 39; 37.1 per cent). Many favoured a more confrontative and active role in the offender's trial: the vast majority of the Israeli victims (N = 80; 76.2 per cent) opted for the idea of letting the victims be a part of the prosecution.

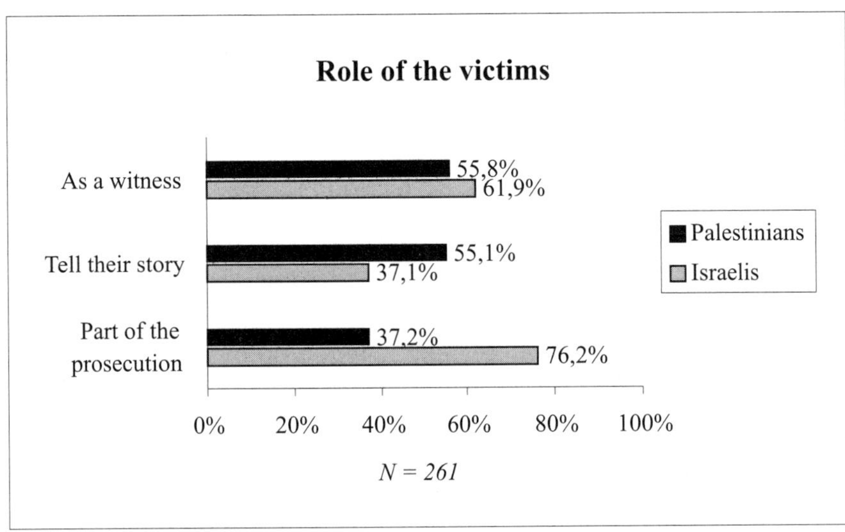

Figure 12.3 Role of the victims

The support for victims to be a part of the prosecution was significantly higher among the Israeli participants than among the Palestinian victims (N = 58; 37.2 per cent).[19] For the Israeli respondents such an active involvement in the prosecution did not exclude the victims' ability to act as witnesses: both items were often combined (N = 34; 32.4 per cent).

To sum up, the Palestinian and Israeli victims expressed their desire to be involved and commonly supported the importance of the victims' testimony. They differed, however, in the degree of narration and the possibility of actively influencing the prosecution as such.

Outcome level

Sanctions

A major aspect with regard to the victims' perspective is their view on punishment and sanctions for those who conducted or backed the particular violence. The Israeli and Palestinian victims were asked to indicate their opinion on what should happen to those who harmed them. In a multiple response set the respondents could also provide an alternative answer. The frequent use of the latter led to the subsequent formation of two extra categories, namely 'execution' and (other) 'retributive measures'.

As displayed in Figure 12.4, the option to put the offender on trial was most supported. This is consistent with the aforementioned

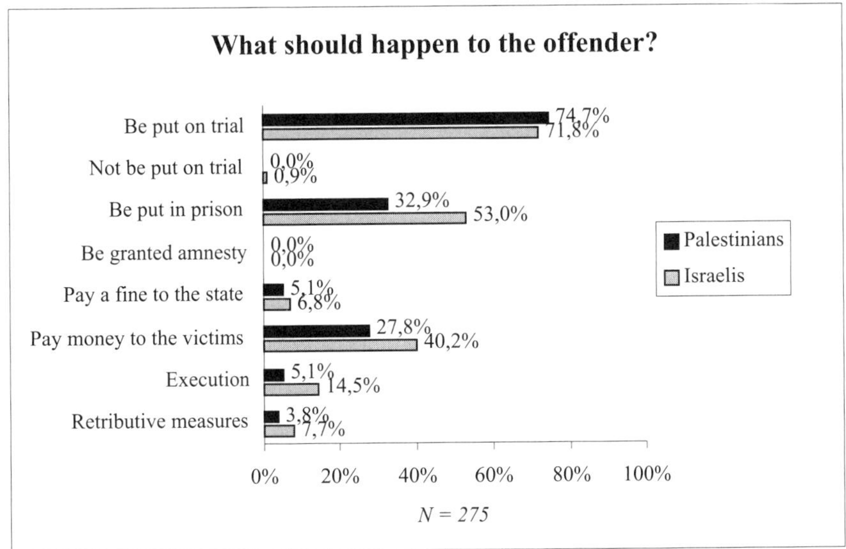

Figure 12.4 Sanctions

strong desire to see the offender prosecuted.[20] Interestingly, a third of the respondents (N = 93; 33.8 per cent) limited their answer to this option without naming a specific form of sanction. The widespread reluctance to name a particular form of punishment could either point to a general indecisiveness in this regard or to the fact that the imposition of punishment was not of primary importance for these victims if only the liable persons were held responsible. Since no respondent opted for the offender's amnesty the data clearly suggest that the victims were not ready to support the offenders' impunity.

The punishment, the majority of victims explicitly supported a certain form of punishment (using the range of the measures offered and adding others). Figure 12.4 shows that the answers in both samples were somewhat congruent: imprisonment as a conventional and comparatively severe punishment received the highest support in both groups. In total, 52 Palestinian respondents (32.9 per cent) and 62 Israeli participants (53 per cent) chose for that option. This was followed by the support of punitive damages payable to the victims. This option was supported by 47 Israelis (40.2 per cent) and 44 Palestinians (27.8 per cent). A considerable number of respondents used the option to indicate further measures to call for the offender's execution. The subsequent formation of the category 'execution' does not allow a direct comparison of answers between the respondent groups. The same is true for the call for other 'retributive measures'. The option to impose a fine on the offender received comparatively low support among both groups, perhaps because from a victim's perspective this form of sanction is too distant and of little value in light of the personal suffering.

In spite of the aforementioned commonalities, Figure 12.4 also reveals some differences between the two victim groups. Overall the Israeli respondents showed a stronger support for the offender's imprisonment[21] as well as for punitive damages payable to the victims[22] than the Palestinian participants. This finding suggests a stronger decisiveness of the Israeli respondents in terms of punishment but could also indicate a stronger punitive desire among them resulting in a cumulative choice of various sanctions. However, these results have to be seen in context with other findings such as the purpose indicated of taking action against the offender(s).

Reparations

From research on conventional crime it is known that victims of such crimes are typically not (only) focused on the offender's punishment (Umbreit *et al.* 1994; Strang 2002: 18). This has been also reported from research in the field of large-scale conflicts (see overview in Kiza *et al.* 2006: 49). Instead, victims often desire various measures in order to overcome the aftermath of violence. This includes also the provision of reparations. Here, the term 'reparation' is used in a wider sense encompassing material restitution as well as symbolic reparation. It also includes other ('autonomous') measures of coping that are not necessarily classified as reparation, namely the victim's desire to forget and to leave behind what happened without any further form of (inter-)action.

Being asked what would be helpful in their situation, most of the victims stressed the material component. However, the support for monetary reparation was rather low given the material losses and financial burdens of recovery that typically follow violent victimisation. Although it was the most frequently chosen item within the Palestinian sample, just about half of them supported this option (N = 70; 47.3 per cent). The support within the Israeli respondent group was somewhat stronger (N = 62; 60.8 per cent).[23] However, among them monetary reparation does not constitute the most favoured category. Instead, the strongest support among the Israeli victims was for an immaterial form of reparation, namely the building of a memorial for the victims (N = 68; 66.7 per cent (see Figure 12.5)). Concerning the latter, there is a clear difference in comparison with the Palestinian victims which is statistically highly significant.[24]

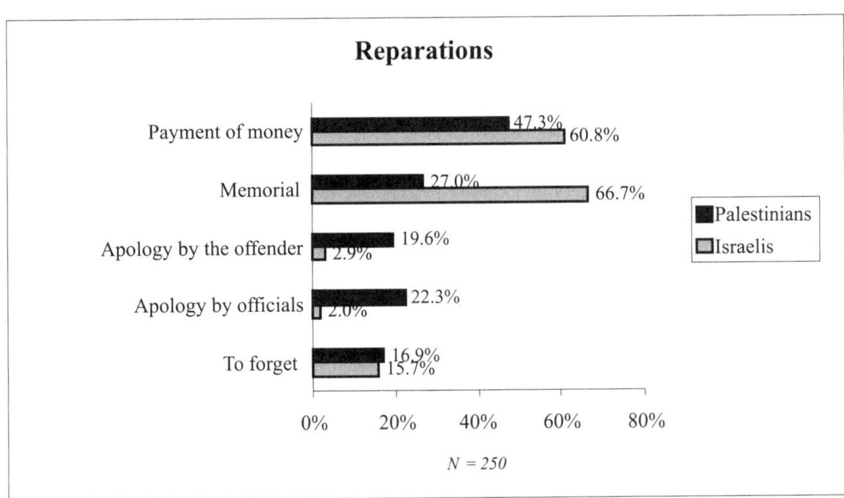

Figure 12.5 Reparations

A noticeable and almost equal number of victims in both groups indicated their desire to forget about what happened; in total 25 Palestinians (16.9 per cent) and 16 Israelis (15.7 per cent) supported this item. A highly significant difference appears with regard to the support of apologies. The survey differentiated between an apology by the offender on the one hand and by officials on the other. When merging both options into a single item ('apology'), the statistical difference between the Palestinian and Israeli respondents inversely resembles what has been observed with regard to the support for memorials.[25] While almost no Israeli respondent viewed an apology by the offender (N = 3; 2.9 per cent) or officials (N = 2; 2 per cent) as being helpful in their situation, the support among the Palestinians was far stronger. This is true for an apology by the offender (N = 29; 19.6 per cent)[26] as well as for an apology by officials (N = 33; 22.3 per cent).[27]

The reasons for the aforementioned differences in terms of intangible forms of reparation are most interesting and point to various influential factors that shaped the attitude of the victims surveyed: in supplementary expert interviews, the interview partners indicated the dependence of the victims' expectations on how probable it is to realise them. In other words, some expectations might latently exist but are possibly suppressed by practical obstacles (Rohne 2007: 278). This might have influenced the answer behaviour of the victims surveyed, especially with regard to the unexpected low support of material reparation: while both sides cannot expect to be compensated by the 'other' side, Israeli victims are generally due to receive a certain but limited material support from state institutions, e.g. national insurance. This might have encouraged their expectation of material alleviation. An equivalent does not exist on the Palestinian side which – according to the aforesaid – might reduce the expectations for material compensation.

But there might be also cultural reasons behind the findings. The traditional role of monetary payment after wrongdoing might be particularly sensitive from a Palestinian point of view (for details see Rohne 2007: 280 and 2006b: 193). As George Irani pointed out in Chapter 11, traditional forms of conflict resolution are still of high relevance for Palestinian society today. Deducing from such traditional forms of conflict resolution – especially the *sulha* procedure – 'blood money' (*diya*) plays a significant symbolic role (see also Rohne 2006b: 192).[28] It is a manifest sign of remorse and, hence, an integral part of the reconciliatory process that cannot be isolated from it. That said, for the majority of Palestinian respondents, a putative Israeli payment might not have (yet) been acceptable given the ongoing conflict they experienced at the time of the survey. Instead, indicating this option in the survey might have carried the notion of trading off the personal suffering for material benefit – a dishonourable and humiliating exchange.

Cultural aspects are probably also influential with regard to the comparatively higher support for apologies among the Palestinian respondents. In traditional approaches to conflict resolution, apologies play a vital role. The aforementioned *sulha* procedure is initiated with and based upon the acknowledgment of guilt from the offender and his family. It is the genuine sign of remorse – typically expressed first by the facilitating committee (*jaha*) on behalf of the offender and later by the offending party itself – that is a prerequisite to restore the victim's honour and to pave the way for the victim's readiness to enter negotiations and dialogue (Jabbour 1996: 31; Rohne 2006b: 190). From an Arab-Islamic perspective, a violent victimisation is not only perceived as violating material goods but is experienced as humiliating and dishonouring the other (Jabbour 1996: 29). It is the sensed 'loss of honour' that is often the motivation for taking action in response to violence (Abu-Nimer 2001: 131; Gräf 1952: 123). A sincere apology can be part of restoring the honour of the victimised. Correspondingly, a *sulha* ceremony traditionally has to be done in public ('from the top of the head', Jabbour 1996: 51). It thereby openly denounces the wrong as such and allows the victim's public rehabilitation (Irani and Funk 2001: 184; Jabbour 1996: 42; Rohne 2006b: 195). This view of apology possibly explains why the option of an apology found far stronger support among the Palestinian victims than within the Israeli respondent group.

The different support for memorials among the Israeli respondents can also be attached to societal or cultural peculiarities: in Israeli society today the collective memory plays an outstanding role. This can be observed in a number of yearly national commemoration ceremonies. These ceremonies are typically characterised by ritualised elements – such as a national silence during a siren signal on the Holocaust Memorial Day or Independence Day – and supplemented by memorials. Memorials have also been implemented for violence stemming from the second intifada, as is the case with the memorial at the site of the Dolphinarium bombing on 1 June 2001 in Tel Aviv. This widespread emphasis on collective remembrance by memorials and other means of commemoration in Israeli society was reflected in the views expressed by the Israeli victims and, hence, most likely explains their strong support for this particular form of reparation.

To sum up, the victims' attitudes to reparations show similarities as well as differences. The latter could be especially attached to cultural and societal peculiarities which gives us reason to believe that such peculiarities significantly shaped the victims' expectations.

Further liabilities

From a victim's perspective it is not only the offender that might be held responsible for the violence but also other persons, especially the political and military leadership. The collective notion of large-scale violence can even result in the perception of a collective guilt, stereotyping the opposing ethnic group (Bar-On 2001: 17; Volkan 1991: 81; Mack 1990: 119; Rohne 2006a: 84). Hence the question of (criminal) liability plays a crucial role in the context of large-scale violence and also for the acceptance of responsive measures (Bassiouni 1996; Ratner and Abrams 1997).

In the present survey the victims were therefore asked about their views on who should be held responsible for their victimisation (see Figure 12.6).[29] Both groups primarily pointed to the responsibility of the political leadership. However, this was more the case within the Israeli sample (N = 94; 84.7 per cent) than among the Palestinian respondents (N = 108; 69.2 per cent).[30] On the Palestinian side, the responsibility of the military leadership was emphasised much more (N = 66; 42.3 per cent) than the respective support among the Israeli

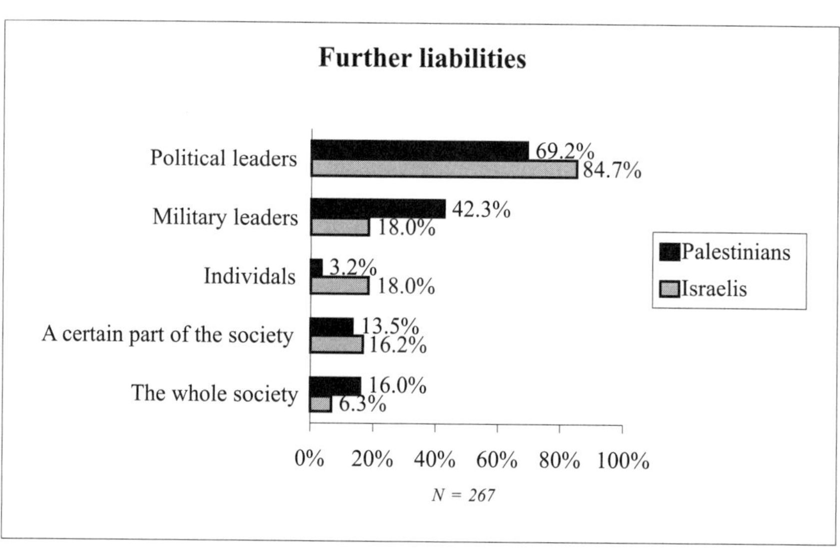

Figure 12.6 Further liabilities

respondents (N = 20; 18 per cent).[31] Both findings were not surprising. As indicated in Chapter 8, from the Israeli perspective there is no clear distinction between the political leadership and the militant players. This is certainly also due to the lack of a regular Palestinian army. The stronger emphasis on the responsibility of the Israeli military leadership is probably based on the fact that most violent operations against Palestinians have been carried out by the Israeli army; this seems to result in an primary attachment of liability to it, notwithstanding its subordination to the Israeli political leadership.

The remaining three response items ('individuals', 'part of the society' and 'whole society') give insight into the victims' perceptions of individual versus collective liability. Although the categories are not further defined, they are helpful in order to identify the respective tendencies. Statistically, significant differences were found with regard to the support of individual liability on the one hand[32] and of the whole collective on the other.[33] The data has to be interpreted very carefully given the relatively small number of persons who opted for these items. Nevertheless, the findings provide for valuable indicators in the perception of individual or collective responsibilities. The present results suggest that these perceptions are also influenced by the respective cultural peculiarities: the tendency to support individual rather than collective liability among the Israeli respondents is probably related to the fact that Israeli society is rather Westernised which includes the 'individualisation' of conflicts and the conflicting parties (Abu-Nimer 2001: 131). It is consistent if liabilities are then also attached to individuals rather than to collectives. In turn, the observed tendency among the Palestinian respondents to agree to collective liabilities corresponds with the collective notion that is culturally attached to conflicts as it was described earlier in this volume (Irani: in this volume, Chapter 11; for further details see below).

Purpose level

Reason for taking action against the offender

Taking actions against the offender can be motivated by various purposes. Accordingly, the reasoning of why to punish war criminals has been fiercely debated in the context of international criminal justice (Drumbl 2007: 59 and 2005: 144; Henham 2003; Alvarez 1999; Bassiouni 1996; Orentlicher 1991: 2541). The victim's perspective is typically not in the focus when discussing the justification of punishment (Henham 2004: 30; Fletcher 1999). To include it, the scope of the discussion has to be widened (Rohne 2007: 79; Kiza *et al.* 2006: 67).

In the present study the victims were asked about their views on why actions should be taken against the offender. The respondents could choose from the following items 'Take revenge', 'Tell the truth about what happened', 'Forget what happened', 'Enable people to live together' and 'Forgive'. In the above mentioned order, these items differ in their retrospective and prospective content (Rohne 2007: 82).

As displayed in Figure 12.7 the majority of both victim groups stated that the main purpose for taking action against the offender was to reveal the truth about what happened to them (N = 87; 56.5 per cent Palestinians and N = 50; 68.5 per cent Israelis). Among the Palestinian victims there were strong statistical correlations with the aim to be actively involved either by testifying[34] or by a narrative involvement[35] pointing to their need to be given a sufficient voice in the process.[36] The option 'take revenge' was also chosen rather frequently among both groups (N = 70; 45.5 per cent Palestinians; N = 25; 34.2 per cent Israelis).

Less support was found for the items to 'forget' (N = 8; 5.2 Palestinians; N = 7; 9.6 per cent Israelis) and to 'forgive' (N = 6; 3.9 per cent Palestinians and N = 2; 2.7 Israelis). Given the ongoing clashes during the time of this survey, this is of little surprise.

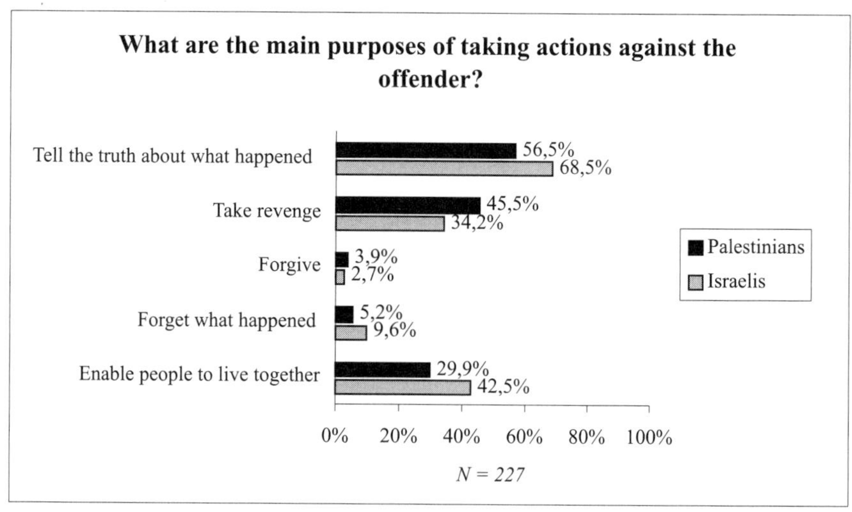

Figure 12.7 Purposes

It is all the more remarkable that almost a third of the Palestinian respondents (N = 46; 29.9 per cent) stated that the measures taken against the offender should serve the purpose of enabling the people to live together again. Among the Israeli group this support was even higher (N = 31; 42.5 per cent).

The purpose of enabling people to live together is indeed a prospective goal. The findings point to the victims' need to take action against the offender *in order to* make coexistence possible. This indicates that taking action against the offender can in fact carry an implicit reconciliatory notion for the victims. It further shows that prospective goals can even be found among those who were extremely affected and personally victimised in the course of the political conflict. This becomes even clearer when further analysing the data: in the Israeli sample, the purpose of enabling people to live together was more likely to be chosen by those who experienced cumulative physical victimisation – the loss of a relative and personal injury.[37]

Albeit there are slight differences between the two victim groups, the support for neither answer revealed statistical differences. It is therefore worth examining the answer combinations (answer profiles). Such a case-wise analysis is also helpful in order to verify the assumed scale of retrospective to prospective purposes (Rohne 2007: 189).[38]

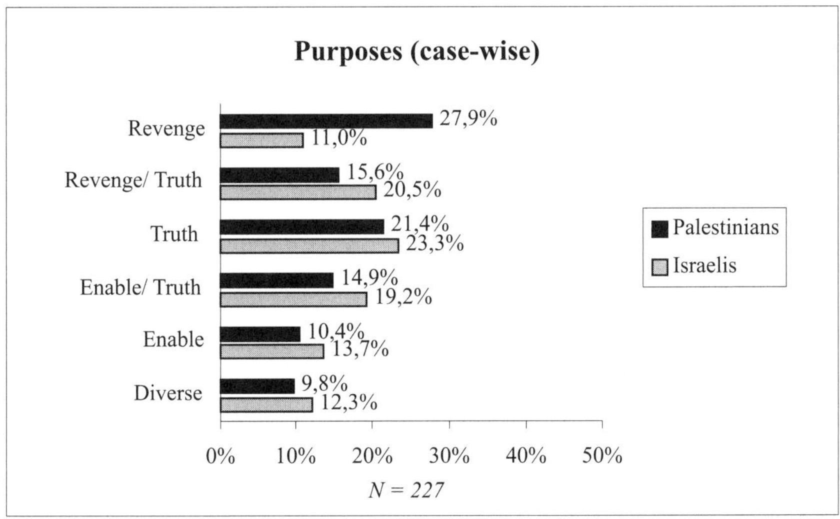

Figure 12.8 Purposes (case-wise)

The answer profiles depicted in Figure 12.8 include only those combinations that were favoured by at least 5 per cent within one or both respondent groups.[39] The relevant profiles were constituted by the items 'take revenge', 'tell the truth' and 'enable people to live together'.[40] The results support the aforementioned assumption of a retrospective-prospective scale that might be useful for a further understanding of the victims' opinions: each of the three relevant items (revenge, truth, live together) appeared either as an isolated option or in combination with (only) one other item. Further, only 'neighbouring' items were combined. Ordering these profiles according to their assumed retro-prospective content reveals – with one exception – an almost normal distribution in both groups. The only exception is the support for 'revenge': we observed above that the overall support for revenge was not significantly different between the victim groups. However, as an *isolated* option it was favoured significantly more often by the Palestinian respondents than within the Israeli group.[41] This might point to another understanding of 'revenge' as a responsive concept and might therefore be explained by cultural notions attached to it (see also Rohne 2007: 188; Valiñas and Arsovska: this volume, Chapter 7).

Apart from this, the case-wise analysis revealed no other statistically significant differences between the victim groups.

Beneficiary

A second aspect with regard to the purpose level is the question of who should actually benefit from such responses taken against the offender. This question becomes especially relevant in the context of collective conflicts.

The violence conducted in the course of these conflicts carries a strong collective notion which has to be considered when searching for appropriate and acceptable responses to it. This is not only because violence in inter-group conflicts affects – and to a certain extent victimises – a whole society (Sebba 2006: 35; Drumbl 2005: 144; Fletcher 2004; Graybill 2002). The collective dimension is also crucial for the coping process of the individual victim. In the aforementioned in-depth interviews with local experts, it became evident that the victims of intifada are in need of social recognition and reintegration (Rohne 2007: 276).

Finally, a sufficient consideration of the victims' views on the beneficiary is also important due to cultural differences and peculiarities. In Western responsive mechanisms the primary assumption is to redress the individual victim. In communally based societies, however, the collective perception of conflicts is likely to be reflected also in terms of communal benefit of conflict resolution (see also Rohne *et al.*: this volume, Chapter 1; Kiza *et al.* 2006: 123; Aukerman 2002: 47; Abu-Nimer 2001).

When asked who should benefit from the criminal prosecution, the Palestinian and Israeli victims revealed remarkable differences in their attitudes. As displayed in Figure 12.9,[42] only about a third in each group supported the idea that individuals as well as the community should benefit from the prosecution (N = 29; 33.7 per cent Israelis and N = 61; 38.4 per cent Palestinians). Instead, the respective majority saw the prosecution as either benefiting individual or communitarian purposes. Among the Israeli group the individual benefit was favoured by almost half of the respondents (N = 39; 45.3 per cent). It is remarkable that within the Palestinian group this option was hardly chosen at all (N = 11; 6.9 per cent). This results in a difference between both groups that is statistically highly significant.[43] In light of the aforementioned individualisation of conflicts and the Westernised shape of Israeli society, the strong(er) support for individual benefit among the Israeli respondents is not surprising.

The majority of the Palestinian victims viewed the offender's prosecution to benefit solely communitarian purposes (N = 87; 54.7 per cent). In comparison to that, support among the Israeli group was

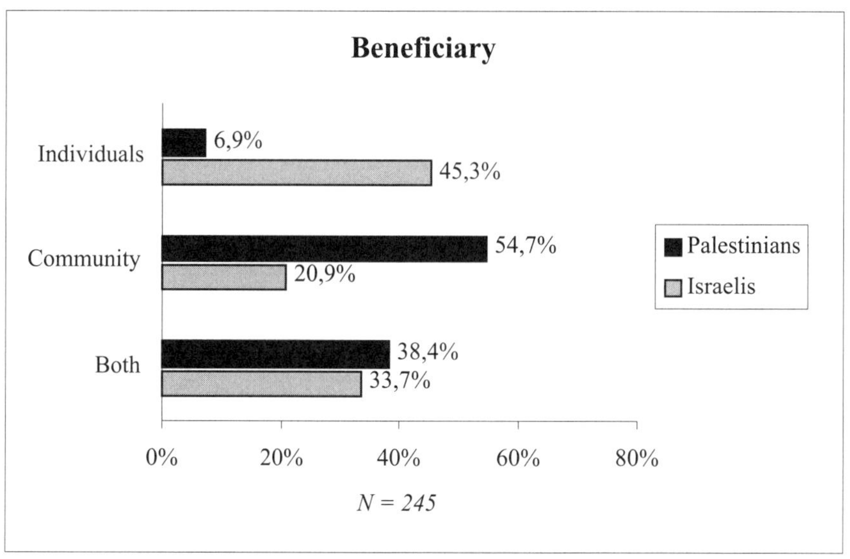

Figure 12.9 Beneficiary

significantly lower, albeit still considerable (N = 18; 20.9 per cent).[44] The results suggest that these victims deemed the individual benefit as not important. This is all the more striking considering the fact that the exclusive communitarian benefit was favoured by persons who were personally victimised. They could have been expected to opt for the benefit of both, the individual and the community. Instead, they subordinated their personal benefit to the community. The strong support for this option among the Palestinian victims can be attached to the aforementioned perception of conflicts as collective disputes that is still prevalent in Arab-Islamic societies (Irani and Funk 2001: 180; Abu-Nimer 2001: 131). If the conflicting party is the collective and not only the individual, it is only consistent that the collective is also deemed to be the beneficiary of the actions taken in response to such a conflict (Rohne 2006b: 202).[45] This collective notion is well reflected in the aforementioned *sulha* ceremony with its public rituals (see also Jabbour 1996: 51; Rohne 2004 and 2006b: 193 and Irani: this volume, Chapter 11) but also shapes the formal justice system: a study at the Birzeit University found that among some judges justice is perceived as the primary collective and the right of the particular victim (Fares and Khalidi 2006: 523).

Apart from this cultural component, the support for this option that could also be observed among a considerable number of Israeli victims indicates that attitudes were not only shaped by the aforementioned cultural differences. Instead, the collective dimension of the overall conflict seems to be influential as well.

Implications for the use of restorative justice

The data provides victimological insights that have not been the subject of empirical research so far. Although the sample size was relatively small and the survey's primary focus was on criminal justice responses, the findings raise various aspects that are also highly relevant in the context of restorative justice. The inclusion of the victims' perspective is crucial when discussing and implementing responsive mechanisms. This is certainly also true for restorative justice approaches. The following discussion aims to elaborate more on these aspects by contrasting the theoretical analysis (Chapters 8–11) and the empirical findings presented above.

This discussion begins with some reflections on the purpose of responding to incidents at the micro level despite the fact that they resulted from the overall (macro) conflict.

Why respond at the micro level

The role of the macro conflict

The profile of restorative justice in the context of large-scale conflicts is not easy to determine. It is tempting to follow a broader understanding of restorative justice that would more resemble approaches from transitional justice or peacebuilding (see Rohne *et al.*: this volume, Chapter 1). Yet, as outlined in Chapter 1, in the present volume the UN Basic Principles serve as a starting point to explore the features of restorative justice and their transferability to such settings. This rather narrow understanding of restorative justice is characterised by its interpersonal facet and therefore poses perhaps the most fundamental challenge to the present debate.

Irani in particular has revealed scepticism with regard to the focus on the micro level instead of the macro level (see Irani: this volume, Chapter 11). Is it useful to focus on a particular incident if the Israeli–Palestinian conflict continues to produce countless other examples of violence and victimisation? The present suggestion to focus (also) on particular cases immediately stimulates a debate that strongly resembles the well-known criminological discourse on 'neutralisation' and 'justification' techniques (Sykes and Matza 1957: 664): in large-scale conflicts a major subject of neutralisation is the referral to the macro level. A deadly incident is then primarily attached to the overall conflict, including its historical, political and religious dimensions. The violence is thereby contextualised and reframed. It is rationalised as 'counter-violence' and justified as being a means for (collective) self-defence. By declaring it a part of the political conflict, the focus fully shifts to the macro level, triggering the discussion on responsibility and competing victimhood.

This view is deficient for various reasons. First, it ignores the fact that large-scale conflicts are often based on prior experiences of war-induced grievances and a persisting sense of victimhood (see Rohne *et al.*: this volume, Chapter 1; Mack 1990; Volkan 1991; Bar-On 2001). It further neglects the fact that large-scale conflicts can only become so violent because of the successful manipulation of individuals. This manipulation often builds upon the aforementioned experience and a sense of victimhood (Braithwaite 2002: 184). If the experience of victimisation is not dealt with effectively, the revitalisation of hostilities can be expected to be more probable even after the political conflict was believed to be solved (van Zyl 2005: 212; Braithwaite 2002: 185). The exclusive attachment of such violence to the political conflict is also insufficient for another reason: although the political dimension is typically the driving force behind actions at the micro level, the background and motivation of recruited suicide bombers typically varies and can be significantly influenced by factors that are detached from the political conflict.[46] Hence it would be misleading to attach the attack in such cases to the political conflict only.

The role of victimisation effects

The typical effects of violent victimisation on the victim are well known from conventional victimology. The experience of violence fundamentally shatters the victims' life- and world-view. It creates a sense of powerlessness, vulnerability and injustice. Victims of violence often suffer of a lowered self-esteem and the development of a social mistrust. They fear a repetition of the victimisation and often perceive others in a disproportionate way as hostile (Schneider 1987: 782; Janoff-Bulman 1992; Orth 2003; Richter 1997: 113). Similar effects have been reported for victims of collective violence at different societal levels (Volkan 1991: 86; Schneider 1993; Jaukovic 2002). It has been argued elsewhere that all aforementioned victimisation effects concern the victims' basic needs for (social) identity and security (Rohne 2006a: 83). Both needs strongly interact with one another in the way that the sense of security reassures and safeguards the sense of identity. In other words, the need for identity requires a sense of security. The experience of victimisation openly negates this security and thereby questions and intrudes into the sphere of 'identity' by, for example, disordering the victim's life- and world-view (see also Rohne 2003). Such a violation typically triggers an intensified search for reassurance and reordering of the concept of the victim's own identity. This is true for violent conflict dynamics at the micro level as well as for those at the macro level: individuals and groups will seek to abolish a threat to their security by all means at their disposal (Burton 1997: 17) – or as Volkan explains: 'we may actually die – or kill the enemy – rather than permit the loss of this sense of self' (Volkan 1991: 87). For the Israeli–Palestinian conflict this means that violence continues as long as an existential threat pervades the respective societies. This threat will be fought against with all means available, be it F-16 attacks or suicide bombings. In the course of the present victim study and particularly the in-depth interviews, it was a striking observation how extremely similar the experts described the perceptions of the Palestinian and Israeli victims with regard to the threat posed by the 'unpredictable other' side (Rohne 2007: 270).

Responding to intifada violence requires a process that allows the restoration of a shattered sense of security and identity. A related need exists at all societal levels but it certainly exists at the individual level, too. This restoration for individuals must not and cannot be left only to developments at the macro level. Healing the wounds from the second intifada is certainly facilitated by a stabile political peace. But as has been demonstrated, for example by the *Parents Circle – Families Forum* (a grassroots organisation of bereaved Palestinians and Israelis) such a process is not necessarily dependent on the existence of a political peace (Auer-Shayan and Cromer 2007). Instead, the individuals need responsive measures at the micro level as well. The results of the survey among intifada victims presented here confirmed this: the surveyed victims repeatedly expressed their desire for an adequate response to their victimisation and their wish to be part of this response.

Although the UN Basic Principles do not stress the restoration of security and identity, the patterns outlined illustrate that its objectives are closely connected to this process: the acknowledgment of responsibility, the possibility for dialogue in a secure environment and the common search for redress are largely contributing to the disturbed sense of security and identity. The same is true for the offender who is aiming to be reintegrated into his community without being stigmatised. When applied in contexts of violence in large-scale conflicts, the restoration of security and identity will certainly remain a major task – and challenge – for restorative justice. But this 'new' context also requires modifications of restorative justice features. On the basis of the Chapters 8–11 and the empirical findings presented above, the following discussion will elaborate on these requirements as well as on the potential and limitation of restorative justice in such settings.

Procedural level

Prosecution and the role of international influence

In Chapter 9, Ghanayim critically reflected on the legality of the violence carried out on both sides. In many cases, the respective actions were questionable from the point of view of international humanitarian law. According to Ghanayim, a major problem in this respect is the use of force against civilians. As I have described in Chapter 8, civilians are indeed suffering most in the violent Israeli and Palestinian hostilities. Ghanayim described various existing international and domestic approaches to prosecute those responsible for attacks. The actual relevance of criminal prosecution for the victims was confirmed by the present survey. It revealed a strong support for prosecution among practically all victims surveyed.

A vast majority in both groups wanted such a prosecution to take place at the international level, or at least with an international involvement. This result was partially surprising due to existing scepticism towards the international community. From the governmental perspective, Ghanayim argued that the support for an international approach is highly selective:[47] on both sides the welcome of international (humanitarian) law seems to be conditioned by and limited to conformity with the respective interests. The victim survey partially confirmed this argument. A large number of Israeli victims who opted for the application of international law also stressed the importance of domestic law as a main source for criminal prosecution. A similar result was found in terms of judicial responsibility. For the surveyed Palestinian victims, the situation was obviously different. Trust in the domestic judicial system was found to be low which correlates with a local scepticism in its integrity and capability to effectively carry out a prosecution. In light of the weakened and mistrusted domestic judicial system, the Palestinian victims were either opting for international involvement or informal – extra-judicial – approaches as favourable alternatives (for details see also Rohne 2007: 138).

That said, in both groups the support for international involvement seems not to be the result of a genuine trust in the international community but rather is – at least in part – strongly shaped by the domestic situation. This phenomenon was also observed in other (post-)conflict regions (Kiza *et al.* 2006: 100). The data suggests that international involvement is not per se perceived as illegitimately 'externalising' domestic matters. This could change, however, if the applied standards were regarded as irreconcilable with local values. Thus, intercultural settings require a common basis that can either be reached by a minimum consensus and/or a certain flexibility of the respective response with regard to cultural peculiarities. In contrast to highly formalised criminal prosecution, restorative justice responses have an advantage in this respect. As was indicated by Alberstein and Irani, an external player might be respected as a facilitating party if he is able to balance the power of the parties, to ensure a sense of security and to demonstrate a nuanced appreciation of local histories and cultural values (see Alberstein: Chapter 10 and Irani: Chapter 11, both in this volume).

The political dimension of the Israeli–Palestinian conflict and the complexity of other interlocking conflicts (Bar-Siman-Tov 2006) requires extreme sensitivity for a third party to appear neutral. This will also be the case at the micro level. In this respect restorative justice has another particular strength to offer: as outlined in Chapter 1 the UN Basic Principles demand a 'fair and impartial' facilitator (Art. I(5)) 'with due respect to the dignity of the parties' (Art. III(18)). More precisely, restorative justice programmes demand an 'all-sided' facilitator rather than a 'neutral' one. It is far more feasible for a facilitator to develop authentic empathy for each side and then to communicate it in a balanced way than to sustain or create a 'neutrality'. At the same time an all-sided third party is more likely to promote a dialogue between the parties if demonstrating the possible (co-)existence of conflicting perspectives and emotions.

Intercultural challenges to the victims' participation and the role of the facilitator

Such a dialogue, however, requires a certain participation by the parties which is typically very limited in criminal trials. According to Ghanayim, the role of victims is also limited in the Israeli legal system (see Ghanayim: this volume, Chapter 9). However, it has increased in recent years (Sebba 2000). A global awareness of the victims' needs is reflected not only in various national legal systems but also at the international level: various integrative approaches have been discussed and introduced (Garkawe 2003: 346; Schabas 2001: 171). At the same time a one-size-fits-all approach is not suitable due to the specific conflict constellations and the diverse cultures involved. As discussed above, the victims' desire to participate varies from victim to victim and from culture to culture. This non-uniformity was also confirmed in the victim survey: the Palestinian and Israeli respondents stressed different aspects of their involvement, namely a narrative and an active role in the prosecution. Both emphasis have in common that they aim to ensure a certain control over the procedure and outcome. The desire for such influence is crucial for each procedure and has to be taken into sufficient account for restorative justice responses as well. The element of 'control' has already been identified by pioneers of procedural justice research: according to John W. Thibaut and Laurens Walker control is a crucial element for participants to perceive a process as 'just' (Thibaut and Walker 1975: 1).[48] Restorative justice approaches offer a remarkable opportunity in this respect. Their emphasis on dialogue on the one hand and the principle of voluntariness and autonomous agreement on the other allow the inclusion of different emphases and victims' expectations with regard to their participation.

On the other hand, restorative justice has to be aware of the fact that victims might prefer not to be involved in the decision-making process. In some cultures, the ability to come up with an acceptable decision and to implement it is seen as proof of the legitimacy of the third party. Other victims might want to tell their story without carrying the responsibility of a decision and expect this to be shouldered by a ('strong') third party. A similar aspect was indicated by Irani for the Israeli–Palestinian context (see Irani: this volume, Chapter 11). He argues that a facilitator needs to guarantee a sense of security (see also Irani 2006: 589).

Restorative justice procedures allow a broader variety of participatory nuances. However, it has to be aware of personal and cultural sensitivities.

In large-scale conflicts like the Israeli–Palestinian dispute, restorative justice faces multicultural challenges. In his paper Irani suggests the application of (modified) *sulha* principles and values. The values applied, however, have to be reconcilable with those of the other side. In *sulha* the participation of victims is subordinated to the representation of socially respected persons (*muslihs*). They are representing in particular the social entity or community that the victim and the offender belong to. The socio-historical function of such a representation was to provide protection for the parties as well as for the social order. Restorative justice, as it is mostly understood and practised in Western or Westernised cultures, follows a different approach. The aforementioned functions are side effects but the main task of the facilitator is not primarily to protect the parties but to provide a protective atmosphere for the parties which allows them to settle their conflict if they want to. It is not the task of the facilitator to represent anybody; a 'representative form' of mediation is – to say the least – a challenging thought for Western restorative justice approaches (for details see Rohne 2006b: 210). As Alberstein indicated in Chapter 10 the latter understanding is also dominant in Jewish-Israeli society as well as in the 'modern' restorative justice programmes found in Israel today (see also Segal 2006; Goldstein 2006).

It goes without saying that a transfer of traditional principles to a restorative justice procedure is conditioned by the relevance that these principles still enjoy among the stakeholders. From the Israeli perspective, Alberstein identified various traditional Jewish elements of restorative conflict resolution describing them as general principles rather than distinct mechanisms (see Alberstein: this volume, Chapter 10). But she also states that these principles are not very widespread within Jewish-Israeli society today. Instead, the formal criminal justice system – and to some extent also modern informal restorative justice programmes – are primarily shaping Israeli views on how to respond to domestic criminal matters (see also Segal 2006; Goldstein 2006). Irani states that the tradition of *sulha* is still relevant for the Palestinian society. As in other Arab societies, the use of *sulha* is widely spread among the Palestinian population (Jabbour 1996: 26). It even influences a considerable number of criminal cases not just before Israeli courts but especially within the Palestinian judicial system (Ghanayim: this volume, Chapter 9, this volume; Tsafrir 2006; Fares and Khalidi 2006: 517). However, the traditional emphasis of authoritarian and hierarchical powers that are underpinning the use of *sulha* (Irani: this volume, Chapter 11) is not undisputed within the Palestinian population due to the inherent danger of power misuse (Fares and Khalidi 2006: 519; Shalhoub-Kevorkian 2006).

Alternative processes: the role of truth commissions

Support for the implementation of truth commissions was far lower than for conducting a criminal prosecution. To some extent this contradicts the theoretical assumption that truth commissions would probably be welcome as a response to violent victimisation among the local population (Alberstein: this volume, Chapter 10). However, the survey results have to be interpreted very carefully due to the low number of respondents included in these questions. Further, among the Palestinian victims the low support for truth commissions was seemingly also caused by the widespread ignorance of 'truth commissions' in general. This dependence corresponds with observations made in other (post-)conflict regions where knowledge of and support for particular responsive mechanisms were sometimes interconnected (Kiza *et al.* 2006: 108; AIHRC 2004: 34; ICTJ 2005: 32). This correlation can be a valuable indicator for responsive mechanisms: the local acceptance and success of responsive mechanisms might strongly depend on the degree the population is familiar with the respective concept. A low acceptance might be increased by also stimulating a general knowledge about the particular mechanism.

Outcome level

Punitiveness and restorative justice

It cannot be discussed here whether punishment can be integrated into a restorative justice paradigm (Duff 2003: 382; see also Rohne *et al.*: this volume, Chapter 1). But a significant challenge to restorative justice in large-scale conflicts is the observation that amnesty or impunity for offenders is largely rejected among victims from various (post-) conflict regions (Kiza *et al.* 2006: 97). A remarkably strong support for prosecution was also found among Palestinian and Israeli intifada victims. While there is a widespread expectation of punishment for those who were responsible for the victimisation, support for a specific form of punishment was comparatively hesitant, especially among the Palestinian victims.

Overall, the data indicated a widespread punitive desire among the intifada victims of both sides. A debate on restorative justice has to deal with these expectations and has to find a way to respond to them. Ignoring an existing punitive demand will probably result in a lack of acceptance of restorative justice approaches among the parties as it leaves these victims unsatisfied. It is possible that punitive desires diminish in the course of a restorative justice process but this can presently only be hypothesised.

Forms of reparation and the role of culture

In terms of reparation we have seen that both material and immaterial reparation received a strong support among the victim groups. This supports general approaches of restorative justice programmes, namely to encourage amends by financial and symbolic reparation (Van Ness 2002: 3). In criminal justice systems, reparation is often a synonym for financial restitution. In the present survey, however, we observed that monetary compensation was not as important as might have been expected. Instead, a great emphasis was put on intangible forms of reparation. Similar results were also found among victim groups in other (post-)conflict regions (Kiza *et al.* 2006: 117).

Especially with regard to the intangible forms of reparation, the results revealed differences *between* the victim groups that could be attached to cultural peculiarities. The Israeli victims clearly favoured the option to build a memorial. This corresponded to the strong emphasis on remembrance and the use of supplementary commemoration ceremonies and sites.[49]

Among the Palestinian respondents there was no such distinct preference for a particular intangible form of reparation. However, the support for apologies was clearly stronger than among the Israeli participants. Although the importance of apologies is well acknowledged in the field of restorative and transitional justice (Strang 2002: 20; Van Ness 2002: 4; Mani 2000: 276; Minow 1998: 112), we found culture to (co-)influence the view on apologies among the intifada victims. The comparatively strong support among Palestinian victims for the use of an apology was attached to a culturally based understanding of 'honour' and its violation in the course of the victimisation.

So, in both victim groups culture was apparently (co-)influencing the attitudes of the respondents. This has to be considered when searching for appropriate responses to violence. Restorative justice programmes encourage the consideration of cultural peculiarities. The flexibility of restorative justice approaches certainly offers a significant potential in this regard. In spite of this flexibility, existing commonalities between the victim groups should also be explored and used where possible.

Further liabilities

As indicated above, the collective dimension of violent attacks in the course of the intifada, is particularly challenging the implementation of restorative justice in such cases. This becomes especially apparent in terms of identifying accountabilities. From a legal perspective Ghanayim described that liability is not only attributed to the actual perpetrators but also to co-perpetrators, instigators and abettors and so forth (Ghanayian: this volume, Chapter 9). This was largely confirmed in the victim survey. In both victim groups the majority did not only regard the actual perpetrator to be responsible for the violence but also desired to see the military and political leadership to be held accountable.

It is at the core of restorative justice approaches that all persons involved in a conflict are brought together (Zehr and Mika 1998: 51; Christie 1977: 8). The extended circle of liabilities can constitute a major obstacle for the implementation of restorative justice in such cases. It is not impossible to connect political and military officials to such a setting; experiences from other contexts might serve as an example here (Savage 2007: 213). The ongoing conflict, however, makes their personal involvement unlikely. Given these difficulties the inclusive principle of restorative justice possibly needs to be reframed and adapted to a certain extent when implementing restorative justice mechanisms at the micro level.

However, it is also possible that victims want the political and military leadership to be held responsible at the political level but not as part of the response to their personal victimisation. The same is true for the observed tendency among parts of the Palestinian victims to hold the Israeli society accountable. If and to what extent the latter assumptions are justified can only be left to further research.

Purpose level

Objectives for taking action

In the context of large-scale conflicts retribution is often deemed to be a predominant desire among the respective populations. Related research confirms this – if at all – only partially (Kiza *et al*. 2006: 123). In the present context, the survey also provided an ambivalent picture among intifada victims. Revenge was named as a main purpose by a considerable number of victims. However, in neither group was it supported by a majority.

Instead, a tendency for favouring rather forward-looking purposes became visible: there was substantial support for such purposes that resemble those pursued by restorative justice, i.e. to reveal the truth about what happened and to enable people to live together again. The data suggested the preference for a more narrative or dialogic process of dealing with the past which goes beyond what is usually pursued by criminal trials. In this respect restorative justice contains a remarkable potential for victims and offenders alike. It is an essential pillar of restorative justice to give sufficient voice to the parties within a protective atmosphere allowing them to express their experiences and views while at the same time learning more about the other's perspective.

Perhaps most encouraging from a restorative justice perspective was the fact that a considerable number of victims named that future coexistence ('enabling people to live together') as a main purpose for taking actions against the offenders. Given the fact that these victims also support the offender's criminal prosecution, the envisaged goal of coexistence seems to interact with the pursuit of 'justice'. But what does justice mean? If this necessarily includes the offender's trial, then restorative justice needs to find ways to cooperate or coexist with a criminal justice response. Given the forward-looking content of the aforementioned purpose, further research in this regard could reveal an underlying willingness to exchange the demand for criminal prosecution for other – possibly more restorative – approaches if the victims find these approaches to offer them the 'justice' they desire. A particular advantage in this regard is the fact that restorative justice is not per se focused on a particular form of restoration (see Rohne *et al*.: this volume, Chapter 1).

In light of the survey results, it cannot be argued that the objectives of restorative justice have no sound basis in situations of large-scale conflicts and the related complex and multidimensional suffering. On the contrary, among the Israeli respondents it was observed that those who suffered the most severe victimisation were more likely to name the forward-looking purpose of 'enabling people to live together' than other victims. This questions the (reasonable) assumption that a high degree of victimisation necessarily decreases the willingness of victims to pursue reconciliatory goals (Alberstein: Chapter 10, this volume).

Beneficiary and the role of culture

As indicated above, the victim survey also questioned the – predominantly Western – assumption that conflicts primarily concern the interests of individuals. While a number of Israeli victims also wanted their community to benefit from the offender's prosecution, a majority of the Palestinian victims fully subordinated an individual benefit to the communitarian benefit. In Chapter 11, this volume, Irani has already pointed to the importance of communal structures that are shaping an Arab-Islamic perception of conflicts and the conflicting parties (see Irani and Funk 2001: 180; Rohne 2006b: 202). These cultural perceptions were also reflected in the responses.

Such evident cultural influences need to be considered – also and especially – in the intercultural setting of the Israeli–Palestinian conflict. This challenges a predominantly Western understanding of restorative justice that is very much based on the individual role of the victimised and the offender.[50] At the same time, restorative justice is in fact well aware of the communitarian aspect of conflicts and the role that a community has in settling the dispute. Thus it can be argued that it is better prepared to meet communal aspects and the involvement of social entities than other mechanisms such as a criminal justice system.

Conclusion

We have seen that although particular incidents cannot be isolated from their political context, they also need to be dealt with at the micro level in order to prepare the ground among the population for sustainable peace and stability. It was argued here that in order to maximise the effectiveness of responsive measures there needs to be a close examination of prevailing attitudes among those who suffered most. Considering these expectations is crucial for the acceptance and, hence, the success of the respective responsive mechanisms.

The chapter has shown various interesting similarities between Israeli and Palestinian victims. But we also observed striking differences many of which could be clearly attached to socio-political and especially cultural influences. They also revealed the need to carefully explore traditional responses to conflict resolution. Depending on their relevance today such responses can greatly help an understanding of culturally based views and perceptions.

Due to its multifaceted and flexible nature, restorative justice offers promising 'tools' to tackle this task. Its emphasis on the parties' autonomy and self-determination provides for a flexibility that appears to be highly advantageous for related intercultural challenges. The victims' basic need for identity and security can be constructively contributed to by restorative justice.

The features of restorative justice as they are outlined in the UN Basic Principles can serve as a useful starting point for understanding the role of restorative justice in large-scale settings. However, violence stemming from large-scale conflicts is in many respects very different from conventional violence. Due to these specifics the features of restorative justice have to be adapted and modified. In doing so, restorative justice has to be aware not to repeat mistakes we know from other contexts, i.e. developing an 'externalisation of justice' (Drumbl 2007: 127). The paradigms outlined in the UN Basic Principles largely reflect a Western view of restorative justice. If restorative justice is to be implemented in other cultures, for example the Israeli–Palestinian context, it needs to make sufficient consideration of cultural perceptions and needs. The flexibility of restorative justice offers a particular advantage in doing so but it needs to make use of this. A related question has to be further explored when profiling restorative justice in the context of large-scale violence: to what extent can restorative justice be transferred to settings that it was not originally designed for?[51]

To sum up, up till now the discussion about the implementation of restorative justice mechanisms in the Israeli–Palestinian context is – if anything – rather theoretical. This paper, however, has revealed a significant potential that restorative justice has to offer should it be used to respond to large-scale violence. The victims' responses can be largely interpreted as encouraging for restorative justice elements – but probably hand in hand with a criminal justice system. There is a need to analyse more deeply the capacities of restorative justice. Furthermore, restorative justice has to adapt its profile according to the specifics of collective violence. This profile will ideally be developed on the basis of the UN Basic Principles. This would promote the implementation of restorative justice in these settings and certainly ensure the quality required of related programmes. I conclude with the wish that the UN Basic Principles will be supplemented soon by the development of 'Basic Principles on the Use of Restorative Justice Programmes in Matters of Violence used in Large-Scale Conflicts'.

Notes

1 Restorative justice programmes share the restorative intention with the aforementioned approaches. However, the features of restorative justice differ significantly from such programmes (see Rohne *et al.*: this volume Chapter 1).

2 The survey is also connected to a broader research project that the author conducted together with colleagues at the Max Planck Institute for Foreign and International Criminal Law (Freiburg, Germany). This pilot project explored the experiences and attitudes of war victims on an international comparative level including eleven (post-)conflict regions in Africa, Asia and Europe (see Kiza *et al.* 2006).

3 The required minimum age was 18 and the cooperating organisations were asked to provide for a balanced gender distribution. Concerning the latter, the Palestinian sample included 105 men (59 per cent) and 73 women (41 per cent). Among the Israelis were 59 female (50.4 per cent) and 58 male respondents (49.6 per cent). In total, three persons did not indicate their gender.

4 Among them were 72 Palestinians and 78 Israelis.

5 This was reported by 72 Palestinians and 77 Israelis.

6 There were no such cases among the Israeli group.

7 In total, 270 respondents provided a decisive answer to this question.

8 These respondents did so notwithstanding a note in the questionnaire to skip this question if not having heard of 'truth commissions' before.

9 For a methodological explanation see Reuband (2000: 27) and Hough and Roberts (1998: 43).

10 Phi = .359, p = .002 (two-tailed).

11 This assumption is confirmed by the case-wise analysis of the answer profiles which show that 74.6 per cent of those Israeli victims who supported prosecution by international courts simultaneously opted for the responsibility of their national courts.

12 Phi = –.217, p = .000 (two-tailed) and Phi = –.523, p = .000 (two-tailed), respectively.

13 More than 70 UN resolutions dealt with the Israeli–Palestinian conflict, many of which sharply criticised Israeli policies; see: http://www.un.org.

14 Phi = 433, p = .000 (two-tailed).

15 Due to the reported religious affiliation the respondents referred to principles stemming from the Jewish religion. Within the Israeli sample, 114 persons (95.8 per cent) reported their affiliation to the Jewish

religion. One person indicated to be agnostic and one person stated to be Muslim. Three others did not indicate their religious affiliation.

16 The statistical difference between the two samples was strong and highly significant (phi = .328, p = .000 (two-tailed)).

17 In the Palestinian sample 176 persons (98.3 per cent) stated they were Muslim. One respondent was reportedly Christian and two others did not indicate their religious affiliation.

18 This support was almost equal within the Palestinian (N = 145; 92.4 per cent) and Israeli samples (N = 97; 89 per cent).

19 Phi = –.383, p = .000 (two-tailed).

20 The lower support in comparison to the preference for prosecution might stem from its design as a multiple response set.

21 The statistical difference between the Israeli and Palestinian samples was noticeable and highly significant (phi = –.202, p = .001 (two-tailed)).

22 The statistical difference between the sample groups was rather weak but significant (phi = –.129, p = .032 (two-tailed)).

23 Phi = –.133, p = .036 (two-tailed).

24 Phi = –.391, p = .000 (two-tailed).

Phi = .313, p = .000 (two-tailed). Among the Palestinian respondents, many (N = 45; 30.4 per cent) opted for both alternatives.

26 Phi = –.245, p = .000 (two-tailed).

27 Phi = .288, p = .000 (two-tailed).

28 At the same time, this money is often returned to the offender which is generally perceived as an honourable gesture (Jabbour 1996: 43).

29 In a multiple response set (including the option for an open answer) the respondents were asked 'Who should be held responsible for the things that happened during the Al-Aqsa Intifada?'

30 Phi = –.177, p = .004 (two-tailed).

31 Phi = .256, p = .000 (two-tailed).

32 In the Israeli sample 20 respondents (18 per cent) supported this item. Compared to five Palestinians (3.2 per cent) who did so, this resulted in a statistically highly significant difference between the two victim groups (phi = –.251, p = .000 (two-tailed)).

33 The statistical values for the latter are relatively weak but still significant (phi = .147, p = .016 (two-tailed)) including 25 respondents (16 per cent) of the Palestinian sample and only seven Israelis (6.3 per cent).

34 Phi = .321, p = .000 (two-tailed).

35 Phi = .228, p = .006 (two-tailed).

36 No such correlation was found among the Israeli victims which supports the aforementioned assumption that for them a main desire was to have a sense of control over the process rather than feeling the need to tell their story (at least in a court setting) – see also Rohne (2007: 141).

37 Cramer's V = .295, p = .047 (two-tailed). This was especially apparent in comparison with those who were solely directly victimised (phi = .308, p = .016 (two-tailed)).

38 The applied method has been borrowed from a more complex procedure known as *configuration frequency analysis*; see Krauth and Lienert (1973); Lautsch and Weber (1990).
39 The remaining answer profiles are condensed into the category 'diverse'.
40 The options 'forget' and 'forgive' do not appear in a case-wise analysis due to their low support.
41 Phi = .190, p = .004 (two-tailed).
42 The respective question was 'Who should benefit from the prosecution?'
43 Phi = –.455, p = .000 (two-tailed).
44 Phi = .326, p = .000 (two-tailed).
45 The referral to the intercollective dimension of the Israeli–Palestinian conflict as an explanation would be insufficient since it cannot explain the observed differences *between* the victim groups.
46 While this has been mainly reported about female suicide bombers (Tzoreff 2006: 19) this is also true for males (Issacharoff 2006: 43). The reported (co-)influential factors included economic distress and personal difficulties as well as family and marital problems etc. See, for example: http://www.telegraph.co.uk/news/main.jhtml?xrnl=/news/2005/06/26/wmid26.xrril.
47 Israeli caution is well expressed in a statement accompanying Israel's signature of the Rome Statute: 'The State of Israel signs the Statute while rejecting any attempt to interpret provisions thereof in a politically motivated manner against Israel and its citizens.' See Kremnitzer and Cohen (2005: 323).
48 The importance of 'control' as the dominating variable was later put into perspective with other factors identified by subsequent research conducted, for example, by Gerald S. Leventhal ('Leventhal scale' – Leventhal 1980) and Allen Lind and Tom R. Tyler ('Group Value Model' – Lind and Tyler 1988). For details about the relevance of procedural justice research in the context of large-scale conflicts, see also Rohne (2006a: 90 and 2007: 67).
49 In the supplementary expert interviews one of the Israeli interview partners put it as follows: 'We learn from when we are small onwards that we have to remember that we cannot forget. This is a society of "the book". Books in general but also of old tradition. [...] We remember. It's part of the Jewish tradition but also a heritage from the holocaust where people were victimised in such a way that their name was stolen. So, remembrance is very, very important. And it's highly respected – people go by these rules.' (For details see Rohne 2007: 167).
50 For a detailed comparative analysis on *sulha* and Western victim–offender mediation, see Rohne (2006b).
51 Experiences from other attempts to implement traditional approaches to collective violence were quite ambivalent; for the implementation of *Gacaca* tribunals in Rwanda, see Drumbl (2007: 85).

References

Abu-Nimer, M. (2001) 'Conflict resolution in an Islamic context: some conceptual questions', in A. Said, N.C. Funk and A.S. Kadayifci (eds), *Peace and Conflict Resolution in Islam*. Lanham, MA: University Press of America, pp. 123–41.

AIHRC (2004) *A Call for Justice*. Afghanistan Independent Human Rights Commission. See: http://www.aihrc.org.af/Rep_29_Eng/rep29_1_05cal!4justice.pdf.

Albrecht, H.-J., Simon, J.-M., Rezaei, H., Rohne, H.-C. and Kiza, E. (eds) (2006) *Conflicts and Conflict Resolution in Middle Eastern Societies – Between Tradition and Modernity*. Berlin: Duncker & Humblot.

Alvarez, J.E. (1999) 'Crimes of states/crimes of hate: lessons from Rwanda', *Yale Journal of International Law*, 24: 365–483.

Auer-Shayan, H. and Cromer, G. (2007) 'The Families Forum: from personal tragedy to political reconciliation among Israeli bereaved parents', in Y. Danieli (ed.), *International Handbook of Multigenerational Legacies of Trauma*. New York: Springer (forthcoming).

Aukerman, M. (2002) 'Extraordinary evil, ordinary crime: a framework for understanding transitional justice', *Harvard Human Rights Journal*, 15: 39–97.

Avruch, K. and Vejarano, B. (2001) 'Truth and Reconciliation Commissions: a review essay and annotated bibliography', *Social Justice: Anthropology, Peace and Human Rights*, 2 (1–2): 47–108.

Bar-On, D. (2001) *Die 'Anderen' in uns: Dialog als Modell der interkulturellen Konfliktbewältigung*. Hamburg: Ed. Körber-Stiftung.

Bar-On, D. (2005) 'Empirical criteria for reconciliation in practice', *Intervention*, 3 (3): 180–91.

Bar-Siman-Tov, Y. (2006) 'Interlocking conflicts in the Middle East structural dimensions', in H.-J. Albrecht, J.-M. Simon, H. Rezaei, H.-C. Rohne and E. Kiza (eds), *Conflicts and Conflict Resolution in Middle Eastern Societies – Between Tradition and Modernity*. Berlin: Duncker & Humblot, pp. 215–28.

Bassiouni, M.C. (1996) 'Searching for peace and achieving justice: the need for accountability', *Law and Contemporary Problems*, 59 (4): 9–28.

Braithwaite, J. (2002) *Restorative Justice and Responsive Regulation*. New York: Oxford University Press.

Burton, J. (1997) *Violence Explained – The Sources of Conflict, Violence and Crime and Their Prevention*. Manchester: Manchester University Press.

Christie, N. (1977) 'Conflicts as property', *British Journal of Criminology*, 17 (1): 1–15.

Cohen, S. (1995) 'Justice in transition? Prospects for a Palestinian-Israeli truth commission', *Middle East Report*, 194/195: 2–5.

Drumbl, M.A. (2005) 'Collective punishment and individual punishment: the criminality of mass atrocities', *Northwestern University Law Review*, 99 (2): 101–79.

Drumbl, M.A. (2007) *Atrocity, Punishment, and International Law*. Cambridge: Cambridge University Press.

Duff, R.A. (2003) 'Restorative punishment and punitive restoration', in G. Johnstone (ed.), *A Restorative Justice Reader*. Cullompton: Willan, pp. 382–97.

Fares, S. and Khalidi, D. (2006) 'Formal and informal justice in Palestine: between justice and social order', in H.-J. Albrecht, J.-M. Simon, H. Rezaei, H.-C. Rohne and E. Kiza (eds), *Conflicts and Conflict Resolution in Middle Eastern Societies – Between Tradition and Modernity*. Berlin: Duncker & Humblot, pp. 507–24.

Findlay, M. and Henham, R. (2005) *Transforming International Criminal Justice – Retributive and Restorative Justice in the Trial Process*. Cullompton: Willan.

Fletcher, G.P. (1999) 'The place of victims in the theory of retribution', *Buffalo Criminal Law Review*, 3 (51): 51–63.

Fletcher, G.P. (2004) 'Collective guilt and collective punishment', *Theoretical Inquiries in Law*, 5 (1): 163–78.

Garkawe, S. (2003) 'Victims and the International Criminal Court: three major issues', *International Criminal Law Review*, 3 (4): 345–67.

Goldstein, A. (2006) 'Family Group Conference (FGC) in Youth Justice in Israel', in H.-J. Albrecht, J.-M. Simon, H. Rezaei, H.-C. Rohne and E. Kiza (eds), *Conflicts and Conflict Resolution in Middle Eastern Societies – Between Tradition and Modernity*. Berlin: Duncker & Humblot, pp. 493–506.

Gräf, E. (1952) *Das Rechtswesen der heutigen Beduinen*. Walldorf: Verlag für Orientkunde.

Graybill, L. (2002) *Truth and Reconciliation in South Africa. Miracle or Model?* Boulder, CO: Lynne Rienner.

Hayner, P. (2004) 'Fifteen Truth Commissions – 1974 to 1994: a comparative study', *Human Rights Quarterly*, 16 (4): 597–655.

Henham, R. (2003) 'The philosophical foundations of international sentencing', *Journal of International Criminal Justice*, 1 (1): 64–85.

Henham, R. (2004) 'Conceptualizing access to justice and victims' rights in international sentencing', *Social and Legal Studies*, 13 (1): 27–55.

Hough, M. and Roberts, J. (1998) *Attitudes to Punishment: Findings from the British Crime Survey*, Home Office Research Study No. 179. London: Home Office.

ICTJ (2005) *Forgotten Voices – A Population-Based Survey on Attitudes about Peace and Justice in Northern Uganda*. International Center for Transitional Justice and Human Rights Center, University of California, Berkeley. See: http://www.ictj.org/downloads/ForgottenVoices.pdf.

Irani, G.E. (2006) 'Lebanese and Arab methods of conflict resolution', in H.-J. Albrecht, J.-M. Simon, H. Rezaei, H.-C. Rohne and E. Kiza (eds) *Conflicts and Conflict Resolution in Middle Eastern Societies – Between Tradition and Modernity*. Berlin: Duncker & Humblot, pp. 575–92.

Irani, G.E. and Funk, N.C. (2001) 'Rituals of reconciliation: Arab-Islamic perspectives', in A. Said, N.C. Funk and A.S. Kadayifici (eds), *Peace and*

Conflict Resolution in Islam. Lanham, MA: University Press of America, pp. 169–91.

Issacharoff, A. (2006) 'The Palestinian and Israeli media on female suicide terrorists', in Y. Schweitzer (ed.), *Female Suicide Bombers – Dying for Equality?* Tel Aviv: Tel Aviv University, pp. 43–50.

Jabbour, E.J. (1996): *Sulha – Palestinian Traditional Peacemaking Process*. Montreal: House of Hope Publications.

Jamal, A. (2006) 'Political and ideological factors of conflict in Palestinian society', in H.-J. Albrecht, J.-M. Simon, H. Rezaei, H.-C. Rohne and E. Kiza (eds), *Conflicts and Conflict Resolution in Middle Eastern Societies – Between Tradition and Modernity*. Berlin: Duncker & Humblot, pp. 229–56.

Janoff-Bulman, R. (1992) *Shattered Assumptions: Towards a New Psychology of Trauma*. New York: Free Press.

Jaukovic, J. (2002) 'The manners of overcoming stress generated by war conflict trauma', *European Journal of Crime, Criminal Law and Criminal Justice*, 10 (2/3): 177–81.

Joutsen, M. (1991) 'Changing victim policy: international dimensions', in G. Kaiser, H. Kury and H.-J. Albrecht (eds), *Victims and Criminal Justice – Particular Groups of Victims*, Criminological Research Reports 52:2. Freiburg: Max Planck Institute for Foreign and International Criminal Law, pp. 765–97.

Kiza, E., Rathgeber, C. and Rohne, H.-C. (2006) *Victims of War – An Empirical Study on War Victimization and Victims' Attitudes towards Addressing Atrocities*. Hamburg: Hamburger Institut für Sozialforschung. See: http://ww.his-online.de/cms.asp?H='79'&T=0&Plugin=10&HE=10&HEP=978-3-936096-73-6.

Krauth, J. and Lienert, G.A. (1973) *Die Konflgurationsfrequenzanalse (KFA) und ihre Anwendung in Psychologie und Medizin*. Freiburg: Verlag Karl Alber.

Kremnitzer, M. and Cohen, M.A. (2005) 'Prosecution of international crimes in Israel', in A. Eser, U. Sieber and H. Kreicker (eds), *National Prosecution of International Crimes*, Vol. 5. Berlin: Duncker & Humblot, pp. 317–409.

Kritz, N.J. (1996) 'Coming to terms with atrocities: a review of accountability mechanisms for mass violations of human rights', *Law and Contemporary Problems*, 59 (4): 127–52.

Landau, S. (2006) 'Settings, factors and phenomena of conflict in the Israeli society', in H.-J. Albrecht, J.-M. Simon, H. Rezaei, H.-C. Rohne and E. Kiza (eds), *Conflicts and Conflict Resolution in Middle Eastern Societies – Between Tradition and Modernity*. Berlin: Duncker & Humblot, pp. 257–74.

Lautsch, E. and Weber, S. von (1990) *Konfigurationsfrequenzanalyse (KFA) – Methoden und Anwendungen*. Berlin: Volk und Wissen.

Leventhal, G.S. (1980) 'What should be done with equity theory? New approaches to the study of fairness in social relationships', in K.J. Gergen, M.S. Greenberg and R.H. Willis (eds), *Social Exchange: Advances in Theory and Research*. New York: Plenum Press, pp. 27–55.

Lind, E.A. and Tyler, T.R. (1988) *The Social Psychology of Procedural Justice.* New York: Plenum Press.
Mack, J.E. (1990) 'The psychodynamics of victimization among national groups in conflict', in V.D. Volkan, D.A. Julius and J.V. Montville (eds), *The Psychodynamics of International Relationships.* Lexington, MA: Lexington Books, pp. 119–29.
Mani, R. (2000) 'Restoring justice in the aftermath of conflict: bridging the gap between theory and practice', in T. Coates (ed.), *International Justice.* Aldershot: Ashgate, pp. 264–99.
Maoz, I. (2004) 'Coexistence is in the eye of the beholder: evaluating intergroup encounter interventions between Jews and Arabs in Israel', *Journal of Social Issues,* 60 (2): 437–52.
Minow, M. (1998) *Between Vengeance and Forgiveness: Facing History after Genocide and Mass Violence.* Boston: Beacon Press.
Orentlicher, D.F. (1991) 'Settling accounts: the duty to prosecute human rights violations of a prior regime', *Yale Law Journal,* 100: 2537–615.
Orth, U. (2003) 'Punishment goals of crime victims', *Law and Human Behaviour,* 27 (2): 173–86.
Ratner, S. and Abrams J.S. (1997) *Accountability for Human Rights Atrocities in International Law: Beyond the Nuremberg Legacy.* Oxford: Oxford University Press.
Reuband, K.-H. (2000) '"Pseudo-opinions" in Bevölkerungsumfragen', *ZA-Information,* 46: 26–38.
Richter, H. (1997) *Opfer krimineller Gewalttaten – Individuelle Folgen und ihre Verarbeitung.* Mainz: Weisser Ring.
Robinson, G.E. (1997a) *Building a Palestinian State: The Incomplete Revolution.* Bloomington, IN: Indiana University Press.
Robinson, G.E. (1997b) 'The politics of legal reform in Palestine', *Journal of Palestine Studies,* 27 (1): 51–60.
Rohne, H.-C. (2003) 'Intracultural Approaches to Violent Conflicts and Their Victimological Significance'. Paper presented on 6 December 2003 at Experts' Seminar on 'Alternative Means to Retributive Justice in Violent Conflicts in the Middle East', 4–7 December, Istanbul (unpublished).
Rohne, H.-C. (2006a) 'Approaches to respond to violent conflicts – victimological reflections in the context of the Al-Aqsa Intifada', in H.-J. Albrecht, J.-M. Simon, H. Rezaei, H.-C. Rohne and E. Kiza (eds), *Conflicts and Conflict Resolution in Middle Eastern Societies – Between Tradition and Modernity.* Berlin: Duncker & Humblot, pp. 79–98.
Rohne, H.-C. (2006b) 'Cultural aspects of conflict resolution – comparing *sulha* and Western mediation', in H.-J. Albrecht, J.-M. Simon, H. Rezaei, H.-C. Rohne and E. Kiza (eds), *Conflicts and Conflict Resolution in Middle Eastern Societies – Between Tradition and Modernity.* Berlin: Duncker & Humblot, pp. 187–214.

Rohne, H.-C. (2007) *Opferperspektiven im interkulturellen Vergleich. Eine viktimologische Studie im Kontext der Al-Aqsa Intifada*. Hamburg: Verlag Dr. Kovač.

Roy, S. (2001) 'Palestinian society and economy: the continued denial of possibility', *Journal of Palestine Studies*, 30 (4): 5–20.

Savage, S.P. (2007) 'Restoring justice. Campaigns against miscarriages of justice and the restorative justice process', *European Journal of Criminology*, 4 (2): 195–216.

Schabas, W. (2001) *An Introduction to the International Criminal Court*. Cambridge: Cambridge University Press.

Schneider, H.J. (1987) *Kriminologie*. Berlin: de Gruyter.

Schneider, H.J. (1993) *Einführung in die Kriminologie*. Berlin: de Gruyter.

Sebba, L. (2000) 'Victims' rights and legal strategies: Israel as a case study', *Criminal Law Forum*, 11 (1): 47–100.

Sebba, L. (2006) 'Formal and informal conflict resolution in international criminal justice', in H.-J. Albrecht, J.-M. Simon, H. Rezaei, H.-C. Rohne and E. Kiza (eds), *Conflicts and Conflict Resolution in Middle Eastern Societies – Between Tradition and Modernity*. Berlin: Duncker & Humblot, pp. 25–44.

Segal, P. (2006) 'Restorative justice in Jewish law and present Israel', in H.-J. Albrecht, J.-M. Simon, H. Rezaei, H.-C. Rohne and E. Kiza (eds), *Conflicts and Conflict Resolution in Middle Eastern Societies – Between Tradition and Modernity*. Berlin: Duncker & Humblot, pp. 525–34.

Shalhoub-Kevorkian, N. (2006) 'Tribal justice and gender: perspectives in the Palestinian society', in H.-J. Albrecht, J.-M. Simon, H. Rezaei, H.-C. Rohne and E. Kiza (eds), *Conflicts and Conflict Resolution in Middle Eastern Societies – Between Tradition and Modernity*. Berlin: Duncker & Humblot, pp. 535–56.

Strang, H. (2002) *Repair or Revenge. Victims and Restorative Justice*. Oxford: Oxford University Press.

Sykes, G. and Matza, D. (1957) 'Techniques of neutralization: a theory of delinquency', *American Sociological Review*, 22 (6): 664–70.

Thibaut, J.W. and Walker, L. (1975) *Procedural Justice – A Psychological Analysis*. Hillsdale, NJ: Erlbaum.

Tsafrir, N. (2006) 'Arab customary law in Israel: sulha agreements and Israeli courts', *Islamic Law and Society*, 13 (1): 76–98.

Tzoreff, M. (2006) 'The Palestinian shahida: national patriotism, Islamic feminism, or social crisis', in Y. Schweitzer (ed.), *Female Suicide Bombers – Dying for Equality?* Tel Aviv: Tel Aviv University, pp. 13–23.

Umbreit, M.S., Coates, R.B. and Kalanj, B. (1994) *Victim Meets Offender: The Impact of Restorative Justice and Mediation*. Monsey, NY: Criminal Justice Press.

UN (2002) *Basic Principles on the Use of Restorative Justice Programmes in Criminal Matters*. UN Economic and Social Council, Resolution 2002/12.

Van Ness, D. (2002) 'The shape of things to come: a framework for thinking about a restorative justice process', in E. Weitekamp and H.-J. Kerner (eds), *Restorative Justice: Theoretical Foundations*. Cullompton: Willan, pp. 1–20.

Van Zyl, P. (2005) 'Promoting transitional justice in post-conflict societies', in A. Bryden and H. Hänggi (eds), *Security Governance in Post-conflict Peacebuilding*. Münster: LIT Verlag, pp. 209–22.

Volkan, V.D. (1991) 'Psychoanalytic aspects of ethnic conflicts', in J.V. Montville (ed.), *Conflict and Peacekeeping in Multiethnic Societies*. New York: Lexington Books, pp. 81–92.

Zehr, H. and Mika, H. (1998) 'Fundamental concepts of restorative justice', *Contemporary Justice Review*, 1 (1): 47–55.

Section 3
The conflict in the Democratic Republic of Congo

Kris Vanspauwen and Tyrone Savage

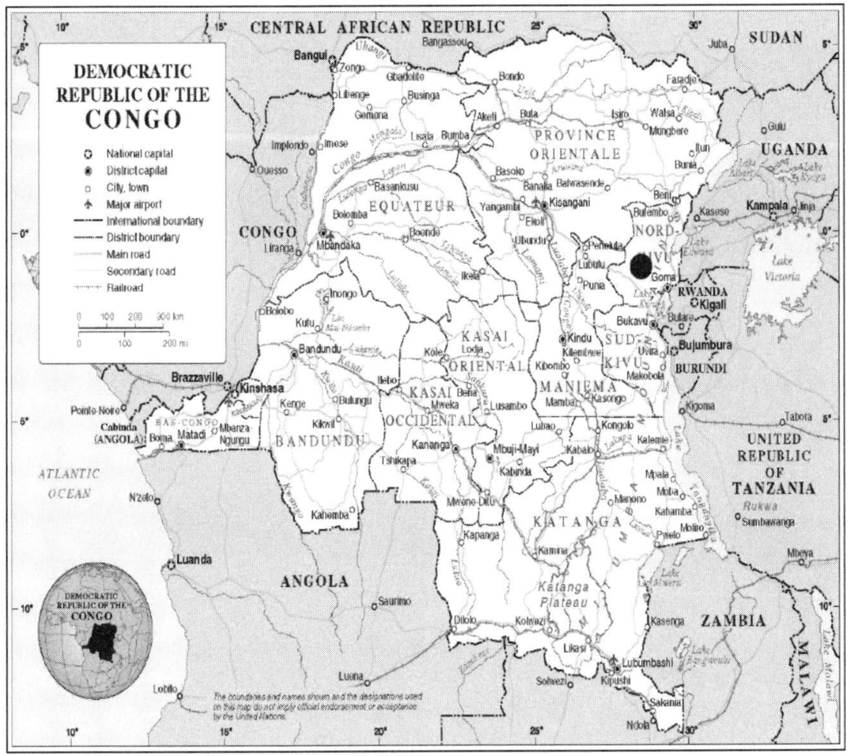

Based on UN map No. 4007 Rev. 8 (January 2004)

Chapter 13

The conflict in the DR Congo: a story of failed transitions and interlocking conflicts[1]

Tyrone Savage and Kris Vanspauwen

Africa, Frantz Fanon once said, has the shape of a gun and its trigger is Congo. Its dense jungles have often been the site of various, interlocked conflicts that seem to come and go, continually, in the African Great Lakes region. Fugitive rebel movements find shelter there, regroup and resume their struggles from well concealed bases. Among them have been the *Interahamwe* from Rwanda – militia that carried out the genocide that, between April and July 1994, left over 800,000 people dead – Burundian rebels, militarised Congolese movements and, in late 2005, the notorious Lord's Resistance Army. Run ragged by Uganda's armed forces, this mysterious cluster of child fighters left the no man's land of northern Uganda and southern Sudan and sought refuge in the sheltering jungles of the Congo. Once again, the vastness of sub-Saharan Africa's largest country, the Democratic Republic of the Congo (DRC, formerly Zaire), had once again attracted fugitive guerrillas – adding further complication to a complex of interlocking regional wars being fought on Congolese soil.

The transitional administration, born out of the peace talks in 2002 and led by President Joseph Kabila, took an array of initiatives to defuse such threats and create the possibility of a thoroughgoing break from entrenched historical patterns of coercion and continual trauma. The formal transition having culminated in the first democratic elections in over 40 years, with Kabila elected as president, the DRC today enjoys a fragile peace. The war that resulted in an estimated death toll of 3.9 million (Coghlan *et al.* 2006: 44) is over. The challenge is to translate the present reprieve into a sustainable peace, in which a robust democracy can take hold. In this context, public debate about tackling the lingering impact of past abuse has grown prolifically.

A variety of dilemmas and obstacles have emerged. Prospects for challenging perpetrators of human rights violations have been hampered by the fact that, historically, the judiciary itself has been part of the conflict, its functioning manipulated for political ends, its infrastructure ravaged; its capacity drastically insufficient to answer the public demand for justice. Questions are also being asked about whether prosecutions would suffice to answer the massive needs resulting from Congo's traumatic past: what would it give survivors of unspeakable abuses and irreparable loss? What should be done with the many children who have been abducted, forced to participate in the fighting and often to commit atrocious acts? How should their twofold status – victim *and* perpetrator – be managed? How does one answer the grief, the rage, the outrage over millions who have died? Justice, in terms of due prosecutorial process, is necessary, obviously; yet equally obviously, it cannot be enough – to provide sufficient redress for victims, to answer the crimes perpetrated, to transform the situation from endemic conflict to sustainable peace, or even to establish enough justice to move on. Such is the scale of the challenge in present-day Congo.

This introduction unpacks the traumatised history of the DRC, highlighting the patterns of coercive rule, failed transition, domestic decay and interconnected conflicts. It thus sets the parameters for the discussions in the following chapters on formal and informal ways of pursing justice amid the peace that has slowly unfolded since 2002.

Systemic abuse in the Congo Basin goes at least as far back as the sixteenth and seventeenth centuries, when European slave merchants operated in the region. The use of coercion escalated dramatically after the Berlin Conference of 1885 when the Belgian king, Leopold II negotiated with his European peers and effectively secured Congo as his personal possession. Though he never set foot in Africa himself, the treatment of Congolese people at the rubber plantations established under his rule were notoriously brutal, becoming such an embarrassment to Belgium that in 1908 the parliament annexed the territory.[2]

The plunder continued, however. State concessions were granted to companies granting them commercial rights as well as extraordinary administrative and judicial prerogatives in all their operations. A quarter of a century after annexing the territory, the colonial power finally took responsibility for matters of local administration. Even then, however, the colonial state as well as the companies saw the Congolese merely as labour to be recruited, by whatever means necessary. In the years that followed, a vast *lumpenproletariat* formed, out of which an elite group emerged that began to resist this 'crude and violent' (SIDA 2004: 159) relationship and agitate for independence and democracy.

As decolonisation movements proliferated through Africa, nationalism and demands for independence from Belgium surged in the Congo. In 1956, a group belonging to an organisation based in the south east of Congo, the Alliance des Bakongo (ABAKO), published a manifesto calling for immediate independence from Belgium. Nationalist sentiment spread through the lower Congo region. An array of similar movements emerged, virtually overnight, throughout the country. The Mouvement National Congolais (Congolese National Movement, MNC), led from 1958 by Patrice Lumumba, stood out.

In January 1959, with social unrest and public protests now prolific, Belgium asserted that its goal in the Congo was eventual independence achieved through a phased process. Nationalist agitation had, however, reached a critical mass and, twelve months later, the Belgian government convened a Round Table Conference in Brussels and invited a broad array of Congolese organisations. Belgium's declared aim was to negotiate conditions for the transition. The result was a framework for rapid decolonisation. On 30 June 1960, Congo formally gained independence. ABAKO leader Joseph Kasavubu was named president and Patrice Lumumba prime minister.

Tragically, the transition soon collapsed. Units of the national army mutinied. A few days later, Katanga, the country's richest province, declared independence from the rest of the country. As the chaos unfolded, Belgium declared that it would intervene to protect the lives of Belgian citizens. To the shock of the fledgling Congolese government, however, the Belgian troops that landed in Katanga proceeded to support the secession. Lumumba asserted that Brussels was seeking to regain control of strategic areas of its former colony.

Less than two weeks into independence, Lumumba and Kasavubu together appealed to United Nations (UN) for assistance. The President and the Prime Minister disagreed, however, on the role and mandate of the UN in the process. Lumumba insisted that the peacekeepers should use force, if necessary, to restore Katanga to the domain of central government. Kasavubu adamantly opposed this option, arguing instead for a measure of local autonomy in the provinces. In his frustration, Lumumba turned to the Soviet Union for assistance.

With this, the crisis – and the next thirty years – in Congo became inextricably tied to the machinations of the Cold War.

Government ground to a halt. President Kasavubu revoked the authority of Prime Minister Lumumba. Lumumba contested his dismissal and dismissed Kasavubu in turn. A constitutional impasse followed, with two groups claiming to be the legitimate government. At the same time, the Katanga rebellion continued, precipitating similar movements in other regions. The country fragmented into four separate areas: Katanga, Kasai, Orientale Province and Léopoldville.

In this chaos, on 14 September 1960, Colonel Joseph Mobutu (later Mobutu Sese Seko) announced that the army, in cooperation with a caretaker government, would now rule the country. In the talks that followed, an agreement was reached with Kasavubu. In October 1960, the General Assembly of the United Nations recognised the government established under Kasavubu. Lumumba, in turn, was apprehended by Kasavubu's forces. On 17 January 1961, in a turn of events that is still unclear, he was handed over to the secessionist regime in Katanga and murdered, reportedly with the collusion of Belgian officers and with the blessing of the United States (De Witte 2000). Two years later, the Katanga secession was finally crushed.

In Léopoldville, on 2 August 1961, a new civilian government was established, with Cyrille Adoula as prime minister. It too lacked the capacity to secure the domain. In 1964, insurgencies engulfed five of the 21 provinces, raising fears of a total collapse of central government. The former leader of the Katanga secession, Moise Tshombe, replaced Adoula and formed another administration that was to be short-lived. On 24 November 1965, for the second time, the head of the military Mobutu seized control of the country.

This time, Mobutu consolidated his rule. He permitted only one political party, the Mouvement Populaire de la Révolution (Popular Revolutionary Movement, MPR), and this he effectively turned into a system that functioned according to patronage. A new constitution was drafted that left Mobutu head of state, head of government, head of foreign policy and – crucially – commander-in-chief of the armed forces and the police. Cabinet ministers were restricted to implementing Mobutu's decisions. Provincial governors, judges of all courts, including the Supreme Court of Justice, and virtually all public offices were subject to Mobutu. The regime lasted until the end of the Cold War, when, under pressure from local opponents and foreign donors, Mobutu agreed to end one-party rule and allow for a shift towards democratic reform.

Public demand for change grew more vocal. In one clash between protesting students and security forces at the University of Lubumbashi, dozens of students were killed. The incident – and moreover Mobutu's refusal to permit an international inquiry – drew strong international censure as well as vigorous domestic opposition. Mobutu was forced to agree to a national forum that would map out a path to thoroughgoing democratic transition.

In August 1991 the Conférence Nationale Souverain (Sovereign National Conference, CNS) was convened, gathering together 2,800 political, religious and civic leaders. In the negotiations that followed, Mobutu agreed to form a transitional government. In terms of the accord, Mobutu named a leading figure among the opposition, Etienne Tshisekedi, as prime minister and agreed to a cabinet comprising five Mobutu loyalists and six opposition leaders. Mobutu fired Tshisekedi within a week when they failed to reach agreement on ministerial portfolios. In November, Mobutu formed a second transitional government with a Tshisekedi rival.

The action was met with demands, to which Mobutu agreed, of a resumption of the CNS. In a major blow for Mobutu, a leading opposition figure, Laurent Monsengwo Pasinya, was elected president of the CNS. As power began to shift away from Mobutu, delegates at the conference asserted the right of the CNS to draft a new constitution and establish a system of multi-party democracy. In August 1992, the CNS passed a Transitional Act allowing for a provisional constitution and a transitional government that would effectively leave the president a mere figurehead. In December, Mobutu declared the process illegitimate, reconvened his abolished legislature and tasked it with drafting a rival constitution.

The transitional arrangements formulated at the CNS remained inchoate and unrealised chiefly as a result of emerging leaders' inability to limit Mobutu's powers except on paper. Mobutu deployed an array of tactics – not least the use of military units loyal to him – to obstruct the operations of the transitional government, to intimidate opposition figures, to promote chaos and to incite violence. Savage comments:

> Some 35 years after the country's independence and nearly nine decades after the demise of the Congo Free State, the Leopoldian quality of the Mobutist state remained evident in its thoroughly centralized power apparatus, highly personalized style of governance, and readiness to use force whenever circumstances required. (Savage 2002: 42)

The domestic challenge took on new dimensions in 1994 as a genocide unfolded in Rwanda. As the Rwandan Patriotic Front (RPF) moved in from Uganda to the north to stop the killing, more than a million Hutu refugees fled into the eastern provinces of Congo. Mobutu agreed, with alacrity, to allow international organisations into the country to receive the refugees. Among the refugees, however, were tens of thousands of members of the genocidal forces. These forces used the camps to replenish, regroup, re-arm and resume killing. The French NGO Médecins Sans Frontières left in protest. The Swedish International Development Agency (SIDA) notes:

> As soon as these forces displayed their intention to mount continuous military incursions back into Rwanda from Congolese soil, the war was there [...] It should have been seen as obvious from the outset that the new Rwandan government would do whatever necessary to remove this security threat. (SIDA 2004: 163)

Mobutu was now the spoiler of domestic transition and the one responsible for allowing the nation to become a massive obstacle to justice and stability in post-genocide Rwanda. In 1997, the Alliance des forces démocratiques pour la libération du Congo-Zaire (AFDL) swept through Congo, finally precipitating Mobutu's overthrow. The AFDL comprised a coalition of forces. Nominally, it was led by veteran Congolese politician Laurent Kabila. It was, however, sponsored by neighbouring states, including Rwanda, with a variety of strategic interests. The aging and now ailing Mobutu eventually fled, opening up the way for the appointment of Kabila as president of the newly named Democratic Republic of Congo. The Mobutu regime was over. Transition, it seemed, was finally possible.

Undoing entrenched patterns of coercion and repression would not be achieved easily, however. Laurent Kabila failed to reconstruct the infrastructure that had been decimated by years of corruption or to manage the interests of neighbours. He postponed democratic reform; centralised executive, legislative and military power in his office; and, crucially, expanded the jurisdiction of military courts to include trials of politically active civilians. Cruel, inhumane and degrading treatment, torture and even execution became widespread, as the regime of Laurent Kabila clamped down on political opposition, the press, civic groupings and the country's human rights organisations. Discontent grew and the transition previously envisaged seemed to slip further away.

Laurent Kabila also failed to manage national interests with those of his foreign backing. In August 1998, he dismissed his foreign advisers. Within days, Congo was at war; within a few weeks, much of the country was occupied by foreign forces (International Crisis Group 1999: ii). In a re-run of the events that led to the overthrow of Mobutu, alliances were hatched between foreign powers and local groupings. When the insurgents besieged Kinshasa, Kabila urged civilians to expose the rebels and rebel sympathisers among them, precipitating numerous summary executions. The attack on the capital was eventually repelled when Angola and Zimbabwe intervened. Rwandan, Ugandan and rebel Congolese forces remained, however, stretched across this vast country, their failed assault deteriorating into occupation. Human rights abuses occurred on a vast scale. Moreover, Kinshasa lost much of the little control it still exerted over the country's natural resources.[3] Soldiers cut off from supply lines found ways to survive that proved extremely profitable for many of them, and utterly devastating for the Congolese population. Martin Meredith observes:

> Like vultures picking over a carcass, all sides [were] engaged in a scramble for the spoils of war. The Congo imbroglio became not only self-financing but highly profitable for the elite groups of army officers, politicians and businessmen exploiting it. [...] For their part, Rwanda and Uganda, having failed to dislodge [Laurent] Kabila from Kinshasa, turned the eastern Congo into their own fiefdom, plundering it for gold, diamonds, timber, coltan, coffee, cattle, cars and other valuable goods. (Meredith 2005: 540).

The chief casualties were civilian. The International Rescue Committee estimated that over three million people died between 1998 and 2002 either as a result of the fighting or from the malnutrition and disease that swept through communities fleeing the fighting (International Rescue Committee Report, 2004). This second, longer conflict to sweep in from the north-east revealed, *inter alia*, the military might of Rwanda as well as the extent to which Congo's history of continual trauma and failed transition had turned the country into something of a no man's land – or rather, an everyman's land.

An agreement was eventually reached in the Zambian capital of Lusaka in July 1999 between the heads of state of Angola, the DRC, Namibia, Rwanda, Uganda and Zimbabwe as well as more than fifty rebel leaders.[4] The Lusaka Peace Accord did little, however, beyond freezing the various military formations in position, and thus leaving the pillage of resources – and local communities – unchecked. The Accord did, however, provide a point of reference that stakeholders in the Great Lakes region would work from when negotiations eventually resumed.

Slave traders, a megalomaniac sovereign, commercial enterprises, Belgian colonisation, African dictatorship and a war of ongoing attrition produced literally millions of casualties. Such was the history of Congo when in January 2001 Laurent Kabila was assassinated. In a move widely denounced as dynastic and undemocratic, his son, Joseph, was made president. The appointment marks the turning point in the conflict – and potentially in the history of Congo's continual trauma and inchoate transitional efforts.

Immediately, Joseph Kabila took steps to resume negotiations with neighbours in the region and announced the revival of the national dialogue on democratic transition that had been established ten years earlier under Mobutu. In early 2002, the Inter-Congolese Dialogue was re-established at Sun City, in South Africa. All significant Congolese political groupings were present: government, opposition parties, civil society, the Mayi-Mayi militia, the Ugandan-backed Mouvement pour la Libération du Congo (MLC), and the various factions of the Rwandan-backed Rassemblement Congolais pour la Démocratie (RCD). Under vigorous South African facilitation, intense negotiations led to consensus and to the historic Sun City Accord, which was signed on 19 April, 2002.[5] Joseph Kabila then turned his attention to neighbouring states. In July, the DRC and Rwanda signed the Pretoria Agreement, in which the DRC agreed to apprehend Rwandan *génocidaires* that had taken refuge in the country; Rwanda agreed to withdraw its troops from the country.[6] In September, Uganda agreed to withdraw its troops in exchange for security guarantees.[7]

By the end of 2002, an agreement integrating these various settlements into a single, all-encompassing document, the Global and All-Inclusive Accord (the *Accord Global et Inclusif sur la Transition en République Démocratique du Congo* 2002), had been signed by all stakeholders. The Accord established a transitional constitution, a transitional government based on a power-sharing arrangement and five transitional institutions: the Truth and Reconciliation Commission, the National Human Rights Observatory, the High Authority of the Media, the Ethics and Anti-Corruption Commission and the Independent Electoral Commission.

The outcomes of the transition have been extremely mixed. Horrific incidents of violence have occurred, particularly in the eastern provinces, but these outbursts have been contained, peace has been restored and the transition process has not been derailed. Despite plenty of jostling for position, privilege and prospects beyond the transition, the signatories to the *Accord Global et Inclusif* have kept to the deal, and a new phase of democratic politics has begun. While many former fighters remain outside the national disarmament, demobilisation and reintegration process, numerous groupings – among them many of the Mayi-Mayi – have signed up (Institute for Security Studies 2006). Threats emanating from the region, including the movement into the DRC of fighters from the Lord's Resistance Army (LRA) in late 2005, have been addressed. The Independent Electoral Commission produced a voters' roll with 25 million registered voters, laying the basis for the country's first democratic elections in almost half a century.

Thoroughgoing transformation is a long way off, however. The transitional institutions have had limited impact. Above all, the massive crimes of the past remained little confronted. The following chapters by Kambala and Savage and by Kamwimbi unpack the obstacles, dilemmas and strategic options that have been raised, in terms of both formal legal and informal processes. Congo's Commission Vérité et Réconciliation (Truth and Reconciliation Commission, CVR) receives a special attention in this regard. Suffice it here to note that the conceptualisation, design and implementation of a strategy for the sort of justice that can restore the violated fabric of relations in Congo have barely begun.

In Focus: The Nyabyondo Massacre*

In December 2004, soldiers of the *Forces Armées de la République Démocratique du Congo* (Congolese National Army, FARDC), attacked civilians, killing at least 100 and moreover raping many women and girls. This occurred in the context of fighting in North Kivu, the province of the Democratic Republic of Congo (DRC) on the border of Rwanda and Uganda. In some cases ethnic Hutu civilians, armed by local authorities, joined the soldiers in committing these crimes. The fighting pitted FARDC forces still loyal to the *Rassemblement Congolais pour la Démocratie-Goma (RCD-Goma)* against other units of the national army. RCD-Goma was arguably the most powerful non-state military grouping to emerge in the fighting before the Sun City Accord, and – by many accounts – was somewhat active during the transitional period. It has been widely believed to have the backing of Rwanda. Soldiers on both sides of this split within the national army attacked, raped and executed civilians in various incidents throughout the province. The armed conflict between the two different factions of the same army illustrates the failure of the Congolese government to integrate the forces of previously belligerent parties at war since 1998. The creation of a single national army was part of the Pretoria Agreement of 2002 that led to the establishment of the transitional government in June 2003.

The fighting in North Kivu can be linked to political struggles in Kinshasa, the capital, where leaders of the former government and rebel groups jostled to position themselves ahead of national elections planned for 2006. But the fighting also reflects local ethnic tensions. Coming after two outbreaks of sharp, ethnic hostility in June and August 2004, the incidents described below – with their further loss of life and the new involvement of armed civilians – raised ethnic fears and antagonisms to greater heights. Furthermore, the possible involvement of neighbouring Rwanda should not be ignored. Integral to the formation of the RCD-Goma, Rwanda threatened to invade Congo in November 2004 to disarm Rwandan rebels it said pose a risk to its security. In response to these threats, as well as to continuing resistance RCD-Goma to any control from the capital, the transitional government sent 10,000 troops east, sparking fears that widespread armed conflict could resume. By mid-December, these FARDC troops under central control clashed with those loyal to RCD-Goma in at least five places in North Kivu. One of these places was Nyabyondo, 150 km North East of Goma (see map).

In mid-December, Mayi Mayi troops loyal to the central government started fighting RCD-Goma troops, in and around Nyabyondo. The Mayi-Mayi troops attacked Hutu villages, killing civilians indiscriminately. One of these incidents was the attack of a nearby Hutu village during a wedding celebration. According to a young Hutu woman injured in the attack, the former Mayi-Mayi threw a grenade at a house where the bride and other women were preparing for the festivities. Three people were killed and some others were injured (See: Human Rights Watch 2005).

Several days later, RCD-Goma troops responded with a coordinated attack on the Mayi-Mayi stronghold at Nyabyondo, also without distinguishing between military and civilian targets.

After the actual combat was over, RCD-Goma troops continued to seek out fleeing Mayi-Mayi fighters. At the same time, they systematically looted the area and moreover beat and sometimes executed the civilians they came across. They also raped many women and girls, terrorized the civilians and prevented them from returning home. Soldiers of RCD-Goma killed at least sixty civilians and raped dozens of others, according to an investigation by the MONUC human rights unit.

In the weeks that followed, RCD-Goma troops of the 11th brigade attacked along three axes approaching Nyabyondo. One of the people they targeted was a Hunde customary leader, Baroki Mine'ene of Bukombo, whom they captured and brought to Mianja, where he was murdered several days later. Another victim was Mbaende Léopold, also a member of Bukombo's customary Hunde elite. Mbaende was in the house and saw soldiers trying to take chickens in his yard. He went out into the yard to stop the soldiers. They shot him in the chest at point blank range, killing him.

FARDC soldiers also committed abuses against civilians, including rape and killing, as they searched for Mayi-Mayi whom they believed were hidden among the rest of the population. One witness reported to Human Rights Watch (2005) that the violence continued for eleven days.

* The case study presented here is based on a report by Human Rights Watch (2005). The authors would like to emphasise that the facts and viewpoints presented in their accounts are subject to controversy. Therefore the authors of this chapter do not necessarily endorse the reading or the wording of these accounts.

Notes

1 Parts of this introduction benefit from work done in preparation for a publication by the Institute for Security Studies. See Savage (2006) "In Quest of a Sustainable Justice: Transitional Justice and Human Security in The Democratic Republic of the Congo" Occasional Paper No. 130 (Pretoria: Institute for Security Studies), accessible through ISS's website, http://www.issafrica.org.
2 See Hochschild (1998) for a detailed history of Leopold II's rule in the Congo.
3 In April 2001, a United Nations inquiry found that Rwanda, Uganda and Burundi were systematically plundering the DRC's mineral resources. See United Nations Security Council, Report of the Security Council Mission to the Great Lakes Region, 15–26 May 2001, S/2001/521.
4 The Ceasefire Agreement, signed in the Zambian capital Lusaka and referred to as the Lusaka Peace Accord, is available from the website of the United States Institute of Peace, at: http://www.usip.org/Hbrary/pa/drc/drcJ37101999_toc.html.
5 The Sun City Accord is available from the website of Afrique Express, at: http://www.afrique-express.com/archive/CENTRALE/rdcongo/rdcongopol/249texteaccord.htm.
6 The peace agreement between the governments of the Republic of Rwanda and the Democratic Republic of Congo on the withdrawal of the Rwandan troops from the territory of the Democratic Republic of Congo and the dismantling of the Ex-FAR and Interahamwe Forces in

the Democratic Republic of Congo (DRC) is available from the website of the United States Institute of Peace, at http://www.usip.org/library/pa/drc_rwanda/drc_rwanda_pa07302002.html.

7 The agreement between the governments of the Democratic Republic of Congo and the Republic of Uganda on withdrawal of Ugandan troops from the Democratic Republic of Congo, cooperation and normalisation of relations between the two countries is available form the website of the United States Institute of Peace, at: http://www.usip.org/library/pa/drc_uganda/drc_uganda_9062002.html.

8 The events described in this case study on Nyabyondo are based on a report issued by Human Rights Watch (2005).

References

Accord Global et Inclusif sur la Transition en République Démocratique du Congo (2002), signé à Pretoria (République d'Afrique du Sud) le 17 décembre 2002 et adopté à Sun City le 1er avril 2003.

Arendt, H. (1968) *Between Past and Future: Eight Exercises in Political Thought*. New York: Viking.

Campbell, H. (n.d.) *The Assassination of Laurent Kabila*. See: http://www.prairienet.org/acas/edge/campbell.html.

Coghlan, B., Brennan, R., Ngoy, P., Dofara, D., Otto, B. and Stewart, T. (2004) *La Mortalité en République Démocratique du Congo: Résultats d'une Enquête Nationale Réalisée d'avril à juillet 2004*. Melbourne and New York: Burnet Institute and International Rescue Committee.

De Witte, L. (2000) *L'Assassinat de Lumumba*. Paris: Karthala.

Hochschild, A. (1998) *King Leopold's Ghost: A Story of Greed, Terror, and Heroism in Colonial Africa*. Boston: Houghton Mifflin.

Human Rights Watch (2005) *Democratic Republic of Congo: Civilians Attacked in North Kivu*, HRW Report A1709, 13 July.

International Crisis Group (1999) *Africa's Seven Nation War*, ICG Democratic Republic of the Congo Report No. 4, 21 May.

International Crisis Group (2005) *Back to the Brink in Congo*, ICG Africa Briefing No. 21, 17 December.

Journal Officiel de la République Démocratique du Congo, Spécial Issue, 5 avril 2003, pp. 51–69.

Meredith, M. (2005) *The State of Africa: A History of Fifty Years of Independence*. London: Free Press.

Sarkin, J. (2004) *Carrots and Sticks: The TRC and the South African Amnesty Process*. Antwerp: Intersentia.

Savage, T. (2002) 'The Democratic Republic of the Congo: inchoate transition, interlocking conflicts', in E. Doxtader and C. Villa-Vicencio (eds), *Through Fire with Water: Understanding the Roots of Division and Assessing the*

Potential for Reconciliation in Africa – 15 Case Studies. Cape Town: David Philip, pp. 129–52.
Savage, T. (2006) *In Quest of a Sustainable Justice. Transitional Justice and Human Security in the Democratic Republic of the Congo*, ISS Paper 130. Pretoria: Institute for Security Studies.
Swedish International Development Agency (2004) *A Strategic Conflict Analysis for the Great Lakes Region*, Report No. SIDA3689. Stockholm: SIDA.
Turner, T. (2000) 'War in the Congo', *Foreign Policy in Focus*, 5: 10.
United Nations Development Programme (2003) *Human Development Report 2003 Millennium Development Goals: A Compact among Nations to End Human Poverty*. New York: United Nations Development Programme.
Wolters, S. and Boshoff, H. (2006) *The Impact of Slow Military Reform on the Transition Process in the DRC*, Situation Report. Pretoria: Institute for Security Studies.

Chapter 14

Decayed, decimated, usurped and inadequate: the challenge of finding justice through formal mechanisms in the DR Congo[1]

Tyrone Savage and Olivier Kambala wa Kambala

At the Inter-Congolese Dialogue, participants in the Peace and Reconciliation Commission debated prospects for prosecutions in the DRC extensively. Among the various arguments they presented were that prosecutions were integral to efforts to combat impunity, they would act as a deterrent against similar crimes in future, and that proceeding with prosecutions would provide the basis for the possibility of a realistic, national reconciliation process. Justice, in other words, would be an integral part of creating a sustainable peace.

Such reasoning is plausible. It resonates deeply with widespread demands in the DRC for some sort of reckoning with past abuses, without which, it is widely felt, attempts to move forward will be stymied by the lingering effects of unaddressed trauma. Yet for all its necessity, post-conflict societies like the DRC generally run into a variety of daunting challenges in their quest for justice. One challenge has to do with the toll a war may have taken on a society. The buildings may have been razed. Records of court proceedings and even copies of the legal code itself may have been burned, lost or stolen. The lawyers may have been caught up in the fighting or found ways to flee the region. Often too the law itself will have been usurped by political agendas, or at least adapted to meet the contingencies of war.

Yet the greatest challenge to obtaining justice in a post-conflict society often has to do with the peace process itself. Throughout history, negotiations to end a conflict have had to tackle demands by belligerents to let bygones be bygones, and to look to the future rather than delve into misdeeds perpetrated amid the desperation and trauma of war. The result has often been an amnesty that has left those who have been victimised during the conflict without any means of finding acknowledgement or redress for their grievances. Particularly since the latter years of the twentieth century, general or blanket amnesties have come under increasing criticism. International efforts to combat impunity have grown an extraordinary momentum, producing international criminal tribunals (for the former Yugoslavia and for Rwanda), hybrid tribunals (in Sierra Leone and in Cambodia), the International Criminal Court (ICC), as well as an array of initiatives designed to rebuild the capacity of justice systems with post-conflict societies. As accountability initiatives have grown worldwide, so have the demands of people who have survived war that abuses committed be confronted.

The dearth of prosecutions for the atrocities committed amid the military escalations of 1996 to 2003, and particularly at Nyabyondo, is at once a sorry reflection of the decayed, decimated, usurped and inadequate justice system in the DRC as well as an indication of the limitations of international justice. Nyabyondo, it should be acknowledged, is but one instance among many massive violations of human rights and international humanitarian law in recent years in Congo, not least at Kasika, Makobola, Sake, Tingi-Tingi and Kenge. In terms of internationally entrenched norms and practices, the acts were a violation of basic human rights.[2] They were also a contravention of the provisions of international humanitarian law that forbid the targeting of civilians during armed conflicts:[3] crimes against humanity as defined in the Rome Statute (Rome Statute of the International Criminal Court 2002: Art. 7), given that they were widespread and systematic; and a contravention of Article 147 of the Fourth Geneva Convention, which includes wilful killing, torture or inhuman treatment, wilfully causing great suffering or serious injury and extensive destruction of property not justified by military necessity (cited in Steiner and Alston 2000: 1135). In short, the abuses committed in and around Nyabyondo constitute a flagrant violation of international law. Yet to date international response has been limited to including Nyabyondo, among an array of other sites of atrocities, to be 'mapped' with the assistance of the international community. Limited though this response has been, it is nonetheless groundbreaking. Negotiated by the government of the DRC and the United Nations during the May 2007 visit of the UN High Commissioner for Human Rights, Louise Arbour, the initiative involves documenting the 'most serious violations of human rights and international humanitarian law committed within the territory of the DRC between March 1993 and June 2003' (address by Louise Arbour, UN High Commissioner for Human Rights, on the occasion of the 5th Session of the Human Rights Council, 11 June 2007, Geneva). The agreement by the government to conduct the exercise, in cooperation with MONUC, is an encouraging step towards the pursuit of accountability in the DRC.

In order to understand the particular failure to address Nyabyondo, or more generally to develop a realistic prosecutorial strategy that can meet the sorts of goals articulated at Sun City, it is necessary to begin with a candid appraisal of the capacity of the legal system to meet public demands for justice. Following this assessment, we examine the role the international community has played in formal justice efforts in the DRC, before turning to alternative means of providing a measure of justice – a justice that may not satisfy the ideals of formal, prosecutorial justice but which may, in its focus on the victims, help inculcate a culture of human rights, entrench respect for the rule of law, help restore the public dignity of victims, and moreover involve a variety of administrative measures – such as lustration and vetting – not least in the military and security services, members of whom are reported to have committed the bulk of the violations.

Domestic prosecutions: incapable, inchoate, inadequate

In a 2000 report to the Security Council, the Secretary-General concluded that, 'the human rights situation [in the DRC] is … aggravated by a justice system controlled at every level by the State, and unable to grant defendants the most elementary procedural guarantees' (United Nations Security Council 2000: para. 48).[4] Establishing an independent, fully functional justice system has, accordingly, been a key dimension of the transition in the DRC. A number of historically embedded patterns have rendered this challenge particularly daunting:

- political manipulation;
- lack of capacity;
- the role of military tribunals;
- amnesty provisions established as part of the peace accord.

Formal justice systems have, throughout the history of Congo, been the plaything of political forces. The ad hoc justice meted out by European overlords in Leopold's time, the judicial powers granted mining companies during colonial times, the machinations of Mobutu, Laurent Kabila's use of the courts to undermine critical opponents – the Congolese judiciary has effectively functioned at the pleasure of the powers-that-be since time immemorial.

In recent years, the dearth of capacity to deal with mass violations has become evident in a number of ways. By the time the peace accord was signed at Sun City, the infrastructure of the judicial system had virtually collapsed, with judges and prosecutors lacking copies of basic legal texts and urgently needing training or retraining. Few jurisdictions have been established in any formal, effective, thoroughgoing way. A massive audit of the justice system in May 2004 found that only about 20 per cent of the population had access to the formal justice system (Altit *et al.* 2004).

The European Union has been supporting a wide range of projects related to the rehabilitation of the rule of law as well as the rebuilding of the judiciary including capacity-building activities for magistrates and lawyers. The United Nations, through MONUC's human rights division, has considerably contributed to reinforcing and supporting the judiciary and the defence councils, particularly in the north-eastern city of Bunia. Non-governmental organisations, such as RCN Justice & Démocratie, Avocats Sans Frontières and Global Rights have substantially contributed to these endeavours. A significant example is the assistance to the rehabilitation of the judiciary in Bunia in 2003, carried out by RCN Justice & Démocratie after the end of the French-led multinational forces operation 'Artemis'. The independence of the judiciary has also been vigorously debated and is being expanded slowly, incrementally, as democratic stability grows and security fears are allayed.[5]

In this context, most formal justice proceedings have been in the form of military tribunals. Although the jurisdiction of military courts is generally restricted to the disciplining of soldiers for military offences, military courts in Congo have, throughout history, been invested with vast powers. Laurent Kabila's military courts, the 'Cour d'Ordre Militaire',[6] achieved particularly notoriety for its brutal suppression of political opposition (United Nations Commission on Human Rights 2003). Moreover, as Borello argues (2004: 20), Congolese penal law does not proscribe war crimes, crimes against humanity or the crime of genocide. The Military Criminal Code addresses these violations – though not, as Wetsh'okonda Koso notes (2005: 60–1), with definitions that correspond to those laid down in the Rome Statute of the International Criminal Court (2002). Key challenges therefore have been to address this serious gap in the ordinary criminal courts

(Krasnor 2004: 184) and to harmonise the role of military courts with the ideals of a democratising society.

That said, the military courts have also taken on functions in the Congolese transition that have been surprisingly attentive to some of the concerns of transitional justice, including mass atrocities and reparations for victims. A series of prosecutions have been carried before military courts for war crimes and serious abuses of international humanitarian law. The Ankoro trial, for example, led to the charging of 22 soldiers for mass human rights violations committed in Ankoro, 800 kilometres from Lubumbashi, in November 2002. From 2005, further prosecutions were organised by the military courts in Mbandaka, Bunia, Katanga and Bukavu that have applied international criminal standards within the domestic legal framework, most notably Articles 5 to 8 of the Rome Statute as well as jurisprudence from the International Criminal Tribunal for the former Yugoslavia and for Rwanda (Avocats sans frontières Belgique 2007).

In April 2006, at Songo Mboyo, the Military Garrison Court sentenced seven military officers of the armed forces to life imprisonment for crimes against humanity. The court moreover ruled that the Congolese government was 'jointly responsible' and had to provide compensation of US$10,000 to the family of a rape victim who died following the attack, US$5,000 to rape survivors, and damages, with interest, of between US$200 and US$500 to families robbed by the soldiers (IRIN News 2006). The ruling applied Article 7 of the Rome Statute, which declares rape a crime against humanity when committed as part of a widespread or systematic attack directed against any civilian population (MONUC Human Rights Division 2006c). The proceedings asserted – in a domestic court – the international principle that mass rape is a crime against humanity. It moreover highlighted the lingering trauma and present needs of the victims. Such trials are intended to help restore public faith in the rule of law in the DRC. They also reflect a growing dialogue between Congolese domestic courts, international humanitarian law and the salient preoccupations of transitional justice.

At the same time, a growing acknowledgement has become evident that military courts generally enjoy little statutory independence and that, as the DRC expands its democratic culture into every dimension of public life, their jurisdiction should therefore be made to harmonise with international norms. As agreed per Inter-Congolese Dialogue Resolution No. DIC/CPJ/06, the reform of the military jurisdictions were promulgated on 18 November 2002.[7] The 'Cour d'Ordre Militaire' established under Kabila the Elder was disbanded in 2004 and it is envisaged that, in time, as the provisions of the Rome Statute are fully implemented in the post-transitional period, all crimes will be tried in civilian courts.

As a signatory to an array of international treaties and agreements, Congolese courts are in a position to directly apply the provisions of international law as well as to draw on international formulations of certain crimes.[8] Moreover, given that the DRC's legal system is monist, international treaties and agreements are automatically incorporated into domestic law and no explicit act of incorporation is needed. However, it would appear Congolese judges have, till now, remained loathe to apply the international treaties unless specific, explicit acts of incorporation mandate them to do so.

There is, however, a need to synchronise the entire Congolese criminal system to international norms, in particular with regard to the Rome Statute, in order to address the issues of definitions of criminal acts, of sentences (the military penal code applies the death penalty for war crimes, crimes against humanity and genocide: Articles 161–175) and of statutory immunities (certain officials, such as the head of state, are immune from civil and criminal liability).

One further problem still to be fully resolved is an amnesty agreed upon during the Sun City negotiations that covers acts of war, political crimes and crimes of opinion. A presidential decree was adopted on 15 April 2003, in conformity with the *Accord Global et Inclusif* (2002: III.8) and the Constitution,[9] stating that:

> Pending adoption of an amnesty law by the National Assembly and its promulgation, all acts of war, political crimes and crimes of opinion committed during the period from 2 August 1998 and 4 April 2003 are provisionally amnestied, excluding war crimes, genocide and crimes against humanity.[10]

The provisional amnesty law of April 2003 was replaced by the amnesty law of acts of war, political and opinion crimes of 29 November 2005,[11] broadening the scope of amnesty to crimes committed since 1996. The adoption of the latter was the subject of persistent controversy, since the parliamentary group representing the head of state boycotted the debates to express dissensions on the interpretation given to political crimes. Specifically, the November 2005 amnesty law considered the assassination of the head of state as a political crime subject to amnesty. This meant that the murderers of Laurent Desire Kabila would benefit from the law.

Debate around amnesty has failed to find closure, however, and formulating a policy on amnesty that can endure in the post-transitional dispensation remains a salient priority. Nonetheless, it will be impossible to prosecute all or even most perpetrators and a '*de facto* amnesty' (Sarkin 2004) is simply inevitable. A nuanced strategy for tackling impunity is going to be needed that combines an array of interests, including, as Savage (2006) notes, 'the public's demands for accountability, the courts' need to re-establish the rule of law, the victims' needs to have lingering trauma and loss redressed, the armed services' ability to apprehend mass criminals, and the nation's need to begin to move on'.

In other words, prosecutions are, inevitably, going to be somewhat selective. What will be crucial in holding the nation together is not whether all crimes are uncovered and punished, but whether the process of establishing criteria for the selection manages to draw the nation together. The detail of such criteria could easily form the subject of much further study; suffice it to note here a few principles that may help inform such discussion:

- Target those most responsible for mass violations, such as public officials, military officers and others involved in orchestrating crimes. While this would risk appearing to condone or at least declare negligible the crimes of less notorious criminals, it would reflect the nation's commitment to breaking patterns of abuse at the root.
- Pursue cases where evidence is readily available and ample, and conviction is likely.
- Prioritise recidivism, again in an attempt to tackle patterns of abuse.[12]

One further option in the application of the law would be to prosecute suspects for underlying crimes rather than the larger systemic crimes with which international law is concerned. The accused would therefore be tried for assault, rape, murder and other crimes covered by the criminal code rather than war crimes or crimes against humanity. The chief advantage of this option is that it would assert the criminality of such acts and so, to some extent, provide victims a measure of vindication. Reducing the focus of the trials to underlying crimes would hold numerous risks, however, not least that of obscuring the systemic character of the crimes, concealing those who held command responsibility by focusing on isolated individuals, and failing to account for the pervasiveness of the abuses. The truth-seeking potential of a prosecutorial process would thus not be maximized.

Despite the various challenges, it is widely accepted that the chief avenue for the pursuit of prosecutions in any post-conflict society should be the domestic courts: 'on principle, it should remain the rule that national courts have jurisdiction, because any lasting solution must come from the nation itself' (United Nations Commission on Human Rights 1997: para. 28). Domestic prosecutions and the reforms usually needed to make them feasible are an integral part of the reconstruction process, giving public vindication to victims and restoring trust in public institutions. Given the magnitude of the challenges and the lingering volatility of the situation in the DRC, however, intervention by international justice mechanisms is obviously crucial. On the ground, Congolese expectations of such interventions have been huge – unrealistically so, according to most commentators. We turn now to examine options that are internationally driven, designed and delivered.

Hybrid mechanisms: international capacity, domestic credibility[13]

At Sun City, demands were made for an ad hoc international criminal tribunal of the sort established for Rwanda and the former Yugoslavia (ICTR and ICTY, respectively). Given the costs involved in these tribunals as well as their seemingly limited efficiency in dealing with mass crimes, the United Nations has become extremely unwilling to establish any further ad hoc tribunals. Discussion has grown rather around two other options for international intervention, namely a 'hybrid' tribunal, which would include a combination of international and domestic lawyers, and intervention by the ICC. We turn to the latter shortly, but first examine the possibility of a 'hybrid' tribunal.

The model usually cited is the Special Court for Sierra Leone (Scharf 2000; Frulli 2000), which includes both international and local lawyers, operates under a strict timeline and runs at significantly less cost that the international tribunals for Rwanda and the former Yugoslavia. Unlike the international ad hoc tribunals, the Special Court is located in the country concerned, Sierra Leone, though admittedly its largest trial – that of Charles Taylor – has been transferred to The Hague as a result of security fears. Holding the proceedings *in situ* has the advantage of enabling justice to be seen, by victims and by the local population more broadly. It also has the effect of helping rebuild the rule of law in the country concerned, by making manifest the principles of justice, such as impartiality and the burden of proof, showing – and growing – the capacity of legal professionals, and helping cultivate public faith in justice mechanisms as a means of addressing past abuses.

There are numerous problems, however, in establishing this option in the DRC. One is the fractured condition of Congolese society. The selection of local participants would, inevitably, be perceived as biased. The continuing instability in the DRC would pose massive security risks. The cost of even a hybrid tribunal is significant. Yet perhaps the chief problem has to do with the international context. Most international justice effort has gone into establishing the ICC, in part because having a permanent court would help resolve precisely these sorts of issues – not least cost. Discussion within the DRC, among both local and international actors, has in consequence focused increasingly on cooperation with the ICC. That said, crimes committed before 2002 will not form part of the temporal jurisdiction of the ICC, given the principle of non-retroactivity. However, the envisaged mapping is likely to suggest realistic, acceptable and timely options to address these crimes within the domestic courts.

The International Criminal Court: impactful but limited

After years of preliminary meetings, the Rome Statute was adopted by 120 nations in 1998, establishing the possibility of a permanent, international criminal court. As momentum built, the minimum of 60 states ratified the statute and, in July 2002, the ICC was formally founded. It currently has jurisdiction over three crimes: genocide, war crimes and crimes against humanity. The principle of complementarity guides the work of the ICC, meaning that the court undertakes investigations and prosecutions only when states are unable or unwilling to do so themselves. Moreover, the ICC may intervene only if the crime occurred in a state that is a party to the Rome Statute (the principle of territoriality) or in which the suspect is a national of a state that is party to the statute (the principle of nationality). These conditions may be waived, however, if a situation is referred to the Chief Prosecutor of the ICC by the Security Council, according to Article 13 of the Rome Statute referrals.

The DRC has participated actively in this development, signing the Rome Statute in September 2000 and then ratifying it on 11 April 2002. In March 2004, it referred the situation in the country to the Chief Prosecutor, opening up the option of ICC intervention. On 19

March 2006, the ICC made its first arrest, apprehending and charging a Congolese militia leader in Ituri province, Thomas Lubanga, with three counts of war crimes involving forcibly recruiting children and making them take part in armed hostilities. The arrest was the culmination of efforts by a multinational team led by Chief Prosecutor, Luis Moreno-Ocampo, to identify and apprehend those most responsible for atrocities in Ituri province.

Against fears that such intervention could escalate the conflict, the arrest of Lubanga had a settling effect, inhibiting similar activities by other warlords and bringing some respite to the traumatised communities of north-eastern DRC. Public response, both in the Congo and abroad, has been supportive and demand for similar arrests is prolific. Following the arrest, the International Center for Transitional Justice (ICTJ) issued a press statement, as follows:

> Much more must be done to ensure justice for victims in that country, ... where countless others accused of war crimes continue to operate with impunity. The ICTJ express[es] the hope that this development is but the first step in a broader and more comprehensive prosecutorial strategy targeting the long list of those responsible for horrific abuses in one of the world's most deadly conflicts. (International Center for Transitional Justice 2006)

While the ICC's intervention has been widely welcomed, it is crucial that this first success be consolidated into strategic thinking about how best to proceed in a situation that remains extremely volatile. Among the challenges that remain are the following:

- unrealistically high expectations among the Congolese population;
- the need for a comprehensive prosecutorial strategy to replace sporadic interventions;
- the formulation of outreach strategies that would harmonise hearings in The Hague and local expectations of the process;
- the necessity for the ICC to investigate across the ethnic lines, especially in Ituri province where local perception still needs to move beyond the apprehension that only Hemas, like Lubanga, are being targeted;
- the relationship between international justice mechanisms and other transitional justice mechanisms, not least the nation's embattled truth and reconciliation commission.

Truth and Reconciliation Commission: ambitious and lacking good governance

Under Resolution No. 20/DIC/2002, the members of the Peace and National Reconciliation Commission of the Inter-Congolese Dialogue instituted the Commission Vérité et Réconciliation (Truth and Reconciliation Commission, CVR) in 2002. This resolution was then approved that same year in the Global and All-Inclusive Accord (*Accord global et inclusif sur la transition en République Démocratique du Congo* 2002) as well as by the Constitution of April 2003 under Resolution No. DCI/CPR/04. Finally the CVR was legally established by Law No. 04/018 of 30 July 2004 (*Loi No. 04/018 du 30 juillet 2004 Portant Organisation, Attribution et Fonctionnement de la Commission Vérité et Réconciliation*) which specifies its composition, its mandate and its functioning (Borello 2004: 39–40).

According to the Preamble of Law No. 04/018, the CVR's general mission was to establish truth and to promote peace, justice, reparation, forgiveness and reconciliation for sustaining national unity. The mandate of this transitional institution as specified under Article 6 of the above mentioned law included establishing the truth about all political crimes and all human rights abuses from Independence, on 30 June 1960, up to the end of the transition, symbolised by democratic elections.[14] Yet, as Tyrone Savage has pointed out:

> From the outset, the CVR has battled. Its work has mostly involved pacifying traumatized communities. It has failed to establish any truthseeking process and appears to have barely glimpsed the role truth recovery could play in the DRC's transition – helping survivors of past abuses gain closure, creating opportunities for perpetrators to acknowledge their actions, entrenching the rule of law and initiating a shared national process. (2006: 9)

The response of the Commission generally points to the difficulty of truth-seeking in a highly volatile situation. CVR President, Bishop Jean-Luc Kuye, has indicated that the CVR has been unable to undertake investigations of human rights violations and instead has focused its work on conflict mediation activities (Borello 2004: 46). Bishop Kuye was also reported in a newspaper interview as saying that the CVR had facilitated coexistence initiatives between ethnic groups in the east and helped pacify communities in several provinces, including the Kivus, Kasai, Bas-Congo, Oriental Province (Kongo 2005: 1). In South Kivu province, for example, the CVR mediated conflict between military soldiers of the FARDC 10th battalion and Mayi-Mayi commanding officers. It also intervened in the resolution of the conflicts concerning Banyamulenge soldiers in the territory of Minembwe. In North Kivu province, the CVR provided support to local structures of mediation and conflict resolution, such as the Barza Intercommunautaire during the electoral period (Wakenge and Bossaerts 2006: 2). In this province, the CVR also collected complaints filed by the victims in order to begin the process of reparations for the harm they suffered (Wakenge and Bossaerts 2006: 7).

These few conciliation activities aside, the CVR has essentially failed in its mandate of recovering the truth and beginning a national reconciliation process. Among the reasons for the CVR's failure to achieve reconciliation, Savage (2006: 9) notes issues like the Commission's problematic composition – it includes in its numbers political appointees rumoured to have been involved in abuses themselves – budget deficiencies, lack of credibility among the Congolese public and a failure of leadership to deal with these problems. In such conditions, it is difficult to imagine a face-to-face process between perpetrators and their victims (Kamwimbi 2006).

The Deputy President of the CVR, Henri-Elie Ngoma Binda (2006), has raised several reasons for the ineffectiveness of the Commission. These include the following:

- an unrealistically large mandate, spanning a 46-year period from 1960 to 2006;
- the lack of professional capacity among the Commission's staff members;
- corruption among magistrates as an obstacle to truth-finding;
- the inability of the Commission to grant amnesty; and
- bad governance within the Commission.

Moreover, an array of questions has not been resolved as to how domestic prosecutions, international prosecutions and a national truth commission should relate to each other. Will there be sharing of information between domestic courts, the ICC and the truth commission? Will perpetrators be willing to participate in truth commission hearings if their testimony can incriminate them in the domestic courts or at the ICC? What of the many who are both perpetrator and victim? How can they present their stories, replete with intimate complexity and inevitable contradictions, under threat of prosecution? What role is possible for reconciliation if truth recovery is inextricably linked to the threat of prosecutions? The tensions evident at Sun City between demands for justice and the compromises involved in negotiating peace eventually led to a fearful hesitancy in the transitional period about uncovering the facts of past abuses. The failure to establish any public process of truth recovery is utterly perilous: it has robbed Congo's victims of their basic right to truth and with that deprived the nation of an opportunity to find meaningful ways to respond to the facts. We turn now to examine the options that avail in post-conflict societies, when a process of truth recovery is established.

Complements to the courts: the indispensability of truth and reparations

Alongside the challenge of prosecutions in Congo has been that of creating conditions in which processes of truth-seeking and truth-telling can unfold. This in turn would offer a basis for an array of further initiatives that could be established to complement formal justice proceedings.

Interest has grown massively in such options in recent years, particularly given the challenge of prosecutions in most post-conflict situations. Seminal works in this regard are the Joinet Principles (United Nations Sub-Commission for Prevention of Discrimination and Protection of Minorities 1996), Bassiouni's *Post-Conflict Justice* – which talks of international and national investigatory commissions, truth commissions, lustration, civil remedies and mechanisms for the reparation of victims (2002: 27) – and 'Defining transitional justice: tolerance in the search for justice and peace?' by former Deputy Chairperson of the South African Truth and Reconciliation Commission, Alex Boraine, which highlights the role of accountability, truth recovery, reconciliation, institutional reform and reparations in helping establish justice in societies seeking transition out of entrenched patterns of conflict (Boraine and Valentine 2006: 22–37). Further studies will doubtless explore more fully the potential such strategies may hold for the DRC. Suffice it here to introduce one that may hold particular pertinence, namely reparations.

The right to reparations is well set out in international law, not least in the *Convention Against Torture and Other Cruel, Inhuman or Degrading Treatment or Punishment* (UN 1987), the *Vienna Declaration* (1993) and in the *Basic Principles and Guidelines on the Right to a Remedy and Reparation for Victims of Gross Violations of International Human Rights Law and Serious Violations of International Humanitarian*

Law (UN 2005), more commonly known as the Bassiouni Principles. The Bassiouni Principles comprise five reparative measures integral to the design of public reparation programmes: restitution (which involves steps to restore what has been lost), compensation (payment of money for economically assessable damages resulting from the abuse), rehabilitation (restoration of health and reputation), satisfaction (public acknowledgement of the wrong committed in the form of memorials, tributes, etc.) and guarantees of non-repetition (such as legislative reforms). The Bassiouni Principles offer a general set of nuanced options for societies seeking to address past violations through reparations. The uses are various. Reparations may contribute – tangibly or at least symbolically – to acknowledging the wrongness of the abuses committed. Reparations often help diminish desires for vengeance – and with that the likelihood of a re-escalation of the conflict. Above all, as de Greiff notes, 'Victims consider them to be the most tangible manifestation of the efforts of the state to remedy the harm they have suffered' (2006: 19). Reparations, in other words, directly address the needs of those who have borne the brunt of abuse, the victims.

In terms of the DRC, concern with victims and the provision of reparations in addressing past abuses have been unprecedented features of the few domestic trials that have been held – the compensatory measures provided for in the verdict of military courts, among others the Songo Mboyo case and the Bavi mass grave case offer two salient examples. The DRC also has strong traditions of symbolic reparations in the form of monuments and memorials. The largest football stadium in Kinshasa, for example, is named 'Stade des Martyrs de la Pentecôte' (Stadium of the Martyrs of Pentecost), in memory of those who lost their lives in the struggle for freedom and democracy. It was built on the site where four were publicly hanged on 2 June 1966.[15] Streets and avenues have been named after other 'martyrs of independence', as those who gave their lives in the struggle for independence from colonial rule are called. The 17th of January is a public holiday recognised as a day of remembrance for the assassination of Patrice Lumumba specifically.

Reparations, it should be noted, have also formed a salient theme within the region more broadly. UN Resolution 1304 (2004) declares that Rwanda and Uganda should pay reparations for loss of life and damage to property resulting from a lengthy battle with each other in Kisangani in 1999, which resulted in casualties among the local population and extensive damage to property. Similarly, the International Court of Justice ruling of 19 December 2005 recognises

Ugandan responsibility in the continuation of armed activities in the eastern DRC and condemns Uganda to pay reparations (International Criminal Court 2004).

A number of problems are evident, however, with formulations of reparations currently being discussed in the DRC. Equating compensation with reparation, for example, runs a number of risks. Attaching a price tag to some gross violations – like gang rape, mutilation, or the loss of a loved one – may be offensive to some victims. Compensation for such wrongs also quickly becomes very expensive, as the experience of countries such as Malawi have proved. Compensation should necessarily be balanced by other reparatory measures – such as public apologies, memorials and legislative measures to combat future repetition. Such initiatives may honour victims in ways that are more satisfying to victims than compensation alone.

The development of a productive reparations package in the DRC is, above all, premised on a process of truth recovery in which victims' testimonies may be given and their heart-rending stories told in a public forum that explores the factual – and often intimate – detail of the many abuses committed and helps produce a history that the DRC can embrace. Without such a process, what may be presented as reparations readily deteriorates into throwing money at the problem – that is, at the victims – and establishing monuments and memorials to already widely acknowledged political figures. Without truth recovery, the restorative potential of complementary justice measures such as – but not limited to – reparations is dramatically eroded.

An interval of opportunity has emerged in the DRC. Against the predictions of many, the transitional process has held – albeit with patchy success in some key areas – and the country has gone through its elections. But the country is not yet at peace. Although the fighting – most of it in the east – is generally sporadic, contained and dealt with expeditiously, the trauma of gross violations remains, unspoken, lingering, waiting, pernicious.

Hannah Arendt talks of a moment appearing in the history of a nation, 'determined by things which are no longer and which are not yet' (Arendt 1968: 9). It is a brief interval of opportunity which, Arendt argues, holds the possibility of truth. In the space created by a transitional process that has held – against all odds, despite its patchy success – it is now crucial that Congolese leaders find the political will to take the first step in establishing the conditions in which a just and sustainable peace can emerge: a public truth-seeking process that prioritises victims, enables perpetrators to acknowledge their misdeeds and becomes a resource for a just restoration.

Notes

1 An earlier version of this contribution was published by Savage (2006) for the Institute for Security Studies. See "In Quest of a Sustainable Justice: Transitional Justice and Human Security in the Democratic Republic of the Congo" Occasional Paper No. 130 (Pretoria: Institute for Security Studies), accessible through ISS's website, http://www.issafrica.org. The research assistance of Theodore Kamwimbi for the present contribution is moreover gratefully acknowledged.

2 The right to life is guaranteed in the following international and regional human rights instruments: the Universal Declaration of Human Rights (1948), United Nations General Assembly, Art. 3; the International Covenant on Civil and Political Rights (1976), United Nations General Assembly, Art. 6(1); the African Charter on Human and People's Rights (also known as the Banjul Charter) (1981), Organisation of African Unity, Art. 4; the American Convention on Human Rights (1969), Inter-American Commission on Human Rights, Art. 4; the American Declaration of the Rights and Duties of Man (1948), Inter-American Commission on Human Rights, Art. 1; and the Convention for the Protection of Human Rights and Fundamental Freedoms (also called the European Convention on Human Rights) (1950), Council of Europe, Art. 2.

3 Article 3 common to the Geneva Conventions (1949) sets out a number of minimum humanitarian standards which are to be respected in cases of conflicts that are not of an international character and enumerates certain acts which 'are and shall remain prohibited at any time and in any place whatsoever'. Among these prohibited acts are: '(a) violence to life and person, in particular murder of all kinds, mutilation, cruel treatment and torture; [...] (c) outrages upon personal dignity, in particular, humiliating and degrading treatment [...]' (cited in Steiner and Alston 2000: 155).

4 See also reports by the Special Rapporteur, Mr Roberto Garretôn, E/CN.4/1998/65, paras 32–37, E/CN.4/1999/31.

5 At the time of going to press, efforts to reform and develop the justice sector in the DRC, with an emphasis on tackling international crimes, were taking on new dimensions. These efforts, which comprise both logistical and substantive elements, are a follow-up of the 2004 audit of the justice system. Tangible results have been achieved, including the establishment of reforms in the Eastern DRC, known as Rejusco (Reform of Justice in Congo), as well as the setting up of a mulilateral committee, the Comité Mixte de Justice, comprising donors and the DRC government, to oversee reforms.

6 Decree No. 019 of 23 August 1997.

7 Laws No. 023/2002 and No.024/2002 on the military judicial code and on the military penal code of 18 November 2002.
8 The DRC has either ratified or acceded to, among others, the International Covenant on Civil and Political Rights, the Convention Against Racial Discrimination, the Convention on Discrimination Against Women, the Convention on the Rights of the Child and its Optional Protocol on the Involvement of Children in Armed Conflict, the Convention against Torture, the Genocide Convention and the Geneva Conventions and both of their Protocols, and the Rome Statute of the International Criminal Court.
9 Section III, point 8 of the Agreement and Article 199 of the Constitution.
10 Article 1 of the *Décret-loi n° 03-001 du 15 avril 2003 portant Amnistie pour faits de guerre, infractions politiques et d'opinion*, cited in Borello (2004: 23).
11 See the report on BBC: http://news.bbc.co.Uk/2/hi/africa/4485916.stm.
12 See Mark Drumbl's argument with respect to preventing a recurrence of genocide in Rwanda in Drumbl (2000: 1324).
13 Adapted from Katshung (2006b: 20–1).
14 This was specified by Article 196 of the transitional Constitution promulgated by President Joseph Kabila on 4 April 2003, which stipulates: 'La durée de la transition est de vingt quatre mois. Elle court à compter de la formation du Gouvernement de transition et prend fin avec l'investiture du Président de la République élu à l'issue des élections marquant la fin de la période transitoire en République Démocratique du Congo. Toutefois, en raison de problèmes spécifiquement liés à l'organisation des élections, la transition peut être prolongée pour une durée de six mois renouvelable une seule fois, si les circonstances l'exigent, sur proposition de la Commission électorale indépendante et par une décision conjointe et dûment motivée de l'Assemblée nationale et du Sénat' (author's translation: 'The transition period is twenty-four months. It takes effect from the time the transitional Government is formed and ends with the investiture of the President of the Republic, duly elected following the elections which mark the end of the transitional period in the Democratic Republic of Congo. However, because of problems specifically linked to the organisation of elections, the transitional period may be extended for a further six months, renewable one more time should circumstances demand, on the advice of the Independent Electoral Commission and by a joint and properly justified decision of the National Assembly and the Senate') (ISS 2003: 51). In fact, 'a joint decision was reached by the two Houses of the Parliament of the DRC on 17 June 2005, to extend for a period of six months, renewable once, the transitional period that was to expire on 30 June 2005, in accordance with the provisions of the Global and All-Inclusive Agreement signed in Pretoria on 17 December

2002 and with Article 196 of the Transitional Constitution' (UN Security Council 2005). Also the current Constitution, approved by the Congolese people in a referendum held on 18 December 2005 and promulgated on 18 February 2006 by President Joseph Kabila, under subparagraph 1 of Article 222, stipulates: 'Les institutions politiques de la transition restent en fonction jusqu'à l'installation effective des institutions correspondantes prévues par la présente Constitution et exercent leurs attributions conformément à la Constitution de la Transition' (author's translation: 'The political institutions of the transition remain in function until the effective installation of the corresponding institutions provided for by this Constitution and they shall perform their functions in accordance with the Constitution of the Transition') (Schröder 2006: 7; PACO and UNOPS 2006: 11). Considering the above mentioned, it is legally clear that the inauguration of the newly elected President puts an end to the transitional period (de l'Arbre 2006). This has also been confirmed by Vircoulon (2007), who agrees that 'the elections have marked the end of the transition period in the DRC and that the inauguration of Joseph Kabila as president in late 2006 and the admission of defeat by his rival Jean-Pierre Bemba removed the uncertainties, and *de facto* put an end to the transition government set up under the 2002 Sun City agreements.'

15 Four opposition leaders from Lumumba's party, Evariste Kimba, Alexandre Mahamba, Jerome Anani and Emmanuel Bamba, known as the 'Conjurés de la Pentecôte' (Conspirators of Pentecost) were publicly hanged on Pentecost Day. They were executed by Mobutu's regime for allegedly being in contact with Colonel Alphonse Bangala and Major Pierre Efomi with the purpose of planning a coup. Mobutu explained the executions as follows: 'One had to strike through a spectacular example, and create the conditions of regime discipline. When a chief takes a decision, he decides – period' (Young and Turner 1985: 57).

References

Accord Global et Inclusif sur la Transition en République Démocratique du Congo (2002).

Altit, E. *et al.* (2004) *Audit organisationnel du secteur de la justice en République démocratique du Congo. Rapport d'État des lieux: synthèse.* Document attached to a Human Rights Watch Statement of 13 October.

Arendt, H. (1968) *Between Past and Future: Eight Exercises in Political Thought.* New York: Viking.

Avocats Sans Frontières Belgique (2007) *Analyse de verdict – Condamnation des militaires de la 1ère brigade intégrée pour crimes de guerre.* Tribunal militaire de Garison de Bunia, RD Congo, 19 February.

Bassiouni, M.C. (2002a) 'Accountability for violations of international humanitarian law and other serious violations of human rights', in M.C. Bassiouni (ed.), *Post-Conflict Justice*. Ardsley, NY: Transnational Publishers, pp. 3–54.

Bassiouni, M.C. (ed.) (2002b) *Post-Conflict Justice*. Ardsley, NY: Transnational Publishers.

Boed, R. (2002) 'The effect of a domestic amnesty on the ability of foreign states to prosecute alleged perpetrators of serious human rights violations', *Cornell International Law Journal*, 33: 297–314.

Boraine, A. and Valentine, S. (2006) *Transitional Justice and Human Security*. Cape Town: International Center for Transitional Justice.

Borello, F. (2004) *A First Few Steps: The Long Road to a Just Peace in the Democratic Republic of the Congo*, International Center for Transitional Justice, October. Available at: http://www.ictj.org/images/content/1/1/115.pdf.

Coghlan, B., Brennan, R.J., Ngoy, P., Dofara, D., Otto, B., Clements, M. and Stewart, T. (2006) 'Mortality in the DRC: a nationwide survey', *The Lancet*, 367: 44–51.

Council of Europe (1950) *Convention for the Protection of Human Rights and Fundamental Freedoms as Amended by Protocol No. 11 (1950)*, European Treaty Series 155 (also known as the European Convention on Human Rights).

Council of Europe (1983) *European Convention on the Compensation of Victims of Violent Crimes*, European Treaty Series No. 116, opened for signature in Strasbourg on 24 November 1983.

De Greiff, P. (ed.) (2006) *The Handbook on Reparations*. Oxford: Oxford University Press.

De l'Arbre, L. (2006) 'Chronique', *Journal d'Afrique Centrale – RDC*, 1:50, 15 December.

'Décret-loi n° 03-001 du 15 avril 2003 portant Amnistie pour faits de guerre, infractions politiques et d'opinion', *Journal Officiel de la République Démocratique du Congo*.

Drumbl, M.A. (2000) 'Punishment, postgenocide. From guilt to shame to "civis" in Rwanda', *New York University Law Review*, 75: 1221–326.

Du Toit, A. (2003) 'The South African Truth and Reconciliation Commission: local history, global accounting', *Politique Africaine*, 92.

Frulli, M. (2000) 'The Special Court for Sierra Leone: some preliminary comments', *European Journal of International Law*, 11 (4): 857–69.

Geneva Convention Relative to the Protection of Civilian Persons in Time of War (1949) Adopted on 12 August 1949 by the Diplomatic Conference for the Establishment of International Conventions for the Protection of Victims of War, held in Geneva from 21 April to 12 August 1949, entered into force 21 October 1950. United Nations Treaty Series, Vol. 75, p. 287.

Hayner, P. (2000) 'Same species, different animal: how South Africa compares to truth commissions worldwide', in C. Villa-Vicencio and

W. Verwoerd (eds), *Looking Back, Reaching Forward: Reflections on the Truth and Reconciliation Commission of South Africa*. Cape Town: UCT Press, pp. 32–41.

Human Rights Watch (2000) *RDC, l'Est du Congo dévasté, civils assassins et opposants réduits au silence*, 12: 3.

Inter-American Commission on Human Rights (1948) *American Declaration of the Rights and Duties of Man*, approved by the Ninth International Conference of American States, Bogotá, Colombia. Washington, DC: Inter-American Commission on Human Rights.

Inter-American Commission on Human Rights (1969) *American Convention on Human Rights*. Adopted at the Inter-American Specialized Conference on Human Rights, San José, Costa Rica, 22 November.

Inter-American Court of Human Rights (1988) *Velasquez Rodriguez Case*. Judgment of 29 July (Ser. C) No. 4.

Internal Displacement Monitoring Centre (n.d.). See http://www.internal-displacement.org.

International Center for Transitional Justice (2006) *Congolese Militia Leader Arrested and Transferred to the ICC: A Positive Development but Further Steps toward Accountability in the DRC Needed*. Press statement. See: http://www.ictj.org.

International Court of Justice (2004) *Armed Activities on the Territory of the Congo (Democratic Republic of the Congo v. Uganda)*. Press release 2004/36. The Hague: International Court of Justice.

International Court of Justice (2005) *Democratic Republic of the Congo* v. *Uganda (Case Concerning Armed Activities on the Territory of the Congo)*. Judgement of 19 December 2005. The Hague: International Court of Justice.

International Rescue Committee (2004) *Mortality in the Democratic Republic of the Congo, December*. New York: International Rescue Committee.

IRIN News (2006) *DRC: Soldiers Jailed for Mass Rape*. UN Office for the Coordination of Humanitarian Affairs. See: http://www.irinnews.org/report.asp?ReportID=52801&SelectRegion=Great_Lakes&SelectCountry=DRC.

ISS (2003) *Democratic Republic of Congo: Draft Constitution of the Transition*. Pretoria. Available at: http://www.iss.co.za/af/profiles/DRCongo/icd/consdraft.pdf.

Kamwimbi, T.K. (2006) 'The DRC elections, reconciliation and justice', *Pambazuka News*. See: http://www.pambazuka.org/en/category/features/36231.

Katshung, J.Y. (2005) 'The Relationship Between the International Criminal Court and Truth Commissions: Some Thoughts on How to Build a Bridge Between Retributive and Restorative Justices'. Unpublished paper, Lubumbashi: Centre for Human Rights and Democracy Studies. See: http://www.iccnow.org/documents/InterestofJustice_JosephYav_May05.pdf?PHPSESSID=4319aee3dOd3eddcb97c8aa3ae5bfe3e.

Katshung, J.Y. (2006a) 'Place et Rôle de la Commission Vérité et Réconciliation Comme Méchanisme de Justice Transitionnelle en RDC'. Unpublished conference paper.

Katshung, J.Y. (2006b) 'Prosecution of grave violations of human rights in light of challenges of national courts and the International Criminal Court: the Congolese dilemma', *Human Rights Review*, 7 (3): 5–25.

Katshung, J.Y. and Djamba, D.W. (2006) 'Towards a legacy of impunity in the Great Lakes region: two militia leaders appointed army colonels in DRC', *ISS Today*, 1 November.

Kongo, V.C. (2005) 'Cinq questions à Mgr Jean-Luc Kuye', *Le Potentiel*, 3359, 25 February.

Krasnor, E. (2004) 'American disengagement with the International Criminal Court: undermining international justice and U.S. foreign policy goals', *Online Journal of Peace and Conflict Resolution*, 6 (1): 179–91.

'Law No. 023/2002 of 18 November 2002', *Journal Officiel de la République Démocratique du Congo*.

MONUC Human Rights Division (2006a) *Human Rights Situation in February 2006*. Kinshasa: MONUC. See: http://www.monuc.org/News.aspx?newsID=10348.

MONUC Human Rights Division (2006b) *Monthly Human Rights Assessment: June 2006*. Kinshasa: MONUC. See: http://www.monuc.org/News.aspx?newsId=11764.

MONUC Human Rights Division (2006c) 'The Fight against Impunity Took a Step Forward in the DRC on 12 April 2006', in *The Human Rights Situation in April 2006*. Kinshasa: MONUC. See: http://www.monuc.org/News.aspx?newsId=11083.

Mugwanya, G.W. (1999) 'Expunging the ghost of impunity for severe and gross violations of human rights and the commission of *delicti jus gentium*: a case for the domestication of international criminal law and the establishment of a strong permanent International Criminal Court', *Michigan State University – DCL Journal of International Law*, 8 (3): 701–79.

Ngoma Binda, H.-E. (2006) Untitled presentation at the conference 'After the DRC Elections: Justice, Reconciliation and Reconstruction in the Great Lakes', Johannesburg, 18–19 November.

Okumu, W. (2003) 'Humanitarian international NGOs and African conflicts,' in F.F.C. Henry and P.R. Oliver (eds), *Mitigating Conflicts – The Role of NGOs*. London: Frank Cass.

Organisation of African Union (1986) *African Charter on Human and People's Rights*, OAU Doc. CAB/LEG/67/3 Rev. 5, 21 ILM 58, adopted in 1982, entered into force 21 October 1986 (also known as the Banjul Charter).

PACO and UNOPS (2006) *International Observer Handbook Presidential and Legislative Elections DR Congo*, Kinshasa.

Paust, J.J. (2000) 'The reach of ICC jurisdiction over non-signatory nationals', *Vanderbilt Journal of Transnational Law*, 33 (1): 1–15.

Roht-Arriaza, N. (1990) 'State responsibility to investigate and prosecute grave human rights violations in international law', *California Law Review*, 78: 451–513.

Rome Statute of the International Criminal Court (2002). Adopted in Rome on 17 July 1998, entry into force 1 July 2002 in accordance with Article 126. United Nations Treaty Series, Vol. 2187.

Sarkin, J. (2004) *Carrots and Sticks: The TRC and the South African Amnesty Process*. Antwerp: Intersentia.

Savage, T. (2006) *In Quest of a Sustainable Justice: Transitional Justice and Human Security in the Democratic Republic of the Congo*, Occasional Paper No. 130. Pretoria: Institute for Security Studies.

Scharf, M. (2000) 'The Special Court for Sierra Leone', *ASIL Insight*. See: http://www.asil.org/insights.htm.

Schröder, J. (2006) 'Delegation to Observe the Presidential and Legislative Elections in the Democratic Republic of Congo', unpublished report. Brussels: European Parliament.

Steiner, H.J. and Alston, P. (2000) *International Human Rights in Context: Law, Politics, Morals – Text and Materials*, 2nd edn. Oxford: Oxford University Press.

Tan, C.J. (2004) 'The proliferation of bilateral non-surrender agreements among non-ratifiers of the Rome Statute of the International Criminal Court', *American University International Law Review*, 19: 1115–63.

United Nations Commission on Human Rights (1997) *Final Report on 'Question of the Impunity of Perpetrators of Human Rights Violations (Civil and Political)'*. Prepared by Louis Joinet for the Commission on Human Rights, E/CN.4/Sub.2/1997/20.

United Nations Commission on Human Rights (2003) *Question of the Violation of Human Rights and Fundamental Freedoms in Any Part of the World. Report on the Situation of Human Rights in the Democratic Republic of the Congo.* Submitted by the Special Rapporteur, Ms Iulia Motoc, in accordance with Commission on Human Rights Resolution 2002/14, E/CN.4/2003/43.

United Nations General Assembly (1948a) *Convention on the Prevention and Punishment of the Crime of Genocide*, adopted by Resolution 260 (III) A on 9 December 1948, entered into force 12 January 1951, in accordance with Article XIII. United Nations Treaty Series, Vol. 78, p. 277.

United Nations General Assembly (1948b) *Universal Declaration of Human Rights*, General Assembly Resolution 217 A (III) of 10 December 1948.

United Nations General Assembly (1976) *International Covenant on Civil and Political Rights*. Adopted and opened for signature, ratification and accession by General Assembly Resolution 2200A (XXI) of 16 December 1966, entry into force 23 March in accordance with Article 49.

United Nations General Assembly (1987) *Convention Against Torture and Other Cruel, Inhuman or Degrading Treatment or Punishment*, General Assembly Resolution 39/46, UN Doc. A/39/51 (1984), entered into force 26 June.

United Nations General Assembly (2005) *Basic Principles and Guidelines on the Right to a Remedy and Reparation for Victims of Gross Violations of International Human Rights Law and Serious Violations of International Humanitarian Law*, UN Doc. A/RES/60/147 (also known as the Bassiouni Principles).

United Nations Security Council (2000) *Third Report of the Secretary-General on the MONUC*, S/2000/566.

United Nations Security Council (2004) *The Rule of Law and Transitional Justice in Conflict and Post-conflict Societies. Report of the Secretary General*, S/2004/616.

United Nations Security Council (2005) *Security Council Notes Decision in Democratic Republic of Congo to Extend Transitional Period until End of 2005: Permitted under Peace Agreement, Transitional Constitution; Aims to allow time to strengthen security, logistics for elections*. Press Release SC/8430, 5218th Meeting 29 June 2005. See: http://www.un.org/News/Press/docs/2005/sc8430.doc.htm.

United Nations Sub-Commission for Prevention of Discrimination and Protection of Minorities (1996) *Set of Principles for the Protection and Promotion of Human Rights Intended to Strengthen Action to Combat Impunity*, E/CN.4/Sub.2/1996/18.

Vienna Declaration (1993) Vienna: World Conference on Human Rights, UN Doc. A/CONF.157/24, adopted on 14–25 June 1993.

Vircoulon, T. (2007) 'DRC-Great Lakes: From War to Development?', unpublished report to the 24th France-Africa Summit held in Cannes, 15–16 February 2007.

Vlassenroot, K. and Romkema, H. (2002) 'The emergence of a new order? Resources and war in Eastern Congo', *Journal of Humanitarian Assistance*, October. See: http://www.jha.ac/articles/a111.

Wakenge, R. and Bossaerts, G. (2006) *La Commission Vérité et Réconciliation en RDC: Le travail n'a guère commencé*. Goma: SNV Kivu.

Wetsh'okonda Koso, M. (2005) 'Why Congo needs the International Criminal Court', in 'Human rights and justice sector reform in Africa: contemporary issues and responses', *Justice Initiatives: Journal of the Open Society Justice Initiative*, February: 58–62.

Young, C. and Turner, T. (1985) *The Rise and Decline of the Zairian State*. Madison, WI: University of Wisconsin Press.

Chapter 15

Between peace and justice: informal mechanisms in the DR Congo

Theodore Kasongo Kamwimbi

Various informal mechanisms have been developed and applied in response to the human tragedy that has taken place in the North Kivu province. This chapter examines the limitations as well as the opportunities of these mechanisms with specific reference to the massacres that took place in 2004 in Nyabyondo. Apart from the massacre described in Chapter 13 of the volume, thousands of other civilians were brutally massacred, women and girls raped and the local infrastructure, including schools, was decimated. While the bodies of most of the victims were dropped into the Loashi and Mbizi rivers, thousands of survivors managed to flee to neighbouring regions such as Pinda, Loashi, Central Masisi and so on. These atrocities occurred during the armed conflict between the Forces Armées de la République Démocratique du Congo (the Congolese National Army Forces, FARDC) and rebel movements backed by Rwanda. The causes of the conflict appear to have been economic and ethnic. All sides sought to control the region's mineral resources and victims seemed to have been targeted mostly along ethnic lines – the victims generally belonged to the Hunde and Nande ethnic groups.

The situation in Nyabyondo was thoroughly confusing, with an array of armed groups endeavouring to take control of it. The Mayi-Mayi considered Nyabyondo to be their territory and resisted attacks by the 11th brigade of the Armée Nationale Congolaise (which is the former national army, the ANC). The Mayi-Mayi militia also resisted attacks by Rassemblement Congolais pour la Démocratie-Goma (RCD-Goma), which was also seeking to control the territory. It is generally acknowledged that all the warring parties had committed mass atrocities on civilians. Human Rights Watch (2005a: 19–21) indicated that the main actors involved in the Nyabyondo massacres were the FARDC, the RCD-Goma troops, Hutu civilians and Mayi-Mayi militia. Among the crimes committed were murder, torture, rape, other forms of sexual violence, abduction, mutilation, forced recruitment of child soldiers, terrorising civilians and looting. These abuses were reported by local and international human rights organisations alike, including Human Rights Watch (HRW), Amnesty International (AI), the International Crisis Group (ICG), the International Rescue Committee (IRC), Watchlist on Children and Armed Conflict, and the Association Africaine des Droits de l'Homme (ASADHO). According to the IRC (cited in Amnesty International *et al.* 2006: 2), it is estimated that between January 2003 and April 2004 almost 400,000 people died in the eastern DRC as a result of the war (Coghlan *et al.* 2004: 12, cited in Amnesty International *et al.* 2006: 2). Moreover, women were specifically targeted for sexual, physical, psychological and social abuse. Perhaps the most harmful and cynical acts in the Nyabyondo case were the massive and systematic rape and killing of women and young girls by the warring parties.

There were many incidents of extreme cruelty and gravity described by Human Rights Watch (2005a: 19–25). On one occasion, Mayi-Mayi militia threw a grenade among civilians preparing for a wedding celebration. The victims were apparently targeted because they were present in a Hutu village and were therefore assumed by Mayi-Mayi militia to be enemies. The same sort of ethnic hatred evidently prompted troops of the FARDC 11th brigade loyal to the RCD-Goma to execute a Hunde traditional leader, Baroki Mine'ene of Bukombo, at Mianja (Human Rights Watch 2005a: 20). The soldiers justified their actions as revenge against someone they believed had collaborated with the enemy, namely Mayi-Mayi and Interahamwe militias. In another scenario, RCD-Goma troops opened fire at a group of civilians – apparently they believed (mistakenly) that Mayi-Mayi militias were hiding among civilians. In addition to what has been described in the Human Rights Watch report, another report by Watchlist on Children and Armed Conflict (2006: 26) describes specific incidents of gender-based violence committed on women and young girls in and around Nyabyondo. In an interview with Amnesty International, a commander of the 11th Brigade of the FARDC, Colonel Bonane, admitted that his troops had raped women and girls in February 2005 during an attack on Nyabyondo. The report (2006: 29) mentions another case, which occurred on 11 October 2005, in which three police officers raped a 14-year-old girl after having detained her on theft charges. UN officials reported that the police officers were later arrested, but noted that *no action* had been taken against them. Another case mentioned in the report (2006: 29) dated December 2004 was about the rape of a ten-year-old girl, Josephine, by two RCD-Goma soldiers after they discovered her hiding in the forest near Nyabyondo. During the same attack, a mother and her twelve-year-old daughter, Colette, were raped in front of their entire village near Nyabyondo by ten RCD-Goma soldiers. After the rape, the soldiers abducted Colette, claiming that she was their possession. Clearly all these violent actions were the result of attacks and counter-attacks between warring parties, with mainly civilians among the victims.

Nyabyondo has been the site of atrocities committed by these different armed groups that clearly constitute gross violations of human rights, war crimes and crimes against humanity – perpetrated moreover on a massive scale and in systematic ways. But given the failure of the state to respond to these serious crimes through formal mechanisms, in the sorts of ways outlined described by, among others, Juan Méndez (1997: 261), alternative mechanism were pursued by local communities seeking to come to terms with these abuses.

Informal accountability mechanisms in the DRC

The following informal mechanisms need to be examined: traditional community courts and the traditional institutions for peace and conflict resolution. The latter include the Barza Intercommunautaire, the Commission de Pacification et de Concorde and the Kyaghanda.

Traditional community courts

It has been argued that because of the DRC's enormous size and the weakness of its administrative system, customary law is the most practicable system for the country – not least because it operates at village, clan and kinship levels (Woodrow Wilson School of Public and International Affairs 2005: 20, hereafter WWSPIA). It is therefore important to analyse the origins, development and rules of these traditional justice mechanisms.

The Congolese judicial system follows a dualist model. It is a mixture of colonial or European law with African customary law and other forms of local practices. Historically, on the one hand, the system provided classic or common law courts. On the other hand, it provided traditional community courts, named 'juridictions coutumières' (customary courts), which were created during the colonial era for judging the indigenous people. Thus, under the Decree of 15 April 1926 (cited in Cigolo 2006: 2), six types of customary courts were legally established in the DRC: Tribunal de Chefferie (Chieftaincy Tribunal), Tribunal de Collectivité (Community Tribunal), Tribunal de Cité (City Tribunal), Tribunal de Zone Urbaine (Urban Zone Tribunal), Tribunal de Zone Rurale (Rural Zone Tribunal) and Tribunal de Ville (Town Tribunal). According to the Decree, customary tribunals apply traditions that are not contrary to the written law, to universal public order, to good morals and to the principles of humanity and equity. Customary courts make use of oral tradition methods in resolving conflicts and contestations of customary nature between citizens. For instance, chieftains and local elders make use of mechanisms of oral tradition – such as fables, myths, genealogies, proverbs, enigmas and even songs – to illustrate precepts when settling disputes between parties (Wikipedia 2007).

After independence in 1960, the legal dualism persisted at the local level, particularly after President Mobutu Sese Seko incorporated 'custom' into the national law under the Ordinance of 10 July 1968. The ordinance moreover provided that customary courts were to be replaced by the Tribunaux de Paix (Peace Courts), meaning that professional magistrates would replace local notables as judges. Eventually, legislation[1] stipulated that the Tribunaux de Paix should replace customary courts. The law says the Peace Courts were instituted by the DRC to bring justice closer to the population for better administration. Nevertheless, in practice this has never become effective because in many parts of the country, especially in rural areas, it is the communal chiefs that serve as judges. Nonetheless, legislation in 1978 provided that there should be one or more Peace Courts in each urban or rural zone. But, 'even in the early 1990s, many areas of the DRC did not have a local court, apparently because of the inability of the government to recruit people with legal training who were willing to work in the countryside, far from urban amenities. Much of the population remained subject to customary justice, as administered by the chiefs and their courts' (CIA World Factbook 1993). Even today, customary tribunals or tribal courts continue to legally operate and offer advantages, particularly their being more accessible to the population covering 80 per cent of the country, as Dimandja clearly recognises (cited in UNHRC 2005).

However, these tribunals – called by some 'mal-aimées' (ill-loved) of the formal judicial system (Adau 2004: 196) – have been criticised for 'being under the control of local chieftains, being based on certain "retrograde" customs and being discriminatory toward women' (UNHRC 2005).

In addition, other scholars and organisations have called for suppression of these customary tribunals in the DRC because they do not enable compliance with standard international principles for better administration of justice. In this respect, Cigolo (2006: 8–9) considers customary law to be an impediment to the just and equitable administration of justice in the DRC. In the same context, the *Resolution on the Right to a Fair Trial and Legal Assistance in Africa* (African Commission on Human and People's Rights 1999 – also called the 'Dakar Declaration') states that 'traditional courts have significant weaknesses, resulting in many instances in a denial of a fair trial' (CHR and UPEACE 2005: 194).[2] On the other hand, some are calling for effective and regular control by first instance courts over the decisions and functioning of customary tribunals (Global Rights 2005b: 15).

Despite all their weaknesses, these tribunals exist and interact with people's needs for justice in the DRC. They can therefore play a role, of some sort, in meting out justice for the violations committed in Nyabyondo and elsewhere. According to Global Rights (2005a, 2005b), this is feasible as 'customary tribunals have discouraged victims in criminal cases such as rape from seeking legal redress before the courts, opting instead to encourage out of court settlements.' And the conclusion is that 'in most cases, these settlements [...] have awarded victims with inadequate (such as a goat or small sum of money) or inappropriate (such as marriage to the perpetrator of the crime) compensation' (Global Rights 2005a: 6). This position was also supported by the WWSPIA report which mentions the case of a villager who, after being found guilty of rape, was ordered by the village council members in North Kivu to award his victim a pig or cow as compensation (2005: 21).

Apart from these tribunals, there are other village-based mechanisms of conflict resolution. Specifically, councils of elders in most communities meet regularly in order to resolve conflicts and disputes between community members. All these traditional institutions focus on reparative justice, forgiveness and reconciliation between parties in conflict. They generally reject impunity while they strengthen social relations within communities and villages (Sonkosi 2004: 97–100).

Do customary tribunals have jurisdiction to prosecute the sort of atrocities committed in the Nyabyondo case? In order to respond to this question, a thorough analysis needs to be made with regard to jurisdictions of customary tribunals and in terms of criminal law. Article 9 of the Decree of 15 April 1926 (Bulletin Officiel du Congo Belge 1926) organising customary tribunals in the DRC contains provisions on their jurisdictions.

- Jurisdiction *ratione materiae*. In accordance with the Decree of 15 April 1926, customary tribunals have jurisdiction to settle contestations, and to mete out punishment accordingly, for matters that cannot be resolved by application of the rules of written law. In addition, customary tribunals have no jurisdiction if the offence is punishable by both customary and written law and for which the sentence is more than five years of fixed-term imprisonment. They also have no jurisdiction if the law stipulates a minimum sentence of less than five years of fixed-term imprisonment, or if the sentence is of more than one month and/or a fine, given the circumstances (Cigolo 2006: 3–4).
- Jurisdiction *ratione personae*. The above-mentioned decree prescribes that customary tribunals have jurisdiction over contestations between Congolese individuals and over nationals from neighbouring countries.
- Jurisdiction *ratione loci*. Customary tribunals are empowered to adjudicate matters in which a defendant is located in the tribunal's jurisdiction and if the offence is committed in the tribunal's jurisdiction.

Yet, for most of the atrocities committed in Nyabyondo the Congolese Penal Code (*Décret du 30 janvier 1940 portant Code Pénal Congolais* 1940) imposes sentences ranging between five years of imprisonment and the death penalty, even if in practice the death sentence is usually commuted to life imprisonment. For instance, those found guilty of murder and assassination as well as of association formed in order to injure individuals and properties face the death penalty according to the Ordinary Penal Code (Articles 44, 45, 157).

The law moreover imposes penalties ranging between five and 20 years of imprisonment on perpetrators for acts of torture, rape, sexual violence, mutilation and pillage (*Loi No. 06/018*, 2006: Articles 110, 170). Thus, legally speaking, customary tribunals in the DRC have no jurisdiction over serious crimes, such as those committed in Nyabyondo, and which are for the most part war crimes and crimes against humanity.

According to general theory, traditional forms of justice are designed to deal with relatively small numbers of cases of minor wrongdoing, such as theft and conflicts between neighbours (Huyse 2003: 113). They also deal with matters relating to witchcraft, which does not constitute a criminal offence under Congolese law. However, human rights organisations have noted, with regret, that a customary tribunal at Tumbwe in Katanga province has sentenced a woman for witchcraft (MONUC Human Rights Division 2006a). In other words, traditional forms of justice have no capacity to deal with serious international crimes, such as genocide, war crimes and crimes against humanity.

Traditional institutions for peace and conflict resolution

It is argued that the most prevalent mechanism for conflict resolution in the DRC is a village-based system in which councils of elders meet on a regular basis in rural villages or towns (WWSPIA 2005: 20). In most cases, these councils have been established in communities where formal courts are inaccessible for various reasons, such as long walking distances. In North Kivu to which the territory of Nyabyondo belongs, a number of traditional dispute mechanisms have been established to resolve conflict among different social communities and ethnic groups. This section aims at examining each of them in more detail.

The Barza Intercommunautaire

The Barza Intercommunautaire, etymologically from the Swahili word 'baraza' meaning council of elders for resolving conflicts and addressing concerns of the community, is an old practice based on the francophone African tradition of *l'arbre à palabre* (Villa-Vicencio *et al*. 2005: 58–9). This inter-communitarian structure in North Kivu was initiated and established in 1998 by community leaders for reducing and preventing ethnic tensions between the community groups. Eight ethnic communities are equally represented in it through customary chiefs and opinion-leaders, namely Nyanga, Nande, Hutu, Kano, Tembo, Hunde, Humu and Tutsi. The Barza has a well elaborated structure and a code of conduct imposed on all the community members. In accordance with the statute, it is for instance forbidden for any community to question the nationality of another community, especially on the basis of physical appearance (WWSPIA 2005: 20). This is probably to prevent tensions between the Hutus and Tutsis, which is well known as one of the major sources of conflict not only in the DRC but throughout the Great Lakes region of Africa. Today, the Barza has been accused of being hijacked, controlled and influenced by some political authorities, and this factor has undermined its originality and effectiveness and caused the failure of attempts to replicate it in other areas such as South Kivu (Huggins and Pottier 2005: 387).

The Barza Intercommunautaire's purpose is reconciliation between divided ethnic communities in North Kivu. Therefore it aims at breaking the barriers between communities to avoid any suspicion between them and to bring them together at the same place. Exclusion, violence, contempt, intolerance and idleness are all categorically banned in the Barza Intercommunautaire and can be punished. The Barza has the responsibility to receive complaints from the victims and create opportunities for resolving the conflict between the victims and the perpetrators for sustainable reconciliation. In facilitating peace and reconciliation between parties in the conflict, 'the Barza involves disputants engaging one another through dialogue and ritual – usually under a tree, sharing food and drinking from a common calabash. Ceremonies also contain the acknowledgment of guilt, the request for forgiveness, the promise not to repeat the offence and rituals of purification' (Villa-Vicencio *et al.* 2005: 59). This reflects the underlying values of the Barza such as sincerity, frankness, transparency, mutual forgiveness and equality of all communities, as enumerated by the President of the Barza Intercommunautaire of the North Kivu province, Mr Kibira Katarungu Thomas (Tegera *et al.* 2000: 6–7). As can be seen, any type of conflict may be dealt with inside the Barza, which does not focus on the perpetrators but on the sources of conflict, which in the Nyabyondo case are ethnic and economic.

It is recognised that together with other complementary initiatives in North Kivu province, the Barza Intercommunautaire has been able to find peaceful and sustainable solutions to some conflicts and to promote peaceful coexistence (Uvin and Bourque 2004: 20). For instance, in 2004 the Pole Institute together with various partners, including the Barza Intercommunautaire, started activities of research and reflection around the question of historical memory (Tegera *et al.* 2004: 10). The objective was to work with the communities impacted by the conflict and to continue their intercultural activities for appropriation by different local communities with a similar common history (Kayser 2004: 2).

The whole work, Kayser (2004: 2) expresses, was essentially 'based on the principle that apparent collective amnesia coupled with a culture of hatred and exclusion of the other, identification of one or several scapegoats including communities and/or entire countries would not make it possible for the Congolese populations to build their future'.

The work of research and memorialisation conducted by the Barza Intercommunautaire for sustainable reconciliation between communities was a challenging task. The investigating team visited sites of massacres and conducted interviews on the spot in several territories of North Kivu. These experimental phases of the work showed above all how deep the wounds in all the communities were, and how difficult it was to speak about reconciliation and learn lessons for a better coexistence of all in the future (Uvin and Bourque 2004).

More recently in December 2006, the members of the Barza Intercommunautaire took a peace initiative and met with the Army Chief-of-Staff in Goma to find ways of resolving the conflict between the rebel commander Laurent Nkunda and the FARDC in the province (United Nations Office for the Coordination of Humanitarian Affairs 2006).

The Barza Intercommunautaire is obviously not the only mechanism for peace and reconciliation. There is also one of the most important mechanisms, which is the Commission de Pacification et de Concorde (Commission for Pacification and Harmony – CPC).

Commission de Pacification et de Concorde

The idea of establishing the CPC in North Kivu emerged from the need to reconcile the major ethnic groups in conflict since July 1997 following the decay of Mobutu's regime (Tegera *et al.* 2000: 32). Upon the request of President Laurent Kabila, a commission of elders from the two Kivu provinces was formed with the mission of establishing the CPC to identify the causes of inter-ethnic violence. Once the delegates of the CPC were appointed by the notables, a decree was signed for legal establishment of the CPC in North and South Kivu, with a national coordination office attached to the Interior Ministry in Kinshasa (Tegera *et al.* 2000: 32). Thereafter, the members of the CPC established a bureau, which comprised at least one representative per community. The CPC managed not only to identify the causes of conflicts, but also to resolve the problems of coexistence and reconciliation between communities and inside the communities. For these reasons they created the 'cells or antennas of peace', which are structures of pacification at the local level and in which the problems of inter-communitarian coexistence are addressed (Tegera *et al.* 2000: 32).

Among its achievements, the CPC has also created opportunities for different communities to engage in dialogue, discuss community problems and achieve reconciliation for peaceful coexistence. The Commission has even achieved a big goal in terms of the disarmament, demobilisation and reintegration of former combatants into society. In this regard, the report (Tegera *et al.* 2000: 39) mentions some significant examples. For instance, the CPC managed to bring back into the community many Hutu and Mayi-Mayi militias from the bush after having talked to them about the process of demobilisation. Among the returnees, the report mentions former Hutu warlords Mayanga and Rugayi along with 1,500 of their child soldiers. Another Mayi-Mayi warlord, Ndoole Fely, was convinced by the CPC to leave his weapons in the bush to join a community in which he is now serving in security intelligence forces to make other Mayi-Mayi militia aware of demobilisation options. In the territory of Kalehe, the CPC managed to reintegrate into the society another warlord together with 300 of his combatants and to collect 200 weapons from them (Tegera *et al.* 2000: 39).

The CPC and Harmony has produced some significant and positive results in terms of peacebuilding, reconciliation, demilitarisation, demobilisation and reintegration – so much so that the Interior Ministry established a Provincial Commission of Pacification, which comprised representatives of each ethnic community of North Kivu (Tegera *et al.* 2000: 32).

In addition to the Commission, the North Kivu province has another key traditional institution for peace and coexistence, namely the Kyaghanda.

The Kyaghanda

The Kyaghanda is a traditional mechanism for conflict resolution in the most populous ethnic group in North Kivu, the Nande. All the Nande people living both inside and outside the DRC are socially organised and interconnected through the Kyaghanda. They speak a common language, the Kinande, which constitutes an element of cohesion and unity among the Nande people for strong and powerful Bunande (being Nande). The Kyaghanda is viewed as a 'traditional veranda' as it serves as the space for meetings, customary rituals and intercommunity dialogues for peaceful coexistence between different social groups (Ansay 2005: 13). As Roger Kasereka Mwana wa vene (2005: 174) points out, the Kyaghanda is a space where everyone is invited to build peace, harmony and social and intercommunity tolerance for addressing differences between individuals and communities.

In terms of procedure, Mwana wa vene (2005: 174) observes that the Kyaghanda dialogue begins with discussion and identification of the nature and sources of the conflict and ends up with reconciliation as the final result. As in many other African traditional mechanisms, the hearings in the Kyaghanda take place under the responsibility of great customary chiefs assisted by the notables, the elders, as well as other wise men who hear the protagonists' arguments and their witnesses on the matter (Mwana wa vene 2005: 174). The case is closed only when compromise, reconciliation, harmony and social peace are achieved. The perpetrator is due to provide the victim with reparation estimated in terms of natural values, such as a chicken (hen) or goats according to the gravity of the offence or harm suffered. At the end of the ceremonies, the protagonists are always invited to share food from the same plate and drink wine or beer from the same calabash as a symbol of restoring the new alliance between the two parties (Mwana wa vene 2005: 175). In some extreme cases, to symbolise and materialise the new covenant, the perpetrator's family offers to the victim or his family a young girl full of virtuosity and fecundity. This has a particular meaning given that in the Kyaghanda women represent political power and strengthen harmony between communities, as reflected in the Nande proverb, 'Without women, no power' (Mwana wa vene 2005: 175). Among the values characterising the Kyaghanda are: mutual understanding, mediation and finding consensual solutions, among others. In resolving conflicts, the Kyaghanda puts emphasis on the satisfaction of the protagonists in reaching a consensual solution. As an adage says, 'every imposed solution is a source of tensions and social disorder' (Mwana wa vene 2005: 175).

Clearly, the Kyaghanda aiming to restore concord and social peace (Ansay 2005: 13) could be considered as one of the best options for dealing with the past in Nyabyondo. However, up to now no report has been recorded on the use of the Kyaghanda for reconciliation between perpetrators, victims and the entire community in Nyabyondo.

Level of operation by the informal mechanisms

From the examples developed in the previous sections, it is somewhat evident that each of the informal mechanisms discussed operate at either the community, national or international level, or at a combination of these levels.

Local/communal mechanisms

In many cases, informal mechanisms operate at the local level where relationships between individuals or communities have been broken. It is within the community that the *notables* or wise men meet in order to resolve conflicts and restore relations. This is the case for all the mechanisms analysed in this study – the Barza Intercommunautaire, the CPC and the Kyaghanda.

National mechanisms

Some of the mechanisms operate at the national level with their structures represented in each province throughout the country. This is the case for customary tribunals, the Barza Intercommunautaire and the CPCs. All are represented in major regions of the DRC with specific and well-established structures. The Barza Intercommunautaire was formally established through an initiative of the transitional government in June 2004 to achieve pacification and reconciliation missions. The project draws on the traditional model for allowing the local communities to resolve their conflicts. The government decided to extend the project throughout the DRC regions, starting with South Kivu, where the Barza was officially installed on 28 March 2005. The project was funded by the government and logistically supported by the United Nations peacekeeping mission in the DRC (MONUC). Crucially, it was fully supported by a number of Congolese and international civil society organisations (Tegera *et al.* 2000: 39).

International mechanisms

It has been demonstrated that some traditional mechanisms operate at the international or regional level. For instance, the Barza Intercommunautaire has been invited to intervene in Uganda and Rwanda in the disarmament, demobilisation and repatriation of Rwandan and Ugandan rebel troops operating in eastern DRC, including the Forces for the Democratic Liberation of Rwanda (FDLR), the *Interahamwe* militias, the Lord's Resistance Army (LRA) and the Ex-Forces Armées Rwandaises (ex-FAR). Similarly, the Kyaghanda has been extended beyond Congolese borders to help resolving conflicts involving the Nande people. As stated above, the Kyaghanda works with Nande people, including those of the diaspora. The purpose is to preserve and promote the Bunande, which is their philosophy.

Combination of local/communal, national and international mechanisms

Some traditional mechanisms operate at the local, national and international levels. This is the case for the Kyaghanda, which is applied in the Nande community where it serves to resolve conflicts between members of the community and facilitate peaceful coexistence between them. Similarly, the Barza Intercommunautaire comprises representatives of eight communities from North Kivu province in order to enable it to contribute meaningfully to peaceful coexistence between different ethnic groups in the region (Pole Institute 2002: 8).

Normative framework of the informal response

African traditional justice systems are widely acknowledged to contain elements of restorative justice (Skelton and Batley 2006: 8–9). They aim at reconciliation and the restoration of peace and harmony. In the context of the DRC, many informal mechanisms of conflict and dispute resolution are based on an array of factors: culture, tradition, religion, universal human rights, national law, international law, to name but a few – and combinations of such factors.

Cultural and religious elements

Most informal mechanisms are inextricably tied to culture and tradition, most notably the culture of *l'arbre à palabre*. They are also based on the African oral tradition, which consists of dialogue and exchange of views on disputed issues within the communities. This applies to mechanisms such as the Barza Intercommunautaire, the CPC and the Kyaghanda. Other informal mechanisms are based on religion to resolve conflicts. Informal judicial mechanisms have been established inside churches, such as the Comités des Sages (Committees of Wise People) and the Communautés Ecclésiales Vivantes (CEV) in the Roman Catholic Church. These structures have the power to collect complaints from the victims and help promote reconciliation. The means used by the main actors to resolve conflicts are generally taken from traditional law: mediation, negotiation, arbitration, conciliation, reparation, reconciliation. Some have called this a 'justice of common sense' (Adau 2004: 196). The Catholic CEV were first established in the DRC in 1961 as a structure of the Church to contribute to evangelisation and development (Kakule Kaparay 2006: 145). With the recrudescence of violence in eastern DRC, the

CEV play the role of conflict prevention and conflict resolution in similar ways to those of the Kyaghanda (Kakule Kaparay 2006: 146). However, it is not clear whether the CEV have played any role in terms of reconciliation and peaceful coexistence in Nyabyondo.

Universal human rights

Amid the grave violations that have taken place in the DRC, it would be controversial to suggest that traditional mechanisms described above could play a significant role in addressing gross human rights violations committed on civilians. Because of the deficiencies they exhibit, these mechanisms would simply not be appropriate to address the likes of wartime and gender-based atrocities and should therefore be considered with much scepticism (WWSPIA 2005: 20–1). Among the deficiencies are a lack of legal competence to address contemporary crimes, the risk of offering punishments grossly incommensurate with the crimes committed, and a lack of adequate representation for both women and ethnic minorities (WWSPIA 2005: 20–1).

That said, a number of associations and human rights organisations have played a remarkable role in resolving conflicts between individuals or communities and in facilitating peaceful coexistence. In this respect, it is argued that civil society organisations in the DRC have played a critical role in promoting peace and stability, in monitoring human rights violations and other abuses against innocent civilian populations and in promoting inter-ethnic dialogue and reconciliation at local and regional levels (Fransiscans International 2006). In so doing, these organisations apply human rights norms and principles. For instance, in their work on reconciliation at the community level, women from two opposed ethnic communities, Banyamulenge and Babembe, developed a network of civil society organisations in South Kivu province and reached an agreement over the issues of sexual violence (International Alert n.d.). For this purpose, they based their agreement on existing universal human rights instruments in order to prevent further sexual violence.

Similarly, in their awareness campaign against sexual and gender-based violence, the Congolese network of women's NGOs in eastern DRC along with human rights NGOs have taken action against all forms of violence committed by armed groups against women (Global Rights 2005a: 5). In order to 'raise the profile of this issue to the attention of the Congolese people, the media, local officials, the international community and many Congolese civil society organisations involved in mediation programmes have integrated women's human rights issues in their work' (Global Rights 2005a: 5). In the process they have made use of human rights instruments related to gender violence.[3] The knowledge of these human rights instruments have helped these organisations immensely in documenting and reporting sexual violence committed during the armed conflicts in the DRC and in combating impunity for such acts. In 2003, for example, these organisations 'applied intense advocacy and pressure to secure the trial of a former RCD soldier for raping an eight-year-old girl in Kabare, South-Kivu. The Conseil de Guerre (Military Tribunal) handed down a 20-year prison sentence against the accused' (Global Rights 2005a: 5).

MONUC Human Rights Division and the Office of the United Nations High Commissioner for Human Rights (UNHCHR) together reported that 'a judicial investigation was opened by the judicial authorities in North Kivu into the December 2004 Nyabyondo massacre and serious human rights violations committed by the FARDC Battalion under the command of Major Kambale' (MONUC Human Rights Division and Office of the UNHCHR 2007: 15). According to the report, 'Major Kambale considered as one of the prime suspects in the Nyabyondo massacre was neither interrogated by a magistrate, nor charged for the crimes committed.' Further reports received by the United Nations Human Rights Integrated Office in the DRC (cited in MONUC Human Rights Division and Office of the UNHCHR 2007: 15) suggest 'that Major Kambale returned to duty in Ituri in December 2006 where he reportedly resumed his functions as Commander of the 2nd Battalion of the 4th Integrated Brigade based in Bavi.' This is clearly a case of impunity characterising the judicial system in the DRC and particularly with regard to the atrocities committed in Nyabyondo, as described by Human Rights Watch (2005a: 31). In order to fight impunity a 'MONUC special investigation team, based in Kinshasa, promptly investigated crimes committed at Nyabyondo and Buramba, near Kanyabayonga and made public their results' (Centre d'Etudes et de Recherches en Education de Base pour le Développement Intégré (CEREBA), cited in Human Rights Watch 2005a: 31). This is an illustration of measures taken by MONUC to face challenges posed by impunity and the weakness of the DRC judicial system. In addition, 'MONUC has created a Rule of Law Task Force with a mandate encompassing human rights and judicial reform and composed of members of all its sections as well as members of other UN agencies and other international institutions' (Tremblay 2004: 67).

National or international law

Basically, the DRC has not implemented the traditional mechanisms described above into its ordinary Penal Code, but in practice these mechanisms intervene to resolve disputes in areas where legal ordinary courts do not exist, such as rural areas. Named by Adau (2004: 198) as the 'informal judicial function', this form of justice seems to respond to the legitimate needs of the people who choose to refer their disputes to informal judges, in the absence of legal and formal tribunals. For instance, in some areas human rights activists have established 'boutiques des droits' (law-shops). In others, peasants created 'comités d'autodéfense populaire' (committees for popular self-defence) for dispute resolution purposes. The judges – who sometimes have never been taught anything about conflict mediation – are chosen by the communities themselves (Adau 2004: 198).

Moreover, in the Congolese legal system, especially in the Family Code (*Code de la Famille* 2003), there is an important mechanism of domestic justice, namely the 'conseil de famille' (family council) which serves as a link between the family and formal judicial instances. The family council intervenes as the formal judge to resolve conflicts inside the family. In order to resolve the conflicts, the family councils apply the rule of law as established by the state.

Many organisations as well as the DRC government have called for the establishment of a Special Tribunal for the DRC for prosecuting perpetrators of massive human rights violations committed in the country during the wartime. It has been suggested that such a tribunal should rely on two basic sources: traditional justice mechanisms, particularly village councils, and the civil law procedures. Obviously, this tribunal should be respectful of Congolese traditions and have jurisdiction over crimes in customary international law and under applicable treaties, including genocide, war crimes and crimes against humanity (WWSPIA 2005: 7). As far as Nyabyondo is concerned, we should refer to the Human Rights Watch report (2005a: 32) which clearly argues that 'most war crimes committed in eastern DRC, especially those documented in the report (including the Nyabyondo massacre) have been neither fully investigated nor prosecuted.'

Role of the parties in the process

Possible parties to the processes of informal mechanisms are the victim(s), the perpetrator(s), the local community, the broader community, the state and the international community. Broad-based engagement is necessary if the goal of restorative justice and rehabilitation is to be met (Villa-Vicencio 2004b: 34).

The victim plays a key role. In many traditional methods, the victim is given the opportunity to tell their side of the story during the hearing under the responsibility of a mediator, who in most cases would be a widely respected wise man. The victim has the opportunity to ask for compensation, if they wish, in reparation for the harm done to them. The victim generally does so in the presence of the perpetrator, another key actor, obviously, in the process.

Traditional mediation-based mechanisms generally bring the perpetrator into the process. The perpetrator is asked to explain the reasons for his/her actions. Emphasis is given to enabling the perpetrator to understand the full impact of what he/she has done. The opportunity is also given to them to tell the truth and seek forgiveness from the victim, to repent, to show remorse and to repair the harm inflicted on the victim. By participating fully in the mediation process, the perpetrator gains an opportunity to be healed and accepted back into community (Sonkosi 2004: 97–9).

The offence or the harm done is generally considered to be a matter for both the victim and the entire community which shares in the suffering of the victim. The local community is involved in the process through its leaders who mediate the confrontation between the protagonists. This applies to all the traditional institutions for peace and conflict resolution analysed in this study. In this regard, in most traditional societies conflicts are dealt with by a group of elders because of their wisdom, integrity and honour, so that their decisions are widely accepted as legitimate. According to the Pole Institute (2002: 8), these wise men are regrouped in a sort of forum known in eastern DRC under the generic name of 'Baraza', or 'Kyaghanda' in Nande culture, 'Bushenge' in Hunde, 'Obushenge' in Havu and 'Inama' in Hutu.

The informal mechanisms of conflict resolution address the tensions and conflicts not only within a particular community, but also throughout the broader society. For instance, the Barza Intercommunautaire assists the broader society to resolve its differences and conflicts. The entire society gets involved in the process. Increasingly, both international organisations and state agencies provide training and financial and logistic support for the traditional leaders to fulfil their mission of restoring relations between the members of the communities. For instance, International Alert working on reconciliation at the community level has provided

Congolese women, through its main partners in the Kivu provinces,[4] with intensive training on gender and conflict resolution techniques and leadership skills (International Alert n.d.). Another example to be mentioned in this respect would be Search for Common Ground (SFCG), known in the DRC as Centre Locale and established in 2001 to promote peace and reconciliation in the country. 'Through media programming and capacity building and outreach activities, SFCG-DRC enhances communication about the political transition process and contributes towards reduction of tensions and development of lasting peace in the East' (Search for Common Ground in the DRC 2006).

Such organisations have been immensely helpful in mediating local conflicts. They have particularly worked with communities divided over the demobilisation and reintegration into society of child soldiers from opposing sides and mediating between antagonistic chiefs. In traditional mechanisms, the perpetrator does not pay compensation to the state but to the victim directly.

The international community's position on the atrocities committed in Nyabyondo has been widely criticised for its timidity. Amnesty International (2005) blames the UN peacekeeping mission in the DRC (MONUC) for having intervened too little and too late, and for essentially having failed to prevent the atrocities. Moreover, the report condemns the impunity characterising the Nyabyondo case, arguing that none of the officers or troops allegedly involved in the abuses have been prosecuted despite having been identified. The Amnesty report does indicate that MONUC at least conducted an investigation on the atrocities and submitted the findings to the Congolese government and military authorities at the national and provincial levels. A commission of enquiry composed of local security officials was established by the Governor of North Kivu province, Eugène Serufuli, to investigate the killings at Buramba. But the report released by the commission in January 2005 (cited in Amnesty International 2005) made no recommendation for prosecution against those suspected of responsibility for the killings.

At the same time, some international organisations have actively sought to support the extension of traditional mechanisms throughout the DRC for dealing with atrocities committed in the country, including in Nyabyondo. Among other events, an expert meeting was convened in late 2004 by the Amsterdam Center for International Law (ACIL) at the University of Amsterdam and No Peace Without Justice (NPWJ), aimed at contributing to a fuller understanding of the alternative options of assigning responsibility for crimes under international law and addressing them.[5] In the discussion, the experts agreed that in order to fill an impunity gap evident in the jurisdiction and practice of the International Criminal Court (the ICC), four alternative accountability mechanisms are necessary: local or traditional mechanisms; domestic proceedings; proceedings before a truth commission; and special internationalised courts and tribunals. The delegates believed that 'these mechanisms have advantages over a purely international accountability mechanism in terms of legitimacy, cost, domestic politics and their ability to promote reform' (NPWJ 2004: 11). Delegates therefore encouraged the DRC (as well as Uganda) 'to analyse in depth these traditional mechanisms of justice in order to determine which mechanisms would be most beneficial to peace and justice' (NPWJ 2004: 11) Logically, this idea should equally prevail in the context of Nyabyondo where sustainable peace, stability and reconciliation are much needed by different communities. It is understandable that in such a situation formal or judicial mechanisms of justice would only undermine any chance of reconciliation and stability given that there is still a risk of relapsing into violence. Moreover, it would be virtually impossible to prosecute all those who committed atrocities in Nyabyondo, given that most of them have joined the new integrated national army while others are serving in leadership position and this of course raises the issue of selectivity as one of the challenges to prosecution. In the case of Nyabyondo, the ideal may be to establish what Alex Boraine (2004: 68) calls a 'just society' in which the most important elements are truth-searching, the restoration of dignity and reconciliation processes. The best option would then be to strengthen the 'council of elders' known as 'baraza' (WWSPIA 2005: 20). On a practical note, and as already noted, the Pole Institute has established a strong partnership with the Barza Intercommunautaire of North Kivu to conduct investigations for truth recovery around atrocities committed in the region as a whole (Tegera *et al.* 2004: 10). Presumably Nyabyondo, being a territory of North Kivu seriously affected by wars and massive human rights violations, is covered by the investigations.

Purpose level of informal mechanisms – justice, truth and redress

Amnesty International points out that the 'three major principles, namely truth, justice and redress, are identified in international human rights standards as the foundations of an effective remedy to serious human rights violations' (Amnesty International 1997: 1). The report also admits that 'together they act as a framework for addressing human rights violations of the past and provide safeguards against their repetition in the future' (Amnesty International 1997: 1). In the Nyabyondo case, traditional mechanisms could be used to achieve a measure of justice, truth and redress, especially for the lesser crimes committed, in a number of ways.

Justice

In the informal mechanisms of conflict resolution in the DRC, and most notably in the Barza Intercommunautaire, perpetrators are invited to face the victims and respond to the allegations laid against them so that the truth may be recovered, reconciliation reached and justice achieved (Villa-Vicencio *et al.* 2005: 58–9). It has been argued by Luc Huyse (2003: 112), most notably, that 'traditional forms of justice might be of great value in post-conflict countries where punitive measures are often risky or simply unattainable strategy'. Like Huyse, Cigolo (2006: 6) attributes a number of advantages to traditional mechanisms of justice with specific pertinence to the DRC. In fact, both Huyse and Cigolo agree that traditional mechanisms of justice are accessible to local and rural people in terms of language, distance and legal representation. It is indeed argued that 'traditional justice mechanisms exist in virtually every village in the DRC – regardless of ethnicity – in which a council of elders meets on a regular basis to discuss topical issues in the community and to adjudicate local disputes, often relating to land use, ownership, or other concerns' (WWSPIA 2005: 7).

They also agree that traditional mechanisms of justice are based on reconciliation, compensation, restoration and rehabilitation and give the victim, the offender and the entire community the opportunity to find a lasting solution to the conflict. This corresponds to a core element of restorative justice, described by Villa-Vicencio (2004b: 35) in the following terms:

> [Restorative justice] necessarily involves victims and survivors, perpetrators and the community in the quest for a level of justice that promotes repair, trust-building and reconciliation.

Another advantage of traditional mechanisms of justice mentioned by Cigolo (2006: 6) concerns the key role these mechanisms play in educating all members of the community about the due process to be followed for peaceful conflict resolution. Lastly Cigolo (2006: 6) argues that 'traditional mechanisms of justice prevent prison overcrowding given the non-custodial nature of the sentences they employ, that they allow offenders to make a contribution to the economy and pay compensation to the victims, and prevent the economic and social dislocation of the family.'

Drawing on the work of memorialisation and reconciliation conducted by a variety of partners that included the Barza Inter-communautaire in North Kivu province, it could be argued that traditional mechanisms of justice are in fact being used in that circumstance to reconcile communities. This important work is considered to be a long-term process involving academics, researchers and specialists on memorialisation and oral history in order to enable North Kivu to deal with its past by recording its memory.

With regard to formal forms of justice, there has been a trial in February 2005 on abuses committed in the neighbourhood of Nyabyondo, at Kanyabayonga (Amnesty International 2005). In this case, 29 FARDC military personnel were found guilty of offences ranging from looting, indiscipline and rape to murder in connection with the Kanyabayonga abuses. Twenty-one of those low ranking-military soldiers were sentenced to death after a summary military trial. They have appealed against the sentences. It was alleged that these soldiers were punished in order to cover up the mismanagement of the Kanyabayonga offensive by the senior FARDC command. The majority of the FARDC commanders, allegedly responsible for the atrocities at Kanyabayonga, have not been brought to justice (Amnesty International 2005). This raises the question of truth.

Truth

As Babu Ayindo (cited in Villa-Vicencio 2000a: 202) suggests, 'Truth telling is at the heart of most "African traditional justice systems" that aim to reintegrate both the offender and the victim back into society.' This is the case for all the mechanisms examined in this study, which aim above all at revealing the whole truth about what happened to the victims. It has been demonstrated from interviews conducted all over the DRC that many Congolese – through civil society organisations – are calling for the prosecution of perpetrators, preferably by international judicial mechanisms. The victims indicate that they needed perpetrators to be brought to them to tell the truth about the atrocities and to pay reparations (Amnesty International 2003).

The DRC's Commission Vérité et Reconciliation (CVR) forms an integral part of another chapter in this volume. Suffice it to note here the overlap between the efforts of the commission with traditional methods of pursuing justice. According to the CVR President, Bishop Jean-Luc Kuye, a CVR team was sent to Goma on a mission of peaceful coexistence and conflict resolution with regard to the situation in the neighbourhood of Nyabyondo, at Kanyabayonga in North Kivu (Kongo 2005). One could presume in this context that the team conducted some interviews with the victims of the atrocities and the witnesses in order to recover the truth about what happened. Unlike Bishop Kuye, Raphael Wakenge and Geert Bossaerts (2006: 7) argue that despite the numerous requests it received for resolving conflicts in the region, the CVR of North Kivu has been unable to respond because of lack of resources and the conflictual relationship it has with the national CVR office based in Kinshasa. It is therefore clear that the truth about the atrocities committed in Nyabyondo will take a long time to emerge, unless there is the political will and a radical change of attitude within the entire government.

Redress

Redress for victims of human rights violations through formal or informal procedures is provided for by relevant international legal provisions at both the universal and regional levels. At the international level, paragraphs 4 and 5 of the *Declaration of Basic Principles of Justice for Victims of Crime and Abuse of Power* (United Nations 1985) contain provisions related to redress for victims. In fact, these provisions specify a legal duty incumbent upon states to provide effective redress to victims of human rights violations. They stipulate that victims are entitled to access to the mechanisms of justice and to prompt redress through formal or informal procedures, according to national legislation, for the harm that they have suffered. At regional level, sections (a) and (d) of paragraph P of the *Principles and Guidelines on the Right to a Fair Trial and Legal Assistance in Africa* (African Commission on Human and People's Rights 2003) reproduce the above-mentioned provisions of the UN *Declaration of Basic Principles*. Moreover, section (g) of paragraph P of these principles (2003) provide that informal mechanisms for the resolution of disputes, including mediation, arbitration and traditional or customary practices, should be utilised where appropriate to facilitate conciliation and redress of victims. In this respect, section (h) of the principles (2003) demands that perpetrators and third parties, where appropriate, make fair restitution to the victims, their families or dependants. Clearly, both international and regional human rights law standards allow use of informal mechanisms for dealing with redress for victims who are surely one of the beneficiaries of justice, truth and redress. However, at this stage there hasn't been any discussion of which the public is aware around this issue with regard to the Nyabyondo case.

Informal mechanisms in the DRC: balancing between peace and justice

The plethora of informal mechanisms available in the DRC – and particularly in the Kivu provinces – have shown to be chiefly focused on conflict resolution and reconciliation. Looking at the transitional process in the DRC through a restorative justice lens, these efforts should have deserved acknowledgment for their crucial contribution to establishing peace between ethnically divided groups and communities, and between communities and former combatants.

With regard to its main goals of truth, justice and redress, the transitional justice process in the DRC has mostly failed to seize the opportunities to deal with the beneficiaries – the victims, the perpetrators and the community – through any of the formal mechanisms of accountability considered. The victims or survivors have not received – with the exception a few notable cases – reparation for the loss and harm done to them. Perpetrators were not given a chance to account for their wrongdoings, and are at the same time still waiting for admission to the national demobilisation and rehabilitation programme that has been announced. And finally, due to the failed attempt of the transitional government to launch victim or community hearings at the TRC the community was not given a chance to recover and keep historical records about what happened in the past. In this regard the preparatory work done by some traditional mechanisms such as the CPC should have been considered by the formal transitional justice process. The establishment of the truth about the past and ensuring justice and adequate redress for victims could have contributed enormously to efforts at finding a long-term and durable solution to the issue.

Notes

1 Article 163 of the *Ordinance-law related to the Code of Organisation and Judicial Competences* (1982).

2 African Commission on Human and People's Rights (1999) *Resolution on the Right to a Fair Trial and Legal Assistance in Africa* ('Dakar Declaration') (1999), in *Compendium of Key Human Rights Documents of the African Union*. Pretoria: Pretoria University Law Press, pp. 194. Available online at: http://www.chr.up.ac.za/pulp/Compendium%20Second%20Edition.pdf.

3 These include, *inter alia*, the *Universal Declaration of Human Rights* (United Nations 1948b), the *International Covenant on Civil and Political Rights* (United Nations 1976a), the *International Covenant on Economic, Social and Cultural Rights* (United Nations 1976b), the *Convention on the Elimination of All Forms of Discrimination Against Women* (United Nations 1981) and the *Convention on the Rights of the Child* (United Nations 1989); they implicitly protect sexual rights by guaranteeing rights to personal freedom, health, non-discrimination, equal opportunity and protection from violence.

4 The Réseau des Femmes pour un Développement Associatif (a collective of 44 women's organisations), the Réseau des Femmes pour la Défense des Droits et la Paix (a local women's network) and two other community-based women's organisations, AFIP and AFEC.

5 The expert meeting 'Accountability Mechanisms for International Crimes: The Cases of the Democratic Republic of Congo and Uganda' was organised at Universiteit van Amsterdam on 14 October 2004 by the Amsterdam Center for International Law (ACIL) and No Peace Without Justice (NPWJ).

References

Accord Global et Inclusif sur la Transition en République Démocratique du Congo (2002), signé à Pretoria (République d'Afrique du Sud) le 17 décembre 2002 et adopté à Sun City le 1er avril 2003, in *Journal Officiel de la République Démocratique du Congo*, Spécial Issue, 5 avril 2003, pp. 51–69.

Adau, P.A. (2004) 'Partenariat entre les initiatives publiques et privées? Et participation citoyenne pour les droits humains', in *Proceedings of the International Seminar on the Transition Process in the DRC (26–28 April 2004)* (original in French: *Séminaire international sur la gestion de la transition en République Démocratique du Congo)*. Kinshasa: International Francophone Organisation and the Ministry of Foreign Affairs of the DRC, pp. 183–208.

African Commission on Human and People's Rights (1999) *Resolution on the Right to a Fair Trial and Legal Assistance in Africa.* (Also known as 'the Dakar Declaration').

African Commission on Human and People's Rights (2003) *Principles and Guidelines on the Right to a Fair Trial and Legal Assistance in Africa*, adopted in 2003, following the appointment of a Working Group on the Right to a Fair Trial per its 1999 Resolution on the Right to a Fair Trial and Legal Assistance.

Amnesty International (1997) *East Timor: Truth, Justice and Redress*, ASA 21/081/1997, 1 November 1997.

Amnesty International (2003) *Democratic Republic of Congo – Addressing the Present and Building a Future: A Memorandum to the DRC Transitional Government of National Unity, Armed Groups and Foreign Governments Involved in the DRC Conflict, and the International Community*, AI Resource Centre Reports, APR 62/050/2003.

Amnesty International (2005) *Democratic Republic of Congo North-Kivu: Civilians Pay the Price for Political and Military Rivalry*, AI Resource Centre Reports, APR 62/013/2005.

Amnesty International (2006) *DRC: Children at War, Creating Hope for the Future*, AI Resource Centre Reports, AFR 62/017/2006.

Amnesty International, Oxfam and IANSA (2006) *The Call for Tough Arms Controls. Voices from the Democratic Republic of the Congo, Report*. London: Oxfam Great Britain.

Amsterdam Centre for International Law and No Peace Without Justice (2004) *Accountability Mechanisms for International Crimes: The Cases of the Democratic Republic of Congo and Uganda*, Conference Report. See: http://www.npwj.org/?q=node/2288.

Ansay, M. (2005) *Sub-Saharan Veterinary Health Recipes and Peace Traditions in Dialog with the Western Countries*. Paper at the International Conference on 'Indigenous Knowledge Systems (IKS) in Africa and Their Relevance for Sustainable Development', VUB Brussels, 31–23 November. Institut de la Vie.

Bhargava, R. (2000) 'The moral justification of truth commissions', in C. Villa-Vicencio and W. Verwoerd (eds), *Looking Back, Reaching Forward: Reflections on the Truth and Reconciliation Commission of South Africa*. Cape Town: University of Cape Town Press, pp. 60–7.

Boraine, A. (2000) *A Country Unmasked*. Oxford: Oxford University Press.

Boraine, A. (2004) 'Transitional justice', in C. Villa-Vicencio and E. Doxtader (eds), *Pieces of the Puzzle: Keywords on Reconciliation and Transitional Justice*. Cape Town: Institute for Justice and Reconciliation, pp. 67–72.

Borello, F. (2004) *A First Few Steps: The Long Road to a Just Peace in the Democratic Republic of Congo*, Occasional Paper Series. New York: International Center for Transitional Justice.

Brittion, S. (1995) 'What price truth in South Africa?', *Peace News*, 2389. See: http://www.peacenews.info/issues/2389/pn238911.htm.

CHR and UPEACE (2005) *Compendium of Key Human Rights Documents of the African Union*. Pretoria: Pretoria University Law Press.

CIA World Factbook (1993) *Democratic Republic of the Congo: The Judiciary and the Courts*, Library of Congress Country Studies. See: http://www.photius.com/countries/congo_democratic_republic_of_the/government/congo_democratic_republic_of_the_government_thejudiciary_and_th~53.html.

Cigolo, J. (2006) *Les juridictions coutumières dans le système judiciaire congolais: une reforme pour la bonne administration de la justice* (*Customary Courts in the Congolese Judiciary System: A Reform for Better Administration of Justice*). ACAT/Sud-Kivu: OSI-Africa Governance Monitoring and Advocacy Project.

Code de la Famille (2003) *Journal Officiel de la République Démocratique du Congo*, Vol. 44, 25 Avril 2003. Loi No. 87/010 du 1 août 1987.

Code Pénal Congolais (2006) *Journal Officiel de la République Démocratique du Congo*, 47, 15. Loi No. 06/018 du 20 juillet 2006 modifiant et complétant le Décret du 30 janvier 1940 portant Code pénal congolais.

Coghlan, B., Brennan, R., Ngoy, P., Dofara, D., Otto, B. and Stewart, T. (2004) *La Mortalité en République Démocratique du Congo: Résultats d'une Enquête Nationale Réalisée d'avril à juillet 2004*. Melbourne/New York: Burnet Institute and International Rescue Committee.

Council of Europe (1950) *Convention for the Protection of Human Rights and Fundamental Freedoms as Amended by Protocol No. 11*, European Treaty Series 155 (also known as 'the European Convention on Human Rights').

De Greiff, P. (2006) 'Introduction – repairing the past: compensation for victims of human rights violations', in P. De Greiff (ed.), *The Handbook of Reparations*. Oxford: Oxford University Press, pp. 1–19.

De l'Arbre, L. (2006) 'Chronique', *Journal d'Afrique Centrale – R.D.C.*, 15 December, 1: 50, 15.

De Lange, J. (2000) 'The historical context, legal origins and philosophical foundation of the South African Truth and Reconciliation Commission', in C. Villa-Vicencio and W. Verwoerd (eds), *Looking Back, Reaching Forward: Reflections on the Truth and Reconciliation Commission of South Africa*. Cape Town: University of Cape Town Press, pp. 14–31.

Décret du 30 janvier 1940 portant Code Pénal Congolais (1940) Issued on 30 January 1940 and entered into force on 30 November 2004. *Journal Officiel de la République Démocratique du Congo*.

Décret-Loi du 15 avril 1926 sur les juridictions coutumières tel que modifié et complété à ce jour (1926) Bulletin Officiel du Congo Belge.

Dimandja, Ellysé, Vice-President of Women as Partners for Peace in Africa and member of the Congolese National Assembly, 14 October 2004. Telephone interview, cited in United Nations High Commissioner for Refugees (2005) *Democratic Republic of the Congo: State Protection (June 2003 – November 2004)*, February.

Doxtader, E. (2004) 'Reparation', in C. Villa-Vicencio and E. Doxtader (eds), *Pieces of the Puzzle: Keywords on Reconciliation and Transitional Justice*. Cape Town: Institute for Justice and Reconciliation, pp. 25–32.

Franciscans International (2006) *Position Paper on Fourth Ordinary Session of the African Commission on Human Rights, 15–29 November 2006, Banjul*. See: http://www.franciscansinternational.org/docs/statement.php?id=475.

Geneva Convention Relative to the Treatment of Prisoners of War (1950) Adopted on 12 August 1949 by the Diplomatic Conference for the Establishment of International Conventions for the Protection of Victims of War, held in Geneva from 21 April to 12 August 1949, entered into force 21 October 1950.

Global Rights in the Democratic Republic of Congo (2005a) 'Global Rights in the Democratic Republic of Congo'. See: http://www.globalrights.org/site/DocServer/Fact_Sheet_DRC.pdf?docID=2683.

Global Rights in the Democratic Republic of Congo (2005b) 'SOS JUSTICE: What Justice is there for Vulnerable Groups in Eastern DRC? Assessment of the Justice Sector in North and South Kivu, Maniema and North Katanga'. See: http://www.globalrights.org/site/DocServer/SOS_ExecutiveSurnmary_ENG_FIN.pdf?docID=4123.

Global Rights in the Democratic Republic of Congo (2006) 'Democratic Republic of Congo'. See: http://www.globalrights.org/site/DocServer/Fact_Sheet_DRC.pdf?docID=2683.

Hamilton, R.J. (2006) 'The responsibility to protect: from document to doctrine. But what of implementation?', *Harvard Human Rights Journal*, 19: 289–97.

Heyns, C. and Killander, M. (eds) (2006) *Compendium of Key Human Rights Documents of the African Union*. Pretoria: Pretoria University Law Press.

Huggins, C. and Pettier, J. (2005) 'Land tenure, land reform and conflict in Sub-Saharan Africa: towards a research agenda', in C. Huggins and J. Clover (eds), *From the Ground Up: Land Rights, Conflict and Peace in Sub-Saharan Africa*. Pretoria: African Centre for Technology Studies, pp. 383–92.

Human Rights Watch (2000) *RDC: l'Est du Congo dévasté, civils assassins et opposants réduits au silence*, Report 12:3. New York: Human Rights Watch.

Human Rights Watch (2004) *Democratic Republic of the Congo: Confronting Impunity*, Background Briefing, 2 May. New York: Human Rights Watch.

Human Rights Watch (2005a) *Democratic Republic of Congo: Civilians Attacked in North-Kivu*, Report 17:9. New York: Human Rights Watch.

Human Rights Watch (2005b) *Mounting Ethnic Tensions in 2004*, Report 17:9. New York: Human Rights Watch.

Huyse, L. (2003) 'Justice', in D. Bloomfield, T. Barnes and L. Huyse (eds), *Reconciliation After Violent Conflict: A Handbook*. Stockholm: International Institute for Democracy and Electoral Assistance, pp. 97–121.

Inter-American Commission on Human Rights (1948) *American Declaration of the Rights and Duties of Man*, approved by the Ninth International Conference of American States, Bogotá, Colombia, 1948. Washington, DC: Inter-American Commission on Human Rights.

Inter-American Commission on Human Rights (1969) *American Convention on Human Rights*, adopted at the Inter-American Specialized Conference on Human Rights, San José, Costa Rica, 22 November 1969.

International Alert (n.d.) 'Inter-ethnic community dialogue between women'. See: http://www.international-alert.org/our_work/regional/great_lakes/drc_1.php.

International Court of Justice (2004) *Armed Activities on the Territory of the Congo (Democratic Republic of the Congo v. Uganda)*, Press Release 2004/36. The Hague: International Court of Justice.

International Court of Justice (2005) *Judgement Democratic Republic of the Congo* v. *Uganda* ('Case Concerning Armed Activities on the Territory of the Congo'), Judgement of 19 December 2005. The Hague: International Court of Justice.

International Crisis Group (2005) *Back to the Brink in Congo*, Africa Briefing No. 21. Brussels: International Crisis Group.

International Rescue Committee (2004) *Mortality in the Democratic Republic of the Congo, December*. New York: International Rescue Committee.

IRIN News (2006) 'DRC: Soldiers jailed for mass rape', UN Office for the Co-ordination of Humanitarian Affairs. See: http://www.irinnews.org/report.asp?ReportID=52801&SelectRegion=Great_Lakes&SelectCountry=DRC.

ISS (2003) *Democratic Republic of Congo: Draft Constitution of the Transition*, Pretoria. Available online at: http://www.iss.co.za/af/profiles/DRCongo/icd/consdraft.pdf.

Kabunda, M. (2000) 'The Role of Multinationals in the Perpetuation of Conflicts in Africa'. Unpublished paper. Madrid: Africa Studies Group, Universidad Autônoma de Madrid.

Kakule Kaparay, C. (2006) 'Finance Populaire et Développement Durable en Afrique au Sud du Sahara: Application à la Région Nord-Est de la République Démocratique du Congo'. Unpublished thesis. Leuven: Catholic University of Leuven.

Kambere, T. (2006) *Prospects for Justice in the Democratic Republic of Congo: A Global Rights Discussion Forum*. Washington, DC: Global Rights.

Kamwimbi, T.K. (2005) 'Transitional Justice in a Regional Context: Case of the Great Lakes Region of Africa'. Unpublished paper. Cape Town: Institute for Justice and Reconciliation.

Kamwimbi, T.K. (2006) 'The DRC elections, reconciliation and justice', *Pambazuka News*. See: http://www.pambazuka.org/en/category/features/36231.

Katshung, J.Y. (2006) 'DRC: healing the wounds of war trough reparations', *Pambazuka News*. See: http://www.pambazuka.org/en/category/features/36471.

Kayser, C. (2004) 'Devoir de mémoire et responsabilité partagée pour l'avenir', *Regards Croisés*, 13. Goma: Pole Institute.

Kongo, V.C. (2005) 'Cinq questions à Mgr Jean-Luc Kuye', *Le Potentiel*, 3359, 25 February.

Krasnor, E. (2004) 'American disengagement with the International Criminal Court: undermining international justice and U.S. foreign policy goals', *Online Journal of Peace and Conflict Resolution*, 6 (1): 179–91.

Kuye, Jean-Luc (2005) *Réconciliation, Paix et Constitution en RDC*. Kinshasa: MONUC News.

Loi modifiant et complétant certaines dispositions du code pénal, du code d'organisation et de la compétence judiciaires, du code pénal militaire et du code judiciaire militaire, en application du statut de la cour pénale internationale (2005) See *Journal Officiel de la République Démocratique du Congo*, September 2005.

Loi No. 04/018 du 30 juillet 2004 Portant Organisation, Attribution et Fonctionnement de la Commission Vérité et Réconciliation (2004) Adopted on 28 August 2003, entered into force 30 July 2004.

Loi No. 06/018 modifiant et complétant le Décret du 30 janvier 1940 portant Code Pénal Congolais (2006) Adopted on 20 July 2006, entered into force 1 August 2005. See *Journal Officiel de la République Démocratique du Congo*, 47 (15): 1–6.

Lyster, R. (2000) 'Amnesty: the burden of victims', in C. Villa-Vicencio and W. Verwoerd (eds), *Looking Back, Reaching Forward: Reflections on the Truth and Reconciliation Commission of South Africa*. Cape Town: University of Cape Town Press, pp. 184–92.

Mbombo, L.B. and Bayolo, C.H. (2002) *Women Rights Violations During the Conflict in the Democratic Republic of the Congo from August 2, 1998 to September 30, 2001*. Kinshasa: International Centre for Human Rights and Democratic Development.

Méndez, J.E. (1997) 'Accountability for past abuses', *Human Rights Quarterly*, 19 (2): 255–82.

MONUC Human Rights Division (2006a) *Human Rights Situation in February 2006*. Kinshasa: MONUC. See: http://www.monuc.org/News.aspx?newsID=10348.

MONUC Human Rights Division (2006b) *Monthly Human Rights Assessment: June 2006*. Kinshasa: MONUC. See: http://www.monuc.org/News.aspx?newsld=l 1764.

MONUC Human Rights Division (2006c) The Fight Against Impunity Took a Step Forward in the DRC on 12 April 2006', in *The Human Rights Situation in April 2006*. Kinshasa: MONUC. See: http://www.monuc.org/News.aspx?newsld=l 1083.

MONUC Human Rights Division and Office of the United Nations High Commissioner for Human Rights (2007) *The Human Rights Situation in the Democratic Republic of Congo (DRC) During the Period of July to December 2006*, United Nations Report, 8 February. Kinshasa: MONUC. See: http://www.globalpolicy.org/security/issues/congo/2007/0307transition.pdf.

Mwana wa vene, R.K. (2005) 'Le Kyanganda, un couloir de paix chez les Nande', in M. Ansay et R.K. Mwana wa vene (eds) *Racines de paix en Afrique: A la rencontre des traditions de paix dans la région des Grands Lacs juin 2004 – juillet 2005*. Bruxelles: Institut de la Vie, pp. 171–6.

Ngoma Binda, H.-E. (2006) Paper presented at the conference 'After the DRC Elections: Justice, Reconciliation and Reconstruction in the Great Lakes', Johannesburg, 18–19 November.

NPWJ (n.d.) *Conference Report: Accountability Mechanisms for International Crimes: The Cases of the Democratic Republic of Congo and Uganda*. Presented at the Expert Meeting, 14–15 October 2004. See: http://www.

npwj.org/2004/11/24/expert_meeting_accountability_mechanisms_international_crimes.

Ordinance-law No 82-020 of 31 March 1982 related to the Code of Organization and Judicial Competences (1982) See: *Journal Officiel de la République Démocratique du Congo*, 1 April 1983, 23 (7): 39–53.

Ordinary Penal Code (Decree of 30 January 1940 pertaining to the Congolese Penal Code as modified several times since) *Journal Officiel de la République Démocratique du Congo*, Special Issue of 30 November 2004.

Organisation of African Union (1986) *African Charter on Human and People's Rights*, OAU Doc. CAB/LEG/67/3 Rev. 5, 211.L.M. 58 adopted in 1982, entered into force 21 October 1986 (also known as 'the Banjul Charter').

Orr, W. (2000) 'Reparation delayed is healing retarded', in C. Villa-Vicencio and W. Verwoerd (eds), *Looking Back, Reaching Forward: Reflections on the Truth and Reconciliation Commission of South Africa*. Cape Town: University of Cape Town Press, pp. 239–49.

PACO and UNOPS (2006) *International Observer Handbook Presidential and Legislative Elections DR Congo*. Kinshasa.

Pole Institute (2002) *La violence, l'Impunité et l'Education (II): Nos Valeurs Traditionnelles peuvent-elles remettre notre société à flot?* Goma: Pole Institute.

Rome Statute of the International Criminal Court (2002) Adopted in Rome on 17 July 1998, entered into force 1 July 2002 in accordance with Article 126. United Nations Treaty Series, Vol. 2187.

Sarkin, J. (2003) 'To prosecute or not to prosecute? Constitutional and legal issues concerning criminal trials', in C. Villa-Vicencio and E. Doxtader (eds), *The Provocations of Amnesty: Memory, Justice and Impunity*. Cape Town: Institute for Justice and Reconciliation, pp. 237–64.

Sarkin, J. (2004) 'The coming of age of claims for reparations for human rights abuses committed in the South', *SUR International Journal on Human Rights*, 1 (1): 66–125.

Savage, T. (2006) *In Quest of a Sustainable Justice: Transitional Justice and Human Security in the Democratic Republic of the Congo*, ISS Occasional Paper No. 130, November 2006. Pretoria: Institute for Security Studies.

Scharf, M.P. (1997) 'The case for a permanent international truth commission', *Duke Journal of Comparative and International Law*, 7 (2): 375–410.

Schröder, J. (2006) 'Delegation to Observe the Presidential and Legislative Elections in the Democratic Republic of Congo', unpublished report. Brussels: European Parliament.

Schwager, E. (2005) 'The right to compensation for victims of an armed conflict', *Chinese Journal of International Law*, 4 (2): 417–39.

Schwager, E. and Bank, R. (2005) *An Individual Right to Compensation for Victims of Armed Conflicts?* Paper prepared for the International Law Association intersessional meeting held in Frankfurt in September 2005. London: International Law Association.

Search for Common Ground in the DRC (2006) *Programme Overview*, Bukavu, March. See: http://www.sfcg.org/Documents/Programs/DRC.pdf.

Shattuck, J., Simo, P. and. Durch, W.J. (2003) *Ending Congo's Nightmare: What the U.S. Can Do to Promote Peace in Central Africa*. Washington, DC: International Human Rights Law Group.

Skelton, A. and Batley, M. (2006) *Charting Progress, Mapping the Future: Restorative Justice in South Africa*. Pretoria: Restorative Justice Centre.

Sonkosi, Z. (2004) 'Traditional and customary law', in C. Villa-Vicencio and E. Doxtader (eds), *Pieces of the Puzzle: Keywords on Reconciliation and Transitional Justice*. Cape Town: Institute for Justice and Reconciliation, pp. 96–101.

Steiner, H.J. and Alston, P. (2000) *International Human Rights in Context: Law, Politics, Morals; Text and Materials*, 2nd edn. Oxford: Oxford University Press.

Tegera, A., Kayser, C. and Sematumba, O. (2004) 'Devoir de mémoire et responsabilité collective pour l'avenir', *Regards Croisés*, No. 13. Goma: Pole Institute.

Tegera, A., Mashanda, M., Kayser, C. and Endanda, K. (2000) 'Le dialogue intercongolais 2: Le travail de paix intercommunautaire au Nord Kivu', *Regards Croisés*, No. 3. Goma: Pole Institute.

Tremblay, P. (2004) *The Transition in the Democratic Republic of Congo: A Historic Opportunity*. Montreal: Rights & Democracy.

United Nations (1948a) *Convention on the Prevention and Punishment of the Crime of Genocide*, General Assembly Resolution 260 A (III) of 9 December 1948, United Nations Treaty Series, Vol. 78, p. 277.

United Nations (1948b) *Universal Declaration of Human Rights*, United Nations General Assembly Resolution 217 A (III) of 10 December 1948.

United Nations (1968) *Convention on the Non-Applicability of Statutory Limitations to War Crimes and Crimes Against Humanity*, UN General Assembly Resolution 2391 (XXIII), adopted and opened for signature, ratification and accession by General Assembly Resolution 2391 (XXIII) of 26 November 1968, entered into force 11 November 1970, in accordance with article VIII.

United Nations (1973) *Principles of International Co-operation in the Detection, Arrest, Extradition and Punishment of Persons Guilty of War Crimes and Crimes Against Humanity*, General Assembly Resolution 3074 (XXVIII), adopted on 3 December 1973.

United Nations (1976a) *International Covenant on Civil and Political Rights* (1976), UN General Assembly, adopted and opened for signature, ratification and accession by General Assembly Resolution 2200A (XXI) of 16 December 1966, entered into force 23 March 1976, in accordance with Article 49.

United Nations (1976b) *International Covenant on Economic, Social and Cultural Rights*, UN General Assembly, adopted and opened for signature, ratification and accession by General Assembly Resolution 2200A (XXI) of 16 December 1966, entered into force 3 January 1976.

United Nations (1981) *Convention on the Elimination of All Forms of Discrimination Against Women*, UN General Assembly Resolution 34/180, 34 UN GAOR Supp. (No. 46) at 193, UN Doc. A/34/46, entered into force 3 September 1981.

United Nations (1985) *Basic Principles of Justice for Victims of Crime and Abuse of Power*, UN General Assembly Resolution 40/34 of 29 November 1985.

United Nations (1987) *Convention Against Torture and Other Cruel, Inhuman or Degrading Treatment or Punishment*, General Assembly Resolution 39/46, UN Doc. A/39/51 (1984), entered into force 26 June 1987.

United Nations (1990) *Convention on the Rights of the Child*, UN General Assembly Resolution 44/25, adopted and opened for signature, ratification and accession on 20 November 1989, entered into force 2 September 1990.

United Nations (2005a) *Basic Principles and Guidelines on the Right to a Remedy and Reparation for Victims of Gross Violations of International Human Rights Law and Serious Violations of International Humanitarian Law*, United Nations General Assembly, UN Doc A/RES/60/147 (also known as 'the Bassiouni Principles').

United Nations (2005b) *World Summit Outcome*, UN General Assembly, A/RES/60/1, 24 October.

United Nations (2005c) *World Summit Outcome Resolution*, United Nations General Assembly, A/RES/60/1, 24 October.

United Nations High Commissioner for Refugees (2005) *Democratic Republic of the Congo: State Protection (June 2003–November 2004)*, February. See: http://www.unhcr.org/home/RSDCOI/430601354.pdf.

United Nations Office for the Coordination of Humanitarian Affairs (2006) *Situation humanitaire en RDC, 16–22 décembre 2006*, Rapport Hebdomadaire. New York: Office for the Coordination of Humanitarian Affairs, 6.

United Nations Security Council (2005) *Security Council notes decision in Democratic Republic of Congo to extend transitional period until end of 2005; Permitted under Peace Agreement, Transitional Constitution; Aims to allow time to strengthen security, logistics for elections*. Press release SC/8430, 5218th Meeting – 29/6/2005. See: http://www.un.org/News/Press/docs/2005/sc8430.doc.htm.

Uvin, P. and Bourque, A. (2004) 'Operationalizing the Dutch Great Lakes Regional Strategy: A Discussion Paper'. Unpublished.

Vienna Declaration (1993) Vienna: World Conference on Human Rights, UN Doc. A/CONF.157/24, adopted on 14–25 June 1993.

Villa-Vicencio, C. (2000a) 'Getting on with life: a move towards reconciliation', in C. Villa-Vicencio and W. Verwoerd (eds), *Looking Back, Reaching Forward: Reflections on the Truth and Reconciliation Commission of South Africa*. Cape Town: University of Cape Town Press, pp. 199–209.

Villa-Vicencio, C. (2000b) 'Restorative justice: dealing with the past differently', in Villa- Vicencio, C. and W. Venvoerd (eds), *Looking Back, Reaching Forward: Reflections on the Truth and Reconciliation Commission of South Africa*. Cape Town: University of Cape Town Press, pp. 69–76.

Villa-Vicencio, C. (2004a) 'Reconciliation', in C. Villa-Vicencio and E. Doxtader (eds), *Pieces of the Puzzle: Keywords on Reconciliation and Transitional Justice*. Cape Town: Institute for Justice and Reconciliation, pp. 3–9.

Villa-Vicencio, C. (2004b) 'Restorative justice', in C. Villa-Vicencio and E. Doxtader (eds), *Pieces of the Puzzle: Keywords on Reconciliation and Transitional Justice*. Cape Town: Institute for Justice and Reconciliation, pp. 33–8.

Villa-Vicencio, C., Nantulya, P. and Savage, T. (2005) *Building Nations: Transitional Justice in the African Great Lakes Region: Burundi, The DRC, Rwanda, Uganda*. Cape Town: Institute for Justice and Reconciliation.

Vircoulon, T. (2007) 'DRC-Great Lakes: From War to Development?' Unpublished report on the 24th France-Africa Summit held in Cannes, 15–16 February 2007.

Wakenge, R. and Bossaerts, G. (2006) *La Commission Vérité et Réconciliation en RDC: Le travail n'a guère commencé*. Goma: SNV Kivu.

Watchlist on Children and Armed Conflict (2006) *Struggling to Survive: Children in Armed Conflict in the Democratic Republic of the Congo*. New York: Watchlist on Children and Armed Conflict. See: http://www.watchlist.org/reports/pdf/dr_congo.report.20060426.pdf.

Wetsh'okonda Koso, M. (2005) 'Why Congo needs the International Criminal Court', in 'Human rights and justice sector reform in Africa: contemporary issues and responses', *Justice Initiatives: Journal of the Open Society Justice Initiative*, February, pp. 58–62.

Wikipedia (2007) *Culture of the Democratic Republic of the Congo*. See: en.wikipedia.org/wiki/Culture_of_the_Democratic_Republic_of_the_Congo.

Woodrow Wilson School of Public and International Affairs (2005) *Balancing Peace, Justice and Stability: A Great Lakes Regional Justice Commission and a Special Tribunal in the Democratic Republic of the Congo. Princeton,* NJ: Princeton University.

Young, C. and Turner, T. (1985) *The Rise and Decline of the Zairian State*. Madison, WI: University of Wisconsin Press.

Chapter 16

Restorative justice and truth-seeking in the DR Congo: much closing for peace, little opening for justice

Kris Vanspauwen and Tyrone Savage

> *Telling the truth about the past undermines the mental foundation of future human rights abuses.*
>
> Luc Huyse (1995)

Looking at ways to embark on a restorative justice model with the aim of finding the truth about abuses committed in a large-scale conflict is always a challenging task. This is particularly so in the DRC. There are at least three factors that militate against such an ambitious approach. First, there is the sheer degree and the scale of violence that has characterised the conflict. The figures of mass victimisation in the DRC are immense: the death toll in the five-year war that began in 1998 was somewhere in the vicinity of four million (Coghlan *et al.* 2007: 44). Is it feasible – or even desirable – for a society massively victimised on this scale to attempt to devise a restorative justice model?

Second, tensions remain high between political rivals, and violent encounters, between armed rebel groups and the local population have continued unabated. The violence in the Kivu provinces and in Ituri in the postwar period has often threatened to annul, at least partially, the achievements of the transitional process – and this is but one of many concrete examples showing how fragile the situation is in the DRC. Is it therefore realistic to aim for the establishment of accountability mechanisms in a country in which the transition is, in effect, still underway, a country still trying to build state structures such as a polity, a military and a police force? Some argue that the DRC has virtually ceased to exist as a state (Reyntjens 2007: 315).

Third, the conflict in the DRC is interwoven with a massive tangle of interrelated regional conflicts (Prendergast and Smock 1999; Savage 2002). With respect to the Nyabyondo massacre, presented in this volume as a case study by Savage and Vanspauwen (Chapter 13), a number of other conflicts – or at least highly problematical relationships – in the Kivu region alone need to be factored into interpretations of violent events: the Congolese government and Congolese rebel groups; the Congolese government and the Rwandan government; the Mayi-Mayi and Rwandan troops as well as those of the Rwandan-backed Rassemblement Congolais pour la Démocratie (RCD). Suffice it to say that peace and security in the Great Lakes region, as a whole, are of vital importance to national peace processes in the DRC, and thus also to initiatives from the DRC to engage in restorative justice projects.

These elements have forced this nascent democracy to confront a thorny problem too often described as the peace versus justice dilemma (Sriram 2004). Rather than making a choice, the challenge is to find the most strategic combination between the two. In this context, it also needs to be ascertained both how much – and what sort of – truth is needed in order provide some justice for victims and, at the same time, how much truth Congo can bear in order to maintain its fragile peace. Stanley Cohen links such choices with modes of controlling the past. The first mode is through truth recovery – truth for justice. The second mode is through truth eradication – truth omission for peace (1995: 47–8).

In this chapter we will try to gain a better understanding of the role and the relationship of these seemingly incompatible goals of peace and justice. How have they affected the transitional process in the DRC? We argue that restorative justice could offer some elements to reconcile peace and justice, or to mutually reinforce one another. To elaborate on this argument, we will take a closer look at the roles that restorative justice principles – through formal and informal justice mechanisms – have played in enhancing or in inhibiting the peace and justice process in the DRC.

The analysis will not comprise an overall evaluation of the transitional justice process in the DRC, but rather a detailed analysis of some significant observations developed by Savage and Kambala (this volume, Chapter 14) and by Kamwimbi (this volume, Chapter 15).

The first observation is quite gloomy. It focuses on the transitional justice process with regard to its goal of achieving the truth about the past. In this respect, we particularly point to the history of criminal justice in the country and the very few successes in establishing the facts about atrocities. We also note the failure to design, implement and deliver a truth recovery process by the Commission Vérité et Réconciliation (Congolese Truth and Reconciliation Commission, CVR).

The second observation has to do, ironically, with the useful developments for victims, particularly as regards compensation, that have emerged before the Congolese military courts. These trials have opened up promising perspectives with regard to redress for victims in individual cases. This shows how restorative justice outcomes can permeate the existing formal justice system and should thus not be restricted to practices that fall outside of the formal justice system.

The last observation is that, despite their availability and relatively popular support, the plethora of existing traditional justice mechanisms in the DRC have not been granted the sort of mandate that would enable them to contribute significantly to the truth-seeking process. While lacking jurisdictional power, credibility and state support, they are at best viewed as local peacebuilding efforts rather than fully-fledged accountability mechanisms.

An integrative truth-seeking process

The chapter will now examine the above-mentioned observations and the extent to which the institutions involved have provided – or could have provided – opportunities for restorative justice principles to be applied in the transition processes of the DRC. As a framework of analysis we use a model (see Figure 16.1) that has been developed earlier by Vanspauwen (2006).[1]

In the heart of any transitional justice strategy lies an integrative truth-seeking process because recovering the truth is an obligation – not an option – for societies seeking to find peace in the aftermath of violent conflict and to prevent future fighting (Bassiouni 1998: 65–6; Méndez 2006: 116–19). It is only on the basis of truth that other processes such as reconciliation and forgiveness can be undertaken in earnest.

An integrative process (Braithwaite 2006) means that the truth should be sought and acknowledged at different levels. The complexity of the concept of truth lays bare the limitations of factual evidence. Factual truth – which could form the starting point for a truth-seeking process – should thus be complemented with other notions of truth, such as the individual stories of victims and perpetrators (narrative truth), the truth that arises through interaction and debate (dialogical

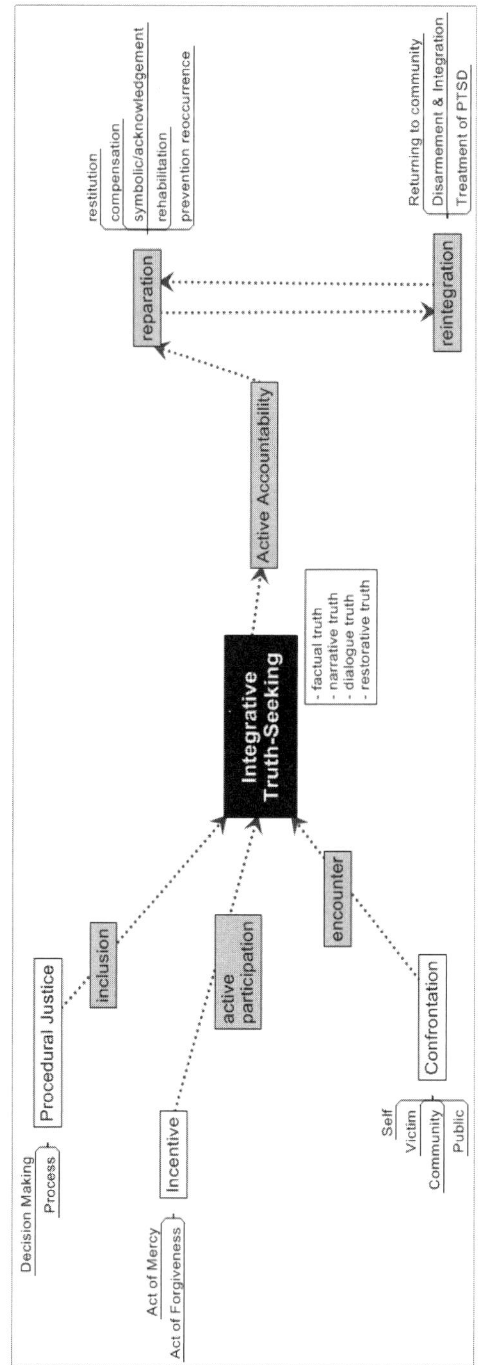

Figure 16.1 Integrative truth-seeking

truth), and the kind of truth that places facts and what they mean within the context of human relationships and thus has the capacity to contribute to reparation (restorative truth). These different notions of truth were articulated during the debates that preceded and then contributed to the form of the South African truth-seeking process, among others (Truth and Reconciliation Commission of South Africa 1998: 109–13).

An integrative truth-seeking process is necessarily a process of active participation of all stakeholders, an inclusive process in which the various parties are not disconnected from the process and the decision-making, and a process in which some sort of 'encounter' should always be an option for the parties. These components can create the necessary conditions for active accountability, conditions in which the perpetrators accept their responsibility and are encouraged to make amends for the harm done to victims. Such accountability forms the first step to reparation. This is in keeping with the five forms of reparation proposed by the Bassiouni Principles (United Nations 2005), which provide a useful point of departure for reparation policies.

Reintegration, as a final element in our model, deserves a more central role than it generally receives now in debates about transitional justice. Large-scale conflicts such as that in the DRC are characterised by a proliferation of armed rebel groups as well as by extremely high numbers of victims, be it casualties in the actual fighting or, as has also been the case in the DRC, those who have fled the familiar territory of home in quest of refuge. The mobilisation of fighters, often through abduction and forcible recruitment, and the mass victimisation of civilians often cause a devastating breakdown of social fabric. The reintegration of perpetrators as former combatants or soldiers and of victims as refugees or displaced persons is therefore of crucial importance to implement any credible programme of social reconstruction. At the same time, a well implemented reparation programme can facilitate this reintegration process.

A gloomy view of the transitional justice process

The peace process

Almost a decade after its own historic peace negotiations, South Africa played a key role in the mediation of the complex negotiations between the various political and armed groups of the DRC, as well as between the DRC government and forces from neighbouring countries. This multi-level diplomacy began to ease the tensions in the Great Lakes region and eventually led to the Global and All-Inclusive Accord (*Accord Global et Inclusif sur la Transition en République Démocratique du Congo* 2002).

Although its implementation has been hotly contested, this key agreement has laid the foundation for transition in the DRC and made a huge contribution to peace in the region. The inclusion of all political and military leaders was a crucial step in securing a cessation of the hostilities, although it has proven not to be a thoroughgoing guarantee of sustainable peace.

Among the further achievements of this peace process that emerge when one examines it through the lens of a restorative justice analysis are the following. First, the peace agreement was a consensus-based process that allowed all major political stakeholders a role in the planning and conceptualisation of a transitional justice framework. Second, in the setting up of the transitional justice process, the DRC has formally acknowledged the importance of establishing a truth-seeking process and providing a reparation programme for victims.

Transitional justice processes are prone, however, to what has been described as a 'geographic' limitation in their mandate (Sriram and Ross 2007). In the context of the DRC, it will be very unlikely that the embryonic nation will be able to deal with gross human rights violations committed by non-Congolese. This situation has, at times, had the effect of paralysing the DRC in its efforts to trigger the active accountability of neighbouring countries such as Rwanda and Uganda. Significant efforts have been undertaken at the level of diplomacy, and a more convivial understanding seems to be emerging on how to go forward. The need to address questions about the past remains urgent, however. The post-transition violence of May 2007 in villages in the north-east Democratic Republic of Congo (IRIN 2007) that involved troops of the Front démocratique pour la libération du Rwanda (FDLR) is a case in point.[2]

Impunity as the glue of a peace process?

The 'success' of the transition in the DRC, meaning there was no major outbreak or resurgence of the conflict since the end of war – a sort of negative peace, could be called a paradox: in order to keep the transition process going smoothly, virtually no one was brought to account for the massive levels of corruption and gross abuses of human rights. This has been aptly described by Stearns (2007: 202), when he states that 'impunity has been to some extent the glue of the peace process'.

As said, the *Accord Global et Inclusif* signed in 2002 formed the start of Congo's transitional process. With elections as the transition's envisaged culmination, the transitional government was tasked with tackling the nation's own deeply embedded history of violence through various mechanisms, including prosecutions and a truth commission. And thus the DRC sought to account for the worst of the gross human rights violations that have taken place since independence. The recent past formed a particular focus. The Pretoria Agreement was highly ambitious in establishing five *institutions d'appui à la démocratie* (institutions in support of democracy).[3] Along with these plans, the Inter-Congolese Dialogue (ICD) also extensively discussed other strategies of accountability, including the prosecution of perpetrators.

Savage and Kambala (this volume, Chapter 14) provide a more detailed overview of the systems that were or could have been envisaged in the DRC. It was clear from the outset, however, that the international community would refrain from establishing a criminal tribunal for the DRC like that which was established in the aftermath of Rwanda's genocide (Zacklin 2004: 545). At the same time, the DRC has battled to produce accountability domestically for several reasons: its weak justice system, the ways in which the rule of law has been usurped by past dictatorial regimes, the large number of perpetrators, the vast numbers of victims and the very fragile peace process. Although the pursuit of prosecutions was supported during the debates in the Peace and Reconciliation Commission at the ICD, the DRC failed, according to Savage and Kambala (this volume, Chapter 14) to develop a realistic prosecutorial strategy that could somehow take into account the almost insurmountable deficiencies that are so common in many post-conflict societies (see also Reyntjens 2007). The ambitious goals laid down in the Sun City Accord were extremely high – unrealistically high, many have argued – and therefore, inevitably, became a source of frustration and even provocation to many victims.

While the DRC was, perhaps, on the verge of becoming the victim of its own intentions, a turning point in the justice process occurred on 19 April 2004, when the Prosecutor of the International Criminal Court (ICC) in the Hague received an official confirmation from the President of the DRC of the country's willingness to cooperate with the ICC in the investigation of crimes committed in the DRC (and more particularly in Ituri province) that fell under the jurisdiction of the ICC.[4] On 17 March 2006, after a warrant was issued against him by the ICC, Thomas Lubanga Dyila was arrested. Lubanga is alleged to have committed war crimes as set out in Article 8 of the Statute, committed in the territory of the Democratic Republic of the Congo since July 2002.[5] This was a major test for the fragile peace process. To the relief of international actors and local communities, the situation in the northern region – where Lubanga mainly operated – didn't escalate as a result. On the contrary, it seems the arrest may have had an immediate deterrent effect: conflict in Ituri ebbed dramatically in the period following Lubanga's arrest.

Notwithstanding this success, the ICC will clearly not be the wide-ranging source of justice that many Congolese victims have been hoping for. The ICC exists as a last resort, and its options are – inevitably – going to be both few and dispersed across post-conflict situations worldwide. It should not therefore be seen as a default option or as a substitute for domestic prosecutorial activities. Moreover, international prosecutorial processes are widely known for having a variety of disadvantages: a high cost and a slow process; a low impact in the places where the crimes were committed because proceedings are generally held at a remote distance; a generally poor record when it comes to involving victims in any meaningful way during proceedings; and providing only little to the development of the local judicial system (see also Borello 2004; Huyse 1995; Wippman 1999).

At the same time, the transitional government has seemed to overlook or ignore a range of alternative options to complement prosecutions with other forms of accountability. With all the obstacles it could have created, one valuable alternative could have been a deliberate and strategic complementary relationship between the international prosecutions and the national truth commission such as eventually emerged in Sierra Leone.[6] Another option that was also raised by some was the inclusion of existing local structures of peace and reconciliation to deal with some types of crimes committed during the conflict, as has been developed in East Timor.[7] In fact, the organic law establishing the CVR has provided the option for the truth commission to 'envisage the organisation of a ritual for certain cases of reconciliation among the parties appearing in front of it' (cited in Borello 2004: 38). These options remained little explored, however, by the CVR.

Truth and Reconciliation Commission

The Commission Vérité et Réconciliation (CVR), as one of the five institutions supporting democracy, was tasked with drawing as complete a picture as possible of the patterns of violence during the DRC conflict. In hindsight, it may have been naive to believe that a truth commission could lay bare the vast responsibility of high-ranked military and political leaders – with many of them still appointed in official positions – and their involvement in the planning, ordering or execution of gross human rights violations. Bassiouni (1998: 69) has described this problem as a 'mediator's dilemma', observing that, on the one hand, the involvement of political leaders is essential for a cessation of hostilities and thus the establishment of peace, while on the other hand their presence in the political settlement processes weighs heavily on the pursuit and integrity of justice processes. Personal ambitions, positioning of power, the degree of public support each possesses, and above all their responsibilities in connection with the initiation of the conflict and the ways in which the war has been waged, particularly when international humanitarian law violations have occurred – these are all factors that make up the 'mediator's dilemma'. In the case of the DRC, as in many others, this dilemma has to some extent already been partly resolved – or rather bypassed – at the expense of justice.

It is perhaps somewhat difficult to make an overall assessment of the operation of the CVR, given that it never came into full operation. Yet the fact that it did not ever really get going is itself a massive failure. Given a rich mandate, the institution's main actors failed to seize a historic opportunity to establish even a starting point for a nation desperately in need of coming to terms with its past. If in fact their hands were tied by political constraints, then it would have been vastly preferable to declare this, to resign with their dignity intact and to suggest conditions necessary for a productive process at some future time. That would at least have given victims' groupings and other local actors a vision around which to mobilise and prepare.

From the beginning, there were tensions when the commission was discussed in the DRC. The commission, as pointed out by Savage and Kambala (this volume, Chapter 14), was marked by a systematic failure in terms of credibility, independence, competence and impartiality. As a consequence, civil society organisations have formulated strong reservations about the institution (Borello 2004: 40). Without going into detail, suffice it here to mention the most problematic elements of the truth commission and specifically to examine them through the analytical lens of restorative justice. Most of the elements discussed here have been elaborated by Savage (this volume, Chapter 14).

The first element was the highly politicised composition of the CVR. The initial eight commissioners were nominated by the respective parties of the transitional government rather than selected after a process of public engagement. They are not figures known for having taken a committed, non-partisan stand on human rights. Under pressure of criticism by Congolese activists and the international community, the Organic Law was amended and provided for the additional appointment of 13 members to be elected from civil society organisations. Although this helped to provide for alternative voices within the commission, a divide has been evident between the original commissioners, nominated by political groupings, and the 'johnnies-come-lately', as they are perceived, from civil society. The measure is therefore not going to prove sufficient to elevate the commission to a status that is beyond political interference and reflects transcendent values of human rights. In order for a truth commission to comply with the rules of procedural justice (Tyler 2006), the impartiality and the ethicality of the process must be guaranteed.

Furthermore, the credibility of the CVR is affected by a dearth of consultation. Victims groups and other representative organisations should have been offered a much greater voice in debates about the design, mandate, objectives and processes of the CVR. For a truth commission to be inclusive – and, indeed, owned by the nation more broadly – issues related to procedural justice and incentive-based provisions such as amnesty have to be discussed during a broad consultation process. The CVR therefore has run the risk of being imposed on victims and inadvertently deterring perpetrators from coming forward.

Finally, there are two provisions that, if they had been adapted to the needs of Congo and installed carefully, could have been deployed by the Congolese commission and produced a groundbreaking, restorative justice-based truth commission. These provisions are the amnesty procedure and the reparation programme.

For its amnesty provision the DRC was drawn to a model used in South Africa, and which provided the truth commission the power to grant amnesty for perpetrators under certain conditions, excluding serious human rights violations.[8] However, it was not clearly articulated how perpetrators should submit their applications, for which crimes they could and could not apply, how the CVR and the judiciary were going to cooperate, what the legal safeguards of the perpetrators were, etc. This lack of clarity doubtless discouraged alleged perpetrators from actively participating in the truth-seeking processes. But even more importantly, this failed attempt to bring the 'less' severe perpetrators to account has clearly disappointed victims hoping for some kind of reckoning process.

As for reparations, the CVR was granted – in a groundbreaking move – the authority to decide over compensation measures for individual victims (Sarkin 2007: 210). Other levels of reparation such as community or national reparations were apparently never proposed. In any case, reparation rested completely in the hands of the CVR. Since the reparations must be decided by agreement of all parties, this would mean that the CVR was given a unique but unrealistic task to act as a mediator in each and every individual case between victims and perpetrators. This would have created huge practical challenges – it would mean that the CVR would have to devise local mediation programmes, recruit mediators, provide training for mediators and establish a code of conduct under which the mediation process could operate. It must be said that this overambitious plan – which the CVR didn't even consider implementing – has further jeopardised the acceptance and credibility of the CVR among the Congolese people. However, the activities of the Barza Intercommunautaire in the North Kivu province (described by Kamwimbi, this volume, Chapter 15) have made sincere attempts to pave the way for the CVR to start its work by organising site visits and interviews with people. The CVR has failed to take advantage of this preparatory work.

According to the scarce information available (Borello 2004: 45), the CVR has focused its efforts largely on conflict mediation and resolution efforts, particularly in the South Kivu province. Notwithstanding the merits of these and other efforts that are mainly related to reconciliation and peace, it shows that the CVR has hardly contributed to the creation of a national truth recovery process where victims could find closure or perpetrators could acknowledge openly their wrongdoings (Savage 2006). The CVR's approach to transitional justice has essentially involved promoting peace by putting out fires rather than pursuing justice. It has effectively closed off transitional justice options rather than opening up truth. It has conciliated parties to particular incidents rather than creating options for sustainable national reconciliation.

Congolese military courts

Although their jurisdiction is usually – and necessarily – restricted to offences of a military nature committed by military personnel (African Commission on Human and People's Rights 2003: para. 5(l)), the military courts in the DRC have, somewhat ironically, played an important role in the prosecution of crimes against humanity, war crimes and genocide. Moreover, they have proved in two remarkable cases, described by Savage and Kambala (this volume, Chapter 14), that compensation measures for victims of these crimes are feasible. The right of victims to receive reparation was honoured in the military court of Mbandaka (the Songo Mboyo case) and in a military court in Ituri (the Kahwa Mandro case). In the former case, victims were granted compensation ranging from US$5,000 to 10,000; in the latter the 14 victims were to receive between US$2,500 and 75,000 compensation. While these compensation measures are certainly positive developments in the jurisdiction of the military courts, it should be noted that it remains doubtful whether all of these victims will actually receive the compensation due from perpetrators, who are often also battling poverty.

Furthermore little has been made public about the level and quality of participation of the victims in these court proceedings. The reparation ruling is not a result of a process of active accountability in which the perpetrator has openly acknowledged the suffering of the victims. It is simply the result of a court ruling.

Traditional justice mechanisms

Justice, according to Biggar (2001: 10–11), should not be about

> the punishment of the perpetrator, but about the vindication of the victim. [...] First it involves the recognition of the injury, and thereby acknowledging the dignity of the victim. [...] Second, [it exists] to give victims support and to seek to repair the damage as far as possible. [...] And third, [it exists] to establish the truth of what happened, why it happened, and who was responsible.

Restorative justice programmes, if based on the six principles mentioned above – namely inclusion, active participation, encounter, active accountability, reparation and reintegration (see grey boxes in Figure 16.1 above) – can serve this purpose in ways that the criminal justice systems – whether domestic or international – simply cannot.

The lack of clarity over the concept often leads many to label any informally-led initiative as restorative justice. The naive assumption that community systems are restorative and Western systems punitive have produced a conceptual gap that both hampers debate and threatens any productive complementarity between the different systems. Due to this conceptual vagueness informally-led and community-based processes are too easily assumed to be 'restorative justice'.

Debate about the use of traditional mechanisms in transitional justice processes is now well under way. Although among the most cited examples in recent history, the Rwandan *gacaca* tribunals remain heavily criticised, and as such make manifest the extent to which the use of traditional mechanisms in transitional societies still remains in the experimental phase.

For the DRC, in the build-up to the transition, traditional justice mechanisms were studied by some (see, for example, the Woodrow Wilson School of Public and International Affairs 2005, hereafter WWSPIA) with a view to their potential to fulfil a role in the transitional justice process. The report states,

> Despite their potential benefits the village councils exhibit significant deficiencies that would render them incapable of addressing severe crimes, such as genocide, crimes against humanity, or war crimes, including mass rape. As a village-based system, the councils often lack the legal competence to address contemporary crimes, offering punishments that may appear grossly incommensurate with the crimes committed. (WWSPIA 2005: 21)

While the blunt classification of these mechanisms as 'not appropriate to address war-time and gender-based atrocities in the DRC' (ibid.: 20) may be well supported, the potential which traditional mechanisms may hold is yet to be realised.

With regards to the peace and reconciliation efforts, and more particularly the process of demilitarising and reintegrating members of armed rebel groups, the community-based Commission de Pacification et de Concorde (CPC) has played a significant role in the North Kivu province (Tegera *et al.* 2000). Kamwimbi reports on a few important achievements in this regard (this volume, Chapter 15). The national programme on disarmament, demobilisation and reintegration was not able to draw on the work done by these locally-based initiatives in any meaningful way. The process has been complicated, with patchy successes, continuing struggles and the last, most sensitive phase – reintegration – largely still ahead. The demobilisation of former combatants and their reintegration into the communities could have created opportunities, however, for local structures to regain the moral authority that was partly eroded during the time of war. In March 2007, many former combatants were still waiting for the national disarmament, demobilisation and reintegration programme to begin (*Africa Research Bulletin* 2007: 17010).

It will be critical for the sustainability of the peace in the DRC – and particularly in the eastern part of Congo – for reconciliation processes to be established between the local populations with the remaining rebel troops. Sriram's empirical research (2004) shows that the level of accountability that is feasible in a transitional process is highly dependent on the power balances between government – which in this case can be adapted to refer to local government – and the oppressive forces. Traditional forms of conflict resolution such as the Barza Intercommunautaire, the CPC and the Kyaghanda have proven to be successful in easing tensions between ethnic communities (this volume, Chapter 15). And hence, the accomplishments of these traditional justice mechanisms could provide the preparatory work for formal accountability mechanisms to be established.

Looking back at the model of integrative truth-seeking (Figure 16.1), we see that the traditional justice mechanisms would be mainly active at the tail-end of the process, when it comes to the implementation of reparation measures and the reintegration of victims and perpetrators. For the traditional justice mechanisms to play a more central role in the truth-seeking process as an accountability mechanism, they would need a clearer mandate.

The political perseverance of the transitional government to institutionalise these traditional justice mechanisms in the transitional justice process was apparently not strong enough. Nor was there any thoroughgoing discussion held on the possibility for traditional justice mechanisms to work in tandem with the CVR. We should mention, however, that the transitional government undertook the initiative in 2004 to establish the Barza Intercommunautaire on a national level in which they were tasked to carry out pacification and reconciliation missions throughout the country (described in more detail by Kamwimbi, this volume, Chapter 15).

The growing body of international law on the duty to prosecute is an inhibiting factor for traditional justice mechanisms seeking to gain support from the international community. The conditions for the DRC to receive international support remain highly dependent on the country's efforts, it may be argued, to comply with the neo-liberal approach of the international community to adopt Western norms of justice.

Prospects for a restorative justice?

The transition in the DRC has produced an array of promising – but somewhat isolated – processes that together have, in turn, led to the first successful democratic elections in the country in almost half a century. It has not, however, produced a thoroughgoing transformation of conflictual relationships through any vision of restorative justice. It never could have. The active accountability of perpetrators at all levels, a comprehensive reparation programme, and above all, a national process of truth recovery remain a long way off. Moreover, it is doubtful whether such projects can ever be expected from the newly established Congolese government. Any policy considerations (Huyse 1995: 78) taken by new governments are tied to the legacy of a regime's past (authoritarian, totalitarian), the international legal context and the mode of transition (overthrow, reform or compromise). A transition shaped around compromise – such as the one established in the DRC – very often involves aiming for enough justice to survive even if this comes at the price of an ideal justice.

Known abusers mingle freely in the civilian life they have re-entered. Others have been integrated into the army.[9] Still others have political aspirations. Victims groups continue to mobilise through civil society, and demands continue for public mechanisms that will unpack the past and provide some sort of redress. Unprecedented prosecutorial processes have been undertaken, but they are few, and discussion about establishing complementary restorative justice options remains a long way off. Moreover, despite the establishment of a truth commission, a public-truth seeking process is yet to begin. Savage describes the mood in Congo as follows:

> Mixed in with the relief, the hope and the sheer novelty of the transition, one may sense above all a waiting among everyday Congolese people: a watchfulness, a restraint, an ambivalence toward internationally driven initiatives, a circumspection towards neighbours with whom they will have to live when

the present, internationally bolstered security is over. (Savage 2006: 10)

It is now widely acknowledged that transitional justice efforts thus far in Congo have been vague, precipitous and massively disappointing. Amid efforts to grow initiatives from the formal transitional period into projects with the capacity to confront and address deeply entrenched patterns of violence and abuse – and on this basis to produce a sustainable peace – victims' demands for truth and justice are likely to grow. The difficulties involved in obtaining either will inevitably become painfully evident.

Yet as long as peace holds, an interval of opportunity for both remains and seizing the opportunity may well prove crucial for creating a sustainable peace. It will necessarily involve precisely the sort of leadership on questions of social transformation that has, so far, been sorely lacking in the DRC. It will also need to be demanded, driven, designed and delivered by the nation, including – and especially – some of its most hurt members.

Notes

1 The model is inspired by one presented by Braithwaite elsewhere (2006), but complemented by six principles of restorative justice (inclusion, active participation, encounter, active accountability, reparation and reintegration) that were identified in earlier research done by the author in collaboration with Marta Valiñas.

2 At the time of going to press, North Kivu appeared to be rapidly turning into a theatre of war between government troops and the rebel forces of Laurent Nkunda.

3 These five institutions were: la Commission électorale indépendante (the Independent Electoral Commission), La Haute autorité des médias (the High Media Authority); la Commission vérité et réconciliation (the Truth and Reconciliation Commission); L'Observatoire national des droits de l'homme (the National Watchdog on Human Rights); and la Commission de l'éthique et de la lutte contre la corruption (Committee on Ethics and the Fight Against Corruption). The *Accord Global et Inclusif* is available from the website of Congo Online, at: http://www.congonline.com/DI/documents/Accord_global_et_inclusif_de_Pretoria_17122002_signed.htm.

4 For details, see the press release issued by the ICC Office on 19 April 2004: http://www.icc-cpi.int/pressrelease_details&id=19&l=en.html.

5 See the press release issued by the ICC Office on 17 March 2006: http://www.icc-cpi.int/press/pressreleases/132.html.

6 For a detailed account, see Schabas (2003).
7 For a detailed account, see Burgess (2004).
8 The original formulation by the ICD of the amnesty provision was inspired by the amnesty procedure of the South African TRC and stated that: 'The Commission is empowered to grant amnesty to any person who accepts to confess and completely denounce, on pain of perjury, all the facts that he/she knows and which have a bearing on the crimes and large-scale violations in which he/she was involved, and whose primary motivation is of a political nature. Such amnesty will have to conform to the relevant international norms, and the Commission will not be empowered to grant amnesty for crimes of genocide or crimes against humanity.' The law, however, granted the following power to the TRC: 'Under reserve of the amnesty law which will be voted by the National Assembly, propose to the competent authority to accept or refuse any individual or collective amnesty application for acts of war, political crimes and crimes of opinion' (Article 8(g) of the Promulgated Law, cited in Borello 2004: 43).
9 Four suspected human rights abusers were appointed in 2005 to serve as generals in the army, to cite but one example.

References

Accord Global et Inclusif sur la Transition en République Démocratique du Congo (2002), signé à Pretoria (République d'Afrique du Sud) le 17 décembre 2002 et adopté à Sun City le 1er avril 2003. See *Journal Officiel de la République Démocratique du Congo*, Spécial Issue, 5 avril 2003, pp. 51–69.

Africa Research Bulletin (2006) 'Democratic Republic of Congo. Foreigners in coup plot', 43 (5): 16652–4.

Africa Research Bulletin (2007) 'Congo. Elusive Peace', 44 (3): 17009–10.

African Commission on Human and People's Rights (2003) *Principles and Guidelines on the Right to a Fair Trial and Legal Assistance in Africa*, adopted in 2003, following the appointment of a Working Group on the Right to a Fair Trial per its 1999 Resolution on the Right to A Fair Trial and Legal Assistance.

Arendt, H. (1968) *Between Past and Future: Eight Exercises in Political Thought*. New York: Viking.

Bassiouni, M.C. (1998) 'Searching for peace achieving justice. The need for accountability', in C.C. Joyner (ed.), *Reining in Impunity for International Crimes and Serious Violations of Fundamental Human Rights: Proceedings of the Siracusa Conference 17–21 September 1998*. Paris: Association Internationale de Droit Pénal, pp. 37–44.

Bassiouni, M.C. (2002) 'Accountability for violations of international humanitarian law and other serious violations of human rights', in M.C. Bassiouni (ed.), *Post-Conflict Justice*. Ardsley, NY: Transnational Publishers, pp. 3–54.

Biggar, N. (2001) 'Making peace or doing justice: must we choose?', in N. Biggar (ed.), *Burying the Past: Making Peace and Doing Justice after Conflict*. Washington, DC: Georgetown University Press, pp. 6–23.

Borello, F. (2004) *A First Few Steps: The Long Road to a Just Peace in the Democratic Republic of Congo*, Occasional Paper Series. New York: International Center for Transitional Justice.

Braithwaite, J. (2006) 'Between proportionality and impunity. Confrontation, truth and prevention', *Criminology*, 43 (2): 283–306.

Burgess, P. (2004) 'Justice and reconciliation in East Timor. The relationship between the Commission for Reception, Truth and Reconciliation and the courts', *Criminal Law Forum*, 15: 135–58.

Coghlan, B., Brennan, R.J., Ngoy, P., Dofara, D., Otto, B., Clements, M. and Stewart, T. (2006) 'Mortality in the DRC: a nationwide survey', *The Lancet*, 367: 44–51.

Cohen, S. (1995) 'State crimes of previous regimes. Knowledge, accountability, and the policing of the past', *Law and Social Inquiry*, 20 (1): 7–50.

Huyse, L. (1995) 'Justice after transition. On the choices successor elites make in dealing with the past', *Law and Social Inquiry*, 20 (1): 51–78.

IRIN (2007) 'DRC: weekend attack prompts villagers to flee in northeast', Kinshasa: *IRIN Report*, 31 May. See: http://www.irinnews.org/Report.aspx?Report!d=72483.

Méndez, J.E. (2006) 'The human right to truth: lessons learned from Latin American experiences with truth telling', in T.A. Borer (ed.), *Telling the Truths: Truth Telling and Peace Building in Post-Conflict Societies*. Notre Dame, IN: University of Notre Dame Press, pp. 115–50.

Prendergast, J. and Smock, D. (1999) *Putting Humpty Dumpty Together: Reconstructing Peace in the Congo*, Special Report. Washington, DC: United States Institute of Peace.

Reyntjens, F. (2007) 'Briefing: Democratic Republic of Congo: political transition and beyond', *African Affairs*, 106 (423): 307–17.

Sarkin, J. (2007) 'Reparations for gross human rights violations in Africa – the Great Lakes', in M. du Plessis and S. Peté (eds), *Repairing the Past? International Perspectives on Reparations for Gross Human Rights Abuses*. Antwerp: Intersentia, pp. 197–230.

Savage, T. (2002) 'The Democratic Republic of the Congo: inchoate transition, interlocking conflicts', in E. Doxtader and C. Villa-Vicencio (eds), *Through Fire with Water: Understanding the Roots of Division and Assessing the Potential for Reconciliation in Africa – 15 Case Studies*. Cape Town: David Philip, pp. 129–52.

Savage, T. (2006) *In Quest of a Sustainable Justice. Transitional Justice and Human Security in the Democratic Republic of the Congo*, ISS Paper 130. Pretoria: Institute for Security Studies.

Schabas, W. (2003) 'The relationship between truth commissions and international courts. The case of Sierra Leone', *Human Rights Quarterly*, 25: 1035–66.

Sriram, C.L. (2000) 'Truth commissions and the quest for justice: stability and accountability after internal strife', *International Peacekeeping*, 7 (4): 91–106.

Sriram, C.L. (2004) *Confronting Past Human Rights Violations. Justice Vs. Peace in Times of Transition*. London: Frank Cass.

Sriram, C.L. and Ross, A. (2007) 'Geographies of crime and justice: contemporary transitional justice and the creation of "zones of impunity"', *International Journal of Transitional Justice*, 1 (1): 45–65.

Stearns, J.K. (2007) 'Congo's peace: miracle or mirage?', *Current History*, May, pp. 202–7.

Tegera, A., Mashanda, M., Kayser, C. and Endanda, K. (2000) 'Le dialogue intercongolais 2: le travail de paix intercommunautaire au Nord Kivu', *Regards Croisés*, No. 3. Goma: Pole Institute.

Truth and Reconciliation Commission of South Africa (1998) *Truth and Reconciliation Commission of South Africa Report*, in five vols. Cape Town: Juta.

Tyler, T.R. (2006) 'Restorative justice and procedural justice: dealing with rule breaking', *Journal of Social Issues*, 62 (2): 307–26.

United Nations (2005) *Basic Principles and Guidelines on the Right to a Remedy and Reparation for Victims of Gross Violations of International Human Rights Law and Serious Violations of International Humanitarian Law*, United Nations General Assembly, UN Doc. A/RES/60/147 (also known as 'the Bassiouni Principles').

Vanspauwen, K. (2006) *Furthering Restorative Justice. How Instrumental Are Restorative Justice Elements within the Framework of Transitional Justice*. Paper presented at the international seminar 'Restoring Justice: Another Way of Dealing with the Post-War Situation in Bosnia and Herzegovina', University of Sarajevo, Sarajevo, 27–28 October.

Wippman, D. (1999) 'Atrocities, deterrence, and the limits of international criminal justice', *Fordham International Law Journal*, 23 (2): 473–88.

Woodrow Wilson School of Public and International Affairs (2005) *Balancing Peace, Justice and Stability: A Great Lakes Regional Justice Commission and a Special Tribunal in the Democratic Republic of the Congo*. Princeton, NJ: Princeton University.

Zacklin, R. (2004) 'The failings of ad hoc international tribunals', *Journal of International Criminal Justice*, 2 (2): 541–5.

Part 3

Conclusion

Chapter 17

Racak, Mahane Yehuda and Nyabyondo: restorative justice between the formal and the informal

Ivo Aertsen

The foregoing contributions in this volume are all written from the common perspective of developing socially constructive and effective ways to deal with 'large-scale state-based conflicts', as defined in Chapter 1. The central question was whether and to what degree restorative justice, as we know it from its applicability to common crime with its focus chiefly at the interpersonal level, can be considered as a relevant and useful framework for understanding and responding to violent inter-group conflicts, forms of mass victimisation and so-called 'new wars' (which are mainly large-scale intra-state conflicts – see Chapter 1). This exercise is conducted through three case studies, which refer to very different types and contexts of large-scale violent conflict: the Kosovo conflict in the former Yugoslavia, the Israeli–Palestinian conflict in the Middle East and the regional conflict in the eastern part of the Democratic Republic of Congo. In the three case studies, both formal and informal approaches were analysed, and this was done – where possible – from the different perspectives coming from local actors with first-hand experience of the conflict and of the justice efforts.

What the editors of this book meant by 'informal' and 'formal' processes and mechanisms was explained to all contributors beforehand. This was done on the basis of two lists of topics, one related to the formal approaches, the other to the informal. Both lists were structured along the elements of the 3-level model as outlined in Chapter 1 in order to identify and elaborate on restorative justice elements. By 'formal' approaches, we refer to processes and mechanisms as they are regulated by official law and handled by judicial authorities. Topics here include: legal assessment of the case; legal responses with regard to punishment and reparation (the outcome level); the type of procedure, its legal basis and the role of parties therein (procedural level); and objectives and beneficiaries of the legal responses (purpose level). The term 'informal approaches' refers to processes and mechanisms that are not strictly regulated by state law (but which can be influenced by legal provisions and can interfere with judicial procedures). Topics here are: interpretation of the case from a cultural perspective; possible informal responses with respect to justice, truth and redress (outcome level); applicability of certain informal procedures at a local, national or international level, the normative framework of the informal response (culture, religion or tradition, universal human rights, national or international law), the role of the parties including the community from the local to the international level (procedural level); and the objectives of the informal responses and beneficiaries (purpose level). By examining and confronting informal and formal ways of dealing with a specific violent event or chain of events, we aimed specifically at finding answers to questions such as:

- Are there restorative justice elements to be identified in formal and/or informal practices in the given case studies at the three levels?
- What, from formal and informal perspectives, is the meaning of concepts like justice, truth and restoration?
- Which factors influence, support or hinder the application of restorative justice elements?
- Are there commonalities to be found between the three case studies?

Obviously – and as will be discussed later – distinguishing the formal and the informal as separate processes can be seen as partly artificial: judicial procedures often give room to and incorporate informal processes; so-called informal mechanisms, in turn, are sometimes highly formalised, even on a legal basis, and often implemented in a top-down way.

In what follows we will deal with some of the general questions related to the applicability of restorative justice to the type of violent conflicts under study. In so doing, we will discuss some of the specific elements, as they emerged in the case studies, in the light of this debate. At the same time, we will try to learn from this research whether and how some of our notions of restorative justice and its principles should be revised or complemented. Otherwise stated, do the findings of our analyses invite a reframing or reformulation of any of the elements or core principles of restorative justice?

The relevance of restorative justice principles

Referring to the methodological approach as developed in Chapter 1, we focus on the framework of the UN Basic Principles (UN Handbook 2006) as well as the 3-level model outlined by Rohne (2006), which are related to each other. Which restorative justice elements are recognisable and applicable within the formal and informal mechanisms as analysed in the case studies? In all three case studies, we find clear indications that restorative justice principles are relevant and are, at least to some extent, even brought into practice. Although formal justice mechanisms contain – to a varying degree and based on various types of arguments – victim-oriented and restorative elements, the potential of restorative justice comes much more to the fore in the wide array of informal mechanisms which are mobilised after violent conflicts.

Restorative justice within formal justice mechanisms

With regard to formal perspectives, Haki Demolli, in his legal analysis of the Racak massacre in Kosovo and the judicial responses towards it at national and international levels (Chapter 4), argues that particular categories should be clear beneficiaries of the action, which is in this case focused on prosecution and punishment: families of the murdered victims; the victims' ethnic, racial, political and religious groups; and the state in its support for the socio-political activities of the victims' groups. These categories of (indirect) victims should all benefit morally from prosecution. Moreover, it is said that family members sometimes can benefit from financial or material reparation ordered by national or international courts. Demolli stresses the importance of prosecution and punishment in a general way. By punishing the perpetrators of war crimes and genocide, 'it will be made clear that justice was on the side of the victims and that human society does not allow their victimisation to go unpunished and unacknowledged'. Prosecution of the criminals would present 'a kind of spiritual relief for the families as well as respect toward the victims'.

The purpose of exposing the truth and acknowledging the harmed person as a victim of crime is aimed at by the Israeli criminal justice system as well, concludes Khalid Ghanayim (see Chapter 9). The judicial denunciation of a crime aims at 'restoring a sense of justice to individuals and society as such'. In a similar way it was reported in the case of the DR Congo by Tyrone Savage and Olivier Kambala wa Kambala (Chapter 14) that 'prosecutions are integral to efforts to combat impunity'; they act as a general deterrent and form the basis for the possibility of a realistic, national reconciliation process. Prosecutions are contrasted with blanket or general amnesty, which would leave victims without any means of finding acknowledgment or redress for their grievances. Demolli (Chapter 4) mentions further benefits of criminal prosecution for the victim and in support of peacebuilding processes: impeaching war criminals would accelerate the process of reconciliation between two nations in conflict; and secondly, punishing the individuals responsible, including political leaders, would prevent stigmatisation of the whole community. But, Demolli argues, officials should also accept responsibility through the public seeking of forgiveness (which might not easily happen as long as a climate of polarisation persists).

Demolli in his analysis puts emphasis on some restorative justice elements, mainly at the outcome and the purpose level: acknowledgment and responsibility, material and symbolic reparation, and some degree of healing through prosecution and punishment. However, the precise contents of this 'spiritual relief for victims' are not elaborated, either in terms of forms of punishment or in the procedures towards it. This leaves the assumed benefits for victims rather at the hypothetical level. Furthermore, processes of well-balanced participation for those involved – victims, perpetrators and others – are not examined in the context of national or international court proceedings, which according to the UN Basic Principles keep these formal mechanisms quite distant from restorative justice. Moreover, at the purpose level, the degree of *relational* restoration that can be obtained through formal justice processes remains extremely limited, since all levels of restoration – from redress to reconciliation – require the activation of horizontal, mutual and consensual dynamics (Rohne 2006, 2007).

Similarly, the Israeli criminal procedural law does not entail a full participatory role of those immediately involved. As can be learnt from Ghanayim's contribution, the law entitles the victim or their relatives to some rights, in terms of submitting a petition to prosecute or appealing against a decision of the public prosecutor not to prosecute. Israeli criminal law does not officially recognise informal responses such as victim–offender mediation, but the Opportunity

Principle allows the public prosecutor to take into account informal outcomes and agreements on indemnification, for example in the context of community processes known as *sulha*. Moreover, the penal code allows the court to order financial reparation to the victim or his family, but in practice this seems not to work for the Palestinian population.

International courts operate in a highly formalised way. This, together with practical and financial restrictions, would not allow for much personal participation from the side of the victims or their families, unless in the status of witness. Nor would this setting give room to forms of interaction with the perpetrator. This type of international procedure is mostly – psychologically and socially – very distant from those directly affected, and, in terms of the 3-level model, little understanding of and support for victims can be expected. Nevertheless, in some contexts, as in the DRC, the potential alleviating, settling and deterrent effects of an international arrest are evident.

Limitations of formal justice mechanisms

With respect to the Israeli–Palestinian conflict, Ghanayim (Chapter 9) argues that the application of domestic criminal law, in particular, is important for Israel with its well established criminal justice system. In the light, then, of an extremely weakened judicial system in the Palestinian territories (as confirmed by the empirical research findings of Rohne with respect to trust in governmental institutions and courts – Chapter 12), Ghanayim challenges Israel to balance and justify the application (and frequent non-application) of both its common criminal law and international humanitarian law. This position is bolstered by the fact Palestinians generally deny the right of the state of Israel to prosecute them in Israeli courts according to Israeli law: the courts are perceived as part of the occupation mechanism and not as an objective judicial institution. Palestinians argue that international humanitarian law, such as the Geneva Conventions, should be applied to them and that they should be considered prisoners of war in a situation of armed conflict and occupation. Furthermore, the author notes that the state of Israel tends to apply international law in a rather casuistic manner, namely when it is advantageous to them and does not impose obligations. Similarly, Israeli criminal law is not always applied in a consistent way when it comes to crimes committed (by Israelis or others) in the Palestinian territories. It is noteworthy that, under Israeli criminal law, not only the direct perpetrator, but all persons who supported the crime materially, logistically or with their know-how can be held criminally accountable. In general, offences committed in the context of the political conflict are treated as crimes under aggravating circumstances, and mitigating factors such as economic distress or remorse by the offender are 'typically given little weight'. The primary consideration at the outcome level of the criminal justice process is general deterrence and hence harsh punishments are the rule.

In their study of formal justice mechanisms in the DR Congo, Savage and Kambala wa Kambala (Chapter 14) present a gloomy picture of a judicial system which is 'decayed, decimated, usurped and inadequate'. Further research is needed in order to understand the failure of a justice system to address atrocities such as that which occurred at Nyabyondo and to develop a realistic prosecutorial strategy. But even the best working criminal justice system would never be able to prosecute all or even most perpetrators, the authors argue. Forms of amnesty are considered inevitable, and careful attention should go to the process of establishing criteria for the selection of prosecutions, for example by targeting those 'most responsible for mass violations'. That formal justice proceedings can meet some of the needs of victims of atrocities has been shown – rather surprisingly and maybe exceptionally – by some military courts operating in the context of the Congolese transition. Remarkably, the military court held the national government jointly responsible and ordered financial compensation to survivors and families. Moreover, from a Congolese perspective, intervention by international justice mechanisms is seen to be crucial (as was emphasised also by a majority of Israeli and Palestinian citizens in the Rohne study). These international courts often create – or at least attract – unrealistically high expectations. In a post-conflict society, the authors argue, prevalence should go to re-establishing domestic courts, eventually in a combination (hybrid form) with contributions by international experts and bodies. According to Savage and Kambala wa Kambala, 'holding the proceedings *in situ* has the advantage of enabling justice to be seen, by victims and by the local population more broadly'.

Formal mechanisms for dealing with the Kosovo conflict are touched on by Vesna Nikolic-Ristanovic in Chapter 6 from a Serbian perspective. She notes considerable shortcomings with regard to justice and redress, and argues that special domestic courts for war crimes can have, for many, more credibility than international ones. But in a general way, formal mechanisms 'are rather slow and not very efficient'. They are seen as not very appropriate instruments to restore relationships and to bring reconciliation.

International courts, in particular, are reported to have clear limitations. The International Criminal Tribunal for the Former Yugoslavia (ICTY) has neither legal mandate nor resources to act as main investigator and prosecutorial agency for all the notorious crimes perpetrated in Kosovo. For this and other international courts, it is simply impossible to arrest and to try all those who ordered and committed massacres. The International Criminal Court (ICC) has restricted competence both territorially and insofar as its prosecutions are limited to certain types of crimes. Theoretically speaking, as Valiñas and Arsovska conclude from their own overview of the Kosovo conflict (Chapter 7), institutions such as the ICTY aim to combine their primarily retributive function with longer-term objectives such as giving victims a voice and preparing a basis for community reconciliation. In practice, however, victims have reported feeling frustrated with regard to the slowness with which actual cases proceed (Chapters 4 and 6). Moreover, relatives of deceased victims have often been sceptical with regard to the level of the pronounced sentences (Chapter 4). Besides these frustrations, the fact is that only a few cases are finally dealt with at the international level.

On the basis of the observations made in the three case studies, some general conclusions can be formulated regarding the relevance of restorative (justice) principles in formal judicial proceedings following large-scale violent conflicts. First, formal justice processes, be it at the national or international level, predominantly focus on denouncement, punishment and deterrence. They do not fundamentally provide room for direct, active participation by the victim, the offender or other affected individuals or community members, and they certainly do not allow for the holding of a meeting of stakeholders in which all participate fully. Therefore, restorative justice as conceived by the UN Basic Principles, in particular in its Articles I(1–5), is not applicable. Also, on the basis of the 3-level model, genuine restorative justice principles are scarce in formal justice proceedings, since they do not allow for interactive processes at the personal level, for certain forms of relational restoration and/or for addressing the community in terms of either its responsibilities or as a beneficiary. Second, this view does not fail to note that both domestic and international criminal proceedings do provide elements of reparation towards victims and their relatives. These elements will mainly take the form of financial compensation or return of property, to be ordered by the court at the sentencing level. However, it is worth mentioning that reparative measures can be taken or ordered by non-judicial, administrative bodies as well (as for the Kosovo case, see Chapter 7). Third, criminal justice procedures, by effecting prosecution, are assumed to bring relief to individual victims and victimised communities, in terms of acknowledgment of the facts and recognition of the harm and injustice done to the victims. Even if sufficient empirical evidence existed to underscore these positive effects, it still remains a question whether prosecution and punishment – on the basis of their limited practical applicability as well as on ethical grounds – are the only or best ways to combat 'impunity' in such cases and to show 'that justice is on the side of the victims'.

Restorative justice within informal mechanisms

Turning to informal mechanisms, the distinction can be made between *traditional* informal processes and *contemporary* informal ones. This delineation is at the centre of the chapter by Marta Valiñas and Jana Arsovska that concludes the Kosovo case study, their aim being to identify retributive and restorative elements present in both forms. Both orientations – the restorative and the retributive – can be observed in the conception and, to a lesser extent, the current practice of the Albanian *Kanun*, a form of customary law which 'formulates the rules upon which the Albanian culture is based, primarily focusing on the concept of honour and hospitality, as well as pride, vengeance and reconciliation'. Valiñas and Arsovska explain the cultural meaning of violence and revenge and, moreover, why so many ethnic Albanians have difficulty in accepting state institutions and institutionalised forms of justice. They also stress the incompatibility that often exists between quickly expanding, Westernised state regulations and laws and informal normative systems. They argue that many of the original elements of the *Kanun* have deteriorated into mere reactions of self-defence, and, partly as a response to oppression under the communist regime, ethnic Albanians in some parts of the Balkans have developed their own interpretation of the *Kanun*, 'focusing more on the concept of revenge and exaggerated sense of honour than on reconciliation'. Nevertheless, as the authors point out, the aim of the original customary laws 'was to gain social order, and the laws contained many restorative elements – seldom practised today – that encouraged reconciliation and mediation as mechanisms for solving conflicts'. Customary processes under the *Kanun* law are described in more detail, focusing on, among other things, the roles of the mediator and of the Council of Elders, as well as the function of asylum in the larger scheme. Although, as indicated, many aspects of traditional *Kanun* law are no longer applied in contemporary Albanian communities, similar customary laws existed in Serbian communities until the end of the second World War – as explained by Rexhep Gashi in Chapter 5 and by Vesna Nikolic-Ristanovic in Chapter 6. Moreover, given that customary courts have also been active in Montenegro, Herzegovina and Kosovo and that they, in particular, have been successful in stopping blood feuds between Serbs and Albanians, it might well be worth considering whether and eventually how some of the mediating and reconciliatory principles and structures of these traditional forms of 'doing justice' can be revitalised and adapted to the current situation.

Customary law provides its own interpretation of the crime, which can differ from official assessment by the authorities and legal interpretations. Knowledge of customary law definitions can thus help in understanding perceptions of crime as well as personal and community reactions to it. This is well demonstrated from the perspective of Albanian customary law in Chapter 5 by Gashi when he analyses the Racak massacre. *Kanun* rules on the basis of cultural values (protection for people's life, health, honour and dignity) and spiritual elements deliver specific qualifications of the crime, taking into account, among other things the circumstances of the event (place, timing, manner and consequences). Also, criminal responsibility is defined under the *Kanun* law in a specific way, taking into account, in the case of murder for example, the responsibility of family members and others who have contributed directly or indirectly. But it must be recalled that under Albanian customary law serious crimes could result in severe punishment, including the death penalty or blood revenge in the case of particularly cruel acts of murder.

Traditional processes of informal justice are also analysed in depth in the case studies on the Israeli–Palestinian conflict and the conflict in the DR Congo. Both Michal Alberstein (from an Israeli perspective, in Chapter 10) and George Irani (from a Palestinian point of view, in Chapter 11) argue how the two communities, as both victims and victimisers, are a 'deformed mirror image' of each other. Through historical and ongoing social and political processes, the other is being 'demonised' constantly and particular perceptions of victimisation, traumatisation, insecurity and threat are being reinforced. Alberstein also deals with cultural perceptions of justice in the Jewish-Israeli society. Specifically, she notes how, in Jewish tradition, the absolute character of the law prevails, yet there is the moral advice to go beyond the law and to strive for peaceful settlement and compromise. Moreover, within Israel nowadays, the diversity of informal conflict resolution mechanisms stemming from different groups and cultural perspectives is remarkable. Some of these mechanisms are based on very old and traditional models from earlier populations or imported and adapted to the context of today. Alberstein presents, for example, the Jewish-Ethiopian figure of the *schmagloth* (mediator), which not only deals with the individual conflict, but at the same time works towards community empowerment and functions as an intermediary between the traditional community and the modern legal system. In this respect, Irani stresses the communal nature of Middle Eastern societies and recalls the entanglement of secular and religious law in both Judaism and Islam. He explains how different types of law coexist (tribal law, religious law and state law) and how, for example, the Arab traditional rituals of *sulh* and *musalaha* are steps in a mediation-arbitration process (*sulha*) which closely link the psychological to the political dimension. The ritual processes of *sulh* and *musalaha* for murder cases is described, and this shows strong similarities with processes under Albanian customary law. Remarkably, the initial role of the mediator focuses also on fact-finding. In *sulh* and *musalaha* too, the process does not merely take place between individuals, but is primarily oriented to restoring communal relationships.

Different types of conflict regulation coexist in the DR Congo as well. Theodore Kamwimbi in Chapter 15 throws light on the dualist nature of the Congolese judicial system, which represents a mixture of state (mostly colonial) law and African customary law and other forms of local practices. He then describes in more detail different types of 'informal accountability mechanisms'. A sketch is drawn of the functioning of the customary courts which were legally formalised in the 1920s under the colonial regime and which – mainly because of their easy accessibility – are still in operation in large parts of the country. These courts – like other models, such as the Councils of Elders in most communities – make use of traditional techniques of conflict resolution and are aiming at pacification and strengthening social relations. However, they have been criticised on grounds of their possibly discriminatory character towards women and their non-compliance with international justice standards. Moreover, these customary courts have no legal competence in the DR Congo for dealing with serious crimes. Finally for the DR Congo, the *Kyaghanda* is described as a traditional mechanism of conflict resolution with the ethnic group of the Nande. This model offers space for dealing with conflicts between social groups as well.

From a restorative justice way of thinking in relation to common crime, traditional informal mechanisms are considered to be useful mainly in terms of personal healing and redress, ensuring offender responsibility and generating community involvement. Applied to large-scale violent conflicts, however, informal mechanisms seem to hold other possible functions as well, such as investigation and 'truth-seeking' on one hand and 'justice' on the other. These functions might not be recognisable at all in practices such as victim–offender mediation or conferencing, where it is often said that mediation is *not* about fact-finding and that the mediation process starts from an objective report on the facts delivered by the police or the justice system (Umbreit 2001: 52). At the very most, the Western victim–offender mediation process offers some room for *interpreting* or redefining the facts, so there might be some place for *narrative* truth (see Vanspauwen and Savage: this volume, Chapter 16). Later we will further explore the – interdependent – notions of 'truth' and 'justice' and their meaning in restorative justice processes in both common crime and large-scale conflicts. It is noteworthy that elements of investigating and uncovering the truth, addressing the family of the victim and repairing damages can also be found in the Albanian customary law. As already mentioned, Councils of Elders played an important role as special trial bodies that sought to make financial compensation and reconciliation possible. The possibility of mediation also for the most serious crimes is regulated and encoded in the *Kanun.* Gashi in Chapter 5 argues that all the informal mechanisms under Albanian customary law – from criminal qualification and investigation to trial and reconciliation – should be applied to cases such as the Racak massacre in ways that complement formal judicial mechanisms at the national and international level.

Apart from the relevance of *traditional* informal mechanisms, the importance of *contemporary* informal processes is demonstrated extensively in all three case studies. Informal mechanisms are not seen merely as useful complements to formal judicial processes, but as approaches with a value of their own – or even sometimes as more appropriate to dealing with violent conflicts in terms of the restoration of relationships and mutual trust. With respect to informal mechanisms and processes, several authors highlight the role of civil society organisations at both the national and the international levels. Some of these represent small grass-roots initiatives, originating from the local community, others are big international NGOs following their own agenda. Also, researchers and scientific organisations seem to play an active role. Restorative justice elements are, again in varying degrees, present in most of these initiatives at the procedural, outcome and purpose level. Some of these projects go to the heart of restorative justice, establishing and developing together with those immediately involved innovative and inspiring practices of acknowledgment, reparation and justice.

The following types of activities undertaken by or in cooperation with civil society organisations can be discerned, according to the analyses offered in different chapters of this volume:

- establishing and acknowledging the facts, either through local experience-sharing initiatives or through large-scale investigations, including those dealing with the issue of missing persons;
- offering technical-legal assistance and psychological support to victims and witnesses in criminal justice proceedings and hearings;
- creating space, developing methods and offering training for contact, dialogue and exchange between members of conflicting parties or different ethnic groups;
- organising or supporting forms of commemoration, such as memorials and other measures of symbolic reparation towards families of victims and communities;
- offering or contributing to measures of rehabilitation for victims, such as health care, assistance in education or employment;
- offering negotiation and mediation.

Most of these types of activities do not reflect restorative processes or outcomes as they are defined by the UN Basic Principles, unless they involve initiatives of direct or indirect mediation or other participatory processes where conflict parties actually meet. However, it can be said that establishing and acknowledging the facts, and providing victim assistance and rehabilitation are essential conditions for making restorative justice possible in concrete, individual cases. Similarly, other types of activities mentioned above can be seen as either necessary conditions or at least supportive elements for the realisation of restorative justice at the collective or community level, which, in the case of large-scale violent conflicts, comes into more prominence than when dealing with common crimes.

All three case studies reveal groundbreaking initiatives of inter-ethnic or inter-group dialogue, often facilitated by non-governmental organisations. Direct encounters have been organised between members of conflicting communities, who at the personal level experience similar suffering or whose personal and family stories are mutually very much recognisable. Examples of encounters are mentioned by Nikolic-Ristanovic with respect to the Kosovo conflict: inter-ethnic seminars were organised; on all sides, organisations of war victims or their relatives as well as organisations of war veterans set up meetings with each other; and mediations were held on the topic of the return of displaced people. Possible hindering factors for participating in such meetings were, however, loyalty to one's own group and fear of reaction from one's own community. Also mentioned in connection with the Kosovo conflict are individual initiatives to meet the other 'side' by women whose husbands were killed or by family members of missing persons. Moreover, for the Israeli–Palestinian case, several programmes and institutions are known that promote dialogue and encounter, such as mothers of killed soldiers meeting each other.

The potential and feasibility of inter-ethnic dialogue is also demonstrated for the DR Congo, where in particular in North Kivu in the late 1990s the 'Barza Intercommunautaire' was started on the initiative of community leaders, along with the 'Commission de pacification et de concorde' at the request of the Congolese president. Both forms focus on engaging one another through dialogue and ritual. Any type of conflict can be dealt with inside the Barza. Acknowledgment of guilt, the request for forgiveness, the promise not to repeat offending and rituals of purification are part of the ceremony. The focus of the *Barza* is not on the perpetrators, but on the sources of conflict. Both the *Barza Intercommunautaire* and the Commissions are found to be effective to some degree in elaborating peaceful inter-ethnic solutions.

In this type of direct, personal encounter, a high level of relational restoration is aimed at, focusing on elements of redress, working through the past, establishing coexistence and promoting reconciliation (Rohne 2007). The role of empathy, which is also seen as an important clue in restorative justice processes with common crime, has been emphasised (see also Pepinsky 2006; Williams 2007). The capacity to develop and to show empathy that leads to 're-humanisation' forms indeed a basic condition in all types of profound conflict resolution. As Alberstein argues from an Israeli-Jewish cultural perspective in Chapter 10, narratives at the micro-level may contribute to deconstructing the stereotypical, binary ideological picture of group conflicts; they may represent a first step to conflict transformation, by showing the diversity of identities within and between ethnic communities. Hence also the prominent place and function of the African 'palabre'. With a view to the further development of encounter models at the inter-community level, mediators and other restorative justice practitioners should bring into the dialogue their know-how and experiences.

Limitations of informal mechanisms

Much more than is the case in formal justice processes, elements of restorative justice seem to be present – directly or indirectly – in informal mechanisms, be they traditional or contemporary. As depicted in the three case studies, the degree and method of integrating restorative justice elements into informal mechanisms at the procedural, outcome and purpose levels vary considerably among practices. But their interventions are mostly guided by the common perspective of social pacification and the philosophy of – what we call – restorative justice. Yet, however promising informal justice models might be, we learn from the three cases studies that in reality no wide use is made of them, and certainly not for violent conflict at a collective level. What is the cause of this limited application? There are a number of obstacles and forms of resistance.

One of the important constraining factors is the limited knowledge, and with that the low degree of acceptance, of restorative justice approaches and mechanisms in society, certainly for more serious crimes. As this is the case in virtually all countries, restorative justice as a general approach to crime has to grow in the minds of people – and has to gain public acceptance – if it is to have significant impact on society. This process of familiarisation can be supported considerably – as we have seen in the case studies – by civil society organisations, governmental bodies and academics. Looking in particular at large-scale violent conflicts between collectivities, Nikolic-Ristanovic identifies two important additional obstacles which are responsible for the 'unused space' for informal processes: firstly, the presence of strongly embedded social distances between the communities, which is often strengthened by a language barrier and absence of physical contact so that people look at each other in a very abstract way; and secondly, the exertion of pressures on the conflict groups by politicians. Vanspauwen and Savage from their side argue that the multitude of existing traditional justice mechanisms in the DR Congo was never sufficiently granted an official mandate that would enable them to contribute significantly to the truth-seeking process. These mechanisms lack judicial power, credibility and state support and therefore remain limited to local peacebuilding efforts. In a similar vein, Irani looks at the Middle East conflict, which is so much embedded in protracted political conflict, and asks how to transfer community based, traditional forms of justice to the national and even international level.

Compared to the application of restorative justice practices to common crime, efforts to deal with large-scale violence and mass victimisation cannot restrict themselves to the individual level. Ethno-cultural differences, group identities, victim self-identities at the group level, political affiliations as well as economic interests can form major obstacles to the application of restorative justice approaches. Compared to intra-group conflicts, inter-group differences are missing a sort of overarching community – as Valiñas and Arsovska conclude in Chapter 7 – which could provide a secure general framework where links can be established. While many informal mechanisms work quite well at the intra-community level, bridging at the inter-community level forms a significant challenge. In this respect, Alberstein in Chapter 10 speaks about the 'ethnocentrism' of restorative principles in Jewish tradition and in modern Zionism: informal approaches are restricted to in-group arrangements, while the other is continuously being presented in a negative way. Identifying and exploring possibilities for different types of personal, political and economic connections should be a priority task not only for governmental and non-governmental organisations at all levels, but also for political parties and groups and for industrial, agricultural and financial corporations.

Another major obstacle for the effective use and broad implementation of informal mechanisms for dealing with large-scale conflicts relates to the possibly vulnerable or precarious situation of the conflict country or region. All three case studies have revealed this impediment, albeit again to different degrees. All three conflict regions are confronted with a manifest or latent threat of violence, sometimes worsened by a catastrophic economic situation, a near total destruction of infrastructure and a weakened or corrupt political system. At the same time, the international community fails either to establish security in the region or to bring any insights or new dimensions to the situation capable of leading to a political solution.

When it comes to large-scale violence and inter-group conflict, informal conflict resolution practices can be criticised – and certainly have been, widely – for their lack of procedural safeguards and legal protection. At the same time, it can be questioned whether Westernised notions of legal protection and legal principle should be copy-pasted onto informal or traditional justice mechanisms or to restorative justice in general (Walgrave 2002b: 216). On the other hand, we should not be blind to the possibly selective or discriminatory functioning and disproportional outcomes of traditional or customary court procedures. Informal practices should be evaluated against widely accepted standards of human rights. Creating a complementary system of judicial review could offer a viable way in this regard. As is shown for the DR Congo, civil society organisations – including women's groups – and human rights organisations can play an important role in supporting traditional informal mechanisms of conflict resolution. But, while restorative justice and informal practices should be scrutinised from a (human) rights perspective, it is also true that human rights approaches and politics can be questioned from a restorative justice point of view. One should not doubt the merits of human rights organisations in disclosing and documenting gross violations of human rights and their ongoing efforts to strive for appropriate legal protection for those involved in proceedings. However, what must be commented on critically is the abstract and dogmatic legal approach of some human rights advocates and organisations. ('Well, we are lawyers …' is a justifying phrase that sometimes can be heard from representatives of human rights organisations.) There is not always sufficient attention given to the concrete complexity of a given conflict situation and to ways of dealing with it. Moreover, human rights discourse often links an absence of 'prosecution' and 'punishment' with the various hazards of 'impunity', without taking into account the possible effects such judicial steps may have on efforts to reach mutual understanding and sustainable solutions in the divided societies. If we are to attain these goals, more attention needs to go to alternative ways to name and firmly denounce the crime – without blocking ways to constructive solutions. Here, we probably can learn a lot from traditional community courts for example in the DR Congo, which combat impunity but strive to strengthen social relations within communities at the same time (see Kamwimbi in Chapter 15). In short, restorative justice practitioners and human rights organisations should sit together in order to learn from one another and to further develop just, safe and effective practices for dealing with these types of conflicts.

The particularity of restorative justice principles

'There is no one commonly accepted definition of restorative justice' is a frequently written sentence amid the proliferation of restorative justice literature of the last ten years. For some, this finding is problematic since the lack of a common definition limits the practical testability and thus credibility of restorative justice as an alternative approach to crime. For others, drafting one fixed definition of restorative justice is not possible, nor is it desirable, since it would hamper flexible adaptation to local needs and continuous growth. Restorative justice is increasingly seen as 'a global social movement with huge internal diversity' (Johnstone and Van Ness 2007: 5). At the same time, a need is evident to at least define the common characteristics of restorative justice programmes and to clarify their basic values, principles and objectives. Such answers are needed to distinguish these programmes sufficiently from other ways of responding to crime (Sharpe 2004). Although consensus exists that restorative justice practices are led by a common set of principles (Marshall 1999), different conceptions of those principles, as well as an array of ideologies, are behind their use (Braithwaite and Strang 2001; Johnstone and Van Ness 2007). Such diversity of thinking applies to criminal justice as well, however, where the existence of differing and sometimes contradictory conceptions, objectives, principles, values and practices is explained by referring to the 'multi-functional' character of criminal justice and the 'open-ended' nature of its underlying principles (see Roach 2000).

Even in the absence of one commonly accepted clear-cut definition of restorative justice, there is, to some degree, a common understanding of what restorative justice stands for. This common understanding is present in international standards and supranational regulations. The most prominent of these are the Council of Europe Recommendation No. R(99)19 concerning mediation in penal matters and the UN Basic Principles on the use of restorative justice programmes in criminal matters (see Chapter 1 of this volume). Restorative justice is, indeed, 'a new type of conflict resolution […] rivalling the traditional approach of legal settlement […] as an alternative to the classical pattern of confrontation' (Council of Europe 2000: 11). What makes restorative justice distinct and unique compared to criminal justice adjudication is – among other things – the inclusive, participatory and deliberately problem-solving nature of its response to crime. Addressing a specific offence implies taking care of – and balancing – the needs of the victim, the offender and the community by actively involving them, as the main stakeholders, in one shared process focused on developing an understanding of what happened, acknowledging the facts, taking responsibility and repairing the harm as far as possible. As Vanspauwen and Savage suggest in Chapter 16, such an all encompassing approach can never be offered by a highly formalised criminal justice system, which must give priority to criminal investigation, the application of legal qualifications, prosecution, establishing guilt and punishment. This having been said, it is also true that criminal justice and restorative justice as distinctive models are more and more recognised in both theory and practice as complementary and even mutually influencing systems (Daly 2000; Duff 2002; Willemsens 2003). The further analysis in this chapter is in line with this idea. But first, we will have a closer look at the UN Basic Principles.

The UN Basic Principles

In order to study the applicability of restorative justice to the handling of large-scale violent conflicts, we have been examining how and to what extent both formal and informal justice processes and mechanisms contain, or give room to, elements which can be considered to be integral to restorative justice, as outlined in the UN Basic Principles and following a conceptual model of restorative justice that focuses on the procedural, outcome and purpose levels. Whereas the 3-level model was explored systematically in several of the preceding chapters, the UN Basic Principles lend themselves to further analysis.

The three case studies made clear the degree to which restorative justice programmes, processes and outcomes, as defined in Section 1 of the UN Basic Principles, are applicable. The inherently flexible, participatory and interactive nature of restorative justice processes according to the Basic Principles restricts the applicability of these processes mainly to settings with a certain degree of informality. Court proceedings can result in restorative outcomes, not least in the context of large-scale violent crimes as we have seen, but not in the form of 'an agreement reached as a result of a restorative process' (UN Basic Principles, Article 3). At least four critical elements can be discerned for a fully restorative process: (1) an identifiable victim; (2) voluntary participation by the victim; (3) an offender who accepts responsibility; and (4) non-coerced participation of the offender (UN Handbook 2006: 8). Like the Council of Europe Recommendation R(99)19, the UN Basic Principles stress three important working principles: the voluntary character of participation by all parties, the neutrality of the facilitator and the confidentiality of the process. Neutrality is defined in terms of an active form of impartiality, where the facilitator shows 'respect to the dignity of the parties', ensures 'that the parties act with respect towards each other' and enables them 'to find a relevant solution among themselves' (Article 18). To show and to foster empathy among the participants is one of the essentials of the mediator's work. Some Western mediators refer to the concept of multi-lateral partiality, a highly relevant concept developed on the basis of the contextual therapy (Böszörményi-Nagy and Krasner 1986). But these same, Westernised mediators follow a very individualising interpretation of the mediator's role, and this must be confronted with the more representative role facilitators have for example in Middle Eastern and African cultures. Furthermore, the requirement of confidentiality is nuanced within the text of the UN Basic Principles, since it only applies to restorative processes 'that are not conducted in public' (Article 14). The latter indicates that the UN Basic Principles, more than the Council of Europe Recommendation, hold a perspective that is open to diverse and community-oriented restorative justice models, which in turn have to be conceived 'taking into account legal, social and cultural circumstances' (UN Basic Principles Preamble, which also refers to traditional and indigenous forms of justice as a basis for restorative justice initiatives).

There is, however, a key element of informal processes, as unpacked in this volume, that does not fit very well with standards of restorative justice as formulated in international regulations. Several of the informal, community-oriented modes, be they traditional or contemporary, have an important investigatory or truth-seeking function. As already mentioned above, restorative justice processes are usually started on the basis of the facts as established by the police or the justice system. If the parties do not 'agree on the basic facts of a case', there will be no mediation process (Article 7, UN Basic Principles; Article 14, Council of Europe Recommendation). The underlying reasons for adopting this principle relate to concern for the practical feasibility of mediation and also for the need to protect the victim from secondary or tertiary victimisation when the offender totally denies the crime. Taking into account, however, the importance of truth-disclosure in cases of violent crime and mass victimisation, the question should be raised whether elements of truth-finding, truth-telling and reinterpretation of the facts should not be given a more prominent place in restorative justice standards.

Although the UN Basic Principles restrict the scope of restorative justice to voluntary and interactive processes, attention is also given to the promotion of restorative values in the context of formal criminal justice proceedings. Where restorative processes are not suitable or possible, 'criminal justice officials should endeavour to encourage the offender to take responsibility vis-à-vis the victim and affected communities, and support the reintegration of the victim and the offender into the community' (Article 11). This perspective relates to a set of broad objectives of restorative justice programmes which might influence options to be taken within formal criminal justice procedures and which, according to the UN Handbook (2006: 9–11), contain the following key elements:

- supporting victims, giving them a voice and enabling their participation;
- repairing the relationships damaged by crime in a consensual way;
- denouncing criminal behaviour as unacceptable and reaffirming community values;
- encouraging all concerned parties to take responsibility, particularly the offenders;
- identifying restorative, forward-looking outcomes as the main focus;
- reducing recidivism by encouraging change in individual offenders and facilitating their reintegration into the community; and
- identifying factors that lead to crime and informing authorities.

It is in its degree of adherence to this set of broad objectives, much more than to a specific practice or process, that makes a particular response to crime a 'restorative' one (UN Handbook 2006: 9). This approach to restorative justice corresponds with the sort of conception Johnstone and Van Ness (2007: 6–8) develop. They emphasise the appraisive, internally complex and open nature of the concept of restorative justice: this implies a need to regularly evaluate the degree to which standards of restorative justice are being met, to continuously clarify its meaning, to ascertain the presence of crucial elements such as 'relatively informal processes', to stress the role of decision-makers, as well as to recognise the evolutionary character of restorative justice models.

This brings us to the already highly debated relationship of restorative justice to criminal justice (von Hirsch *et al.* 2003; Walgrave 2002a), and the issue of possible forms of mutual interference. The UN Basic Principles show an awareness of the delicate relationship, but do not offer much clarification. Restorative justice programmes and the criminal justice system are presented each on their own as more or less separate, autonomous entities. This division of fields of competence is even more visible in the Council of Europe

Recommendation, where this distinction was based on the recognition that the European Convention on Human Rights, and more precisely Article 6 on the right to a fair trial, should apply to mediation practices in criminal cases (Explanatory Memorandum, commentary on Article 6 of the Recommendation – see Aertsen *et al.* 2004: 107–8). The UN Basic Principles deal with the connection of restorative justice to the criminal justice system in several places, for example in its discussion of referring a case back to criminal justice authorities when no restorative justice process is possible (Article 11) or no agreement is reached (Article 16), as well as in the sections on judicial supervision and on the incorporation of the results of agreements reached in restorative processes into judicial procedures (Article 15). These rules, however, do not say anything about the more dynamic relationship and possible interactions between the two systems. What can we learn about these dialectics on the basis of the case studies on large-scale violent conflicts, where we have analysed informal and formal mechanisms in greater depth?

Lessons from the formal–informal dialectics

Valiñas and Arsovska start Chapter 7 in conclusion to Section 1, by pointing out that 'Kosovo is perhaps one of the best examples today, at least in Europe, where formal and informal mechanisms of dealing with conflict coexist but do not communicate with each other'. The same might apply to the two other conflict regions under study. Both in the Middle East and in the DR Congo, traditional and contemporary informal mechanisms of dealing with violent conflict operate parallel to the formal, judicial system. Less clear is whether and to what degree, in these two conflict regions, the two types of process are in any active relationship with one another. Let us further explore the interactive character of the relationship between the formal and the informal. We will do so by looking more closely at the way of functioning of the two systems, and then, more content wise, at the role of identity and dignity, truth, restoration and, finally, justice.

Complementary systems

Irani in Chapter 11 describes how, in some Middle Eastern societies, private modes of conflict control and reduction are invoked simultaneously with official justice processes in order to foster reconciliation. Both systems seem to share a common goal, which is more likely to happen in communal societies where the understanding of 'private' relates to a less liberal, more societal conception of citizenship. Moreover, in the Congolese context the private–public divide might well be less pronounced than in Western industrialised countries. This might at least partly explain why in Congo customary courts were acknowledged and legally established by the colonial state in the 1920s, as Kamwimbi informs us in Chapter 15. Keeping social order was in the interest of both the colonial power and the indigenous populations. Customary courts could operate on the basis of traditional justice principles, as long as they did not obstruct written law, universal public order, good morals and principles of humanity and equity. Such a conditional autonomy implies a supervisory and corrective mechanism from the side of the state law. More recently, modern forms of informal justice were established in the DR Congo, focusing on inter-group conflicts but still based on traditional culture. The *Barza Intercommunautaire* is well know as a bottom-up initiative, recently extended and funded by the national government and supported by the UN and a group of civil society organisations. This model of justice might be an example of synergy between the informal and the formal at the level of administration and implementation. This integration does not seem to exist at the judicial level, since traditional mechanisms are not really incorporated into the DR Congo criminal law.

In the sphere of dealing with large-scale violent conflicts and gross violations of human rights, the insight has been growing that relying on just one type of conflict handling can rarely integrally meet the objectives of social peace under the rule of law (Huyse 2006). For each case, the utility of different approaches must be assessed and, in practice, combined in a flexible way. This concerns the local, national and international level, as well as different types of informal, formal and in-between mechanisms. Vanspauwen and Savage in Chapter 16 refer to the example of East Timor to include existing local structures of peace and reconciliation in dealing with some types of crime officially. According to them, informal mechanisms such as the *Barza Intercommunautaire* could have a preparatory function towards the establishment of formal accountability mechanisms. This is fully in line with the UN Handbook (2006: 30), where it is said that African customary law 'may provide a basis for rebuilding the capacity of the justice system'. Another example, in a Western society this time, of dealing with ongoing violent crime informally but against the background of and in interaction with political changes and police and judicial reforms, is Northern Ireland. Here, community-based restorative justice programmes were set up in the late 1990s as alternatives to paramilitary punishment violence. McEvoy and Mika (2002) reply to old but renewed critiques on informalism and describe how community based programmes can work effectively in the aftermath of the Northern Irish troubles if a number of well specified conditions is fulfilled, such as the localisation of the initiative in politically organised and dynamic communities and also the guidance provided by locally developed standards of practice that, in turn, are based upon accepted human rights principles.

Identity and dignity

Much attention is given, in each of the three case studies in this book, to the cultural context in which the conflicts emerged and developed, and in which context solutions have to be elaborated. Insight into the broader cultural context is, of course, of utmost importance for a deeper understanding of these types of community-based conflicts. In a more familiar, Western environment too, where restorative justice practitioners are mainly intervening at the inter-individual level, knowledge of cultural meanings becomes more and more important. As referred to in Chapter 1, 'cultural identity' with respect to values, language, religion, history, social or ethnic group is more and more part and parcel of modern conflict and needs to be considered when determining the nature of specific instances of hostility. Identity formation can have a beneficial or a destructive effect on ongoing threats, moreover. Communities can be empowered in either direction.

Even when we admit that many large-scale conflicts cannot be reduced to mere cultural, identity-based conflicts, and that more factors are in play – at the historical, political and economic levels – it remains necessary to take into account the cultural background, whether we are working with informal or formal processes. Knowledge of the degree of cultural determination of the conflict can help in choosing the most appropriate, informal mechanism or in adapting existing formal ones. Moreover, insight into the cultural context can assist in understanding and coordinating informal and formal procedures – and thus in bridging the two forms. Know-how developed in the framework of restorative justice practices, with their sensitivity towards and 'good understanding of local cultures and communities' (UN Basic Principles, Article 19) should be mobilised for designing such an overall approach to the conflict.

Examining the concept of dignity might offer a helpful example of the potential contribution a restorative justice approach can make.

Dignity can hardly be understood without descending to the micro-level of personal experience. The same goes for honour, pride and hospitality, which are found to be other crucial, interrelated values in Albanian as well as in African cultures, and which might result in either vengeance or reconciliation, depending on how these values are recognised and awarded in practice. Dignity is, according to the analysis by Finn Tschudi in Chapter 2, a central concept in human rights approaches and therefore a core value of restorative justice. Tschudi clarifies the meaning of dignity by describing possible reactions to its antonym: humiliation. 'Losing one's dignity means being excluded from the family of humankind', which implies that the concept of dignity connects the individual with the community. Restoring dignity in restorative justice practices thus entails including the community perspective by the experience of being part of a joint humanity (such as that upheld in the African concept *ubuntu*) and the experience of empowerment as 'a social process where people believe that their story is worth telling'. The latter refers to an important insight from procedural justice theory where 'standing' – the value of being a member of the group – is identified as one of the determining factors in evaluating a process as fair (Tyler 1989).

Tschudi in his chapter further explores the relevance of cultural factors for the development of restorative justice and peacebuilding practices. He does so by demonstrating, among other things, the importance of the culturally determined understanding of time and by showing how, in Bougainville, thousands of people were trained in restorative justice at a pace that allowed them to examine the concepts fully, in light of contextual concerns, and on that basis to combine local traditions with Western influences.

Truth

Another notion of high relevance for restorative justice – and one which, like old-fashioned 'dignity', is often forgotten in Westernised practices – is truth. Like dignity, formulations of truth contain an inherent link between the individual and the community as well as, moreover, between the informal and the formal. Our three case studies on large-scale, violent conflicts provided overwhelming evidence of the importance and central role of truth in attempts to restore justice and peace. It has been said already that, unlike most restorative justice practices for common crime, informal as well as more formalised mechanisms (such as truth commissions, which deal with large-scale victimisation) include forms of fact-finding, truth-seeking, truth-telling and truth-recovery as crucial ingredients of the process. In these gatherings, truth will often be dealt with at both the individual and the community or political level.

Whereas facts and fact-finding might be characterised by some degree of objectivity ('factual truth'), truth and truth-seeking are much more subject to interpretation. Establishing the truth about a violent incident can be extremely difficult, argues Nikolic-Ristanovic for the Kosovo conflict in Chapter 6, taking into account the historical precedents of giving opposite and stereotypical meanings to the same events. Truth-dichotomy relates to identity-dichotomy, where, as a consequence of listening to the truth of the other, one would give up their own identity. In this field of tension, there is a strong intermingling of the micro- and the macro-level in which, according to Nikolic-Ristanovic, politicians play an important role. Therefore, 'informal mechanisms need to be accompanied by advocacy for political action, i.e. for the proper use of formal mechanisms'. This also means that disputing the truth might not always be the best way of resolving conflict, she concludes.

The latter conclusion puts strong emphasis on *how* the truth about a conflict is discussed, hence the importance of truth-telling or 'narrative truth'. Truth-telling is at the heart of most African traditional justice systems, as Kamwimbi in Chapter 15 notes, but might have important functions in other settings as well. The potential of narratives at the individual level – complementary to political processes – is recognised by Alberstein for the Israel–Palestinian case in Chapter 10: 'The truth about the Mahane Yehuda event can be revealed by exploring the private life histories of the victims involved and understanding the perpetrator's motivations and needs as well as by discussing the damage to and horror of the families and the broader community.' Besides factual and narrative truth, Vanspauwen and Savage (Chapter 16) discern dialogical truth: the truth that arises through conversation and debate. Finally, they consider restorative truth, where facts and their meanings are placed in the perspective of restoration. Some of these alternative ways of discussing the truth might assist in overcoming a truth-dichotomy.

Vanspauwen and Savage place the different modes of truth in the very centre of a restorative justice model, based on 'integrative truth-seeking'. Integrative truth-seeking in the context of a post-conflict society requires a process of active participation by all stakeholders, an inclusive process and the ongoing possibility of encounter. Such a form of integrative truth-seeking invites active accountability, resulting in different types of reparation and reintegration. In this way, restorative justice could offer elements to reconcile the tension between peace and justice – and even to mutually reinforce one another.

In light of the above, truth may be understood to be an integral element in processes towards social pacification and justice, and informal restorative justice practices may be seen to emphasise the values of peace and justice in a variety of ways. The relationship between truth-seeking by informal, bottom-up, ascending processes and truth-recovery by more static, top-down, descending judicial mechanisms should be subject to further research. One example of an element of that relationship not discussed here concerns the use of coercion, which in some stages of the process might be instrumental to truth-finding as well. An example of the latter has been the South African Truth and Reconciliation Commission, where the threat of prosecution underpinned the system of conditional amnesty. In general, however, the role of judicial mechanisms and trials in seeking truth in cases of mass victimisation has been criticised. Trials, according to Drumbl (2000: 293–5), create simplistic categories of 'innocent' and 'guilty', which are binary and mutually exclusive notions, substitutes for 'good' or 'evil' and often reflecting bipolarities of the national political culture. Drumbl refers to Sachs, who calls truths emerging from trials microscopic and logical truth. This gives rise to selective story-telling and selective truths. Public enquiries and truth commissions, by contrast, create experiential and dialogic truths. This phenomenological approach goes to the core of restorative justice.

Restoration

Truth is linked, through the active accountability it allows, to different types of restoration. It has been shown in our case studies that responsibility has to be extended from the individual offender to many others, including politicians as well as – often – the community as a whole (see also Cunneen 2006). Involving the different levels of addressees requires an integrated approach by both informal and formal mechanisms in society. 'Restoration' in the case of large-scale conflict also focuses on different types of reparation, which can be categorised at the public level according to the Bassiouni Principles (see Chapter 14). In Chapter 1, in an attempt to conceptualise restorative justice, four levels of *relational restoration* were distinguished: redress (including material reparation), working through the past, coexistence and reconciliation. It goes without saying that this multi-level approach also presupposes the activation of an array of community-based informal mechanisms. The perspective of *relational* restoration is deemed to be important from a restorative justice point of view. Considering restoration only from its financial or material side can – for these type of conflicts – work negatively: victims, for example, might feel offended, as was argued for the DR Congo by Savage and Kambala wa Kambala in Chapter 14. This means that restoration by itself has an open-ended structure as well, and that, depending on the needs of the specific situation, different reparatory measures must be combined, including public apologies, memorials and legislative measures. In other words, restoration should take place along the informal–formal line, where different forms of restoration influence each other.

Justice

The benefits of such an interplay between informal and formal processes is not restricted to restoration. It can also contribute to the realisation of 'justice' in cases of massive, violent conflict. Both restoration and justice may be seen to be extremely limited compared with what is possible when a functioning complementarity is established between informal and formal approaches. The complementarity consists of both mutual reinforcement and reciprocal challenge. Establishing a system where informal mechanisms can interrogate and question formal procedures constantly, and vice versa, should contribute to a more democratic system of overall justice.

Justice according to Biggar – as quoted by Vanspauwen and Savage (Chapter 16) – should not be focused only on prosecution and punishment, but on the vindication of the victim. This requires recognising the injury caused as well as acknowledging the dignity of the victim, offering support to victims, repairing the damage as far as possible and establishing the truth of the event in ways that include explanations of its reasons and circumstances. Hence, dignity, truth and restoration form cornerstones for a system of justice that relies on – and can only be realised through – active participation by those affected. In other words, through the informal–formal dialectics and following Braithwaite and Parker (1999) (as well as Braithwaite 2003), a system is created for continuous bottom-up value clarification, where 'the justice of the people bubbles up to reshape the justice of the law' and where the justice of the law percolates down to the world of citizens and then more legitimately is able to constrain and influence the justice of the people. What is envisioned here is a form of inter-legality in the tradition of the so-called new legal pluralism (Merry 1988), where the study focuses on the complex and evolving interactions between state law and different forms of non-official law or regulatory systems in society. In this perspective of interactive settings, justice is conceived not so much as a series of separate, ideal typical models, but as a continuum: 'the informal is an integral part of the totality of law and not an alternative to it' (Henry 1983: 46). This brings us back to our starting point on restorative justice, namely that restorative justice is not simply a matter of taxonomy (Johnstone and Van Ness 2007: 6), but a matter of evaluation of whether a particular practice meets certain standards, objectives and principles (UN Handbook 2007: 9).

Conclusion

In this chapter, we have reflected on the three case studies that were based on, respectively, the Racak, the Mahane Yehuda and the Nyabyondo incidents. We analysed, in a comparative way, the degree of applicability of restorative justice principles. We did so by contrasting the informal and the formal processes of dealing with these atrocities, as described by the groups of contributors, mainly local, with first-hand knowledge of the situation on the ground. We discovered an array of informal mechanisms that show a high similarity between the three conflict regions. In particular, informal processes based on traditional forms of justice and social pacification resonated strongly throughout. Taking into account also the existence of these – very similar – traditional kinds of informal justice on all the sides of the respective conflicts, the question emerges whether this community potential shouldn't be called on and revitalised in a more proactive way. International, regional, governmental and non-governmental organisations could act in coordinated ways as a kind of 'overarching community' for a given conflict region in order to support local initiatives and to build a shared framework. The international community could also be responsible for leading efforts to balance the various tensions: the informal with the formal, and the national with the international.

What certainly also became clear in this study was the necessity of developing multi-level strategies in response to cases of large-scale violence as well as to post-conflict situations. The objectives, the constituents, the stakeholders and the leading principles for developing and implementing these strategies have been discussed above. The option for an integrated approach embraces a variety of seemingly paradoxical developments taking place in different parts of the world, where far-reaching forms of international homogenisation and control take place, while at the same time local differentiation, revitalisation and expansion of informal and traditional regulatory forms can be observed. These new developments are part of a broader tendency towards changes in the configuration of plural legal orders (von Benda-Beckmann *et al.* 2002–2003; Huyse 2006: 201).

Our study on the applicability of restorative justice principles and values to large-scale violent conflict resulted, finally, in some lessons for the further conception of restorative justice in general. Firstly, the nature of the conflicts studied forced us to critically look at the UN Basic Principles on the use of restorative justice programmes in criminal matters. Although the UN Basic Principles do focus on the role of the broader community in non-Western societies as well (more so, at least, than does the Council of Europe Recommendation R(99)19 concerning mediation in penal matters), the element of truth and truth-finding and its possible place in the Basic Principles should be raised for further discussion. Furthermore, a number of methodological issues of restorative justice processes, as applied to common crime, have to be nuanced or further reflected on as a result of our comparative study. One of these issues is how to involve the community effectively in restorative justice practices. Finally, we situated the field of restorative justice, as well as its future conceptualisations, in the context of formal–informal relationships and the core elements that, the analysis showed, emerge when dealing with large-scale conflict, specifically identity and dignity, truth, restoration and justice. Analysing the interrelationships of these constitutive elements in the particular conflicts cases will, it is hoped, invite restorative justice practitioners and researchers to further reflect on the central notion of 'justice' in general.

References

Aertsen, I. (2004) 'Victim-offender mediation with serious offences', in *Crime Policy in Europe. Good Practices and Promising Examples*. Strasbourg: Council of Europe Publishing, pp. 75–86.

Aertsen, I., Mackay, R., Pelikan, C., Willemsens, J. and Wright, M. (2004) *Rebuilding Community Connections – Mediation and Restorative Justice in Europe*. Strasbourg: Council of Europe Publishing.

Böszörményi-Nagy, I. and Krasner, B.R. (1986) *Between Give and Take*. New York: Brunner/Mazel.

Braithwaite, J. (2003) 'Principles of restorative justice', in A. von Hirsch, J. Roberts, A.E. Bottoms, K. Roach and M. Schiff (eds), *Restorative Justice and Criminal Justice. Competing or Reconcilable Paradigms?* Oxford: Hart, pp. 1–20.

Braithwaite, J. and Parker, C. (1999) 'Restorative justice is republican justice', in G. Bazemore and L. Walgrave (eds), *Restorative Juvenile Justice: Repairing the Harm of Youth Crime*. Monsey, NJ: Criminal Justice Press, pp. 102–26.

Braithwaite, J. and Strang, H. (2001) 'Introduction: restorative justice and civil society', in H. Strang and J. Braithwaite (eds), *Restorative Justice and Civil Society*. Cambridge: Cambridge University Press, pp. 1–13.

Council of Europe (2000) *Mediation in Penal Matters. Recommendation No. R(99)19 and Explanatory Memorandum*. Strasbourg: Council of Europe Publishing.

Cunneen, C. (2006) 'Exploring the relationship between reparations, the gross violation of human rights, and restorative justice', in D. Sullivan and L. Tifft (eds), *Handbook of Restorative Justice*. New York: Routledge, pp. 355–68.

Daly, K. (2000) 'Revisiting the relationship between retributive and restorative justice', in H. Strang and J. Braithwaite (eds), *Restorative Justice: Philosophy to Practice*. Aldershot: Ashgate, pp. 33–54.

Drumbl, M. (2000) 'Sclerosis: retributive justice and the Rwandan genocide', *Punishment and Society*, 2 (3): 287–307.

Duff, R.A. (2002) 'Restorative punishment and punitive restoration', in L. Walgrave (ed.), *Restorative Justice and the Law*. Cullompton: Willan, pp. 82–100.

Henry, S. (1983) *Private Justice: Towards Integrated Theorising in the Sociology of Law*. London: Routledge & Kegan Paul.

Huyse, L. (2006) *Alles gaat voorbij, behalve het verleden*. Leuven: Uitgeverij Van Halewyck.

Johnstone, G. and Van Ness, D.W. (2007) 'The meaning of restorative justice', in G. Johnstone and D.W. Van Ness (eds), *Handbook of Restorative Justice*. Cullompton: Willan, pp. 5–23.

McEvoy, K. and Mika, H. (2002) 'Restorative justice and the critique of informalism in Northern Ireland', *British Journal of Criminology*, 42: 534–62.

Marshall, T.F. (1999) *Restorative Justice: An Overview*. London: Home Office.

Merry, S.E. (1988) 'Legal pluralism', *Law and Society Review*, 5: 869–96.

Pepinsky, H. (2006) 'Empathy and restoration', in D. Sullivan and L. Tifft (eds), *Handbook of Restorative Justice*. New York: Routledge, pp. 188–97.

Roach, K. (2000) 'Changing punishment at the turn of the century: restorative justice on the rise', *Canadian Journal of Criminology*, 2 (3): 249–80.

Rohne, H.-C. (2006) 'Conceptualizing Restorative Justice in the Context of Large-Scale Conflicts.' Unpublished paper presented at COST Action A21 symposium 'Restorative Justice Development in Europe', 2–3 March.

Rohne, H.-C. (2007) *Opferperspektiven im interkulturellen Vergleich. Eine viktimologische Studie im Kontext der Al-Aqsa Intifada*. Hamburg: Verlag Dr Kovač.

Sharpe, S. (2004) 'How large should the restorative "tent" be?', in H. Zehr and B. Toews (eds), *Critical Issues in Restorative Justice*. Monsey, NY: Criminal Justice Press, pp. 17–31.

Tyler, T.R. (1989) 'The psychology of procedural justice: a test of the group-value model', *Journal of Personality and Social Psychology*, 57 (5): 830–8.

Umbreit, M. (2001) *The Handbook of Victim Offender Mediation: An Essential Guide to Practice and Research*. San Francisco: Jossey-Bass.

UN Handbook on Restorative Justice Programmes (2006) Vienna: United Nations Office on Drugs and Crime.

Von Benda-Beckmann, F., von Benda-Beckmann, K., Eckert, J., Pirie, F. and Turner, B. (2002–2003) 'Vitality and revitalisation of tradition in law: going back into the past or future-oriented development?', in *Max Planck Institute for Social Anthropology Report 2002–2003*. Halle/Saale: Max Planck Institute for Social Anthropology, pp. 296–306 (online at: http://www.eth.mpg.de/pubs/jb-02-03/jb2003-009projectgroup3.pdf).

Von Hirsch, A., Roberts, J., Bottoms, A.E., Roach, K. and Schiff, M. (eds) (2003) *Restorative Justice and Criminal Justice: Competing or Reconcilable Paradigms?* Oxford: Hart.

Walgrave, L. (ed.) (2002a) *Restorative Justice and the Law*. Cullompton: Willan.

Walgrave L. (2002b) 'Restorative justice and the law: socio-ethical and juridical foundations for a systemic approach', in L. Walgrave (ed.), *Restorative Justice and the Law*. Cullompton: Willan, pp. 191–218.

Willemsens, J. (2003) 'Restorative justice: a discussion of punishment', in L. Walgrave (ed.), *Repositioning Restorative Justice*. Cullompton: Willan, pp. 24–42.

Williams, B. (2007) 'Empathy for victims, offending and attitudes', in R. Mackay, M. Bošnjak, J. Deklerck, C. Pelikan, B. van Stokkom and M. Wright (eds), *Images of Restorative Justice Theory*. Frankfurt am Main: Verlag für Polizeiwissenschaft, pp. 225–33.

Chapter 18

From micro to macro, from individual to state: restorative justice and multi-level diplomacy in divided societies

Jana Arsovska, Marta Valiñas and Kris Vanspauwen

> *More than an end to war, we want an end to the beginning of all wars – yes, an end to this brutal, inhuman and thoroughly impractical method of settling the differences [...]*
>
> Franklin D. Roosevelt

We began this book arguing that the twentieth century will be remembered as a century that burdens us with its legacy of mass destruction and violence inflicted on a scale never seen in human history. We tried to show that violence and conflicts pervade the lives of many people around the world, and touch all of us in some way. Yet it often happens that individuals feel helpless and unable to change this trend; hence many remain silent regarding the harm done to them, keeping their anger within themselves. Some choose to take justice into their own hands and seek revenge, adding to the vicious cycle of violence. For others, as Gro Harlem Brundtland, Director of the World Health Organisation, argues, staying out of harm's way is a matter of locking doors and avoiding dangerous places. Yet for those living in the midst of war and conflict, violence permeates every aspect of life and it often seems difficult to find an 'easy escape' (Krug *et al.* 2002). Although we noted that violence and conflicts have always been part of human experience, one has to understand that they are not inevitable. We can do much to address, resolve and further prevent such hideous phenomena. Nelson Mandela, who wrote the preface of the World Report on Violence and Health (2002), explains:

> Many who live with violence day in and day out assume that it is an intrinsic part of the human condition. But this is not so. Violence can be prevented. Violent cultures can be turned around. In my own country and around the world, we have shining examples of how violence has been countered. Governments, communities and individuals can make a difference. (Krug *et al.* 2002)

What states and individuals must eventually start realising is that they have to put an end to war and violent conflict, or war and conflict will put an end to humankind. An eye for an eye policy might leave the world blind, hence revenge and retribution are obviously not the long-term solution for these deeply rooted problems. A policy based on pre-emptive wars and military interventions solely to reach political and economic goals is detrimental if we aim at achieving long-lasting peace in the world. Violence – as noted in the beginning of this book – is only a 'temporary relief of hopelessness' (Kingman Brewster: this volume, Chapter 1).

It causes much more harm than good. Also isolation and seclusion are equally damaging for the individuals that have been victimised. Hence, in this book we have argued that constructive ways for dealing with large-scale violent conflicts are certainly needed if we want 'an end to the beginning of all wars', or if we want at least to minimise the devastating effects of violent conflicts on human lives. However, is there a ground for such 'constructive ways' to flourish? Is there a place for restorative justice mechanisms in this context? What could restorative principles bring to the resolution of the atrocities of the past and the tensions between various conflicting parties? How to extend the practice of these restorative mechanisms in order to achieve sustainable and long-term peace within the broader societies? These are some among many questions that the authors of this book tried to deal with by pointing out the possibilities and limits for a restorative approach within various conflict regions. In this concluding chapter we will not present again a comprehensive overview of overarching themes and questions, but we will simply raise several points that we believe deserve attention in order to enhance better policy-making. How can individuals, communities and states further contribute to the effective prevention and resolution of violent large-scale conflicts? What is the role of the international community in this context? What do restorative justice principles have to add to these prevention/resolution efforts? How can we, as researchers and academics, help victims raise their voice in a constructive way and, hence, hinder further escalation of wars and conflicts worldwide?

Enhancing contacts and multi-level diplomacy in divided societies

The recent literature on social capital, focusing chiefly on the effects of social interaction, has served to strengthen the traditional notion that voluntary associations play a major role in generating civic virtues among the citizens of liberal democracies (Hooghe 2003; Putnam 1993, 2000; Seligman 1992; Warren 2001). According to Hooghe (2003: 151) due to their interaction with other members, citizens are expected to interiorise an attachment to tolerance and other democratic principles. Hooghe (2003: 152) argues that among the values that are expected to be promoted by civic interaction, tolerance can be considered as the most important because it is a prerequisite for the peaceful coexistence of various comprehensive doctrines. Briefly stated, he claims, 'democratic systems will only be able to function if citizens tolerate and respect those with whom they disagree' (see also Rawls 1999).

As we noted at the beginning of this book, existing of research has shown that interaction with others in cross-cutting networks might reduce hostile feelings toward other groups within the population (Mutz 2002: 111–14). According to Hooghe (2003) one approach implies that 'repeated interaction with fellow citizens having different convictions and opinions, or coming from different cultural, ethnic or religious backgrounds, will increase one's capacity to understand the perspective of opponents' (see also Mutz 2002). This argument basically links to the sociology of knowledge which postulates that scientific thought, particularly thought on social and political matters, does not proceed in a vacuum but in a socially conditioned environment. It is influenced by unconscious or subconscious elements which – as Karl Popper explains (1993: 218) – stay concealed from the thinker's observing eye because they form the exact place that he/she inhabits, his/her social habitat. As we could observe throughout this book, the social habitat of the thinker determines a whole system of values and theories, which emerge to him/her as self-evident. It is usually preposterous for the thinker to test the validity of such 'common-sense' statements, since they are considered 'true' in his/her own cultural and socio-political habitat (Arsovska 2006). However, one can notice that these statements are nothing but assumptions when comparing them with arguments put forward by a thinker from a different social habitat. As this book clearly shows, the other thinker, most likely, will also proceed from a certain system of apparently incontestable assumptions that may be very different from the first.

There is a lot of empirical evidence suggesting that interaction, contact and dialogue between such opposing groups and/or individuals within a population, if carried out under specific conditions and in a safe environment, might reduce significantly prejudice towards the 'other group' and promote understanding (Allport 1954; Duckitt 1992; Sniderman et al. 2000; Verba et al. 1995: 506).[1] In this respect, Putnam (2000) further argues that 'bridging' social capital can be much more effective in promoting and installing democratic values in a society than 'bonding' social capital (e.g., interaction between people from different social cleavages is more valuable that interaction between people sharing same demographic characteristics) (see also Hooghe 2003).

Dialogue, interaction across social cleavages and voluntary participation of conflicting parties in a mediated and safe environment are core values of restorative justice (Van Ness and Strong 2002) that could promote peace and tolerance within societies. Very often peace deals are limited to top-level diplomacy (Reychler 1997), which often overlooks the interests of significant (minority) groups in a society. Restorative justice argues for inclusive processes with the active participation of all stakeholders, thus also from different layers in society. Restorative justice also stands for multi-level diplomacy (Braithwaite 2002). Hence, more regular contacts between different conflicting parties (groups or individuals) within one society and across different societies have to be encouraged in order to resolve problems in a constructive way. As noted throughout the chapters in this book, meetings between families of war victims coming from both conflicting parties, between mothers who lost children during a conflict, between war veterans from both sides, between victims and offenders, as well as between antagonistic chiefs, are just some among many examples of social interaction between groups with seemingly opposing views. By enhancing interaction such programmes could possibly reduce stereotyping and promote a somewhat greater degree of tolerance, as well as forgiveness and/or reconciliation between people who eventually have to learn how to live together.

Hence, instead of political compromises/deals, broader horizontal and vertical consultation processes should be the starting point for transitional justice processes to develop. The reason for this argument is twofold. Firstly, broader consultation processes could lead to a higher acceptance by the public of any proposed (post-conflict) justice processes installed by the transitional government. In this respect, the failure of the implementation of the Truth Commission in the DRC is partly due to the fact that the civil society was not actively engaged in the setting up of the commission (Vanspauwen and Savage: this volume, Chapter 16).

Secondly, various horizontal and vertical consultation processes might contribute to creating a culture of human rights and democracy. Through long-term diversified strategies, multi-level diplomacy, international cooperation in different spheres, educational exchange programmes, media campaigns and continuous exchange of information, people should be encouraged to understand that the ideas of monolithic cultures and ethnically clean territories are not realistic, nor do they serve their best interest in the long run. No 'nation-state' can remain wholly monocultural today and if it does it will be culturally stagnant. Not only are modern states mixed; the majority of societies throughout history also have been multicultural (Spencer 1998: 31). According to William McNeill (quoted in Spencer 1998: 31) until our historical epoch, high civilisations were generally polyethnic societies while homogeneity was typical only for isolated barbarian societies. Wars and bloody conflicts that turn people against each other often tend to serve the interests of smaller groups of manipulative individuals, who find their ways to profit out of them, but the evil wars are causing is permanent and the consequences are devastating. It is our assertion that, in the long run, the more meaningful interaction there is between various social groups (under certain conditions, following a specific philosophy), the more difficult it will be for political agitators and leaders to use diversities in order to stimulate collective stereotyping, divisions within societies and further hostilities. The role of NGOs and civil society is essential in this respect, but also the role of communities, governments, international organisations and the media.

Upsurge of international activism: pros and cons

Throughout this book the authors have extensively scrutinised the role of the international community in responding to, exposing, and dealing with state-based large-scale conflicts. Also, as noted in Chapter 1, in the last two decades there has been some research done in this particular field (Finch 1947; Dugard 1991; Gayner 1977; Meron 1995; Friedrichs 1998; Bjelic and Savic 2002; Ramet 2005). Scholars have pointed out either that the role of the international community in (post-)conflict situations is crucial (Reisman 1990; Smith 1999; see Ramet 2005 on debates about intervention), or that it just adds fuel to the fire (Koskenniemi 2001; Bjelic and Savic 2002; Burg and Shoup 1999; Chomsky 2002; Jackson 2000). The authors in this book have also been divided regarding this politically sensitive question.

Let us have a closer look at the recent developments regarding the upsurge of international activism. We cannot dispute that since the end of the 1980s, the UN – on behalf of the international community – has played a very important, however often unclear, tentative and misunderstood role in conflict management and prevention, as well as in post-conflict peacebuilding activities throughout the world. Various actors such as the World Bank, donor states and regional security organisations, as well as thousands of NGOs, have complemented UN activities or played independent peacebuilding roles (Human Security Report 2005: 153). According to the Human Security Report (2005: 153) in recent years there has been an increase in preventive diplomacy that has helped prevent a number of 'hidden' conflicts worldwide, while the rise in peacemaking activities has been associated with a major increase in negotiated peace settlements.[2] There has also been an increase in complex peace operations led by the UN or other regional organisations (2005: 155). These missions have involved a great number of various ambitious peacebuilding activities that have been designed in part to prevent the recurrence of conflict.[3] Also the number of truth and reconciliation commissions, supported by the international community has doubled since the end of the Cold War – from one in 1989 to seven in 2003 (2005: 154). According to various reports, reconciliation has also started to become one of the major aims of most peacebuilding programmes (2005: 155). Hence, generally speaking, this surge of international activism has most likely brought some positive developments as well as a decrease in civil wars around the world, particularly in the period between 1992–2003.

Nevertheless, practice shows that the role of the international community has also been highly criticised and debated. It often happens that international organisations and individuals operating in (post-)conflict regions are seen as intruders who want to impose Western values, without having respect for traditions and local cultures. It is quite common that in these 'diverse, fragmented and internally divided societies' at least one of the conflicting parties believes that the 'egoistic West' which characterises itself as the dominant 'individualistic genius' – celebrating the emergence of possessive individualism modelled on the ownership of material property – is unjust and biased (Herzfeld 2002: ix). Hence, more regular interaction between external experts and individuals from various (post-)conflict regions is also greatly needed because it enables people with seemingly 'different' value systems to exchange information and understand each other better. As noted in the previous section, lack of contact and direct dialogue – on an individual, community, national and/or international level – could encourage negative stereotyping of the West as 'the other'. For example, with regard to the atrocities committed in Nyabyondo, the international community has been widely criticised for its inadequate intervention (Kamwimbi: this volume, Chapter 15). Also the intervention in Kosovo and the bombings on Serbia have been highly criticised by the Serbian side which raises the issue of double standards (Nikolic-Ristanovic: this volume, Chapter 6). A similar situation can be observed in the Israeli–Palestinian conflict where the Palestinian side is highly critical of the 'partial and unjust' involvement of the international community (Irani: this volume, Chapter 11). Moreover, it seems that the international community is not only criticised for its intervention, but also for its lack of intervention (Kamwimbi: this volume, Chapter 15).

Therefore, the international community must become much more cautious regarding whether, when and to what extent it should intervene in other countries' affairs because of the danger of taking away the responsibility of the concerned society to deal with its own past and present hurdles, of creating significant imbalances between groups, and of hampering the creativity of societies to find ways to deal with the past that are more socio-culturally meaningful to them. Hence, internationals should have a solid knowledge of local history and culture before engaging in any international projects promoting peace, democracy and reconciliation in foreign countries. Regular interaction and consultations between internationals and local people are necessary in order to avoid prejudices on both sides and to enhance more effective policies. In this respect cultural norms must be dealt with sensitively and respectfully in all prevention/resolution efforts – sensitively because of people's passionate attachment to their traditions, and respectfully because culture can be often a source of protection against the further escalation of violence (Krug *et al.* 2002: 16).

Moreover, foreign powers should be very careful regarding issues related to impunity and support for criminal agents of former regimes or of paramilitary structures. In general perpetrators who use violent means to achieve their goals should not be led to believe that they will never be brought to justice because they can get impunity in the name of 'peace'. The role of restorative justice in this context is crucial. However, these same rules regarding the use of violence should also apply to the international community in order to avoid double standards. Recently there has been much more willingness on behalf of the international community to use force and violence, which might be sending a wrong message to the conflicting parties in various affected societies (e.g. the Kosovo conflict).

In general, further research is required to determine which precise activities and mechanisms of the international community have been most effective in bringing some improvements in global security – and under what specific conditions.

Complementary forms of justice: combining tradition and modernity

Bringing justice in the context of ongoing conflicts seems to be a challenge faced with many dangers to jeopardise the sustainability of fragile peace accords (Moreno Ocampo 2007: 8–9). Too often peace is then promoted at the expense of justice (for example, we could see in the preceding chapters that this is the strong feeling among the Congolese and Kosovars). Hence, in recent years there has been an increasing consensus regarding the need to have complementary mechanisms of justice in order to address the complex and varied needs of post-conflict societies and individuals affected by mass violence. There is a growing consensus among experts on this issue (see, for example, Bassiouni 2002) supported by empirical research increasingly done in post-conflict societies (e.g. Kiza *et al.* 2006). The challenge for all concerned actors is to strike the right balance between these different approaches and to integrate them into a holistic process of dealing with the past which at the same time remains open to the evolving needs of that particular society and to the needs of specific groups within it (e.g. former combatants, victims, second-generation victims and so forth). Hence mutual understanding, flexibility and creativity in this respect are greatly needed in order to deal most effectively with the problems at stake.

For example, throughout the chapters in this book we could observe that in general the contributors have been quite supportive of ensuring accountability through the judicial mechanisms of criminal justice (courts) at the national and international levels, but we have also found an increasing interest, need and support for other forms of accountability in the aftermath of conflict. These mechanisms are less concerned with retribution (punishment) and more with restoration of the harm done to individuals both in emotional and material terms. Such mechanisms often have a higher degree of informality regarding the participation of the conflicting parties and are sometimes connected to traditional forms of dealing with conflict in a given society.

This leads us to the importance of both the international community and the societies concerned to be open to consider different options when formulating their strategies for dealing with the aftermath of a conflict. More specifically, this means that it should be avoided that the whole focus in the fight against impunity be placed on retributive accountability mechanisms. In general, the subsequent investment of resources in these retributive mechanisms should not lead to closing the doors to other possible mechanisms and approaches which may be as – or even more – relevant to the needs of that specific society. For example, restorative justice, as an accountability model, could create opportunities to achieve justice within a society while contributing to peacebuilding as well. Locally-based initiatives in the DRC – although often not acknowledged as such – have shown to be of crucial importance to the lowering of tensions between ethnic groups on the one hand, and between former combatants and communities on the other (Kamwimbi: this volume, Chapter 15). So one of the major challenges to post-conflict societies and to the international community trying to assist them is the high demand for multifaceted creative solutions which may respond to the needs of the society and its individuals. However, these possible solutions should always take into account the particular historical and socio-cultural context as well as the valuable experiences and guidelines developed in recent years in this field.

One particular area where creativity is highly required is precisely in the use of classical Western mechanisms of criminal justice. Important developments have taken place with the creation of the International Criminal Court and its concerns with victims' rights, namely of participation and reparation, and in other recent experiences of international ad hoc or hybrid tribunals where communication with and the involvement of the affected groups and communities has been improved through outreach programmes. Such developments demonstrate to some degree that the core values or principles of restorative justice such as reparation and participation are increasingly permeating responses to violent conflict which remain primarily retributive. It is argued here that it would be beneficial for the individuals and societies concerned if such developments could be furthered. Moreover, for example, in Congo, increasingly both international organisations and state agencies have been providing training, financial and logistic support for the traditional leaders to fulfil their mission of restoring relations between the members of the communities. Experience has shown that it is important to conduct early and ongoing consultations with religious and traditional leaders, lay groups and prominent figures in the community, such as traditional healers, when designing and implementing programmes (Krug *et al.* 2002: 17). Some contributors in this book have suggested strengthening the 'Council of Elders' or other similar traditional justice systems that have been present in the various (post-)conflict regions (North and South Kivu, Kosovo, and even on Palestinian territories) in order to reduce inter-ethnic clashes. Also the role of the media in this context can be very powerful since it can reduce or enhance tensions between groups and promote reconciliation. Different NGOs through media programming, capacity building and outreach activities should try to enhance communication about the political transition process and contribute towards the reduction of tensions and the development of lasting peace in the various post-conflict regions (see, for example, the Search for Common Ground Project in Congo from 2006).

Adding to what was said before, it is not only important that the choice of retributive mechanisms does not close the door to other parallel approaches, but also that these different approaches and mechanisms may feed each other whenever possible and relevant. However, for that to happen there needs to be awareness of the existence of different mechanisms and a willingness to establish channels of communication between them. After all, highly demanding goals such as those of justice, peace and reconciliation have a better chance of being achieved through concerted efforts.

Accountability and truth-seeking

At the same time, the outcome of the contributions in this book is that complex situations such as those of mass violence require a broad understanding of accountability which goes beyond mere individual criminal responsibility. 'Accounting' for a violent past will include not only a recognition of what happened and the responsibilities associated with it, but also a commitment to make up for those wrongs and to prevent them in the future.

Accountability in this sense is strictly connected to acknowledgment and to a broad process of truth-seeking. Moreover, there can be no comprehensive accountability if there is no comprehensive knowledge, understanding and recognition of what happened in the past. Pointedly, at the cost of 'peace', not all wrongdoers are held accountable for their crimes, and often there is no acknowledgment regarding the crimes and suffering that these perpetrators have caused to the people in their communities. In the introductory chapter we have already stated that the conceptual issues in the area of state-based crime are very daunting precisely because of the problems of bias, the establishment of 'truth', 'peace' and 'justice', double standards and political power. Nevertheless, all these uncertainties often have a very negative impact on the general population causing further tensions and hostilities between opposing groups. Hence, in post-conflict situations the strict connection between 'truth' and 'accountability' brings into the picture the restorative justice discourse – a renewed focus on the role of truth-seeking and truth-telling. An inclusive truth-seeking and truth-telling process will lead to more acceptable and realistic claims for justice and accountability on behalf of the victims. Restorative justice provides the building blocks for this (Valiñas and Vanspauwen 2006). Some reports on the community-based reconciliation process in East Timor provide good evidence of the possible direct effects of such inclusive accountability mechanisms (Pigou 2003). Moreover, as we could observe in the different chapters, a comprehensive truth-seeking process also often requires a combination of formal and informal mechanisms in order to achieve best outcomes.

From micro to macro

Another important element which surfaced throughout the work done for this book was the essential and unavoidable connection between macro and micro levels of the conflict. As acknowledged by the editors and demonstrated by the contributors, it is very difficult if not impossible to reflect upon the micro level (interpersonal relation/conflict) without necessarily reflecting on the macro level. These are intrinsically linked in cases of widespread atrocities. The implications of this for the application of a restorative justice approach to dealing with the aftermath of large-scale conflicts need to be further explored. However, this book has already provided us with some ideas of what those implications are. For example, the encounter or dialogue that in conventional settings may take place between the individual victim and the individual perpetrator must be opened up to the involvement of groups of people who, albeit not direct perpetrators/victims, regard each other with mistrust because they have been on 'opposing sides' during the conflict. The work done at this community/group level may be of crucial importance. In fact, often in post-conflict situations, the macro level is not favourable to processes of accountability and acknowledgment, not to mention of rebuilding empathy between individuals. The processes that take place at the interpersonal/micro level are highly dependent on the macro level. As argued by Fletcher and Weinstein (2002), initiatives of rebuilding trust and empathy at the interpersonal level are ultimately dependent on the overall context to have a significant impact. This is where the role of leadership and civil society is absolutely crucial, especially when the political leadership is primarily divisive.

Opting for a better future: exchange of information in a globalised world

No single factor explains why some individuals behave violently toward others, why violence is more prevalent in some communities than in others, and why there is a continuous eruption of violent conflicts and wars around the world. As we can see in this book, violence is the result of a highly complex interaction of individual, interpersonal, social, cultural, political, historical, economic and other environmental factors. Understanding how these factors are related to violence and conflict is one of the most important steps in order to prevent further escalation of conflicts worldwide. However, because violence is a multifaceted problem with psychological, social, cultural, political, economic and environmental roots, it needs to be confronted in an interdisciplinary manner. We have already shown the need for the use of various complementary forms/mechanisms of justice in order to address the wide-ranging needs of post-conflict societies and individuals affected by mass violence. We have also tried to show how restorative justice can enhance the cooperation between various groups of people and can reduce tensions in divided societies. However, what can we, as researchers and academics, add further to the efforts of conflict prevention/resolution in this globalised world?

First of all, we need to grasp the reality that violence can no longer remain safeguarded by national politics, but must be enthusiastically addressed at the global level as well – not only through international agencies and networks of governmental and non-governmental organisations, but also via networks composed of academics and researchers. Such international efforts must aim to exploit the positive aspects of globalisation for the common good, but should always greatly respect local cultures and traditions. The exchange of information and ideas between academics from all over the world could be one of the strongest tools to address the problems at stake. Academics can help victims raise their voice via different methods (e.g. publications, seminars and workshops, influencing policy-makers, doing empirical research on sensitive issues such as state crimes and human rights violations that is still lacking, finding creative unbiased ways to deal effectively with conflicts and victimised people) and could try to bring conflicting parties closer to each other by pointing out the similarities rather than the differences between these groups. Research networks can help the 'opposite others' to get to know each other better and could also help the international community to create just and long-lasting strategies to fight violence, conflicts and wars in different socio-cultural contexts. Only through group efforts and joint diversified strategies can we assist people living in (post-)conflict societies to deal with their past and start collecting the fruits that a non-violent future might bring to them. Only through cooperation and integration, rather than isolation and seclusion, might these people be able to understand that violence is not inevitable and that forgiveness is the attribute of the strong, not of the weak (Mahatma Ghandi). Understanding and dialogue might enable victimised people and societies to continue with their lives and eradicate manipulative, unjust and repressive governments.

However, enhanced contacts, multi-level diplomacy and joint efforts are the only way to achieve this goal. Individually, it seems that none of these diversified policies and strategies has had a great impact on global security. Sadly, most have achieved only modest success, mainly in terms of their own goals (Human Security Report 2005: 155). But taken together and over a longer period of time, their impact could be highly significant and powerful. This book is one such effort. It tries to show the different perspectives that people from diverse socio-cultural contexts hold dear. Hence, bringing these people from different social contexts together in a safe environment in order to promote a constructive dialogue and better understanding for the sake of reducing further escalation of violence is one among many important messages that this book tries to pass across. We encourage more such positive efforts in order to help in the building of a better and safer future for all.

Notes

1 This effect is known as the 'contact mechanism' or 'contact hypothesis': increased contact and interaction within different groups will lead to the abandonment of prejudices. The WG4 had an opportunity to attend a workshop in Israel entitled 'Restorative Justice and the Contact Hypothesis in Managing Ethno-national Conflicts' (financed by COST within the framework of COST Action A21). The workshop (see workshop programme) attempted to assess the viability of the widespread application of the contact hypothesis: 'The contact hypothesis generally speaking is perceived conventionally as embedded in the application of restorative justice in ethnic and international protracted conflicts, without having been researched in this specific area. The topic under discussion was precisely the link between the contact hypothesis and restorative justice in dealing with large-scale conflicts and mass victimisation. The four cases of conflicts chosen for analysis in the workshop were the Israeli–Palestinian conflict, the conflict in Cyprus, the Northern Ireland conflict and the conflict in the former Yugoslavia. Hence, while the contact hypothesis began with Allport in the 1950s, with respect to race relations, its tenets underlie many of the conflict management and mediation projects in other spheres – ethno-national conflict, religious-secular, community, and perhaps even at the micro-level, in family situations. Dialogues, attentive listening, narrative sharing, reconciliation efforts, restorative justice frameworks, etc. are common to a wide range of conflict management and resolution concepts, theories, and research. Many of the key authors in the field, such as Herbert Kelman, Joseph Montville, Louis Kriesberg, etc., as well as Israeli academics like Ifat Maoz also rely in their studies, often implicitly, on the contact hypothesis. Similarly, attempts to apply theories of reconciliation and restorative justice in ethno-national conflict situations are also linked in many respects to the foundations of the contact hypothesis. Given the lack of substantive outcomes in many of these efforts with some possible exceptions (Northern Ireland), it is high time to ask probing questions about the viability of the widespread and all-purpose application of the contact hypothesis as a technique used by restorative justice theories. In a broader sense, these questions are also important in evaluating reconciliation approaches' (see workshop programme: 'Restorative Justice and the Contact Hypothesis in Managing Ethno-national Conflicts', The Conflict Management and Negotiation Program of Bar Ilan University, Ramat Gan, 5 March 2006).

2 Approximately half of all the peace settlements negotiated between 1946 and 2003 have been signed since the end of the Cold War. The average number of conflicts terminated per year in the 1990s was more than twice the average of all previous decades from 1946 onwards (Human Security Report 2005).

3 The number of UN peacekeeping operations more than doubled between 1988 and 2004 – from seven to 16 (Human Security Report).

References

Allport, G. (1954) *The Nature of Prejudice*. Reading, MA: Addison-Wesley.

Arsovska, J. (2006) 'Understanding a "culture of violence and crime": the Kanun of Lek Dukagjini and the rise of the Albanian sexual-slavery rackets', *European Journal of Crime, Criminal Law and Criminal Justice*, 14 (2): 161–84.

Bassiouni, M.C. (2002) 'Accountability for violations of international humanitarian law and other serious violations of human rights', in M.C. Bassiouni (ed.), *Post-Conflict Justice*. Ardsley, NY: Transnational Publishers, pp. 3–54.

Bjelic, D. and Savic, O. (eds) (2002) *Balkan as Metaphor. Between Globalization and Fragmentation*. London: MIT Press.

Braithwaite, J. (2002) *Restorative Justice and Responsive Regulation*. Oxford: Oxford University Press.

Burg, S. and Shoup, S.P. (1999) *The War in Bosnia-Herzegovina: Ethnic Conflict and International Intervention*. Armonk, NY: M.E. Sharpe.

Chomsky, N. (2002) *Pirates and Emperors, Old and New: International Terrorism in the Real World*. Cambridge, MA: South End Press.

Duckitt, J. (1992) *The Social Psychology of Prejudice*. New York: Praeger.

Dugard, J. (1991) 'The role of international law in the struggle for liberation in south Africa', *Social Justice*, 18: 83–94.

Finch, A.H. (1947) 'The Nuremberg Trial and international law', *American Journal of International Law*, 41: 20–37.

Fletcher, L.E. and Weinstein, H. (2002) 'Violence and social repair. Rethinking the contribution of justice to reconciliation', *Human Rights Quarterly*, 24 (3): 573–639.

Friedrichs, O.D. (ed.) (1998) *State Crime. Defining, Delineating and Explaining Crime*. Aldershot: Ashgate, Vol. 2.

Gayner, B.J. (1977) 'The genocide treaty', *Journal of Social and Political Studies*, 2: 235–45.

Herzfeld, M. (2002) 'Foreword', in D. Bjelic and O. Savic, *Balkan as Metaphor. Between Globalization and Fragmentation*. Cambridge, MA: MIT Press, pp. ix–xii.

Hooghe, M. (2003) 'Value congruence and convergence within voluntary associations: ethnocentrism in Belgian organizations', *Political Behaviour*, 25 (2): 151–75.

Human Security Report (2005) *War and Peace in the 21st Century*. New York: Canadian Human Security Centre/Oxford University Press.

Jackson, R. (2000) *The Global Convenant: Human Conduct in a World of States*. Oxford: Oxford University Press.

Kiza, E., Rathgeber, C. and Rohne, H.-C. (2006) *Victims of War: An Empirical Study on War-Victimization and Victims' Attitudes towards Addressing Atrocities*. Hamburg: Hamburger Institut für Sozialforschung. See: http://www.his-online.de/cms.asp?H='79'&T=0&Plugin=10&HE=10&HEP=978-3-936096-73-6.

Koskenniemi, M. (2001) 'Human rights, politics and love', *Nordic Journal of Human Rights*, 4: 33–45.

Krug, E.G., Dahlberg, L., Mercy, J.A., Zwi, A. and Lozano, R. (eds) (2002) *World Report on Violence and Health*. Geneva: World Health Organisation.

Meron, T. (1995) 'International criminalization of international atrocities', *American Journal of International Law*, 89: 554–77.

Moreno Ocampo, L. (2007) 'Transitional justice in ongoing conflicts', *International Journal of Transitional Justice*, 1 (1): 8–9.

Mutz, D. (2002) 'Cross-cutting social networks. Testing democratic theory in practice', *American Political Science Review*, 96: 111–26.

Pigou, P. (2003) *Crying Without Tears. In Pursuit of Justice and Reconciliation in Timor-Leste: Community Perspectives and Expectations*, Occasional Paper Series. New York: International Center for Transitional Justice.

Popper, K. (1993) *The Open Society and Its Enemies*, 4th edn [1945]. London: Routledge Kegan Paul, Vol. 2.

Putnam, R. (1993) *Making Democracy Work*. Princeton, NJ: Princeton University Press.

Putnam, R. (2000) *Bowling Alone. The Collapse and Revival of American Community*. New York: Simon & Schuster.

Ramet, S. (2005) *Thinking about Yugoslavia*. Cambridge: Cambridge University Press.

Rawls, J. (1999) *Collected Papers*, ed. S. Freeman. Cambridge, MA: Harvard University Press.

Reisman, W.M. (1990) 'Sovereignty and human rights in contemporary international law' *American Journal of International Law*, 84 (4): 886.

Reychler, L. (1997) 'Field diplomacy: a new conflict prevention paradigm?', *Peace and Conflict Studies*, 4 (1).

Seligman, A. (1992) *The Idea of Civil Society*. Princeton, NJ: Princeton University Press.

Smith, M. (1998) 'Humanitarian intervention: an overview of the ethical issues', *Ethics and International Affairs*, 12: 63–76.

Sniderman, P., Peri, P., de Figueiredo, R. and Piazza, T. (2000) *The Outsider. Prejudice and Politics in Italy*. Princeton, NJ: Princeton University Press.

Spencer, M. (1998) 'When states divide', in M. Spencer (ed.), *Separatism: Democracy and Disintegration*. Lanham, MD: Rowman & Littlefield, pp. 7–41.

Valiñas, M. and Vanspauwen, K. (2006) *The Promise of Restorative Justice in the Search for Truth after a Violent Conflict. Experiences from South Africa and Bosnia-Herzegovina*. Paper presentation at the Fourth Conference of the

European Forum for Restorative Justice, 'Restorative Justice and Beyond – An Agenda for Europe', Barcelona, Spain, 14–17 June.

Van Ness, D.W. and Strong, K.H. (eds) (2002) *Restoring Justice*, 2nd edn. Cincinnati: OH: Anderson.

Verba, S., Schlozman, K.L. and Brady, H. (1995) *Voice and Equality. Civic Voluntarism in American Politics*. Cambridge, MA: Harvard University Press.

Warren, M. (2001) *Democracy and Association*. Princeton, NJ: Princeton University Press.

Index

Added to a page number 'f' denotes a figure, 't' denotes a table and 'n' denotes notes.